Gavin Rees QC

'8

GW01459482

COMMERCIAL FRAUD IN CIVIL PRACTICE

COMMERCIAL FRAUD IN CIVIL PRACTICE

Paul McGrath

Barrister, Essex Court Chambers

OXFORD

UNIVERSITY PRESS

OXFORD
UNIVERSITY PRESS

Great Clarendon Street, Oxford OX2 6DP

Oxford University Press is a department of the University of Oxford.
It furthers the University's objective of excellence in research, scholarship,
and education by publishing worldwide in

Oxford New York

Auckland Cape Town Dar es Salaam Hong Kong Karachi
Kuala Lumpur Madrid Melbourne Mexico City Nairobi
New Delhi Shanghai Taipei Toronto

With offices in

Argentina Austria Brazil Chile Czech Republic France Greece
Guatemala Hungary Italy Japan Poland Portugal Singapore
South Korea Switzerland Thailand Turkey Ukraine Vietnam

Oxford is a registered trade mark of Oxford University Press
in the UK and in certain other countries

Published in the United States
by Oxford University Press Inc., New York

© Oxford University Press, 2008

The moral rights of the author have been asserted

Crown copyright material is reproduced under Class Licence
Number C01P0000148 with the permission of OPSI
and the Queen's Printer for Scotland

Database right Oxford University Press (maker)

First published 2008

All rights reserved. No part of this publication may be reproduced,
stored in a retrieval system, or transmitted, in any form or by any means,
without the prior permission in writing of Oxford University Press,
or as expressly permitted by law, or under terms agreed with the appropriate
reprographics rights organization. Enquiries concerning reproduction
outside the scope of the above should be sent to the Rights Department,
Oxford University Press, at the address above

You must not circulate this book in any other binding or cover
and you must impose the same condition on any acquirer

British Library Cataloguing in Publication Data
Data available

Library of Congress Cataloging in Publication Data
Data available

Typeset by Cepha Imaging Private Ltd, Bangalore, India
Printed in Great Britain
on acid-free paper by
CPI Antony Rowe Ltd, Chippenham

ISBN 978-0-19-929057-4

1 3 5 7 9 10 8 6 4 2

FOREWORD

This is a book for practitioners, and in particular for those who are presenting or defending a case in the civil courts based on fraud. The claimant may be seeking compensation from the fraudster himself for the loss he has caused or to recover the proceeds of fraud from third parties who have, whether innocently or dishonestly, received or handled them.

The sophistication of the modern fraudster and the ease and speed with which he can transmit the proceeds to other jurisdictions and conceal or launder them make the facts complex and their discovery difficult. Once the facts have been unravelled, the application of the law should be straightforward. But that is not the case. English law provides a bounteous array of interlocking causes of action, and their relationship and different requirements are not universally agreed. The claimant may bring an action at common law or he may invoke the jurisdiction of equity; he may seek a personal remedy or a proprietary one. It may be questioned whether so many different and overlapping remedies should continue to be available for the same misapplication of property. But while they are available, the practitioner must familiarize himself with their different requirements, and this is no easy matter when scholars, and even Law Lords, disagree; when terminology has changed over the years and is at best confusing and at worst misleading; when the same expression (such as constructive trust) has different meanings in different contexts; and when judges, constrained by precedent, are compelled to express a view of the law which they later repudiate when promoted to a position which enables them to do so.

The author is to be congratulated on providing a guide through this minefield. It is not a context in which certitudes, which is what the practitioner really needs and which the law ought to provide, are possible. It is rather one of choices, and the best that can be done is to provide the practitioner with a series of informed choices. This the present book does.

Lord Millett

PREFACE

From the moment my interest in this area of the law was first kindled by the intense weekly BCL seminars held by that giant of an academic, the late Professor Birks, together with Professor Burrows and Professor McKendrick, commercial fraud litigation has held a fascination for me. There is no doubt in the early days that restitution was the driving force behind this interest but gradually over time it became clear that commercial fraud litigation traverses many different areas of the law including injunctive relief, contract and tortious claims, conflict of laws and insolvency, to name but a few.

My interest received some early nurturing when I spent several months on secondment to Walkers, Attorneys in the Cayman Islands. It was here where I was exposed to high quality commercial fraud litigation on a daily basis. Beatles fans will understand it if I say that the Cayman Islands was my Hamburg. In recent years, I have had the pleasure of returning to the Cayman Islands, along with the British Virgin Islands, on work-related trips.

OUP's original idea was for a book on the law of tracing. I wanted to expand it to include commercial fraud litigation generally as I perceived this was not an area where practitioners were well served with texts. Many of the materials that are or should be relied upon come from obscure texts, articles or monographs, few of which are readily found in practitioners' libraries let alone an individual practitioner's bookshelf. It is this material which has driven the development of many aspects of commercial fraud litigation in the last decade or so. My aims were (i) to bring that material into one book for ease of access and (ii) to try and bring together, in one book, many of the areas in which a commercial fraud litigator might be asked to litigate. It is hoped this book can at least be a starting point for most issues, even if resort is needed to more specialist texts on certain issues.

In writing this book, I hope I have done justice to those that have taught and inspired me in the law over the years. From my undergraduate tutors at University College, Oxford (John Finnis, Adrian Zuckerman and Martin Matthews) to my BCL tutors including Francis Reynolds, Peter Birks, Andrew Burrows, Adrian Briggs and Ewan McKendrick. They have all contributed greatly to my understanding of, and interest in, the law.

A special set of thanks must go to Graham Virgo, who did not teach me, but who took time out of his busy schedule to read some of the early chapters and ensure

I was on the right track. His inciteful remarks greatly improved those chapters and as anyone who has read his *The Principles of the Law of Restitution* (2nd edn, Butterworths, 2006) would already appreciate, his many different ideas provide a much needed counter-balance to the Birksian approach.

The staff, past and present, at OUP deserve a special mention for having to put up with so many delays and late changes caused by my trying, on many occasions unsuccessfully, to juggle a full-time practice with writing a book. I received nothing but full support from them: Rachel Mullaly, Rebecca Howes, and Fiona Stables.

I would also like to thank Lord Millett for agreeing to provide a foreword to the book. Anyone practising in this area will be well aware of the tremendous contribution he has made to the development of so many topics, ranging from the law of tracing, knowing receipt and dishonest assistance, the relationship (or not) between unjust enrichment and proprietary relief and the conflict of laws. His judgments or articles feature in almost every chapter. Whilst the reader will become aware that my views differ from Lord Millett's on occasion, there can be no doubting that his contribution to this and other areas of the law has been peerless.

My biggest set of thanks are reserved to those closest to me. First and foremost, to my parents, Peter and Sheila, and to Peter, Eric, Maria and Theo, for their unstinting support throughout this process. Finally, but certainly not least, I would like to thank Angi for all her help during the writing of the book. She provided practical support, in arranging my research materials into files (something that would not otherwise happen with me) and ensuring that my recent-cases file was right up to date. More recently, she has shouldered much of the burden of putting up with me as I tried to meet publishing deadlines whilst maintaining a full-time practice.

All comments or observations on the book gratefully received at pmcgrath@ essexcourt.net.

Paul A McGrath
Essex Court Chambers

CONTENTS—SUMMARY

CONTENTS

VII CONFLICT OF LAWS

VIII TRACING, DISCLOSURE AND INJUNCTIONS

21. Tracing

TABLE OF CASES

TABLE OF STATUTES

TABLE OF STATUTORY INSTRUMENTS

TABLE OF EUROPEAN REGULATIONS

TABLE OF INTERNATIONAL TREATIES
AND CONVENTIONS

PART I

FRAUD—OVERVIEW

1

OVERVIEW

Fraud is notoriously difficult to define. That is because it is not in itself an activity. **1.01**
X does not *do* fraud. It cannot be equated with buying or selling as an activity and
yet it may form part of any such activity. It is effectively not an activity as such but
the manner in which an activity is performed. It tells us *how* someone went about
an activity. The most obvious consequence to flow from this observation is that
fraud potentially pervades most commercial activity and as such is a diverse subject of study.[1] In many ways, a fraud litigator will find himself dipping into many
different areas of law.

It is not the purpose of this book to provide guidance on each of these areas as **1.02**
such. Indeed, to attempt to do so would be impractical. Rather, the focus is on
those issues which touch most aspects of a fraud claim, e.g. early disclosure and
pre-emptive relief; jurisdictional and choice of law issues; tracing and following
the proceeds of the fraud; and finally the claims which may be asserted in common
law, equity and statute.

A. Fraud—Alive and Well

Commercial fraud is big business and it is only getting bigger, cleverer and more **1.03**
complex. Fraudsters are typically ahead of the market when it comes to taking
advantage of new technology and whilst one can sometimes read that fraud levels

---

[1] *Reddaway v Banham* [1896] AC 199, 221.

are reducing in one area,[2] that is only because the fraudsters have moved on to other areas in which there is a corresponding increase in levels of fraudulent activity. The overall trend is in one direction only.

1.04 Fraud comes in all shapes and sizes. The last decade or so has seen the collapse of huge conglomerates such as Enron and Worldcom through fraudulent accounting and business practices. Much of the work that forms the core of commercial fraud litigation is generated either internally within a company (e.g. the finance director misappropriating funds) or arises between companies or wealthy individuals out of contractual arrangements that have not worked out as planned. At the other end of the scale, identity fraud has been increasing at an exponential rate[3] given our greater willingness to make payments over the internet and increased involvement of organized crime units in this activity. Phishing attacks[4] increased from 3,394 in the first quarter of 2007 to 10,235 in the first quarter of 2008. Bank account takeovers via information obtained from emails have more than doubled in the first quarter of 2008. The internet and banking conducted other than face to face create unique opportunities for the fraudster.

1.05 Fraud responds to economic conditions. The recent 'credit crunch' problems have fuelled fraud relating to all types of loan and mortgage applications and that is only likely to increase over the next year or so. According to the UK fraud prevention service, CIFAS, the first three months of 2008 have seen a 10% leap in fraud cases, with the number of falsely filled-in application forms up 13% from 19,239 in the first three months of 2007 compared to 21,780 in the first quarter of 2008. In a survey conducted in 2005, the insurer Norwich Union concluded that fraud cost the UK some £16bn in 2004, which represented 1.4% of the UK's entire economic output or £650 per household.[5]

1.06 Major law firms now have specialist departments focusing on fraud and a whole new industry has developed surrounding IT and identity fraud. KPMG's annual fraud barometer, which tracks cases of more than £100,000 in the UK Crown Court system found that 277 fraud cases worth a total of £837m in 2006 (compared to 222 cases worth £942m).[6] The increasing ability and ease with which

---

[2] According to APACS, card fraud in face to face transactions has reduced in the last two years by two-thirds, down from £218.8m in 2004 to £73m in 2006 and to £56.2m in 2007. This reduction is attributable to the introduction of chip and pin. But at the same time, card fraud abroad has increased by 77% since fraudsters have directed their attention to the overseas market where chip and pin has yet to be introduced.

[3] ID theft is up 66% on 2006 according to Experian's Annual Report. Those earning over £50,000 per annum were considered most at risk.

[4] Phishing takes place when an email, purporting to be an official email from the bank, is received asking for bank account details, when in fact it is from a would-be fraudster.

[5] £4bn of this was in the private sector and £10bn against the government relating to benefit fraud, customs fraud or tax evasion.

[6] These are obviously figures for criminal cases only.

money can be transferred around the world only assists the fraudster keen to launder his ill-gotten gains. Such has been the increase in fraud, and the concern that the present legal system cannot cope with major city frauds, that the UK government, after long consultation,[7] has felt the need to introduce legislation, the Fraud Act 2006, simplifying fraud offences in criminal law. So we can rest assured that fraud and fraudulent activity is very much alive and well and likely to darken our court-doors, both civil and criminal, for the foreseeable future.

B. Aim of the Book

The aim of this book is to identify and bring before practitioners the necessary **1.07** materials and arguments for commercial fraud litigation. This process has been twofold.

- Fifteen years' experience in this area has convinced me that many of the more important materials are not readily to hand in most practitioner's bookcases. That is because this area of the law, probably more than any other, has been influenced by academic and extra-judicial writing, especially on matters relating to unjust enrichment and equity. These writings have been cited in court and have had, and continue to have, a significant impact on the development of the law. But often these articles and essays are to be found in obscure monographs which rarely find themselves on to a practitioner's bookshelf. What this book aims to do is to identify some of the more important arguments out there so that a busy reader can rapidly identify and understand the arguments. This is particularly the case in respect of issues relating to unjust enrichment and equity. That is not to pretend that this book is an adequate substitution for reading the underlying material: it is not and does not pretend otherwise. At least, however, the reader might be better informed as to the arguments and, if relevant to their particular case, can read the underlying material.

- As indicated above, the fraud litigator will be expected to pray in a broad church. An important aspect of that is understanding topics which are dealt with in excellent texts such as *Dicey, Morris & Collins* (14th edn, Thomson/Sweet and Maxwell, 2006—hereinafter *Dicey, Morris & Collins* (14th edn)) (for conflict of laws) and Professor Goode's *Principles of Corporate Insolvency Law* (3rd edn, Thomson/Sweet and Maxwell, 2005) (for insolvency law). The litigator in this area must have a command of these topics and it is hoped that the level of information provided in this book will suffice for most purposes. No doubt, should the reader need more detailed information, regard can be had to these specialist texts but at least that will be done from a position of knowledge.

---

[7] See Law Commission, *'Fraud'* No. 276.

C. Stucture of the Book

1.08 Following this overview, the book begins with Part II on fraud at common law. It deals with the discrete but important claim in deceit, which is the closest tort comes to a claim in fraud.

1.09 The next three Parts all relate to liability for the receipt of the proceeds of fraud. Part III is concerned with two claims based upon receipt at common law: unjust enrichment and conversion.

1.10 Chapter 3 (on unjust enrichment) draws a sharp distinction between itself as a claim and restitution as a remedy. It is for that reason it has been called unjust enrichment and not restitution. The chapter examines the difficult question of the relationship between proprietary claims and unjust enrichment after *Foskett v McKeown*.[8] As set out there, the unjust enrichment lawyers continue to debate the point. The chapter also examines the view, expressed by Professor Birks just prior to his untimely death, that the civilian law approach to 'absence of consideration' may be preferable to the more traditional list of unjust factors such as mistake, undue influence, etc. It will be seen that whilst it has not so far been adopted in the cases, it has received a warm welcome at the highest judicial level.

1.11 A short chapter on conversion has been included (Chapter 4). As with the claim in unjust enrichment, this is a claim based on strict liability. As will be said many times throughout the book: the fact that the client has been a victim of fraud does not mean that recovery can only be on the basis of alleging dishonesty and other serious allegations. The chapter does note, however, the limitations of the claim when dealing with money as currency (which is the typical position in a commercial fraud).

1.12 Part IV deals with receipt-based claims in equity. These raise some of the most controversial topics in the whole book. Knowing or unconscientious receipt is a very useful claim in a fraud. It has the advantage of the flexible rules on equitable tracing, enabling the claim to extend beyond the initial recipient, something which limits the common law claims based upon receipt. The latest position of unconscientious receipt, as set out in the Court of Appeal in *BCCI v Akindele*,[9] is examined. It remains to be seen whether such a flexible concept creates the uncertainty feared by commentators.

1.13 The three chapters on constructive trust (Chapters 6, 7 and 8) aim, as far as possible, to assist the practitioner in understanding a very difficult but important area of the law. Chapter 6 is designed to touch on various topics raised about constructive

---

8 [2001] 1 AC 102, HL.
9 [2001] Ch 437.

trusts and explain them as briefly as possible. The aim is not to dwell on them but to remove the mystery that sometimes surrounds constructive trusts. It also aims to identify topics which are, for practical purposes, now closed, such as the remedial constructive trust. Chapter 7 identifies specific instances of wrongdoing that typically give rise to a constructive trust. Finally, Chapter 8 examines such trusts arising from a pre-existing fiduciary relationship.

Part V covers the statutory provisions which relate to attempts to spirit funds away **1.14** from a company with a poor financial status. Although they have limitations (e.g. some can only be brought by the liquidator and then only on behalf of all creditors), they represent a discrete area of insolvency law with which a commercial fraud litigator should be familiar.

Part VI contains four chapters loosely collated under the title 'multi-party liabil- **1.15** ity'. Chapter 14 covers conspiracy in its two forms. The comparisons and contrasts with dishonest assistance in Chapter 16 are drawn. The latter chapter examines the debacle that was *Twinsectra's*[10] attempts to re-interpret Lord Nicholls' test of dishonesty in *Royal Brunei v Tan*. If ever the phrase, 'if it ain't broke don't fix it' applied, it was here. Thankfully, the Privy Council in *Barlow Clowes v Eurotrust*[11] has restored the orthodox position, leaving practitioners only with an issue of precedent. Chapter 15 on inducing a breach of contract is based entirely upon the reasoning of the recent House of Lords decision in *OBG v Allan*.[12] The final chapter in this Part is Chapter 17, Bribery. This has deliberately been given its own chapter because it gives rise to several different causes of action and so cannot be pigeon-holed into the Constructive Trusts Part II—Abuse of Fiduciary Position. That ignores the tort and unjust enrichment element to the claim.

Part VII is concerned with the jurisdictional and choice of law issues arising out of **1.16** commercial fraud. Specific focus is given to the types of claim which typically arise in a commercial fraud. It will be seen that both the jurisdictional and choice of law issues in relation to various unjust enrichment and equitable wrongdoing claims are still very much in the process of development. The text has attempted to provide as much guidance from various sources as possible but it is an area likely to cause practitioners some concern for a while yet.

Part VIII begins with a chapter on tracing and following (Chapter 21). This is now **1.17** recognized as a process of identifying the location of value. It is a crucial part of the ability to claim, whether in personam or in rem, against subsequent recipients of the proceeds of the fraud. It is the weapon against the laundering of the proceeds of the fraud. It will be seen that there is a fair amount of criticism to be levelled at

---

[10] [2002] AC 164.
[11] [2006] 1 WL 1476.
[12] [2008] 1 AC 1.

the rules as they presently exist. It is to be hoped that favourable dicta in the House of Lords will soon be followed by a binding decision that there is just one set of rules for tracing.

1.18   Chapter 22 focuses on pre-action disclosure, including *Norwich Pharmacal* relief. The ability to obtain, at the earliest opportunity, information relating to the location of the alleged fraudsters, the proceeds of the fraud, any bank accounts the fraudsters may use, etc. is one of the most important tasks in litigation involving fraud allegations. Although the CPR did introduce certain grounds for pre-action disclosure, the reality appears to be a greater court willingness to employ the *Norwich Pharmacal* order and to employ it as a weapon against fraud and general wrongdoing.

1.19   Chapter 23 deals with search orders, or Anton Piller orders as they used to be called. Such orders have rightly been called one of the nuclear weapons of English civil procedure. It represents an effective but expensive means of obtaining documents crucial to the determination of issues at trial. Chapter 24 covers various types of injunctive relief including freezing or Mareva relief, as well as proprietary injunctions. Although last in order in the book, very often this injunctive relief will be one of the first steps undertaken in any fraud litigation so as to secure, as best possible, the client's position pending trial. The requirements for the freezing injunctions are carefully examined and, in the case of the criteria of risk of dissipation, re-asserted. It does not mean simply that a judgment may go unsatisfied, as some interpret *The Ninemia*.[13] It is concerned with *unjustifiable* dissipation: see Mr Justice Walker in *Mobil Cerro Negro Ltd v Petroleos de Venezuela SA*.[14]

1.20   Finally, the reader will see that where appropriate, extracts and quotations taken from the case law or articles have been used. This has been done so that the reader can make up his own mind as to whether the interpretation of the extract portrayed in the text is correct. The danger of paraphrasing, which is necessary sometimes, is that something important may well be left out which alters its meaning. It is hoped also that the ready availability of the quotation may be more user-friendly for the busy practitioner reader.

---

[13] [1983] 1 WLR 1412.
[14] [2008] EWHC 532 (Comm).

Part II

FRAUD AT COMMON LAW

2

DECEIT[1]

A. Summary of Requirements

A claim in the tort of deceit arises in the following circumstances: **2.01**

- X makes a representation [of fact] to Y;[2]
- X knows the representation is false, or has no belief in its truth or is reckless as to whether or not it is true;[3]
- X intends Y to rely upon the representation;[4]
- Y does rely upon the representation;[5]
- Y is caused loss and damage as a result of such reliance.[6]

---

[1] See *Clerk & Lindsell on Torts* (18th edn, Thomson/Sweet and Maxwell, 2006, hereinafter *Clerk & Lindsell*), ch 18; Hazel Carty, *An Analysis of the Economic Torts* (Oxford University Press, 2001, hereinafter *Economic Torts*), ch 6; McBride and Bagshaw, *Tort Law* (2nd edn, Longman Law Series, 2005), ch 22.

[2] E.g. *Bradford Trust Equitable Benefit Building Society v Borders* [1941] 2 All ER 205; *Gross v Lewis Hillman Ltd* [1970] Ch 445.

[3] *Derry v Peek* (1889) 14 App Cas 337.

[4] *Peek v Gurney* (1873) LR 6 HL 377.

[5] *Smith v Chadwick* (1884) 9 App Cas 187.

[6] *Derry v Peek* (1889) 14 App Cas 337.

B. Introduction

2.02 Deceit is the closest the English law of tort comes to a claim in fraud. As its name suggests and as one might expect of a claim based on fraudulent conduct, a claim in deceit requires that the claimant be deceived by the words or conduct of the defendant resulting in loss or damage being sustained. Deception causing loss to the claimant is at the heart of any claim for deceit.

2.03 This chapter is concerned solely with the tort of deceit insofar as it arises from a fraudulent misrepresentation satisfying the elements identified above. Some texts include a discussion about bribery in the context of this tort,[7] whilst recognizing that bribery does not meet the typical requirements of a false misrepresentation. Whether or not bribery properly falls within a wide definition of deceit which also includes the fraudulent misrepresentation claims is an exercise in taxonomy which is of no relevance to a commercial fraud litigator. For ease of exposition and explanation, therefore, the elements of the tort of bribery will be dealt with in an entirely separate chapter.[8]

2.04 It will be readily apparent that the elements of the tort of deceit impose a high evidential burden on the claimant.[9] Further, a pleader can only properly plead an allegation of fraud on the basis of reasonably credible material (not necessarily evidence)[10] which, without more, establishes a prima facie case of fraud: Bar Code of Conduct, para 708(c): Law Society's Code for Advocacy, para 6.6(c).[11]

2.05 It must always be remembered that to plead such a claim without appropriate supporting material exposes the drafter to potential professional ethical difficulties, not to mention exposing the whole legal team to a possible wasted costs order should the court subsequently conclude the allegations should not have been made in the first place. The only way confidently to withstand the typical pressure applied by the client to plead out such a case is to know precisely what is required to do so and to be confident that the facts as known satisfy those requirements.

2.06 It is therefore essential that proper enquiries and investigations are undertaken prior to commencing a claim alleging deceit. To persuade a client to await the outcome

---

[7] Carty, *Economic Torts*, 133–6; *Clerk & Lindsell* (18th edn) at para 18-051.

[8] See Ch 17.

[9] Although it remains the civil burden of proof, the court works on the principle that the more serious the allegation the less likely it is that it happened and hence the more it will need persuading that it did happen: see Lord Nicholls in *R H (Minors)* [1996] AC 563, 586–7; *Clerk & Lindsell* (18th edn) at para18-03.

[10] *Metcalf v Mardell* [2001] Lloyd's Rep PN 146.

[11] See also *Mason v Clarke* [1955] AC 778, 794.

of the investigation, rather than rush headlong into commencing a claim, can be a difficult task but it is one which the commercial fraud litigator must not shy away from in appropriate circumstances. This is particularly important when considering whether to pursue claims in deceit.

C. Analysis of Requirements

(1) X makes a false representation [of fact] to Y

(a) Must it be a representation of fact?

There are two schools of thought on this issue. Both will be outlined briefly here **2.07** so that the practitioner is aware of the arguments, but we need not dwell on them since both schools ultimately lead to the same answer in all cases, whether the representation is characterized as one of fact or of intention or opinion.

The first or traditional school of thought is that only representations of fact suffice **2.08** for the tort of deceit. Representations of intention or opinion in themselves do not suffice for the tort of deceit, but they usually contain an implied representation that the maker of the representation in fact holds the intention or opinion expressed and that does suffice. This approach, endorsed by *Clerk & Lindsell*,[12] finds ready support in the case law (see below).

Another way of looking at the traditional analysis is to maintain that a representa- **2.09** tion may be made directly, where the representation expressly states the relevant facts, or it may be made indirectly, where it is possible to derive from an otherwise irrelevant statement about intention or opinion, a representation of fact that the maker genuinely holds such an intention or opinion. In the indirect representation situation, the active representation is not the statement about intention or opinion but the implied statement which says that such an intention or opinion is in fact genuinely held by the maker.

The second school of thought,[13] whilst recognizing that it is possible to reconstrue **2.10** representations of intention or opinion in the manner advocated by the traditional analysis, suggests that the preferable approach is to discard the rule altogether and accept that deceit applies to 'any fraudulent statement which was intended to be acted upon by the representee'.[14]

---

[12] *Clerk & Lindsell on Torts* (19th edn, Thomson/Sweet and Maxwell, 2007), paras 18-09–18-13.

[13] That proposed by J Cartwright in his excellent *Misrepresentation, Mistake and Non-Disclosure* (2nd edn, Thomson/Sweet and Maxwell, 2006), para 3.33.

[14] ibid (2nd edn), para 5.08. The attraction of this approach, which does away with fine distinctions between fact and opinion, is that the rule focuses on the crucial issue which is whether the claimant has been deceived by what has been said. That really is the only issue worth considering and

2.11 The basis for this approach appears to lie in the fact that there is some case support for the proposition that even before the House of Lords decision in *Kleinwort Benson Ltd v Lincoln City Council*[15] had removed the bar on actionable mistakes of law, the courts had been willing to act on fraudulent misstatements of the law, since the fraudulent conduct of the maker of the statement prevents the parties from being *in pari delicto* (i.e. equally at fault for getting the law wrong). So, for example, in *Hirshfeld v The London, Brighton and South Coast Railway Co.*[16] the court allowed an action to proceed based upon a fraudulent misrepresentation of the legal consequences of a deed of release.[17] In *Andre & Cie S A v Ets Michel Blanc & Fils*[18] Geoffrey Lane LJ stated that whatever the arguments in favour of limiting misrepresentations to ones of fact and not law, he was unwilling to extend such reasoning to fraudulent misrepresentations of foreign law.[19]

2.12 While there is much merit in the Cartwright approach, and if it is necessary to choose between the two approaches, then the traditional analysis is probably to be preferred on the basis it has greater support. As set out below, it has the greater support in the authorities and the examples drawn upon by Cartwright in support of his suggestion that representations need not be of fact are all limited to fraud in the context of misstatements of the law as opposed to intention or opinion. That said, whichever analysis is favoured is unlikely to lead to different conclusions in any given case.

2.13 The requirement is that the representation must be made *to* Y. This is usually readily established in two-party situations in which the fraudster is dealing directly with the victim. But what happens if the fraudster is running an investment scam, such as a 'ponzi' scheme.[20] If the fraudster misrepresents the scheme directly to Y, then Y will have a clear claim. If Y happens to go off and tell some friends who then

---

it should matter not a jot the manner in which the deceiver went about his business. Any concerns of the court on whether the claimant should have been swayed or influenced by what the deceiver said can be dealt with by placing the burden on the claimant to establish he was so influenced in fact or, if the court wished to limit the availability of such claims to an objective test of what would influence an objective reasonable by-stander. It is doubtful whether the latter is a route we should go down in the case of deceit and, as for the former, so what if the claimant turns out to be gullible—that is hardly an argument that can come from the mouth of the deceiver.

15 [1999] 2 AC 349 HL.

16 (1876) 2 QBD 1.

17 See *Rashall v Ford* (1866) LR 2 Eq 750; *British Workman's and General Assurance Co Ltd v Cunliffe* (1902) 18 TLR 502; *Hughes v Liverpool Victoria Legal Friendly Society* [1916] 2 KB 482 CA.

18 [1979] 2 Lloyd's Rep 427 CA.

19 [1979] 2 Lloyd's Rep 427, 434. This case is not clear support for Cartwright's approach since the question of foreign law has always taken on a peculiar status as an issue of fact to be proved before the English court: see generally *Dicey, Morris & Collins* (14th edn), Rule 18.

20 A 'ponzi' scheme involves unusually high rates of returns which in fact are nothing more than monies taken from subsequent capital investors. The misrepresentation is that the investor is being paid *interest* rather than capital. If they knew it was the latter, they would immediately realize that the scheme was entirely dependent on constantly finding new investors.

decide to invest themselves without the fraudster repeating the misrepresentations, the issue arises whether they have been misled *by the fraudster* as such. There is no doubting that on the facts no misrepresentation has in fact been made to them by the fraudster but then equally likely is the fact that they are attracted to the investment scam because and only because Y happens to have innocently repeated the misrepresentations to them. It is submitted that if the court can be persuaded (and it is likely on the facts to be somewhat open to persuasion) that the fraudster knew or wanted Y to go off and tell his friends so that they would join, then the court can give a much wider interpretation to the class of individuals intended to act upon the misrepresentations.[21]

(i) Representations of intention As set out above, the main authorities favour **2.14** the traditional school of thought. The leading authority on misrepresentations relating to intention is *Edgington v Fitzmaurice*[22] where Bowen LJ remarked:

> The state of a man's mind is as much a fact as the state of his digestion. It is true that it is very difficult to prove what the state of a man's mind at a particular time is, but if it can be ascertained it is as much a fact as anything else.[23]

This case concerned a prospectus which invited subscriptions for debentures indicating that the monies raised were intended to be used to expand the business premises and purchase additional machinery. In fact, the directors intended to use the monies raised to pay off or reduce existing debts. The Court of Appeal held that there was a relevant misrepresentation of fact (as to the present intention to use the subscription monies) giving rise to the tort of deceit. So in a typical Nigerian advance fee fraud, the fraudster represents that the equivalent of several million pounds is wrongly being held in Nigeria (or some other country) and that if the victim is willing to pay over £50,000 to help with the process of releasing the monies, he will receive the grand sum of £1m. Typically, if the money (i.e. the £50,000) is paid over, the fraudsters invent additional scenarios to justify increasing the amount to be paid over. Whatever those scenarios, the fraudster has no intention of paying over any money and his representation (of intention) otherwise to the victim is actionable.

(ii) Representations of opinion Similarly, in the context of representations **2.15** about opinions, Lord Evershed MR in *Brown v Raphael*[24] stated that 'a statement

---

[21] Goldspink and Cole, *International Commercial Fraud* (Sweet and Maxwell, 2002) at para 2-16.

[22] (1885) 29 Ch D 459. The position differs under criminal law: *Reg v Dent* [1955] 2 QB 590, where the Court of Appeal (Crim Div) refused to apply the reasoning in *Edgington v Fitzmaurice*.

[23] ibid, 483.

[24] [1958] Ch 636. The matter proceeded in front of Lord Evershed MR on the basis of it being an innocent misrepresentation which induced the claimant to enter into a contract.

of opinion is always to this extent a statement of fact, that it is an assertion that the [maker] does in fact hold the opinion which he states'.[25]

2.16   **(iii) Representor in better state of knowledge than representee**   Further, if the maker of the statement is considered to be in a better state of knowledge of the matters contained within the representation than the recipient, a statement of opinion has also been taken impliedly to represent that the maker has good factual grounds for making it.[26] In reaching this conclusion in *Barings Plc (In Liquidation) v Coopers & Lybrand*,[27] Mr Justice Evans-Lombe emphasized that the *Brown v Raphael* test was to be applied to a representation by a professional man in a position where he would be expected to have significantly greater knowledge of the facts represented than did the representee.

2.17   On the facts, Evans-Lombe J found that the finance director had a far more detailed understanding of the financial statements of the company than its auditors could possibly have acquired after two to three weeks of investigation. Accordingly, the Court held that the finance director's representations included the implied representation that he had reasonable grounds for making the statements he did.

2.18   One might question how to interpret the reasoning of Evans-Lombe J consistently with that of the Court of Appeal in *Economides v Commercial Assurance*[28] where the Court of Appeal held that the maker of the statement of belief does not need to show he has an objectively reasonable basis for that belief. The test is one of honesty and not one based upon the existence of any form of duty of care.[29]

---

[25] ibid, 641. In *Bisset v Wilkinson* [1927] AC 177, Lord Merrivale remarked (at 182): 'A representation of fact may be inherent in a statement of opinion and at any rate the existence of the opinion in the person stating it is a question of fact.'

[26] See *Smith v Land and House Property Corporation* (1894) 28 Ch D 7 where Lord Evershed MR, following the approach of Bowen LJ in *Smith v Land and House Property Corporation* (1884) 28 Ch D 7, went on to find that in circumstances where the maker was in a better position of knowledge than the recipient, a statement of opinion also contained the representation that existed some good reason to believe that the opinion is true (643). In *Smith v Land and House Property Corporation*, the Court of Appeal found that the statement that X was a most desirable tenant contained an implied assertion that the maker of the statement knew of no facts suggesting otherwise; *Brown v Raphael* [1958] Ch 1636; *Clerk & Lindsell* (19th edn), para 18-12.

[27] [2002] EWHC (Ch) 461; [2002] PNLR 823, at paras 48–52.

[28] [1998] QB 587. Simon Brown LJ went on to add that if the insurers had wanted the assured to undertake detailed inquiries to support the valuations requested, they should have spelt out that requirement clearly (599–600).

[29] '. . . the plaintiff had to have some basis for his statement of belief in his valuation; he could not simply make a blind guess: one cannot believe to be true that which one has not the least idea about. But . . . the basis of belief does not have to be an objectively reasonable one . . . he was under a duty of honesty, not a duty of care' per Simon Brown LJ [1998] QB 587, 598.

Evans-Lombe J distinguished *Economides* on the grounds that the Court of Appeal **2.19** was there concerned with a representation made by a layman with no particular skills, as opposed to a representation made by a professional who could be expected to be in a better state of knowledge in respect of the matters relating to the representation.[30] Further, a lay person, unless expressly asked so to do, will not be expected to undertake the type of research which one can reasonably expect to underpin an answer or statement given by a professional.

(iv) Representations of law   All parties were originally expected to know the **2.20** law. The court therefore considered the representor and the representee to be *in pari delicto* (i.e. on an equal footing and equally responsible for any misunderstanding of the law) when considering whether to act on a misrepresentation of the law. In the absence of fraudulent intent, the court would refuse to act.

Such a position must now be re-assessed in the light of the House of Lords deci- **2.21** sion in *Kleinwort Benson Ltd v Lincoln City Council*[31] to remove the bar on recovery based upon a mistake of law (as opposed to fact). Given the removal of such a bar in the case of mistake, logically the same attitude must be shown to any misrepresentations relating to matters of law as well. This is indeed the case as held by the court (Rex Tedd QC) in *Pankhania v Hackney LBC*:[32]

> I have concluded that the 'misrepresentation of law' rule has not survived the decision in the *Kleinwort Benson* case. Its historical accident is as an off-shoot of the 'mistake of law' rule, created by analogy with it, and the two are logically interdependent . . . The distinction between fact and law in the context of relief from misrepresentation has no more underlying principle to it than it does in the context of relief from mistake. Indeed, when the principles of mistake and misrepresentation are set side by side, there is a stronger case for granting relief against a party who has induced a mistaken belief as to law in another, than against one who has merely made the same mistake himself. The rules of the common law should, so far as possible, be congruent with one another, and based on coherent principle. The survival of the 'misrepresentation of law' rule following the demise of the 'mistake of law' rule would be no more than a quixotic anachronism. Its demise rids this area of the law of a series of distinctions, such as the 'private rights' exception, whose principal function has been to distinguish the 'mistake of law' rule, and confine it to a very narrow compass, albeit not to extinguish it completely.

The judgment of Rex Tedd QC was quoted with approval by Maurice Kay LJ in *Brennan v Bolt Burdon (a firm)*[33] where it was described as a 'lucid and trenchant judgment'. It has been endorsed by the editors of *Halsbury's Laws of England*

---

[30]   See Peter Gibson LJ in *Economides v Commercial Assurance* [1998] QB 587, 606.
[31]   [1999] 2 AC 349.
[32]   [2002] EWHC 2441 (Ch), [2002] All ER (D) 22, [2002] NPC 123.
[33]   [2005] QB 303 at para10. See also Bodey LJ at para 25.

(4th edn re-issue (1999)), vol 32, para11 and *Chitty on Contracts* (29th edn, 2004), para 5-018.

2.22 Accordingly, it is unlikely now that a deceit claim would fail simply because the fraudulent statement was in relation to an issue of law as opposed to a pure representation of fact.

(b) In what way(s) can a representation be made? Words and conduct

2.23 A representation can be made in a variety of ways. The most obvious and uncontroversial is by way of an express statement of fact, which can, subject to one exception, be made orally, in writing or by conduct. The one exception relates to statements as to a third party's creditworthiness which, pursuant to s 6 of the Statute of Frauds Amendment Act 1828, has to be in writing and signed by the person against whom the action is brought. A recent example of this requirement is the Court of Appeal's decision in *Contex Drouzhba Ltd v Wiseman*[34] where a director signing a contract on behalf of the company containing a clear promise to make certain payments was held to have impliedly represented that the company had the capacity to meet its obligations under that contract. The director knew that to be untrue and was liable for deceit (along with the company).[35] The requirements of s 6 of the 1828 Act were satisfied.

2.24 Instead of uttering the representation himself, the defendant may simply adopt something said by a third party. That will suffice for the purpose of making a representation. In *Bradford Third Equitable Benefit Building Society v Borders*,[36] Viscount Maugham stated that a representation of fact is established 'where the defendant has manifestly approved and adopted a representation made by some third person'.[37]

2.25 Further, it may be possible to make a representation, not by uttering any words or adopting the words of others, but by clear and unequivocal conduct.[38] The oft-cited example is that of the defendant who dressed up as a student of a university in order to gain credit. He was convicted of obtaining by false pretences.[39] Similarly, by agreeing to appear in a scooter commercial, it was held that the *Spice Girls* had impliedly represented that they would not split up as a group during the running of that campaign.[40]

---

[34] [2007] EWCA Civ 1201.
[35] *Standard Chartered Bank v Pakistan National Shipping Corp (No 2)* [2002] UKHL, [2003] 1 AC 959.
[36] [1941] 2 All ER 204.
[37] ibid, 211.
[38] See e.g. *Gordon v Selico Ltd* (1986) 18 HLR 219 (taking steps to disguise presence of rot in a flat in order to encourage others to rent it).
[39] *R v Barnard* (1837) 7 C & P 784.
[40] *Spice Girls Ltd v Aprilia World Service BV* [2002] EWCA Civ 15, [2002] EMLR 510.

More recently, the act of pledging goods carried with it the implied representation **2.26**
that one is the owner of the goods and/or otherwise entitled or authorized to
pledge those goods. If, in fact, the goods belong to a third party and the [pledgor]
had no authorization to enter into any pledge arrangements, the [pledgor] may be
liable in deceit.[41]

An individual who had succeeded in an earlier auction for the purchase of goods **2.27**
and who decides to take those goods away from the auction impliedly represents
that he intends to pay for them.[42] Similarly, a defendant who enters a restaurant,
sits down at a table and orders from the menu impliedly represents that he has the
intention and ability to pay for the meal to be ordered.[43] The use of a forged signature on a mortgage application form or a bank transfer form is an actionable misrepresentation to the bank as to the true identity of the mortgage applicant or the
person wanting to transfer money.

Although the above examples illustrate that it may be possible to derive a repre- **2.28**
sentation from conduct without needing to rely upon the use of express words,
mere silence alone is not generally sufficient to give rise to deceit. So, for example,
the essence of an actionable deceit is that the defendant has *caused* the deception
and not simply that the defendant has failed to correct any misunderstanding it
knows the claimant is acting under.[44]

A claim in deceit may arise, however, in a situation where the defendant owes a **2.29**
duty to disclose and a failure to disclose is properly considered to be an implied
representation that there was nothing to disclose.[45]

**(2) X knows the representation is false, or has no belief in its truth or is
reckless as to whether or not it is true**

There are two aspects to this element. First, the representation must in fact be **2.30**
false. Secondly, the representor must know it is false or have no belief in its truth
or be reckless as to whether or not it is true.

(a) What is the relevant time to assess the falsity of such a representation?

For an actionable claim in deceit, the representation must be false at the time the **2.31**
representee relied upon it and was thereby caused loss.

---

[41] *Advanced Industrial Technology Corporation Ltd v Bond Street Jewellers Ltd* [2006] EWCA Civ
923, [2006] All ER (D) 21 (July).
[42] *Ex p Whittaker* (1875) LR 10 Ch App 446.
[43] See e.g. *DPP v Ray* [1974] AC 370 HL, such conduct sufficing for the purposes of criminal
'deception'. Although one might add the caveat that the diner is willing to pay for the meal 'so long
as it is as ordered and properly cooked'.
[44] *Peek v Gurney* (1873) LR 6 HL 377. Unless, of course, that misunderstanding is a direct result
of something said or done by the defendant.
[45] *Paul Simms v Michael Conlon & Ors* [2006] EWCA Civ 1749.

2.32 If the representation was false when made, but had become true by the time it was relied upon by the claimant, there is no deceit.[46]

2.33 If the representation was true when made but had become false by the time the claimant sought to rely upon it, that would give rise to a deceit unless it could be established that the representor had limited the effectiveness of his original representation to the time when made and not to any time thereafter.[47] However, in the latter case, the representor will only be liable for deceit if it can be shown, applying a subjective test, that the defendant's failure to correct the statement was dishonest conduct.[48] In other words, if the defendant does not in fact know that what he has said in the representation could be understood in the manner alleged by the claimant, he may have been careless in making the statement but he would not have acted dishonestly.

2.34 **(i) Representor's state of mind—representation made by the representor himself**

We are here concerned with a claim in deceit. It requires fraudulent conduct on the part of the representor. Mere carelessness does not suffice for deceit. This was settled in the House of Lords in *Derry v Peek*[49] where Lord Herschell set out clear guidance:

> First, in order to sustain an action of deceit, there must be proof of fraud, and nothing short of that will suffice. Secondly, fraud is proved when it is shewn that a false representation has been made (1) knowingly, or (2) without belief in its truth, or (3) recklessly, careless whether it be true or false. Although I have treated the second and third as distinct cases, I think the third is but an instance of the second, for one who makes a statement under such circumstances can have no real belief in the truth of what he states. To prevent a false statement being fraudulent, there must, I think, always be an honest belief in its truth. And this probably covers the whole ground, for one who knowingly alleges that which is false, has obviously no such honest belief. It matters not that there was no intention to cheat or injure the person to whom the statement was made.[50]

2.35 It is important to appreciate that the state of the representor's mind is directed towards the question of the falsity of the statement and not to whether he wishes to injure or cheat the claimant. Whilst it may appear a little striking at first, the latter is irrelevant to a claim in deceit.

2.36 The use of the word 'careless' by Lord Herschell is apt to confuse: it is being used in the 'had no care' sense—complete indifference to the truth—and not as a

---

[46] *Ship v Crosskill* (1870) LR 10 Eq 73.

[47] E.g. *Incledon v Watson* (1862) 2 F & F 841; *With v O'Flanagan* [1936] Ch 575; *Bradford Third Benefit Building Society v Borders* [1941] 2 All ER 205. See generally *Clerk & Lindsell* (19th edn), para 18-16.

[48] See Cartwright, *Mistake, Misrepresentation and Non-Disclosure* (2nd edn), para 5.18.

[49] (1889) 14 App Cas 337.

[50] ibid, 374.

means of incorporating some form of negligence into the test for deceit. Negligence has nothing to do with a claim in deceit.

The burden is on the representee to establish the representor's dishonesty and so **2.37** must prove that he did not have an honest belief in the representation's truth.[51]

(ii) **Representor's state of mind—representation made by employee** An **2.38** entirely innocent employer will be vicariously liable for a deceit committed by its employee in the course of his employment.[52] However, as made clear in *Credit Lyonnais Nederland NV v Export Credits Guarantee Department*[53] it is essential that all the elements of the tort of deceit are performed by the employee in the course of his employment. So if the employee was only liable for the deceit by combining acts within the course of his employment with those committed outside his course of employment, then the employer could not be vicariously liable. Such an approach makes sense since there is no basis for rendering an employer liable for *certain* acts undertaken by an employee outside the terms of his employment.

On the facts, in *Credit Lyonnais Nederland NV v Export Credits Guarantee* **2.39** *Department*,[54] the House of Lords held that the employee's acts of authorizing the guarantee with an intent to assist in a wrongful act did not amount to an actionable tort committed in the course of his employment, and therefore his employer was not vicariously liable for any loss caused to the bank.

(iii) **Representor's state of mind—representation made by an agent** One of **2.40** the main issues when determining whether and to what extent a principal is to be liable for the deceit of its agent is deciding how to deal with the state of mind requirement for this tort.

Based upon the guidelines provided by the Court of Appeal in *Armstrong v Strain*,[55] **2.41** *Bowstead & Reynolds*[56] has set out a series of propositions.

(a) The principal is liable if he authorized the agent to make the false representation which he (the principal) knew to be untrue (or did not believe to be true), whether the agent knew the truth or not.
(b) The principal is liable if, while not expressly authorizing the agent to make the false representation, he knew it to be untrue and was guilty of some positive

---

[51] *Derry v Peek* (1889) 14 App Cas 337, 374; *Glasier v Rolls* (1889) 42 Ch D 436, 458.
[52] *Lloyd v Grace, Smith and Co* [1912] AC 716; *Barings plc (in Liquidation) v Coopers & Lybrand* [2003] EWHC 1319, [2003] PNLR 639.
[53] [2000] 1 AC 486.
[54] ibid.
[55] [1952] 1 KB 232.
[56] *Bowstead & Reynolds on Agency* (17th edn, Sweet and Maxwell, 2001), para 8-185. See also Cartwright, *Misrepresentation, Mistake and Non-Disclosure* (2nd edn), para 5.21.

wrongful conduct, as by consciously permitting the agent to remain ignorant of the true facts, so as to prevent the disclosure of the truth to the third party, if the third party should ask the agent for information, or in the hope that the agent would make some false representation. The agent's representation when made would of course require to be within the scope of his actual or apparent authority.

(c) The principal is liable if the agent made the false representation fraudulently, it being within the scope of his actual or apparent authority and within the course of his employment, to make such a representation, sometimes even where the representation reached the third party by way of another agent, or by way of the innocent principal himself, because in such a case the innocent second agent or principal may be no more than a conduit for the fraud of the guilty agent.

(d) The principal is not liable if the agent made the false representation innocently, the principal knowing the true facts but not having authorized the agent to make the representation, nor knowing that it would be made, nor being guilty of fraudulent conduct as in (b) above.

(e) Conversely, the principal is not liable if he himself made the false representation innocently, notwithstanding that the agent knew the true facts.

2.42 A principal is liable in deceit in circumstances where his agent, acting within his actual or ostensible authority, knowingly or recklessly, makes a false statement intending that it be relied upon by the claimant.[57]

(3) X intends Y to rely upon the representation

2.43 In addition to having knowledge of the falsity of the statement, the representor must also be shown to have an intention that Y actually relies upon the false statement in the manner which caused loss or damage.[58] It is the knowledge of the falsity coupled with the intention that the representee rely upon the false statement that gives rise to the dishonest conduct required for deceit.

2.44 The relevant intention includes not only the obvious category of a desire by the representor that the representee will rely upon the false statements but also the situation where the representor is well aware that in the absence of unforeseen circumstances the representee will actually rely upon it. So, for example, where a purchaser is content to sign receipts for goods he knows have not been delivered and where he knows that the seller will be using those signed receipts to obtain bank finance, that suffices to establish liability on the part of the purchaser to the bank.[59]

---

[57] *Briess v Woolley* [1954] AC 333; *Bowstead and Reynolds on Agency* (18th edn, Thomson/Sweet and Maxwell, 2006), para 8-185.

[58] E.g. *Peek v Gurney* (1873) 6 LR HL 377, esp Lord Cairns at 411–13; *Bradford Equitable Building Society v Borders* [1941] 2 All ER 205, 211; *Kitcher v Fordham* [1955] 2 Lloyd's Rep 705; *Barton v County Natwest Ltd* [1999] Lloyd's Rep Bank 408.

[59] *Shinhan Bank Ltd v Sea Containers Ltd* [2000] 2 Lloyd's Rep 406.

This category of intention is likely to be relevant when considering the liability of **2.45** professionals. To open bank accounts, obtain finance, release funds or assets, transfer property, etc. it is usually necessary that certain forms are signed by professionals. If the professional is aware or reckless as to the truth of the contents of the document he is willing to sign or certify, he runs the real risk that he may subsequently be found to have deceived another professional who would typically rely upon the document so signed or certified in determining whether to act. On this approach, there is no requirement that the first professional in fact have any intention to deceive the second.

It is not necessary to establish that a particular individual was intended to rely **2.46** upon the statement, as opposed to an individual forming a particular category of individuals.[60] So for example, if documentation necessary for opening a bank account contains fraudulent misrepresentations there is no need to show that any particular individual within the bank was intended to rely upon them. It suffices that the completion of the bank forms and the sending them off to the bank indicates that an employee within the bank charged with the responsibility of dealing with account openings was intended to rely upon the misrepresentations contained within the documentation.

In *Goose v Sandford*[61] the Court of Appeal emphasized that the tort of deceit **2.47** required that the representee establish that the representor intended his statement to be understood by the representee in the sense in which it is false.[62] Where there is no ambiguity in the language used, that is unlikely to present any difficulty. The problems potentially arise where the statement is ambiguous. The Court of Appeal stated that in such circumstances, the representee is required to prove more than simply that on its ordinary meaning the representation was false.

The difficulty is illustrated by the facts of *Akerhielm v De Mare*.[63] The defendant **2.48** had made a representation (C) that 'one third of the share capital had been subscribed in Denmark'. This was not true as some had been allotted to persons resident in Kenya for services rendered in Denmark. Lord Jenkins, delivering the Speech of the Privy Council, made the following observations:

> The Court of Appeal construed the language of representation (c) as they thought it should be construed according to the ordinary meaning of the words used, and having done so went on to hold that on the facts known to the defendants it was impossible that either of them could ever have believed the representation, as so construed, to be true. Their Lordships regard this as a wrong method of approach.

---

[60] Viscount Maughan in *Bradford Equitable Building Society v Borders* [1941] 2 All ER 205, 211 talked in terms of 'a class of persons which will include the plaintiff'.

[61] [2001] Lloyd's Rep P N 189.

[62] See also *Barton v County Natwest Ltd* [1999] Lloyd's Rep Bank 408, 416, para 32; *Gross v Lewis Hilman Ltd* [1970] Ch 445, 459G–H.

[63] [1959] AC 789 PC.

The question is not whether the defendant in any given case honestly believed the representation to be true in the sense assigned to it by the court on an objective consideration of its truth or falsity, but whether he honestly believed the representation to be true in the sense in which he understood it albeit erroneously when it was made. This general proposition is no doubt subject to limitations. For instance, the meaning placed by the defendant on the representation made may be so far removed from the sense in which it would be understood by any reasonable person as to make it impossible to hold that the defendant honestly understood the representation to bear the meaning claimed by him and honestly believed it in that sense to be true . . . (For the general proposition that regard must be had to the sense in which a representation is understood by the person making it, see *Derry v Peek*;[64] . . . *Angus v Clifford*[65] . . .; *Lees v Tod*[66] . . . which authorities must in their Lordships' view be preferred to *Arnison v Smith*[67] . . . so far as inconsistent with them).[68]

(4) Y relies upon the representation

2.49 It suffices to show that a false representation is *a* cause of the representor acting in a certain way. It is not necessary to show it was *the* cause of the representor so acting or indeed that it was the main cause thereof.[69] If the representee would have acted in the same manner even without the misrepresentation, then reliance is not established.[70]

2.50 To assist in establishing whether there has been reliance, the court has devised certain presumptions to remove the need to be dependent entirely and solely upon the oral evidence of the representee and any material adduced in cross-examination. Cartwright expresses the position as follows:

A broader enquiry is therefore necessary and if the representation was 'material' in the sense that it is of such a nature that it would be likely to induce a person in the representee's position to take the action he claims he took, the court is entitled to infer that the representation was an inducement to his action, unless the representor can show the contrary. The materiality of the statement places on the representor the burden of adducing evidence to rebut the inference.[71]

---

[64] (1889) 14 App Cas 337.
[65] [1891] 2 Ch 449.
[66] (1882) 9 Rettie 807, 854.
[67] (1889) 41 Ch D 348.
[68] [2001] Lloyd's Rep P N 189, para 41.
[69] *Barton v County NatWest Ltd* [1999] Lloyd's Rep Bank 408, 421. The Australian decision of *Australian Steel & Mining Corpn Pty Ltd v Corben* [1974] 2 NSWLR 202, cited with approval by the Court of Appeal in *Barton v County NatWest*, makes it clear that the reliance need not take the form of a positive step. It is equally established where an individual, in reliance upon a false statement, maintains a course of conduct determined prior to receiving the representation.
[70] *Smith v Chadwick* (1883–84) 9 App Cas 187; *Nash v Calthorpe* [1905] 2 Ch 237 (omission to mention a company contract in a prospectus not shown to have any bearing on a shareholder's decision to purchase shares: reliance not established).
[71] Cartwright, *Misrepresentation, Mistake and Non-Disclosure* (2nd edn), para 5.25.

Accordingly, once it is established that a false representation is material (in the **2.51** sense that it was of a nature likely to induce the claimant to take the action he did), a presumption arises that the false representation was in fact relied upon unless and until the representor can show otherwise[72]—the presumption effectively shifts the burden of proof on to the representor that there has been no reliance at all.

(5) Y is caused loss and damage in reliance on the false statement[73]

Damage is at the heart of any claim in deceit. Without it, no claim could be pur- **2.52** sued. It is often called the *gist* of the action.[74]

As *McGregor on Damages*[75] correctly warns, it is necessary to be careful when **2.53** assessing damages for deceit. Very often the factual context will be that the deceit has resulted in the claimant having entered into a contract at a price he would not otherwise have paid. In these circumstances, it would be very easy to confuse the tortious and contractual measures of damages. A claim in deceit gives rise to tortious damages which are assessed on the basis, of the representation not having been made and not on a contractual basis, namely the representation which was made being true. So if the deceit led to the claimant entering into a contract for the purchase of shares, the settled rule is that the measure of damages is the price paid less the value received.[76] The value received is not necessarily the actual market price at the time of purchase if it can be shown that that market is a false one, having been misled by the deceit as well. If so, the proper approach, as per the House of Lords in *Smith New Court Securities v Scrimgeour Vickers*[77] is to work out the actual value of the shares in the market if the defendant's fraud was made known to the market and all relevant facts, previously concealed, known.

The correct measure of damages for a claim in deceit is the loss directly flowing **2.54** from the representee's reliance on the false statement—typically a sum sufficient to put the representee in the same position *as if he had not relied upon it.*[78]

---

[72] *Barton v County NatWest Ltd* [1999] Lloyd's Rep Bank 408. Both Morritt and Roch LJJ appeared to be under the misapprehension that such a presumption only arises if the statement is fraudulent. This is not so: see general discussion in Cartwright, *Misrepresentation, Mistake and Non-Disclosure* (2nd edn), para 3.53 citing *Mathias v Yetts* (1882) 46 LT 497.

[73] Treitel, 'Damages for Deceit' (1969) 32 MLR 556; *McGregor on Damages* (17th edn, Thomson/Sweet and Maxwell, 2003), paras 41-002–41-038; *Clerk & Lindsell* (19th edn), paras 18-36–18-44.

[74] *Smith v Chadwick* (1884) 9 App Cas 187, 190 (Lord Blackburn); *Diamond v Bank of London & Montreal Ltd* [1979] QB 333, 349 (Stephenson LJ).

[75] *McGregor on Damages* (17th edn), at para 41-002.

[76] See the CA decision in *Peek v Derry* (1887) 37 Ch D 541. Reversed by HL only on issue of liability. See also *McConnell v Wright* [1903] 1 Ch 546 CA.

[77] [1997] AC 254 HL.

[78] *Doyle v Olby (Ironmongers) Ltd* [1969] 2 QB 158, 167; *Clerk & Lindsell*, para 18-37.

2.55   Crucially, the claimant is not entitled to damages assessed on the basis that the false statement was in fact true. So, if the claimant has been misled into buying something he was told was worth £1m, when in fact it was only worth £300,000, and he paid £900,000 in the purchase price, his damages in a claim for deceit would be assessed at £900,000 minus the £300,0000, being £600,000.[79]

2.56   Similarly, the claimant cannot usually seek to recover by way of damages profits expected to be achieved had the statement been true.[80] The one exception to this general principle appears to be where it can be shown that had the statement been true, the claimant would have taken steps to carry out the same task albeit this time without a defective machine or object. So, in *BHP Biliton Ltd v Dalmine SpA*[81] the quality control employees of a subcontractor supplying pipes falsely certified those pipes as being sound. The pipes later leaked. The court allowed damages based on the pipes in fact being sound since had there not been a false certificate of the pipes, the defects would have been discovered and the defective pipes replaced by sound pipes.

2.57   Further, in limited circumstances, it may be possible to include loss of profits in a deceit damages claim. So, if the claimant can show that by virtue of relying upon the fraudulent statement, he has foregone profitable investment elsewhere, such profits would be recoverable as damages.[82] Such an avenue of recovery is also available in circumstances where it is not possible to show that the transaction into which the claimant has been fraudulently induced is itself loss-making.[83]

2.58   The relevant time for calculating damages will be important in a moving market. The general rule is that such damages are measured as at the date of reliance upon the representation.[84] Another date can be chosen if special factors arise such as the claimant being considered locked into the transaction, then damages can be assessed by reference to the later time.[85]

---

[79] *Doyle v Olby (Ironmongers) Ltd* [1969] 2 QB 158; see also *Pearson v Wheeler* (1825) Ry & M 303; *Saunders v Edwards* [1987] 1 WLR 1116 at 1121; *Smith New Court Securities Ltd v Citibank NA* [1997] AC 254, 282–382.

[80] *East v Maurer* [1991] 1 WLR 461.

[81] [2003] EWCA Civ 170, [2003] BLR 271.

[82] *East v Maurer* [1991] 1 WLR 461 where the claimant was able to recover profits he would have made had he purchased an alternative profitable business. See also *Clef Aquitaine SA v Laporte Minerals (Barrow) Ltd* [2001] QB 488. More recently, in *4 Eng Ltd v Roger Harper & Ors* [2008] EWHC 915 (David Richards J), the court allowed a claim based upon a loss of a chance that had the claimant not been deceived into purchasing a worthless company, X, there was an 80% chance it would have been able to purchase another company T, and it was therefore allowed income profits and a capital profit that would have been realizable by it on a sale.

[83] *Clef Aquitaine SA v Laporte Minerals (Barrow) Ltd* [2001] QB 488.

[84] *Twycross v Grant* (1877) 2 CPD 469; *McConnell v Wright* [1903] 1 Ch 546; *Smith New Court Securities Ltd v Scrimgeour Vickers (Asset Management) Ltd* [1997] AC 254, 267.

[85] ibid, 266

Although damages are considered at large in a deceit claim, there are precious few **2.59**
authorities dealing directly and expressly with recovery of consequential losses.
McGregor on Damages[86] provides:

> The wealth of authority on measure of damages disappears when it comes to conse-
> quential losses. Indeed, the measure as stated in the cases dealt with in relation to nor-
> mal measure would exclude consequential losses entirely. It is submitted that it is for
> this reason that Lord Atkin in *Clark v Urguhart*[87] suggested that the rule [i.e. price paid
> less actual value] as stated in *McConnell v Wright*[88] '*may be expressed in too rigid terms*'.
> In his view the measure of damages should be 'based on the actual damage directly
> flowing from the fraudulent inducement.' This formulation would easily include con-
> sequential lossess, and the propriety of recovery for such losses is supported by the
> decisions where conclusion of contracts other than the purchase of shares has been
> induced by the deceit; support is also derived from the expanding number of cases
> where negligent misrepresentation has brought about the conclusion of contracts and
> where it is now established that the same tortious measure applies as with deceit.

The recent decision of David Richards J in *4 Eng Ltd v Roger Harper & Ors*[89] is a
good illustration of the range of remedies potentially available to a victim of deceit.
The claimant company had been deceived by H into purchasing share capital in a
worthless company (X). The claimant obtained summary judgment on its claim
in deceit. The court held that the claimant was entitled to (i) damages based upon
the loss of the purchase price; (ii) recovery of costs and expenses incurred in making share acquisition; (iii) recovery of costs of investigating the extent of the fraud
by the claimant's managers. These costs were expressly stated to be recoverable as
compensation for cost of the investigation and not as an award of damage for business disruption under *Aerospace Publishing Ltd v Thames Water Utilities Ltd*;[90]
(iv) it was generally accepted that a claimant was in principle entitled to recover
damages for loss of profits based upon a missed alternative investment which is
established on the balance of probabilities: *East v Maurer*.[91] The court held that
the same approach should be adopted for such a claim based upon loss of a chance
so long as the loss of a chance claim was directly caused by the deceit. It was not
necessary to establish the foreseeability of the head of loss so long as it was caused
by the deceit. The court allowed the claim for presumed loss of income based on
loss of income profits up to the date of trial and thereafter loss of capital profits on
resale of alternative investment as at the date of trial, both subject to 20% discount
since it was assessed that there was an 80% chance the claimant would have been
able to purchase the alternative investment shares.

---

[86] *McGregor on Damages* (17th edn), para 41-20.
[87] [1930] AC 28.
[88] [1903] 1 Ch 546.
[89] [2008] EWHC 915 Ch.
[90] [2007] EWCA Civ 3.
[91] [1991] 1 WLR 461.

2.60 *Clerk & Lindsell* is more forthright in its view that deceit damages do indeed include, in principle, the right to recover consequential losses.[92] So, if a person has been forced to borrow money to be used as the purchase price for shares which he has been fraudulently induced to buy, he is entitled to recover the interest charged on the money borrowed.[93]

2.61 There has been some suggestion that it may be possible to obtain restitution of profits made through the deceit,[94] but the position remains unclear after the Court of Appeal decision in *Murad v Al-Saraj*[95] which suggested that the account of profits awarded by Etherton J was based upon the existence of a breach of fiduciary duty and not the deceit as such. It is also to be noted that in *Smith New Court Securities Ltd v Citibank NA*[96] Lord Steyn emphasized that the settled rule for deceit damages was the loss flowing from the victim having entered the transaction.

2.62 The Court of Appeal in *Halifax Building Society v Thomas*[97] was concerned with a mortgage fraud. Having discovered the deceit, the claimant building society exercised its contractual rights to sell the property. There was a surplus left after repayment of the loan. The claimant asserted an entitlement to the surplus but this was rejected by the Court of Appeal on the grounds that the claimant had affirmed the contract by exercising its contractual rights in selling the property. There are two possible routes to the surplus for the claimant. The first, and one which is generally considered as having been rejected by the Court of Appeal, is the assertion of a proprietary interest in the surplus—such a proprietary claim having got off the ground after rescission of the fraudulently induced loan transaction. But, on the facts, the claimant did not rescind: it affirmed the contract by exercising its contractual rights with knowledge of the fraud. The other potential route is to say that to allow the defendant to retain the surplus would be to allow him to become unjustly enriched by virtue of his own wrongdoing (fraud on the bank). This does not involve an assertion of a proprietary interest but does run up against the problem, as noted by Virgo,[98] that the

---

[92] *Clerk & Lindsell* (19th edn), para 18-42; *Cemp Properties (UK) Ltd v Dentsply Research and Development Corp* [1991] 34 EG 62.

[93] *Archer v Brown* [1985] QB 401. See also *Hornal v Neuberger Products Ltd* [1957] 1 QB 247.

[94] Goff and Jones, *The Law of Restitution* (7th edn, Thomson/Sweet and Maxwell, 2007), para 36-005 citing *Hill v Perrott* (1810) 3 Taunt 274; *Abbots v Barry* (1820) 2 Brod & B 369. Reliance was also placed on the comment, at first instance, by Etherton J in *Murad v Al-Saraj* [2005] EWCA Civ 959, that this was 'well established'. However, the majority of the Court of Appeal, considered that the account of profits was awarded not because of the deceit but because the defendant had breached his fiduciary relationship: see [2005] EWCA Civ 959 per Arden LJ at [46]. The relevance of fraud was to the allowances which would be made on an account of profits case for breach of fiduciary duty. For further discussion, see G Virgo, *The Principles of the Law of Restitution* (2nd edn, Oxford University Press, 2006), 473–4.

[95] [2005] EWCA Civ 959.

[96] [1997] AC 254, 283.

[97] [1996] Ch 217.

[98] *The Principles of the Law of Restitution* (2nd edn), 474–5.

surplus may be considered too remote to be recoverable. It is not at all clear that policy or principle dictate such a conclusion, after all the profits have only been obtained directly on the back of the purchase and subsequent sale of the house.

D. Miscellaneous Issues

(1) Contributory negligence as a defence

It is clear that contributory negligence under the Law Reform (Contributory **2.63** Negligence) Act 1945 is not available as a defence to a claim in deceit.[99] It is no defence to a claim in deceit for the defendant to say that the victim could have discovered the truth or even was careless in failing to discover the truth. The only issue that really matters is whether the victim in fact relied upon the false statement. If he did, then foregone or missed opportunities to discover the falsity of that statement will not give rise to any defence.[100] This remains the case even if the victim has been told the truth by a third party.[101]

(2) Civil Liability (Contribution) Act 1978

The court has jurisdiction to apportion losses as between more than one defend- **2.64** ant where each is jointly and severally liable to the claimant for the same damage even if not for the same deceit or tort.

(3) Limitation periods

A claim in deceit is subject to the usual tort limitation period of six years from the **2.65** accrual of the cause of action.[102] However, the fraud element of a claim in deceit means that the limitation period will not commence to run until the claimant has in fact discovered the fraud or could with reasonable diligence have discovered it.[103]

The test for whether or not a fraud has been discovered is whether the claimant is **2.66** aware or could with reasonable diligence have become aware of sufficient material facts in order to plead out such a claim.[104]

---

[99] *Standard Chartered Bank v Pakistan National Shipping Corp'n (Nos 2 and 4)* [2002] UKHL 43, [2003] 1 AC 959; *Alliance & Leicester Building Society v Edgestop Ltd* [1993] 1 WLR 1462; *Corporacion Nacional del Cobre de Chile v Sogemin Metals Ltd* [1997] 1 WLR 1396.

[100] *Attwood v Small* (1838) 6 Cl & Fin 232, 502–3.

[101] *Flack v Pattinson* [2002] EWCA Civ 1820 CA (claimant purchases a vintage car relying on representations it used to operate in Formula 1, notwithstanding evidence that a third party had previously told the claimant the car had not done so).

[102] Limitation Act 1980, s 2.

[103] Limitation Act 1980, s 32(1)(a).

[104] *Law Society v Sephton* [2004] EWCA Civ 1627, [2005] QB 1013. The burden is on the claimant to show he could not have discovered the fraud: *Paragon Finance Plc v D B Thakerar & Co* [1999] 1 All ER 400.

PART III

RECEIPT-BASED LIABILITY—AT COMMON LAW

3

UNJUST ENRICHMENT

A. Overview of Claim

The basic requirements for a claim in unjust enrichment may be summarized as follows:[1]   **3.01**

(1) Has the defendant ('D') been enriched?
(2) Was that enrichment at the expense of the claimant ('C')?
(3) Was the enrichment unjust?
(4) Are there any defences?
(5) What remedies are available to the claimant?

These five questions form the basic structure of any claim in unjust enrichment.   **3.02**
That is not to say, of course, that there is no debate as to whether these are the correct

---

[1] The structure of a claim in unjust enrichment involving the first four questions has been endorsed by Lord Steyn in *Banque Financiere de la Cite v Parc (Battersea) Ltd* [1999] 1 AC 221 (HL); Lightman J in *Rowe v Vale of White Horse DC* [2003] EWHC 388 (Admin), [2003] 1 Lloyd's Rep 418; Mance LJ in *Cressman v Coys of Kensington* [2004] EWCA Civ 47, [2004] 1 WLR 2775, CA. The fifth question comes from Sir Peter Millett in 'Restitution and Constructive Trusts' in Cornish, Nolan, O'Sullivan and Virgo (eds), *Restitution: Past, Present & Future* (Hart Publishing, 1998), 208.

questions to ask and if so how to answer them but there is, in general, a consensus about this approach.

B. Introduction

3.03   This is a practitioner's text on commercial fraud litigation. It is not a treatise on the law of unjust enrichment. It follows from that observation that the reader will not find in these pages a detailed treatment of the development of this area of the law. That development is well mapped-out in the leading texts.[2]

3.04   The purpose of this chapter is to identify the role to be played by the law of unjust enrichment in a typical commercial fraud setting. It is an important role precisely because, unlike most claims arising out of a commercial fraud, a claim in unjust enrichment is a matter of strict liability, where any fault on the part of the recipient is relevant only to the availability of defences.[3]

3.05   An examination of unjust enrichment fits neatly into one of the aims of this book which is to show that even if a case involves actual fraud, it may be in the client's better interests to pursue a claim which obviates the need to plead and prove the more difficult aspects of a fraud claim. Depending on the facts, of course, such a claim is likely to be more easily proved. Fault will only become relevant, if at all, as an issue in relation to the availability of defences such as change of position. So if the defendant is considered good for enforcement of any money judgment, serious consideration needs to be given to whether the benefits of pursuing the more difficult, time-consuming and undoubtedly more expensive fraud claim justify adopting that course of action rather than one in unjust enrichment.

3.06   A claim in unjust enrichment has certain advantages over the alternative common law claim of conversion.[4] It is wider in scope and includes the ability to recover money, when used as currency, which cannot form the basis of a conversion claim.[5] That said, unjust enrichment claims are subject to the defence of change of position which does not apply to conversion claims.

---

[2]   Charles Mitchell, 'Unjust Enrichment', in Burrows (ed), *English Private Law* (2nd edn, Oxford University Press, 2007), ch 18; Goff and Jones, *The Law of Restitution* (7th edn, Thomson/Sweet and Maxwell, 2007) (hereinafter *Goff & Jones*), ch 1; Birks, *Unjust Enrichment* (2nd edn, Clarendon Press, 2005); Burrows, *The Law of Restitution* (2nd edn, Butterworths, 2002), ch 1; G Virgo, *The Principles of the Law of Restitution* (2nd edn, Oxford University Press, 2006).

[3]   See e.g. *Kelly v Solari* (1841) 9 M&W 54. More generally, see Birks, 'The Role of Fault in the Law of Unjust Enrichment' in Swaddling and Jones (eds), *The Search for Principles: Essays in Honour of Lord Goff of Chieveley* (Oxford University Press, 2000).

[4]   See Ch 4.

[5]   Ordinary money does not fall within 'goods' for the purposes of the Torts (Interference with Goods) Act 1977, s 14(1); see para 4.18 *et seq*.

The limits of this chapter should be noted. It is concerned with unjust enrichment **3.07** and only a small part of that topic is directly relevant to a commercial fraud setting. Our principal concern lies with claims based upon mistake and/or ignorance, which are the most obvious candidates in a commercial fraud. Other examples where unjust enrichment may arise but which are not directly relevant to a commercial fraud case include duress, undue influence, necessity and payment under compulsion. None of these areas will be addressed in any detail but the five issues which need to be answered in any unjust enrichment claim will be closely examined in the text, enabling this claim structure to be imposed on any fact scenario.

Further, given this chapter is concerned with unjust enrichment, it will not be deal- **3.08** ing with topics which typically fall within the category of restitution for wrongs. A great deal of confusion has arisen by a failure properly to distinguish these two different types of claims. A claim in unjust enrichment focuses on the transferor and whether he had the necessary and proper intention to transfer the relevant assets. At the liability stage, there is no focus at all on the conduct of the defendant recipient. In a claim for restitution for wrongs, the focus is entirely upon the defendant (i) to establish the relevant 'wrong' he has committed, which can arise under any one of several different causes of action, e.g. breach of contract,[6] or in tort[7] or for breach of fiduciary duty[8] and (ii) to see what benefits or enrichment he has received as a result of that wrong. It is immediately evident that the reason for the claim is the commission of the wrong which has led to his being enriched. Accordingly, restitution for wrongs is an entirely different juridical concept to a claim in unjust enrichment.

In *Macmillan Inc v Bishopsgate Investment Trust plc (No 3)*,[9] Millett J drew the fol- **3.09** lowing distinction between these two types of claim:

> The English law of restitution makes a fundamental distinction between the unjust enrichment of the defendant which is occasioned by depriving the plaintiff of his

---

6 Birks, 'Misnomer' in Cornish et al (eds), *Restitution: Past, Present & Future*, 9–10.

7 ibid, commented on by McInnes, 'Misnomer: A Classic' [2004] RLR 79; Birks, *Unjust Enrichment* (2nd edn).

8 *Goff & Jones* (7th edn), n 1 explains that at the date of the first edition, 1966, the topic was unknown in England and they took the title of the book from the American Law Institute and called it *The Law of Restitution*. The learned editor (Professor Jones) recognizes the arguments in favour of the use of 'unjust enrichment' but concludes that they decided not to abandon their title which has become synonymous with unjust enrichment whilst recognizing that such a title may call for greater explanation in any given case. The problem with this approach is when readers come across bold statements such as 'Foskett v McKeown leads to the firm conclusion that English law does not recognize a restitutionary proprietary claim' (*Goff & Jones*, 86). It would have been more accurate to have said the House of Lords did not recognize a proprietary claim based upon unjust enrichment.

9 In *Macmillan Inc v Bishopsgate Investment Trust plc (No 3)* [1995] 1 WLR 978, 988, Millett J stated that restitution for wrongs is not based upon the principle of unjust enrichment.

property and enrichment which results from a wrong done to the plaintiff by the defendant. In the first category of case the plaintiff's restitutionary claim is said to have a proprietary base. The enrichment of the defendant is at the direct expense of the plaintiff and is matched by a corresponding diminution of his assets. The plaintiff brings the claim in order to recover his own property and must succeed, if at all, by virtue of his own title. In the latter class of case his claim arises from a breach of fiduciary or other obligation on the part of the defendant.[10]

C. Terminology

(1) Unjust enrichment v restitution

3.10 The reader might, not unreasonably, have expected this chapter to be called 'Restitution' rather than 'Unjust Enrichment' and some brief explanation is therefore merited.

3.11 Unjust enrichment is a cause of action, like contract or tort, which, if proven, will give rise to a remedy of restitution. This chapter is called 'Unjust Enrichment' because it is focusing on a particular cause of action which may arise in a commercial fraud. Restitution is not a cause of action but rather the remedy for a cause of action and that cause of action need not, in fact, lie in unjust enrichment. Focus on the nature of the cause of action gives a better understanding of the claim rather than focusing on the remedy to which that claim might give rise.

3.12 The use of 'unjust enrichment' over 'restitution' mirrors the approach adopted by Professor Birks in his later works, although it is accepted that many of the leading texts still utilize the name of restitution in their titles. There is nothing wrong with that approach in principle so long as the real nature of the underlying cause of action is understood.

3.13 By clearly distinguishing 'unjust enrichment' from 'restitution', it is hoped that additional clarity may find its way into the manner in which these claims are pleaded. There seems little point now to hark back to the old language of forms of action (i.e. money had and received, etc). It would be preferable to set out the claim including all material facts and clearly identify whether it is one in unjust enrichment by subtraction or in restitution for wrongdoing. And if it is the former, what unjust factor is being relied upon, what enrichment received, etc? At the moment, however, there appears to be some reticence on the part of the courts to recognize fully unjust enrichment as a separate cause of action. The view appears to be that it is nothing more than the principle underpinning certain established categories of claim, such as money had and received and so should not be separately

---

[10] ibid, 988.

pleaded as such.[11] In *South Tyneside Metropolitan BC v Svenska International Plc*, Clarke J said that unjust enrichment was not a new cause of action and 'is simply another way of describing the same thing'.

It is submitted that whilst it is correct that unjust enrichment underpins claims **3.14** such as money had and received, now that is expressly recognized, the principle should be allowed to come to the fore and be expressly pleaded. It is somewhat ironic that the courts are hanging onto the old language of quantum meruit, etc when pleaders are constantly being told elsewhere to use plain English language— for example, that a plaintiff now needs to be called a claimant and 'among others' to be used instead of 'inter alia'.

It is further suggested, with respect to the views expressed in these authorities, the **3.15** sooner unjust enrichment is expressly pleaded as a claim the better it will be for a more coherent development of the claim. The problem in some of these cases may well have been the manner in which the claim was pleaded. So long as the relevant issues are addressed in the pleading, it will be very difficult for a court to strike out such a claim.

Finally, there has been a gradual but clear move in the case law to adopting openly **3.16** the language of unjust enrichment ever since this cause of action was first recognized in English law in *Lipkin Gorman v Karpnale Ltd*[12] and *Woolwich Equitable Building Society v Inland Revenue Commissioners*.[13]

D. Unjust Enrichment and Contract

One of the difficulties to be faced when dealing with commercial fraud is the **3.17** potential overlap between contractual and unjust enrichment claims. Most commercial frauds involve some form of a contract. This gives rise to a difficult question: when is a claimant constrained to find his remedy within the law of contract and when is he permitted to bring a claim outside the contractual regime, making use of the law of unjust enrichment? Surprisingly, with some notable exceptions,[14] there is not as much guidance as one might expect in the leading texts on the interrelationship between contract and claims in unjust enrichment.

---

[11] *Uren v First National Home Finance Ltd* [2005] EWHC 2529, Ch [16] (Mann J); *Primlake Limited (In Liquidation) v Matthews Associates & Ors* [2006] EWHC 1227 (Ch); [2007] 1 BCLC 666 at [335].
[12] [1991] 2 AC 548.
[13] [1993] AC 70.
[14] Virgo, *The Principles of the Law of Restitution*, ch 2; Birks, *Unjust Enrichment*, 89–93; G McMeel, 'Unjust Enrichment, Discharge for Breach, and the Primacy of Contract' in A Burrows and Lord Rodger (eds), *Mapping the Law: Essays in Memory of Peter Birks* (Oxford University Press, 2006).

3.18 In short, where the law of contract and the law of unjust enrichment collide, it is the law of contract which prevails.[15] This well established proposition was confirmed in the recent decision of Cooke J in *Taylor v Motability Finance Ltd*:[16]

> Not only is it true that, historically, restitution has emerged as a remedy where there is no contract or no effective contract, but there is no room for a remedy outside the terms of the contract where what is done amounts to a breach of it where ordinary contractual remedies can apply and payment of damages is the secondary liability for which the contract provides.[17]

3.19 In *Taylor v Motability*, the court was concerned with an employment contract which had been terminated by the defendant. The claimant had fully performed his side of the contract. He argued that the termination by the defendant amounted to a repudiatory breach by the defendant entitling the claimant to seek relief outside the contract terms. Cooke J held otherwise, maintaining that the claimant was entitled to damages for having provided services for which he had not been paid. That was a contractual matter.

3.20 Cooke J went on to say:

> [24] . . . The decisions of the House of Lords in *Johnson v Agnew* [1980] AC 367, *Photo Products v Securicor Transport* [1980] AC 827 and *Lep Air Services Limited v Rollswin Investments Limited* [1973] AC 331 establish the position where there is a repudiation of the contract which is accepted or which is effective to bring the contract to an end. In those circumstances the contract is not rescinded ab initio, but future obligations are discharged from the moment the contract comes to end. All accrued rights remain in being and, so far as executor elements are concerned, the primary obligation to perform is replaced by a secondary obligation to pay damages.
>
> [25] The position is wholly different from that where money is paid for a consideration which wholly fails. In such a case there is a total failure of consideration and the money is recoverable. Although this means the payer may escape from the consequences of a bad bargain, there is no room for extending this to a situation where

---

[15] *Thomas v Brown* (1876) 1 QBD 714; *Dimskal Shipping Co Ltd v International Transport Workers Federation* [1992] 2 AC 152, 165 per Lord Goff; *Taylor v Bhail* (1995) 50 Con L R 70, 77 per Millett LJ; *Pan Ocean Shipping Co v Creditcorp Ltd ('The Trident Beauty')* [1994] 1 All ER 470, 473–4, per Lord Goff.

[16] [2004] EWHC 2619, Comm. See also, Virgo, *The Principles of the Law of Restitution* (2nd edn), 40–2; Grantham and Rickett, 'On the Subsidiarity of Unjust Enrichment' (2001) 117 LQR 273; Burrows, *Understanding the Law of Obligations* (Hart Publishing, 1998), ch 2.

[17] [2004] EWHC 2619, Comm, para 23. Cooke J was influenced by the comments of Lord Goff in *Henderson v Merrett* [1995] 2 AC 145 at 193 where Lord Goff said there could be no concurrent liability in contract and tort if the tortious liability was so inconsistent with the contractual liability that it must be taken to have been excluded by the parties. The same approach applied with contract and restitution. But see A Tettenborn, 'Subsisting Contracts and Failure of Consideration' [2002] RLR 1 where Professor Tettenborn argues that there are at least three circumstances where it may be possible to raise a restitutionary claim notwithstanding the fact that the contract has not been terminated. The author of *Goff & Jones* (para 1-063, n 89) is not convinced.

both parties have performed substantially and there is a full and adequate remedy for breach of contract which will compensate the claimant for any loss suffered. The point is clearly set out in *Goff & Jones* . . . paragraphs 20-007 and between paragraphs 20-019 and 20-023. The authors there say that there is no English authority to suggest that an innocent party, who has rendered services or supplied goods, may elect to sue in restitution if he has performed or substantially performed his part of the contract. If therefore he can claim under the contract whether in debt or in damages, that is the true measure of his entitlement, because it is that which he bargained for. If it were otherwise, not only would the claimant be able to recover more than his contractual entitlement in respect of bonus, but he could also seek to establish that he was underpaid in terms of salary despite his agreement thereto.

[26] Moreover, . . . there can also be no justification, even if a restitutionary claim is available, for recovery in excess of the contract limit. Such recovery in itself would be unjust since it would put the innocent party in a better position than he would have been if the contract had been fulfilled. In deciding any quantum meruit regard must be had to the contract as a guide to the value put upon the services and also to ensure justice between the parties . . .

It is essential that the relationship between the existence of a contract and the **3.21** entitlement to bring a claim in unjust enrichment is properly understood. In essence, a claim in unjust enrichment must not interfere with the ability of the law of contract, and the remedies available thereunder, to deal with a contractual situation. Accordingly, in a time charter dispute concerning the recovery of overpaid hire, the House of Lords held in *Pan Ocean Shipping Ltd v Creditcorp Ltd* [18] that the existence of a contractual regime to deal with the issue of overpayments negated any resort to unjust enrichment. Lord Goff observed: ' . . . as between shipowner and charterer, there is a contractual regime which legislates for the recovery of the overpaid hire. It follows that, as a general rule, the law of restitution has no part to play in the matter; the existence of the agreed regime renders the imposition by the law of a remedy in restitution both unnecessary and inappropriate. Of course, if the contract is proved never to have been binding, or if the contract ceases to bind, different considerations may arise . . . '

It is sometimes said that the availability of claims in unjust enrichment must await **3.22** the termination of the contract. It is certainly true that a claim in unjust enrichment will not arise whilst the contract is afoot. However, it is not every case where the contract has been terminated that the door is open to a claim in unjust enrichment. It may well be that the contract has stipulated liquidated damages or restricts the entitlement to recover damages generally. It may be that damages are due for partial performance as Cooke J indicated above.

---

[18] [1994] AC 161.

3.23 The following guidance can be suggested.[19]

- If the breach of contract occurs after both parties have substantially performed their contractual obligations, any remedies will be a matter for the law of contract and not the law of unjust enrichment.[20]

- If the contract's terms provide for post-termination restriction on damages those terms will determine the appropriate remedy.

- If the breaching party has conferred a benefit on the other contracting party who has yet to provide any benefits under the contract, then no issue of unjust enrichment can arise. In this example, the only benefit received is that given *to* the claimant.

- If the breaching party has not performed any of its obligations, whilst the claimant has done so, then, so long as the breach is of sufficient importance to qualify as repudiatory, then the claimant can terminate the contract and pursue a claim in unjust enrichment (failure of consideration).

- If the contract is found to be void, then a claim in unjust enrichment may arise for any benefits transferred thereunder.[21]

E. Elements of Liability

3.24 In *Banque Financiere de la Cite v Parc (Battersea) Ltd*,[22] Lord Steyn, effectively adopting Birks' structure for a claim in unjust enrichment, laid down the following guidelines:

- Has D been enriched?
- Was D's enrichment at the expense of C?
- Was the enrichment unjust?
- Are there any defences?[23]
- What remedies are available?

---

19 Virgo, *The Principles of the Law of Restitution* (2nd edn), 41.
20 *Taylor v Motability Finance Ltd* [2004] EWHC 2619, Comm at [25].
21 *Westdeutsche Landesbank Girozentrale v Islington LBC* [1996] AC 669 (swaps litigation where contracts were void and the unjust enrichment claim arose from total failure of consideration).
22 [1999] 1 AC 221, 227 per Lord Steyn.
23 This structure has also been endorsed in *Rowe v Vale of White Horse DC* [2003] EWHC 388 (Admin), [2003] 1 Lloyd's Rep 418 (Lightman J); *Cressman v Coys of Kensington (Sales) Ltd* [2004] EWCA Civ 47, [2004] 1 WLR 2775 (CA). See also Lord Millett, writing *extra-judicially* in 'Restitution and Constructive Trusts' in Cornish et al (eds), *Restitution: Past, Present and Future*.

(1) Has D been enriched?[24]

The core allegation at the heart of a claim in unjust enrichment is that D has been **3.25**
enriched at the expense of the claimant, C. In the context of commercial fraud, it
is unlikely that this will represent much of a problem since the type of activities
which are the focus typically, although not always, operate around the illicit receipt
and transfer of money.

Receipt of money is undoubtedly a benefit or enrichment of D, regardless of D's **3.26**
actual attitude towards money.

The question of D's enrichment can be a difficult question, however, when the **3.27**
form of enrichment is other than a money payment. As stated above, this is
unlikely to feature heavily in commercial fraud scenarios and so there is no need
for the reader to dwell on the complex issues arising from examples such as a window cleaner who performs the task of cleaning without having first obtained the
property owner's agreement so to do.[25] Modern international commercial fraud
fortunately involves few window cleaners.

What is proposed is to make the reader aware of the various differing arguments **3.28**
which are at play, some having the authority of case law to support them, others
being based solely on academic opinion. So long as the reader is aware of the range
of arguments on this issue and has been pointed towards further reading on them,
that will enable him to pursue further lines of enquiry in the event that the issue
of enrichment proves troublesome on the facts of any given case.

The principal issue arising when the form of enrichment is not money is the **3.29**
extent to which D can refuse to pay on the grounds that those goods or services
were not something he would otherwise have purchased himself. This entitlement
to refuse to pay or perhaps to reduce the amount D might otherwise have to pay
is said to derive from the fact D did not himself request any of the goods and services which are said to have enriched D. In such circumstances, D is said to be
entitled to subjectively devalue the goods or services.

This issue has generated a great deal of debate amongst academics as to how one **3.30**
properly goes about the process of subjective devaluation. The more important of
such arguments will be identified briefly below. However, they will all need to be
placed in their proper context, namely a commercial fraud. Whilst the advantage
of a claim in unjust enrichment is that it is a matter of strict liability, the fraudulent aspect of D's conduct is unlikely to be ignored when it comes to any attempt

---

[24] For a most comprehensive and lucid account of the issues relating to the question of enrichment, see Virgo, *The Principles of the Law of Restitution* (2nd edn), ch 4.
[25] The famous example employed by Professor Birks to discuss the issue of free acceptance: *An
Introduction to the Law of Restitution* (revised paperback edn, Clarendon Press, 1989), ch VIII.

by D to rely upon the principle of subjective valuation. Perhaps the best way to sum up the position is simply to record that it will be very difficult for D, if proven to be involved in fraudulent or unconscionable conduct, to be able to rely upon the principle of subjective devaluation in an attempt to deny or reduce the level of liability for unjust enrichment.

(a) Receipt of money

3.31 This is the most likely form of enrichment in a commercial fraud and equates with the common law claim of money had and received. It gives rise to no difficulties of assessing enrichment since money is always considered to be an enrichment in the hands of D. Subjective devaluation is not available to D in respect of receipt of money. D can always simply return the enrichment received to meet his obligations under the law of unjust enrichment. In the event that this is no longer possible, D will need to rely upon the change of position defence discussed below.

3.32 This was made clear by Robert Goff J in *BP Exploration Co (Libya) Ltd v Hunt (No. 2)*,[26] where his Lordship stated:

> . . .[I]t is always necessary to bear in mind the difference between awards of restitution in respect of money payments and awards where the benefit conferred by the plaintiff does not consist of a payment of money. Money has the peculiar character of a universal medium of exchange. By its receipt, the recipient is inevitably benefited; and (subject to problems arising from such matters as inflation, change of position and the time value of money) the loss suffered by the plaintiff is generally equal to the defendant's gain, so that no difficulty arises concerning the amount to be repaid. The same cannot be said of other benefits, such as goods or services. By their nature, services cannot be restored; nor in many cases can goods be restored, for example when they have been consumed or transferred to another. Furthermore the identity and value of the resulting benefit to the recipient may be debateable. From the very nature of things, therefore, the problem of restitution in respect of such benefits is more complex than in cases where the benefit takes the form of a money payment . . .

3.33 Whilst we are no longer constrained by the old forms of action method of pleading, it is perhaps worth recalling that attempts to shoe-horn into the claim for money had and received claims based upon receipt of benefits other than money but which can be objectively valued have proved fruitless.[27] The court typically insisted that such claims fell within the other forms of action, quantum valebat, quantum meruit and money paid to the use of a third party, which all involved some element of request on the part of D. As will be discussed below, the request element plays an important role in whether or not a non-money benefit can be subjectively devalued.

---

[26] [1979] 1 WLR 783 (QBD), [1983] 2 AC 352 (HL).
[27] *Nightingall v Devisme* (1770) 5 Burr 2589, 2 Wm Bl 684.

(b) Non-money receipt

Once one moves away from the receipt of money, one moves immediately into an **3.34** area of uncertainty with competing and differing judicial and academic opinions. Central among these theories is the idea of choice. The moment one begins talking about a benefit other than in money is the moment the recipient is able to say he or she would not have chosen to have purchased that object or service. Others may place a value upon that matter but the actual recipient does not. As will be seen there is much force in this argument and it can, if fully proven, refute the suggestion that a particular non-money benefit represents an enrichment. On the other hand, there exists certain types of non-money benefit (e.g. incontrovertible benefit) where the recipient is not permitted to deny enrichment on the basis he would not himself have chosen the benefit.

In no particular order, the following theories should be noted:[28]   **3.35**

- *Incontrovertible benefit.*[29] An incontrovertible benefit is said to be one where there is no scope for a subjective devaluation.[30] If the recipient has been saved an inevitable expense, he can hardly complain that he would not have been called upon at some point to pay that bill. This concept has received the support of Robert Goff J in *BP Exploration Co (Libya) Ltd v Hunt (No 2)*[31] in the context of the Law Reform (Frustrated Contracts) Act 1943.

  Other examples of incontrovertible benefit include payment of another's debt under compulsion of law[32] and circumstances where an individual seeking to recover his own property is required to discharge a lien imposed over those goods due to another's debt.[33]

  Although both *Goff & Jones* and Birks endorse the concept of incontrovertible benefit, there is a subtle but important difference in approach. The former favour an approach based upon realizable benefits so that the non-monetary benefit need not first be converted into cash in order to ascribe a value to it.[34]

---

[28] For an excellent overview of these theories, see Burrows, *The Law of Restitution* (2nd edn), 18–25.

[29] *Goff & Jones* (7th edn), paras 1-023–1-026.

[30] In *Regional Municipality of Peel v Her Majesty* (1992) 98 DLR (4th) 159, 160, McLachlin J remarked: '[an] "incontrovertible benefit" is an unquestionable benefit, a benefit which is demonstrably apparent and not subject to debate and conjecture . . . [it] is limited to situations where it is clear on the facts (on balance of probabilities) that had the plaintiff not paid, the defendant would have done so. Otherwise, the benefit is not incontrovertible.'

[31] [1979] 1 WLR 783 (Robert Goff J). See also Hirst J in *Proctor & Gamble Philippine Manufacturing Corpn v Peter Cremer GmbH* [1988] 3 All ER 843.

[32] *Goff & Jones* (7th edn), ch 15.

[33] *Kleinwort Benson plc v Vaughan* [1996] CLC 620 CA. For a detailed treatment of this particular issue, see Sutton, 'Payments of Debts Charged Upon Property' in Burrows (ed), *Essays on the Law of Restitution* (Clarendon Press, 1991).

[34] *Goff & Jones* (7th edn), para 1-023.

Birks is of the view that it cannot represent an actual benefit in the hands of the recipient until it has been exchanged for cash.[35]

- *Free acceptance.* This view found favour in English law prior to any notion of incontrovertible benefit. The courts considered that a request was necessary before a defendant could be expected to pay for a non-monetary benefit. Otherwise, there was a real risk that the recipient would be obliged to pay for benefits he did not want. As Pollock CB once famously remarked:

> One cleans another's shoes. What can the other do but put them on?[36]

Goff & Jones explains the principle thus:

> In our view, he will be held to have benefited from the services rendered if he, as a reasonable man, should have known that the claimant who rendered the services expected to be paid for them, and yet he did not take a reasonable opportunity open to him to reject the proffered services. Moreover, in such a case, he cannot deny that he has been unjustly enriched.[37]

It has been pointed out,[38] however, that a failure to speak up when the opportunity arises is not necessarily determinative that the silence amounts to an acceptance that it would be appropriate to charge the individual for the unrequested work. The recipient may be entirely ambivalent to the work, not caring one way or the other as to whether it is done. Such an argument simply leads to the question whether it is appropriate that one person should allow another to continue to provide services, expecting to be paid, when the recipient does not value those services. It is submitted that the conduct of the homeowner who refuses to speak up when he knows that the window cleaner is expecting payment is not the kind of conduct that merits protection or indeed encouragement. It is not onerous or burdensome for him to make his views known to the cleaner who can then decide whether to continue or not. If he has a ready opportunity to inform the cleaner, it is not burdensome for him to take up that opportunity and inform the cleaner, and he chooses not to do so, he should be taken to have accepted the work done and that it needs to be paid for. It would be otherwise if the work was completed before the homeowner had an opportunity to express his view. In those circumstances, there would be nothing untoward in the conduct of the homeowner and the cleaner simply runs foul of the risk he openly chose to undertake.

Whilst recognizing the force of Burrows' comments as to ambivalence, Birks has nevertheless defended the concept of free acceptance as being relevant to the determination of the receipt of benefits on the grounds that the recipient's conduct,

---

[35] Birks, *An Introduction to the Law of Restitution* (Clarendon Press, 1985), 121.
[36] *Taylor v Laird* (1856) 25 LJ Ex 329, 332.
[37] *Goff & Jones* (7th edn), para 1-019.
[38] Burrows, 'Free Acceptance and the Law of Restitution' (1988) 104 LQR 576, 577–80.

amounting to free acceptance, bars him from raising arguments based upon subjective devaluation.[39]

The principle of free acceptance has received some recent judicial endorsement by Lightman J in *The Queen (On the application of Charles Rowe) v Vale of White Horse FC*,[40] and by Mance LJ in *R McDonald v Coys of Kensington*,[41] though in both cases the argument failed on the facts.

In the context of a commercial fraud, it is difficult to imagine many situations in which a fraudster who has deceived a claimant into parting with a non-monetary asset will be able to say that he has not freely accepted that asset such as to bar him from raising subjective devaluation arguments.

- *Bargained-for test.* It was noted above that Burrows rejected the notion of free acceptance espoused by *Goff & Jones* and Birks. The heart of his rejection of this principle was the fact that free acceptance did not establish that the recipient *valued* the benefit received. He could equally be entirely neutral as to whether he received it or not. To overcome this, Burrows argues that the principle of free acceptance should be replaced by a bargained-for test. If a party receives even part only of what he had bargained for then he cannot claim he has not been enriched. But even this test can be questioned. If the bargain was for a shed to be built in my garden and only half a shed is built, Burrows would say that since I bargained for a shed I cannot complain that half a shed has no value to me. Certainly I cannot deny I wanted a shed but I have not got a shed, I have received a half botched job. Of itself, it has no value to me—I never bargained for a half-done job, would never have agreed to pay the other party to build me half a shed and then disappear, hoping I might be able to get someone else to finish it off. The bargain was for a full shed.

  It remains to be seen how far the courts will go to endorse this theory. Burrows himself accepts that it has not been expressly approved in any case but maintains it provides a ready explanation for many of the cases in this area.[42]

- *Reprehensible seeking-out test.* It will be recalled that one of the criticisms laid at the door of the free acceptance principle by Burrows was the fact that it includes the situation where an individual simply stands by and does nothing and yet he would be taken to value the benefit received by him. As Burrows has pointed out, such an individual could equally be indifferent to the receipt of the benefit.

---

[39] Birks, 'In Defence of Free Acceptance' in Burrows (ed), *Essays on the Law of Restitution*, 105–46. See also Virgo, *The Principles of the Law of Restitution* (2nd edn), 87–8, although Virgo recognizes that here free acceptance is acting along the lines of an estoppel without the usual representation and/or reliance element being satisfied.

[40] [2003] 1 Lloyd's Rep 418 at [12].

[41] [2004] EWCA Civ 47; [2004] 1 WLR 2775 at para 32.

[42] Burrows, *The Law of Restitution* (2nd edn), 23.

In other words, as far as Burrows is concerned, free acceptance does not necessarily establish value being ascribed to the non-monetary benefit by the recipient and on Birks' revised position (see above), there is a blurring between issues of enrichment and whether that enrichment is unjust. Burrows maintains none of these difficulties arise with the reprehensible-seeking out test:

> Clearly this test runs close to free acceptance. But it is crucially distinct because in requiring a 'seeking-out' of the benefit rather than a 'standing-by' it overcomes the indifference argument. Moreover this test is a test of benefit only. It is not intended to establish that the enrichment is unjust.[43]

In the reprehensible seeking-out test, the recipient has positively taken steps to obtain the benefit received and thus cannot logically assert a general indifference to its value (thereby avoiding the criticisms of the free acceptance principle). So benefits obtained by duress or with a gun held to one's head would fall within such a test.

Again, it is worth the practitioner noting that this test has been devised to overcome what some consider are the pitfalls of the free acceptance test of benefit, namely that it equally includes neutral valuation. To date, it has not received express support in any case law. There is little doubt that should a recipient pass the 'reprehensible seeking-out' test it is unlikely that he will be permitted to raise arguments based upon subjective devaluation. That said, whilst accepting the force of much of what Burrows says about free acceptance, it is submitted that it is not an onerous burden to place a positive duty on an individual to say he does not want a service that is being performed and for which he knows the performer intends to charge.

So, going back to the famous Pollock CB example of a man cleaning another's shoes, it is, with respect, not a great deal to ask for the owner of the shoes to tell the cleaner to stop or make it clear that there would be no payment should he continue to clean. If the owner forgoes that clear opportunity, he cannot expect to pay nothing for his cleaned shoes.

(2) Was D's enrichment at the expense of C?

3.36 This question has nothing to do with quantum and everything to do with the issue of proper title to sue.[44] It establishes the nexus as between payee and payor so as to justify the claimant payor being able to say that the payee has been unjustly enriched at the payor's expense.

---

[43] Burrows, *The Law of Restitution* (2nd edn), 25.

[44] *Kleinwort Benson plc v Birmingham City Council* [1997] QB 380 CA. At 393, Evans LJ stated: ' "At his expense" in my judgment, serves to identify the person by or on whose behalf the payment was made and to whom repayment is due . . .'.

(a) Privity

The requirement of 'at the expense of' also introduces a somewhat controversial **3.37**
restriction on the availability of a claim in unjust enrichment—namely, that a
claim in unjust enrichment will generally only arise in respect of direct recipients
of the enrichment.[45] As Morritt LJ confirmed in *Kleinwort Benson v Birmingham
City Council,* the phrase 'at the expense of' does:

> no more than point to the requirement that the immediate source of the unjust
> enrichment must be the claimant.[46]

But what is the justification for this limitation on this claim? Some commentators **3.38**
say that the argument in favour of a claim is simply stronger as against an immediate recipient than as against a subsequent recipient, who may know nothing of the
original transferor.[47] In itself, it is difficult to see that this gives any principled justification for the rule. Others have contended that the subsequent recipient is in
lawful receipt of the enrichment received from the immediate recipient and the
original transferor cannot now interfere with that receipt.[48]

It would appear that the restriction is premised upon a mistaken assumption that **3.39**
a claimant would only have title to sue as against an immediate recipient and not
any subsequent recipient. In order to bring a claim in common law for unjust
enrichment, a claimant must show that the recipient received assets which
belonged, at law, to the claimant. This is readily satisfied in a typical two-party
scenario. But, as illustrated by the facts of *Lipkin Gorman v Karpnale Limited*[49] it
is not limited to a two-party scenario.

The facts are well known but can be briefly summarized as follows. **3.40**

- Cass, a partner in a firm of solicitors, wrongly withdrew monies from the client
  accounts and gambled it away at a club. The solicitors brought a claim for
  money had and received against, *inter alia*, the club. The difficulty for the solicitors was to show that the monies that the club received *legally* belonged to
  the solicitors. If not, no common law claim could be maintained. The problem
  was that there was strong authority that Cass, as a partner in the solicitors,
  obtained good title to the monies upon their unauthorized withdrawal from the
  bank.

---

[45] *Colonial Bank v Exchange Bank of Yarmouth, Nova Scotia* (1885) 11 App Ca 84, 85; Sir P
Millett, 'Tracing the Proceeds of Fraud' (1991) 107 LQR 71, 79.
[46] Morritt LJ in *Kleinwort Benson v Birmingham City Council* [1997] QB 380, 400.
[47] Virgo, *The Principles of the Law of Restitution* (2nd edn), 106–7.
[48] Tettenborn, 'Lawful Receipt—A Justifying Factor' (1997) 5 RLR 1. Virgo welcomes
Tettenborn's approach: *The Principles of the Law of Restitution* (2nd edn), 106–7.
[49] [1991] 2 AC 548, HL.

- The House of Lords refused to overrule the problematic authorities[50] and instead held that whilst the monies were in the bank account, the solicitors had a chose in action against the bank in the relevant amount; when the monies were wrongly withdrawn, Cass may have legally obtained good title to the cash, but nevertheless that cash represented the exchange-product for the solicitors' original chose in action against the bank.

- By adopting an analysis which draws a distinction between cash and chose in action, the House of Lords was able to provide a remedy to the solicitors where none might otherwise have existed had the focus been entirely on the cash.

- However, it is an approach which has opened the door to many further issues. It rather suggests that both the solicitors and the rogue partner held title to the cash withdrawn from the client's account at one and the same time. This clearly could not be the case, but the true nature of the solicitors' interest in the cash remains unclear. This issue is discussed in more detail in the section dealing with the problems of geometric progression.[51]

(b) The problem of geometric multiplication of title

3.41 This issue has been touched upon already in our discussion of *Lipkin Gorman*. This problem is best considered by way of an example. A thief (X) steals £5,000 from the claimant and uses it to purchase a painting from Y, who knows that X is using stolen monies. In these circumstances, prima facie, the claimant is entitled to trace both the £5,000 in the hands of Y (who cannot rely upon a defence of bona fide purchaser for value without notice) and also the painting received by X. But can it really be correct to say that the claimant owns both the £5,000 *and* the painting? Must he elect? What is the position of ownership prior to election?

3.42 The authorities are not consistent in their approach. There are those, such as *Cave v Cave*,[52] *Jones v Jones*[53] and *Boscawen v Bajwa*,[54] which suggest the immediate vesting of full ownership (i.e. no need for any election) without really examining the problems that conclusion may cause in other factual situations. Others see decisions such as that of the House of Lords in *Lipkin Gorman* as consistent with an approach which did not support the immediate vesting of full ownership, but rather one which advocated in some form a clear election by the claimant as to which asset full title was being claimed.

---

[50] Ie those that established that title in the withdrawn cash vested in the partner: *Union Bank of Australia Ltd v McClintock* [1922] 1 AC 240; *Commercial Banking Co of Sydney Ltd v Mann* [1961] AC 1.

[51] See Professor Birks' analysis in 'Mixing and Tracing: Property and Restitution' (1992) 45 CLP 69.

[52] (1880) 15 Ch D 639, a case dealing with equitable interests.

[53] [1997] Ch 159.

[54] [1995] 4 All ER 769.

The problem of geometric progression is said to be particularly acute for those **3.43** proponents of the theory, now fully endorsed by the House of Lords in *Foskett v McKeown*, that proprietary claims are based upon the vindication of pre-existing property rights and have nothing to do with the law of unjust enrichment. For these, it is difficult not to be forced to the conclusion that the claimant owns both the £5,000 and the painting at the same time on the basis that it is the act of substitution, without more, which gives rise to the proprietary interest in the substitute product.

Those, such as Burrows, who hold to the view that the true reason for the claimant **3.44** being able to assert ownership over the substitute is the fact that the defendant would otherwise be unjustly enriched, are able to point to the fact that a claimant, who brings a claim based upon unjust enrichment after tracing, is to be taken to have elected that his title in the original asset has been transferred to the substitute.[55] Election is thus the means by which the problems of geometric progression are avoided.

It is by no means clear why the option of an election to circumvent these difficul- **3.45** ties should not also be available to those who favour the view that proprietary claims arise in the law of property and not the law of unjust enrichment. Rescission is one example where a party's proprietary interest can be held to be a mere 'equity', something less than an equitable interest, unless and until the transaction or contract is rescinded, wherein the full title in the object which has been transferred under that transaction or contract may become vested in the claimant.

Similarly, it is submitted that the proprietary interests of the claimant can hover **3.46** over the various assets, from the original to the final substitute and it is only upon the claimant electing to assert ownership over one of them that full title vests therein. Until the point of election, the claimant might be said to have merely a 'power in rem'—a power to alter the proprietary interest in the various assets from the original asset to the final substitute asset.

The main proponent of the 'power in rem' analysis is Birks.[56] Although he accepts **3.47** the phrase 'power in rem' was never used by the House of Lords in *Lipkin Gorman*, nevertheless the reasoning adopted by Lord Goff is entirely consistent with a power in rem analysis of the problem. His Lordship stated that the claimant's right depended upon a definite act manifesting an election on their part akin to but not quite a ratification.

Unfortunately, given the somewhat conflicting state of the authorities, together **3.48** with the relatively recent endorsement of the law of property analysis of proprietary claims, it remains unclear how the courts propose to deal with the problem

---

[55] Burrows, *The Law of Restitution* (2nd edn), 92–3.
[56] See Birks, 'Mixing and Tracing: Property and Restitution' (1992) 45 CLP 69, 89–95.

of geometric progression. Such uncertainty at the heart of proprietary claims is not to be welcomed and it is to be hoped that the courts are given an opportunity to deal with this issue directly sooner rather than later. If so, it is suggested that the best way forward would be to adopt a power in rem analysis.

(3) Was D's enrichment unjust?

3.49 The starting point is to remove the suggestion that a claim in unjust enrichment is in any way dependent upon vague notions of 'doing justice' as between the parties. It is not. Nor is it an approach determined by the exercise of court discretion. An enrichment will be considered 'unjust' based upon the proper application of legal principle.

> The recovery of money in restitution is not, as a general rule, a matter of discretion for the court. A claim to recover money at common law is made as a matter of right; and even though the underlying principle of recovery is the principle of unjust enrichment, nevertheless, where recovery is denied, it is denied on the basis of legal principle.[57]

3.50 There are essentially two competing theories as to what makes an enrichment unjust. The first and most orthodox view is that there is a range of unjust factors which, if present, determine a claimant's entitlement to recover the enrichment. The second and far more controversial view is that there is simply one legal principle rendering an enrichment unjust, namely the absence of any legal basis for the transfer.[58] Both will be examined below but practitioners should note that as matters presently stand the former has greater support in the authorities than the latter, although there has been an invitation from one House of Lords judge for the academic world seriously to consider the benefits of Professor Birks' revised position.

(a) A range of unjust factors

3.51 This is the approach pioneered by *Goff & Jones* and was the mainstay of Professor Birks' tremendous contribution to this area of the law.[59]

3.52 Whilst it is not suggested that the list of unjust factors is exhaustive or closed, the following are generally accepted as being unjust factors: mistake, ignorance, duress, undue influence, legal compulsion, necessity, failure of consideration, incapacity, illegality and ultra vires demands by public authorities. Each of these factors merit a chapter on their own for proper analysis.

---

[57] Lord Goff in *Lipkin Gorman v Karpnale Ltd* [1991] 2 AC; see also Evans LJ in *Kleinwort Benson Ltd v Birmingham City Council* [1997] QB 380, 387.
[58] This is Professor Birks' revised position: *Unjust Enrichment* (2nd edn), chs 5 'Changing Direction' and 6, 'Absence of Basis'.
[59] As will be seen, the second theory was proposed by Professor Birks in *Unjust Enrichment* (2nd edn) which was published shortly before his untimely death in 2004.

The importance for present purposes is not to examine each head of unjust factor **3.53** in detail—that is something that can be left to the specialist texts on unjust enrichment—but rather to recognize situations which arise in a commercial fraud setting as entitling the claimant to bring a claim for unjust enrichment.

(a) Behind many commercial frauds is a claim for recovery of monies paid over by mistake. So, for example, a claim in unjust enrichment will arise where a victim has been persuaded by a fraudster to transfer money to a third party on the basis that the fraudster wrongly represented that a debt was due and owing to a third party. Such a claim can be characterized as a payment by way of a mistake: *Re Jones Ltd v Waring and Gillow*.[60]

(b) Even in complex frauds such as *Agip (Africa) v Jackson*[61] it is possible to simplify the complaint of having been defrauded to one of having paid by way of a mistake.[62] The problem, however, is that the present-day limitations on the common law rules on tracing make it exceedingly unlikely that any claim at common law for unjust enrichment will survive beyond the initial transfers of an international commercial fraud. In *Agip* itself, the relevant monies had been mixed in a bank account and sent via the CHAPS system, thus defeating the conventional view of the common law ability to trace.

(c) If X has been the victim of a 'ponzi' scheme or has been in some way deceived into putting his money into an investment scam, he will, in addition to having available claims based upon deceit, be able to plead a claim in unjust enrichment based upon a mistake. As stated above, such a claim would not require establishing any intention to deceive or be dishonest: it would simply rest on the factual difference between what X was told he was investing in and what in fact he was investing in.

(d) Other cases which previously might have been considered under the rubric of mistake are now considered by some commentators[63] to fall more naturally within a category known as 'ignorance'. This is an important area for commercial fraud. It typically involves a third party misappropriating the assets of the claimant. So, for example, consider the common situation of the finance

---

60 [1926] AC 670, HL.

61 [1990] Ch 265 (Millett J), [1991] Ch 547, CA.

62 It may well be better categorized as an example of payment in ignorance: see Burrows, *The Law of Restitution* (2nd edn), 190.

63 Professor Birks is the main advocate for the recognition of ignorance as an unjust factor. His relevant writings include *An Introduction to the Law of Restitution* at 140–6; 'Misdirected Funds: Restitution from the Recipient' [1989] LMCLQ 296; 'The English Recognition of Unjust Enrichment' [1991] LMCLQ 473; 'Trusts in the Recovery of Misapplied Assets: Tracing, Trusts and Restitution' in McKendrick (ed), *Commercial Aspects of Trusts and Fiduciary Obligations* (Clarendon Press, 1992); Birks (ed), *Restitution—The Future* (Federation Press, 1992), 27–8. See also Burrows (ed), *English Private Law* (2nd edn) paras 18.46–18.49; McKendrick, 'Tracing Misdirected Funds' [1991] LMCLQ 378, who argues in favour of ignorance being the relevant unjust factor in *Agip (Africa) Ltd v Jackson* [1991] CH 547, CA.

director re-directing cheques into an account other than one belonging to his company. Whilst it may be possible to shoe-horn the case into the mistake category, it more neatly and appropriately fits into this category of 'ignorance'. The monies were transferred away from the claimant without that claimant having any knowledge of what was happening.

(e) The rationale behind this new category is compelling: if X can recover payments made by mistake *a fortiori* X must be entitled to recover payments made using his monies without him having any knowledge about the payments at all.[64] Although the House of Lords did not expressly endorse this unjust factor in *Lipkin Gorman v Karpnale*,[65] Birks and others consider this is the answer to why restitution was available in that case.[66]

(b) Absence of legal basis

3.54 Just before his untimely death, Professor Birks began exploring the possibility of an entirely different approach to the structure of a claim in unjust enrichment.[67] The starting point was a dissatisfaction with the approach based upon unjust factors. This approach was initially premised upon showing that a claim in unjust enrichment could arise wherever there could be shown to be a problem with the transferor's intent to transfer the benefit received by the defendant. It was thought that this area was covered by three categories—no intent to transfer, a vitiated intent to transfer or a qualified intent to transfer. This would include unjust factors such as ignorance, mistake, duress, undue pressure.

3.55 It soon became clear, however, that this approach failed to explain all instances where a claim in unjust enrichment was permitted. In addition to these areas, there were also those occasions when there could be no questioning of the validity of the intent to transfer, but there existed some policy reason which justified a claim in unjust enrichment e.g. illegal transactions. At a time when unjust enrichment was not fully recognized by English law, and there was a great deal of scepticism about whether it should be, this failure to be able to present a coherent theory as to the structure of the claims considerably undermined the force of the arguments in favour of recognition of this area of the law.[68] Even Birks accepted that '[t]he single term "policy-motivations" did no more than confess the miscellany.

---

[64] Birks, 'Misdirected Funds: Restitution from the Recipient' [1989] LMCLQ 296. Not all commentators agree on the analogy between mistake and ignorance: see Grantham and Rickett, *Enrichment & Restitution in New Zealand* (Hart Publishing, 2000), ch 12.

[65] [1991] AC 512, HL.

[66] Burrows (ed), *English Private Law* (2nd edn), para 18.47.

[67] Birks, *Unjust Enrichment* (2nd edn), 101–60.

[68] I Jackman, *The Varieties of Restitution* (Federation Press, 1998), ch 1.

It left an unbridged gap between "miscellaneous other reasons" and non-voluntary transfer.'[69]

There then followed a series of cases known as the Swaps Litigation in which con- **3.56** tracts of swaps entered into by public authorities were held to be void, giving rise to repayment obligations under the law of unjust enrichment. It has always been difficult to discern from the relevant judgments what the court considered to be the unjust factor. According to Birks, these authorities, including *Kleinwort Benson Ltd v Sandwell BC*,[70] *Guinness Mahon & Co Ltd v Kensington & Chelsea Royal London BC*[71] illustrate the new approach based upon an 'absence of any legal basis for the transfer' rather than an approach based upon the existence of certain unjust factors. Birks interprets these cases and others such as *Westdeutsche Landesbank v Islington BC* and *Kleinwort Benson v Lincoln CC*,[72] as revealing the true basis for the claim in unjust enrichment being the invalidity of the relevant swap contract itself.

In commenting on *Kleinwort Benson v Lincoln*, in *Lessons of the Swaps Litigation*,[73] **3.57** Birks observed:

> The disagreement between the majority and the minority turns on whether one can be retrospectively mistaken in any sense relevant to restitutionary relief. The major- ity holds that one can, and in so holding it appears to have approved a notion of operative mistake of law which is not only broader than operative mistake of fact but broader than the rationale underlying relief for mistake. Without saying so expressly, it has moved English law towards a civilian condictio indebiti. 'Condictio indebiti' means 'Claim in respect of something not due'.

Whilst Birks contends that this approach gives a tighter unity to the structure of **3.58** the law of unjust enrichment, it has not met with universal approval and does rest on controversial interpretations of some of the authorities, whilst ignoring adverse comments in others. So, for example, not everyone would interpret *Kleinwort Benson v Lincoln* as resting on the absence of any legal basis for the payment, as opposed to mistake of law. Similarly, the theory fails to deal with the comments of Lord Goff in *Woolwich Equitable BS v IRC*,[74] rejecting the notion that English law had embraced the civilian system's view of unjust enrichment.

---

[69] Birks, *Unjust Enrichment* (2nd edn), 107.

[70] [1994] 4 All ER 890.

[71] [1999] QB 215 (CA).

[72] [1999] 2 AC 349 (HL), applied in *Nurdin & Peacock plc v DB Ramsden & Co Ltd* [1999] 1 WLR 1249 (Ch D).

[73] Birks and Rose (eds), *Lessons of the Swaps Litigation* (Mansfield Press, 2000), ch 1, 14.

[74] [1993] AC 70, 172. English law 'might have developed so as to recognize a *condictio indebiti* – an action for the recovery of money on the ground that it was not due . . . it did not do so'.

3.59 More recently, in *Deutsche Morgan Grenfell plc v IRC*[75] the House of Lords felt it was necessary to go and examine the precise state of mind with which the payor had made a particular payment, notwithstanding the fact that an earlier decision had made it clear that the Inland Revenue was not entitled to receive it. Although the search for a 'mistake' in the making of the payment was in order to bring the payment within the terms of the relevant statutory provision which allowed relief for such a mistaken payment, it is quite clear that the House of Lords was unwilling, at this stage, to embrace the 'absence of legal basis' theory.

3.60 Lord Hoffmann explained the reason for this approach as follows:

> 21 The answer, at any rate for the moment, is that unlike civilian systems, English law has no general principle that to retain money paid without any legal basis (such as debt, gift, compromise etc) is unjust enrichment. In the *Woolwich* case [1993] AC 70, 172 Lord Goff said that English law might have developed so as to recognise such a general principle – the condictio indebiti of civilian law – but had not done so. In England, the claimant has to prove that the circumstances in which the payment was made come within one of the categories which the law recognizes as sufficient to make retention by the recipient unjust. Lord Goff provided a list in the *Woolwich* case, at pp 164 – 165, and the decision itself added another. One such category, long recognised, is payment by mistake: see *Kelly v Solari* (1841) 9 M & W 54. The late Professor Birks argued, in the second edition of his book on *Unjust Enrichment* (2005), that the trend of recent English decisions meant that, for the purpose of entitling a claimant to recover, the categories were now superfluous. The fact that the money had not been due was, in the absence of some other causa for payment, a sufficient ground for recovery. We have now developed a condictio indebiti.[76] The absence of a basis for the payment is a ground which generalises and subsumes all the separate categories of situation in which a payment of money not due was recoverable.
>
> 22 I do not think it is necessary for us to decide this question about the fundamental basis of enrichment liability because the question before the House is not the fundamental juridical basis of DMG's cause of action but whether the action can be described as being "for relief from the consequences of a mistake" within the meaning of section 32(1)(C) of the 1980 Act. The *Kleinwort Benson* case [1999] 2 AC 349 is recent authority for the proposition that an action for restitution of money paid under a void contract can fall within this description . . .

---

75 [2006] UKHL 49, [2007] 1 AC 558. C Mitchell, 'Unjust Enrichment' ch18 in Burrows (ed), *English Private Law* suggests that the House of Lords in *Deutsche Morgan* held that the revised Birks' approach was not a part of English law [18.43]. In fact the extracts reveal that their Lordships were not interested in resolving such a fundamental issue when they were in fact concerned to identify a relevant 'mistake' for the purposes of bringing the claim within the terms of the relevant statutory provision. It was not something they needed to decide in this case. It is interesting to note Lord Walker's encouragement for academics to consider the suggestion put forward by Birks and identify what advantages or disadvantages it may entail for the development of this area of the law.

76 'Claim in respect of something not due.'

Lord Walker also took advantage of the opportunity afforded in *Deutsche Morgan* **3.61**
Grenfell plc v IRC to set out his views on Birks' revised position. Having explained
that Birks' revised views derived from his interpretation of the swaps cases, and
identifying various academic articles and books which no doubt also influenced
Birks to adopt the civilian law approach on this issue, Lord Walker went on to
make the following observations. They merit being set out in full as they indicate
an agreement with the logic of much of what Birks has said in his revised position,
but a desire not to rush headlong into accepting that position without further
consideration by the courts and academics:

> . . . The choice as to the way forward which restitution scholars identify is between
> continuing to view unjust enrichment as depending on the presence of one or more
> of a variety of 'unjust factors' and adopting the single test of 'absence of basis'.
>
> 155   My Lords, the House is being invited (much more pressingly, it must be said,
> by scholars than by counsel for the parties) to make a choice at a very high level of
> abstraction. Most scholars would take the view (though Professor Birks himself
> would not, I suspect, have agreed, since he regarded taxonomy as very important)
> that the choice is one which will rarely make much if any practical difference to the
> outcome of any particular case before the court. For several reasons I doubt whether
> this is the right time for your Lordships to decide whether to rebase the whole law of
> unjust enrichment on a highly abstract principle which (although familiar to civil-
> ians and to Scottish lawyers, and discussed in the speech of my noble and learned
> friend Lord Hope of Craighead in the *Kleinwort Benson* case [1999] 2 AC 349, 408-
> 409) would represent a distinct departure from established doctrine.

After discussing the problems created by the single principle of voluntary assump-   **3.62**
tion of responsibility in the law of negligence, Lord Walker continued:

> 157 By contrast the English law on unjust enrichment has in the space of a decade
> seen four very important developments, all informed by the learning of Lord Goff:
> *Lipkin Gorman v Karpnale Ltd* [1991] 2 AC 548 in 1991, the *Woolwich* case [1993]
> AC 70 in 1992, *Westdeutsche Landesbank Girozentrale v Islington London Borough
> Council* [1996] AC 669 in 1996, and the *Kleinwort Benson* case [1999] 2 AC 349 in
> 1998. The change in the views of Professor Birks is a recent development (which
> sadly he could not pursue further) and it has not yet been fully considered by other
> legal scholars. There is, it seems to me, much to be said for a period of reappraisal.
>
> 158 Nevertheless I would add that my tentative inclination is to welcome any ten-
> dency of the English law of unjust enrichment to align itself more closely with
> Scottish law, and so to civilian roots. I see attractions in the suggestion made by
> Professor Birks in *Unjust Enrichment*, 2nd ed, p116, under the heading 'The Pyramid:
> A Limited Reconciliation':
>
> > 'A pyramid can be constructed in which, at the base, the particular unjust factors
> > such as mistake, pressure, and undue influence become reasons why, higher up,
> > there is no basis for the defendant's acquisition, which is then the master reason
> > why, higher up still, the enrichment is unjust and must be surrendered.'
>
> I would be glad to see the law developing on those lines. The recognition of 'no basis'
> as a single unifying principle would preserve what Lord Hope refers to as the purity

of the principle on which unjust enrichment is founded, without in any way removing (as this case illustrates) the need for careful analysis of the content of particular 'unjust factors' such as mistake.[77]

3.63 Lord Walker's comments show that the new approach of Professor Birks may not represent the present state of English law but yet cannot be dismissed lightly. It may have the disadvantage of marking a departure from the approach hitherto adopted in the cases or most of them, but, as Lord Walker observed, it has the benefit of aligning English law of unjust enrichment with that of Scottish law and that of civilian legal systems. It is to be hoped that the scholars and academics will take up the challenge laid down by Lord Walker to closely examine this new theory and highlight the advantages and disadvantages of adopting it.[78]

F. Personal and Proprietary Remedies

(1) Personal remedy

3.64 It is essential to begin this section with a reminder about language. This chapter is concerned, and solely concerned, with the law of unjust enrichment (by subtraction). It is not concerned with the restitution remedy generally. So, claims for wrongdoing, such as for breach of fiduciary duty, fall outwith the terms of this discussion.[79]

3.65 A claim in unjust enrichment is concerned with the recovery of the benefit received by the defendant and not concerned with compensating the claimant for loss caused.[80] Such a claim is personal in nature. It imposes a personal obligation on the part of the recipient of the enrichment to return to the transferor—make restitution of—the *value* of the enrichment received. In shorthand, it might be said that the defendant must make restitution of the enrichment but this should not be confused with any obligation to return the very asset received.

---

[77] See also Lord Hope's observations in *Sempra Metals Ltd v IRC* [2007] UKHL 34; [2007] 3 WLR 354 at [23]. See also the comments of Lawrence Collins J in *Primlake Limited (In Liquidation) v Matthews Associates & Ors* [2006] EWHC 1227 (Ch); [2007] 1 BCLC 666 at [335] where his Lordship appeared to endorse an 'absence of legal basis' approach.

[78] For those who were privy to the excellent series of Saturday seminars on restitution at All Souls College, Oxford, chaired by Professor Birks in the 1990s, one might contemplate something of this nature would be a fitting way to take up Lord Walker's challenge.

[79] See Ch 6 on constructive trusts.

[80] Save in the sense of the benefit which was received by the defendant may (but need not: see Birks, *Unjust Enrichment* (2nd edn), 167–8) correspond with a loss suffered in the same amount by the claimant: but see Lord Hope in *Sempra Metals Ltd v IRC* [2007] UKHL 34; [2007] 3 WLR 354, 367, paras [28]–[29], commenting on the views of Birks: 'So the remedy of restitution differs from that of damages. It is the gain that needs to be measured, not the loss to the claimant. The gain needs to be reversed if the claimant is to make good his remedy.' For an argument that there should be corresponding loss to gain: M McInnes, 'Interceptive Subtraction, Unjust Enrichment and Wrongs—A Reply to Professor Birks' [2003] CLJ 697.

In traditional pleading language, a claim in unjust enrichment may lead to bring- **3.66**
ing a claim for:

- money had and received. This is the traditional common law claim for, say, a
  payment by way of a mistake;
- quantum valebat—reasonable value paid for goods;
- quantum meruit—reasonable value paid for services rendered;

However, it must surely have come time, given the express recognition of the **3.67**
cause of action in unjust enrichment, that the claims be properly pleaded in the
language of unjust enrichment. This not only updates the position, it ensures that
each element which is material to the existence or otherwise of a claim in unjust
enrichment is expressly pleaded out in the Particulars of Claim.

But as the House of Lords recognized in *Sempra Metals Ltd v IRC*,[81] the return of **3.68**
the monies paid over by way of mistake may not constitute 'full restitution' of the
recipient's unjust enrichment. In that case, the court recognized the need to take
into account the time value of the premature tax payment. This was prima facie
the reasonable cost to the claimant of borrowing the same sum over the same
period.[82] Simple interest was rejected as being inconsistent with everyday business
where interest is compounded.

> 34. All this points to the conclusion . . . that, for restitution to be given for the time
> value of the money which was paid prematurely, the principal sum to be awarded in
> this case should be calculated on the basis of compound interest.[83]

The Court of Appeal decision in *Trustee of the Property of F C Jones & Sons (A firm)* **3.69**
v Jones[84] requires careful consideration. It was a claim by the trustees based on its
having retained legal title to recover the exchange product of the money wrongly
taken from the trust. That money had been given to the wife of one of the partners
who invested it well. Given the English common law has no equivalent to the
Roman law claim of *vindication*, the claim had to be framed as one in debt.
Notwithstanding that the claim was one in debt, and that the exchange product
was worth more than the original money taken, the Court of Appeal allowed a
personal claim against the wife up to the level inclusive of profits. For a difficult
interpretation of the case based upon unjust enrichment, see Birks, 'At the Expense
of the Claimant: Direct and Indirect Enrichment in English Law' in Johnston and

---

[81] [2007] UKHL 34, [2007] 3 WLR 354. See C Nicoll, 'Compound Interest for late payment of
insurance claims' (2008) 124 LQR 199; *Westdeutsche Landesbank v Islington LBC* [1996] AC 669,
not followed.

[82] Compound interest would not be awarded if the defendant could show that he had gained no
such benefit himself or per Lords Scott and Mance compound interest would only be charged if the
money had been proved to have actually earned interest in the hands of the defendant.

[83] [2007] 3 WLR 354, 368 at [34] per Lord Hope.

[84] [1997] Ch 159, CA.

Zimmermann (eds), *Unjustified Enrichment* (Cambridge University Press, 2002) and for criticism of this approach: *Goff & Jones* (7th edn), para 2-030, n 72a.

(2) Proprietary remedies

(a) The decision in Foskett v McKeown

3.70 The short answer for practitioners is that on the present state of the law claims in unjust enrichment do not give rise to proprietary relief. Whether or not a proprietary claim arises is entirely dependent upon the law of property and not the law of unjust enrichment. So held the House of Lords in *Foskett v McKeown*.[85]

3.71 The debate that led to the decision in *Foskett v McKeown* merits close analysis in order (i) that the decision be fully understood and (ii) that practitioners are aware of the arguments which are persisted with in some academic quarters. It may take some time for them to be raised again in courts, given the strong views echoed in the House of Lords, but it would be wrong to conclude they will simply go away.

3.72 The starting point for understanding this debate is the distinction between tracing and following.[86] This is dealt with in detail in Chapter 21 on tracing and following. This brief introduction should enable the point to be understood.

3.73 If X hands over his pen to Y who hands it over to Z, the process of identifying where the pen is now and through whose hands it has passed is known as following. The object of the identification process, the pen in our example, does not alter. We were focused on the pen when it was in X's hands and we remain focused on the pen now it is in Z's hands. It is the same pen but now in different hands. That is following. If anyone were to ask why X can assert ownership over the pen in the hands of Z it is because it was his pen at the start of the story and, subject to any possible defences, it remains his pen in the hands of Z. We can explain the assertion of ownership over the pen in the hands of Z by reference to the fact that the story began with the pen being owned by X and nothing in fact has happened to transfer that ownership.

3.74 Now tweak the example a little. X transfers the pen to Y who exchanges it for a ruler from Z who in turn exchanges the pen for a pad of paper. Putting aside possible defences, upon what basis, if at all, can X assert ownership in the pad of paper in the hands of Z?

- Those who favour the law of property theory say X can assert ownership in the pad of paper because X originally owned the pen and the pad of paper is the

---

[85] [2001] 1 AC 102.
[86] See Lord Millett in *Foskett v McKeown* [2001] 1 AC 102, 127B–D.

traceable substitute for that pen. The ownership in the pen justifies, via satisfactory tracing, the proprietary claim to the paper.[87]

- Those who favour an explanation in the law of unjust enrichment say that this property explanation cannot work. They maintain that the only basis upon which ownership can be asserted in the pad of paper is the fact that without such a claim Z would be unjustly enriched, having received the pen and having exchanged it for the pad of paper.

In *Foskett v McKeown*,[88] the House of Lords emphatically came out in favour of **3.75** the law of property explanation. The facts may be summarized as follows:

- A trustee misappropriated trust money belonging to the beneficiaries and used it to pay for the fourth and fifth premiums on his own life insurance policy.
- The trustee committed suicide, giving rise to a payment under the policy of £1m.
- The beneficiaries claimed a proportionate share of this £1m (£400,000 in fact) on the basis that the trust money had been used to pay two of the premiums under the policy.
- The Court of Appeal limited the beneficiaries' recovery to a lien over the trust funds for the recovery of the misappropriated funds.
- The House of Lords (3–2) held that the beneficiaries were entitled to a proportionate share of the policy proceeds, being £400,000.
- In so doing, their Lordships rejected the theory that any such claim was based upon unjust enrichment.

Lord Millett, giving the leading speech, said: **3.76**

> The transmission of a claimant's property rights from one asset to its traceable proceeds is part of our law of property, not of the law of unjust enrichment. There is no 'unjust factor' to justify restitution (unless 'want of title' be one, which makes the point). The claimant succeeds if at all by virtue of his own title, not to reverse unjust enrichment . . . [89]

His Lordship went on to add that this conclusion had important consequences **3.77** since the two claims (one in property, one in law of unjust enrichment) had different requirements and even different defences (change of position arising for unjust enrichment and bona fide purchaser for value without notice for property claims).

---

[87] One of the main proponents of this view prior to *Foskett v McKeown* is Professor Virgo: see *The Principles of the Law of Restitution*, ch 20.
[88] [2001] 1 AC 102.
[89] ibid, 127.

As I have already pointed out, the plaintiffs seek to vindicate their property rights, not to reverse unjust enrichment . . . A plaintiff who brings an action in unjust enrichment must show that the defendant has been enriched at the plaintiff's expense, for he cannot have been unjustly enriched if he has not been enriched at all. But the plaintiff is not concerned to show that the defendant is in receipt of property belonging beneficially to the plaintiff or its traceable proceeds. The fact that the beneficial ownership of the property has passed to the defendant provides no defence; indeed it is usually the very fact which founds the claim. Conversely, a plaintiff who brings an action like the present must show that the defendant is in receipt of property which belongs beneficially to him or its traceable proceeds, but he need not show that the defendant has been enriched by its receipt. He may, for example, have paid full value for the property, but he is still required to disgorge it if he received it with notice of the plaintiff's interest.[90]

3.78 Lord Browne-Wilkinson was of similar opinion:

The contrary view appears to be based primarily on the ground that to give the purchasers a rateable share of the policy moneys is not to reverse an unjust enrichment but to give the purchasers a wholly unwarranted windfall . . . But this windfall is enjoyed because of the rights which the purchasers enjoy under the law of property. A man under whose land oil is discovered enjoys a very valuable windfall but no one suggests that he, as owner of the property, is not entitled to the windfall which goes with his property right. We are not dealing with a claim in unjust enrichment.[91]

3.79 Lord Hoffmann was equally decisive in rejecting the unjust enrichment theory. Having agreed with the conclusion that Mr Murphy's children and the trust beneficiaries whose money Mr Murphy used were entitled to share in the proceeds of the insurance policy in proportion to the value which they respectively contributed to the policy, Lord Hoffmann said:

This is not based upon unjust enrichment except in the most trivial sense of that expression. It is . . . a vindication of proprietary right.[92]

3.80 In any event, on the facts, there was no enrichment, let alone unjust enrichment. It was found as a fact that although misappropriated trust monies had been used to make the last two payments of premium under the policy, the entitlement to the £1m had already crystallized prior to the payment of these premiums. In other words, the £1m would have been paid out under the policy even if these last two premiums had not been paid. Accordingly, there was no basis, in fact, to say that the defendants had been unjustly enriched.

*(b) Lord Millett's post-*Foskett *explanation*

3.81 One thing that the decision in *Foskett* is clear on is the rejection of the unjust enrichment approach in favour of one based on the law of property. So far, so good.

---

90 ibid, 129E–G.
91 ibid, 110.
92 ibid, 115.

Where the speeches fall down a little, with respect to their Lordships, is in any detailed analysis of the reasoning underpinning this decision. There is, with respect, more assertion than reasoning in the various speeches.

Fortunately, Lord Millett has set out that very reasoning extra-judicially.[93] It is, as one would expect, tightly reasoned and compelling and merits a close read. **3.82**

- The law of property governs the question of the creation, acquisition, disposal and transmission of property rights. It determines the ownership of property in any dispute and protects pre-existing property rights. One rule of the law of property is that the owner of a thing can assert ownership in the traceable proceeds of that thing.[94] None of this requires invoking unjust enrichment theories.
- The convoluted analysis based on unjust enrichment has no direct support in the authorities (even pre-*Foskett*).
- Applying Lord Millett's approach:
  - In a case, such as total failure of consideration, where the payor intends to divest himself of both the legal and equitable interest in the money/property, there can be no proprietary remedy (no resulting trust). For Lord Millett, the reason is because the payor relinquished all beneficial interest in the goods when he supplied them or made the payment. He has no remaining title and therefore cannot raise a proprietary claim. The decision is the same for those favouring unjust enrichment, but because the unjust factor supervened afterwards.
  - At the other extreme are the examples where the beneficial (or perhaps even the legal) title does not pass. This may be because the transaction itself is void and so no title passes or, more commonly, the transfer to the recipient has taken place as part of a three-party case. Here a fiduciary, in breach of fiduciary duty, without his principal's knowledge, pays away his money. Equity says that a transfer in breach of trust or fiduciary duty does not dispose of the beneficial interest unless the recipient is a bona fide purchaser for value without notice. No rescission is necessary because, as far as equity is concerned, the beneficial interest never left the payor. He can call for the return of his property based on his beneficial interest.
  - Finally, there are those cases where the payment is fully intended to be made but the relevant consent to transfer has been vitiated by some form of fraud, mistake or misrepresentation. In these cases, as intended, the beneficial interest is fully transferred. A right to rescind arises and, by analogy with specific

---

[93] Lord Millett, 'Proprietary Restitution' in S Degeling and J Edelman (eds) *Equity in Commercial Law (*Law Book Co of Australasia, 1996).

[94] Birks calls this the 'fiction of persistence': *Unjust Enrichment* (2nd edn), 198.

performance, Lord Millett's view appears now to be that rescission will only affect a proprietary remedy in cases of land or other property of unique or special value to the claimant.

> What distinguishes this third category of case from the second is not the absence of a fiduciary relationship. It may be present. It is the distinction between property obtained, whether by a fiduciary or not, by means of a voidable transaction, and property obtained by a fiduciary in breach of fiduciary duty. Put another way, the distinction is between property obtained with the knowledge and consent of the beneficial owner, but whose consent is vitiated by some unjust factor; and property obtained without his knowledge or authority by a fiduciary exploiting his position for his own benefit.[95]

- Therefore, the only practical difference between Lord Millett's property approach and that of unjust enrichment lies in the example where payment is voidable for mistake, duress, legal compulsion, etc. Here, those favouring unjust enrichment support the decision in *Chase Manhattan*. Lord Millett does not.

(c) Change of position defence after Foskett v McKeown

3.83 It has been said that one very practical consequence of the decision in *Foskett v McKeown* is that the defence of change of position is not available to a claim to a proprietary remedy.[96] However, the matter is not free from doubt.

3.84 Lord Millett, writing *extra-judicially*, maintains that the issue of whether this defence is available to the property based restitutionary claim is not yet resolved and certainly was not determined by the decision in *Foskett v McKeown*.[97] He chastised one commentator for saying that it followed from the fact tracing was part of the law of property that the change of position defence was not available in the context of actions contingent on this process. Lord Millett's response is clear:

> I chose my words with great care; and it is very irritating to see how widely they have been misunderstood . . . I said no such thing. I drew no distinction between the misappropriated asset and its traceable proceeds. On the contrary, I was concerned to say that a claimant has the same interest in the proceeds as he had in the property which they represent.
>
> Nor did I say that a property based action for a personal remedy (eg a claim for knowing receipt) was not subject to the change of position defence. I said that 'an action like the present' (ie a claim to a *proprietary* remedy) did not depend on showing that

---

[95] Lord Millett, 'Proprietary Restitution' in Degeling and Edelman (eds), *Equity in Commercial Law*, 321.

[96] Burrows, 'The English Law of Restitution: A Ten Year Review' in J Neyers, M McInnes and S Pitel (eds), *Understanding Unjust Enrichment* (Hart Publishing, 2004), 11, 26 '. . . and most important in practice, change of position has been rejected by their Lordships in respect of proprietary remedies after tracing, whereas, in principle and policy, it should be a defence'.

[97] Lord Millett, 'Proprietary Restitution' in Degeling and Edelman (eds), *Equity in Commercial Law*, 309, 319.

the defendant had been enriched, and (inferentially) was not subject to the defence. And I did not say that the change of position defence invariably operates by reducing or extinguishing the element of enrichment. I said that it *usually* does so.

In my opinion, there are only two kinds of case where the change of position defence is not available: (i) where the claimant seeks a proprietary remedy (where it is not needed); and (ii) where the defendant is the original wrongdoer (who is an accounting party and in any case could hardly plead an innocent change of position.) But it is available where the claimant seeks a personal remedy against a successor in title, whether the defendant parted with the original asset or its traceable proceeds; and whether the action is brought to reverse unjust enrichment, when it reflects the fact that the defendant is no longer enriched, or to recover the value of the claimant's property, when it has a different rationale, viz to mitigate the harshness of the rule that all restitutionary liability restitution is strict.[98]

(d) The debate continues

3.85

Unjust enrichment academics are hardy souls. They are not about to allow one decision of the House of Lords to end this debate. The practitioner should at least be aware of the arguments remaining on both sides post-*Foskett v McKeown*.

3.86

(i) Advocates of unjust enrichment-based proprietary claims[99] One of the major arguments put forward to criticize the decision in *Foskett v McKeown* is that it fails to give any relevance or significance to the distinction between tracing and following set out above. The fact that the claimant had title to the original asset does not provide, so it is said, any explanation or justification for the claimant's entitlement to assert ownership in another asset, even after tracing. This is the assertion of a new proprietary right and not simply the original proprietary right.

3.87

It is said that given this is a new proprietary right, one cannot rely upon ownership of the original asset to justify its creation. The fact X owns the pen says nothing as to X's entitlement to own the ruler. The two are distinct items of ownership. It is necessary to justify creating a new proprietary right in this asset and that the only justification for doing so is the unjust enrichment which would otherwise ensue if the claimant were denied a proprietary right.

3.88

Birks argues that it is important to recognize the distinction between events and responses.[100] He maintains the law recognizes four events: consent, wrongs, unjust enrichment and other events. He does not accept that property rights or their vindication constitutes an event to which restitution is the response. On that analysis,

---

[98] ibid, 325.

[99] Birks, 'Property, Unjust Enrichment and Tracing' (2001) 54 CLP 231. See also Burrows, 'Proprietary Restitution: Unmasking Unjust Enrichment' (2001) 117 LQR 412.

[100] Birks, 'Equity in the Modern Law: An Exercise in Taxonomy' (1996) 26 Univ WALR 1; 'Property, Unjust Enrichment and Tracing' [2001] CLP 231.

property rights cannot be competing with unjust enrichment to be the event to trigger proprietary restitutionary remedies. If there are only four events and restitution, as a response, must respond to one of these events, it can only be responding to one of the four events (and not to property rights) in any given fact-situation.

3.89 Birks may well be correct that property rights *per se* are not events to which restitution responds in the same manner as for unjust enrichment. But no one is asking restitution to respond to property rights *per se*—rather, restitution is being asked to respond to interferences with those property rights. It is not entirely clear why *interference* with property rights cannot amount to an event to which restitution is the response.[101]

3.90 Professor Burrows has criticized the reasoning in *Foskett v McKeown* as being 'flawed and [relying] on the fiction that tracing involves the continuation of proprietary rights into substitute property'.[102] Nevertheless, he goes on to say that the decision itself may be correct and could have been reached applying the unjust enrichment analysis.[103] On this basis, Professor Burrows maintains that *Foskett v McKeown* cannot be the last word on the relationship between unjust enrichment and proprietary claims.

3.91 One difficulty which has always undermined the argument in favour of unjust enrichment being the basis of a proprietary claim is that until relatively recently, there has been no consistent theory presented, within those arguing in favour of unjust enrichment, as to when the law of unjust enrichment gives rise to a proprietary claim. Since no one argues in favour of every example of unjust enrichment justifying a proprietary claim, it is essential that a clear dividing line be drawn between those that do and those that do not.

3.92 In *Unjust Enrichment*,[104] Birks puts forward a view which substantially mirrors that advocated by Robert Chambers:

> [T]he best interpretation of the English cases is that they should be divided between those in which there is no moment in which the enrichment is held free of any claim, and those in which for however short a time the enrichee holds the enrichment freely at his own disposition. This distinction almost exactly corresponds with the line between initial and subsequent failure of basis. In the former case, where the enrichment is never freely at the enrichee's disposition, there is always a proprietary response alongside the common or garden right *in personam*. In the latter case, where the value

---

[101] This argument is most developed by Graham Virgo, *The Principles of the Law of Restitution* (2nd edn), 15, and chs 20 and 21.
[102] Burrows, *The Law of Restitution* (2nd edn), 65.
[103] ibid, 20.
[104] *Unjust Enrichment* (2nd edn), 181–2.

in question has been freely at the disposition of the defendant before the basis of the enrichment fails, there is no proprietary response.

With one additional observation, Burrows has indicated his general agreement **3.93** with the Birks/Chambers approach:

> According to their view, wherever an unjust enrichment at the claimant's expense triggers personal restitution, so too it should trigger proprietary restitution provided two additional conditions are satisfied. These conditions are: (i) the enrichment subtracted from the claimant exists, if necessary by applying tracing rules, in an asset to which the proprietary right can attach; and (ii) the injustice arose at the moment the defendant was entitled to the enrichment. Applying this approach, mistake, duress, and undue influence, for example, should and do all trigger proprietary restitution, whether through a trust or a power to revest title by rescission. On the other hand, failure of consideration, which concerns a subsequent injustice, does not and should not trigger proprietary restitution.[105] So, according to Birks and Chambers, *Re Goldcorp*[106] and *Westdeutsche Landesbank*[107] were correct in denying proprietary restitution through a resulting or constructive trust precisely because the injustice was subsequent only: the ground for restitution was failure of consideration.

> I essentially agree with Birks and Chambers' theory, although I do think that, as a matter of policy, a good reason why one would not want to allow proprietary restitution for a subsequent failure of consideration is because, at least normally, this is the classic situation where we would say that the payor has taken the risk of the payee's insolvency.[108]

(ii) Overview of present position   A good illustration of the difficulties facing **3.94** practitioners trying to give clear advice to clients on the availability of proprietary relief is the treatment handed out to the first instance decision of Goulding J in *Chase Manhattan v Israel-British Bank*.[109] It may be recalled that in this case the bank payor made in error a second transfer of US\$2m to the recipient bank in New York. Goulding J found that the monies paid over by mistake were held on trust.

This has always been a controversial and much-maligned decision to some. To **3.95** others, it has proved an invaluable authority, particularly at the early stages of a fraud case, where there is a need to get certain pre-emptive relief off the ground but the facts are not fully known. To be able to say, at the interlocutory stage, that

---

[105] Unless the payment was 'ring-fenced' so that the defendant was not free to use it, as in *Barclays Bank Ltd v Quistclose Investments Ltd* [1970] AC 567.

[106] [1995] 1 AC 74.

[107] [1996] AC 669.

[108] A Burrows, 'The English Law of Restitution: A Ten Year Review' in Neyers, McInnes and Pitel (eds), *Understanding Unjust Enrichment*, 11, 27.

[109] [1981] Ch 105.

there clearly has been a mistake and so under this authority there is every prospect of a proprietary claim, has proved extremely helpful over the years.

3.96 But it is anything but clear what the present status of this authority is and that does none of us involved in this area of the law any good.

- In *Westdeutsche*, Lord Browne-Wilkinson says the reasoning is flawed but the decision correct. He says the trust was imposed because of the recipient's knowledge of the true position at a time before the monies had been mixed with its other assets. At that point, the recipient held on trust, his conscience having been affected by his knowledge of the mistake.

- In *Westdeutsche*, Lord Goff refused to express any view on the validity of the decision.[110]

- *Extra-judicially*, Lord Millett has rejected Lord Browne-Wilkinson's suggested re-interpretation based upon conscience and says the decision is simply wrong.[111]

- Burrows, applying the Birks and Chambers approach to proprietary restitution, maintains *Chase Manhattan* was correctly decided. The mistaken payment constitutes a vitiation and not simply a qualification of consent[112] such that there was never a time the recipient was in fact entitled to the enrichment. Given the existence of the mistake, the claimant had not taken the risk of the recipient's insolvency.[113]

- At the same time, Burrows has argued that Lord Browne-Wilkinson's suggested re-interpretation of *Chase Manhattan* is flawed, being based upon the assertion that a trust is only imposed where the defendant's conscience is affected: 'If an aunt puts shares in the name of her niece and the niece knows nothing of what she has done, there is a resulting trust irrespective of when the niece acquires the requisite knowledge.'[114]

- Perhaps one of the most forceful arguments in favour of *Chase Manhattan* is that any overruling of that decision must take into account and deal with the analogous position involving voidable transactions.[115]

3.97 The disparate nature of the views on just this one case perfectly illustrates the wider difficulties faced by the practitioner in this area. It can be seen that the

---

110 [1996] 1 AC 669, 690G.

111 Lord Millett, 'Proprietary Restitution' in Degeling and Edelman (eds), *Equity in Commercial Law*, 318. See also Sir Peter Millett, 'Restitution and Constructive Trusts' in Cornish et al (eds), *Restitution: Past, Present & Future*, 212.

112 It is a vitiation because the basis failed *ab initio* in that there existed no contractual obligation to make the second payment.

113 Burrows, 'The English Law of Restitution: A Ten-Year Review' in Neyers, McInnes and Pitel (eds), *Understanding Unjust Enrichment*, 28–9.

114 Burrows, ibid, 29.

115 Birks, *Unjust Enrichment* (2nd edn), ch 8, 'Rights *in rem*'.

debates continue on the issue of a role for unjust enrichment but it is questionable whether any such arguments will, in the near future, have much practical input into submissions before the court given the manner in which the House of Lords rejected the unjust enrichment analysis in *Foskett v McKeown*.

G. Defences

Four defences will be examined: (i) change of position; (ii) bona fide purchaser for value without notice; (iii) ministerial receipt; and (iv) limitation. **3.98**

(1) Change of position

(a) Introduction[116]

It was the express recognition of this defence in *Lipkin Gorman* which really **3.99** opened the doors to the development of the law of unjust enrichment on a strict liability basis. Indeed, it is the defence which makes the strict liability claim more palatable than it otherwise would be.

Lord Goff was careful in *Lipkin Gorman* not to lay down some over-arching gen- **3.100** eral principle which would apply in all circumstances as opposed to encouraging a case-by-case development of the defence.

> I am most anxious that, in recognising this defence to actions of restitution, nothing should be said at this stage to inhibit the development of the defence on a case by case basis, in the usual way. It is, of course, plain that the defence is not open to one who has changed his position in bad faith, as where the defendant has paid away the money with knowledge of the facts entitling the plaintiff to restitution; and it is commonly accepted that the defence should not be open to a wrongdoer. These are matters which can, in due course, be considered in depth in cases where they arise for consideration.[117]

He went on to say:[118] **3.101**

> I do not wish to state the principle any less broadly than this: that the defence is available to a person whose position has so changed that it would be inequitable in all the circumstances to require him to make restitution, or alternatively to make restitution in full. I wish to stress however that the mere fact that the defendant has spent the

---

[116] *Goff & Jones* (7th edn), ch 40; Birks, 'Disenrichment and Disimpoverishment', ch 9 in *Unjust Enrichment* (2nd edn); Birks, 'Change of Position: The Nature of the Defence and its Relationship to other Restitutionary Defences' in McInnes (ed), *Restitution: Developments in Unjust Enrichment* (Law Book Co of Australasia, 1996); Virgo, *The Principles of the Law of Restitution* (2nd edn), 689 *et seq.*; Virgo, 'Change of Position: The Importance of Being Principled' [2005] RLR 34; Nolan, 'Change of Position' in Birks (ed), *Laundering and Tracing* (Clarendon Press, 1995), C Mitchell, 'Unjust Enrichment' in Burrows (ed), *English Private Law* (2nd edn), paras 18.222–18.242.

[117] [1991] 2 AC 548, 579.

[118] ibid, 580.

money, in whole or in part, does not of itself render it inequitable that he should be called upon to repay, because the expenditure might in any event have been incurred by him in the ordinary course of things. I fear that the mistaken assumption that mere expenditure of money may be regarded as amounting to a change of position for present purposes has led in the past to opposition by some to recognition of a defence which in fact is likely to be available only on comparatively rare occasions. In this connection, I have particularly in mind the speech of Lord Simonds in *Ministry of Health v Simpson* [1951] AC 251, 276.

So, the mere spending of the money will not suffice. There is a need to examine the defendant's spending habits to determine whether such spending would have taken place in any event. If so, then it cannot amount to a change of position.

3.102   Lord Goff was, however, keen to ensure that the development of the defence of change of position was not inextricably linked with the doctrine of estoppel and the consequential need for a representation and reliance thereon.

3.103   Having identified that often the facts do not give rise to any representation at all, Lord Goff continued:

> Considerations such as these provide a strong indication that, in many cases, estoppel is not an appropriate concept to deal with the problem . . . It is not however appropriate in the present case to attempt to identify all those actions in restitution to which change of position may be a defence. A prominent example will, no doubt, be found in those cases where the plaintiff is seeking repayment of money paid under a mistake of fact; but I can see no reason why the defence should not also be available in principle in a case such as the present, where the plaintiff's money has been paid by a thief to an innocent donee, and the plaintiff then seeks repayment from the donee in an action for money had and received. At present I do not wish to state the principle any less broadly than this: that the defence is available to a person whose position has so changed that it would be inequitable in all the circumstances to require him to make restitution, or alternatively to make restitution in full.[119]

3.104   Two theories of this defence emerged.[120]

3.105   The first, called the narrow view, categorizes change of position as a form of estoppel but without the need for an actual representation. It suffices if there has been detrimental reliance. Based on this narrow view, it would be more difficult to establish a relevant change of position based upon something having to have happened to the defendant, rather than the defendant having done something. So, for example, events such as fire or theft may not qualify under this narrow view, where detrimental reliance is required.

3.106   The second, called the wide view, distinguishes the change of position defence from the estoppel doctrine and the need for any detrimental reliance. Under this

---

[119]   ibid, 579–80.
[120]   Burrows, *The Law of Restitution* (2nd edn), 512–17 for a discussion of these two theories.

view, it suffices if the recipient has, consequent upon receipt of the relevant funds, so changed his position that it would now be inequitable to require him to repay the monies wrongly paid over. Although the test is wide enough to include monies stolen from the recipient,[121] it is nevertheless premised upon a causal link existing as between the receipt of the funds and the change of position.

In addition to apparently being adopted in *Lipkin Gorman* (see extracts above) **3.107** and more clearly so in *Scottish Equitable v Derby*,[122] the wide view has received the endorsement of Burrows,[123] and *Goff & Jones*.[124] In *Commerzbank AG v Gareth Price-Jones*[125] Munby LJ also adopted the wide view and went on to state:

> The consequence is that, as a matter of law, the defence of change of position is not dependent upon proof of some representation by the payer, nor is it dependent upon the proof of any detrimental reliance on the part of the payee. There will, no doubt, be certain factual circumstances where absent proof of detrimental reliance it will be unlikely, or perhaps even impossible, for the defence to be made out.[126]

It is submitted that Munby LJ's reasoning is correct. There is no reason why a defendant should not be able to rely upon the enrichment having been stolen in order to raise a change of position defence. The crucial issue is whether it remains available to be returned without the defendant having to use his own monies. If the money is stolen, or destroyed in a fire, then it is gone and can only be replaced by the defendant's own monies—a key indication that change of position has been established.

(b) Payments which would never otherwise have been made

Lord Goff used the example of the charitable donation which would not have **3.108** been made but for the receipt of the enrichment. To require the defendant, having made that charitable donation, to repay the money mistakenly paid over would be to require the defendant to dig into his own money and repay the defendant using his own money, which he might have been saving up for something of interest. If he would have made the donation, irrespective of his mistaken enrichment, he cannot rely upon the same as representing a change of position.

(c) Payments which were made earlier than would otherwise have been the case

More difficult perhaps is the situation where the recipient would have had to **3.109** make the relevant payment or transfer *at some point* but because of his receipt of additional sums, he makes the transfer earlier than planned. Just such a situation

---

121 *Rose v AIB Group (UK) plc* [2003] EWHC 1737 (Ch); [2003] 1 WLR 2791 at [49].
122 [2001] 3 All ER 818.
123 Burrows, *The Law of Restitution* (2nd edn), 515–17.
124 *Goff & Jones* (7th edn), para 40-008.
125 [2003] EWCA Civ 1663.
126 ibid, at [54].

arose in *Scottish Equitable plc v Derby*[127] where the Court of Appeal dismissed an appeal against the decision not to allow a recipient to rely upon monies transferred to pay off a mortgage debt as a change of position. Robert Walker LJ stated:

> [35] [Counsel] submitted that the payment-off of the mortgage was a change of position, but I cannot accept that submission. In general it is not a detriment to pay off a debt which will have to be paid off sooner or later: *RBC Dominion Securities Inc v Dawson* (1994) 111 DLR (4th) 230. It might be if there were a long term loan on advantageous terms, but it was not suggested that that was the case here; and as the judge said ([2000] 3 All ER 793 at 803) the evidence was that the house was to be sold in the near future.

3.110   Similarly, in *Credit Suisse (Monaco SA) v Attar*,[128] the Court of Appeal went on to consider the availability of the change of position defence under English law, although it was common ground that Monegasque law applied and no such defence existed under that law.

3.111   The Court began by recognizing the following principles were applicable to the change of position defence:

- that *Scottish Equitable v Derby* established the need to show a causal link between the mistaken receipt of the overpayment and the recipient's change of position;

- that *Lipkin Gorman* required any change of position to be *bona fide;* and also

- that *Lipkin Gorman* established that the defence would not be available in circumstances where the expenditure would be incurred by the recipient in the ordinary course of events;

- that *Scottish Equitable* also established that it would not be a detriment in general to pay off a debt which would have to be paid off sooner or later, at least unless the debt related to a long-term loan on advantageous terms;

- that negligence by the payor does not bar recovery of money mistakenly paid.

3.112   Applying these principles to the various forms of change of position defence raised by the defendants, the Court dismissed the appeal.

- Mrs Attar knew nothing of the existence of the relevant payment prior to her alleged change of position. She could thus not establish any causal link.

- The credit and store card payments would have been paid in any event and some of the later payments were made after the problems associated with the enrichment had already emerged.

---

[127] [2001] EWCA Civ 369, [2001] 3 All ER 818, CA.
[128] [2004] EWHC 374.

- The £50,092.70 used to reduce the mortgage did not amount to change of position since (i) Mrs Attar simply increased her equity stake in the house and (ii) those debts would have been paid off in any event.

- No change of position arose in respect of the use of the monies to buy shares, particularly since it was a successful investment.

- Other payments were made by Mr Attar acting in bad faith and so do not qualify for the change of position defence.

(d) Across the board increase in standard of living

A difficult situation often facing defendants is where they have, as a result of receiv- **3.113** ing the windfall, generally raised the standards of their living. So, one might imagine examples where the weekly shopping ceases to take place at the local Aldi low-cost supermarket and instead takes place at the higher priced Waitrose. In these circumstances, it might be difficult evidentially to show what additional expenditure has been caused as a result of the windfall receipt. The court has adopted a more relaxed approach to such situations, removing the need to prove each and every additional payment.[129] As Jonathan Parker J recognized in *Philip Collins Ltd v Davis:*[130]

> it may well be unrealistic to expect a defendant to produce conclusive evidence of change of position, given that when he changed his position he can have had no expectation that he might thereafter have to prove that he did so, and the reason why he did so in a court of law.[131]

Further, the Canadian case of *RBC Dominion Securities Inc v Dawson et al*[132] illustrates that there is no need for all the items purchased on this general increased level of living need to have been used up in order to give rise to a change of position defence: the 'mere fact that [the defendant] continues to benefit from the money does not defeat the defence of change of circumstances'. A little later, the court held the defence 'is not limited to those situations where the money is spent and there is nothing to show for it'.

(e) Court will scrutinize the facts of each case to determine extent of change of position

In *National Westminster Bank v Somer*,[133] a company's account was mistakenly **3.114** credited with additional funds. The company considered that these funds were the dilatory payments of an outstanding creditor and in reliance thereon the

---

[129] *Philip Collins Ltd v Davis* [2000] 3 All ER 808, 829–30; *Scottish Equitable plc v Derby* [2001] EWCA Civ 369; [2001] 3 All ER 818, [30]–[31].

[130] [2000] 3 All ER 808.

[131] ibid, 827. See also *National Westminster Bank plc v Somer International UK Ltd* [2002] 1 All ER 198 (CA).

[132] (1994) 11 DLR (4th) 230, 233, 240.

[133] [2001] EWCA Civ 970, [2002] QB 1286.

company released further goods to the non-paying customer. The Court of Appeal held that the company was able to rely upon such release of goods as a change of position. However, the failure to chase for the remaining payment from the outstanding creditor did not amount to a change of position as there was no causal connection between the receipt of the mistaken payment and the recipient's lost opportunity to chase its debtor for payment.

(f) A causal link must exist between the receipt of funds and the change of position

3.115 So far most of the examples have all included instances where it can be shown that the recipient has taken some step to make a transfer out of his funds as a consequence of receipt of the funds. Take the example of a recipient who suffers an illness. As counsel in *Scottish Equitable v Derby* submitted and the Court of Appeal accepted:

> The fact that the recipient may have suffered some misfortune (such as the breakdown in his health, or the loss of his job) is not a defence unless the misfortune is causally linked (at least on a 'but for' test) with the mistaken receipt.[134]

So there must be a causal connection, in the sense of 'but for', between the receipt of the payments and the event relied upon for change of position. This would include the monies being stolen, since without having received them, they could not be stolen. Similarly, with a fire. But the same cannot so readily be said for an illness to the recipient. There is no causal connection between the illness and the receipt of the enrichment and so nothing upon which to base a change of position defence.

(g) Anticipatory change of position a good defence

3.116 There has been a divergence of opinion as between decisions of the English High Court and that of the Privy Council on whether or not anticipatory change of position amounts to a good defence. It is likely that the Privy Council's view in favour of such conduct amounting to a good change of position will be followed in the English courts in the future.

3.117 In two High Court decisions, *Kleinwort Benson Ltd v South Tyneside MBC*[135] and *South Tyneside Metropolitan BC v Svenska International plc*[136] it has been held that the conduct relied upon as a change of position must *generally* take place after the receipt of payment. Clarke J in *South Tyneside* remarked:

> save perhaps in exceptional circumstances, the defence of change of position is in principle confined to changes which take place after receipt of the money . . . It does

---

[134] [2001] EWCA Civ 369; [2001] 3 All ER 818, [30].
[135] [1994] 4 All ER 972, 984–7 (Hobhouse J).
[136] [1995] 1 All ER 545 (Clarke J), [1995] LMCLQ 313 (Nolan) and criticized in *Goff & Jones* (7th edn) at paras 40-009–40-010.

not however follow that the defence of change of position can never succeed where the alleged change occurs before the receipt of the money.[137]

This statement was picked up by Jonathan Parker J in the *Philip Collins* case, lead- **3.118**
ing to his conclusion that:

> whether or not a change of position may be anticipatory, it must . . . have been made as a consequence of the receipt of, or (it may be) the prospect of receiving, the money sought to be recovered.[138]

The stance adopted by Jonathan Parker J in the *Philip Collins* case and that **3.119**
of Clarke J in *South Tyneside* was the subject of criticism by Munby J sitting in the Court of Appeal in *Commerzbank AG v Gareth Price-Jones*.[139] According to Munby J, Jonathan Parker J's comments were not 'particularly clear' and the views expressed in *South Tyneside* as to 'exceptional circumstances' were only likely to lead to detailed and distracting analysis of exactly what amounts to such circumstances—'a jurisprudence which, if allowed to flourish, would likely service only to distract attention away from the true question identified by Lord Goff'.[140]

By contrast, in *Dextra Bank and Trust Company Ltd v Bank of Jamaica*,[141] the Privy **3.120**
Council was prepared to find a change of position defence was established notwithstanding the fact that the defendant had changed his position in reliance on the future receipt of a payment.

Lords Goff and Bingham observed: **3.121**

> Here what is in issue is the justice or injustice of enforcing a restitutionary claim in respect of a benefit conferred. In that context, it is difficult to see what relevant distinction can be drawn between (1) a case in which the defendant expends on some extraordinary expenditure all or part of a sum of money which he has received from the plaintiff, and (2) one in which the defendant incurs such expenditure in the expectation that he will receive the sum of money from the plaintiff, which he does in fact receive. Since ex hypothesi the defendant will in fact have received the expected payment, there is no question of the defendant using the defence of change of position to enforce, directly or indirectly, a claim to that money. It is surely no abuse of language to say, in the second case as in the first, that the defendant has incurred the expenditure in reliance on the plaintiff's payment or, as is sometimes said, on the faith of the payment. It is true that, in the second case, the defendant relied on the payment being made to him in the future (as well as relying on such payment, when made, being a valid payment); but, provided that his change of position was in good faith, it should provide, pro tanto at least, a good defence because it would be inequitable to require the defendant to make restitution, or to make restitution in full. In particular it does not, in their Lordship's opinion, assist to rationalise the defence of

---

137 [1995] 1 All ER 545, 565e.
138 [2000] 3 All ER 808, 827g.
139 [2003] EWCA Civ 1663, [61]–[62].
140 ibid, [61].
141 [2002] 1 All ER (Comm) 193 (PC) (Lords Goff and Bingham delivering the PC Opinion).

change of position as concerned to protect security of receipts and then to derive from that rationalisation a limitation on the defence. The defence should be regarded as founded on a principle of justice designed to protect the defendant from a claim to restitution in respect of a benefit received by him in circumstances in which it would be inequitable to pursue that claim, or to pursue it in full. In any event, since . . . the context of a restitutionary action requires that the expected payment has in any event been received by the defendant, giving effect to 'anticipatory reliance' in that context will indeed operate to protect the security of an actual receipt.[142]

3.122 The Privy Council's view is to be preferred. It can make no significant difference whether the conduct upon which the change of position defence is founded is caused by the actual receipt of a mistaken payment or the expectation that such a payment is to be received. According to the Privy Council, *Svenska* can be confined to its own special facts and is not of general application.

(h) Relevance of fault to the defence of change of position

3.123 Self-evidently this is an important topic when considering the application of the defence of change of position in the context of a commercial fraud. Whilst the advantage of pursuing a claim in unjust enrichment is that the claimant need not overcome the hurdle of establishing fraud to succeed (the claim being one of strict liability), the conduct of the defendant will become relevant when it comes to whether he can rely upon the defence of change of position. In short, if the case is one of commercial fraud, whatever the view taken of the present state of the law (see below), it will be very difficult for a defendant to establish a good faith change of position.

3.124 Lord Goff in *Lipkin Gorman* was clear that the defence of change of position was not available to a defendant who had acted in bad faith.[143] In this context, bad faith obviously includes proceeding to change one's position notwithstanding having knowledge of the facts entitling the claimant to recover the monies paid over.[144] It will be readily appreciated that a fraudster will have difficulty overcoming this requirement.

3.125 It is also clear that negligence does not amount to bad faith.[145]

---

[142] [2002] 1 All ER (Comm) 193 (PC) at [38].

[143] [1991] 2 AC 548, 580.

[144] *McDonald v Coys of Kensington* [2004] WCA Civ 47; [2004] 1 WLR 2775, 2792 (Mance LJ).

[145] *Dextra Bank & Turst Co Ltd v Bank of Jamaica* [2001] UKPC 50, [2002] 1 All ER 193 (Comm); *Niru Battery Manufacturing Co v Milestone Trading Ltd* [2002] EWHC 1425, [2002] 2 All ER (Comm) 705, 738; *Papamichael v National Westminster Bank plc* [2003] 1 Lloyd's Rep 341, 368 (a wilful and reckless failure to make such inquiries as a reasonable person would make amounts to bad faith); *Maersk Air Ltd v Expeditors International (UK) Ltd* [2003] 1 Lloyd's Rep 491, 499; *Abou-Rahman v Abacha* [2006] 1 Lloyd's Rep 484 at [88] where the point was accepted by both parties.

Unfortunately, the more this area has been subjected to judicial scrutiny, the greater has become the confusion. For a general overview of the criticism, see *Goff & Jones* (7th edn) at paras 40-012–40-015. In particular, the learned authors criticize the Court of Appeal in *Niru Battery Manufacturing Co v Milestone Trading Ltd*[146] for misinterpreting Lord Goff in *Lipkin Gorman* and, with Lord Bingham, in *Dextra Bank and Trust Co Ltd v Bank of Jamaica* and seeking to apply the 'widest of principles' to the issue of bad faith. **3.126**

As such, the Court of Appeal in *Niru* moved away from the simple divide between good and bad faith and began to employ notions, more akin to the doctrine of unconscionability as employed for knowing receipt claims by the Court of Appeal in *BCCI v Akindele*.[147] Some of the more important conclusions reached by the Court of Appeal in *Niru* include: **3.127**

- Neither Lord Goff nor Lord Templeman indicated in *Lipkin Gorman* that the defence of change of position would only be lost on showing dishonesty or other wrongdoing [147].

- The underlying principles to be derived from Lord Goff in *Lipkin Gorman* were (i) the question is whether it would be unjust to allow restitution, or restitution in full; (ii) it will be unjust to allow restitution where an innocent defendant's position has so changed that the injustice of requiring him to repay outweighs the injustice of denying the claimant's restitution; (iii) the defence of change of position is not available to a defendant who has changed his position in bad faith, as where he has paid away the money with knowledge of the facts entitling the claimant to restitution; (iv) nor is it available to a wrongdoer; (v) in general terms, the defence is available to a defendant whose position has so changed that it would be inequitable to require him to make restitution or to make restitution in full.

In the Court of Appeal, Clarke LJ summarized the above principles into: 'the essential question is whether it would be inequitable or unconscionable, and thus unjust, to allow the recipient of money paid under a mistake of fact to deny restitution to the payer'[149]. This had nothing to do with good or bad fath. **3.128**

What this involved was a balancing exercise between the interests of the payor and those of the payee. Clarke LJ considered this was consistent with *BCCI v Akindele* [154]. **3.129**

It remains to be seen whether this will provide the sort of guidance that Lord Goff anticipated when he first expressly recognized the defence in *Lipkin Gorman*. **3.130**

---

[146] [2003] EWCA Civ 1446, [2004] QB 985. The decision of Moorebick J at first instance is at [2002] EWHC 1425, Comm, [2002] 2 All ER (Comm) 705.
[147] [2001] Ch 437 (CA).

Notable commentators have serious doubts that it has achieved anything other than the obsfucation of the law in this area.[148]

(i) Relevance of wrongdoing to defence of change of position

3.131 This section is concerned only with wrongdoing connected with the conduct amounting to change of position. It is assumed that the recipient was acting entirely innocently in receiving and retaining the monies. So, an example might be where the recipient innocently receives monies which he then uses in an illegal exchange control scam. Can he rely upon his conduct in the illegal exchange control scam as giving rise to change of position?

3.132 Lord Goff in *Lipkin Gorman* said that the defence of change of position would not be available to a wrongdoer. Whether this was intended simply to refer to that category of restitutionary claims based on wrongdoing, as opposed to unjust enrichment, remains unclear. Some commentators at least considered the comments to refer to restitution for wrongdoing.[149]

3.133 The general view is in favour of denying a claim in unjust enrichment if the defendant has committed a criminal offence. So, in *Barros Mattos Junior v General Securities & Finance Ltd*,[150] Laddie J held that defendants, who had breached foreign exchange rules, but who had otherwise acted in a bona fide manner, were not entitled to take advantage of this defence. In *Equiticorp Industries Group Ltd v R (No 47)*,[151] Smellie J held that the change of position defence could not be relied upon where the relevant payments making up that defence contravened legislation prohibiting a company purchasing its own shares.[152]

3.134 Laddie J in *Barros* had indicated that the court had no discretion as to whether to disallow the change of position on the ground of wrongdoing, even if this resulted in rather a harsh result. Charles Mitchell has suggested that the result in *Barros* itself—namely that the defendants were facing a US$8m liability simply because they had changed the money into naira before paying it on to a third party when such liability would not have remained had they simply made the payment in US dollars—indicates that Laddie J's approach is unduly rigid.

---

[148] Burrows, 'Clouding the Issues on Change of Position' [2004] CLJ 277.

[149] Burrows, *The Law of Restitution* (2nd edn), 526; Tettenborn, *Law of Restitution in England and Ireland* (3rd edn, Taylor and Francis Routledge, 2003), 278; see also Tettenborn, 'Bank Fraud, Change of Position and Illegality: The Case of the Innocent Money-Launderer' [2005] LMCLQ 6.

[150] [2004] EWHC 1188, [2005] 1 WLR 247.

[151] [1998] 2 NZLR 481.

[152] See also the Supreme Court of Canada, *Garland v Consumers' Gas Co Ltd* [2004] 1 SCR 629, [63]–[66]. These cases are discussed in Burrows, *English Private Law* (2nd edn), at paras 18.237–18.238.

*(j) Availability of defence post-*Foskett v McKeown

Much to his irritation,[153] Lord Millett's carefully chosen words in *Foskett v* **3.135**
McKeown have been misinterpreted by some commentators, leading to erroneous
conclusions as to when he says a change of position defence would be available.

Foskett v McKeown involved a claim to a proprietary remedy. Such a claim has **3.136**
nothing to do with enrichment as such and everything to do with assertion of title.
Such a claim would not be subject to the change of position defence.

But just because the change of position defence is not available for a proprietary **3.137**
claim does not mean that it has no role to play in respect of in personam claims
which are dependent upon establishing that the recipient received assets belonging to the claimant. *Lipkin Gorman* was just such a claim.

Such claims are typically dependent upon the invocation of the tracing rules. The **3.138**
fact that the tracing rules need to be employed does not mean that there can be no
change of position defence.

Lord Millett summarized his position as follows: **3.139**

> In my opinion, there are only two kinds of case where the change of position defence
> is not available: (i) where the claimant seeks a proprietary remedy (where it is not
> needed); and (ii) where the defendant is the original wrongdoer (who is an account-
> ing party and in any case could hardly plead an innocent change of position). But it
> is available where the claimant seeks a personal remedy against a successor in title,
> whether the defendant parted with the original asset or its traceable proceeds; and
> whether the action is brought to reverse unjust enrichment, when it reflects the fact
> that the defendant is no longer enriched, or to recover the value of the claimant's
> property, when it has a different rationale, viz to mitigate the harshness of the rule
> that all restitution is strict.[154]

(2) Bona fide purchaser for value without notice

The relationship between this defence and a claim in unjust enrichment is **3.140**
chequered and uncertain. There is a marked divergence of opinion as to whether
this defence should have any role to play at all in a typical claim in personam for
unjust enrichment.

The difficulties stem from the juxtaposition of two issues: **3.141**

- the fact this defence has nothing to do with enrichment issues and everything
  to do with title to assets; and

---

[153] See Lord Millett, 'Proprietary Restitution' in Degeling and Edelman (eds), *Equity in
Commercial Law*, 324–5 criticizing C Rotherham, 'Tracing Misconceptions in *Foskett v McKeown*'
(2003) 11 RLR 57 at 71.
[154] Lord Millett, 'Proprietary Restitution' in Degeling and Edelman (eds), *Equity in Commercial
Law*, 325.

- the fact there is a significant debate ongoing as to when, if at all, it is appropriate to grant a proprietary remedy for a claim in unjust enrichment.

3.142 So the answer to whether the defence is available is tied up with the more general question of the availability of proprietary claims in unjust enrichment and/or claims in personam which are based upon a vindication of existing property rights.

3.143 In his excellent book, *The Principles of the Law of Restitution*, Virgo observes:

> The function of the *bona fide* purchase defence is to make good defects in the defendant's title to property. The defence constitutes an exception to the *nemo potest dare quod non habet* principle by virtue of which the transferee cannot obtain rights to property which are better than those of the transferor. Consequently, where the transferor of property does not have good title to that property the transferee can be considered to have obtained good title if the conditions for the *bona fide* purchase defence have been satisfied. It is for this reason that the operation of the defence is confined to those restitutionary claims which involve the vindication of the claimant's property rights.[155]

3.144 This reasoning mirrors that of Lord Millett in *Foskett v McKeown*:[156]

> As I have already pointed out, the purchasers seek to vindicate their property rights, not to reverse unjust enrichment. The correct classification of the purchasers' cause of action may appear to be academic, but it has important consequences . . . [A] claim in unjust enrichment is subject to a change of position defence, which usually operates by reducing or extinguishing the element of enrichment. An action like the present is subject to the bona fide purchaser for value defence, which operates to clear the defendant's title.[157]

So, to summarize the position:

(a) In an ordinary claim in personam for unjust enrichment against the direct recipient, the defence of bona fide purchaser for value without notice has no application. Change of position defence is available.

(b) In a proprietary claim, the defence of bona fide purchaser applies because the claim is all about title to assets and not unjust enrichment.

(c) In a claim in personam for unjust enrichment where the claim, although personal in nature, is based upon a vindication of property rights (e.g. *Lipkin Gorman*, where the recipient is indirect), it is maintained by several commentators[158] that the defence must apply.

---

[155] Virgo, *The Principles of the Law of Restitution* (2nd edn), 656.
[156] [2001] 1 AC 102.
[157] ibid, 129.
[158] Burrows, *The Law of Restitution* (2nd edn), 586.

(3) Ministerial receipt

Where an individual, acting as an agent for his principal, receives an enrichment **3.145** paid over by, say, mistake, and before that individual becomes aware of the mistake, he pays[159] it over to his principal, no claim in unjust enrichment can be made against the agent.[160] This defence is available to all manner of agents including bankers[161] and solicitors.[162] The burden is on the agent to establish the defence.[163]

We are focused on claims which might arise in the commercial fraud setting. So **3.146** long as the agent has no knowledge of the claimant's entitlement to make a claim in unjust enrichment (in other words, knows nothing about his principal's fraud), he will be able to take advantage of this defence.

The defence is not available to an agent of an undisclosed principal.[164]   **3.147**

If the agent has notice of the activities of his principal, prior to handing over the **3.148** money, and nevertheless continues to do so, a claim in unjust enrichment can be brought directly against him as though he was acting as principal.[165]

If the agent has participated in some form of wrongdoing and/or received the **3.149** money as a consequence of wrongdoing of which he had knowledge, no defence of ministerial receipt can be established.[166] It does not matter whether the agent was acting on his own behalf[167] or took part in the wrongdoing on behalf of his principal.[168] In both circumstances, he will not be able to take advantage of this defence.

Although the defence has similarities with the change of position defence, it has **3.150** developed a separate body of authorities and recent case law suggests the two

---

[159] The agent needs to have: 'paid over the money which he received to the principal, or settled such an account with the principal as amounts to a payment, or done something which so prejudiced his position that it would be inequitable to require him to refund.' *Kleinwort, Sons & Co v Dunlop Rubber Co* (1907) 97 LT 263, 265; *Goff & Jones* (7th edn), para 40-028; *Buller v Harrison* (1777) 2 Cowp 565.

[160] ibid; *Stevenson v Mortimer* (1778) 2 Cowp 805, 806 per Lord Mansfield.

[161] *Gowers v Lloyds* [1938] 1 All ER 766.

[162] *Davys v Richardson* (1888) 21 QBD 202.

[163] The only possible caveat to this is the suggestion by the High Court of Australia that given the well known operation of banks in crediting payments to customers, the burden should perhaps be on the paying bank to show that the agent had not paid the money over to his principal: see *Australia and New Zealand Banking Group v Westpac Banking Corp* (1988) 62 ALJR 292 cited in *Goff & Jones* (7th edn), para 40-028.

[164] *Gurney v Womersley* (1854) 4 E & B 133 (agent discounts bills which he pays over to his principal; bills turn out to be forged and discounter has claim against agent for failure of consideration); *Baylis v Bishop of London* [1913] 1 Ch 127.

[165] *Continental Caoutchouc & Gutta Percha v Kleinwort* (1904) 90 LT 474, 477 per Romer LJ; *Goff & Jones* (7th edn), para 40-030.

[166] *Snowdon v Davis* (1808) 1 Taunt 359; *Goff & Jones* (7th edn), para 40-031.

[167] *Smith v Sleap* (1844) 12 M&W 585; *Wakefield v Newbon* (1844) 6 QB 276.

[168] *Oates v Hudson* (1851) 6 Ex 346.

defences are distinct. In *Portman Building Society v Hamlyn Taylor Neck (A firm)*,[169] Millett LJ said he did not:

> regard the agent's defence in such a case as a particular instance of the change of position defence, nor is it generally so regarded. At common law the agent recipient is regarded as a mere conduit for the money, which is treated as paid to the principal, not to the agent. The doctrine is therefore not so much a defence as a means of identifying the proper party to be sued. It does not, for example, avail the agent of an undisclosed principal; though today such an agent would be able to rely on a change of position defence.

(4) Limitation of actions

3.151 It is a matter of regret that given the slow development and recognition of the distinct cause of action known as unjust enrichment, the relevant statutory provision dealing with limitation periods, notably the Limitation Act 1980, does not expressly deal with claims in unjust enrichment.

3.152 This could lead one to conclude that in the absence of an express provision dealing with limitations, no limitation period applies at all. This would be unsatisfactory and single out unjust enrichment as against the better established claims which all have periods laid down in the Act.

3.153 Instead, the courts have applied the six-year period for simple contract claims to those arising under unjust enrichment. This view began with the 1939 Limitation Act which was interpreted by Lord Greene MR in *Re Diplock*[170] as including claims for money had and received. More recently, this approach was endorsed by Hobhouse J in *Kleinwort Benson Ltd v The Sandwell BC*.[171]

3.154 Whilst this is a throwback to the bad old days of labels such as quasi-contract,[172] it does nevertheless provide a clear and consistent approach to the determination of limitation issues for claims in unjust enrichment.

3.155 In general, time for such a claim starts to run from the moment of receipt of the enrichment. It is not when there is a demand for repayment.[173]

---

[169] [1998] 4 All ER 202, 207–8. See also *Bowstead & Reynolds on Agency* (18th edn, Thomson/Sweet and Maxwell, 2006), [9-104].

[170] [1948] Ch 465, 475.

[171] [1994] 4 All ER 890, 943.

[172] It does appear that examination of Hansard relating to the 1939 Act under the *Pepper v Hart* [1993] AC 593 principle reveals that the Solicitor-General did intend 'contract' to include 'quasi-contract'.

[173] *Fuller v Happy Shopper Markets Ltd* [2001] 1 WLR 1681 where Lightman J said that the principle set out in *Freeman v Jeffries* (1869) LR 4 Ex 189, that a demand for repayment was necessary before any cause of action accrued, must be understood against the fact that that case concerned a claim in rescission. It is accepted one needs to give notice of rescission. Otherwise, there is no general rule requiring such notice.

4

CONVERSION[1]

A. Overview of Elements of Conversion

The act of conversion can take place in so many different ways that it is quite diffi-   **4.01**
cult to provide a general definition which includes all elements of the claim. Lord
Nicholls attempted to provide an overview of the elements in *Kuwait Airways
Corporation v Iraqi Airways Co*:[2]

> Conversion of goods can occur in so many different circumstances that framing a
> precise definition of universal application is well nigh impossible. In general, the basic
> features of the tort are threefold. First, the defendant's conduct was inconsistent with
> the rights of the owner (or other person entitled to possession). Second, the conduct
> was deliberate, not accidental.[3] Third, the conduct was so extensive an encroachment
> on the rights of the owner as to exclude him from use and possession of the goods. The
> contrast is with lesser acts of interference. If these cause damage they may give rise to
> claims for trespass or in negligence, but they do not constitute conversion.[4]

---

[1] See *Clerk & Lindsell* (19th edn), ch 17 for a detailed treatment of this tort and its historical
background.

[2] [2000] 2 AC 883.

[3] But be careful not to confuse the need for a deliberate act as indicating a requirement that there
be an intention to interfere. The claim is one of strict liability.

[4] *Kuwait Airways Corporation v Iraqi Airways Co* [2000] 2 AC 883, at [39].

4.02 In the earlier case of *Lancashire and Yorkshire Railway Co v MacNicoll*,[5] Atkin J suggested the following definition:

> It appears to me plain that dealing with goods in a manner inconsistent with the right of the true owner amounts to a conversion, provided that it is also established that there is also an intention on the part of the defendant in so doing to deny the owner's right or to assert a right which is inconsistent with the owner's right.

It is necessary to be clear as to the role to be played by intention. The tort is one of strict liability, but the defendant must intend to assert a right inconsistent with that of the true owner, although the defendant need not be aware of the existence of any other true owner. The point is illustrated by an example. X attempts to sell what he believes to be his car. In fact, it belongs to someone else. The very act of offering it for sale and deliberately so, is an act contrary to the rights of the true owner if X is not the true owner.

B. Introduction

4.03 The tort of conversion is a common law claim of strict liability intended to protect proprietary interests (more accurately, possessory interests) in tangible assets usually by the award of damages, although very occasionally it may be possible to obtain an award of specific restitution.

4.04 As we have already seen, the tort of conversion is very difficult to define with any precision:

> I have frequently stated that I never did understand with precision what was a conversion . . . I find it impossible to give an exhaustive description as to what was or was not a conversion, per Bramwell LJ in *Hiort v The London and North Western Railway Company*.[6]

4.05 In *Kuwait Airways Corpn v Iraqi Airways Co (Nos 4 and 5)*,[7] the House of Lords appeared willing to accept as an accurate description of the tort of conversion that is contained in *Clerk & Lindsell*:[8]

> . . . conversion is an act of deliberate dealing with a chattel in a manner inconsistent with another's right whereby that other is deprived of the use and possession of it.

4.06 Conversion is confined to tangible assets.[9] Whilst it has a very limited role to play where money is treated as a bag of coins, in most situations of commercial fraud,

---

[5] (1918) 88 LJKB 601. This definition was approved by the Court of Appeal (Scrutton LJ) in *Oakley v Lyster* [1931] 1 KB 148.

[6] (1879) 4 Ex D 188, 194.

[7] [2002] UKHL 19; [2002] 2 AC 883, [427]–[429].

[8] (19th edn), para 17-07.

[9] *OBG v Allan* [2007] UKHL 21, [2008] 1 AC 1. See also *Halsbury's Laws of England* (4th edn, reissue vol 45(2) 1999), para 547: 'The subject matter of conversion or trover must be specific personal property, whether goods or chattels.'

where money is placed in the banking system and treated as currency, no claim in conversion can arise. In that respect, therefore, this claim will not be available to a victim of a fraud involving the misappropriation of funds. The victim will be left with his common law claim for money had and received, or unjust enrichment as it is now called.

That said, negotiable instruments such as cheques and bills of exchange can be the subject of conversion, since they are tangible assets whose value is treated as being their stated value. So, in the case of a cheque, its value will be taken to be the amount in which the cheque is drawn. This may appear a little anomalous but it is well established in the authorities.[10] **4.07**

Space does not permit a detailed account of the historical development of this claim, nor is one strictly required in a practitioner's text. It suffices, perhaps, simply to make clear that the Torts (Interference with Goods) Act 1977 (the 1977 Act) removed some of the anachronistic claims, such as detinue, and only tinkered with some aspects of the common law claim for conversion. The 1977 Act limited conversion to 'goods' which it defines to include: 'all chattels personal other than things in action and money.'[11] **4.08**

The main alteration was the introduction of a claim against bailees in respect of the destruction or loss of goods for which the bailees owed duty of care to the bailor. That was the only new statutory tort created by the 1977 Act. A further important change introduced by the 1977 Act was the introduction, in certain circumstances, of a claim for specific restitution rather than damages, which had, at common law, been limited only to claims for detinue. **4.09**

Finally, the 1977 Act clarified the position that a mere denial of title, without any actual dealing with the property itself, did not amount to an act of conversion.[12] **4.10**

Whilst for completeness, this chapter will provide an outline of the various methods of conversion and those assets which might be susceptible to such a claim, it will at the end focus on, and provide an overview in relation to, banks, cheques and conversion claims. More detailed treatment of the position with banks is to be left to the specialist texts.[13] **4.11**

This chapter is divided into the following sections: **4.12**

- what conduct may amount to conversion?
- what assets may be the subject matter of a claim in conversion?

---

[10] *Lloyds Bank Ltd v Chartered Bank of India, Australia and China* [1929] 1 KB 40, 55–6 per Scrutton LJ. See para 4.45 *et seq.*

[11] Torts (Interference with Goods) Act 1977, s 14(1).

[12] Torts (Interference with Goods) Act 1977, s 13(3).

[13] M Hapgood QC, *Paget's Law of Banking* (13th edn, Butterworths, 2006); M Brindle QC and R Cox QC, *Law of Bank Payments* (3rd edn, Sweet and Maxwell, 2004).

- who can sue in conversion?
- what remedies exist for a claim in conversion?
  - how does the court value the damages claim?
  - when might the court award specific restitution?
- consideration of banks, cheques and conversion.

C. What Conduct may Amount to Conversion?

(1) A strict liability claim

4.13   Conversion is a strict liability claim.[14] Subject to certain exceptions,[15] it does not require to be established that the defendant had any intention to deprive the owner of its possessory interest. It suffices that the defendant's conduct in fact achieves that effect, irrespective of whether it was actually intended by the defendant.

4.14   As Diplock LJ in *Marfani & Co Ltd v Midland Bank Ltd*[16] remarked:

> At common law one's duty to one's neighbour who is the owner, or entitled to possession, of any goods is to refrain from doing any voluntary act in relation to his goods which is a usurpation of his proprietary or possessory rights in them. Subject to some exceptions, it matters not that the doer of the act of usurpation did not know, and could not by the exercise of any reasonable care have known of his neighbour's interest in the goods. This duty is absolute; he acts at his peril.[17]

The relevant intention consists in the doing of the act and not in usurping another's possessory or proprietary rights.

4.15   This is, therefore, another one of those claims which may be available in a commercial fraud scenario which will not require the claimant to plead and establish fraud, which is always a high burden to overcome.

(2) Conduct amounting to conversion

4.16   It has already been noted that conversion is not a claim of ready or fixed definition or description. As such, it is important to appreciate that the various means by which conversion may take place are not closed. That said, a useful indication of

---

[14] *Kuwait Airways Corpn v Iraqi Airways Co (Nos 4 and 5)* [2002] 2 AC 883, [77], [78] and [80].

[15] These exceptions include a bailee acting on the bailor's instructions, an agent dealing with custody only, an involuntary bailee and various statutory exceptions, the most important of which for present purposes is s 4 of the Cheques Act 1957 (discussed below). For a detailed treatment of these exceptions, see *Clerk & Lindsell* (19th edn) at para 17-70 *et seq.*

[16] [1968] 1 WLR 956.

[17] ibid, 970–1.

the type of conduct which would be required is given by the list proposed by *Clerk & Lindsell* (19th edn) at para 17-08, namely:

(1) when property is wrongfully taken or received by someone not entitled to do so

(a) The taking or receiving must constitute an act inconsistent with the rights of the actual owner.

(b) It is sometimes said that the defendant must act with an intention to assert a right inconsistent with that of the actual owner. Care must be taken with this. It is not intended to introduce, by the back-door, a fault-based approach to conversion but rather to highlight that the kind of relevant conduct must involve some form of assertion of right which is in fact inconsistent with that of the actual owner.

(c) The point is made good by example. If D purchases goods which did not belong to the vendor, that would be an example of conduct on the part of D inconsistent with the rights of the actual owner. D intended to obtain title and possession of those goods but, crucially, it is not necessary to show that D was aware that the vendor was not the true owner.[18]

(d) In *Kuwait Airways Corpn v Iraqi Airways Co (Nos 4 and 5)*[19] Lord Nicholls said: 'To constitute conversion, detention . . . must be accompanied by an intention to keep the goods.'

(e) The need to show an intention to assert a right inconsistent with that of the actual owner is the means to distinguish trespass (which does not require such an intention) from conversion (which does).[20]

(f) The presentment and collection of the proceeds of a cheque by a collecting bank on behalf of a person who is not the true owner of the cheque will, subject to statutory defences, be conduct amounting to a conversion.[21]

> The bank so dispose of the chattels, the cheques, as to deprive both themselves and the true owners of the dominion over them, and in exchange for the pieces of paper constituted themselves the debtors of the customer. I cannot imagine a plainer case of conversion.[22]

(2) when property is wrongfully parted with

(a) If D, without lawful justification, delivers to a third party by way of a sale, pledge or simply by way of gift, a tangible asset belonging to another, D has committed an action of conversion.

---

[18] E.g. *The Saetta* [1993] 2 Lloyd's Rep 268.

[19] [2002] UKHL 19; [2002] 2 AC 883, [42].

[20] *Fouldes v Willoughby* (1841) 8 M & W 540; *Sanderson v Marsden* (1922) 10 Ll L Rep 467, 472.

[21] *Underwood v Bank of Liverpool* [1924] 1 KB 775.

[22] [1924] 1 KB 775, 795 per Atkin LJ. See also *Honourable Society of the Middle Temple v Lloyds Bank plc* [1999] Lloyd's Rep Bank 50 (Rix J); *Kleinwort, Sons and Co v Comptoir National D'escompte de Paris* [1894] 2 QB 157; *Morison v London* [1914] 3 KB 356.

(b) The mere act of sale itself, without delivery into the possession of the third party, will not amount to a conversion.[23]

(3) when, in breach of his duty, the bailee loses bailed property

    (a) This is the only new statutory act of conversion introduced by the 1977 Act. It circumvents the common law requirement to show a voluntary act before conduct could amount to conversion.

    (b) It is now established that if a bailee loses or allows goods bailed to him to be destroyed, that will amount to conversion (s 2(2) of the 1977 Act).

(4) when property is wrongfully sold so as to pass good title to the buyer

    (a) It has already been shown that a sale by a non-owner, coupled with delivery to the purchaser, will amount to conversion, notwithstanding the fact that the sale is ineffective to pass title to the buyer.

    (b) If the sale by the non-owner in fact is effective, without delivery, to transfer title to the purchaser, by way of exception to the *nemo dat quod non habet* rule,[24] the non-owner seller commits an action of conversion.

(5) when property is wrongfully retained upon demand

    (a) If D wrongfully retains property after the actual owner or an individual with an immediate right to possession demands its return, that will amount to a conversion.[25]

    (b) The statutory conversion (Torts (Interference with Goods) Act 1977, s 2(2)), which corresponded with the common law claim in detinue, does require a demand for the goods to be returned and an unequivocal refusal so to do.[26]

(6) when property is wrongfully misused or destroyed

    (a) The deliberate misuse of property in possession can amount to a conversion, such as the wrongful use of a hire-car for smuggling.[27]

    (b) Similarly, the use of property in circumstances where D has no lawful entitlement so to do will also amount to conversion. The example often used is that of D borrowing a horse for a ride. Although D returns the horse, the true owner has a claim for conversion.[28]

(7) when the claimant is denied access to property by the defendant, without the defendant physically interfering with it

---

[23] *Marcq v Christie's* [2004] QB 286, [19] citing with approval *Consolidated Company v Curtis & Son* [1892] 1 QB 495; see also *Lancashire Waggon Co v Fitzhugh* (1861) 6 H & N 502, 158 ER 206.

[24] E.g. Sale of Goods Act 1979, s 21(1), where the actual owner is estopped from denying the vendor's power to pass good title.

[25] *Barclays Mercantile Finance Ltd v Sibec Developments Ltd* [1992] 1 WLR 1253.

[26] *Helga Henriette Schwarzschild v Harrods Ltd* [2008] EWHC 521 (QB) (Eady J) applying *Clayton v Le Roy* [1911] 2 KB 1031 (CA).

[27] *Moorgate Mercantile Co Ltd v Finch* [1962] 1 QB 701 CA.

[28] *Rolle, Abridgement,* Action sur Case p 5. This example can fall under this heading or under the first example of conversion by taking or receiving property.

(a) This is best illustrated by way of an example. A sells property to B, which is presently located on C's land. D prevents B from collecting that property. D is liable to B in conversion even though he was never in possession of the property sold to B.[29]

(b) In *Kuwait Airways Corpn v Iraqi Airways Co*[30] Kuwait, aircraft were forcibly removed by the Iraqi army to Iraq in order that D take them over. D repainted them, re-registered and obtained insurance in respect of these aeroplanes. The House of Lords found such conduct amounted to a conversion.

These are simply some specific examples of the type of conduct which may **4.17** amount to an act of conversion. In a commercial fraud context, it will be important to keep open the possibility of a claim in conversion, perhaps against some of the peripheral participants in the fraud through whose hands property has passed or been channelled. If it can be shown that their conduct was inconsistent with the rights of the actual owner of the property, then it may be possible to bring a claim in conversion against them, without needing to prove knowledge on their part of the overall fraud. The difficulty for such a claim is that such individuals are unlikely to assert ownership rights over such assets if they are simply passing through their hands.

D. What Property may be the Subject of a Claim in Conversion?

The tort of conversion is limited to dealings in respect of corporeal personal prop- **4.18** erty i.e. tangible movable assets. Land is not capable of being the subject of an action in conversion.

It does not apply to choses in action, such as contractual rights,[31] or to intellectual **4.19** property rights.[32]

It does not apply to documents stored in electronic form. Any claim under the **4.20** 1977 Act is limited to the hard disk of a computer and does not include the files stored on it: *Dunn & Bradstreet v Typesetting Facilities Ltd*;[33] *St Alban's City & District Council v International Computers Ltd.*[34]

Whilst the claim may have a very limited role to play in respect of money, such as **4.21** a bag of coins, it will cease to have any role to play at all when that money is treated

---

[29] *Oakley v Lyster* [1931] 1 KB 148.
[30] [2002] UKHL 19, [2002] 2 AC 883.
[31] *OBG v Allan* [2007] UKHL 21, [2008] 1 AC 1.
[32] *Stewart v Engel* [2000] BCC 741 (no conversion relating to copyright).
[33] [1992] FSR 320.
[34] [1996] 4 All ER 481.

as currency, such as whenever it is placed into the banking system.[35] So, if a thief steals A's cash and pays it over to B, a claim in conversion may arise against the thief in respect of its dealings with the stolen cash[36] but no such claim will arise in respect of the money in the hands of B.[37]

4.22 If money has been handed over to an individual with specific responsibility to hold *that money* and to return *that money* to the owner upon demand then a wrongful refusal by the recipient may amount to conversion, such money not having been treated as currency.[38]

4.23 Whilst there is a very limited role for conversion in respect of money, it does apply to negotiable instruments, cheques, guarantees, insurance policies and bonds. Indeed, it extends to any document, prepared in the ordinary course of business, as evidence of a debt or obligation to pay and which remains valid and enforceable[39] e.g. share certificates.[40]

4.24 In *Lloyds Bank Ltd v Chartered Bank of India, Australia and China*[41] Scrutton LJ sought to provide an explanation for the legal fiction whereby a valid cheque is deemed to have the value equal to the amount in which it is drawn:

> Conversion primarily is conversion of chattels, and the relation of bank to customer is that of debtor and creditor. As no specific coins in a bank are the property of any specific customer there might appear to be some difficulty in holding that a bank, which paid part of what it owed its customer to some other person not authorised to receive it, had converted its customer's chattels; but a series of decisions . . . culminating in *Morison v London County and Westminster Bank Ltd* [1914] 3 KB 356 and *A L Underwood Ltd v Bank of Liverpool* [1924] 1 KB 775, have surmounted the difficulty by treating the conversion as of the chattel, the piece of paper, the cheque under which the money was collected, and the value of the chattel converted as the money received under it: see the explanation of Phillimore LJ in *Morison's* case.[42]

---

[35] *Lipkin Gorman v Karpnale Ltd* [1992] 2 AC 548, 559 (per Lord Templeman).
[36] *Hall v Dean* (1600) Cro. Eliz 841. It remains interesting to see how this area will develop given the willingness of the courts to find that a thief is a fiduciary in order to afford the victim of the theft the advantage of the equitable rules on tracing. If this results in the victim of the theft having only an equitable interest in the stolen proceeds, that will not suffice for the purposes of a claim in conversion: *MCC Proceeds Inc v Lehman Bros International (Europe)* [1998] 4 All ER 965 CA.
[37] *Lipkin Gorman v Karpnale Ltd* [1992] 2 AC 548.
[38] *Orton v Butler* (1822) 5 B & A 652, 106 ER 1329.
[39] Pursuant to the Bills of Exchange Act 1882, s 64, if the conduct towards the cheque has rendered it invalid, on the basis of unauthorized alteration, the cheque becomes a worthless piece of paper for which no damages are recoverable: *Smith v Lloyds TSB plc* [2001] QB 541 CA.
[40] *Malkins Nominees Ltd v Societe Financiere Mirelis SA* [2004] EWHC 2631; see also *MCC Realisations Ltd v Lehman Bros* [1998] 4 All ER 675 where the claim failed because the claimant only had an *equitable* interest in the shares. That was not enough to give rise to a title to sue which required either actual possession or an immediate *legal* right to possession.
[41] [1929] 1 KB 40.
[42] ibid, 55–6.

In *Morison v London County and Westminster Bank Ltd* [43] Phillimore LJ stated: **4.25**

> That the damages for such conversion are (at any rate where the drawer has sufficient funds to his credit and the drawee bank is solvent) the face value of the cheques is . . . so well established that it is not necessary to inquire into the principle which may underlie the authority. But the principle probably is that, though the plaintiff might at any moment destroy the cheques which remained in his possession, they are potential instruments whereby the sums they represent may be drawn from his bankers, and, if they get into any other hands than his, he will be the loser to the extent of the sums which they represent. It may be also that any one who has obtained its value by presenting a cheque is estopped from asserting that it has only a nominal value. [44]

This principle will only apply where the paper has a stated value attached to it. If,   **4.26** for example, the drawer's signature on the instrument has been forged, it is no longer a valid instrument. [45] Similarly, if a cheque is stolen and materially altered it becomes a worthless piece of paper incapable of giving rise to substantial damages. [46]

E . Who has Title to Sue in Conversion? [47]

In order to have title to sue in a claim for conversion a claimant must establish that   **4.27** at the time of the conversion he had either actual possession of the property or alternatively an immediate (legal) right to possess the property. [48]

It is not necessary to prove full ownership (whatever that actually means under   **4.28** English law) and in fact, ownership will not suffice without either of the conditions of actual possession or an immediate (legal) right to possess. [49] Often the possessory right has been given to an agent or pledgee or some other individual, thus depriving the actual owner of having title to sue in conversion. If so, it will be the agent or pledgee who would have title to sue in those circumstances.

An employee does not typically have 'actual possession' of his employer's property   **4.29** and is therefore not entitled to bring a claim in conversion in respect of that property. So if a cheque is stolen from an employee, it is his employer who will be

---

[43] [1914] 3 KB 356.

[44] ibid, 379.

[45] *Arrow Transfer Co Ltd v Royal Bank of Canada, Bank of Montreal and Canadian Imperial Bank of Commerce* [1971] 2 WWR 241, aff'd on appeal: [1972] 4 WWR 70.

[46] *Smith v Lloyds TSB Group plc* [2001] QB 541.

[47] Curwen, 'Title to Sue in Conversion' [2004] Conv 308; M Bridge, *Personal Property Law* (3rd edn, Clarendon Press, 2002), 62–71.

[48] *Bute (Marquess) v Barclays Bank Ltd* [1955] 1 QB 202, 211.

[49] *Kahler v Midland Bank Ltd* [1950] AC 24 (HL).

deemed to be in actual possession (through the employee) of the cheque and therefore entitled to bring the conversion claim.[50]

4.30 In the case of an 'immediate right to possession', it has already been established that the right must be a legal and not an equitable right to possession.[51] An equitable interest will not suffice.[52] Any other conclusion would ride a coach and horses through equity's Darling defence of *bona fide purchaser for value without notice*.

4.31 Whether the drawer or the payee of a cheque has an immediate right to its possession will depend on the rules as to when a cheque has been delivered.[53] Section 2 of the Bills of Exchange Act 1882 defines 'delivery' as being the transfer of possession, actual or constructive, from one person to another. If X, the drawer of the cheque, hands the cheque over to Y, the named payee, that will amount to a delivery. Y, as named payee properly in receipt of the cheque, would have title to sue. If the cheque is stolen from X and transferred to Y, that will not suffice as delivery.[54] In such event, the title to sue would remain vested in X.

4.32 A contractual right to possession would appear to suffice for the purposes of title to sue in conversion. In *Iran v Bakarat Galleries Ltd*[55] the Court of Appeal considered the following issue: where 'A', who is in possession of a chattel, or who is entitled to immediate possession of the chattel, agrees that another ('B') may enter into possession of the chattel, can B rely upon his contractual right to immediate possession to found an action in conversion against C who wrongly interferes with the chattel? If by the agreement A has transferred to B not merely the right to enter into possession, but the ownership that A enjoyed, so that B enjoys both proprietary title and an immediate right to possession, he will be entitled to sue in conversion. If, however, A has retained his proprietary title, can B rely on his contractual right to enter into immediate possession to found a claim in conversion?

4.33 The Court of Appeal noted that there was support for a contractual right sufficing from the following:

- *Halsbury's Laws of England* (4th edn, reissue) vol 45(2), para 560.
- Salmond, *Law of Torts* (21st edn, 1996), 108.
- Winfield and Jolowicz, *Tort* (17th edn, 2006), 762.
- Markesinis and Deakin, *Tort Law* (5th edn, 2003), 436.
- F H Lawson, *Remedies of English Law* (2nd edn, 1980), 122.

---

[50] Gleeson, *Personal Property Law* (Sweet and Maxwell, 1997), 26 *et seq.*

[51] *MCC Proceeds Inc v Lehman Bros International (Europe)* [1998] 4 All ER 965 CA; Tettenborn [1996] CLJ 36.

[52] Notwithstanding suggestions to the contrary in *International Factors Ltd v Rodriguez* [1979] QB 351, 359 CA.

[53] The issues surrounding any claim in conversion arising from a cheque are examined in some detail in Brindle and Cox (eds), *The Law of Bank Payments* (3rd edn, Sweet and Maxwell, 2004), ch 7.

[54] *Arnold v Cheque Bank* (1876) 1 CPD 578.

[55] [2007] EWCA Civ 1374, [2008] 1 All ER 1177.

Against this view is *Clerk & Lindsell* at para 17-59: '. . . it seems that the immediate   **4.34**
right to possession on which the owner relies must be a proprietary right; a mere
contractual right will not do.' In support of this view, *Clerk & Lindsell* cites two
cases: *Jarvis v Williams*[56] and *International Factors v Rodriguez*.[57]

The Court of Appeal in *Iran v Bakarat* noted that the Court of Appeal in *MCC*   **4.35**
Proceeds Inc v Lehman Brothers International (Europe)[58] interpreted *International*
Factors v Rodriguez in a manner which was inconsistent with *Jarvis v Williams*. To
reconcile the position the Court of Appeal in *Iran v Bakarat* held:

> Where the owner of goods who has an immediate right to possession of them,
> albeit that they are in the possession of a third party, by agreement transfers his
> title to a new owner, the new owner can bring a claim in conversion against the
> person in whose possession they are. Where the owner of goods with an immediate
> right to possession of them by contract transfers the latter right to another, so that
> he no longer has an immediate right to possession but retains ownership, it would
> seem right in principle that the transferee should be entitled to sue in conversion.
> *A fortiori* if the contract provides that when the transferee enters into possession,
> ownership will be transferred to him. We consider that this accords with the
> weight of academic opinion and can be reconciled with the facts of *Jarvis v*
> *Williams*.[59]

F. What Remedies Exist for a Claim in Conversion?

The tort of conversion is focused on wrongful interference with a person's posses-   **4.36**
sory rights over chattels and yet the main remedy for this claim is not recovery of
the chattel, but damages. The 1977 Act did introduce, for the first time outside of
claims for detinue, a remedy of specific restitution but it will only be granted by
the courts in limited circumstances.

(1) Assessment of damages[60]

Section 3 of the Torts (Interference with Goods) Act 1977 provides: **4.37**

> (1)   In proceedings for wrongful interference against a person who is in possession or
>   in control of the goods relief may be given in accordance with this section, so far
>   as appropriate.

---

56   [1955] 1 WLR 71.
57   [1979] 1 QB 351.
58   [1998] 4 All ER 675.
59   [2007] EWCA Civ 1374; [2008] 1 All ER 1177 at [30].
60   See Tettenborn, 'Damages in Conversion' [1993] LJ 128; Hudson, 'Money Claims for the
Misuse of Chattels' in McKendrick and Palmer (eds), *Interests in Goods* (Lloyd's of London Press,
1993), 548; *McGregor on Damages* (17th edn, Thomson/Sweet and Maxwell, 2003), ch 33.

(2) The relief is—

    (a) an order for delivery of the goods, and for payment of any consequential damages, or

    (b) an order for delivery of the goods, but giving the defendant the alternative of paying damages by reference to the value of the goods, together in either alternative with payment of any consequential damages; or

    (c) damages.

(3) Subject to rules of court—

    (a) relief shall be given under only one of paragraphs (a), (b) and (c) of subsection (2).

    ...

(4) ...

(5) Where an order is made under subsection (2)(b) the defendant may satisfy the order by returning the goods at any time before execution of judgment, but without prejudice to liability to pay any consequential damages.

4.38   The statutory scheme for relief in a conversion claim is therefore an award based upon the delivery of the goods and the payment of any consequential damages, an option to pay damages based upon the value of the goods instead of returning them, again with liability to pay for consequential damages, or finally simply an award of damages.

4.39   The normal award is ultimately one of damages rather than return of the specific object.

4.40   In *Kuwait Airways Corpn v Iraqi Airways Co (Nos 4 and 5)*[61] Lord Nicholls was keen to stress that there is nothing special or artificial about the method of calculating damages for conversion:

> The fundamental object of an award of damages in respect of this tort, as with all wrongs, is to award just compensation for loss suffered. Normally ('prima facie') the measure of damages is the market value of the goods at the time the defendant expropriated them. This is the general rule, because generally this measure represents the amount of the basic loss suffered by the plaintiff owner. He has been dispossessed of his goods by the defendant. Depending on the circumstances some other measure, yielding a higher or lower amount, may be appropriate. The plaintiff may have suffered additional damage consequential on the loss of his goods. Or the goods may have been returned.[62]

4.41   The aim of the damages award is to compensate the claimant for his loss caused by the conversion. Accordingly, damages will be assessed by reference to the value of the property converted at the time of conversion,[63] together with any consequential

---

[61] [2002] 2 AC 883.

[62] ibid, [67]. See also *Hall v Barclay* [1937] 1 All ER 620 CA.

[63] *Solloway v McLoughlin* [1938] AC 247 (PC). Lord Atkin (delivering the PC Opinion) said (257–8): 'As to the deposited shares, in the circumstances of the case the company never had any right to deal with them . . . Their disposal of the deposited shares amounted to nothing short of conversion, and the client on each occasion on which the shares were sold had vested in him a right to a right to damages for conversion which would be measured by the value of the shares at the date of the

damages reasonably foreseeable at the time of conversion.[64] That is when, typically, the claimant would be expected to go into the market to purchase alternative goods. The House of Lords in *Kuwait Airways Corpn v Iraqi Airways Co* held that where the defendant had acted in good faith, the appropriate remoteness test was the test of foreseeability whereas if the defendant had acted in bad faith, he would be liable for all the direct and natural consequences of his act.[65]

If the value of the converted property has risen after the date of conversion and the **4.42** claimant is not at fault for having failed to mitigate his losses earlier, then the court may award damages based upon the additional loss caused by the increase in market price after the date of conversion.[66] If the claimant had been warned to collect his goods and he unjustifiably delayed such that the goods were (wrongfully) sold, the claimant would be unable to claim any increase in value of the goods after they had been sold.[67]

If the value of the converted property falls after conversion, the claimant will be **4.43** entitled to recover damages assessed as at the date of conversion.[68] This ensures that the defendant does not profit from his wrongdoing and has been described in *Kuwait Airways Corpn v Iraqi Airways Co*[69] as a form of gain-based damages akin to those awarded in *Attorney-General v Blake*.[70]

(2) When might a court award specific restitution?

This is an award entirely in the discretion of the court. Specific restitution under **4.44** the 1977 Act will not be awarded for the return of assets or property which are readily available in the market. The court is likely to need to be persuaded that there is something unique in the particular property such that an award of damages

---

conversion . . . . not knowing of the conversion, he received from the wrongdoer, and has retained, the very goods converted or their equivalent . . . the only effect is that he must give credit for the value of what he has received at the time he received it, and . . . the damages are reduced by this amount.' See also *Caxton Publishing Co v Sutherland Publishing Co* [1939] AC 178; *Brandeis Goldschmidt v Western Transport Ltd* [1981] QB 864; *BBMM Finance (Hong Kong) Ltd v Eda Holdings Ltd* [1990] 1 WLR 409; *VFS Financial Services (UK) Ltd v Euro Auctions (UK) Ltd* [2007] EHWC 1492.

[64] *Saleslease Ltd v Davis* [1999] 1 WLR 1664 (CA); *Hillesden Securities Ltd v Ryjack Ltd* [1983] 1 WLR 959.

[65] [2002] UKHL 19; [2002] 2 AC 883, [95]–[104].

[66] *The Playa Larga* [1983] 2 Lloyd's Rep 171.

[67] *Sachs v Micklos* [1948] 2 KB 23; *BBMB Finance (Hong Kong) Ltd v Eda Holdings Ltd* [1990] 1 WLR 409. If the appreciation was foreseeable, the claimant should have made an equivalent purchase and thereby complied with his obligation to mitigate.

[68] *Rhodes v Moules* [1895] 1 Ch 236; *Solloway v McLoughlin* [1938] AC 247 (PC); *BBMB Finance (Hong Kong) Ltd v Eda Holdings Ltd* [1990] 1 WLR 409.

[69] [2002] 2 AC 88.

[70] [2001] 1 AC 268, 278–80.

will not adequately compensate the claimant for his loss, but even then it remains a matter of court discretion whether to make such an award.[71]

G. Banks, Cheques and Conversion

4.45 So far we have looked at the requirements for a claim in conversion generally. In this section, we will focus on a claim in conversion in respect of a 'collecting bank's' handling of cheques and how the general requirements set out above apply in this banking context.

4.46 A bank that collects a cheque for a person who has no title to that cheque, or whose title is in some way defective, runs the risk of a claim in conversion by the true owner of the cheque.[72]

(1) The cheque must have value and be valid

4.47 It has been seen above that the court has come to assess damages based upon valuing the paper cheque at its stated value. One commentator has observed:

> The true object of treating a converted cheque as having its face value is to enable the 'true owner' to sue for the proceeds under the guise of an action brought in tort. The fictive element in the conclusive presumption that a cheque has a value equal to the amount for which it is drawn becomes apparent when one reflects on the true value of a cheque issued by an impecunious customer whose account is heavily overdrawn. The instrument is bound to be dishonoured by the drawee bank, and an action against the penniless customer is hopeless. The real value of the cheque involved is, therefore nil. Why, then, should it be regarded at law as having its face value?[73]

4.48 But the court will only award the stated value for so long as the cheque remains a valid instrument. If the cheque bears a forged signature or has been materially altered in an unauthorized manner, and has been avoided, it will be considered a nullity and no substantial damages will be awarded. In *Smith v Lloyds TSB Group plc*[74] the Court of Appeal was dealing with a fraudster having altered the name of the payee on the cheque. Given such alteration rendered the cheque void,[75] the 'true owner' could not recover the full stated value from the collecting bank.

---

71 *Clerk & Lindsell* (18th edn), para 14-95.

72 In addition, the true owner can sue for money had and received. Such a claim is defeated by any payment over by the bank acting as agent in good faith: e.g. *Admiralty Commissioners v National Provincial and Union Bank of England Ltd* (1922) 127 LT 452; *Gowers v Lloyds and National Provincial Bank Ltd* [1937] 3 All ER 55. See generally para 3.145 *et seq*.

73 Ellinger, Lomnicka and Hooley, *Modern Banking Law* (3rd edn, Oxford University Press, 2003), 564.

74 [2001] QB 541, affirming [2000] Lloyd's Rep. Bank 58.

75 Bills of Exchange Act 1882, s 64.

Decisions such as *Smith v Lloyds TSB Group* have led *Clerk & Lindsell* to remark **4.49**
that the awarding of damages based upon the stated value of the cheque is simply
a presumptive rule. The editors recognize the oddity of saying a cheque drawn for
£1m by a pauper should be treated as worth £1m when there was no possibility at
all of the bank paying out that amount. Accordingly, it can be seen that the test for
damages involves a combination of factors. First, whether the instrument remains
valid. If not, and no payment remains due thereunder, then conversion of it cannot logically lead to the award of anything other than the value of the paper.
Secondly, even if the instrument is valid, it may be necessary for the court to take
into account the likelihood of payment being made under the cheque. It is unlikely
that this second situation will be allowed to become a detailed investigation into
the likelihood of a customer's standing being good enough with a bank that it
would pay out, but if the matter can be established clearly one way or the other,
the court is likely to take that into account.

(2) Claimant must have immediate right to possession[76]

The general requirement remains unaltered in the context of banks collecting **4.50**
cheques.

So, if X draws a cheque and hands it over to the payee, and it is thereafter con- **4.51**
verted by the bank, X has no title to sue the bank because the act of handing over
the cheque to the payee resulted in X losing any right to possession thereof.[77] Such
delivery is presumed unless and until the contrary is proved.[78]

If a fraudster rips a cheque out of a cheque book and forges the signature on it, the **4.52**
party entitled to immediate right to possession is the true owner of the cheque
book.[79]

If a cheque drawn in favour of X and delivered to X is subsequently wrongly **4.53**
taken from X (before it has been presented for collection) and altered to be made
payable to a third party, the party entitled to sue is X, and not the drawer of the
cheque.[80]

---

[76] *The Marquis of Bute v Barclays Bank* [1955] 1 QB 205. For a detailed treatment, see
Hapgood, *Paget's Law of Banking* (13th edn), 573–6.
[77] *Surrey Asset Finance Ltd v National Westminster Bank plc* 8 September 2000, unrep. Aff'd on
appeal: [2001] EWCA Civ 60.
[78] Bills of Exchange Act 1882, s 21(3). An exception might be proof that the payee was acting
fraudulently in his receipt of the cheque: see Australian authority: *Australian Guarantee Corporation
v Commissioners of the State Bank of Victoria* (1989) Victoria Reports, 608, 632 and 634–6. The
argument failed on the facts in *Surrey Asset Finance Ltd v National Westminster Bank plc* at p 13 of the
transcript of Anthony Temple QC's judgment.
[79] *Morison v London County and Westminster Bank* [1914] 3 KB 356; *Marquess of Bute v Barclays
Bank Ltd* [1955] 1 QB 205.
[80] *Lacave & Co v Credit Lyonnais* [1897] 1 QB 148; Ellinger, Lomnicka and Hooley, *Modern Law
of Banking* (3rd edn), 567.

4.54 If, however, X has endorsed the cheque in blank, it becomes a bearer instrument which can be transferred on mere delivery. Insofar as a third party takes such a cheque from the rogue in good faith and for value, he will become a holder in due course and therefore entitled to sue.[81]

4.55 The general rule in relation to cheques is that the true owner is the party to whom the cheque was validly transferred last.

(3) Statutory protection for banks: Cheques Act 1957, s 4

4.56 The position of banks renders them vulnerable to claims in conversion, particularly given the strict liability basis of the claim. To ameliorate the banks' position, they have been afforded certain statutory defences. In their most recent form they are to be found in s 4(1) of the Cheques Act 1957:

> (1) Where a banker, in good faith and without negligence,—
>   (a) Receives payment for a customer of an instrument to which this section applies; or
>   (b) Having credited a customer's account with the amount of such an instrument, receives payment thereof for himself;
>
> And the customer has no title, or a defective title, to the instrument, the banker does not incur any liability to the true owner of the instrument by reason only of having received payment thereof.

4.57 The Cheques Act 1957, s 4, in essence provides banks with a defence based on good faith and non-negligent conduct. While the concept of 'good faith' is not difficult to understand, the lack of good faith will rarely be established against a main street bank.

4.58 The other aspect of the defence is that the bank must not act negligently in its dealings with the cheque. This necessarily brings into play the bank's good practice and code of conduct which varies and alters over time. What may have been negligent conduct 20 years ago may not be viewed as such these days. The true test is laid down by the Court of Appeal in *Marfani & Co Ltd v Midland Bank Ltd*[82] where Diplock LJ stated:

> [W]ere those circumstances such as would cause a reasonable banker possessed of such information about his customer as a reasonable banker would possess, to suspect that his customer was not the true owner of the cheque?[83]

4.59 Such a question can only properly be answered by reference to banks' general conduct and practice covering all aspects of their business. Was the bank negligent in

---

[81] *Smith v Union Bank of London* (1875) 1 QBD 31.
[82] [1968] 1 WLR 956.
[83] ibid, 973.

opening up the account in the first place by failing to make obvious enquiries?[84] It is likely that any negligence in this area would have serious ramifications on potential criminal liability in respect of the money laundering legislation. Was the bank negligent in the actual way it went about collecting the cheque. For example, was there any indication that the cheque may have been forged or stolen? Was it an employer cheque made out to the employee but not for wages? If the cheque was altered in any way, should this have given rise to cause for concern or at least further inquiry?

Banks have become increasingly loaded with duties about knowing their customers and customers' business via the money laundering requirements and it is likely that such onerous duties have only served to tighten the banks' duties such that they may now be more susceptible to having acted negligently than would have been the case some 20 or 30 years ago. **4.60**

H. Limitation[85]

As a claim in tort, the usual limitation period for a conversion claim is six years from the act constituting the conversion. **4.61**

If there is more than one individual involved and more than one act constituting conversion, a separate six-year limitation period would arise for each act of conversion. So, for example, A loses his watch in the park. B finds it and sells it to C who, in turn, sells it to D. Then A will have a claim in conversion against B and C, who both converted the watch. Without the Act, each new conversion would give rise to a fresh start of six years of the limitation period. To avoid this, the Limitation Act 1980, s 3(1) provides that the six years start from the first act of conversion and once completed, all future claims are statute-barred. **4.62**

If, however, the first act of conversion also amounted to theft, then time does not start to run until the asset is first acquired by a good faith purchaser (s 4). **4.63**

---

[84] *Ladbroke v Todd* (1914) 30 TLR 433—a rogue stole a cheque made out to an Oxford undergraduate and sought to open a new account and deposit the cheque. He told the bank he was trying to hide his gambling debts from the University. The bank failed to take up his references, including the alleged Master of his college and were held negligent in not doing so.

[85] Prime and Scanlan, *The Law of Limitation* (2nd edn, Oxford University Press, 2001), 154–60; M Bridge, *Personal Property Law* (3rd edn, Clarendon Press, 2002), 78–9.

PART IV

RECEIPT-BASED LIABILITY—IN EQUITY

5

KNOWING RECEIPT

A. Overview

A claim for knowing receipt requires the following to be established:[1]   **5.01**

- assets held under a trust or fiduciary relationship;
- a transfer of those assets in breach of that trust or fiduciary relationship;
- to a third party who beneficially receives those assets (i.e. for its own sake and not as agent for others);
- in circumstances where it would be unconscionable to permit that third party to retain those assets.

B. Introduction

Liability for knowing receipt is an equitable claim giving rise to personal liability   **5.02**
on the part of a defendant who receives assets transferred to him in breach of trust
in circumstances where the defendant's knowledge of events is such as to render it
unconscionable for him to retain those assets.

---

[1] *El Ajou v Dollar Land Holdings plc* [1994] 1 All ER 685, 700 (Hoffmann LJ); *BCCI v Akindele* [2001] Ch 437, 448 CA.

5.03 This claim has its origins in the law of trusts and can still be located in the standard texts on trusts in the section dealing with intermeddling with trusts. It has traditionally been considered alongside the claim for dishonest assistance.[2] More recently, however, it has been recognized that the two claims are distinct and merit separate consideration. The relationship between the two claims is discussed in para 5.10 *et seq.* below.

5.04 There can be little doubt that with the explosion of commercial fraud from the late 1980s onwards, the knowing receipt claim has come to be viewed as a significant head of liability, offering the victim of a commercial fraud opportunities to recover funds which might not otherwise have been available. The extended role for knowing receipt claims derives principally from the fact that this claim can take advantage of the wide-ranging tracing rules in equity. This coupled with the fact that there has been a greater willingness to find fiduciary relationships within commercial contexts has meant that the knowing receipt claim has become a powerful weapon in the fight against commercial fraud. No longer is it confined to express formal trusts but it has, instead, been adapted to meet the demands of commercial fraud litigation.

5.05 By virtue of its expanded role in commercial fraud litigation, the knowing receipt claim has been subjected to a great deal of examination by those seeking to adapt it to the requirements of a modern fraud. In so doing, as we shall see, some of the traditional requirements (or restrictions) imposed on this claim have been questioned or abandoned in favour of a more flexible model better suited to the intricacies of a complex fraud. The process is not yet complete.

5.06 One of the features of this claim attractive to commercial fraud litigators is the fact that, unlike the common law claim of unjust enrichment, it is not limited to direct recipients but extends to all recipients who, via the rules on tracing, can be shown to have received the assets or their traceable proceeds. Given a knowing receipt claim can invoke Equity's more liberal rules on tracing (as compared to the common law claim for unjust enrichment) this greatly expands the number of potential defendants to such a claim. In particular, it enables the victim to look beyond the immediate recipient of the proceeds of the fraud and, subject to the satisfaction of the other requirements of the claim, enquire into the potential liability of all those through whose hands the fraud proceeds have passed.

5.07 That said, this claim requires the defendant to have a certain level of knowledge before any personal liability is imposed on him for receipt of trust assets wrongly transferred. In this way, it imposes an additional hurdle over that required for the common law claim of unjust enrichment (or money had and received in old

---

[2] C Harpum, 'The Stranger as Constructive Trustee' (1986) 102 LQR 114, 162 where it is suggested that the failure properly to distinguish these two heads of claim has resulted in a confusion over the distinct requirements of each claim.

parlance) which is a matter of strict liability. The relationship between the two claims is discussed in para 5.19 *et seq.* below. It will be evident that the relationship (or not) between these two claims has had an influence on the debate as to the correct level of knowledge for a knowing receipt claim. It suffices to say, by way of a preliminary observation, that the judicial tide appears to have turned away from subsuming the knowing receipt claim into the law of unjust enrichment. The debate nevertheless rumbles on, is instructive and so will be briefly examined below.

It is important to clarify that knowing receipt gives rise to a personal liability **5.08** to account on the part of the defendant. In itself, it does not give rise to any proprietary relief. If, however, the defendant retains the assets or traceable proceeds then his knowledge coupled with the possession of the relevant assets may well give rise to a constructive trust. The language of constructive trust or liability as a constructive trustee is inappropriate when applied to a knowing receipt claim *simpliciter*. It is no more than an awkward shorthand for the personal obligations imposed on the individual found to have knowingly received trust property: 'nothing more than a formula for equitable relief': *Selangor United Rubber Estates Ltd v Cradock (No 3).*[3] As Lord Millett has advised, it may be preferable to use the language of 'accountable in equity' rather than 'accountable as constructive trustee'.[4]

C. Nature of Liability

A better understanding of the nature of liability for knowing receipt can be gained **5.09** by examining the relationship between this head of liability and that for (i) dishonest assistance, and (ii) unjust enrichment.

(1) Knowing receipt and dishonest assistance claims

It is perhaps understandable that historically these two heads of claim have, until **5.10** recent times, been considered together. They both arise out of a similar fact scenario, namely a third party's involvement in a breach of trust or fiduciary duty and they are both instances of accessory liability. However, that is where the similarity ends. The basis for the imposition of liability in each head of claim is different and requires consideration of factors not relevant to the other head of liability.

---

³ [1968] 1 WLR 1555, 1582 per Ungoed-Thomas J.
⁴ *Dubai Aluminium Co Ltd v Salaam* [2003] 2 AC 366, [140]–[142]. It is to be hoped that both the bar and the bench will take on board Lord Millett's advice. The area is difficult enough without having to clear the clutter created by inappropriate language.

5.11   The distinction between these two heads of claim is that in a knowing receipt claim, liability is imposed for the (beneficial) receipt of the proceeds of a fraud,[5] whereas in a dishonest assistance claim, liability is imposed because of the defendant's *participation* in a fraud. It may, of course, be possible for the receipt of the fraud proceeds to amount to assistance for the purpose of a dishonest assistance claim. But given that the receipt must be the defendant's *beneficial* receipt (i.e. for his own purpose/own benefit) it does not so readily fall into the category of assistance to the main perpetrator by way of receipt of some of the fraud proceeds.[6]

5.12   If one strives to understand the nature of a knowing receipt claim only from the perspective of a dishonest assistance claim then one will end up ignoring the fact that the defendant in the receipt claim, but not in the assistance claim, has ended up beneficially receiving some of the fraud proceeds. Common sense dictates these additional factors merit a different approach. The reason why each is liable is different and obviously so. Such a conclusion does not, however, necessarily drive one into the arms of those who maintain that this requires knowing receipt to be understood only from an unjust enrichment perspective and therefore should properly be considered a matter of strict liability.

5.13   The focus of any meaningful inquiry in a knowing receipt claim is the requirement that the defendant must return the value of the assets received. That is an analytically distinct question from the inquiry which is conducted in a dishonest assistance claim where the focus is on the circumstances in which the defendant should be liable for participating in the breach of trust or fiduciary duty (or, in shorthand, the fraud). When these two areas of focus are clearly identified, there is every reason to believe that the two claims are distinct and no reason at all for contending that questions of knowledge or dishonesty should be treated the same for both claims. The immediate response to such a suggestion would be: why? Why should we expect the circumstances in which the court will require the return of assets transferred as part of a fraud to be the same as when the court will find a defendant liable for participating in a fraud? Logically, there is no reason to treat the two claims the same.

5.14   If further proof were needed, one need only examine the different factors at play in each claim. The answer to the question when a defendant should return any assets knowingly received will involve consideration of matters such as security of

---

[5] The phrase 'proceeds of fraud' is used as a shorthand for 'proceeds of a breach of trust and/or fiduciary duty'. Given the readiness of the courts to find fiduciary duties in the context of commercial frauds, it is considered that the shorthand is appropriate.

[6] See below for a discussion based on recent attempts by Lord Nicholls, followed by Professor Birks, to re-interpret the knowing receipt claim as potentially giving rise to two separate heads of claim: (i) dishonest receipt, to be equated with the equitable wrongdoing of dishonest assistance and (ii) receipt of assets, based upon the strict liability approach of the common law of unjust enrichment.

receipt and title, certainty in commercial transactions etc, none of which is likely to arise in any determination of whether a defendant has knowingly or dishonestly participated in a fraud.

The two heads of claim also give rise to distinct remedies. Liability for knowing **5.15** receipt is an in personam liability to account to the beneficiary for the value received by the defendant. So if there was a breach of fiduciary duty involving the misappropriation of £1,000 and X received £100 himself, X's liability to the beneficiary would, absent interest, be £100, being the amount he had beneficially received. For those who favour an unjust enrichment approach to knowing receipt, the fact that liability is £100 and not £1,000 supports the unjust enrichment argument. It is certainly consistent with it. But then others will say that the £100 is equally consistent with a compensation for loss as opposed to a disgorgement of gain argument.

In dishonest assistance, liability is again in personam in nature but unlike where a **5.16** knowing receipt claim is limited to the amount received, liability for dishonest assistance extends to all losses caused by the breach of trust which has been assisted.[7] One does not look to see what loss was caused by the defendant's particular assistance.[8]

Although we have identified that one major distinction between the two claims is **5.17** the beneficial receipt of assets in the case of knowing receipt, that discovery does not require us to accept, in their entirety, the arguments put forward that knowing receipt is merely an example of unjust enrichment and should therefore be a matter of strict liability. That is the subject of the next section.

Finally, it should be acknowledged in this section that examination of the relation- **5.18** ship between knowing receipt and dishonest assistance claims has led some notable commentators[9] to the conclusion that the claim for knowing receipt involves two separate heads of liability—one based solely on the receipt of proceeds of the

---

[7] It may even extend to an account of profits obtained by the party liable for dishonest assistance: see Bribery at para 17.59 below.

[8] See *Lewin on Trusts* (18th edn, Thomson/Sweet and Maxwell, 2008), [40-40]. The authors point out that liability for the assistance may even be more onerous than for the express trustee since if the assistance has been provided *dishonestly* it may give rise to compound interest in equity. Thomas and Hudson, *The Law of Trusts* (Oxford University Press, 2004), whilst recognizing the general principle that the assistor is liable for all loss caused by the breach (and is not limited to that caused by the assistance per se), argue that it may be possible to persuade the court, consistent with *Target Holdings v Redferns* [1996] 1 AC 421, that liability should be limited to that which has in fact been caused by the assistance provided: [30.51].

[9] Lord Nicholls, 'Knowing Receipt: The Need for a New Landmark' in Cornish, Nolan, O'Sullivan and Virgo (eds), *Restitution: Past, Present and Future* (Hart Publishing 1998), ch 15; Professor Birks, 'Receipt' in Birks and Pretto (eds), *Breach of Trust* (Hart Publishing 2002), 223–4; see also Lord Walker, 'Dishonesty and Unconscionable Conduct in Commercial Life—Some Reflections on Accessory Liability and Knowing Receipt' (2005) 27 Sydney LR 187.

fraud and one based upon participation in a fraud. Such claims will be examined below.

(2) Knowing receipt and unjust enrichment

5.19 In the aftermath of *Lipkin Gorman v Karpnale Ltd*,[10] and the express recognition in English law of a category of claim based upon unjust enrichment,[11] there has been a growing chorus in favour of subsuming the knowing receipt category of claim within the general umbrella of unjust enrichment. It is anomalous, they say, that equity should employ a fault-based approach to receipt of assets whereas the common law under the law of unjust enrichment applies a strict liability regime subject to a change of position.

5.20 The chief proponent of this view was Professor Birks.[12] The thrust of Professor Birks' approach was to re-examine a series of knowing receipt cases in the hope that he might be able to persuade the reader that references in such cases to questions of fault were limited to the factual inquiries as to whether or not a defence of bona fide purchaser for value without notice could be made out. Professor Birks was too brilliant a lawyer genuinely to believe that these authorities were intended by the courts to be read that way and ultimately his attempt must be viewed as one to re-invent judicial reasoning. If successful, it would no doubt have helped smooth the path on the road to strict liability but it would have caused a great deal of uncertainty as to the manner in which a host of authorities are to be interpreted.

5.21 In *Twinsectra Ltd v Yardley*,[13] Lord Millett added further support to the argument in favour of a strict liability approach based upon receipt of assets:

> Liability for 'knowing receipt' is receipt-based. It does not depend on fault. The cause of action is restitutionary and is available only where the defendant received or applied the money in breach of trust for his own use and benefit . . . There is no basis for requiring actual knowledge of the breach of trust, let alone dishonesty, as a condition of liability. Constructive notice is sufficient, and may not even be

---

10 [1991] 2 AC 548.

11 Or, at least, if it is not a new claim, it is the newly recognized principle underlying other established claims: *Uren v First National Home Finance Ltd* [2005] EWHC 2529, Ch [16] (Mann J); *Primlake Limited (In Liquidation) v Matthews Associates & Ors* [2006] EWHC 1227 (Ch); [2007] 1 BCLC 666 at [335].

12 Birks, *An Introduction to the Law of Restitution* (Clarendon Press, 1985), 140–6; Birks, *Restitution: The Future* (Federation Press of Australia, 1992), 26–42; 'Misdirected Funds: Restitution from the Recipient' [1989] LMCLQ 296; Birks, 'The English Recognition of Unjust Enrichment' [1991] LMCLQ 473; Birks, 'Trusts in the Recovery of Misapplied Assets: Tracing, Trusts and Restitution' in McKendrick (ed), *Commercial Aspects of Trusts and Fiduciary Obligations* (Clarendon Press, 1992), 149, 159–61; 'Persistent Problems in Misdirected Money: A Quintet' [1993] LMCLQ 218. For a different view see N McBride and P McGrath, 'The Nature of Restitution' (1995) 15 OJLS 33.

13 [2002] UKHL 12, [2002] 2 AC 164.

necessary. There is powerful academic support for the proposition that the liability of the recipient is the same as in other cases of restitution, that is to say strict but subject to a change of position defence.[14]

As with many of the more recent authorities on this issue, the dicta may point towards a strict liability approach but the older authorities have not been overturned by such comments, leaving the practitioner with a clear obligation, below the House of Lords, to follow the authorities on the very issue and not simply the dicta, however logical and persuasive in their reasoning.

5.22 Professor Burrows also appears to favour a strict liability approach. In his excellent *The Law of Restitution*,[15] Professor Burrows laments that the Court of Appeal in *BCCI v Akindele* regarded Lord Nicholls' extra-judicial comments[16] as being unattractive both as a matter of authority and principle. Professor Burrows expressly rejected the Court of Appeal's concerns that a strict liability approach would be practically unworkable, arguing that if that was truly the case, that would mean the whole of the law of restitution would similarly be unworkable and no one has ever said that. It is difficult to understand why the Court of Appeal viewed strict liability in equity as unworkable when it works perfectly well at common law for claims in unjust enrichment. So long as the defences are in place, there should be little concern.

5.23 In his thought-provoking article, 'Knowing Receipt: The Need for A New Landmark',[17] Lord Nicholls remarked:

> In this respect equity should now follow the law. Restitutionary liability, applicable regardless of fault but subject to a defence of change of position, would be a better-tailored response to the underlying mischief of misapplied property than personal liability which is exclusively fault-based. Personal liability would flow from having received the property of another, from having been unjustly enriched at the expense of another. It would be triggered by the mere fact of receipt, thus recognising the endurance of property rights. But fairness would be ensured by the need to identify a gain, and by making change of position available as a defence in suitable cases when, for instance, the recipient had changed his position in reliance on the receipt.

5.24 One of the major arguments employed by those who favour a strict liability approach in equity is that equity has already accepted the principle of strict liability for receipt of property relating to the administration of deceased persons'

---

[14] ibid, 194. See also *Grupo Torras SA v Al Sabah (No 5)* [2001] Lloyd's Rep Bank 36, 62 where the Court of Appeal held that the knowing receipt claim may be either 'a vindication of persistent property rights or a personal restitutionary claim based upon unjust enrichment by subtraction'.

[15] *The Law of Restitution* (2nd edn, Butterworths, 2002), 203.

[16] Lord Nicholls, 'Knowing Receipt: The Need for a New Landmark' in Cornish et al (eds), *Restitution: Past Present and Future*, 230–45. This was not the first time that Lord Nicholls had referred to the restitution-based nature of the claim in knowing receipt. He had described the knowing receipt claim as 'recipient liability [that] is restitution-based' in *Royal Brunei v Tan* [1992] 2 AC 378, 382.

[17] *Restitution: Past Present and Future*, 231.

estates.[18] This is known usually as the *Diplock* principle, although the relevant case name (in the House of Lords) is actually *Ministry of Health v Simpson*.[19]

5.25 Under this principle, anyone who mistakenly receives property as a distribution of a deceased's estate, even a fault-free recipient, is liable to repay those to whom the property should have been distributed. Few accept that there is any compelling reason why the *Diplock* principle must be restricted to the law of administration of estates.[20] In the absence of any such reason, it provides compelling force to arguments in favour of a strict liability approach in equity. However, it is unlikely to provide a general strict liability restitutionary remedy. First, even assuming it can be extended to a trust scenario (rather than limited to the administration of estates), the beneficiary must first exhaust its remedy against the wrongful trustee before seeking to enforce any such secondary remedy against an innocent recipient of the estate's or trust's monies.[21] Secondly, the unpaid beneficiary cannot recover all the amounts received by the innocent recipient, only that amount which, had the beneficiary been paid what was due to him, he would have received.[22]

5.26 Whilst advocating a strict liability approach to liability for the receipt of proceeds of a fraud, Lord Nicholls developed the argument that had hitherto been presented by Professor Birks by suggesting that there might well be scope for the imposition of equitable liability for wrongdoing if the recipient *dishonestly* received the proceeds of the fraud—such liability to be equated with dishonest assistance and requiring the same level of knowledge/dishonesty. Lord Nicholls remarked:

> The law is perhaps now sufficiently mature to dispense with an ill-fitting deemed trusteeship as the source of liability. A more direct approach is to recognise that breach of trust and dishonest participation in a breach of trust are two species of equitable wrongs. Dishonest participation in a breach of trust, whether by receiving trust property or otherwise, is itself an equitable wrong, rendering the participants accountable in equity. It is the equitable counterpart of the common law tort of interfering with contractual relations.[23]

5.27 The attraction of Lord Nicholls' argument is that it does not seek to jettison all questions of fault from the analysis of this head of liability, recognizing perhaps

---

[18] Underhill and Hayton, *The Law of Trusts and Trustees* (17th edn, Lexis Nexis, 2006) at para 100.80; *Lewin on Trusts* (18th edn), [42-13].

[19] [1951] AC 251. The House of Lords confirmed the approach of the Court of Appeal's decision sub-nom *Re Diplock* [1948] Ch 465, hence the name of the principle.

[20] It has been suggested this remedy might be available in respect of the distribution of company assets on insolvency but for the various statutory remedies: see *Butler v Broadhead* [1975] Ch 97, 107 (Templeman J); *Re Leslie Engineering Co* [1976] 1 WLR 292, 299 (Oliver J).

[21] *Lewin on Trusts* (18th edn), [42-16].

[22] ibid, [42-17].

[23] 'Knowing Receipt: The Need for a New Landmark', 244. To similar effect, see Lord Walker, 'Dishonesty and Unconscionable Conduct in Commercial Life—Some Reflections on Accessory Liability and Knowing Receipt' (2005) 27 Sydney LR 187 at 202.

that to do so has the very unattractive feature of equally jettisoning a substantial number of established authorities on the issue. It gives a role to be played for a fault-based approach—that role being to equate dishonest receipt of proceeds with dishonest assistance as a single form of equitable wrongdoing. The established authorities can be said to be dealing with the fault-based approach whilst saying nothing about a strict liability approach based on unjust enrichment.

Lord Nicholls' argument appeared to persuade Professor Birks to accept a role for **5.28** a fault-based approach to knowing receipt claims in addition to a strict liability claim. Professor Birks accepted:

> Although I have myself strenuously argued that 'knowing receipt' should be regarded as a claim in unjust enrichment, and should therefore discard the incongruous requirement of fault implicit in the word 'knowing', the courts appear to have set their face against that view. It now seems right to abandon that analysis once and for all. It was a mistake to insist that 'knowing receipt' was simply a species of unjust enrichment which had been slow to understand itself and, in particular, slow to understand that liability in unjust enrichment is strict though subject to defences.

> The better way of proceeding is to accept that the ambiguities and uncertainties in the case law of knowing receipt arise from its having failed to distinguish between two very different kinds of liability, one wrong-based and the other based on unjust enrichment. The task is then, not to force 'knowing receipt' into one or other category, but to demonstrate that both kinds of liability are necessary and that neither renders the other redundant. Within the law of obligations the recipient of trust property can, on appropriate facts, be made liable for the wrong of misappropriation or he can be compelled to make restitution of his unjust enrichment.[24]

Similarly, Lord Millett would appear also to be persuaded as to Lord Nicholls' **5.29** dual approach. He returned to this theme in *Dubai Aluminium Co Ltd v Salaam*,[25] where he held:

> Dishonest receipt gives rise to concurrent liability, since the claim can be based on the defendant's dishonesty, treating the receipt itself as incidental, being merely the particular form taken by the defendant's participation in the breach of fiduciary duty; but it can also be based simply on the receipt, treating it as a restitutionary claim independent of any wrongdoing.

So what can be said about the arguments in favour of a strict liability approach? It **5.30** is clear that there is a groundswell of academic and some notable judicial support for such an approach, attracted by the logic of the analysis by way of comparison with the common law approach. The force of this argument is clear and its thesis logical. The problem for this approach lies not in its merits but rather in the historical accident that the English law did not expressly recognize the law of unjust enrichment until *Lipkin Gorman*, allowing a library of authoritative precedents to

---

[24] Birks, 'Receipt' in Birks and Pretto (eds), *Breach of Trust*, 223–4.
[25] [2002] UKHL 48; [2003] 2 AC 366 at para 87.

be created all advocating some form of fault-based approach to liability in equity.[26] Attempts by Professor Birks to re-interpret such cases have not worked and in fact have served only to highlight the obstacles of precedent in the way of a strict liability approach. Notwithstanding the forceful dicta coming from Lord Millett in *Twinsectra* and *Dubai Aluminium,* the Court of Appeal's rejection of this approach in *BCCI v Akindele* renders it unlikely to be adopted in the very near future.

5.31   This would also appear to be the position under Australian law as well in light of the recent decision of the High Court of Australia in *Farah Constructions Pty Ltd v Say-Dee Pty Ltd*[27] where the High Court expressly overruled the Court of Appeal's decision to adopt strict liability as the basis for knowing receipt. The High Court described such an approach as 'a grave error'.[28]

5.32   It would take a Herculean effort to re-write the authorities, or simply overrule them, so as to favour a strict liability approach. There is no doubt that Lord Nicholls' more developed argument—that knowing receipt may well give rise to two distinct claims, one based upon receipt and the other upon equitable wrongdoing—enables some lip service to be paid to the library of authorities suggesting a fault-based approach. However, Lord Nicholls' approach, as well as the last position of Professor Birks just before his death, is that knowledge for the equitable wrongdoing claim had to be the same as for assistance, i.e. dishonesty. Very few of the authorities favour such a high threshold test and the trend is, if anything, in the opposite direction.

5.33   In other words, Lord Nicholls' approach still runs into the problem of having to deal with the numerous cases where the court has held that something less than dishonesty needs to be shown. It therefore fails to provide an answer that works both on a common sense and logical level as well as fits in with precedent in this area.

5.34   One can readily see a time when the House of Lords has had an opportunity to remove the distinction between legal and equitable rules on tracing, that the logic of the arguments in favour of strict liability might be given greater freedom to be employed and developed. A unified system of tracing is likely to foster a greater overlap in the application of the common law and equitable claims, rendering any

---

[26] Judges, such as Millett J, at first instance, were not in a position to advocate a strict liability approach to knowing receipt, as a matter of precedent and hence one sees reference to constructive notice. Indeed, until the House of Lords introduced the defence of change of position in *Lipkin Gorman v Karpnale Ltd* [1991] 2 AC 548, the use of 'constructive notice' was the best means of avoiding injustice in knowing receipt cases. Once change of position was adopted, Millett LJ stated in *Boscawen v Bajwa* [1996] 1 WLR 328, 334: 'The introduction of this defence not only provides the court with a means of doing justice in future, but allows a re-examination of many decisions of the past in which the absence of the defence may have led judges to distort basic principles in order to avoid injustice to the defendant.'

[27] [2007] HCA 22; Matthew Conaglen and Richard Nolan, 'Recipient Liability In Equity' [2007] CLJ 515; Hugh Atkin, '"Knowing Receipt" Following *Farah Constructions Pty Ltd v Say-Dee Pty Ltd*' (2007) 29 Sydney LR 713.

[28] [2007] HCA 22, 131.

duplication in liability, and differences in approach, the subject of closer scrutiny. This, coupled with the arguments based upon expanding the strict liability approach in equity adopted in *Re Diplock*,[29] might well be enough to see this approach eventually accepted. Much work remains to be done before that occurs and practitioners must therefore approach these claims from the perspective of the present state of the law, as exemplified by the Court of Appeal in *BCCI v Akindele*. As with the law relating to the rules on tracing, we know where the law wishes to go but it has not yet got there and the practitioner must abide by the existing authorities unless and until they are overturned or explained in a different manner.

D. Elements of Claim

The elements of a claim for knowing receipt were summarized by Hoffmann LJ **5.35**
in *El Ajou v Dollar Land Holdings plc*[30] as follows:

> For this purpose, the plaintiff must show, first, a disposal of his assets in breach of duty; secondly, the beneficial receipt by the defendant of assets which are traceable as representing the assets of the plaintiff; and thirdly, knowledge on the part of the defendant that the assets he received are traceable to a breach of fiduciary duty.

For a greater understanding of what the claim requires, these three categories can **5.36**
be further divided into the following categories:

- assets held under a trust or fiduciary duty;
- disposal of those assets in breach of that trust or fiduciary duty;
- beneficial receipt of those assets[31] by the defendant;
- the defendant having sufficient knowledge to render it unconscionable for it to retain the assets.

Each element requires careful consideration. **5.37**

(1) Assets held under a trust or fiduciary relationship

Equity will only provide a remedy in circumstances where the assets, which are the **5.38**
subject of the knowing receipt claim, were originally held under some form of trust or fiduciary relationship. It is the breach of that trust which triggers equity's willingness to find a remedy against the recipient who receives with a sufficient level of knowledge.

Traditionally, the asset would be held subject to a formal express written trust **5.39**
instrument. As we shall see, however, equity has moved on from this position to

---

[29] *Ministry of Health v Simpson* [1951] AC 251.
[30] [1994] 2 All ER 685, 700.
[31] Or traceable proceeds thereof.

one where a liberal attitude is adopted as to what kind of trust or fiduciary relationship suffices for these purposes.

5.40 This requirement sub-divides into two distinct issues:

- what type of trust or fiduciary relationship suffices?
- what type of asset suffices?

5.41 The analysis set out below mirrors that developed in Chapter 16 (para 16.33) in respect of this requirement in the context of dishonest assistance claims. On this issue, there is no distinction between the two claims.

(a) What type of trust or fiduciary relationship suffices?

5.42 The need for the knowing receipt claim to develop to meet the demands of modern commercial frauds has already been highlighted. This issue perfectly illustrates equity's response.

5.43 Equity could have said that knowing receipt claims were only to be available in the circumstances of a breach of a formal express written trust. If it had adopted such an approach, this head of claim would quickly have ceased to have much relevance to the commercial fraud litigator. Instead, equity has allowed the requirements of the knowing receipt claim to develop with the demands of modern-day frauds. So, instead of adopting a very traditional and restrictive attitude as to what breach of trust qualifies for the purposes of this claim, equity is content to permit any form of breach of trust or fiduciary relationship, whether it arises under a formal written trust instrument, resulting or constructive trust, or simply amounts to a breach of a fiduciary duty.

5.44 (i) **Express written trust instrument** Although it suffices, it is not necessary that the assets be held subject to an express written trust instrument. While one can readily foresee factual situations in which the abuse of such a written instrument gives rise to a commercial fraud claim, such instruments are in fact unlikely to figure significantly in the context of commercial fraud litigation.

5.45 (ii) **Resulting trusts** Similarly, it is known from the House of Lords' decision in *Twinsectra Ltd v Yardley*,[32] that a resulting trust (in that case a *Quistclose* trust) will also suffice for the purposes of dishonest assistance and there is no reason to believe a different approach is justified in the context of a knowing receipt claim.[33] Indeed, it would be odd for a different approach to be adopted given that Lord Millett's analysis of the *Quistclose* trust[34] emphasized that the monies were transferred over to the solicitor to be used only for a particular purpose. The solicitor could not

---

[32] [2002] UKHL 12, [2002] 2 AC 164.
[33] *Lewin On Trusts* (18th edn), [43-33].
[34] Although dissenting, all agreed with Lord Millett's general analysis of the *Quistclose* trust.

make general use of the assets for his own purposes or interests—usually a very good indicator of the existence of some form of trust or fiduciary relationship.

(iii) Fiduciary relationships More commonly, a commercial fraud is likely to be perpetrated outside the context of express written trusts. Take a typical example of a commercial fraud. A finance director (D) misappropriates monies in the company bank account and transfers the same to another account. Can it be said that the first requirement for a knowing receipt claim is satisfied on these facts? The answer is a clear yes.[35] **5.46**

In *Selangor United Rubber Estates Ltd v Craddock (No 3)*[36] Ungoed-Thomas J examined whether a director amounted to a trustee of the company's assets for these purposes. His Lordship noted there was disagreement as to whether and to what extent directors were trustees but went on to point out that both directors and trustees had one thing in common: they were only able to apply the trust or company assets for a particular purpose and that any misapplication of those assets would, in both cases, amount to a breach of trust.[37] **5.47**

So, applying the reasoning of Ungoed-Thomas J, an asset may be considered as being held under a trust in circumstances where those assets are held or controlled by an individual who is obliged to use those assets only for a particular purpose.[38] There is no actual requirement that the legal title to the assets vests in the individual as would usually be the case if that individual were formally a trustee. **5.48**

This wider notion of assets held under a trust includes assets which are controlled by solicitors or accountants[39] for and on behalf of their clients. These are clear examples of fiduciary relationships. **5.49**

In other commercial relationships, it is notoriously difficult to establish with any certainty whether a fiduciary relationship exists. On the one hand, the practitioner is told that there is only a limited role to be played by the fiduciary relationship in **5.50**

---

[35] Absent the availability of a derivative action, any such claim would vest in the company as claimant and not in its shareholders.

[36] [1968] 1 WLR 1555.

[37] ibid, 1573–4; see also *Karak Rubber Co v Burden (No 2)* [1972] 1 WLR 602, 633C-D. In *Ultraframe (UK) Ltd v Fielding* [2005] EWHC 1638 (Ch), Lewison J said at [1487]: 'Although a company is the legal and beneficial owner of its own assets, there is no difficulty in classifying property belonging to a company as trust property for the purpose of knowing receipt, where the company's property has been alienated by its directors in breach of their fiduciary duty.' He went on to say at [1488]–[1489] that relevant company property included (i) property already belonging to the company and purchased from the company by a director who had failed to disclose planning permission: *JJ Harrison (Properties) Ltd v Harrison* [2002] 1 BCLC 162 and (ii) property which the fiduciary should have acquired if at all for the company: *Keech v Sandford* (1726) Sel Cas Ch 61.

[38] This reasoning is not dissimilar to that employed to justify *Quistclose* trusts.

[39] *Agip (Africa) Ltd v Jackson* [1990] Ch 265, 290; on appeal to CA, [1991] Ch 547, 566–8.

arm's-length commercial relationships and, on the other, general definitions or descriptions of what amounts to a fiduciary relationship would appear, on their face, to cover many such situations.

5.51 The reality is that in modern commercial litigation, the fiduciary relationship has become a tool, to be employed as and when considered necessary in order to ensure that some form of remedy is available to the victim of a fraud. This is made all the more obvious once it is realized that even a thief can be considered a fiduciary,[40] notwithstanding the obvious inconsistency between such an approach and the English law on theft and its effect (or not) on legal title.[41]

5.52 Perhaps the clearest definition or description of a fiduciary relationship is that given by Millett LJ in *Bristol and West Building Society v Mothew*:[42]

> A fiduciary is someone who has undertaken to act for or on behalf of another in a particular matter in circumstances which give rise to a relationship of trust and confidence. The distinguishing obligation is the obligation of loyalty. The principal is entitled to the single-minded loyalty of his fiduciary. This core liability has several facets. A fiduciary must act in good faith; he must not make a profit out of his trust; he must not place himself in a position where his duty and his interest may conflict; he may not act for his own benefit or the benefit of a third person without the informed consent of his principal. This is not intended to be an exhaustive list, but it is sufficient to indicate the nature of fiduciary obligations. They are the defining characteristics of the fiduciary. As Dr Finn pointed out in his classic work *Fiduciary Obligations* (1977) p.2, he is not subject to fiduciary obligations because he is a fiduciary; it is because he is subject to them that he is a fiduciary.

5.53 On its face, this is a potentially wide-ranging description or definition of who might be a fiduciary. It involves an agreement to act for another but with the crucial addition of single-minded loyalty. The relationship is typically one which engenders trust and confidence in the individual who is the fiduciary. Often that trust and confidence can be evident from the degree of control afforded the would-be fiduciary in dealing with and/or generally handling the other party's assets or finances. Indeed, it is that ready access to those assets which often creates the temptation leading to the fraud.

5.54 One difficult question is what happens if the defendant receives property transferred to him in breach of fiduciary but being property which the fiduciary never held on trust. The point has been considered at least arguable in *Carlton v*

---

[40] This conclusion has been accepted elsewhere: *Black v Freedman & Co* (1910) 12 CLR 105, 108–9, per Griffith CJ; *Australian Postal Corp v Lutak* (1991) 21 NSWLR 584, 589 per Bryson J.
[41] See e.g. S Worthington, *Proprietary Interests in Commercial Transactions* (Clarendon Press, 1996), 128.
[42] [1998] Ch 1, 18.

Halestrap[43] although the High Court of Australia in *Farah Construction v Say-Dee*[44] rejected such an approach, noting that it always remained possible to bring a claim for dishonest assistance.

(iv) Constructive trust So far we have looked at the situation where there is a **5.55** pre-existing trust or fiduciary relationship which is then broken by the conduct of the fraudster. What if there is no pre-existing fiduciary relationship between the initial wrongdoer and the victim of the fraud? So, for example, an individual, not employed by the company, steals money belonging to the company and transfers the same to another account from where monies are distributed to various third parties. Is it possible to say, on these facts, that the first requirement of monies held on trust or fiduciary relationship has been satisfied?

As indicated above, in order to ensure the effectiveness of equity's armoury against **5.56** commercial fraud, the courts are prepared to find that a thief holds the monies as a fiduciary for and on behalf of the company. It has been suggested that the very act of theft itself creates the fiduciary relationship existing as between the thief and the victim of the theft, the company.[45]

Whilst no doubt according with a good deal of common sense, and consistent with **5.57** the desire to deploy all possible remedies to the assistance of the victim of the theft, this approach is not in accordance with a strict legal analysis of the events. It is trite law, or so we are told, that a thief does not get *any title* to the stolen assets. The act of theft has no effect, at all, on the title of the true legal owner, let alone create a fiduciary relationship existing as between the thief and the true legal owner. It is for that reason why the legal owner remains entitled to bring a claim in conversion.

The driving force behind this subversion of strict legal principle (and that undoubt- **5.58** edly is what is going on here) is a desire not to create a lacuna in remedies whereby someone who has been defrauded by an existing employee may be in a better position than the victim of a simple theft. Potter LJ in the Court of Appeal in *Twinsectra v Yardley* remarked:

> It seems to me that, whatever the legal distinction between 'theft' and 'fraud' in other areas of the law, the distinction of importance here is that between non-consensual transfers and transfers pursuant to contracts which are voidable for misrepresentation. In the latter case, the transferor may elect whether to avoid or affirm the transaction

---

[43] (1988) 4 BCC 538, 540.

[44] [2007] HCA 22. This decision has been described as 'doctrinally sound': see M Conaglen and R Nolan, 'Recipient Liability in Equity' [2007] CLC 515, 517. It is, however, difficult to see a principled difference between this scenario and that which arises as between company and director and yet there is little difficulty in allowing knowing receipt claims in the latter situation.

[45] *Westdeutsche Landesbank Girozentrale v Islington London Borough Council* [1996] AC 669, 716 per Lord Browne-Wilkinson (obiter).

and, until he elects to avoid it, there is no constructive (resulting) trust; in the former case, the constructive trust arises upon the moment of transfer.[46]

5.59 (v) **Liens**   Finally, it is worth noting that the wrongful transfer of an asset held under a lien will not qualify as a transfer in breach of trust or fiduciary duty as required to kick-start a claim in knowing receipt. A lien operates by way of the creation of a security interest (charge) over an asset and not an ownership interest.

(b) What type of asset suffices?

5.60 The preceding section dealt with the courts' willingness to apply a liberal concept of trust or fiduciary duty in the context of knowing receipt claims. The issue in this section is what type of assets can be the subject of a knowing receipt claim. In particular, whether confidential information may amount to assets for the purposes of a knowing receipt claim.

5.61 The reader is referred to Chapter 16, para 16.33. The same points made there apply in the context of a knowing receipt claim.

(2) Transfer in breach of trust or fiduciary relationship

5.62 It is an essential requirement of the knowing receipt claim that the transfer of the assets into the hands of a third party must itself amount to a breach of trust or fiduciary duty.[47] Two inter-related aspects of this requirement call for greater consideration.

- It is the transfer itself which must amount to a breach of trust or fiduciary duty. The fact that the transfer happens to take place sometime after a previous breach of trust or fiduciary duty will not suffice.
- Not all wrongful transfers of assets by a trustee or fiduciary will amount to a breach of trust or fiduciary duty. It is possible for a trustee or fiduciary to be negligent without necessarily breaching any trust or fiduciary duty owed to the claimant.

Both aspects focus on the need to establish that any transfer must itself have been in breach of trust to qualify for a knowing receipt claim.

(a) Transfer itself must amount to breach of trust

5.63 On the traditional understanding of the claim for knowing receipt, it is a claim categorized as one intermeddling in a trust. As such, it is an essential requirement

---

46 [1999] Lloyd's Rep Bank 438, 461 (CA).

47 See *Brown v Bennett* [1999] BCLC 649, 655 where the Court of Appeal stressed that 'the receipt must be the direct consequence of the alleged breach of trust or fiduciary duty of which the recipient is said to have notice'.

that the transfer which is complained of must itself amount to a breach of trust. Without such a breach, title in the transferred asset will properly and fully vest in the recipient such that no claim for knowing receipt will arise.

So it is important that there be a careful assessment of the actual transfer of the **5.64** asset to determine whether it amounts to a breach of trust. A good illustration of this requirement is the Court of Appeal decision in *Brown v Bennett*[48] where it was found that the trustees permitted a property under their control to fall into a state of disrepair. Thereafter, the trustees sold the property at its then reduced market price (reflecting the state of disrepair of the property) to the defendant. The Court found that the sale itself to the defendant did not amount to any breach of fiduciary duty, since it was a sale which took place at the true market price of the property. Knowledge on the part of the defendant purchaser of the trustee's failure to keep the property in good repair did not give rise to a claim for knowing receipt. The consequence of that prior failure was a matter to be determined between the beneficiaries and the trustees and it did not concern or involve the third party purchaser.

On the facts the prior breach of duty, allowing the property to fall into a state of **5.65** disrepair, was not itself a breach of the trustee's fiduciary duties although it obviously was a breach of their duty of care. It is submitted that even if the prior breach had amounted to a breach of fiduciary duty but the transfer itself did not, that would not suffice to render the recipient liable for knowing receipt, even if the recipient had the requisite level of knowledge of the prior breach of fiduciary duty. Such a conclusion is in line with the fact that the causative event, triggering equity's involvement in the third party's receipt of the assets, is that they were transferred to the third party in breach of trust. The breach of trust affects the validity of the transfer. That would not exist where the breach of trust occurs at a distinct point prior to any transfer to the third party.

This point is well made by the example used by Morritt LJ in *Brown v Bennett*. His **5.66** Lordship said:

> The matter, I think, can be tested in this way. Let us assume a mansion house is vested in trustees. The trustees fail to perform their fiduciary duties and allow it to fall into appalling disrepair. They are then replaced by other trustees who decide that the matter has gone too far and decide to sell the property. They sell the property to a next-door neighbour, who for the previous 40 years has watched the mansion house falling into disrepair. The sale by the new trustees to the neighbour is entirely proper, at a proper price. The neighbour unquestionably has notice of the previous breaches of duty, because he watched them happen, but the breaches of duty did not give rise to any receipt by the neighbour; the neighbour was not in any way responsible for them and he paid the full value for what he received from the new trustees when he bought.

---

[48] [1998] EWCA Civ 1881, [1999] BCLC 649 (CA).

I can see no reason why in those circumstances there should be any constructive trust liability imposed upon the neighbour merely because he watched the house fall into disrepair before he was enabled to buy it.[49]

(b) Distinction between breach of duty and breach of fiduciary duty

5.67   Typically, in the context of a complex commercial fraud, the fraudster may owe different types of duties to the victim of the fraud. The fraudster may well be an employee of the victim company, owing duties in contract and tort as well as possible fiduciary duties. In these circumstances, it is necessary to establish that any complained of transfer amounts to a breach of fiduciary duty and not simply to a breach of contractual or tortious duty. If it is either of the latter two alternatives, then no claim for knowing receipt can arise.

5.68   It is not possible to provide a definitive list of all the defining features of a fiduciary relationship and the duties to which it can give rise.[50] In *Henderson v Merrett Syndicates Ltd*[51] Lord Browne-Wilkinson provided the following guidance on fiduciary duties:

> The phrase 'fiduciary duties' is a dangerous one, giving rise to a mistaken assumption that all fiduciaries owe the same duties in all circumstances. That is not the case. Although, so far as I am aware, every fiduciary is under a duty not to make a profit from his position (unless such profit is authorised), the fiduciary duties owed, for example, by an express trustee are not the same as those owed by an agent.[52]

5.69   Millett LJ endorsed Lord Browne-Wilkinson's views in *Bristol and West BS v Mothew*,[53] a case involving the conflicting nature of the fiduciary duties owed by an estate agent.

5.70   What can be said is that carelessness has more to do with contractual or tortious duties than it does with fiduciary duties. A failure to sign a required document may well amount to a breach of contract but without more is unlikely to give rise to a breach of fiduciary duty.

5.71   It has been said that the defining feature of the fiduciary relationship is the duty of loyalty which divides into the following core elements:

- a fiduciary must act in good faith;
- he must not make a profit out of his trust;
- he must not place himself in a position where his duty and his interest may conflict;

---

[49] [1999] 1 BCLC 649, 655f–h.
[50] It being recalled that not all fiduciaries owe the same fiduciary duties. The nature and extent of the duties are, to a certain extent, context-dependent.
[51] [1995] AC 145 HL.
[52] [1995] AC 145, 205.
[53] [1998] Ch 1, CA.

- he may not act for his own benefit or the benefit of a third person without the informed consent of his principal.[54]

Whilst not exhaustive, this list identifies several core elements of the fiduciary **5.72** relationship. It also reveals that a commercial fraud is very likely to involve a breach of one or perhaps more than one of these duties. In this regard, whilst it is essential that the claim be framed in terms of breach of a fiduciary duty, this is unlikely to present an insurmountable problem in the case of most fraud situations, where the fraudulent act is almost always going to strike at the heart of one or more of these characteristics.

In *Hilton v Barker*,[55] whilst considering a firm of solicitors which had become **5.73** embroiled in owing conflicting duties to two different clients, Lord Walker remarked:

> The relationship between a solicitor and his client is one in which the client reposes trust and confidence in the solicitor. It is a fiduciary relationship. But not every breach of duty by a fiduciary is a breach of fiduciary duty: see the observations of Millett LJ in *Bristol and West Building Society v Mothew (t/a Stapley & Co)* [1996] 4 All ER 698 at 710-711, [1998] Ch 1 at 16-17. If a solicitor is careless in investigating a title or drafting a lease, he may be liable to pay damages for breach of his professional duty, but that is not a breach of a fiduciary duty of loyalty; it is simply the breach of a duty of care. This may have practical consequences, for instance in relation to causation, as in the *Mothew* case.[56]

Commercial fraud often occurs in the context of commercial contracts and the **5.74** use of various agents. Care must be taken not to rush to try and establish the requirements of a knowing receipt claim before understanding the position from the common law perspective.

So, for example, if a director or directors have acted contrary to their company's **5.75** best interests in agreeing to bind their company to a contract with X, there is little point in rushing to argue that any benefits received by X have been knowingly received without first checking whether or not the company is in fact bound by the contract notwithstanding the directors' conduct. If so, X is entitled to receive whatever benefits accrue under that contract since the company is bound by the contract. If not, then that opens the door to consideration of whether X has the relevant level of knowledge or unconscionability to be liable for any sums received.

It is precisely this lesson that was learnt in *Criterion Properties plc v Stratford UK Prop-* **5.76** *erties LLC*[57] although not before an expensive trip all the way to the House of Lords.

---

[54] *Bristol and West Building Society v Mothew* [1998] 1, 18 per Millett LJ. See also the helpful discussion in Thomas and Hudson, *The Law of Trusts* (Oxford University Press, 2004), para 29.05 *et seq.*
[55] [2005] 1 All ER 651.
[56] ibid, at para 29.
[57] [2004] 1 WLR 1846 HL.

5.77 The claimant company had entered into a limited liability partnership with the defendant company on terms which included what is known as a 'poison pill' agreement whereby the defendant was entitled to its share of the partnership bought out on favourable terms in the event that the claimant was taken over or its managing director dismissed. The claim was treated as a knowing receipt claim right up to the House of Lords but their Lordships were clear that the case, properly analysed, was first and foremost concerned with company law and the law of agency before any possibility of liability for knowing receipt could arise.

5.78 Their Lordships were unanimous in their view that the central issue was one of the authority on the part of the two directors of the claimant company to enter into the agreement and not the conscionability or otherwise of the defendant company. It was not possible, on the evidence available, to resolve that issue of authority and so the matter had to be remitted to trial.

5.79 Lord Nicholls offered the following explanation for their Lordships' approach:

> If a company (A) enters into an agreement with B under which B acquires benefits from A, A's ability to recover these benefits from B depends essentially on whether the agreement is binding on A. If the directors of A were acting for an improper purpose when they entered into the agreement, A's ability to have the agreement set aside depends upon the application of familiar principles of agency and company law. If, applying these principles, the agreement is found to be valid and is therefore not set aside, questions of 'knowing receipt' by B do not arise. So far as B is concerned there can be no question of A's assets having been misapplied. B acquired the assets from A, the legal and beneficial owner of the assets, under a valid agreement made between him and A. If, however, the agreement is set aside, B will be accountable for any benefits he may have received from A under the agreement. A will have a proprietary claim, if B still has assets. Additionally, and irrespective of whether B still has the assets in question, A will have a personal claim against B for unjust enrichment, subject always to the defence of change of position. B's personal accountability will not be dependent upon proof of fault or 'unconscionable' conduct on his part. B's accountability in this regard, will be 'strict'.[58]

5.80 The logic of this approach is indubitable. There can be no question of B having knowingly received any assets belonging to A if B received those assets pursuant to the terms of a contract which is valid and legally binding on A. So the first question in these situations is to always enquire whether, notwithstanding the conduct of, say, the directors, the contract is binding on their company. If so, a claim for knowing receipt cannot get off the ground.

5.81 Interestingly, Lord Nicholls went on to say that in the event that the underlying agreement was set aside, B might be personally accountable in equity without proof of any fault on B's part:

> If, however, the agreement *is* set aside, B will be accountable for any benefits he may have received from A under the agreement. A will have a proprietary claim, if B still

---

[58] [2004] UKHL 28; [2004] 1 WLR 1846, para 4.

has the assets. Additionally, and irrespective of whether B still has the assets in question, A will have a personal claim against B for unjust enrichment, subject always to a defence of change of position. B's personal accountability will not be dependent upon proof of fault or 'unconscionable' conduct on his part. B's accountability, in this regard, will be 'strict'.

Again, the practitioner must take note.[59] First, Lord Nicholls' view is *obiter dicta* **5.82** since on the facts it was not known whether the particular underlying contract was in fact valid and binding on the company. Secondly, while it is another indication where the House of Lords may wish to go, it should not yet be assumed we have got there. Nothing in *Criterion* should be used to cast doubt on *BCCI v Akindele* and the claim for unconscionable receipt. Thirdly, as pointed out by Graham Virgo,[60] Lord Nicholls' view in favour of strict liability is premised upon the claim being based upon unjust enrichment and yet there is little or no analysis of the various elements of a typical claim in unjust enrichment.

(3) Beneficial receipt of assets by defendant

The characteristic requirement of a claim for knowing receipt is the defendant's **5.83** receipt of the trust property transferred in breach of trust. It is not every example of receipt of trust property which will suffice for these purposes. What needs to be shown is that the defendant *beneficially* received the trust property for its own use and not for and on behalf of another.[61] Classic examples of the latter include receipt by agents or nominees. Particularly difficult issues arise in respect of receipt by corporate entities and banks. These require more detailed investigation.

(a) What amounts to beneficial receipt?

The concept of beneficial receipt is satisfied when an individual or entity receives **5.84** funds for his/its own use and is not required to hold those funds for the benefit of someone else.

So if a fraudster asks a friend to allow him to use her bank account to launder **5.85** £75,000 only for £74,250 to be transferred out of that account the next day, leaving £750 as 'commission' for use of the account, the friend has only beneficially received £750 and not the full £75,000. If any claim is to lie in respect of the latter, it must sound in dishonest assistance and not in knowing receipt.[62]

---

[59] See G Virgo, *The Principles of the Law of Restitution* (2nd edn, Oxford University Press, 2006), 652–4.

[60] ibid, 653.

[61] *Barnes v Addy* (1874) 9 Ch App 244, 254–5; *Staniar v Evans* (1886) 34 Ch D 470, 478; *International Sales and Agencies Ltd v Marcus* [1982] 3 All ER 551, 557; *Agip (Africa) Ltd v Jackson* [1990] Ch 265, 291–2; *Polly Peck International plc v Nadir (No 2)* [1992] 4 All ER 769, 777; *El Ajou v Dollar Land Holdings plc* [1994] 2 All ER 685, 700g.

[62] *Bank of America v Arnell & Ors* [1999] Lloyd's Rep Bank 339.

5.86 The authorities do not provide any clearer guidance on what amounts to beneficial receipt. In *International Sales and Agencies v Marcus*[63] the court emphasized that the receipt must be for the recipient's own use or own purposes.

5.87 It has been suggested that Millett J in *Agip v Jackson*[64] and the Court of Appeal in *Polly Peck International v Nadir (No 2)*[65] support a wider notion of beneficial receipt, one based upon possession or control and not ownership, such that a bank through whose hands money has passed will, with the requisite knowledge, be liable for knowing receipt.[66] But, with respect, neither case appears so to do.

5.88 It is quite clear that Millett J in *Agip v Jackson* was not suggesting a test of receipt of trust property for the purposes of a knowing receipt claim on a basis other than beneficial receipt by that person. This point is made clear in his judgment when he said:

> The essential feature of the first class is that the recipient must have received the property for his own use and benefit. This is why neither the paying nor the collecting bank can normally be brought within it. In paying or collecting money for a customer the bank acts only as his agent. It is otherwise, however, if the collecting bank uses the money to reduce or discharge the customer's overdraft. In doing so it receives the money for its own benefit.[67]

5.89 The section of Millett J's judgment which appears to have caused some confusion comes earlier in the judgment, when he is talking generally about fiduciary relationships being readily found when a company director embezzles company funds. It is in that context that Millett J remarked:

> There is clear authority that there is a receipt of trust property when a company's funds are misapplied by a director and, in my judgment, this is equally the case when a company's funds are misapplied by any person whose fiduciary position gave him control of them or enabled him to misapply them.[68]

It is submitted that the references to control or ability to misapply the assets are references to the characteristics arising from the fiduciary position as opposed to determining the nature of the receipt of trust property for the purposes of a knowing receipt claim.

5.90 Similarly, the Court of Appeal in *Polly Peck* did emphasize the need for funds to be received for the bank's own use in order to qualify for a knowing

---

    63 [1982] 3 All ER 551, 558 per Lawson J.
    64 [1990] Ch 265; aff'd [1991] Ch 547.
    65 [1992] 4 All ER 769.
    66 This interpretation of *Polly Peck International v Nadir (No 2)* [1992] 4 All ER 769 is to be found in Thomas and Hudson, *The Law of Trusts*, para 30.56.
    67 [1990] 1 Ch 265, 292.
    68 ibid, 290E–F. This is the section cited and relied upon in Thomas and Hudson, *The Law of Trusts*, para 30.56, although it is cited as coming from p 286.

receipt claim.[69] It is submitted that there is nothing in *Polly Peck* which suggests a more relaxed approach to establishing beneficial receipt of assets for the purposes of knowing receipt. The only difference between the Court of Appeal and Millett J at first instance on this issue is that the Court of Appeal considered that where the bank was involved in providing exchange of currency it beneficially received the Turkish lire which was exchanged into sterling.

(b) Receipt by agents

It has already been discussed that one distinguishing feature between the common law claim for money had and received and that in equity for knowing receipt is that the former is traditionally limited to the initial direct recipient,[70] whereas the latter can extend to any beneficial recipients so long as the equitable rules on tracing are satisfied. In a complex commercial fraud, the potential number of hands through which the money might pass is large and raises the complicated issue of receipt of funds by agents. **5.91**

The involvement of agents raises two distinct issues, each of which merits discussion: **5.92**

- Does receipt by an agent qualify as beneficial receipt by the agent's principal for the purposes of knowing receipt?

- In what circumstances will receipt by an agent qualify as receipt for the purposes of knowing receipt against that agent?

(i) Receipt by agent—receipt by principal   Receipt by an authorized agent of monies transferred in breach of trust will amount to receipt by the agent's principal, without the need to show that at some subsequent point the agent in fact transferred the relevant assets to his principal.[71] **5.93**

Such an approach is in line with the position at common law in respect of money had and received, where receipt by the agent suffices for the principal's liability.[72] **5.94**

(ii) Can an agent be liable for knowing receipt?   Ordinarily, where an agent receives funds on behalf of its principal, the agent will not have beneficially received the assets and so no question of knowing receipt liability can arise. Although it is sometimes said that in these circumstances, the agent can raise the **5.95**

---

[69] *Polly Peck International v Nadir (No 2)* [1992] 4 All ER 769, 777 (Scott LJ).

[70] With the possible rider that there may be some discussion whether the fraudster himself qualifies as the first recipient or whether it is only the first recipient from the fraudster.

[71] *Lewin on Trusts* (18th edn), [42-33] citing *El Ajou v Dollar Land Holdings plc* [1993] 3 All ER 717, 738 (Millett J).

[72] *Goff & Jones* (7th edn), para 40-027; *Butler v Harrison* (1777) 2 Cowp 565. In such circumstances, the agent has a defence of ministerial receipt to a claim for restitution: see generally, Virgo, *The Principles of the Law of Restitution* (2nd edn), 685–9.

defence of ministerial receipt, it is perhaps more accurate simply to say that one essential element of a claim for knowing receipt, being the beneficial receipt of the trust assets, is absent in this scenario.

5.96 If, however, the agent becomes aware that the property in its possession has been transferred in breach of trust, the agent's level of knowledge being consistent with the Privy Council's definition of dishonesty in *Royal Brunei v Tan*, then whilst the agent cannot be liable for knowing receipt (since it has not beneficially received the assets for its own purpose), it nevertheless runs the real risk of being liable for dishonest assistance in the event that it seeks to carry out its instructions by transferring the assets to its principal after it has acquired the relevant knowledge.[73]

(e) Use of corporate entities

5.97 Corporate entities are commonly used in commercial frauds as a means of disguising the initial transfer of funds from the claimant and, possibly, the identity of the ultimate recipient of the proceeds of fraud. The English court is astute to ensure that the principle of the separate legal nature of the corporate entity is not abused so as to hide the ultimate receipt of the fraud proceeds. If the corporate entity is a sham or is being used to facilitate a fraud then the court will allow the lifting of the corporate veil, such that receipt by the subsidiary is to be treated as receipt by a parent company or the individual controlling the subsidiary.[74]

5.98 Knox J in *Cowan de Groot Properties Ltd v Eagle Trust plc* declined to lift the corporate veil on the grounds that the 100% wholly-owned subsidiary (Pinepad) was not acting as agent of Cowan de Groot (its parent company) and there was no evidence of dishonesty or want of probity on the part of Pinepad.[75]

5.99 In *Trustor v Smallbone (No 2)*,[76] the Court of Appeal was willing to find that receipt of funds by a corporate entity (Introcom Ltd) amounted to receipt of funds by a defendant who was a beneficiary of the trust which controlled Introcom Ltd. The exception to the standard reluctance to lift the veil was the fact that the structure had been used as a façade to disguise the true facts (namely, that the defendant was a recipient of the proceeds of the fraud) coupled with evidence of dishonesty or want of probity.[77]

---

[73] *Bowstead & Reynolds* (18th edn), Article 116, Rule 2; Underhill and Hayton, *The Law of Trusts and Trustees* (17th edn), para 100.62; see *Agip (Africa) Ltd v Jackson* [1990] Ch 265, 291–2 (Millett J).

[74] See e.g. *Adams v Cape Industries Plc* [1990] Ch 433 (Scot J), [1990] 2 WLR 657 CA.

[75] [1992] 4 All ER 700 CA.

[76] [2001] 1 WLR 1177 CA.

[77] [2001] 1 WLR 1177, 1184.

The Court's approach is well illustrated in *El Ajou v Dollar Land Holdings plc*[78]   **5.100**
where Millett J remarked:

> ... The sum of £270,000 was never received by DLH. It was paid into Grangewoods'
> client account, and their client at the time must be taken to have been DLH London.
> DLH London was not a nominee or agent for DLH. As had previously been agreed
> between Roth and Mr Stern, it was the intended contractual purchaser of the site,
> and the money was to be used exclusively for the payment of the deposit on exchange
> of contracts. In my judgment, DLH did not receive the money at all, and DLH
> London did not receive it beneficially but upon trust to apply it for a specific pur-
> pose. DLH London used the money, as it was bound to do, to pay the deposit on site,
> and thereby acquired for its own benefit a corresponding interest in the site which it
> subsequently sold and transferred to DLH. The plaintiff can follow his money
> through these various transactions, but the relevant asset capable of being identified
> as having been received by DLH is an interest in the site corresponding to the
> payment of the deposit.[79]

(f) Position of banks

Banks play a special role in commercial frauds. They provide the means by which   **5.101**
the proceeds of any fraud are distributed amongst the fraudsters. At the same
time, the banks are operating a business and therefore are providing various services to their customers and charging for those services. It is perhaps fair to say that
the circumstances in which a bank might be found to have beneficially received
any proceeds of fraud (and therefore potentially be liable for knowing receipt)
have not, with one exception,[80] been the subject of detailed and sustained
examination.

In *Agip (Africa) Ltd v Jackson*[81] Millett J, at first instance, drew a distinction   **5.102**
between an account which is in credit and one which is in overdraft.[82] A bank is
said not to receive beneficially in the case of an account in credit into which fraud
proceeds are deposited since those monies are received by and credited to the
bank's customer who holds the relevant account. By contrast, it is said that a bank
will have beneficially received funds which are paid into an account which is overdrawn and those funds are used to reduce or extinguish that overdraft:

> The ['knowing receipt' claim] is concerned with the person who receives for his own
> benefit trust property transferred to him in breach of trust . . . The essential feature
> of [this] class is that the recipient must have received the property for his own use

---

[78] [1993] 3 ALL ER 717 (Millett J).
[79] ibid, 734.
[80] The one exception being the unpublished Oxford D.Phil thesis of Jonathan Moore,
'Restitution from Banks' (2000—on file with the author).
[81] [1990] Ch 265.
[82] ibid, 292; see also *Stephens Travel Service International Pty Ltd v Qantas Airways
Ltd* (1988) 13 NSWLR 331; *Citadel General Assurance Co v Lloyds Bank Canada* (1997) 152 DLR
(4th) 411.

and benefit. This is why neither the paying nor the collecting bank can normally be brought within it. In paying and collecting money for a customer the bank acts only as his agent. It is otherwise, however, if the collecting bank uses the money to reduce or discharge the customer's overdraft. In doing so it received the money for its own benefit.[83]

5.103 It can be seriously questioned how this analysis equates with an understanding of the banker–customer relationship and how it operates on an everyday basis.[84] It is accepted that absent any express trust agreement, the relationship between the bank and its customer is one of creditor–debitor and not trustee and beneficiary. If £100 is deposited into X's account and that account is in credit, that £100 is exchanged for a chose in action, being a debt owed by the bank to the customer in the amount standing to its credit in the account. The debt exists because the account is in credit and the additional £100 has been loaned from the customer to the bank for whatever purposes the bank wishes to use it for. On this analysis, there can be no real doubt that the £100 that was deposited into the account in credit has been received by the bank free to be used as the bank sees fit, leaving a debt owed by the bank to the customer.

5.104 If, however, the account is overdrawn by £150 and £100 is deposited into it, the debt owed by the customer to the bank is reduced by the amount deposited. Prior to the deposit, the bank was owed £150 by its customer. It is now owed just £50, having received the other £100 in part-payment of the overdraft facility. It is precisely because the overdraft has been reduced that there are those who argue that this constitutes beneficial receipt by the bank.

5.105 Yet if receipt of monies for one's own use is a definition of beneficial receipt then receipt by the bank even in the context of an account in credit still represents receipt of monies freely available to the bank. In both cases, the deposited money becomes the property of the bank and in both cases the bank is free to use those monies for whatever investments it chooses, subject only to its contractual obligation to repay the customer upon demand.

5.106 The main distinguishing factor is not the bank's freedom to use the monies deposited, which is the same whether the account is overdrawn or in credit, but rather whether it creates any additional debt relationship. In the example of the £150 overdraft, the deposit of £100 reduces that overdraft to £50. The £100 is used to pay off the debt owed by the customer to the bank, at least in the amount of £100. There is no contractual obligation to repay attached to that deposited £100 whereas when the account is in credit, the £100 becomes the bank's property

---

83 [1990] Ch 265, 292 (Millett J).
84 See E Cranston, *Principles of Banking Law* (2nd edn, Oxford University Press, 2002), 193–4 criticizing the present approach as 'sitting ill' with legal principle and banking practice.

but the bank also incurs a debt owed to its customer in the same amount. It is difficult, as a matter of legal principle, to see why the creation of an additional debt from the bank to the customer should have any bearing on whether the bank can be said to have beneficially received the monies.

Similar criticisms can be made of other instances where it has been said that a bank **5.107** has beneficially received assets. One example often cited is the exchange of currency by the bank.[85] Here it is said that the bank has beneficially received the money in order for it to be exchanged into the foreign currency. But, again, such analysis defies reality. Irrespective of whether the bank is providing an exchange currency service, receipt of the monies by the bank places the bank in a position to do with that money what it, the bank, chooses to do. There are no restrictions on how the bank can invest that money. It belongs legally to the bank, subject only to a debt being owed by the bank to its customer to repay the same amount.

In his seminal article, 'Tracing the Proceeds of Fraud'[86] Sir Peter Millett returned **5.108** to this issue and refined his view from that given in *Agip*. He saw merit in distinguishing between an ordinary account in overdraft and one which was closely monitored:

> The mere continuation of a running account in overdraft should not be sufficient to render the bank liable as recipient; there must probably be some conscious appropriation of the sum paid into the account in reduction of the overdraft.[87]

This view mirrors that of Professor Cranston who believes that beneficial receipt **5.109** 'must be confined to situations of real benefit, for example, to the bank pressing the customer to reduce its indebtedness under a facility when the customer is of doubtful solvency'.[88] Professor Cranston is driven to this conclusion because the ordinary test of beneficial receipt would apply too widely in the case of a bank, thus exposing it potentially to a large number of claims for knowing receipt.

Whilst fully sympathizing with Professor Cranston's concerns about applying the **5.110** usual test of beneficial receipt in the context of banks, the problem with his suggested approach is that it applies a different test to beneficial receipt by banks than by other entities and it is questionable whether there really exist meritorious grounds for applying the knowing receipt claim differently in these contexts. It is perhaps best remembered that banks are now subject to a great deal of additional

---

[85] E.g *Polly Peck International v Nadir (No 2)* [1992] 4 All ER 769, 777 per Scott LJ.
[86] (1991) 107 LQR 71.
[87] ibid, 83 n 46. See also C E F Rickett, 'Banks and Knowing Receipt' [1999] NZLJ 40.
[88] *Principles of Banking Law* (2nd edn), 194; see also M Bryan, 'When Does a Bank Receive Money?' [1996] JBL 165; C Rickett, 'The Banker's Liability for Receipt in Equity and at Common Law' (1995) 16 Co L 35. See also *Westpac Banking Corp v Savin* [1985] 2 NZLR 41 and *Anderson v Chilton* (1993) 4 NZBLC 103, 375.

scrutiny and potential liability under the various money laundering regimes than they have ever previously been.

5.111 So long as knowing receipt retains its fault-based approach, it is questionable why a bank should not be liable for knowing receipt in circumstances of ordinary beneficial receipt coupled with the appropriate level of knowledge on the bank's part. It is highly likely that such conduct will place the bank in difficulties in respect of its money laundering obligations and so there is little justification for exempting it from any liability in equity for knowing receipt.

5.112 It is respectfully suggested that there is little merit in seeking to adopt an approach to determining when a bank has beneficially received deposits based upon a notion of how closely monitored customers' accounts are. What real difference does it make if the bank was pressing the customer to reduce its overdraft facility? Such a reduction might well calm nerves at a bank concerned at the solvency of a customer but it provides no principled basis upon which to conclude that the bank must have beneficially received those funds.

(4) Defendant's knowledge

5.113 This is the issue which has drawn the focus of the courts and commentators alike. The most recent position is that it is necessary to show that the defendant had such knowledge as to render it unconscionable for that defendant to retain the assets so received. In reaching this conclusion, the Court of Appeal in *BCCI v Akindele*[89] (i) rejected dishonesty as a suitable test for knowing receipt; (ii) rejected strict liability and the unjust enrichment analysis of knowing receipt; (iii) cast further doubt on the usefulness of the five-level *Baden Delvaux* scale; and (iv) recognized that a test based upon unconscionability swapped difficulties of definition for difficulties of application.

5.114 Fortunately, given the absence of any detailed guidance from the Court of Appeal as to what amounts to unconscionability, coupled with the myriad of conflicting authorities, it is not possible to conclude that *BCCI v Akindele* represents the last word on this subject. Nor is it possible, however desirable it might be, to jettison examination of the earlier case law in favour of an approach based solely on the guidance contained within *BCCI v Akindele*. This decision is no *Royal Brunei v Tan*.

5.115 Finally, by way of introduction to *BCCI v Akindele*, the test for knowing receipt may gain some guidance from the recent cases on change of position defence, which also appear to favour a test based upon unconscionable conduct.[90]

---

[89] [2001] Ch 437. See R Nolan (2000) CLJ 447; J Penner (2000) 14 Trust Law International 229.

[90] 'Unconscionability' has been adopted in various authorities as being relevant to the defence of change of position: see *Niru Battery Manufacturing Co v Milestone Trading Ltd* [2003] EWCA Civ 1446, [2004] QB 985 CA; *Criterion Properties plc v Stratford UK Properties LLC* [2003] 1 WLR 2108—the House of Lords was silent on this point.

The facts of this case can be summarized as follows.   **5.116**

- The claimants were the liquidators of two Cayman Island companies ('A' and 'B') both controlled by the same holding company, and both licensed to carry on banking business.

- In 1985, employees of company A procured company B, which was already in severe financial difficulties, to enter into various dummy loan agreements with the defendant, Mr Akindele, a Nigerian businessman.

- US$10m was paid by Mr Akindele to company B in return for 250,000 shares in the holding company. It was a term of this arrangement that after two years company B would arrange for the sale of the shares at a price which would be equivalent to Mr Akindele receiving 15% annual return on his investment.

- In 1988, the shares were sold and Mr Akindele received US$16.679m.

- The claimants sued Mr Akindele for dishonest assistance and knowing receipt in respect of the additional US$6.679m.

- Carnwath J held that dishonesty was central to both claims and on the facts Mr Akindele had acted honestly.

- On appeal, the Court of Appeal held the judge was entitled to reach his conclusion on the honesty of Mr Akindele and so dismissed the appeal in respect of the dishonest assistance claim.

- In respect of the claim for knowing receipt, the Court of Appeal held dishonesty was not a prerequisite of liability and that the crucial test was one of unconscionability. Given the judge had found that Mr Akindele had acted honestly in entering into the 1985 agreement, those factual findings supported the conclusion that the defendant's knowledge both in 1985 and in 1988 was not such as to make it unconscionable for him to retain the benefit of the receipt of US$6.679m.

With that in mind, we shall approach this topic by way of a discussion of the fol- **5.117**
lowing issues which were each examined in some detail in the judgment of Nourse
LJ in *BCCI v Akindele*:

- dishonesty;
- strict liability;
- *Baden Delvaux* scale of knowledge;
- unconscionability.

(a) Dishonesty

The Court of Appeal in *BCCI v Akindele*[91] soundly rejected the suggestion that **5.118**
dishonesty might be required to impose liability for knowing receipt claims.[92]

---

[91] [2001] Ch 437.
[92] The Court of Appeal rejected Carnwath J's analysis, at first instance, that the same test of dishonesty should apply to both dishonest assistance and knowing receipt: ibid, 448F–G. Nourse LJ

In so doing, the Court chose not to equate the test laid down in *Royal Brunei v Tan* for dishonest assistance with that for knowing receipt. There is no reason why they should have, given the separate nature of these respective claims.

5.119 The Court of Appeal was heavily influenced in reaching this conclusion by the decision in *Belmont Finance v Williams Furniture (No 2)*.[93] The relevant facts of this somewhat complex case can be summarized as follows.

- Belmont was a wholly-owned subsidiary of the second-defendant, City, which was, in turn, a wholly-owned subsidiary of the first defendant, Williams. Mr James was chairman and general controlling influence over all three companies. A third party company, Maximum, offered to sell its shares to Belmont for £500,000 and to purchase Belmont's share capital from City for £489,000.

- This was a transaction in breach of s 54 of the Companies Act 1948 which prohibited the provision of financial assistance to a company to enable it to purchase its own shares and thus involved a misapplication of Belmont's funds.

- It turned out, after the appointment of an independent valuer by the receiver of Belmont, that the Maximum shares were worth only £60,000 and not the £500,000 paid by Belmont.

- Belmont's receiver brought a claim against Mr James, Williams and City for conspiracy to defraud and liability as constructive trustee for both knowing assistance (as it was then called) and knowing receipt.

- At the trial, Foster J found as a fact that Mr James (and the other directors of City) genuinely believed that the purchase of Maximum's shares at £500,000 price was in the commercial interests of Belmont. They were not acting dishonestly in so doing.

- On appeal, the Court of Appeal found that the directors of City, whilst not acting dishonestly, nevertheless did receive £489,000 out of the £500,000 misapplication of Belmont's funds when they had knowledge of all the circumstances. The knowing receipt claim therefore succeeded. The Court of Appeal dismissed the claim for knowing assistance on the grounds that Foster J had found that none of City's directors had acted dishonestly.

5.120 Thus, as Nourse LJ in *BCCI v Akindele*, pointed out, *Belmont Finance* 'is clear authority for the proposition that dishonesty is not a necessary ingredient of liability for knowing receipt'.[94]

---

commented: 'While a knowing recipient will often be found to have acted dishonestly, it has never been a prerequisite of the liability that he should' (448G–H).

[93] [1980] 1 All ER 393.

[94] [2001] Ch 437, 450C–D.

To similar effect is the conclusion of Vinelott J in *Eagle Trust plc v SBC Securities* **5.121**
Ltd:[95]

> What the decision in *Belmont (No 2)* [1980] 1 All ER 393 shows is that in a 'knowing
> receipt' case it is only necessary to show that the defendant knew that the moneys
> paid to him were trust moneys and of circumstances which made the payment a mis-
> application of them. Unlike a 'knowing assistance' case it is not necessary, and never
> has been necessary, to show that the defendant was in any sense a participator in a
> fraud.

The decision of Vinelott J in *Eagle Trust* on this point is a little difficult to discern, **5.122**
as recognized by other commentators who have tentatively suggested the decision
may stand as authority for the proposition that dishonesty is in fact required.[96]

What is clear is that although the Court of Appeal in *BCCI v Akindele* has chosen **5.123**
to focus on *Belmont* in support of its view that dishonesty has never been a requirement for knowing receipt, there are numerous other authorities which do suggest
that dishonesty is required for this claim.[97]

In addition to these authorities, as explained earlier, there is the relatively recent **5.124**
suggestion, put forward by Lord Nicholls *extra-judicially*[98] and taken up by
others,[99] that there may well be an equitable wrongdoing aspect to the knowing
receipt claim based upon dishonest receipt of the proceeds. Such liability would
be imposed on similar grounds to that for dishonest assistance. The requirement
for dishonesty is said to be justified because equity intervenes, not because of the
defendant's receipt of proceeds of the fraud, but because of his dishonesty in so
doing.

It can be surmised that the Court of Appeal in *BCCI v Akindele* rejected dishon- **5.125**
esty because they wished to give effect to the fact that the defendant had actually
received assets which were the proceeds of the fraud. There was no need to go so
high as to require dishonesty to place liability on the defendant for receiving fraud
proceeds. At the other extreme, Lord Nicholls' recent suggestion ignores entirely

---

95 [1993] 1 WLR 484, 497.

96 A Burrows, E McKendrick and J Edelman, *Cases and Materials on the Law of Restitution* (2nd
edn, Oxford University Press, 2005), 231.

97 *Carl-Zeiss Stiftung v Herbert Smith (No 2)* [1969] 2 Ch 276 (CA); *Competitive Insurance
Co Ltd v Davies Investments Ltd* [1975] 1 WLR 1240 (Goff J); *Re Montagu's Settlement Trusts* [1987]
Ch 264 (Sir Robert Megarry VC); *Cowan de Groot Properties Ltd v Eagle Trust plc* [1992] 4 All ER 700
(Knox J, commercially unacceptable conduct may amount to dishonesty in a commercial setting);
Eagle Trust plc v SBC Securities Ltd (No 2) [1996] 1 BCLC 121 (Arden J). See also, less forcefully, the
views expressed by Scott LJ in *Polly Peck International plc v Nadir (No 2)* [1992] 4 All ER 769.

98 'Knowing Receipt: The Need for a New Landmark' in Cornish et al (eds), *Restitution: Past,
Present and Future*, ch 15.

99 Professor Birks, 'Receipt' in Birks and Pretto (eds), *Breach of Trust*, 223–4; see also Lord Walker,
'Dishonesty and Unconscionable Conduct in Commercial Life—Some Reflections on Accessory
Liability and Knowing Receipt' (2005) 27 Sydney LR 187.

the fact of receipt of the assets and simply wishes to equate the conduct of the defendant with that of the dishonest assistor. This is not a surprising position for Lord Nicholls to adopt. Indeed, it is entirely logical, since if he gives any relevance to the fact of the receipt of the proceeds it would force him to argue for strict liability only.

5.126 In conclusion, the Court of Appeal in *BCCI v Akindele* was correct to reject the high threshold of dishonesty for the purposes of knowing receipt claims. Yet, in so doing they ignored certain authorities to the contrary and that will only ever increase uncertainty in this already uncertain part of the law, but ultimately it is difficult to see any logical argument requiring the same level of knowledge or wrongdoing in the case of someone participating in a fraud as for someone receiving the proceeds of a fraud.

5.127 The ingenious attempt by Lord Nicholls to deal with the authorities requiring a fault-based approach whilst advocating a strict liability approach by trying to equate *dishonest* receipt with dishonest assistance is, at its heart, flawed by the failure to take into account the crucial factor which has always distinguished the receipt claims from the assistance claims, namely the fact of receipt in the former which is absent in the latter. Unless in the new version of the claim, receipt is to be equated with mere assistance, it is likely the court would always wish to give some effect to this important feature of the claim.

(b) Strict liability

5.128 Having rejected any suggestion that dishonesty was necessary, the Court of Appeal in *BCCI v Akindele* also dismissed a test based upon strict liability for knowing receipt claims.[100] The arguments in favour of a strict liability approach derive from the views of highly-respected restitutionary lawyers and judges who have contended that liability for knowing receipt is based upon the unjust enrichment of the recipient and that since claims in unjust enrichment are strict liability (subject to defences), so should liability for knowing receipt. This specific argument is dealt with in some detail above.[101]

5.129 Whatever the merits of the general debate on this issue, the reality is that there is very little support for such a contention in the relevant authorities. The decision in *Re Diplock* [1948] Ch 465 (CA) would, if extended beyond the confines of the limited area of administration of estates, provide some support for a strict liability approach to recipient liability in equity. Similarly, *G L Baker Ltd v Medway*

---

[100] It would in fact appear that no submissions in favour of strict liability were advanced in front of the Court of Appeal but reference was made to the general arguments in favour of strict liability towards the end of Nourse LJ's judgment: see [2001] 1 Ch 437, 456.

[101] See para 5.19 *et seq.*

Building and Supplies Ltd,[102] at first instance, supports the strict liability approach. See also the decision of Hansen J in *Koorootang Nominees Pty Ltd v Australia and New Zealand Banking Group Ltd*.[103]

In rejecting the approach based upon strict liability, it is important to recall those **5.130** cases where the court was content to impose liability on the recipient for knowing receipt for something falling short of dishonesty. These are the numerous cases which favour the approach that the recipient is liable if he knew or ought to have known that the assets were being transferred in breach of trust.[104]

Further, a valiant but ultimately futile attempt was made by Prof Birks to re-inter- **5.131** pret the standard authorities on the question of knowing receipt.[105] He attempted to limit the relevance of fault or knowledge to questions of the availability of the defence of bona fide purchase for value without notice. With respect, a careful reading of these authorities, uninfluenced by a desire to spread the strict liability approach of unjust enrichment, does not support such a contention. Indeed, it is quite evident that the enquiry into knowledge and fault in each of these cases was specifically directed to the primary liability of the recipient and not, as contended by Birks, to the availability or otherwise of potential defences.

Not only was the strict liability approach devoid of a great deal of support in the **5.132** authorities, the Court of Appeal in *BCCI v Akindele* was also concerned that it would have a detrimental effect in respect of commercial transactions. Nourse LJ commented as follows:

> We must continue to do our best with the accepted formulation of the liability in knowing receipt, seeking to simplify and improve it where we may. While in general it may be possible to sympathise with a tendency to subsume a further part of our law of restitution under the principles of unjust enrichment, I beg leave to doubt whether strict liability coupled with a change of position defence would be preferable to fault-based liability in many commercial transactions, for example where, as here, the receipt is of a company's funds which have been misapplied by its directors. Without having heard argument it is unwise to be dogmatic, but in such a case it would appear to be commercially unworkable and contrary to the spirit of the rule in *Royal British Bank v Turquand* (1856) 6 E & B 327 that, simply on proof of an internal misapplication of the company's funds, the burden should shift to the recipient to defend the receipt

---

102 [1958] 1 WLR 1216, 1220 (Danckwerts J). The actual decision was overturned on appeal on a specific pleading point but, importantly, the Court of Appeal cast no doubt on the strict liability approach adopted by Danckwerts J: CA in [1958] 1 WLR 1225.

103 [1998] 3 VR 16, although on the facts Hansen J did not need to reach any decision on the issue.

104 E.g. *Houghton v Fayers* [2000] Lloyd's Bank Rep 145 (CA); *Belmont Finance Corpn v Williams Furniture Ltd* [1979] Ch 250; *International Sales and Agencies v Marcus* [1982] 3 All ER 551; Millett J in *Agip (Africa) v Jackson* [1990] Ch 265.

105 Birks, 'Misdirected Funds: restitution from the recipient' [1989] LMCLQ 296; Birks, 'Trusts in the Recovery of Misapplied Assets: Tracing, Trusts and Restitution' in McKendrick (ed), *Commercial Aspects of Trusts and Fiduciary Obligations* (Clarendon Press, 1992), 149, 159–61; Birks, 'Problems in Misdirected Money: A Quintet' [1993] LMCLQ 218.

either by a change of position or perhaps in some other way. Moreover, if the circumstances of the receipt are such as to make it unconscionable for the recipient to retain the benefit of it, there is an obvious difficulty in saying that it is equitable for a change of position to afford him a defence.

5.133   It is evident from this quotation that Nourse LJ's main reason for rejecting strict liability had less to do with any principled disagreement on the issue of unjust enrichment underlying knowing receipt claims and more to do with the practical consequences which might ensue for commercial transactions. In his Lordship's words, an approach based upon strict liability would be 'commercially unworkable'. This view echoes that given by Lord Shand in *Thomson v Clydesdale Bank Limited*[106] over 100 years earlier.

5.134   Lionel Smith has similarly expressed concerns at the practical effect a strict liability approach may have on institutions such as banks.[107] He states:

> The strict liability approach would contemplate that a plaintiff need only allege that a bank received trust property, not that the bank knew or should have known of the trust; with no more than that, the bank would be required to prove its good faith as a defence, or to account for what it had done with this money. In other words, there is no procedure which a bank, be it ever so honest, can adopt in order to ensure that it is not prima facie liable for the receipt of trust funds.[108]

5.135   Although Dr Smith's last sentence would be correct under a strict liability regime, it is questionable whether such a regime would in fact lead to greater instances of liability on the part of banks than is seen under the present fault-based approach.[109] Ultimately, whether liability is imposed and/or defences available (whether change of position or bona fide purchaser for value without notice) will depend on whether the bank carried out the transaction with a certain level of knowledge of the wrongdoing. If so, the bank will be liable under either regime. If not, then the prima facie liability under the strict liability regime would be met with a defence of change of position or bona fide purchaser for value without notice. It is of course accepted that there is a distinction in the burden of proof, which may have a bearing in a very small number of cases, but generally few cases will turn on this issue.

5.136   Given the Court of Appeal's clear attitude in *BCCI v Akindele*, it will take a landmark House of Lords' decision to overrule existing authorities and re-position the knowing receipt claim in a strict liability category. There have been encouraging dicta in support of such an approach by senior judges, most recently by Lord Nicholls in *Criterion Properties plc v Stratford UK Properties LLC*.[110] However, as

---

[106]   [1893] AC 282, 292–3.
[107]   L Smith, 'Unjust Enrichment, Property, and the Structure of Trusts' (2000) 116 LQR 412.
[108]   ibid, 434.
[109]   See also, Jonathan Moore, 'Restitution from Banks' (unpublished Oxford D.Phil thesis), 56–8.
[110]   [2004] UKHL 28; [2004] 1 WLR 1846, 1848, para 4.

with the unification of the rules on tracing, we have a good idea where at least some of the senior judges wish to go on this issue, but dicta is of little use to the practitioner in the face of clearly binding authorities.

(c) The Baden Delvaux *scale*

The well-known and oft-criticized *Baden Delvaux* scale derives from the epony-   **5.137**
mous case of *Baden v Societe Generale pour Favoriser le Developpment du Commerce et de l'Industrie en France SA (Note)*.[111] Peter Gibson J's scale includes the following five categories of knowledge: (i) actual knowledge; (ii) wilfully shutting one's eyes to the obvious; (iii) wilfully and recklessly failing to make such inquiries as an honest and reasonable man would make; (iv) knowledge of circumstances which would indicate the facts to an honest and reasonable man; (v) knowledge of circumstances which would put an honest and reasonable man on inquiry.

One obvious point to make is that the *Baden Delvaux* scale is concerned with lev-   **5.138**
els of knowledge as opposed to being a scale to determine levels of dishonesty and carelessness. That said, levels (i) to (iii) are often equated with actual knowledge and such knowledge will readily lead to a conclusion of want of probity or dishonesty[112] (although this depends ultimately on what is meant by dishonesty i.e. subjective or objective test). Levels (iv) and (v) are concerned with constructive knowledge and might be said to equate to levels of carelessness.

Nourse LJ made the following observations as to the suitability and applicability   **5.139**
of the *Baden Delvaux* scale to knowing receipt claims.

- The scale was the subject of agreement amongst counsel in a case concerned with dishonest assistance and not knowing receipt. It would not therefore have been formulated with the requirements of knowing receipt in mind.

- Both Millett J in *Agip (Africa) Ltd v Jackson*[113] and Knox J in *Cowan de Groot Properties Ltd v Eagle Trust plc*[114] have given warnings about treating the scale like a statute and/or too readily assuming that categories (iv) and (v) are categories of constructive knowledge only.

- Lord Nicholls in *Royal Brunei v Tan* believed that the scale had no role at all to play in respect of dishonest assistance claims. By contrast, in *BCCI v Akindele*, Nourse LJ believed the scale has a greater role to play in dishonest assistance claims than in knowing receipt claims. This view appears premised upon the fact that the usefulness of any categorization depended on whether it served its purpose.

---

[111] [1993] 1 WLR 509.
[112] It will ultimately be dependent, however, on what is meant by 'dishonesty' and whether it is taken to have a subjective or objective meaning.
[113] [1990] Ch 265, 293.
[114] [1992] 4 All ER 700, 761G.

Nourse LJ could see little point in arguing about which category of (i) to (v) any particular case fell within when the answer would not in itself determine the relevant question for the receipt claims, namely whether the recipient's conscience was so affected as to justify imposing a duty to return the assets received.

5.140 So where does this leave the *Baden Delvaux* scale? It was rejected and considered 'best forgotten' by Lord Nicholls in the context of dishonest assistance claims in *Royal Brunei v Tan* and has received similar treatment at the hands of Nourse LJ in the context of knowing receipt claims. Although Nourse LJ considers there may be some scope for its continued use in the context of dishonest assistance claims, it is difficult to see this as likely given the strong views expressed by Lord Nicholls in what has been a universally-accepted Privy Council Opinion. No doubt it will continue to surface in discussions on the authorities of both assistance and receipt claims given the need to understand the scale in order to comprehend the decision reached in many of the authorities. Other than that, it is unlikely to be much of a practical aid to the practitioner in future claims.

(d) Unconscionability[115]

5.141 The Court of Appeal favoured a test of unconscionability for the knowing receipt claim. In doing so, Nourse LJ was under no misapprehension that he was providing practitioners with clear and definitive guidance:

> . . . I have come to the view that, just as there is now a single test of dishonesty for knowing assistance, so ought there to be a single test of knowledge for knowing receipt. The recipient's state of knowledge must be such as to make it unconscionable for him to retain the benefit of the receipt. A test in that form, though it cannot, any more than any other, avoid difficulties of application, ought to avoid those of definition and allocation to which the previous categorisations have led. Moreover, it should better enable the courts to give commonsense decisions in the commercial context in which claims in knowing receipt are now frequently made, paying equal regard to the wisdom of Lindley LJ[116] on the one hand and of Richardson J[117] on the other.[118]

---

[115] S B Thomas, 'Goodbye Knowing Receipt. Hello Unconscientious Receipt' (2001) 21 OJLS 239, applying an economic analysis to this test.

[116] This is a reference to Lindley LJ's well-known dicta in *Manchester Trust v Furness* [895] 2 QB 539, 545: 'In dealing with estates in land title is everything, and it can be leisurely investigated; in commercial transactions possession is everything, and there is no time to investigate title; and if we were to extend the doctrine of constructive notice to commercial transactions we should be doing infinite mischief and paralysing the trade of the country.'

[117] This is a reference to the decision of Richardson J in *Westpac Banking Corpn v Savin* [1985] 2 NZLR 41, where Richardson J who had expressed a provisional preference for constructive knowledge, said at 53: 'Clearly courts would not readily import a duty to inquire in the case of commercial transactions where they must be conscious of the seriously inhibiting effects of a wide application of the doctrine. Nevertheless there must be cases where there is no justification on the known facts for allowing a commercial man who has received funds paid to him in breach of trust to plead the shelter of the exigencies of commercial life.'

[118] See also Thomas J in *Powell v Thompson* [1991] 1 NZLR 597, who had earlier proposed a similar test based upon unconscionability: 'Once a breach of trust has been committed, the commission

This decision provides little practical guidance on when a recipient might be **5.142** found to have acted unconscionably in receiving the proceeds. We can surmise that something short of dishonesty, given the Court of Appeal's rejection of assimilation of the receipt and assistance claims, and that something more than strict liability, is required before liability can be imposed. The merit which the Court of Appeal saw in this approach is that it left plenty of room for the court to use its own common sense. But what the Court of Appeal sees as the advantage of this approach—its flexibility—is the cause of difficulties amongst practitioners seeking to provide clear guidance to clients.

Professor Birks commented that the test of unconscionability is based on unrea- **5.143** sonable conduct:

> What it requires is unreasonableness and, in particular, unreasonable failure to appreciate the trust provenance of the assets in question.[119]

It might seriously be questioned whether unreasonableness truly encompasses **5.144** all that is intended to be covered by the term 'unconscionable'. Behaving unreasonably does not necessarily carry with it the undertones of moral turpitude which appear to fall within 'unconscionable' conduct. Indeed, the court should not quickly forget Lord Nicholls' observations in *Royal Brunei v Tan*, obviously in the context of dishonest assistance but equally applicable to knowing receipt, that unconscionability, without a clear definition, is too vague a test to be applied:

> Unconscionable is a word of immediate appeal to an equity lawyer. Equity is rooted historically in the concept of the Lord Chancellor, as the Keeper of the Royal Conscience, concerning himself with conduct which was contrary to good conscience. It must be recognised, however, that unconscionable is not a word in everyday use by non-lawyers. If it is to be used in this context, and if it is to be the touchstone for liability as an accessory, it is essential to be clear on what, *in this context*, unconscionable *means*. If unconscionable means no more than dishonesty, then dishonesty is the preferable label. If unconscionable means something different, it must be said that it is not clear what that something different is. Either way, therefore, the term is better avoided in this context.[120]

It is nothing short of remarkable that just a few years later the Court of Appeal **5.145** is content to invoke the use of this term without providing the clear definition called for in the Privy Council. Parties can hardly be blamed if they are now going

---

of which has involved a third party, the question which arises is one as between the beneficiary and that third party. If the third party's conduct has been unconscionable, then irrespective of the degree of impropriety in the trustee's conduct, the third party is liable to be held accountable to the beneficiary as if he or she were a trustee' (613).

119 Birks, 'Receipt' in Birks and Pretto (eds), *Breach of Trust,* 227.
120 *Royal Brunei v Tan* [1995] 2 AC 378, 392D–F.

to be forced to spend significant costs litigating the ambit of this new test in the courts.

5.146   Having said that, it is worth pointing out that there have been several cases, principally involving Lawrence Collins J as judge, which have applied *BCCI v Akindele* without apparently having any difficulty in so doing and without having to engage in any detailed discussion of what is meant by unconscionable receipt. The matter was dealt with en passant by Mr Justice Collins in an otherwise lengthy judgment in *Primlake Ltd (In Liquidation) v Matthews Associates & Ors*.[121] Similarly, the test was applied without any difficulty by Tugendhat J in *Ali v Al-Basri*,[122] and by Paul Morgan AC (sitting as a deputy judge) in *Quarter Master UK v Pyke*[123] where the judge imputed the knowledge of two wrongdoing directors to their company and held that certain assets received by that company could not be retained.

5.147   None of the cases recently applying the unconscionability test appeared to involve any detailed argument as to what that test entailed. Some of the cases, such as *Quarter Master v Pyke*, appear quite straightforward and unlikely to generate much debate in any event. The difficulties will develop at the extreme positions, and that is where the lack of real guidance will be most acutely felt.

5.148   It may well be necessary to look to the recent cases in respect of the availability of the change of position defence for guidance on the test for knowing receipt liability. In *Niru Battery Manufacturing Co v Milestone Trading Ltd*,[124] the Court of Appeal was concerned, in part, with the correct level of fault which would bar an individual from being able to rely upon the defence of change of position. Having examined the authorities from *Lipkin Gorman* onwards, Clarke LJ, giving the lead judgment, concluded that although dishonesty and wrongdoing would suffice to bar the defence, they were not in fact necessary. The essential question is whether on the facts of a particular case it would in all the circumstances be inequitable or unconscionable, and thus unjust, to allow the recipient of money paid under a mistake of fact to deny restitution to the payer.[125]

---

[121] [2006] EWHC 1227, para 334. See also Lawrence Collins J in *Commerzbank Aktiengesellschaft v IMB Morgan Plc* [2004] EWHC 2771. Similarly, Lawrence Collins J appeared to have no difficulty in applying the reasoning in *BCCI v Akindele* in *Re Loftus (deceased)* [2005] EWHC 406; [2005] 2 All ER 700, para 168: 'Dexter had the requisite knowledge/notice of the breaches, sufficient to render it unconscionable that he should retain the yard . . .'

[122] [2004] EWHC 2608, [2004] All ER (D) 290 (Nov).

[123] [2005] 1 BCLC 245, 272.

[124] [2004] QB 985 (CA).

[125] The most troubling aspect of the Court of Appeal's approach is their desire to adopt some form of weighing up approach as between claimant and defendant before determining whether full restitution should be made. The danger in such an approach is that it may come perilously close to applying vague concepts of justice, as opposed to a claim being available if certain hard facts can be established.

Clarke LJ went on to hold that a lack of good faith is not to be equated with the **5.149**
existence of bad faith and then endorsed the following passage from Moore-Bick
J at first instance on how one goes about establishing a lack of good faith:

> I do not think that it is desirable to attempt to define the limits of good faith; it is a
> broad concept, the definition of which, in so far as it is capable of definition at all, will
> have to be worked out through the cases. In my view it is capable of embracing a failure
> to act in a commercially acceptable way and sharp practice of a kind that falls short of
> outright dishonesty as well as dishonesty itself. The factors which will determine
> whether it is inequitable to allow the claimant to obtain restitution in a case of mis-
> taken payment will vary from case to case, but where the payee has voluntarily parted
> with the money much is likely to depend on the circumstances in which he did so and
> the extent of his knowledge about how the payment came to be made. Where he knows
> that the payment he has received was made by mistake, the position is quite straight-
> forward: he must return it. This applies as much to a banker who receives a payment
> for the account of his customer as to any other person . . . Greater difficulty may arise,
> however, in cases where the payee has grounds for believing that the payment may have
> been made by mistake, but cannot be sure. In such cases good faith may well dictate
> that an inquiry be made of the payer. The nature and extent of the inquiry called for
> will, of course, depend on the circumstances of the case, but I do not think that a per-
> son who has, or thinks he has, good reason to believe that the payment was made by
> mistake will often be found to have acted in good faith if he pays the money away with-
> out first making inquiries of the person from whom he received it.[126]

It is likely that similar reasoning may come to apply to determine the question of **5.150**
liability for knowing or unconscientious receipt.

E. Remedies for Knowing or Unconscientious Receipt[127]

Although some of the older cases talk of liability for knowing receipt 'as a con-   **5.151**
structive trustee', it has been shown convincingly that such language detracts
rather than adds to our understanding of this claim.[128] The knowing recipient is
not a trustee in any meaningful sense of the word. The fact that liability arises
upon receipt of property does not mean it is necessary to characterize that liability
as some form of trust liability. It is not.

It is preferable to talk in terms of a personal liability to account for the value of the   **5.152**
benefit received. It matters not if the recipient has subsequently divested himself
of the benefit knowingly received. Retention of the benefit is not part of liability
for knowing receipt—another reason why the language of the constructive trust
was inappropriate.

---

[126] [2002] EWHC 1425; [2002] 2 All ER (Comm) 705, [135].
[127] *Lewin on Trusts* (18th edn) at [42-71].
[128] See e.g. Millett LJ in *Paragon Finance plc v DB Thakerar and Co* [1999] 1 All ER 400, 408.

6

CONSTRUCTIVE TRUSTS—AN OVERVIEW

A. Introduction

To aid discussion, we must, as far as possible, understand our terms better and distinguish the constructive trust from the express trust and the resulting trust. **6.01**

• Unlike the express trust, which is created based on the settlor's intention, both a constructive trust and a resulting trust are imposed by operation of law. But in a constructive trust, the trust is imposed by operation of law to protect the fiduciary relationship or prevent general wrongdoing or unconscionable conduct, whereas for the resulting trust, it is imposed to give effect to intention[1] or, for some,[2] more accurately the absence of any intention to benefit the recipient.

---

[1] Per Lord Browne-Wilkinson in *Westdeutsche Bank v Islington LBC* [1996] AC 669 at 708C–D.
[2] E.g. those who champion the relationship between restitution and the resulting trust (see below).

- A constructive trust arises whenever the circumstances are such that it would be unconscionable for the owner of the legal title to assert his own beneficial interest and deny the beneficial interest of another. The relevant events must be known to the legal owner so his conscience can be affected. It may arise in answer to a catalogue of different types of wrongdoing (see Chapter 7) or, more commonly, in response to a breach of fiduciary duty (see Chapter 8).[3]

- Conscience being affected is of central importance to the existence of a constructive trust. It does not feature at all in relation to resulting trusts.

- For some, such as Birks,[4] Chambers,[5] and Lord Millett,[6] a resulting trust arises whenever there has been a transfer from X to Y and X does not intend to pass the beneficial interest to Y. It is the absence of an intention to pass the beneficial interest which grounds the resulting trust and not any intention to create a trust. So if X knew nothing about the transfer to Y that would suffice to give rise to a resulting trust since X could not be said to have intended to benefit Y by such a transfer. There is an attractive logic and simplicity about this view. It is sometimes wrongly accused of allowing too much proprietary relief but that is premised on the view that a mistaken payor does not intend to benefit the payee.[7] He does: an intention to transfer should not be confused with an intention to benefit. A mistake about the former does not alter the latter.[8] However, whatever the attractive logic of this view of the resulting trust, it cannot be said to be the present state of the law: see *Westdeutsche Landesbank*.[9]

- Lord Browne-Wilkinson in *Westdeutsche* rejected the 'absence of intention' approach to resulting trusts in favour of an approach based upon intention.[10] A resulting trust arises:

  - Where A makes a voluntary payment to B or pays (wholly or in part) for the purchase of property which is vested either in B alone or in the joint names of A and B, there is a presumption that A did not intend to make a gift to B; the money or property is held on trust for A (if he is the sole provider of the

---

[3] Sir Peter Millett, 'Restitution and Constructive Trusts' in Cornish, Nolan, O'Sullivan and Virgo (eds), *Restitution: Past, Present & Future* (Hart Publishing, 1998), 201.

[4] Birks, 'Restitution and Resulting Trusts' in Goldstein (ed), *Equity: Contemporary Legal Developments* (Hebrew University of Jerusalem, 1992).

[5] *Resulting Trusts* (Clarendon Press, 1997).

[6] Sir Peter Millett, 'Restitution and Constructive Trusts' in Cornish et al (eds), *Restitution: Past, Present & Future*, 201.

[7] G Virgo, *The Principles of the Law of Restitution* (2nd edn, Oxford University Press, 2006), 596–9. He recognizes some problems with this approach, principally the need to limit the availability of proprietary relief but ultimately recognizes it is not presently English law: House of Lords in *Westdeutsche Landesbank v Islington London Borough Council* [1996] AC 669.

[8] Sir Peter Millett, Review Article, 'Resulting Trusts' by Robert Chambers 1997: [1998] RLR 283, 284.

[9] *Westdeutsche Landesbank Girozentrale v Islington London Borough Council* [1996] AC 669 (HL).

[10] Lord Browne-Wilkinson's analysis is dealt with in more detail later in this chapter at para 6.42 *et seq.*

money) or in the case of a joint purchase by A and B in shares proportionate to their contributions. The presumption is just that and can be countered by evidence.

- Where A transfers property to B on express trusts, but the trusts declared do not exhaust the whole beneficial interest.
- In both examples, Lord Browne-Wilkinson contends the resulting trust is imposed by law to give effect to the parties' intentions.

The focus of any inquiry into whether an event gives rise to a constructive trust, **6.02** on the other hand, is on the defendant recipient, his knowledge of the circumstances of his receipt of the asset and whether such knowledge prevents him from denying the interest of another. But, whether one adopts the Lord Browne-Wilkinson approach, or the Chambers approach, the resulting trust inquiry is focused on the transferor, not the recipient/transferee, and whether he intended to create a trust (as Lord Browne-Wilkinson would have it) or whether there is an absence of any intention to benefit the recipient (as Birks, Chambers and Lord Millett would have it). In this way, one can see the attraction of the resulting trust to the unjust enrichment lawyer whose focus is always on the transferor and not the transferee. But it also shows just how different the constructive trust is from whatever form of the resulting trust ultimately finds favour with the courts.

The law of constructive trusts is undoubtedly one of the more complex and diffi- **6.03** cult areas of law with which a commercial fraud litigator must grapple. As will be seen, part of its complexity arises from the lack of any clear uniform principle governing when such a trust should arise which, in turn, is a reflection of the fact that the term 'constructive trust' is used in more than one sense.

It may arise in support of the restrictions placed on a fiduciary's conduct, however **6.04** honest and well meaning the fiduciary may have been, or it may respond to certain identified categories of wrongdoing, where the wrongdoing is considered to be such as to justify the imposition of a trust. Finally, the term has also been used inaccurately as a shorthand for personal liability to account.

In addition, the greater willingness of commercial lawyers to invoke equitable **6.05** principles and concepts in commercial settings so as to provide a remedy where none would otherwise exist has resulted in each of these uses of the term 'constructive trust' being pushed and pulled in various directions and ultimately, perhaps, out of shape.

None of this bodes well for the busy practitioner who must get to grips with the **6.06** concept of the constructive trust in order to see if it may provide a practical solution to a particular client's problem. The purpose of this overview chapter is to assist the practitioner to clear a path through the myriad of arguments and debates which surround this topic. Those arguments and debates, particularly over the last 15 to 20 years, have generated an inordinate amount of academic material on all aspects of the constructive trust. Much of this material has been helpful, identifying the nature and extent of relief arising under a constructive trust—other material has been helpful in a different manner, indicating a particular line of argument as fruitless. So long as the practitioner is aware that time has been spent on that argument and it has been rejected that in itself is useful.

6.07 Where such arguments have now been firmly rejected, this chapter will say so and move on. Where such arguments have been adopted and accepted, this chapter will focus on them and attempt to present them as clearly as possible. Where the door has not entirely closed on certain arguments, the reader will be informed of the arguments for and against, so that the reader can make an informed decision whether there is any merit in that line of argument.

6.08 This overview chapter focuses on five principal arguments or topics each of which, no doubt with others, plays their part in making this area slightly more confusing and obscure than perhaps it really needs to be. Those five arguments or topics are:

- constructive trusts within the law of trusts;
- attempts at a uniform principle;
- misuse of language;
- remedial v institutional constructive trust;
- unjust enrichment and resulting trust.

B. Constructive Trusts within the Law of Trusts

6.09 One way of examining the place of the constructive trust in the law of trusts is to examine the usual requirements for an express trust (i.e. the three certainties) and then seeing to what extent, if at all, such requirements apply to the constructive trust. In addition, this section will examine (at (4) below) the duties arising under a constructive trust and finally examine (at (5) below) various statutory regimes and the constructive trust.

(1) Certainty of intention

6.10 It is in respect of this requirement that a marked divergence between an express private trust and a constructive trust is evident. Although no specific language or wording is required, an express private trust does require evidence of the settlor's intention to create a trust. This may be done without using the word 'trust' and conversely using the word 'trust' will not guarantee that such intention will be found.[11]

---

[11] *Tito v Waddell (No 2)* [1977] Ch 106, where the word 'trust' was considered to be used in a governmental sense and not as giving rise to fiduciary duties. Accordingly, no relief was available from the courts in that case.

This is not the settlor's subjective intention but rather his objective intention— **6.11** the intention that an objective bystander would ascribe to the settlor on hearing or reading the words used to create the trust. So long as the settlor intended to enter a specific arrangement, so long as he knew about the arrangement and intended to enter it, it matters not that he did not consider that arrangement to amount to a trust.[12]

Constructive trusts, on the other hand, are imposed by operation of the law and **6.12** not as a result of the express intention of the settlor. The law responds to certain situations in which it is considered inappropriate that the legal owner assert his beneficial ownership of the property whilst at the same time denying another's beneficial interest in that property.

So constructive trusts, unlike other trusts, do not adhere to the requirement of **6.13** certainty of intention.

(2) Certainty of subject matter

An express private trust requires that its subject matter be certain. This is hardly **6.14** surprising since a trustee has specific obligations in respect of property and must therefore know precisely which property is the subject of the trust.

Certainty of subject matter remains as applicable to a constructive trust as it does **6.15** to any other trust. So, if the relevant property is part of gold bullion stored in bulk but unascertained and not segregated then no constructive trust can arise in respect of it: *Re Goldcorp Exchange Ltd.*[13]

There was some suggestion by Lord Browne-Wilkinson in *Westdeutsche Landesbank* **6.16** *v Islington LBC*[14] that the constructive trusteeship imposed on a dishonest assistant in a breach of fiduciary duty represented an exception to the usual requirement for certainty of subject matter. It does not and, with respect, to hold otherwise does nothing to advance the law or our understanding. We shall see, and disagree with, those who have wrongly used the language of constructive trusteeship to explain the personal liabilities of someone liable for dishonest assistance (see para 6.57 *et seq* below).

(3) Certainty of objects: identifiable beneficiaries

Putting aside charitable trusts and certain exceptional trusts for purposes, the **6.17** general rule is that an express private trust must have identifiable beneficiaries.[15]

---

12 *Twinsectra Ltd v Yardley* [2002] 2 AC 164, [17].
13 [1995] 1 AC 74.
14 [1996] AC 669 (HL).
15 *Re Vandervell's Trusts (No 2)* [1974] Ch 269, 319 per Lord Denning. The test varies depending on whether it is a fixed trust (trust is void unless every beneficiary is able to be identified) or a

6.18　This is also the case with constructive trusts. There must be an identifiable individual or group of individuals or entities to which the property held under a constructive trust must be delivered. They will be the beneficiaries under the trust and typically the claimant in the action seeking recovery of the property.

(4) Duties arising under a constructive trust

6.19　An express trustee voluntarily undertakes the responsibility to act as trustee. The duties of such an express trustee are extensive and derive from the general law (both case law and statute) coupled with the terms of the trust deed. The express trustee will enjoy the full range of administrative duties and powers associated with his office.[16]

6.20　A constructive trust is typically a bare trust, where the only obligation on the part of the constructive trustee is to return to the beneficiary the assets of the trust. It would seem a little odd to impose any other substantive obligations on such a constructive trustee. So, for example, one would not expect a constructive trustee to be subject to investment duties since such duties suggests an entitlement to continue to hold the assets when the only obligation arising under the constructive trust is forthwith to transfer to the true owner.

(5) Constructive trusts and statutory regimes

6.21　Some statutes are drafted to include only express private trusts and others to include constructive trusts as well.

6.22　A constructive trust over land will be subject to the Trusts of Land and Appointment of Trustees Act 1996 (s 1(2)). But the formal requirements for writing in respect of a trust over an interest in land under s 53(1)(b)(2) of the Law of Property Act 1925 do not apply to constructive trusts.

6.23　A constructive trustee cannot take advantage of the protection of the statutory defence for honest and reasonable trustees set out in s 61 of the Trustee Act 1925.[17]

6.24　The Limitation Act 1980, s 21(1) provides that no time period will apply in respect of a claim by a beneficiary in respect of any fraud or fraudulent breach of trust to which the trustee was a party or privy or to recover from the trustee trust property or proceeds thereof in the possession of the trustee, or previously received

---

discretionary trust (can it be said with any certainty whether any individual is or is not a member of the class? *McPhail v Doulton* [1971] AC 424 (HL)).

　16　Trustee Act 2000; J McGhee QC (ed), *Snell's Equity* (31st edn, Thomson/Sweet and Maxwell, 2005), para19-08.

　17　Underhill and Hayton, *Law of Trusts and Trustees* (17th edn, Butterworths Law, 2006), para 95.2.

by the trustee and converted to his use.[18] The problem is that this section has been held only to apply to one type of constructive trust, namely that which arises out of a pre-existing fiduciary relationship between the parties ('Class 1 constructive trust'). It does *not* apply where the constructive trust is imposed only because of wrongdoing or unconscionable behaviour ('Class 2 constructive trust').[19] This is an important point. It may be made clearer by examples.

(a) In *JJ Harrison (Properties) Ltd v Harrison*[20] the defendant was a director in the claimant company which was involved in property business. The company obtained a valuation on a property it owned and the valuation report stated, in addition to giving a valuation, that the property may have some developmental potential which had not been included in the actual valuation given. The defendant did not disclose this fact to the company. One year later, the defendant bought the property without disclosing the development potential to the company. He later made a significant profit in an onward sale. More than 6 years later, the company claimed against the defendant for an account of the sale proceeds. The defendant's limitation defence failed in the Court of Appeal on the basis he was within Class 1 category of constructive trust. Chadwick LJ stated:

> [29] There is no doubt that Millett LJ regarded it as beyond dispute that a director who obtained the company's property for himself by misuse of the powers with which he had been entrusted as a director was a constructive trustee within the first category. He referred to 'directors and other fiduciaries' in that context . . . There is also no doubt, if I may say so, that he was correct to do so—see *Re Sharpe, Re Bennett, Masonic and General Life Assurance Co v Sharpe* [1892] 1 Ch 154 at 172, *Soar v Ashwell* [1893] 2 QB 390 at 398. The reason is that a director, on appointment to that office, assumes the duties of a trustee in relation to the company's property. If, thereafter, he takes possession of that property, his possession 'is coloured from the first by the trust and confidence by means of which he obtained it.' His obligations as a trustee in relation to that property do not arise out of the transaction by which he obtained it for himself. The true analysis is that his obligations as a trustee in relation to that property predate the transaction by which it was conveyed to him. The conveyance of the property to himself by the exercise of his powers in breach of trust does not release him from those obligations. He is trustee of the property because it has

---

[18] *Lewin on Trusts* (18th edn, Thomson/Sweet and Maxwell, 2008), ch 44; Underhill and Hayton, *Law of Trusts and Trustees* (17th edn), Article 96. For a more general discussion on the topic, see William Swaddling, 'Limitation' in Birks and Pretto (eds), *Breach of Trust* (Hart Publishing, 2002).

[19] See *Paragon Finance plc v DB Thakerar & Co* [1999] 1 All ER 400, 408–14 per Millett LJ; *Cia De Seguros Imperio v Heath (REBX) Ltd* [2001] 1 WLR 112, 122; *JJ Harrison (Properties) Ltd v Harrison* [2001] EWCA Civ 1467; [2002] 1 BCLC 162 at [27]–[29]; *Halton International Inc v Guernroy Ltd* [2006] EWCA Civ 801 (where the relevant shares were obtained as part of the impugned transaction and therefore the trust was held to be a Class 2 trust which fell outside of s 21(1)(a) of the Limitation Act 1980. Accordingly, the claim was statute-barred).

[20] [2002] 1 BCLC 162.

become vested in him; but his obligations to deal with the property as a trustee arise out of his pre-existing duties as a director; not out of the circumstances in which the property was conveyed.[21]

Accordingly, s 21(1)(b) of the Limitation Act 1980 applied and the defendant could not establish a limitation defence.

(b) By contrast, in *Gwembe Valley Development Co Ltd v Koshy*[22] the defendant was both managing director and shareholder in the claimant company ('the company'). The defendant was also the majority shareholder and controller of another company, Lasco, which lent money to the company. As a result of various loans, the company acknowledged a debt due to Lasco in the amount of US$5.8m, which was based upon a loan advanced of 56.4m kwacha (Zambian currency) being the equivalent of US$5.8m. In fact, it was worth only US$1m. The claim against the defendant was based upon his failure to disclose his interest in Lasco or the profit that Lasco made on the loans to the company. Mummery LJ held that the trust imposed was a category 2 constructive trust:

> . . . The judge made no finding that any payments made by [the company] to Lasco, or any payments made out of the current account, were improperly made. The only thing wrong with them was Mr Koshy's failure, in his separate capacity as director of [the company], to make full disclosure to that Board of the nature and extent of his own financial interest.
>
> . . .
>
> If that is the correct analysis, then it is clear in our view that any trust imposed on Mr Koshy is a class 2 trust, within Millett LJ's classification . . . [In *Harrison*] the director transferred to himself property which had previously belonged to the company, and in relation to which he had 'trustee-like responsibilities' before the transaction in question. By contrast, Mr Koshy's liability to account for undisclosed profits, and any constructive trust imposed on those profits, do not depend on any pre-existing responsibility for any property of the company. They arose directly out of the transaction which gave rise to those profits, and the circumstances in which it was made. The fact that Mr Koshy was in a pre-existing fiduciary relationship with the company was not enough, by itself, to bring the case within class 1 . . .[23]

6.25 To conclude on limitation:

- Class 1 constructive trusts are likely to include trustees de son tort, executors de son tort, secret trustees, professionals such as solicitors receiving trust property and then misappropriating it. Many but perhaps not all examples falling within Chapter 8 will be Class 1. The caveat is placed because, as seen in *Gwembe*,

---

[21] *JJ Harrison (Properties) Ltd v Harrison* [2002] 1 BCLC 162, 175 [29].
[22] [2004] 1 BCLC 131.
[23] ibid, 165 [118]–[119].

the existence of a pre-existing fiduciary is not determinative of whether it is a Class 1 or Class 2 trust; what is crucial is such a pre-existing fiduciary relationship in respect of the relevant asset.

- Class 2 constructive trusts are likely to include those examples dealt with in Chapter 7, where the fiduciary duties and constructive trust arise out of the impugned transaction and are not considered to be pre-existing.

C. Attempts at a Uniform Principle

For present purposes, we shall put aside the debate about constructive trusts and unjust enrichment. That is dealt with in para 6.57 *et seq* below. There have been many attempts at trying to find one uniform principle which accurately and adequately covers the situations in which a constructive trust will arise. **6.26**

The attempt to identify one overarching general principle underlying constructive trusts is a laudable task and one peculiarly suited to academic input but it is, at the same time, a somewhat daunting task. If the principle is to serve a real purpose it must provide some practical guidance as to when a constructive trust will be imposed. If not, and it is so wide as to be abstract, it is questionable whether it is doing anything useful at all.[24] The problem in this area is that constructive trusts are imposed in a whole range of factual situations such that it is extremely difficult to encapsulate all those situations into one or two general principles. **6.27**

Furthermore, as made clear above, the constructive trust is used in different ways to achieve different aims, making it all the more difficult to have one general principle underlying the imposition of all constructive trusts. **6.28**

(1) D W M Waters—a Canadian perspective

Professor Waters is a leading Canadian academic on the nature of constructive trusts. In his textbook, *The Law of Trusts in Canada*[25] he has usefully summarized his view as to the relevant principles governing the imposition of a constructive trust under English law as follows: **6.29**

> In England . . . the constructive trust is still in search of a raison d'etre. In the United States it has one, the prevention of enrichment. The reason for this difference is largely historic. In England, the first use of the term, constructive trust, occurs in the seventeenth century; then and thereafter English equity courts were clear that, if a person is subject to an obligation to hold specific property for the benefit of another, whatever the source of that obligation, his position is comparable with that of a person appointed to administer a settlement or testamentary provision for successive lives.

---

[24] G Elias, *Explaining Constructive Trusts* (The Lawbook Exchange Ltd, 2002), 3.
[25] (2nd edn, Carswell, 1984), 379–80.

Though he has not been appointed a trustee, the duty of such an obligated person to recognize the interests of another puts him in a similar position in terms of what can be expected of him. The equity courts therefore 'construed' his position as that of a trustee, a fiduciary with regard to the property in question. As for what those obligations were which led to the imposition of the trustee status, they reflected the whole spectrum of remedies that were available in the equity jurisdiction . . . English courts did not seriously examine what the constructive trust as a concept was 'for', and without the direction that this inquiry would have given they fell into describing what the position of a person is 'like', who is vested with property the benefit of which he is obligated to hold for another. It was like the express trust; there was a trustee and a beneficiary; there was trust property and duties with regard to that property which fell upon the trustee. The name, constructive trust, 'described' the existence of an independent obligation; it neither created that obligation, nor was it itself a remedy. This was the approach taken to the constructive trust and it has survived to the present day in the older common law jurisdictions of the Commonwealth.

6.30 As will be seen, it remains as true today as it was in 1984 when Waters wrote his comments, that English law is still searching for the raison d'être of the constructive trust. But it would be wrong to think little had altered since these observations from Waters. The principles underlying the constructive trust have been subjected to sustained and detailed investigation by both the English courts and academics. Various views, including unjust enrichment, have been put forward to be discarded by some and endorsed and argued for by others. There is no doubt we have a better understanding of the proper use of the term constructive trust and we are better identifying the hard cases—the cases on the periphery—and these are being subjected to detailed examination. One only has to think of all that has been written about one first instance decision of Goulding J in *Chase Manhattan v Israel-British Bank*.[26] So it is not for the want of trying that English law has not yet adopted a single-principled approach to constructive trusts.

(2) The new model constructive trust[27]— Lord Denning MR

6.31 In the 1970s there was a series of Court of Appeal decisions on the availability of constructive trusts which would have reasonably led to the conclusion that such trusts were *remedial* in nature[28] and available whenever required by equity, justice and good conscience. Established legal principles were not to undermine the flexibility of this new model constructive trust.

6.32 Lord Denning MR was very much the driving force behind this attempt to adopt a more flexible approach to the grant of a proprietary remedy where justice

---

[26] [1981] Ch 105.

[27] *Eves v Eves* [1975] 1 WLR 1338.

[28] The distinction between remedial and institutional trust will be discussed in paras 6.64–6.72 below.

required it. In this regard, he was very much influenced by the approach adopted by the celebrated American Judge, Cardozo J, whom he quoted in *Binions v Evans*:[29]

> A constructive trust is the formula through which the conscience of equity finds expression. When property has been acquired in such circumstances that the holder of the legal title may not in good conscience retain the beneficial interest, equity converts him into a trustee.

For example, in *Hussey v Palmer*,[30] Lord Denning MR held that a constructive trust: **6.33**

> is a trust imposed by law whenever justice and good conscience require it . . . it is an equitable remedy by which the court can enable an aggrieved party to obtain restitution.[31]

Whilst such an approach has been adopted in other jurisdictions, in particular **6.34** Canada,[32] albeit with modifications and amendments over time, it was rejected in others, such as Australia and New Zealand. No doubt picking up on Lord Denning MR's comment that 'Equity is not past the age of child bearing' in *Eves v Eves*,[33] one Australian case remarked, somewhat harshly, that Lord Denning MR's new approach was 'a mutant from which further breeding should be discouraged'.[34]

As far as the English courts were concerned, this new model trust was unlikely to have **6.35** a long shelf-life. English law eschews the concept that proprietary rights can be granted (not simply recognized) whenever justice requires it. Such rights are a matter of clear and firm principles and not discretionary considerations of justice and fairness.[35] This is all the more so where the granting of such proprietary rights would, in an insolvency, have a detrimental effect on other unsecured creditors. Depriving an unsecured creditor of his fair share of the proceeds can only take place pursuant to clearly established principles of law and not vague and ill-defined notions of fairness.[36]

As a tool, to fashion the outcome in a given case, it may have proved useful to the court, but it would have ridden a coach and horses through traditional English **6.36** property law. It was soon rejected in the 1980s.[37]

---

[29] [1972] Ch 359, 386. The Cardozo J quotation comes from *Beatty v Guggenheim Exploration Co* 225 NY 380 (1919) at 386.

[30] [1972] 1 WLR 1286, 1290.

[31] See also *Heseltine v Heseltine* [1971] 1 All ER 952.

[32] See *Soulos v Korkontzilas* 146 DLR (4th) 214, 222 (1997) per McLachlin J: 'Canadian courts have never abandoned the principles of constructive trust developed in England. They have however, modified them.'

[33] [1975] 1 WLR 1338, referring to the new model constructive trust.

[34] *Allen v Snyder* [1977] 2 NSWLR 685, 700.

[35] *Pettit v Pettit* [1970] AC 777 (HL). Property rights are not to be determined by reference to what is reasonable and fair or just in the circumstances.

[36] See Lord Millett, 'Restitution and Constructive Trusts' in Cornish et al (eds), *Restitution: Past, Present and Future*.

[37] *Burns v Burns* [1984] Ch 317; *Grant v Edwards* [1986] Ch 638; *Ashburn Anstalt v Arnold* [1989] Ch 1.

(3) Elias—explaining constructive trusts

6.37 One of the most sustained attempts at providing some form of rationale for the imposition of constructive trusts was that of Gbolahan Elias in his text, *Explaining Constructive Trusts*.[38] He denied he was trying to discover a general principle applicable to all cases— indeed he questioned whether such was possible given the heterogeneous and wide-ranging nature of the rules permitting constructive trusts. Instead, he was attempting to identify the relevant rationale or rationales underlying constructive trusts.

6.38 He rejects the North American thesis that the principle of restitution or unjust enrichment underlies all constructive trusts.[39] This is dealt with in detail in para 6.57 *et seq.* below. At the other extreme, he rejects the idea that there was probably no general rationale or rationales as to when the English court imposes a constructive trust.[40]

6.39 Elias rejects these two theses in favour of a third thesis:

> The third thesis is that the rules should be regarded basically as means for the rational furtherance of three good aims. The three aims are to ensure that (1) one who has chosen to dispose of his options in favour of another person should abide by that choice; (2) one who has made a pecuniary gain through another person's loss gives up the gain to the other person; and (3) one who has caused loss to another repairs the loss. These three aims will henceforth be called 'the perfection aim', 'the restitution aim', and 'the reparation aim' respectively . . .[41]

6.40 Elias' attempts at discovering the underlying rationale of constructive trusts are to be welcomed, irrespective of whether one agrees with his ultimate conclusions. They represent one of the first sustained efforts at identifying a coherent theme or themes to the availability of constructive trusts under English law.

6.41 It is impossible to do justice to his thesis in this summary, but it is suggested that it should be rejected for at least two distinct reasons.

- The first is that none of the aims provide the sort of practical guidance we have been seeking in a general principle. They are so widely stated, no doubt to incorporate the wide-ranging instances which fall within each aim and exemplified in the authorities, that they tell one little of the actual parameters of each aim. To talk of giving up a gain obtained through another's loss is as wide as it

---

[38] (The LawBook Exchange Ltd, 2002).

[39] ibid, 4

[40] He cites Oakley as the main proponent of this view (1973) 26 Current Legal Problems 17. It is noted that Oakley remains of the same view: *Constructive Trusts* (3rd edn, Sweet and Maxwell, 1997), 1–2, n 4. The reality is that most of the leading textbooks on trusts simply deal with constructive trusts in the recognized categories without necessarily trying to find an overall principle to cover all examples when such a trust will be imposed by the law.

[41] Elias, *Explaining Constructive Trusts*, 4.

can get and potentially includes every bad bargain entered into. It presumably does not intend to include such situations yet there is nothing on its face which would exclude them.

• Secondly, and more fundamentally, the third aim is not one that should be assimilated with constructive trusts at all. As we have seen above, constructive trusts are trusts with trust property and obligations (albeit bare ones) to return that property to the rightful owner. Constructive trusts, properly so-called, are imposed on property which represents a gain in the hands of the constructive trustee. That gain is said to be held by the constructive trustee for and on behalf of the claimant. The focus is very much on identifying the (wrongful) benefit which must be returned to the wife. Constructive trusts are not concerned with making good losses to an individual which have no correlation to the gain in the hands of the wrongdoer. So we must reject Elias's third thesis since it includes within it the central error of the continued use of the language of constructive trusteeship to claims based upon liability to account for losses caused such as by dishonest assistance. It is accepted that such language was in general usage at the time Elias wrote his text but things have moved on considerably on this issue in the intervening years and for the better.[42]

(4) Lord Browne-Wilkinson in *Westdeutsche*—a general test of unconscionability

In the landmark case of *Westdeutsche Landesbank Girozentrale v Islington London*   **6.42**
Borough Council[43] (where the House of Lords rejected the argument that a proprietary claim, whether under constructive or resulting trust, arose from a void contract), Lord Browne-Wilkinson set out his theory of the relevant principles of law. At the heart of Lord Browne-Wilkinson's approach is a theory that equity acts on the conscience of the holder of the legal estate:

   (i) Equity operates on the conscience of the owner of the legal interest. In the case of a trust, the conscience of the legal owner requires him to carry out the purposes for which the property was vested in him (express or implied trust) or which the law imposes on him by reason of his unconscionable conduct (constructive trust).

   (ii) Since the equitable jurisdiction to enforce trusts depends upon the conscience of the holder of the legal interest being affected, he cannot be a trustee of the property if and so long as he is ignorant of the facts alleged to affect his conscience, ie, until he is aware . . . in the case of a constructive trust, of the factors which are alleged to affect his conscience.

---

[42] It is, of course, true that Lord Browne-Wilkinson in *Westdeutsche Landesbank Girozentrale v Islington London Borough Council* [1996] AC 669 at 705 stated that liability for dishonest assistance was an exception to the usual requirement that trust property be identifiable, that view, with respect, must be wrong: see para 6.57 *et seq* below.
[43] [1996] AC 669.

6.43 The problem with Lord Browne-Wilkinson's analysis is that it is predicated upon notice being both a necessary and sufficient reason for the existence of a proprietary claim. This is most evident in Lord Browne-Wilkinson's re-interpretation of *Chase Manhattan Bank NA v Israel-British Bank (London)Ltd.*[44]

6.44 The facts of this much-maligned authority are well known. A bank in London mistakenly duplicated a payment of US$2m to a bank in New York. Goulding J held that where money was paid under a mistake of fact the receipt of such money without more constituted the recipient a trustee on the basis that the payer 'retains an equitable property in it and the conscience of [the recipient] is subjected to a fiduciary duty to respect his proprietary right'.[45]

6.45 Lord Browne-Wilkinson rejected Goulding J's reasoning but contended that the decision might well be correct on the ground that the bank in New York became aware of the existence of the mistaken double payment before they had paid that sum out to third parties and 'the retention of the moneys after the recipient bank learned of the mistake may have well given rise to a constructive trust'.[46]

6.46 On this basis, it was the recipient bank's knowledge of the mistaken nature of the payment, discovered two days after receipt of the monies, which, according to Lord Browne-Wilkinson, justified imposing a constructive trust on the bank. If correct, this would elevate every claim for unjust enrichment to one for a proprietary claim if the demand for repayment is not immediately met and the monies remained identifiable in the hands of the recipient.

6.47 Sir Peter Millett, writing extra-judicially, has accurately described the difficulties with Lord Browne-Wilkinson's approach:

> I agree with Lord Browne-Wilkinson that *Chase Manhattan Bank NA v Israel-British Bank (London) Ltd* was wrongly decided, but it was wrongly decided, not because the defendant had no notice of the plaintiff's claim before it mixed the money with its own, but because the plaintiff had no proprietary interest for it to have notice of . . . The fact that the money was paid by mistake afforded a ground for restitution. By itself notice of the existence of a ground of restitution is obviously insufficient to found a proprietary remedy; it is merely notice of a personal right to an account and payment. It cannot constitute notice of an adverse proprietary interest if there is none.[47]

6.48 Graham Virgo[48] has analysed Lord Browne-Wilkinson's approach and whilst recognizing that it has the benefit of at least purporting to be principled—with all

---

[44] [1981] Ch 185.

[45] ibid, 119.

[46] [1996] AC 669, 715B–C. Lord Goff expressly held that he saw no reason to opine on the validity of *Chase Manhattan*.

[47] Sir Peter Millett, 'Restitution and Constructive Trusts' in Cornish et al (eds), *Restitution: Past, Present & Future*, 212–13.

[48] *The Principles of the Law of Restitution* (2nd edn, Oxford University Press, 2006), 608–13.

categories of constructive trust being linked by the concept of unconscionability—
he has nevertheless identified certain flaws in it which were not and have not yet
been addressed by the courts.

- Lord Browne-Wilkinson's approach fails to explain (or even recognize as a
problem) the fact that claims which would fall within his new constructive trust
would ordinarily not involve the wrongdoer obtaining legal title to the relevant
property. So, to take the obvious example, a thief gains no title at all to the
stolen property. Accordingly, the full legal title remains with the true owner
with the consequence there has been no splitting of legal and equitable ownership in the property. Rimer J in *Shalson v Russo*[49] was not willing to adopt Lord
Browne-Wilkinson's approach to stolen monies:

  > . . . a thief ordinarily acquires no property in what he steals and cannot give a title
  > to it even to a good faith purchaser: both the thief and the purchaser are vulnerable
  > to claims by the true owner to recover his property. If the thief has no title in the
  > property, I cannot see how he can become a trustee of it for the true owner: the
  > owner retains the legal and beneficial title . . .

  Virgo is of course correct in his criticism but the difficulty he faces is that Lord
  Browne-Wilkinson is not alone in construing a thief as a constructive trustee. It
  has long been the position in Australia[50] and is endorsed here in *Goff & Jones*.[51]

- Lord Browne-Wilkinson suggests that a constructive trust arises from the moment
of unconscientious receipt. Virgo points out that this draws what he contends
is an inappropriate distinction between contractual and non-contractual transfers: the former being required to rescind the contract whereas the latter is not.[52]
The only possible explanation for this distinction is a recognition of the primacy of contracts over restitutionary remedies.

- Given the manner in which Lord Browne-Wilkinson re-interpreted *Chase
Manhattan*, it would appear that it suffices that the recipient's conscience be
affected at any time prior to the assets becoming untraceable. But, if correct,
this would likely lead to *Sinclair v Brougham*[53] having been correctly decided
after all since the discovery of the lack of capacity to receive the deposits took
place at a time when the deposits were still traceable. Yet, as Birks points out, we
know that Lord Browne-Wilkinson could not have intended that consequence
since he expressly overruled *Sinclair v Brougham*.[54]

---

[49] *Shalson v Russo* [2005] Ch 281, [110].
[50] See e.g. *Black v Freedman & Co* (1910) 12 CLR 105, 108–9 per Griffith CJ.
[51] *Goff & Jones* (7th edn), para 2-033. The authors go on to say that the holder of both the legal
and equitable titles should be able to invoke the equity tracing rules.
[52] Unless it can be shown that the contractual arrangement itself has been impugned with the
fraud: *Halley v The Law Society* [2003] EWCA Civ 97.
[53] [1914] AC 348.
[54] Birks, 'Trusts Raised to Reverse Unjust Enrichment: The *Westdeutsche* Case' [1996] RLR 3, 22.

6.49   Notwithstanding these obvious difficulties, Lord Browne-Wilkinson's approach has received some support in subsequent cases.

- In *Papamichael v National Westminster Bank Plc*[55] Judge Chambers QC, sitting as a deputy judge of the High Court, was willing to apply the reasoning of Lord Browne-Wilkinson as to mistaken payments and unconscientious receipt. The judge indicated that in his view it did not matter when knowledge of the mistake arose save that the later the acquisition of knowledge the less the chance a trust will arise.[56]

- In *Halley v The Law Society* [2003] EWCA Civ 97, Carnwath LJ sought to deal with the problem raised above as to the distinction between contractual and non-contractual transfers. He relied upon the trial judge's finding that the relevant transaction was 'no more than a vehicle for obtaining money . . . by false pretences'. In those circumstances, Carnwath LJ could see no point in requiring the transaction to be rescinded before any proprietary relief could be obtained:

  > 48. In such a case, it is meaningless to impose a requirement for the fraudster to be notified of 'rescission'. From the fraudster's point of view there is nothing to rescind; for practical purposes, he has parted with nothing of value and incurred no obligations; the victim is left with some documents which, from the outset, were known and intended by the other party to be worthless. The 'election' to which Potter LJ referred [in *Twinsectra v Yardley*] is not a real option. Although the case does not fit neatly into Potter LJ's binary classification, he was not dealing with these facts. Subject to any direct authority, I see no reason why it should not be regarded as a simple case of 'property obtained by fraud', in Lord Browne-Wilkinson's terms.

- In *Commerzbank AG v IMB Morgan plc*,[57] Lawrence Collins J (as he then was) was content to apply Lord Browne-Wilkinson's reasoning in *Westdeutsche* both generally, that property received as a result of fraud was held on constructive trust and specifically, that *Chase Manhattan*, as re-interpreted by Lord Browne Wilkinson, held that a constructive trust arose from a mistaken payment where the recipient was aware of the mistake.[58]

- In *Sinclair Investment Holdings SA v Versailles Trade Finance Limited*[59] Arden LJ recognized that Lord Browne-Wilkinson's comments had not been followed in some cases, including *Halifax Building Society v Thomas*[60] where Peter Gibson LJ

---

[55] [2003] EWHC 164 (Comm), [2003] 1 Lloyd's Law Rep 341.
[56] ibid, 232.
[57] [2004] EWHC 2771 (Ch).
[58] ibid, [36].
[59] [2005] EWCA Civ 722.
[60] [1996] Ch 217.

had cast doubt on the merit of this approach.[61] Nevertheless, Arden LJ was willing to distinguish *Thomas* on the basis that *Sinclair* was not concerned with a typical theft as such:

> This is a more refined situation where . . . the alleged wrongdoer made a profit out of monies vested in TPL as a trustee for Sinclair. Mr Cushnie was, on this part of the case, a stranger to the trust, and indeed the trustee (TPL) was a stranger to the profit. Moreover, this is not a case of what one might call constructive unconscionability. This is a case where actual fraud on the part of Mr Cushnie is alleged, and it is alleged that fraud commenced before the profit was made; not after it was received. In those circumstances, it may well be that the dictum of Peter Gibson LJ in the *Thomas* case is distinguishable. In my judgment, it is in any event not binding. Moreover, the passages relied on from the *Paragon* case are not, in my judgment, authority for the proposition that there is no arguable course of action on this alternative claim. It is not desirable, as it seems to me, that I should say more than that it seems to me that there is an arguable cause of action.

• In *Campden Hill Ltd v Fazil Chakrani*[62] Hart J was willing to rely upon Lord Browne-Wilkinson's comments regarding the bag of stolen coins being held on constructive trust, as well as the Court of Appeal's decision in *Halley v The Law Society*, in support of his conclusion that where the claimant has advanced money on the basis of forged documentation and where it has done so by paying it to a solicitor to hold against production of genuine documents, the money is held on constructive trust.[63]

(5) Millett LJ in *Paragon Finance plc v DB Thakerar & Co*[64]

It is perhaps fair to say that Millett LJ is not here attempting to identify the under-**6.50** lying principle or principles of the English constructive trust so much as to give a *description* of when such a trust is typically imposed. In *Paragon Finance plc*, Millett LJ set out his description of the constructive trust:

> A constructive trust arises by operation of law whenever the circumstances are such that it would be unconscionable for the owner of the property (usually though not necessarily the legal estate) to assert his own beneficial interest in the property and deny the beneficial interest of another.

---

[61] In summary, Peter Gibson LJ noted that Lord Browne-Wilkinson relied upon the dictum of Lord Westbury in *McCormick v Grogan* (1869) LR 4 HL 82, 97 in support of the proposition that property obtained by fraud is held on constructive trust for the true owner. Peter Gibson LJ said: 'But that statement must be read in the context in which it was made, namely the jurisdiction where a secret trust is alleged. It cannot be elevated into a universal principle that wherever there is personal fraud the fraudster will become a trustee for the party injured by the fraud' ibid, 227.
[62] [2005] EWHC 911 (Ch).
[63] ibid, [74].
[64] [1999] 1 All ER 400.

6.51 In a similar vein, Aldous LJ, in a case dealing with an executor de son tort, held in *James v Williams*[65] that the executor knew he was not solely entitled to the inherited property and that others were entitled to share in the estate and that accordingly the executor de son tort held that property on constructive trust. Having been unable to establish that the facts of the present case fall within any of the existing recognized categories of constructive trust as set out in the then current edition of Underhill and Hayton, *The Law of Trusts and Trustees* (15th edn), Aldous LJ held the issue had to be decided as a matter of general principle:

> As a general rule a constructive trust attaches by law to property which is held by a person in circumstances where it would be inequitable to allow him to assert full beneficial ownership of the property.[66]

6.52 This wording is very similar to that of Millett LJ in *Paragon Finance*.

6.53 At first blush, one might question what the difference is between the statements of principle deriving from Millett LJ and Aldous LJ, on the one hand, and those heavily criticized coming from Lord Browne-Wilkinson in *Westdeutsche*. For Millett LJ, unlike Lord Browne-Wilkinson, knowledge of the in personam right is not sufficient to give rise to a constructive trust. What is needed is knowledge of the proprietary interest of the other party coupled with conduct aimed at denying that interest on the part of the defendant. If the transaction has not resulted in the other party having a proprietary interest in the property, then knowledge of any personal claim he may have will not convert that claim into a proprietary claim.

(6) Edmund Davies LJ in *Carl-Zeiss Stiftung v Herbert Smith (No 2)*[67]

6.54 In *Carl-Zeiss*, and admittedly before the recent explosion of interest in this area, Edmund Davies LJ remarked:

> English law provides no clear and all-embracing definition of a constructive trust. Its boundaries have been left perhaps deliberately vague, so as not to restrict the court by technicalities in deciding what the justice of a particular case may demand.[68]

6.55 Whilst one might question the purported justification for the lack of a proper definition, namely a desire to keep the boundaries fluid and open, as opposed to a reflection of the reality of the disparate circumstances in which such trusts presently arise, there can be little doubting that Edmund Davies LJ's conclusion is correct. One can really search in vain for an all-embracing general definition of constructive trusts.

---

[65] [1999] 3 WLR 451.
[66] ibid, 458F–G.
[67] [1969] 2 Ch 276.
[68] ibid, 300.

The closest one gets is perhaps that of Millett LJ in *Paragon Finance* and Aldous **6.56** LJ in *James v Williams*. Yet neither of these provide, nor are they probably intended to provide, the sort of guidance a practitioner seeks as to whether a constructive trust may arise in any given fact-situation. For that, resort must be had to the established categories where constructive trusts have been granted in the cases. Those categories having any relevance to commercial fraud litigation will be analysed in some detail in the two chapters to follow.

D. Misuse of Language

We have already seen that, with the exception of certainty of intention, a construct- **6.57** ive trust must fulfil the normal requirements of a trust including having identifiable trust property.[69] Indeed, in commercial fraud, where the proceeds of the fraud have been dissipated, quite often the existence or otherwise of identifiable trust property will determine whether it will be possible to bring a claim for constructive trust.

Against that understanding, there is no point at all[70] in using the language of con- **6.58** structive trustee to describe the personal liability to account which may arise as a result of being involved in dishonest assistance. Dishonest assistance does not require the defendant to hold let alone retain any trust property and in the absence of such a requirement there can be no sensible discussion of a constructive trust liability.

Lord Browne-Wilkinson in *Westdeutsche* was willing to consider the liability for **6.59** dishonest assistance may fall within that of a constructive trustee, albeit with the exception that no trust property need be held.

> (iii) In order to establish a trust there must be identifiable trust property. The only apparent exception to this rule is a constructive trust imposed on a person who dishonestly assists in a breach of trust who may come under fiduciary duties even if he does not receive identifiable trust property.[71]

But why? What drives Lord Browne-Wilkinson to reach such a conclusion? The **6.60** fact that the language of constructive trusteeship has been misapplied for some time to cases of dishonest assistance is no justification for continuing to misapply it and thereby be forced to drive a coach and horses through the traditional requirements for a trust, namely the need for identifiable trust property. Far simpler to recognize the problem and solve it by jettisoning the inappropriate language. It has been done successfully with quasi-contract, it can be done with constructive trust.

---

[69] *Re Barney* [1892] 2 Ch 265, 273.
[70] This includes suggestions that 'liability to account as a constructive trustee' is a useful shorthand to describe the personal liabilities of the defendant. It is not.
[71] [1996] AC 669.

6.61 Writing extra-judicially, Sir Peter Millett criticized the use of the language of constructive trustee to describe the personal liability to account for dishonest assistance:

> While we still insist on the institutional character of the constructive trust, however we undoubtedly use it as a remedial instrument. This has the unfortunate consequence that we employ the expression 'constructive trust' in two different senses without distinguishing between them. The resulting confusion is a disgrace to our jurisprudence. I should like to begin by trying to clear the ground.

One source of confusion arises when equity lawyers use the expressions 'constructive trust' and 'constructive trustee' in relation to the equitable duty to account. The accessory, charged with 'knowing assistance' in the misapplication of the plaintiff's money, is said to be 'liable to account as constructive trustee'. These last three words add nothing except confusion. There is no trust fund, or at least none in the defendant's possession. He is not a trustee at all, constructive or otherwise.[72]

6.62 Lord Millett returned to this theme in *Dubai Aluminium Co v Salaam*[73] where he made his position quite clear:

> Equity gives relief against fraud by making any person sufficiently implicated in the fraud accountable in equity. In such a case, he is traditionally (and I have suggested unfortunately) described as a 'constructive trustee' and is said to be 'liable to account as a constructive trustee'. But he is not in fact a trustee at all, even though he may be liable to account as if he were. He never claims to assume the position of trustee on behalf of others, and he may be liable without ever receiving or handling the trust property . . . In this second class of case the expressions 'constructive trust' and 'constructive trustee' create a trap . . . I think that we should now discard the words 'accountable as constructive trustee' in this context and substitute the words 'accountable in equity'.[74]

6.63 Few would disagree with this view. It is now time that all talk of constructive trust or constructive trustee be banished from claims in dishonest assistance. The liability to account in such claims is personal in nature and has nothing to do with the existence or otherwise of a trust being imposed on the defendant.

E. Remedial v Institutional Constructive Trusts

6.64 Few issues can have generated as much confusion within the law and yet have contributed so little to its proper development as the arid debate between the remedial and institutional constructive trust. As far as the practitioner need be

---

[72] Sir Peter Millett, 'Restitution and Constructive Trusts' in Cornish et al (eds), *Restitution: Past, Present & Future*, 200.

[73] [2002] UKHL 48, [2003] 2 AC 366.

[74] ibid, [141]. See also Millett J in *Agip (Africa) v Jackson* [1990] Ch 265, 291; 114 LQR (1998) 399, 399–400.

concerned, all semblance of meaningful debate on this topic is now over. English law does *not* recognize the remedial constructive trust: it only recognizes the institutional constructive trust.

We should define our terms. **6.65**

- A remedial constructive trust is one imposed by the court in its discretion whenever the court thinks it is just and proper to do so. No rights arising under such a trust exist unless and until the court imposes the trust over the property.

- An institutional constructive trust arises by way of the operation of law as and when certain specified events take place. It is not a matter of court discretion.[75]

Apart from Lord Denning MR's authorities in the early 1970s, the high water- **6.66** mark for the advocates of the remedial constructive trust came in two cases, one Court of Appeal, *Metall und Rohstoff v Donaldson Lufkin & Jenrette*,[76] and one from the House of Lords, *Westdeutsche Landesbank v Donaldson*.[77]

In *Metall und Rohstoff*, the Court of Appeal, in the context of a service out applica- **6.67** tion, was content to find there existed a good arguable case that 'a further category of constructive trust may arise beyond the three referred to above, that is to say where the court imposes a constructive trust de novo on assets which are not subject to any pre-existing trust as a means of granting equitable relief in a case where it considers it just that restitution should be made. [Counsel] contended that when B wrongfully takes A's property by way of a tort and then converts it into money, B will become in equity a constructive trustee of the proceeds by virtue of the tort itself.'[78] The Court of Appeal was content to call such a trust a 'remedial constructive trust'.[79]

It is true that this isolated remark was picked up on by Lord Browne-Wilkinson in **6.68** *Westdeutsche Landesbank* and used to provide a re-interpretation of the reasoning employed in *Chase Manhattan* where the decision is justified on the basis that the recipient became aware of the mistaken payment at a time prior to mixing the monies with its own monies and from that point onwards held the monies on constructive trust for the mistaken payor.

More generally, in *Westdeutsche*, the House of Lords was faced with an argument **6.69** that the resulting trust was the proper vehicle to effect proprietary restitution.[80]

---

75 There are, of course, variations on the theme of both the remedial and institutional constructive trust: see *Lewin on Trusts* (18th edn) at 7-08 *et seq.*
76 [1990] QB 391.
77 [1996] AC 669.
78 [1990] QB 391, 478.
79 ibid, 479.
80 This idea began, it would appear, in Birks, 'Restitution and Resulting Trusts' in Goldstein (ed), *Equity: Contemporary Legal Developments*, 335, a copy of which was made available to the House

In rejecting that argument, Lord Browne-Wilkinson suggested that the 'remedial constructive trust, if introduced into English law, may provide a more satisfactory road forward'. It is important to stress, however, that Lord Browne-Wilkinson was clear: he was only talking about the remedial constructive trust '*if introduced into English law*' (emphasis added). At present it is not. This point was made clear by his Lordship when he stated: 'whether English law should follow the United States and Canada in adopting the remedial constructive trust will have to be decided in some future case when the point is directly in issue.'[81]

6.70 That this is the position under English law has been underlined in a series of Court of Appeal decisions. In *Re Polly Peck (No 2)*[82] the Court of Appeal rejected an attempt to introduce the remedial constructive trust into English law and thereby undermine the application of the *pari passu* principle. Mummery LJ made his position quite clear:

> The insolvency road is blocked off to remedial constructive trusts, at least when judge driven in a vehicle of discretion.[83]

Similarly, at the heart of Nourse LJ's views, was that the remedial constructive trust permitted the courts 'a discretion to vary proprietary rights'.[84]

6.71 To make good the point that such an approach does not form part of English law, have regard for Lord Browne-Wilkinson's more recent observations in *Foskett v McKeown*,[85] where the House of Lords was examining whether beneficiaries under a trust were able to trace misappropriated trust money into a life insurance policy and ultimately to the payment out of that policy:

> Therefore the critical question is whether the assets now subject to the express trusts of the purchasers trust deed comprise any part of the policy moneys, a question which depends on the rules of tracing. If, as a result of tracing, it can be said that certain of the policy moneys are what now represent part of the assets subject to the trusts of the purchasers trust deed, then as a matter of English property law the purchasers have an absolute interest in such moneys. There is no discretion vested in the court. There is no room for any consideration whether, in the circumstances of this particular case, it is in a moral sense 'equitable' for the purchasers to be so entitled. The rules establishing equitable proprietary interests and their enforceability against certain parties have been developed over the centuries and are an integral part of the property law of England. It is a fundamental error to think that, because certain

---

of Lords after submissions had ended, together with counter-arguments from William Swaddling, 'A New Role for Resulting Trusts?' (1996) 16 LS 110, 133. This idea of the resulting trust effecting proprietary restitution was thereafter taken up and developed by R Chambers in *Resulting Trusts* (Oxford University Press, 1997).

81 [1996] AC 669, 716.
82 [1998] 3 All ER 812.
83 ibid, 827.
84 ibid, 831.
85 [2001] 1 AC 102 (HL).

property rights are equitable rather than legal, such rights are in some way discretionary. This case does not depend on whether it is fair, just and reasonable to give the purchasers an interest as a result of which the court in its discretion provides a remedy. It is a case of hard-nosed property rights.[86]

6.72 In the circumstances, the concept of remedial constructive trust is not one accepted in English law and that any attempt to introduce it would require a trip all the way to the House of Lords.

F. Unjust Enrichment and Resulting Trust

6.73 This section is concerned with the issue whether English law recognizes the principle of unjust enrichment as being at the heart of the imposition of a constructive trust. That is a distinct question from whether unjust enrichment per se should give rise to a proprietary remedy and if so in what circumstances. We may sensibly conclude that constructive trusts have nothing to do with unjust enrichment as far as English law is concerned but then go on to consider, separately, whether another vehicle exists which better performs the task of providing a proprietary remedy for claims in unjust enrichment. This second question is dealt with in Chapter 3 on unjust enrichment. This section will focus only on the first issue.

(1) North America

6.74 North American jurisprudence has embraced the principle of unjust enrichment as underpinning the existence of the constructive trust. This began with the American Law Institute's *Restatement on the Law of Restitution* in 1937 which provided:

> Where a person holding title to property is subject to an equitable duty to convey it to another on the ground that he would be unjustly enriched if he were permitted to retain it, a constructive trust arises.

This view has been confirmed, time and again, in leading articles and texts.[87] It does not necessarily mean that the court will grant a constructive trust for every case of unjust enrichment. Rather, and this is where the remedial nature of the North American constructive trust plays an important role, the court will have a choice to do so if it considers such relief appropriate on the facts. It is that very discretion on the part of the courts which is alien to the English law of property, particularly in the insolvency context (which is where such issues take on greater importance).

---

[86] [2001] 1 AC 102, 109B–D.
[87] See e.g. W A Seavey and A W Scott, (1938) 54 LQR 29, 42.

6.75   Canada has now followed a similar although not identical path,[88] with the Supreme
Court of Canada confirming in *Pettkus v Becker*[89] that the principle of unjust
enrichment lies at the heart of the constructive trust. The leading academic proponent of this type of constructive trust in Canada is Professor Donovan Waters,
who has summarized the position in Canada as follows:

> The remedial constructive trust . . . connotes the type of redress which a claimant
> receives by way of a court order, and in the manner decreed by that order, when the
> claimant is successful in establishing that the defendant to that claim has breached
> an obligation owed to the claimant. In Canada that obligation is that the defendant
> shall not be unjustly enriched, ie at the expense of the claimant. The constructive
> trust is the terminological vehicle for conferring specific property upon the claimant.
> It matters not whether the claimant has a pre-existing right of a proprietary nature in
> the specific property awarded; 'the imposition of a constructive trust can both recog-
> nize and create a right of property.'[90] Nor . . . does the law in common law Canada
> necessarily provide that the grant of a constructive trust by a court recognizes in that
> property any interest of a claimant that allegedly arose at the time when the unjust
> enrichment, so found, took place or commenced. Were the law so to provide, the
> claimant might effectively demand the recognition of the property interest when the
> court is of the view that the appropriate remedy would be damages or some other
> form of personal relief. Were that to be possible, the law would have found its way
> back to what Canadians see—at least for their purposes—as the barren state of the
> institutional constructive trust.[91]

6.76   The remedial nature of the Canadian approach to constructive trusts is clear from
this extract, as is the fact that the existence of such a trust is entirely dependent upon
the claimant establishing that the defendant has been unjustly enriched at its
expense. As we shall see, none of this represents the present position of English law.

(2) English law

6.77   English law has never adopted an unjust enrichment-based approach to constructive trust. This is perhaps not that surprising. When English law was adopting its
most liberal attitude to the existence and nature of the constructive trusts, in the
cases involving Lord Denning MR in the early 1970s, English law had not even
recognized the existence of any separate cause of action based upon unjust enrichment, let alone given any thought to whether it was the principle underlying the
constructive trust. That did not come until the 1990s, by which point the courts
had already turned their back on the flexible 'just and convenient' approach of the
early 1970s new model trust, and those proponents of the newly established

---

[88] Canada employs the principle of unjust enrichment alongside the established categories of
constructive trust whereas in the USA the principle is the only basis for a constructive trust.
[89] (1980) 117 DLR (3d) 257.
[90] *Lac Minerals v International Corona Resources* (1989) 61 DLR (4th) 14, 50 per Le Forest J.
[91] In Birks (ed), *Frontiers of Liability* Vol II (Oxford University Press, 2002), 165, 183.

unjust enrichment were keen to emphasize that it was a principle-based cause of action and not some example of palm-tree justice.

Thereafter, notwithstanding one or two unsuccessful flirtations with the idea that **6.78** unjust enrichment lay behind the constructive trust,[92] unjust enrichment was subjected to the most sustained and detailed analysis, both in the courts and class-room, with the consequence that the view began to circulate that perhaps the con-structive trust, with its connotation of conscious wrongdoing, was not the most appropriate vehicle through which to effect proprietary restitution and that in fact the resulting trust was preferable.

The leading exponent of this view was Professor Birks whose idea was picked up **6.79** and fully developed by Robert Chambers.[93] In typical style, Professor Birks first suggested that proprietary restitution might best be effected via the resulting trust in his controversial paper, 'Restitution and Resulting Trusts'.[94]

> The proposition at the heart of this paper is that, within the field of subtractive unjust enrichment, if and so far as personal restitutionary claims—viewed from the other side, restitutionary obligations—are backed by equitable proprietary claims, we should learn to attribute those proprietary rights to the resulting trust, not the constructive trust . . .

> The partnership between restitutionary obligations and the resulting trust may, it seems, turn out to operate over a considerable number of the causes of action within the field of subtractive unjust enrichment. In the great majority of cases within that sector the 'unjust' factors turn out to be, if the matter is stated at a rather high level of generality, that the plaintiff did not intend or did not fully and freely intend that the defendant should have the enrichment in question in the events which have hap-pened. This is merely a different way of describing non-beneficial transfer: in the events which have happened the transfer was not intended to enure to the benefit of the recipient.

> . . . If it is true that the resulting trust is equity's response to non-beneficial transfer, then, subject to the definitional limit that a resulting trust must carry the interest back whence it came and cannot therefore be concerned with capturing value obtained from others, the resulting trust rests on an inquiry of exactly the kind as the action for money had and received . . .

> If this is right, it cannot be far from the truth to say that the result trust, not the con-structive trust, is equity's principal contribution to the independent law of unjust

---

[92] See e.g. the Court of Appeal in *Halifax Building Society v Thomas* [1996] Ch 217. The mort-gage was provided as a result of the fraudulent misrepresentations of the borrower. The house was sold and the mortgage was paid off entirely, leaving a surplus of monies. It was argued that the defendant should not be entitled to retain the benefits of the increase in property value as this would be equivalent to him benefiting from his wrongdoing. Peter Gibson LJ (229) held that English law had not followed other jurisdictions where the constructive trust had become a remedy for unjust enrichment and declined to hold the surplus after full payment of the mortgage.

[93] *Resulting Trusts* (Clarendon Press, 1997).

[94] Goldstein (ed), *Equity and Contemporary Legal Developments*.

enrichment.... If proprietary restitution in respect of subtractive unjust enrichment is seen to be both the work of and the definitive limit upon the resulting trust, both the law of restitution and the law of trusts will be more easily intelligible. Only more complex tasks—in particular the fulfillment of reasonable expectations, which is naturally the work of contract and is certainly beyond the scope of any law of unjust enrichment—will need to invoke the constructive trust, though in jurisdictions in which proprietary restitution for wrongs is encouraged the constructive trust will continue to have a role in that purely remedial sector of the subject.

6.80 It is apparent that the driving force behind Birks' and Chambers' move away from the constructive trust towards the resulting trust is a realization that both unjust enrichment (by subtraction) and the resulting trust operate in circumstances where the transferor did not intend beneficial receipt by the recipient. 'I paid over by mistake. I did not intend you to have it.'[95] 'I was pressured into transferring the payment. I did not truly intend you to have it.'[96] 'I had no idea that the transfer was being made to you. I certainly did not intend you to have it. I did not know anything about it at all.'[97]

6.81 All the various attempts at describing a constructive trust involve some notion of wrongdoing known to the legal owner in asserting his beneficial interest vis-à-vis a third party. Unjust enrichment by subtraction is not about wrongdoing. Indeed, a tremendous amount of literature has been generated on the issue in its early days, much was said and written about the strict liability approach to unjust enrichment.[98] Such an approach, which focuses on the nature, existence and quality of the intention to transfer on the part of the transferor and not on any wrongdoing on the part of the transferee sits uneasily with the concept of a constructive trust imposed by law because of wrongdoing. No such wrongdoing arises in the case of the resulting trust.

6.82 The dual proposition that the principle of unjust enrichment may give rise to proprietary claims and that its best vehicle is the resulting trust was dealt two severe if

---

[95] Mistake as the unjust factor.

[96] Duress as the unjust factor.

[97] More controversially, before championing the cause of the adoption of the civilian approach of 'absence of basis', Professor Birks argued in favour of ignorance as an unjust factor: if mistake is a ground for recovery of payments so must also be ignorance: 'Misdirected Funds: Restitution from the Recipient' [1989] LMCLQ 296; 'Trusts in the Recovery of Misapplied Assets: Tracing, Trusts and Restitution' in E McKendrick (ed), *Commercial Aspects of Trusts and Fiduciary Obligations* (Clarendon Press, 1992); Burrows agrees: *The Law of Restitution* (2nd edn, Butterworths, 2002), ch 4; *Goff & Jones* does not: para 4-001.

[98] Birks, 'The Role of Fault in the Law of Unjust Enrichment' in W Swaddling and G Jones (eds), *The Search for Principle: Essays in Honour of Lord Goff of Chieveley* (Oxford University Press, 1999); 'Receipt' in P Birks and A Pretto (eds), *Breach of Trust* (Hart Publishing, 2002); Virgo, 'The Role of Fault in the Law of Unjust Enrichment' in Burrows and Lord Rodger (eds), *Mapping the Law: Essays in Memory of Peter Birks* (Oxford University Press, 2006). For a different theoretical analysis, see NJ McBride and P McGrath, 'The Nature of Restitution' (1995) 15 OJLS 33.

not fatal blows by the House of Lords in two landmark decisions, *Westdeutsche Landesbank Girozentrale v Islington LBC*[99] and *Foskett v McKeown*.[100] The former rejected entirely the suggestion that the resulting trust may be the best vehicle to effect proprietary claims based upon unjust enrichment and the latter case rejected the proposition that the law of unjust enrichment had anything at all to do with existence or otherwise of proprietary claims under English law.

Each decision will be examined. There is no doubt that the academic world of **6.83** unjust enrichment has been dealt a heavy body-blow by these decisions. Up to this point, most if not all of the developments in the law of unjust enrichment have been driven by academic input, matched by the willingness of the judiciary to consider and be influenced by that input. These decisions represent one of the major occasions when the courts have steadfastly refused to follow the route laid out by some of the academics.[101] It may be an indication of the maturing of the courts' understanding of this area and with that new-found maturity comes a greater willingness to debate and disagree on points. Or it may well be no more than a reflection of the courts' concern that unjust enrichment lawyers must not try to be territorially ambitious.

(a) Westdeutsche Landesbank v Islington LBC [102]

The first decision is *Westdeutsche Landesbank Girozentrale v Islington LBC* in which **6.84** the House of Lords emphatically rejected the new resulting trust theory. The facts of this case are well known. They can be summarized for present purposes as follows.

• This case came from the interest-rate swaps debacle, where it had been declared[103] *ultra vires* for local authorities to enter into swaps transactions which were therefore void *ab initio*.

• The local authority had made four payments under this arrangement (since the interest rates had favoured the banks) but then refused to make any further payments.

• The bank claimed the remainder of the initial sum lent together with compound interest.

• Both Hobhouse J and the Court of Appeal allowed compound interest.

---

[99] [1996] AC 669.
[100] [2001] 1 AC 102.
[101] It should not be forgotten that the House of Lords in *Westdeutsche Landesbank* appeared to be influenced by William Swaddling's 'A New Role for Resulting Trusts?' (1996) 16 LS 110.
[102] [1996] AC 669. See Swaddling, 'A New Role for Resulting Trusts' (1996) 16 LS 110; P Birks, 'Trusts Raised to Reverse Unjust Enrichment: The *Westdeutsche* Case' [1996] RLR 3.
[103] At first instance, *Hazell v Hammersmith and Fulham London BC* [1992] 2 WLR 17 and aff'd by the House of Lords: [1992] 2 AC 1.

- On appeal to the House of Lords, by a majority of 3–2, the appeal was allowed on the grounds that the local authority was not holding the remaining sum as trustee or fiduciary and accordingly there was no basis for awarding compound interest.[104]

6.85 The relevant trust that the bank contended existed was the resulting trust. Counsel for the bank correctly disavowed any attempt to rely upon a constructive trust since, as Lord Browne-Wilkinson recognized, the local authority had no relevant knowledge sufficient to raise a constructive trust at any time before the monies, upon the bank account going into overdraft, became untraceable. It has already been shown that constructive trusts must comply with the requirement that there exists an identifiable trust fund and once there ceased to be an identifiable trust fund prior to knowledge, there could be no trust.[105] The only possible option was therefore the resulting trust.

6.86 After oral submissions had concluded, their Lordships were provided with copies of Professor Birks' article, 'Restitution and Resulting Trusts'[106] and William Swaddling's reply article, 'A New Role for Resulting Trusts?'.[107]

6.87 Lord Browne-Wilkinson rejected the general submissions of the existence of a resulting trust. He said in the absence of an express trust, there could be no resulting trust based upon a failure to exhaust the whole beneficial interest under an express trust. He also rejected the presumption of intention resulting trust on the ground that the bank intended the monies paid to the local authority become the local authority's absolutely. He then rejected the view put forward by Professor Birks:

> As one would expect, the argument is tightly reasoned but I am not persuaded. The search for a perceived need to strengthen the remedies of a plaintiff claiming in restitution involves, to my mind, distortion of trust principles. First, the argument elides rights in property (which is the only proper subject matter of a trust) into rights in 'the value transferred:' see 361. A trust can only arise where there is defined trust property: it is therefore not consistent with trust principles to say that a person is a trustee of property which cannot be defined. Second, Professor Birks' approach appears to assume (for example in the case of a transfer of value made under a contract the consideration for which subsequently fails) that the recipient will be deemed to have been a trustee from the date of his original receipt of money, ie the trust arises at a time when the 'trustee' does not, and cannot, know that there is going to be a

---

[104] It was at the time considered necessary to establish an equitable proprietary claim in order to be entitled to claim compound interest. On this point, *Westdeutsche* was distinguished in the HL in *Sempra Metals Ltd v Inland Revenue Commissioners & Ors* [2007] UKHL 34 which held that it was possible to claim compound interest at common law where the claimant sought a restitutionary remedy for the time value of money paid under a mistake.

[105] *In re Goldcorp Exchange Ltd* [1995] 1 AC 74.

[106] Goldstein (ed), *Equity: Contemporary Legal Developments.*

[107] (2006)16 LS 110, 133.

total failure of consideration. This result is incompatible with the basic premise upon which all trust law is built, viz that the conscience of the trustee is affected. Unless and until the trustee is aware of the factors which give rise to the supposed trust, there is nothing which can affect his conscience. Thus neither in the case of a subsequent failure of consideration nor in the case of a payment under a contract subsequently found to be void for mistake or failure of condition will there be circumstances, at the date of receipt, which can impinge on the conscience of the recipient, thereby making him a trustee. Thirdly, Professor Birks has to impose on his wider view an arbitrary and admittedly unprincipled modification so as to ensure that a resulting trust does not arise when there has only been a failure to perform a contract, as opposed to total failure of consideration: see 356, 359 and 362. Such arbitrary exclusion is designed to preserve the rights of creditors in the insolvency of the recipient. The fact that it is necessary to exclude artificially one type of case which would logically fall within the wider concept casts doubt on the validity of the concept.

. . . I do not think it right to make an unprincipled alteration to the law of property (ie the law of trusts) so as to produce in the law of unjust enrichment the injustices to third parties which I have mentioned and the consequential commercial uncertainty which any extension of proprietary interests in personal property is bound to produce.[108]

Although those who support the resulting trust as the vehicle for proprietary claims in unjust enrichment continue to champion the cause, the position, as far as practitioners need be concerned, is pretty straightforward and clear following this decision. The principles underpinning the law of unjust enrichment do not establish the existence of a resulting trust. **6.88**

(b) Foskett v McKeown[109]

To say that the law of unjust enrichment is the, or one of the general principles underlying the imposition of a constructive trust, necessarily involves a more general proposition that the law of unjust enrichment has something to do with the availability of proprietary claims. If the latter does not hold true, then the former must also collapse. Any other conclusion must rest on the use of the term 'constructive trust' to denote personal obligations—something which has itself been soundly rejected. **6.89**

It has already been seen that the House of Lords in *Westdeutsche* emphatically rejected the idea of the resulting trust being the relevant proprietary vehicle for unjust enrichment. *Foskett v McKeown* went one stage further and rejected the more general proposition that unjust enrichment has anything at all to do with the availability of property claims, however they are brought (ie whether constructive or resulting trust). **6.90**

---

[108] [1996] AC 669, 709.
[109] [2001] 1 AC 102.

6.91 The facts of *Foskett v McKeown* may be summarized as follows.

- A trustee misappropriated trust money belonging to the beneficiaries and used it to pay for the fourth and fifth premiums on his own life insurance policy.

- The trustee committed suicide, giving rise to a payment under the policy of £1m.

- The beneficiaries claimed a proportionate share of this £1m (£400,000, in fact) on the basis that the trust money had been used to pay two of the premiums under the policy.

- The Court of Appeal limited the beneficiaries' recovery to a lien over the trust funds for the recovery of the misappropriated funds.

- The House of Lords held (3–2) that the beneficiaries were entitled to a proportionate share of the policy proceeds, being £400,000.

- In so doing, their Lordships rejected the theory that any such claim was based upon unjust enrichment.

6.92 Indeed, on the facts, the beneficiaries could not allege that the recipients of the insurance proceeds were unjustly enriched.[110] The stolen monies had been used to make the fourth and fifth premiums but those premiums were not causally linked to the payment out of the policy which would have happened without such premiums having been made. Lord Steyn was clear that 'the stolen moneys were not causally relevant to any benefit received by the children'.[111] His Lordship went on to point out that '[g]iven that the stolen moneys from the purchasers did not contribute or add to what the children received, in accordance with their rights established before the theft by Mr Murphy, the proprietary claim of the purchasers is not in my view underpinned by any considerations of fairness or justice'.[112]

6.93 On the basis of *Foskett v McKeown* there could not be a much clearer rejection of unjust enrichment underpinning the availability of proprietary claims, let alone constructive trust claims. This theme is dealt with in more detail in Chapter 3. It will be seen there that commentators favouring unjust enrichment will continue to push the arguments. It suffices for present purposes to conclude by noting that hitherto the law of unjust enrichment has not been accepted as the basis for the English constructive trust and that given the rejection by the House of Lords in *Foskett v McKeown* of its role in proprietary claims more generally, it is unlikely to feature more prominently in the near future.

---

[110] Their Lordships were clear on this point. Extra-judicially, Lord Millett has described the assumption as 'questionable.' See Lord Millett, 'Proprietary Restitution', Ch 12, Degeling and Edelman (eds), *Equity in Commercial Law*.

[111] [2001] 1 AC 102, 114F–G.

[112] ibid, 115D–E.

7

CONSTRUCTIVE TRUSTS—
UNCONSCIONABLE CONDUCT

A. Introduction

Before embarking on a category by category examination of the examples when **7.01** English law has imposed a constructive trust, it would be sensible to recap where we have got to in terms of understanding when and in what circumstances English law may grant a *proprietary* remedy.[1] The following points, some overlapping and some inconsistent, have emerged.

(1) *Foskett v McKeown* rejected any concept that unjust enrichment lay at the heart of proprietary claims in English law. That is a matter for the law of property.

(2) *Westdeutsche Landesbank* rejected failure of consideration in the swaps cases giving rise to a proprietary claim. Their Lordships also rejected the resulting trust theory increasingly adopted by some unjust enrichment lawyers.

---

[1] This is a more general question than when English law will impose the constructive trust on an individual.

(3) Lord Browne-Wilkinson in *Westdeutsche* did espouse a controversial theory of trusts based upon the knowledge and conscience of the recipient being affected. Under this theory, actual knowledge of the mistaken payment, for example, would suffice to give rise to a proprietary claim in the nature of a constructive trust.

(4) Some unjust enrichment lawyers disagree with this controversial theory of trusts. For them, knowledge of a personal right does not, without more, convert that right into a property right. The crucial issue is not actual knowledge or fault but a question of timing. Was the asset free to be used for any purpose whilst in the hands of the recipient? If the answer is yes, then no proprietary claim. If the answer is no, then, for some, a resulting trust should be imposed. It remains unclear whether, outside of wrongs, any proponent of unjust enrichment contends for the constructive trust rather than the resulting trust as the vehicle for proprietary restitution.

7.02 So where does a practitioner go faced with these varying and apparently inconsistent approaches to a fundamental issue of English law? The following can be said.

(1) The unjust enrichment approach to proprietary claims has been rejected in the House of Lords and has no clear and unequivocal support in the authorities more generally. If it is not the basis of a proprietary claim, *a fortiori* it cannot be the basis of a constructive trust claim.

(2) In further support of the conclusion in (1), it is noted that unjust enrichment advocates point to the resulting trust rather than the constructive trust as the means of effecting proprietary claims. So they are not even arguing in favour of a relationship between unjust enrichment and the constructive trust. Their argument as to the role to be played by the resulting trust was expressly rejected in *Foskett*.

(3) So far, therefore, on the present state of precedent, the practitioner can safely put to one side the unjust enrichment arguments as a basis for constructive trust claims in English law.

(4) Where the law of property analysis espoused in *Foskett v McKeown* applies, Lord Millett contends for a resulting and not a constructive trust. He contends for a constructive trust only when it would be unconscionable for the owner of the legal title to assert his own beneficial interest and deny the beneficial interest of another. It arises from circumstances which are known to the legal owner and so his conscience is affected. He also accepts that the relevant circumstances are 'many and various'.[2]

---

[2] Sir Peter Millett, 'Restitution and Constructive Trusts' in Cornish, Nolan, O'Sullivan and Virgo (eds), *Restitution: Past, Present & Future* (Hart Publishing, 1998) at 201.

(5) As an alternative to Lord Millett's narrower view of the availability of constructive trust, there is the much wider view of Lord Browne-Wilkinson set out in *Foskett v McKeown* based upon whether the recipient's conscience is affected. The distinction between these two views appears premised upon the willingness of Lord Browne-Wilkinson to give a proprietary claim based upon the recipient's knowledge that the payment should not have been paid as opposed to Lord Millett's view which appears premised upon the recipient's knowledge that as a result of the particular transaction, the transferor has retained a beneficial interest in that which was transferred and it would be unconscionable for the recipient to seek to assert his own beneficial interests in the transferred asset and, at the same time, deny the transferor's.

The purpose of this chapter is to try to identify those categories of claim in which **7.03** the court has imposed a constructive trust. Some categories may be clear-cut, with ample authority in support, whilst others may be based on only one or two authorities. Given the above, not all categories will receive the support of all commentators and some categories may have more than one suggested explanation. In order to render the debate in this chapter intelligible and to avoid the reader having to refer to other chapters, there will inevitably be an element of overlap in material cited here and that dealt with elsewhere.

It should also be noted that the aim of this text is to provide assistance to practi- **7.04** tioners when dealing with commercial fraud cases. It is not the function of this text to provide some all-embracing unifying theory as to when proprietary claims may be available. A practitioner cannot and must not be expected to sacrifice the interests of his client in gaining a result in an individual case on the altar of the search for consistency in the court's overall approach to such claims. So, for example, if *Chase Manhattan* represents the best way forward in a given case, it is entirely appropriate the practitioner use that authority as best he can.

We are of course, as ever, focused on commercial fraud litigation. Accordingly, we **7.05** make no apologies for excluding from this chapter any discussion of mutual wills, secret trusts or trusts of the family home under the *Lloyds Bank v Rosset* principles. All important topics, but not in commercial fraud scenarios.

B. Unconscionable Conduct

This chapter has various examples of particular categories of conduct which have **7.06** led to the imposition of constructive trusts. Each such category could be said to give rise to unconscionable conduct. What we are here concerned with, however, is whether there exists a general category of unconscionable conduct which leads to the court imposing a constructive trust. In other words, a category which is not constrained by the particular factual features which arise in the specific categories of conduct highlighted below.

7.07   The main proponent of such a general category based upon unconscionable conduct is Lord Browne-Wilkinson in *Westdeutsche Landesbank v Islington LBC*.[3] His Lordship held that:

> when property is obtained by fraud, equity places a constructive trust on the fraudulent recipient.

7.08   Lord Browne-Wilkinson's general theory has already been subjected to detailed analysis: see paras 6.42–6.53. Most of the criticism has come from the academic world and the occasional extra-judicial observation.[4] It would, however, be wrong to say that his theory has been universally rejected. There are a fair number of decisions which are based on or influenced by Lord Browne-Wilkinson's reasoning in *Westdeutsche*: see *Papamichael v National Westminster Bank plc*;[5] *Halley v The Law Society*;[6] *Commerzbank AG v IMB Morgan plc*;[7] *Sinclair Investment Holdings SA v Versailles Trade Finance Limited*;[8] *Niru Battery Manufacturing Co v Milestone Trading Ltd*[9] and *Campden Hill Ltd v Fazil Chakrani*.[10]

7.09   The problem with Lord Browne-Wilkinson's approach is that, taken at face value, it does too much. It would appear to include those cases of voidable transactions, where it is recognized that it is necessary first to rescind the transaction before it is possible to impose a constructive trust.[11] It is inconceivable that Lord Browne-Wilkinson could have intended his views to sweep away the whole raft of case law dealing with voidable transactions—certainly not without saying something about it.

In the circumstances, there is little to be gained and perhaps much, by way of analysis to be lost, by adopting a general theory based on unconscionable conduct. It includes too much and by so doing rides roughshod over the principle of the need to rescind before bringing any proprietary claim. It also gives the wrong impression that all instances of unconscionable conduct may lead to the imposition

---

3   [1996] AC 669.

4   *See* G Virgo, *The Principles of Law of Restitution* (2nd edn, Oxford University Press, 2006), 608–13; Birks, 'Trusts Raised to Reverse Unjust Enrichment: The *Westdeutsche* Case' [1996] RLR 3; Sir Peter Millett, 'Restitution and Constructive Trusts' in Cornish et al (eds), *Restitution: Past, Present & Future*.

5   [2003] EWHC 164 (Comm), [2003] 1 Lloyd's Law Rep 341.

6   [2003] EWCA Civ 97.

7   [2004] EWHC 2771 (Ch).

8   [2005] EWCA Civ 722.

9   [2002] EWHC 1425 (Comm), [2002] All ER (Com) 705.

10   [2005] EWHC 911 (Ch).

11   *Box, Brown & Jacobs v Barclays Bank* [1998] Lloyd's Rep Bank 185 (Ferris J); *Sinclair Investment Holdings SA v Versailles Trade Finance Ltd* [2004] All ER (D) 158.

of a constructive trust. That is not so. Indeed, to emphasize once again the difference between Lord Browne-Wilkinson and Lord Millett on this issue, the fact that one party has notice of a personal right of another may well give rise to unconscionable conduct but does not, on Lord Millett's analysis at least, justify the imposition of a constructive trust. What practitioners are left with are the recognized disparate categories of unconscionable conduct examined herein below.

C. Mistaken Payments

In *Chase Manhattan Bank v Israel-British Bank*[12] a bank mistakenly made two transfers of US$2m instead of one on 3 July 1974 to another New York bank for the account of the defendant British bank. On 5 July 1974, it was found that the defendant knew or should have known about the clerical error. Soon thereafter, the defendant became insolvent. Goulding J granted a declaration that the defendant bank became a constructive trustee of the second (mistaken) payment on receipt of it on 3 July 1974. It remained to be proved (which it was) that the monies remained identifiable.   **7.10**

As decided, *Chase Manhattan* stands as authority for the proposition that a payment made by way of mistake can give rise to a constructive trust without needing to establish any knowledge on the part of the recipient.[13]   **7.11**

In *Nesté Oy v Lloyds Bank plc*[14] the claimant shipowners, from time to time, employed PSL whenever one of the vessels was to enter a UK port. PSL would be put in funds to discharge liabilities incurred by the vessels such as jetty, river dues, pilotage and berth fees. The claimant shipowners made five advance payments for services not provided prior to deciding to cease trading. Thereafter, one further payment was received. The question was whether any of the payments were subject to a trust.   **7.12**

Bingham J held that the first five payments did not give rise to any trust, express or otherwise. As regards the last payment, he held that this was received in circumstances   **7.13**

---

12 [1981] Ch 105.

13 In *Bank of America v Arnell* [1999] Lloyd's Law Rep Bank 399, Aikens J, on an application for summary judgment, refused to apply *Chase Manhattan v Israel-British Bank* and hold that a mistaken payment gives rise to a constructive trust after Lord Browne-Wilkinson had cast doubt on its reasoning in *Westdeutsche Landesbank v Islington LBC* [1996] AC 669. It is implicit in Aikens J's reasoning that had the recipient in *Bank of America v Arnell* been aware of the mistake, he would have followed Lord Browne-Wilkinson's reasoning and found a constructive trust: see 405. In *Bank Tejarat v Hong Kong and Shanghai Banking Corporation Ltd* [1995] 1 Lloyd's Law Rep 239, the defendant accepted that *Chase Manhattan* was correctly decided and it was on that basis that Tuckey J applied its reasoning: see 248, col 1.

14 [1983] 2 Lloyd's LR 658.

giving rise to a constructive trust. The claim was not made on the basis of mistake, since counsel had been refused permission to amend his claim so to allege a payment by mistake. Rather, counsel relied upon the statement of Mr Justice Cardozo in *Beatty v Guggenheim Exploration Co*:[15]

> . . . A constructive trust is the formula through which the conscience of equity finds expression. When property has been acquired in such circumstances that the holder of the legal title may not in good conscience retain the beneficial interest, equity converts him into a trustee.

7.14 Counsel also relied upon Goulding J's reliance on an extract from Story's *Commentaries on Equity Jurisprudence* in *Chase Manhattan Bank*:

> 1255. One of the most common cases in which a Court of Equity acts upon the ground of implied trusts in invitum, is where a party has received money which he cannot conscientiously withhold from another party. It has been well remarked, that the receiving of money which consistently with conscience cannot be retained is, in Equity, sufficient to raise a trust in favour of the party for whom or on whose account it was received. This is the governing principle in all such cases. And therefore, whenever any controversy arises, the true question is, not whether the money has been received by a party of which he could not have compelled the payment, but whether he can now, with a safe conscience, ex aequo et bono, retain it. Illustrations of this doctrine are familiar in cases of money paid by accident, or mistake, or fraud.

7.15 Based upon these submissions, Bingham J held that the last payment was received and held on constructive trust:

> . . . any reasonable and honest directors of that company (or the actual directors had they known of it) would, I feel sure, have arranged for the repayment of that sum to the plaintiffs without hesitation or delay. It would have seemed little short of sharp practice for PSL to take any benefit from the payment, and it would have seemed contrary to any ordinary notion of fairness that the general body of creditors should profit from the accident of a payment made at a time when there was bound to be a total failure of consideration. . . .It . . . seems to me that at the time of its receipt PSL could not in good conscience retain this payment and that accordingly a constructive trust is to be inferred.[16]

7.16 *Nesté Oy* was followed in *Re Farepak Food and Gifts Ltd (in admin)*.[17] This case concerned the typical tote or annual savings scheme where monies are paid in throughout the year in order to provide sufficient funds to purchase Christmas goods and vouchers at the year end. By October 2006, the directors of Farepak had decided they could no longer continue to trade and ordered their agents to stop collecting the regular payments. Notwithstanding those instructions, certain money kept coming in and the administrators sought directions as to how best to

---

[15] 225 NY 380 (1919), 386.
[16] [1983] 2 Lloyd's LR 658, 666.
[17] [2006] EWHC 3272, [2007] 2 BCLC 1.

deal with these funds. It was argued, based upon *Neste Oy*, that those payments received after the date upon which the directors had agreed to cease trading, must be held on constructive trust. Mann J held it was not that simple.

- Mann J recognized that *Nesté Oy* had been criticized by Lord Browne-Wilkinson in *Westdeutsche*.

- Mann J was referred to Ferris J in *Box v Barclays Bank*[18] who also recognized Lord Browne-Wilkinson's criticism and said 'it would now be dangerous to rely upon a principle of the kind applied by Bingham J in the *Nesté Oy* case'.[19] It is clear that Ferris J was characterizing the *Nesté Oy* case as being akin to if not a remedial constructive trust, which has no place in English law.

- In *Shalsun v Russo* [2003] EWHC 1637; [2005] Ch 281 at [118], Rimer J said that he 'respectfully share[s] the caution with which Ferris J regarded the existence of the general principle which Bingham J applied in the *Nesté Oy* case'.

- On the other hand, Mann J was influenced by the fact that the Court of Appeal in *Friends' Provident v Hillier Parker May & Rowden* [1997] 1 QB 85 were willing to proceed on the basis it was arguable that *Nesté Oy* was good law.[20]

- Similarly, in *Re Japan Leasing (Europe) plc*,[21] Nicholas Warren QC, sitting as deputy judge of the High Court, having rejected the existence of an express trust, went on to consider *Nesté Oy*:

  > The constructive trust is imposed because it would be unconscionable for the Company, as agent, to receive money as agent knowing that it could not account for it to its principal.[22]

- Mann J was also referred to the Privy Council decision in *Re Goldcorp Exchange Ltd*[23] where the Privy Council accepted the *Nesté Oy* case as being justifiable as giving rise to a proprietary interest 'where to the knowledge of the payee no performance at all could take place under the contract for which the payment formed the consideration'.[24]

---

[18] [1998] Lloyd's Rep Bank 185.
[19] ibid, 200.
[20] [1997] 1 QB 85, 106 per Auld LJ: 'In my view, if it is arguable that the developers knew at the time of receipt that they were not entitled to all or part of the notional interest, it is arguable that such receipt made them trustees of one sort or another: see *Nesté Oy v Lloyds Bank* [1983] 2 Lloyd's Rep 658, 665–66, per Bingham J.' Even in the absence of knowledge, Auld LJ was even willing to consider the case arguable based upon the Court of Appeal's support for *Chase Manhattan* in *Westdeutsche*. This latter view would of course have to be revisited in the light of the House of Lords' comments on *Chase Manhattan* in *Westdeutsche*.
[21] [1999] BPIR 911.
[22] ibid, [39].
[23] [1995] 1 AC 74.
[24] ibid, 104.

- Mann J was able to conclude that the authorities generally showed that *Neste Oy* could be justified as an instance of an institutional constructive trust.[25] He went on to apply Lord Browne-Wilkinson's re-interpretation of *Chase Manhattan* to the facts of *Nesté Oy*:

  > If that is right then one might categorise the payment in the *Neste Oy* case as having been made under a mistake (as to whether the recipient intended to fulfil the contract), so that at the moment of receipt the recipient, himself knowing that he would not fulfil the contract and obviously appreciating that the payer must understand otherwise, could not in good conscience keep the money . . . It is not just the pricking of the conscience that gives rise to the constructive trust; there is something more.[26]

- Ultimately, Mann J concluded the factual evidence as to the timing of receipt of payments was not sufficiently clear to apply the principles of *Nesté Oy*.

7.17 The *Nesté Oy* principle was considered by the Court of Appeal in *Triffit Nurseries (a firm) v Salads Etcetera Ltd (in admin rec)*.[27] This case concerned claimant producers of vegetables which were marketed via an agent, SE Ltd, who distributed the produce, billed customers and then remitted the proceeds to the claimants, deducting appropriate commission. In October 1998, SE Ltd went into administrative receivership. At that time, amounts were outstanding in respect of sales of the claimant's vegetables and the receivers subsequently recovered these sums from customers. The issue was whether such sums fell to be dealt with as part of SE Ltd's general assets and subject to the debenture or whether they were held on trust for the claimant producers.

7.18 Rather surprisingly, the Court of Appeal refused to impose a constructive trust over the sale proceeds. There was nothing to indicate conduct a 'little short of sharp practice'. The claim of the disappointed principal will succeed if and only if the circumstances are such that it would be wholly unconscionable for the receivers or the bank to oppose the claim. The Court of Appeal went on: 'If the receivers had, after their appointment, accepted any further consignments of produce or sold further produce (whenever consigned) to customers, the position would no doubt be different (although probably on the basis of the receivers having adopted [SE's] contracts with the claimants, rather than because of a constructive trust).'

7.19 Disappointingly, the Court of Appeal's judgment in *Triffit Nurseries* fails to explain why a distinction should be drawn (if that indeed is what they are inviting us to do) between agents who receive monies to be handed on to their principal and where debts are collected by the administrative receivers of the agent. There would appear to be no difference in principle. Some have interpreted the decision as saying

---

25 [2007] 2 BCLC 1, 16f–g.
26 ibid, 16h–17a.
27 [2000] 1 BCLC 761.

there was an insufficient degree of improbity to convert the company into a constructive trustee.[28] Three brief points can be made.

First, it is not at all clear that the Court of Appeal was seeking to raise the threshold of unconscionable conduct. If it was, that can only be derived from its stating a requirement that it must be 'wholly unconscionable' for the receivers to oppose the claim to the monies in order to impose a constructive trust. One can perhaps debate another day whether 'wholly unconscionable' is wider in ambit than the test applied in *Nesté Oy*. **7.20**

Secondly, the somewhat odd decision may have something to do with how the case was in fact pleaded: see p 773e where Robert Walker LJ said that counsel was right not to pursue this line of argument in the light of the fact that neither the pleaded case nor the judge's findings of fact laid a foundation for a 'conviction' that the receivers or SE Ltd had been involved in 'sharp practice'. **7.21**

Thirdly, Robert Walker LJ appeared to approach the issue by finding that immediately prior to the appointment of the receivers the customers' debts were assets of SE Ltd and therefore charged to the bank under the debenture. He could not see why the appointment of receivers or cessation of trading could alter that. He did however make clear that he would have reached a different conclusion had the receivers continued to accept further consignments after being appointed, although the answer then might lie in adoption of the contract and not constructive trust. **7.22**

In conclusion, there is no doubt that *Chase Manhattan*, as actually decided by Goulding J, is much-maligned and of questionable practical significance.[29] **7.23**

Those who favour unjust enrichment-based proprietary claims support the decision as an example of the consideration failing *ab initio* i.e. the second payment was never available to be freely used by the bank recipient. For these commentators, the crucial issue is timing, not fault.[30] **7.24**

Given the decision in *Foskett v McKeown,* practitioners may have a tall order seeking to persuade a court of the unjust enrichment approach to these cases. **7.25**

The alternative explanation of *Chase Manhattan* is that it is a case (such as *Nesté Oy*) involving knowledge of the mistake on the part of the recipient. Such an argument has greater support in the authorities but appears to elevate notice of a personal right to a proprietary claim without any apparent justification. **7.26**

---

[28] Birks and Mitchell, 'Unjust Enrichment' in Burrows (ed), *English Private Law* (2nd edn, Oxford University Press, 2007), [18.189]; Birks, *Unjust Enrichment* (2nd edn, Clarendon Press, 2005), 187.

[29] Although it has previously been noted that those in favour of unjust enrichment as the bedrock for proprietary claims do consider the case worth maintaining.

[30] Birks, *Unjust Enrichment* (2nd edn), 187.

D. Fraudulent Misrepresentation[31]

7.27 Commercial fraud typically involves large sums of money and parties do not readily relieve themselves of such large sums without the binding promise of something better in return. To be confident of obtaining that promised return, the parties will usually require the matter to be the subject of a contractual arrangement. In this way, contracts play an important role in commercial fraud litigation.

7.28 So this section focuses on when, if at all, might a party obtain a proprietary remedy by way of constructive trust in circumstances where they have been deceived into entering into a contractual arrangement.

(1) Contractual and non-contractual transfers: role for rescission

7.29 A clear distinction must be kept in mind between non-consensual transfers of property and transfer of property pursuant to a contractual arrangement, albeit one induced by fraud.

7.30 Observations, such as those from Lord Browne-Wilkinson in *Westdeutsche Landesbank v Islington LBC*[32] that property obtained by fraud is held on constructive trust have no application to the property transferred pursuant to contract. As Potter LJ made clear in *Twinsectra Ltd v Yardley & Ors*:[33]

> It seems to me that, whatever the legal distinctions between 'theft' and 'fraud' in other areas of the law, the distinction of importance here is that between non-consensual transfers and transfers pursuant to contracts which are voidable for misrepresentation. In the latter case, the transferor may elect whether to avoid or affirm the transaction and, until he elects to avoid it, there is no constructive (resulting) trust; in the former case, the constructive trust arises upon the moment of transfer. The result, so far as third parties are concerned, is that, before rescission, the owner has no proprietary interest in the original property; all he has is the 'mere equity' of his right to set aside the voidable contract. That equity binds volunteers and those taking with notice of the equity, but not purchasers for value without notice.

7.31 Accordingly, a contractual transfer must first be rescinded before any issue of a proprietary remedy arising will be entertained. While the voidable contract may well give rise to a defeasible title, that will make no legal or practical difference in circumstances where no rescission takes place.

---

[31] The whole area of rescission has been subjected to a detailed examination in the excellent D O'Sullivan, S Elliott and R Zakrzewski, *The Law of Rescission* (Oxford University Press, 2007).

[32] [1996] AC 669, 716: 'Although it is difficult to find clear authority for the proposition, when property is obtained by fraud equity imposes a constructive trust on the fraudulent recipient: the property is recoverable and traceable in equity.'

[33] [1999] Lloyd's Law Rep Bank 439, 461 CA.

Whilst it may appear anomalous that trusts do not arise immediately in the con- **7.32**
tract setting but they do where there is no contract, the explanation possibly lies
in the traditional pre-eminence afforded contractual remedies.[34] It has been noted
elsewhere that one cannot obtain a restitutionary remedy unless and until the relevant contract has been terminated; the same view may well be said to apply to
voidable contracts.

(2) Prior to rescission

A contract induced by fraud is voidable but not void. Being voidable, it is valid **7.33**
unless and until it is set aside. A voidable contract passes title to property at law
and in equity.[35] Accordingly, unless and until rescission takes place, any transfer of
assets or property under the voidable contract will be valid to pass good title at law
and in equity to the recipient, leaving the transferor with no proprietary interest
in that property.

In the absence of a proprietary interest, it is said that the transferor has an 'equity' **7.34**
or 'mere equity'. This equity binds volunteers including any trustee in bankruptcy
and unsecured creditors.[36] This equity is not, however, to be confused with either
an interest in the relevant property or a chose in action.[37]

One issue which has arisen relates to whether the absence of an equitable propri- **7.35**
etary interest or a fiduciary relationship, prior to rescission, prevents the rescinding party from being able to trace through transactions which took place prior to
rescission. As we shall see below, such tracing is in fact possible.[38]

---

[34] S Worthington, *Proprietary Interests in Commercial Transactions* (Clarendon Press, 1996),
164–5.

[35] *Lonrho plc v Fayed (No 2)* [1992] 1 WLR 1, 11–12 per Millett J; *El Ajou v Dollar Land Holdings
plc* [1993] 3 All ER 717, 734, per Millett J. See also *Daly v Sydney Stock Exchange Ltd* (1986) 160
CLR 371, 387–90 (Brennan J).

[36] *Tilley v Bowman Ltd* [1910] 1 KB 745, 750 per Hamilton J citing and relying upon *Re Eastgate*
[1905] 1 KB 465, 467, per Bingham J; *Gladstone v Hadwen* (1813) 1 M&S 517, 526–7. F Oditah,
'Assets and the Treatment of Claims in Insolvency' (1992) 108 LQR 459, 474: '. . . there are other
limitations which wipe out the asset *ab initio*. One example is the right to rescind a contract induced
by fraud. Provided *restitution in integrum* is still possible, the defrauded creditor's right of rescission is a powerful contractual remedy, for when exercised it has the effect of withdrawing the asset
transferred under the vitiated contract from the fund of assets available for distribution. Although,
in one sense, the creditor is an unsecured creditor, yet ever since 1813 when *Gladstone v Hawden* was
decided . . . it has been the position in equity . . . that title to rescind a voidable disposition prevails
over the transferee's unsecured creditors.'

[37] *Investors Compensation Scheme Ltd v West Bromwich Building Society* [1998] 1 LR 896 (HL)
915, 916.

[38] *Lonrho v Fayed (No 2)* [1992] 1 WLR 1; *El Ajou v Dollar Land Holdings plc* [1993] 3 All ER
717.

(3) Upon rescission

7.36 Upon rescission of a voidable contract obtained by fraud, the equitable interest in the assets transferred under that contract *may*[39] (re-)vest in the rescinding party.

7.37 The starting point is the influential decision of the High Court of Australia in *Alati v Kruger*:[40]

> Equity has always regarded as valid the disaffirmance of a contract induced by fraud even though precise *restitution in integrum* is not possible, if . . . it can do what is practically just between the parties, and by so doing restore them substantially to the *status quo* . . . Rescission for misrepresentation is always the act of the party himself: *Reese River Silver Mining Co v Smith* (1869) LR 4 HL 64 at 73. The function of a court in which proceedings for rescission are taken is to adjudicate upon the validity of the purported disaffirmance as an act avoiding the transaction *ab initio*, and, if it is valid, to give effect to it and make appropriate consequential orders . . . Of course a rescission which the common law courts would not accept as valid cannot of its own force revest the legal title to property which had passed, but if a court of equity would treat it as effectual the equitable title to such property revests upon rescission.

7.38 The contribution of Sir Peter Millett in this area has been immense: see the decisions of Millett J in *Lonrho pc v Fayed (No 2)*;[41] *El Ajou v Dollar Land Holdings plc*[42] and of Millett LJ in *Bristol and West Building Society v Mothew*.[43] These are the main authorities that one goes to in English law on this topic. That said, it must be recognized that as is often the case with a leading light in a particular area, a wrong path or two might be taken from time to time. The consequence can sometimes be a change of view which may leave some uncertainty in its wake.

7.39 What these authorities clearly establish is that a contract induced by fraud is voidable and not void and gives rise to no proprietary interest unless and until rescinded. In addition, they deal with two specific points relating to the manner in which the rescission might affect prior conduct.

- It is not possible to use the doctrine of rescission so as retrospectively to subject parties to obligations or duties of a fiduciary nature:

  > A contract obtained by fraudulent misrepresentation is voidable, not void, even in equity. The representee may elect to avoid it, but until he does so the representor is

---

[39] The word 'may' has been inserted although such a qualification does not tend to appear in any of the leading texts dealing with the proprietary consequences of rescission. However, as will be seen, Lord Millett, extra-judicially, has suggested certain limitations and so the word 'may' has been used in the event the courts adopt those limitations.

[40] (1955) 94 CLR 216, 224. See also *O'Sullivan v Management Agency and Music Ltd* [1985] QB 428 where (at 457) the Court of Appeal approved the quoted extract from *Alati v Kruger* set out in the text.

[41] [1992] 1 WLR 1.

[42] [1993] 3 All ER 717.

[43] [1998] Ch 1 CA.

not a constructive trustee of the property transferred pursuant to the contract . . . :
see *Daly v Sydney Stock Exchange Ltd* (1986) 160 CLR 371, 387-390, per Brennan J.
It may well be that if the representee elects to avoid the contract and set aside a
transfer of property made pursuant to it the beneficial interest in the property will
be treated as having remained vested in him throughout, at least to the extent necessary to support a tracing claim. But the representee's election cannot retrospectively subject the representor to fiduciary obligations of the kind alleged. It is a
mistake to suppose that in every situation in which a constructive trust arises the
legal owner is necessarily subject to all the fiduciary obligations and disabilities of
an express trustee. Even after the representee has elected to avoid the contract and
reclaim the property, the obligations of the representor would in my judgment be
analogous to those of a vendor of property contracted to be sold, and would not
extend beyond the property actually obtained by the contract and liable to be
returned.[44]

Whether or not there is a retrospective vesting for tracing purposes it is clear that
on rescission the equitable title does not revest retrospectively *so as to cause an
application of trust money which was properly authorized when made to be afterwards
treated as a breach of trust*. In *Lipkin Gorman v Karpnale Ltd*[45] Lord Goff of
Chieveley said, at p 573:

> Of course, 'tracing' or 'following' property into its product involves a decision by the
> owner of the original property to assert his title to the product in place of his original
> property. This is sometimes referred to as ratification. I myself would not so describe
> it, but it has, in my opinion, at least one feature in common with ratification, that it
> cannot be relied upon so as to render an innocent recipient a wrongdoer (cf *Bolton
> Partners v Lambert* (1889) 41 Ch D 295, 307, per Cotton LJ: 'an act lawful at the
> time of its performance [cannot] be rendered unlawful, by the application of the
> doctrine of ratification'.[46]

This must be correct since it cannot be right and proper to determine the wrongfulness or otherwise of a party's conduct based upon a subsequent decision whether
or not to rescind the relevant contract.

- If the contract is rescinded, it is possible to trace through those transactions
  which had taken place prior to rescission and, ultimately, to assert an equitable
  interest:

  > [where a transfer is induced by fraud, the claimants] are entitled to rescind the
  > transaction and revest the equitable title to the purchase money in themselves . . .
  > and . . . can then invoke the assistance of equity to follow property of which he is
  > the equitable owner.[47]

---

44 [1992] 1 WLR 1, 11–12.

45 [1991] 2 AC 548.

46 *Bristol and West Building Society v Mothew* [1998] Ch 1, 23C-D.

47 *El Ajou v Dollar Land Holdings plc* [1993] 3 All ER 717, 734. It is worth noting that in *Lonrho*
Millett J thought the relevant trust was a constructive trust whereas in *El Ajou* he stated it to be a
resulting trust.

> In *El Ajou v Dollar Land Holdings Plc* . . . I suggested that on rescision the equitable title might revest in the representee retrospectively at least to the extent necessary to support an equitable tracing claim. I was concerned to circumvent the supposed rule that there must be a fiduciary relationship or retained beneficial interest before resort may be had to the equitable tracing rules.[48]

These extracts illustrate perfectly the extent to which judges will go to alleviate any difficulties which may be created by the anomalous requirement that there should be a fiduciary relationship before it is possible to trace in equity. Millett J's reasoning appears to be that when a contract is rescinded for fraudulent misrepresentation, it is treated thereafter as void *ab initio* and any transfers that were made under that (now) void contract should never have been and so equity will permit the transferor to trace into any substituted products.

7.40 The analysis of Millett LJ that one can rescind a contract induced by fraud and thereafter trace the proceeds of sale was confirmed by Peter Gibson LJ in *Halifax Building Society v Thomas*[49] although the claim in that case failed on the facts.

7.41 For our present purposes, one of the most important aspects of the rescission of a fraudulently induced contract is the proprietary consequences of so doing by way of the imposition of a trust, whether resulting or constructive. It is here where it is necessary to read Lord Millett's dicta with great care because the availability of proprietary relief may not be quite so widely available as had previously been thought.

7.42 In *Lonrho v Fayed (No 2)*[50] Millett J said:

> *When appropriate*, the court will grant a proprietary remedy to restore to the plaintiff property of which he has been wrongly deprived, or to prevent the defendant from retaining a benefit which he has obtained by his own wrong. It is not possible, and it would not be desirable, to attempt an exhaustive classification of the situations in which it will do so. Equity must retain what has been called its 'inherent flexibility and capacity to adjust to new situations by reference to the mainsprings of equitable jurisdiction'.

Pausing there, it is unfortunate that Millett J did not consider he could provide a little more guidance on when proprietary relief might be available without infringing equity's desire to retain flexibility. After all, such flexibility serves no purpose if the principles guiding its exercise are not promulgated in the authorities so as to assist when advising clients. Further, we are in the realm of proprietary rights where certainty and clear principles should reign superior to concerns about flexibility.

---

[48] *Bristol and West Building Society v Mothew* [1998] Ch 1, 23A–B.
[49] [1996] 1 Ch 217.
[50] [1992] 1 WLR 1, 9 (emphasis added).

Similarly, in *Re Goldcorp*[51] Lord Mustill rejected the submission that: **7.43**

> in every case where a purchaser is misled into buying goods he is automatically en-
> titled on rescinding the contract to a proprietary right superior to those of all the
> vendor's other creditors exercisable against the whole of the vendor's assets.

Lord Mustill also said that misrepresentation 'would only ground a personal claim
to recover a sum equivalent to the amount paid'.[52]

So, if it is not to be every case of rescission which leads to a proprietary remedy,   **7.44**
which ones will? The answer, from Lord Millett, is not to be found in any judgment but in his extra-judicial writings. It is a perfect illustration of one of the driving forces behind writing this text—the desire to bring to the practitioner those
views which might not be readily available. In a section in 'Restitution and
Constructive Trusts',[53] Lord Millett well encapsulates his general view on the
question of rescission and the availability of proprietary relief:

> If he elects to rescind it, it is usually assumed that the beneficial title revests in the
> plaintiff, and the authorities suggest that it does so retrospectively. But the recipient
> cannot anticipate his decision. Pending the plaintiff's election to rescind, the recipi-
> ent is entitled, and may be bound, to treat the payment as effective. It is well settled
> that the plaintiff's subsequent rescission does not invalidate or render wrongful
> transactions which have taken place in the meantime on the faith of the receipt.[54] In
> the meantime, the plaintiff's right to rescind has been classified as a mere equity.[55]
> Although this has been criticised[56] there is much to commend it. Pending rescission
> the transferee has the whole legal and beneficial interest in the property, but his bene-
> ficial title is defeasible. There is plainly no fiduciary relationship. The defeasible
> nature of the transferee's title should not inhibit his use of the property. Any right
> which the transferor may have to a reconveyance after rescission, is best regarded, not
> as a response to a constructive or resulting trust, but as part of the working out of the
> equitable remedy of rescission, which is tightly controlled and subject to special
> defences. It is not inappropriate to describe the transferee as holding property on a
> constructive trust for the purchaser but only after the parties have entered into a spe-
> cifically enforceable contract for sale. If so, the right to reconveyance is a form of spe-
> cific performance (or 'specific unperformance') which equity makes available because
> a money judgment is an inadequate remedy. If this is right, then the remedy should
> be confined to cases of land or other property of special value to the transferor.[57]

---

51 [1995] 1 AC 74, 103.

52 In *Shalson v Russo* [2005] Ch 281, Rimer J held that these dicta were not consistent with
Banque Belge pour L'Etranger v Hambrouck [1921] 1 KB 321 or *El Ajou v Dollar Land Holdings plc*
[1993] 3 All ER 717. *Goff & Jones* (7th edn) agrees with Rimer J: [2-018].

53 'Restitution and Constructive Trusts' in Cornish et al (eds), *Restitution: Past Present & Future*, 216.

54 *Bolton Partners v Lambert* (1889) 41 h D 295, 307 (Cotton LJ); *Lipkin Gorman v Karpnale Ltd*
[1991] 2 AC 548, 573 (Lord Goff); *Bristol & West Building Society v Mothew* [1996] 4 All ER 698.

55 *Phillips v Phillips* (1892) 4 De GF & J 208, 218 (Lord Westbury).

56 See R Chambers, *Resulting Trusts* (Oxford University Press, 1997), 172 onwards.

57 See to similar effect, Lord Millett, 'Proprietary Restitution' in Degeling and Edelman (eds),
Equity in Commercial Law (Law Book Co of Australasia, 2005), 320.

7.45 On this approach, rescission of a fraudulently induced contract will only lead to a proprietary remedy in circumstances where the underlying agreement relates to the transfer of land or otherwise relates to a unique object, for which specific performance would be available. It remains to be seen to what extent these restrictions on the availability of proprietary relief after rescission prove influential in the courts.

E. Stolen Property

7.46 This is undoubtedly a controversial topic.

- On the one hand, standard principles of English law hold that a thief gains no title at all to the stolen property. The theft has no effect at all on the true owner's existing title to the stolen property. On this basis, it is simply impossible for the thief to be a trustee (constructive or otherwise) over the stolen property.

- On the other hand, there are those who are concerned that to leave the victim of a theft to the limited range of remedies at common law and the easily defeasible rules on tracing at common law, places that victim at a severe disadvantage.

(1) Proprietary consequences of theft[58]

7.47 A thief acquires no legal title to the stolen property. The true owner remains the legal owner and can sue the thief in conversion. Since the thief cannot gain a legal title, it cannot transfer such a title to third parties, who remain liable for conversion.[59]

7.48 If the true owner retains his full legal title to the stolen property, there has been no splitting of ownership in terms of legal and beneficial title. On that analysis, there can be no trust involvement. Indeed, if there had been, and the victim of the theft was left with only an equitable interest, he would not be able to sue in conversion.[60]

(2) Lord Browne-Wilkinson's bag of stolen coins

7.49 In *Westdeutsche Landesbank v Islington LBC*[61] Lord Browne-Wilkinson addressed the issue of the ability of a legal owner to trace in equity monies stolen from him. Lord Browne-Wilkinson's reasoning merits being set out in full:

> The argument for a resulting trust was said to be supported by the case of a thief who steals a bag of coins. At law those coins remain traceable only so long as they are

---

[58] See Glanville Williams, 'Mistake in the Law of Theft' [1977] CLJ 62.
[59] S Worthington, *Proprietary Interests in Commercial Transactions* (Clarendon Press, 1996), 128.
[60] See para 4.30.
[61] [1996] AC 669.

kept separate: as soon as they are mixed with other coins or paid into a mixed bank account they cease to be traceable at law. Can it really be the case, it is asked, that in such circumstances the thief cannot be required to disgorge the property which, in equity, represents the stolen coins? Moneys can only be traced in equity if there has been at some stage a breach of fiduciary duty, ie if either before the theft there was an equitable proprietary interest (eg the coins were stolen trust moneys) or such interest arises under a resulting trust at the time of the theft or the mixing of the moneys. Therefore, it is said, a resulting trust must arise either at the time of the theft or when the moneys are subsequently mixed. Unless this is the law, there will be no right to recover the assets representing the stolen moneys once the moneys have become mixed.

I agree that the stolen moneys are traceable in equity. But the proprietary interest which equity is enforcing in such circumstances arises under a constructive, not a resulting trust. Although it is difficult to find clear authority for the proposition, when property is obtained by fraud equity imposes a constructive trust on the fraudulent recipient: the property is recoverable and traceable in equity. Thus, an infant who has obtained property by fraud is bound in equity to restore it: *Stocks v Wilson* [1913] 2 KB 235, 244; *R Leslie Ltd v Sheill* [1914] 3 kb 607. Moneys stolen from a bank account can be traced in equity: *Bankers Trust Co v Shapira* [1980] 1 WLR 1274, 1282C-E: see also *McCormick v Grogan* (1869) LR 4 HL 82, 97.

Although much of what Lord Browne-Wikinson had to say in *Westdeutsche* has **7.50** attracted criticism, few appear willing to depart from his view on the ability to trace in equity stolen monies. It has received the support of *Goff & Jones*,[62] Thomas and Hudson in *The Law of Trusts*,[63] and many other commentators.[64]

Lord Browne-Wilkinson's views are consistent with Lord Templeman's discussion **7.51** in *Lipkin Gorman v Karpnale*,[65] particularly where Lord Templeman cited *Banque Belge pour L'Etranger v Hambrouck*[66] as a case based on following trust assets. *Banque Belge* is a difficult case which can be and has been interpreted many different ways. One interesting issue to arise out of *Banque Belge* is the concern on the part of the Court of Appeal that the arguments suggested there as to why no relief could be granted against the mistress who had received from the thief were not to be allowed to hamper the court's ability to find appropriate relief. In *Banque Belge*,[67] Bankes LJ responded to the suggestion that the mistress obtained good

---

[62] *Goff & Jones* (7th edn), [2-033].
[63] *The Law of Trusts* (Oxford University Press, 2004), [27.21]; see also A Hudson, *Equity and Trusts* (5th edn, Cavendish, 2007), 514–16.
[64] *Lewin on Trusts* (18th edn, Thomson/Sweet and Maxwell, 2008), [7-26]; Pearce et al, *The Law of Trusts and Equitable Obligations* (4th edn, Oxford University Press, 2006), 271–2.
[65] [1991] 2 AC 548.
[66] [1921] 1 KB 321.
[67] ibid.

title to the stolen monies and could not be traced into the bank account, by the following:

> To accept either of the two contentions with which I have been so far dealing would be to assent to the proposition that a thief who has stolen money, and who from fear of detection hands that money to a beggar who happens to pass, gives a title to the money to the beggar as against the true owner—a proposition which is obviously impossible of acceptance.[68]

7.52 Similarly, it is a line which had already found favour with the High Court of Australia. In *Black v S Freedman & Co*,[69] O'Connor J stated:

> Where money has been stolen, it is trust money in the hands of the thief, and he cannot divest it of that character. If he pays it over to another person, then it may be followed into that other person's hands. If, of course, that other person shows that it has come to him bona fide for valuable consideration, and without notice, it then may lose its character as trust money and cannot be recovered. But if it is handed over merely as a gift, it does not matter whether there is notice or not.

7.53 Lord Browne-Wilkinson did not go into detail as to the principles underlying his approach to stolen monies. One way of examining it would be to apply the equitable maxim of 'equity treats that which ought to be done as done', as it was in the case of *A-G of Hong Kong v Reid*.[70] There Lord Templeman held that the defendant, the Acting Director of Public Prosecutions, only received the bribe monies on behalf of his employer, the government of Hong Kong and therefore if the defendant did what he was supposed to do, i.e. pay the monies over, the Hong Kong government would have title to the monies. Applying the maxim, the Hong Kong government was considered to have title to the monies before payment was in fact made and that provided the basis for finding that the defendant held on constructive trust:

> As soon as the bribe was received it should have been paid or transferred instanter to the person who suffered from the breach of duty. Equity considers as done that which ought to have been done. As soon as the bribe was received, whether in cash or in kind, the false fiduciary held the bribe on a constructive trust for the person injured.[71]

(3) Profits obtained with stolen monies

7.54 If, following Lord Browne-Wilkinson, the claimant has a proprietary claim to the stolen monies, does he similarly have such a claim to any profits obtained from the

---

[68] ibid, 327. Note also that the judgments in *Banque* Belge rather suggest that the case was being treated in the same vein as the voidable cases where rescission is necessary. The commencement of the action was treated as implied rescission in *Banque Belge*.

[69] (1910) 12 CLR 105 at 110 (O'Connor J).

[70] [1994] 1 AC 324: see a Hudson, *Equity and Trusts* (5th edn), 514–16 for a more detailed discussion of this explanation.

[71] [1994] 1 AC 324, 331.

use of those monies? It is suggested that if the claimant is to be permitted to raise a proprietary claim to the stolen monies, logically it should follow that he be entitled to the profits obtained from the use of those monies. Such profits naturally follow a proprietary claim.

That said, in *Lewin on Trusts* (18th edn)[72] the learned editors state that the true **7.55** owner cannot recover by way of constructive trust more than he has lost. Two cases are cited in support. *Halifax Building Society v Thomas*[73] and *Lonrho v Fayed (No 2)*. It is not clear that they in fact support the proposition for which they are cited.

In *Halifax Building Society*, the Court of Appeal was dealing with a building soci- **7.56** ety which had chosen to affirm the mortgage and claim under its security rights. They were thus a secured creditor. The building society could not therefore bring any claim in constructive trust for the profits made on the property purchased with the mortgage advances. The position was identical to that which faced Hoffmann J in *Chief Constable of Leicestershire v M*.[74] As the Court accepted in *Halifax Building Society*, '[c]ases where a fiduciary is required to account for a profit are plainly distinguishable from the facts of the present case.' [75] It is submitted, therefore, that *Halifax Building Society* does not support an embargo on recovery profits under a constructive trust.

It is true that Millett J said, in *Lonrho plc v Fayed (No 2)*:[76] **7.57**

> Even after the representee has elected to avoid the contract and reclaim the property, the obligations of the representor would in my judgment be analogous to those of a vendor of property contracted to be sold, and would not extend beyond the property actually obtained by the contract and liable to be returned.[77]

However, Millett J's comments in *Lonrho* must be seen in the context of a claim **7.58** based upon rescission. It is accepted that in that context it would not be appropriate retrospectively to subject the other contracting party to duties of a fiduciary nature in respect of their conduct prior to rescission. After all, the contract may be voidable but unless and until rescinded it remains as valid and binding as any other contract and importantly the other contracting party is entitled so to act. This remains so even if they have fraudulently induced the first contracting party to enter into the contract. It is the act of rescission which takes matters back to the start and the court has rightly eschewed any suggestion that conduct which has

---

[72] At [7-26].
[73] [1996] Ch 217 CA.
[74] [1989] 1 WLR 20, 21: 'None of the lenders have made any claim by way of constructive trust or otherwise to the profits made on the houses bought with their money. They have preferred to affirm the advances and enforce their rights under the mortgages'(Hoffmann J).
[75] *Halifix Building Society v Thomas* (1996) Ch 217 CA, 226 (Peter Gibson LJ).
[76] [1992] 1 WLR 1.
[77] ibid, 12.

already taken place on the basis the contract is valid should, post-rescission, be subjected to a different analysis and perhaps different duties.

7.59 But with theft, there is no sanctity of contract that needs protecting. There is no rescission. The constructive trust arises, or not, from the moment of receipt of the stolen property and not from a subsequent decision to rescind. The property is never free in the hands of the thief for the thief to say, subsequently, I was entitled to do what I liked with the property. The thief knows he has stolen the property. He has no right of security of a transaction to hide behind—there is no transaction at all, simply the taking away of money belonging to others. In that context, it is difficult to see why any profits obtained by the thief with the stolen property should not also be the subject of the constructive trust.

F. Unconscionable Conduct in Commercial Joint Ventures

7.60 In recent years, the Court of Appeal has shown a remarkable keenness to impose proprietary relief by way of constructive trust in commercial settings, where one party has acquired property for himself when, to that party's knowledge, the other party has withdrawn from negotiations on the understanding or expectation (but not necessarily a binding contract) that any land acquired would be split between them. The relief has generally been held to derive from the *Pallant v Morgan* doctrine. It is very difficult to characterize these cases other than property rights granted because of the unconscionable conduct of another. That is a small step away from saying because it would be just and fair to grant them. It is hard to see the House of Lords in *Foskett v McKeown* being content with that justification.

7.61 The starting point is the decision of Harman J in *Pallant v Morgan*.[78] Here, a parcel of land was to be sold by auction and the agents of two neighbouring landowners agreed one only would bid at the auction and if successful the land would be divided between them. There was no binding contract as such since the parties had not reached agreement on the percentage split between them. One party was successful in the auction but thereafter refused to divide the land. Harman J held the property was acquired and held on trust and in the event of no agreement being reached as to how to divide the property, it would be sold and the proceeds split 50:50.

7.62 In *Banner Homes Group plc v Luff Developments*[79] the commercial parties were negotiating to purchase and develop together a particular site through a joint-venture company. One party decided to proceed on its own, purchasing the site

---

[78] [1953] Ch 43.
[79] [2000] Ch 372 CA.

through its wholly-owned subsidiary. It was found by the judge that this party had led the other to believe it intended to enter into the joint venture and had not informed the other party of its second thoughts through a concern a rival bid may come for the property. Blackburne J held there was no contract between the parties and rejected any equitable claim, on the basis that it would turn an arrangement, which permitted either party to withdraw as and when they wanted, into an unqualified undertaking.

The Court of Appeal allowed the appeal, finding that Banner had suffered a detriment in being kept out of the bidding. Chadwick LJ undertook an extensive review of the first instance decisions relating to *Pallant v Morgan* since it was the first time the matter had properly been before the Court of Appeal. Chadwick LJ concluded that the *Pallant v Morgan* doctrine did exist and was firmly established. He also agreed with Millett J in *Lonrho Plc v Fayed (No 2)*[80] that it was an example of the wider equity principles: **7.63**

> Equity will intervene by way of constructive trust, not only to compel a defendant to restore the plaintiff's property to him, but also to require a defendant to disgorge property which should have acquired, if at all, for the plaintiff. In the latter category of case, the defendant's wrong lies not in the acquisition of the property, which may or may not be lawful, but in his subsequent denial of the plaintiff's beneficial interest. For such to be the case, however, the defendant must either have acquired property which but for his wrongdoing would have belonged to the plaintiff, or he must have acquired property in circumstances in which he cannot conscientiously retain it against the plaintiff.[81]

Chadwick LJ also referred, with approval, to Millett LJ in *Paragon Finance Plc v D B Thakerar & Co*:[82] **7.64**

> [The defendant's] possession of the property is coloured from the first by the trust and confidence by means of which he obtained it, and his subsequent appropriation of the property to his own use is a breach of that trust.[83]

Mindful of the need not to restrict the development of equity principles, Chadwick LJ nevertheless advanced the following propositions in respect of the *Pallant v Morgan* doctrine: **7.65**

> (1) A *Pallant v Morgan* equity may arise where the arrangement or understanding on which it is based precedes the acquisition of the relevant property by one party to that arrangement. It is the pre-acquisition arrangement which colours the subsequent acquisition by the defendant and leads to his being treated as a trustee if he seeks to act inconsistently with it. Where the arrangement or understanding is reached in relation to property already owned by one of the parties, he may (if the arrangement

---

80 [1992] 1 WLR 1.
81 ibid, 9–10.
82 [1999] 1 All ER 400.
83 ibid, 409.

is of sufficient certainty to be enforced specifically) thereby constitute himself trustee on the basis that 'equity looks on that as done which ought to be done,' or an equity may arise under the principles developed in the proprietary estoppel cases. As I have sought to point out, the concepts of constructive trust and proprietary estoppels have much in common in this area. *Holiday Inns Inc v Broadhead* 232 E G 951 may, perhaps, best be regarded as a proprietary estoppels case; although it might be said that the arrangement or understanding, made at the time when only the five acre site was owned by the defendant, did, in fact, precede the defendant's acquisition of the option over the 15-acre site.

(2) It is unnecessary that the arrangement or understanding should be contractually enforceable. Indeed, if there is an agreement which is enforceable as a contract, there is unlikely to be any need to invoke the *Pallant v Morgan* equity; equity can act through the remedy of specific performance and will recognize the existence of a corresponding trust. On its facts *Chattock v Muller* 8 CH D 177 is, perhaps, best regarded as a specific performance case. In particular, it is no bar to a *Pallant v Morgan* equity that the pre-acquisition arrangement is too uncertain to be enforced as a contract—see *Pallant v Morgan* [1953] Ch 43 itself, and *Time Products Ltd v Combined English Stores Group Ltd* 2 December 1974—nor that it is plainly not intended to have contractual effect—see *Island Holdings Ltd v Birchington Engineering Co Ltd,* 7 July 1981.

(3) It is necessary that the pre-acquisition arrangement or understanding should contemplate that one party ('the acquiring party') will take steps to acquire the relevant property; and that, if he does so, the other party ('the non-acquiring party') will obtain some interest in that property. Further, it is necessary that (whatever private reservations the acquiring party may have) he has not informed the non-acquiring party before the acquisition (or, perhaps more accurately, before it is too late for the parties to be restored to a position of no advantage/no detriment) that he no longer intends to honour the arrangement or understanding.

(4) It is necessary that, in reliance on the arrangement or understanding, the non-acquiring party should do (or omit to do) something which confers an advantage on the acquiring party in relation to the acquisition of the property; or is detrimental to the ability of the non-acquiring party to acquire the property on equal terms. It is the existence of the advantage to the one, or detriment to the other, gained or suffered as a consequence of the arrangement or understanding, which leads to the conclusion that it would be inequitable or unconscionable to allow the acquiring party to retain the property for himself, in a manner inconsistent with the arrangement or understanding which enabled him to acquire it. *Pallant v Morgan* [1953] Ch 43 itself provides an illustration of this principle. There was nothing inequitable in allowing the defendant to retain for himself the lot (Lot 15) in respect to which the plaintiff's agent had no instructions to bid. In many cases the advantage/detriment will be found in the agreement of the non-acquiring party to keep out of the market. That will usually be both to the advantage of the acquiring party—in that he can bid without competition from the non-acquiring party—and to the detriment of the non-acquiring party—in that he loses an opportunity to acquire the property for himself. But there may be advantage to the one without corresponding detriment to the other. Again, *Pallant v Morgan* provides an illustration. The plaintiff's agreement (through his agent) to keep out of the bidding gave an advantage to the defendant— in that he was able to obtain the property for a lower price than would otherwise have

been possible; but the failure of the plaintiff's agent to bid did not, in fact, cause detriment to the plaintiff—because, on the facts, the agent's instructions would not have permitted him to outbid the defendant. Nevertheless, the equity was invoked.

(5) That leads, I think, to the further conclusions: (i) that although, in many cases, the advantage/detriment will be found in the agreement of the non-acquiring party to keep out of the market, that is not a necessary feature; and (ii) that although there will usually be advantage to the one and correlative disadvantage to the other, the existence of both advantage and detriment is not essential—either will do. What is essential is that the circumstances make it inequitable for the acquiring party to retain the property for himself in a manner inconsistent with the arrangement or understanding on which the non-acquiring party has acted. Those circumstances may arise where the non-acquiring party was never 'in the market' for the whole of the property to be acquired; but (on the faith of an arrangement or understanding that he shall have a part of that property) provides support in relation to the acquisition of the whole which is of advantage to the acquiring party. They may arise where the assistance provided to the acquiring party (in pursuance of the arrangement or understanding) involves no detriment to the non-acquiring party; or where the non-acquiring party acts to his detriment (in pursuance of the arrangement or understanding) without the acquiring party obtaining any advantage therefrom.

7.66 In *London & Regional Investments Ltd v TBI plc*[84] the Court of Appeal refused to apply the *Pallant v Morgan* and *Banner Homes* reasoning to commercial negotiations which were expressly stated to be 'subject to contract'. A distinction was to be drawn between 'no contract' cases, where the parties have not yet reached a binding agreement and a 'subject to contract' situation, where the parties had made it quite clear that no binding arrangement would be reached until formal terms had been agreed. The 'subject to contract' stamp negatives any suggestion the parties were intending to create legal relations prior to entering into a formal legal agreement. The Court of Appeal held the effect of finding a constructive trust in *London & Regional* would be to invoke equity not to counter unconscionable conduct by one party which would defeat the understanding of both parties, but rather to reverse the effect of the express agreement they have made and replace it with a state of affairs (joint ownership of the land with no joint development) which was never contemplated.

7.67 It thus can be seen that the courts will be astute not to allow what might be called sharp practice or unconscionable conduct between negotiating commercial men to result in one acquiring property which should have been acquired if at all for two. As mentioned above, it is difficult to see such cases falling squarely within those statements from e.g. *Foskett v McKeown* that property rights are not to be imposed on the grounds that it is just and fair so to do.[85]

---

84 [2002] EWCA Civ 355.
85 For similar criticism, see W Swaddling, 'Property: General Principles' in A Burrows (ed), *English Private Law* (2nd edn, Oxford University Press, 2007), ch 4, [4.325].

G. Specifically Enforceable Contracts for Sale

7.68 We can deal with this topic briefly. Where X enters into a specifically enforceable sale contract with purchaser P, X becomes a constructive trustee of the relevant property until the contract is completed by transfer of the property to P.[86]

7.69 This is a further example of the operation of the equitable doctrine of conversion i.e. equity treats that as done which ought to be done.

H. Constructive Trust Imposed on Benefits Acquired by Murder

7.70 Given we are focusing on commercial fraud litigation, it is unlikely this category of imposing constructive trust on an individual is likely to feature highly. Some discuss criminal conduct. However, it be would be wrong if it was thereby considered that all criminal conduct will result in any benefits being the subject of the imposition of a constructive trust.[87] The relevant public policy is limited to someone who unlawfully kills another (whether murder,[88] manslaughter,[89] incitement to murder,[90] suicide pacts[91] and, a little more surprising, cases involving findings of diminished responsibility).[92] Some discuss this topic under the more general heading, such as benefits acquired by criminal conduct.

---

[86] *Wall v Brights* (1820)1 Jac & W 494, 503; Underhill and Hayton, *Law of Trusts and Trustees* (17th edn, LexisNexis, 2006), [36.1]; Hanbury and Martin, *Modern Equity* (17th edn, Thomson/Sweet and Maxwell, 2005), ch 24, [12-035] 7.

[87] There are, of course, various statutory routes to the recovery of the proceeds of criminal conduct: see T Millington and M Sutherland Williams, *The Proceeds of Crime: Law and Practice of Restraint, Confiscation, Condemnation and Forfeiture* (2nd edn, Oxford University Press, 2007).

[88] *Bridgeman v Green* (1755) 2 Ves Sen 627; *Beresford v Royal Insurance Co Ltd* [1938] AC 586.

[89] *Re Giles* [1972] Ch 544; *Davitt v Titcumb* [1990] Ch 110.

[90] *Evans v Evans* [1989] 1 FLR 351.

[91] *Dunbar v Plant* [1997] 4 All ER 289.

[92] *Re Giles* [1972] Ch 544.

8

CONSTRUCTIVE TRUSTS—ABUSE OF FIDUCIARY DUTY

A. Introduction

This chapter is solely concerned with the imposition of a constructive trust over **8.01** assets in the hands of an individual having the *pre-existing status* of a fiduciary. We are not concerned with the technique, of questionable principle, but laudable pragmatism, where the court deems an individual to be a fiduciary as a result of some form of wrongdoing so as to take advantage of the more flexible equitable rules on tracing. In this chapter, the fiduciary status precedes any form of wrongdoing.

To that extent, therefore, this chapter's focus is on what has been described as **8.02** Class 1 constructive trusts. In *Paragon Finance plc v DB Thakerar & Co*[1] Millett LJ drew the following distinction:

> Regrettably, however, the expressions 'constructive trust' and 'constructive trustee' have been used by equity lawyers to describe two entirely different situations. The first covers those cases . . . where the defendant, though not expressly appointed as trustee, has assumed the duties of a trustee by a lawful transaction which was independent of and preceded the breach of trust and is not impeached by the plaintiff. The second covers those cases where the trust obligation arises as a direct consequence of the unlawful transaction which is impeached by the plaintiff . . .

One important consequence of the pre-existing nature of the fiduciary duties is **8.03** that breach of such duties does not require proof of fraud or bad faith. It is a matter

---

[1] [1999] 1 All ER 400, 408.

of strict liability and that will greatly assist the victim of a fraud in being able to establish the claims it wants without necessarily having to resort to proving fraud or bad faith. Again, it is stressed that the fact the client may be a victim of a fraud does not necessarily mean it is necessary to plead and prove fraud for the victim to be adequately compensated.

8.04 Further, if the commercial fraud is committed by a party which is considered by the courts to be in a fiduciary relationship with the victim of the fraud, that breaching party will be subject to the strict application of the core duties of a fiduciary and whatever the conduct amounting to the underlying fraud, it is inherently likely to breach one or more of those core duties with the consequence that the breaching party will face the full penalties equity imposes on breaching fiduciaries. As we shall see, equity is harsh in its application of penalties even for a fiduciary who has, however innocently and without bad faith, breached one of the core duties.

B. Who is a Fiduciary?

8.05 One hesitates to start a section with such a question since it raises the expectation that the reader will be given the answer by the end of the section. The reality is that, rather like the concept of constructive trust itself, there is no one succinct and all-embracing definition of a fiduciary. That is perhaps of little surprise, since it is a concept which is used for so many different purposes. In one instance, it is used to describe a special relationship between two parties which gives rise to additional duties on one of the parties vis-à-vis the other. In another instance, we are content to attach the term fiduciary as a label or tag to a thief and his relationship with the victim of his theft activities simply as a device to invoke equity's rules on tracing. It is little wonder that a single definition eludes us still.

(1) Defining characteristics

8.06 As Sir Antony Mason stated:

the fiduciary relationship is a concept in search of a principle.[2]

In similar vein, Professor I Kennedy has said:

of ancient pedigree, and somewhat shrouded in mystery, it cannot be an overstatement that the fiduciary relationship is a legal concept of indistinct features and defining characteristics.[3]

---

[2] Sir Anthony Mason, 'Themes and Prospects' in P D Finn (ed), *Essays in Equity* (Law Book Company, 1985).

[3] I Kennedy, 'The fiduciary relationship—doctors and patients' in P Birks (ed), *Wrongs and Remedies in the 21st Century* (Clarendon Press, 1996) 111, 120. Professor Kennedy goes on to

The best that one can obtain is a description of particular instances or categories **8.07**
of relationship which are accepted to give rise to fiduciary duties and some observations as to various factors said to play differing roles of importance in the definition of a fiduciary relationship.

So we start with the famous description of the fiduciary relationship given by **8.08**
Mason J in *Hospital Products Ltd v United States Surgical Corp*:[4]

> The accepted fiduciary relationships are sometimes referred to as relationships of
> trust and confidence or confidential relations (cf *Boardman v Phipps*[[1967] 2 AC 46
> at 127; [1996] 3 All 721 at 758–9]) viz trustee and beneficiary, agent and principal,
> solicitor and client, employee and employer, director and company, and partners.
> The critical feature of these relationships is that the fiduciary undertakes or agrees to
> act for or on behalf of or in the interests of another person in the exercise of a power
> or discretion which will affect the interests of that other person in a legal or practical
> sense. The relationship between the parties is therefore one which gives the fiduciary
> a special opportunity to exercise the power or discretion to the detriment of that
> other person who is accordingly vulnerable to abuse by the fiduciary of his position.
> The expressions 'for', 'on behalf of', and 'in the interests of' signify that the fiduciary
> acts in a 'representative' character in the exercise of his responsibility, to adopt an
> expression used by the Court of Appeal.

In *Reading v R*,[5] the Court of Appeal was concerned with a soldier who had taken **8.09**
commissions to ride in his uniform in a lorry in which illegal transportation of
spirits or drugs would take place. Asquith LJ suggested a fiduciary relationship
arose in the following circumstances:

> A consideration of the authorities suggests that *for the present purpose* a 'fiduciary
> relation' exists (a) whenever the plaintiff entrusts to the defendant property, includ-
> ing intangible property as, for instance, confidential information, and relies on the
> defendant to deal with such property for the benefit of the plaintiff or for purposes
> authorised by him, and not otherwise (for instances, *Shallcross v Oldham (2)* and
> *Attorney-General v Goddard (3)*) and (b) whenever the plaintiff entrusts to the defend-
> ant a job to be performed, for instance, the negotiation of a contract on his behalf or
> for his benefit, and relies on the defendant to procure for the plaintiff the best terms
> available (for instance *Lister v Stubbs (4)* and *Powell Thomas v Even Jones (5)*).

It is unclear whether Asquith LJ intended his description to be all-embracing
given his use of 'for the present purposes'. It leaves one with the impression, however wrong it may be, that the court was simply using the uniform as a device to
render the soldier liable in equity.

---

examine whether such an indistinct and ill-defined concept can be moulded to the best interests
of medical law.

⁴ (1984) 156 CLR 41, 96–7.
⁵ [1949] 2 KB 232, 236.

8.10 Professor Finn, who has done more than most to find a principled understanding of the fiduciary obligation, has put forward a possible description of a fiduciary, which he says is no more precise than a description of the tort of negligence:

> A person will be a fiduciary in his relationship with another when and in so far as that other is entitled to expect that he will act in that other's interests or (as in a partnership) in their joint interests, to the exclusion of his own several interest.[6]

As far as Finn is concerned, the central idea or concept in a fiduciary relationship is service of another's interests—to procure loyalty in service.

8.11 In the solicitor case of *White v Jones*[7] Lord Browne-Wilkinson described a fiduciary relationship as being:

> The paradigm of the circumstances in which equity will find a fiduciary relationship is where one party, A, has assumed to act in relation to the property or affairs of another, B.

This description is fine, so far as it goes, but it does not go quite far enough. The problem with it is that A can perfectly properly assume such obligations towards another and yet not be a fiduciary. There is nothing in this definition about A not being able to act in accordance with his own interests or that B was entitled to expect that A would always provide disinterested advice and information as to how to handle his property. These factors form a major part of most descriptions of the fiduciary relationship.

8.12 In *Bristol and West Building Society v Mothew*,[8] Millett J suggested the following:

> A fiduciary is someone who has undertaken to act for or on behalf of another in a particular matter in circumstances which give rise to a relationship of trust and confidence. The distinguishing obligation of a fiduciary is the obligation of loyalty. The principal is entitled to the single-minded loyalty of his fiduciary.

It is submitted that the phrase that the principal is entitled to the 'single-minded loyalty of his fiduciary' is a useful short-hand for the obligations which tend to form the core duties of a fiduciary and which separate an agent, whose duties arise in common law and are limited to skill and care, from a party who must suppress his own interests in favour of those of the principal.

8.13 Lord Millett, writing extra-judicially,[9] has set out a more developed line of thought on the topic of defining or describing fiduciary relationships.

- He tells us that English law has, typically, avoided a definition in favour of muddling through without one. He suggests that recent cases illustrate that approach has been optimistic.

---

[6] Paul Finn, 'Fiduciary Law and the Modern Commercial World' in E McKendrick (ed), *Commercial Aspects of Trusts and Fiduciary Obligations* (Clarendon Press, 1992), 9.

[7] [1995] 2 AC 207, 271.

[8] [1998] Ch 1, 18.

[9] 'Equity's Place in the Law of Commerce' (1998) 114 LQR 214.

- He dismisses the benefit of looking for an all-embracing definition and instead suggests the focus should be on defining the characteristics of the fiduciary relationship(s).
- Fiduciary relationships are of many types and, echoing Lord Browne-Wilkinson in *Henderson v Merrett Syndicates Ltd*,[10] not all fiduciary relationships give rise to the same fiduciary duties.
- There are three kinds of fiduciary relationship which possess different characteristics and give rise to different duties.
  - *Relationship of trust and confidence.* 'Such a relationship arises whenever one party undertakes to act in the interest of another, or where he places himself in a position where he is obliged to act in the interests of another. The core obligation of a fiduciary of this kind is the obligation of loyalty.'[11]
  - *Relationship of influence.* The defining characteristic is vulnerability and equity is keen to prevent any exploitation of that vulnerability. There is no need for any express undertakings since the fiduciary duties derive from the nature of the relationship between the parties—being a 'relationship of ascendancy and dependency'.[12]
  - *Relationship of confidentiality.* This fiduciary relationship arises whenever an individual obtains confidential information.
- These fiduciary relationships are not mutually exclusive. For example, the solicitor–client relationship exhibits all three relationships as well as the ordinary commercial relationship based upon the contract of retainer.
- The key distinguishing feature between common law duties and fiduciary duties is that the former are prescriptive whereas the latter are proscriptive.[13] Fiduciary duties do not stipulate what must be done for the principal (i.e. nothing like act with reasonable care and skill), only what the fiduciary must *not* do.

It is evident from the above, that it is perhaps fruitless to search for one general **8.14** definition of a fiduciary and that it is preferable to focus on the characteristics which are present when we say that someone is a fiduciary. In searching for those characteristics, we need to recognize that there may be more than one type of fiduciary relationship and therefore those defining characteristics may alter from one type to another. There is nothing preventing one relationship including more than one basis for the imposition of a fiduciary relationship. The relationship may also be contractual in nature and so not every breach of duty will be a breach of the fiduciary duty, it may simply be a breach of a contractual term by a fiduciary.

---

[10] [1995] 2 AC 145, 206: '. . . the phrase "fiduciary duties" is a dangerous one, giving rise to a mistaken assumption that all fiduciaries owe the same duties in all circumstances. This is not the case.'
[11] (1998) 114 LQR 214, 219.
[12] ibid.
[13] See *Breen v Williams* (1996) 186 CLR 71.

(2) Established categories of fiduciary relationships

8.15   A commercial litigator will have no difficulty in establishing the existence of a fiduciary relationship if he can show that the facts of his case fall within one of the recognized categories of fiduciary relationships:[14]

8.16   *Trustee and beneficiary.* This is the paradigm example of the fiduciary relationship. It is predominantly based upon a traditional written express trust deed. It is unlikely such a formal trust arrangement will be in place in many of the fact-scenarios leading to a commercial fraud and so this category is unlikely to assist a litigator much.

8.17   *Solicitor and client.*[15] There is no real surprise as to the inclusion of this relationship. This is a relationship which has all the hallmarks of a fiduciary relationship: a solicitor agreeing to act in the best interests of the client and receiving confidential information in that capacity. There is also a sense of vulnerability as between solicitor and client in the sense of the client looking up to the solicitor for help and advice as to what to do.

8.18   *Agent and principal.*[16] It is generally accepted that the typical principal and agent relationship, where the agent has undertaken to act in the principal's interests in respect of certain tasks or dealings with money or investments, will give rise to fiduciary duties. This approach is premised upon the fact that the core principal and agent relationship contains one of the defining characteristics of a fiduciary, namely the power to alter the principal's legal position.

8.19   This approach is no more than a reflection of the fact that there are many different types of principal and agent relationship, many of which will give rise to fiduciary duties, albeit not the same fiduciary duties, and a few may give rise to no fiduciary duties at all.[17] Of course, as one moves away from the core principal and agent relationship, the responsibilities imposed on the agent reduce such that they may become so limited, such as with an introducing agent, that it may well be questionable that they give rise to any fiduciary duties at all. Little is to be learnt from seeking to characterize the principal and agent relationship by

---

[14] *Hospital Products Ltd v United States Surgical Corp* (1984) 156 CLR 41, 96–7; *Goff & Jones* (7th edn), ch 33.

[15] *Nocton v Lord Ashburton* [1914] AC 932; *McMaster v Byrne* [1952] 1 All ER 1362 (PC); *Brown v IRC* [1965] AC 244.

[16] See *Bowstead and Reynolds on Agency* (18th edn, Thomson/Sweet and Maxwell, 2006), Article 43; *English v Dedham Vale Properties Ltd* [1978] 1 WLR 93. See also *Lowther v Lowther* (1806) 13 Ves 95, 103 (Lord Erskine).

[17] This issue is addressed in some detail in *Gummow, Meagher & Lehane's Equity Doctrines and Remedies* (4th edn, Butterworths, 2002), [5-190] *et seq*. See also F E Dowrick, 'The Relationship of Principal and Agent' (1954) 17 MLR 24, 31–3.

reference to these peripheral examples as opposed to the core or paradigm examples. As one leading text put the matter '[e]ven if it remains possible to identify cases in which non-fiduciary agencies have been recognised, they are of so special a character as not to merit significant qualification of the general rule that agency is fiduciary.'[18]

If the circumstances of a fraud claim derive from the fact that one party has **8.20** entrusted another with a particular task or responsibility for receiving or holding onto certain assets, then it is likely that reliance will want to be placed on this category in order to establish the existence of fiduciary duties.

Company directors and the company.[19] This category is likely to feature highly in **8.21** many examples of commercial fraud litigation. Reference in this category to 'director' is to a *de jure* director, one who has been formally appointed director. Difficult questions arise as to whether a *de facto* director or a shadow director similarly owe such duties.

A *de facto* director is one who has not been formally appointed but who claims **8.22** to act and purports to act as a director to the company.[20] It is suggested a *de facto* director owes fiduciary duties to the company.[21] Certainly a *de facto* director would fall within s 741(1) of the Companies Act 1985, being the definition of a director. A *de facto* director can be considered analogous to a trustee de son tort i.e. someone who, whilst not actually appointed a trustee, places himself in a position where he acts as a trustee and therefore has the responsibility and duties of a trustee.

A shadow director, however, does not fall within s 741(1) of the Companies Act **8.23** 1985. A shadow director operates not by occupying the position of a director, as

---

[18] *Gummow, Meagher & Lehane's Equity Doctrines and Remedies* (4th edn), [5-200].

[19] *Selangor United Rubber Estates Ltd v Craddock (No 3)* [1968] 1 WLR 1555; *Regal (Hastings) Ltd v Gulliver* [1967] 2 AC 134n, 159 (Lord Porter): 'Directors, no doubt, are not trustees, but they occupy a fiduciary position towards the company whose board they form.' See generally, Sinclair, Vogel and Snowden (eds), *Company Directors: Law and Liability* (Thomson/Sweet and Maxwell, Looseleaf Publication), ch 3. In *Bairstow v Queen's Moat House* [2001] 2 BCLC 531 Robert Walker LJ said at [53]: 'the fiduciary obligations undertaken in this case by the former directors involved heavy and continuing responsibilities for the stewardship of the company's assets. They were not strictly speaking trustees, as title to the assets was not vested in them; but they had trustee-like responsibilities, because they had the power and the duty to manage the company's business in the interests of all its members.'

[20] A *de facto* director falls within the definition of a director within s 741 of the Companies Act 1985.

[21] *Yukong Line of Korea Ltd v Randsburg Corp Investments of Liberia Inc* [1998] 1 WLR 294; *Re Hydrodam (Corby) Ltd* [1994] 2 BCLC 180; *Canadian Aero Services Ltd v O'Malley* (1973) 40 DLR (3d) 371.

such, but rather by influencing those who are properly directors. It is a one-stage removed position.[22] In *Re Hydrodam (Corby) Ltd*[23] Millett J stated:

> A *de facto* director . . . is one who claims and purports to act as a director, although not validly appointed as such. A shadow director, by contrast, does not claim or purport to act as a director. On the contrary, he claims not to be a director. He lurks in the shadows, sheltering behind others who, he claims, are the only directors of the company to the exclusion of himself. He is not held out as a director by the company. To establish that a defendant is a shadow director of a company it is necessary to allege and prove: (1) who are the directors of the company, whether de facto or de jure; (2) that the defendant directed those directors how to act in relation to the company or that he was one of the persons who did so; (3) that those directors acted in accordance with such directions; and (4) that they were accustomed so to act. What is needed is first, a board of directors claiming and purporting to act as such; and secondly, a pattern of behaviour in which the board did not exercise any discretion or judgment of its own, but acted in accordance with the directions of others.[24]

8.24 A shadow director is unlikely to be held to owe fiduciary duties to the company unless it can be shown that the shadow director has had direct dealings with the company's assets.[25]

8.25 In *Foster Bryant Surveying v Bryant*[26] Rix LJ cited with approval the following principles relating to the nature and extent of a director's fiduciary duties:

> 1. A director, while acting as such, has a fiduciary relationship with his company. That is he has an obligation to deal towards it with loyalty, good faith and avoidance of the conflict of duty and self-interest.
>
> 2. A requirement to avoid a conflict of duty and self-interest means that a director is precluded from obtaining for himself, either secretly or without the informed approval of the company, any property or business advantage either belonging to the company or for which it has been negotiating, especially where the director or officer is a participant in the negotiations.
>
> 3. A director's power to resign from office is not a fiduciary power. He is entitled to resign even if his resignation might have a disastrous effect on the business or reputation of the company.
>
> 4. A fiduciary relationship does not continue after the determination of the relationship which gives rise to it. After the relationship is determined the director is in general not under the continuing obligations which are the feature of the fiduciary relationship.

---

[22] Insolvency Act 1986, s 251, defines 'shadow director' as 'a person in accordance with whose directions or instructions the directors of the company are accustomed to act . . .'.

[23] [1994] 2 BCLC 180.

[24] ibid, 182.

[25] *Paragon Finance plv v Thakerar & Co* [1999] 1 All ER 400; *Dubai Aluminium Co Ltd v Salaam* [2003] AC 366; *Ultraframe (UK) Ltd v Fielding (No 2)* [2005] EWHC 1638 (Ch) (Lewison J).

[26] [2007] EWCA Civ 200.

5. Acts done by the directors while the contract of employment subsists but which are preparatory to competition after it terminates are not necessarily in themselves a breach of the implied term as to loyalty and fidelity.

6. Directors, no less than employees, acquire a general fund of skill, knowledge and expertise in the course of their work, which is plainly in the public interest that they should be free to exploit it in a new position. After ceasing the relationship by resignation or otherwise a director is in general (and subject of course to any terms of the contract of employment) not prohibited from using his general fund of skill and knowledge, the 'stock in trade' of the knowledge he has acquired while a director, even including such things as business contacts and personal connections made as a result of his directorship.

7. A director is however precluded from acting in breach of the requirement at 2 above, even after his resignation where the resignation may fairly be said to have been prompted or influenced by a wish to acquire for himself any maturing business opportunities sought by the company and where it was his position with the company rather than a fresh initiative that led him to the opportunity which he later acquired.

8. In considering whether an act of a director breaches the preceding principle the factors to take into account will include the factor of position or office held, the nature of the corporate opportunity, its ripeness, its specificness and the director's relation to it, the amount of knowledge possessed, the circumstances in which it was obtained and whether it was special or indeed even private, the factor of time in the continuation of the fiduciary duty where the alleged breach occurs after termination of the relationship with the company and the circumstances under which the breach was terminated, that is whether by retirement or resignation or discharge.

9. The underlying basis of the liability of a director who exploits after his resignation a maturing business opportunity of the company is that the opportunity is to be treated as if it were the property of the company in relation to which the director had fiduciary duties. By seeking to exploit the opportunity after resignation he is appropriating to himself that property. He is just as accountable as a trustee who retires without properly accounting for trust property.

10. It follows that a director will not be in breach of the principle set out as point 7 above where either the company's hope of obtaining the contract was not a 'maturing business opportunity' and it was not pursuing further business orders nor where the director's resignation was not itself prompted or influenced by a wish to acquire the business for himself.

11. As regards breach of confidence, although while the contract of employment subsists a director or other employee may not use confidential information to the detriment of his employer, after it ceases the director/employee may compete and may use know-how acquired in the course of his employment (as distinct from trade secrets—although the distinction is sometimes difficult to apply in practice).

Partnership.[27] This is one of those relationships in which two or more individuals **8.26** have bound themselves together to pursue a common business aim. As such, each

---

[27] *Bentley v Craven* (1853) 18 Beav 75.

partner has the ability to alter the financial and legal position of the other partners. It is a classic fiduciary relationship.

8.27 *Joint ventures.* Closely allied to the partnership, but not so clearly established, is the joint venture relationship. Unlike a partnership the existence of which and certain terms and duties are statutorily based, the nature and extent of joint ventures vary from one agreement to the next. It is a question of fact in respect of each agreement whether the relationship is likely to give rise to a fiduciary relationship and if so the precise nature of the duties to which it gives rise.

Indeed, the joint venture relationship is a perfectly good example of the principle that the existence of a fiduciary relationship does not determine the nature and extent of any fiduciary duties arising thereunder. Typically, the joint venture is formed between two commercial entities or individuals who would not otherwise owe each other duties of a fiduciary nature. It is the fact that they are combining together with a common aim or aims in which each will have certain responsibilities towards the other that a fiduciary relationship arises. However, that is only the start of enquiries. The nature and extent of the fiduciary duties must match the obligations undertaken by each other towards each other as part of the joint venture. So, as occurred in *Global Container Lines Ltd v Bonyad Shipping Co*,[28] where one party to the joint venture was already conducting independent business prior to the joint venture, it could not be said that such business was within the terms of the joint venture, in the absence of any agreement to include it. Having referred to the estate agents' case of *Kelly v Cooper*,[29] Rix J stated:

> It seems to me that the present case is if anything clearer cut than *Kelly v Cooper*, for even though in many respects they may have been acting as agents or sub-agents on behalf of the joint venture, and even though as joint venturers themselves they may have been acting in the role of quasi partners, Global were essentially businessmen, with an existing business to conduct, as was fully known to Bonyad, and were acting in a competitive business environment. If in such a context, there was no express agreement that Global would give up their existing business in favour of the joint venture, I do not see how such an agreement can be implied under the general rubric of a fiduciary relationship. It may be that in performing some of their agency duties, Global were fiduciaries or owed fiduciary duties, e.g. to account: but in conducting their own and their joint venture businesses side by side, they were merely doing what Bonyad knew about and, as I have found, consented to, and in any event must be regarded as consenting to.[30]

---

[28] [1998] 1 Lloyd's Law Rep 528.

[29] [1993] AC 205.

[30] At 546. See also *New Zealand and Netherlands Society 'Oranje' Inc v Kuys* [1973] 1 WLR 1126; *Bristol and West Building Society v Mothew* [1996] 4 All ER 698. See generally, G Bean, *Fiduciary Obligations and Joint Ventures: The Collaborative Fiduciary Relationship* (Oxford University Press, 1995).

That joint ventures may give rise to fiduciary obligations also appears accepted in Australia. In *United Dominions Corporation v Brian Pty*,[31] the court said:

> In particular a fiduciary relationship may, and ordinarily will, exist between prospective parties who have embarked upon the conduct of the partnership business or venture before the precise terms of any agreement have been settled. Indeed, in such circumstances, the mutual confidence and trust which underlie most consensual fiduciary relationships are likely to be more readily apparent than in the case where mutual rights and obligations have been expressly defined in some formal agreement. Likewise, the relationship between prospective partners or participants in a proposed partnership to carry out a single joint undertaking will ordinarily be fiduciary if the prospective partners have reached an informal arrangement to assume such a relationship and have proceeded to take steps to be involved in its establishment or implementation.[32]

There are numerous other instances of different relationships where the courts have shown a willingness to find within that relationship the existence of fiduciary duties. Such miscellaneous categories are considered in the various texts.[33] **8.28**

It is, of course, important to appreciate that the categories of fiduciary relationships set out above are not intended to be exhaustive and that they are not closed.[34] Yet, it must be accepted that the English courts have not shown any great desire to expand this list of categories, preferring, if possible, to recognize particular fiduciary relationships on the particular facts of each case. **8.29**

C. Nature of Fiduciary Duties

It will have become clear by now that fiduciary relationships can take many different forms and depending on that form and the nature of the obligations undertaken by one party to the other, will give rise to different types of fiduciary duties. In this regard, the reader will do well to heed the comments of Fletcher Moulton LJ in *Coomber v Coomber*:[35] **8.30**

> Fiduciary relations are of many different types; they extend from the relation of myself to an errand boy who is bound to bring me back my change up to the most intimate and confidential relations which can possibly exist between one party and

---

[31] (1985) 157 CLR 1 (High Court of Australia).

[32] Cited with apparent approval by Etherton J in *Murad v Al Saraj* [2004] EWHC 1235 Ch; *Sintra Homes Ltd v Beard & Ors* [2007] EWHC 3071 (Ch). Of course, not all joint venture relationships give rise to fiduciary duties: *Cayzer v Beddow* [2007] EWCA Civ 644; *Button v Phelps* [2006] EWHC 53 (Robert Englehard QC).

[33] See e.g. *Gummow, Meagher & Lehane's Equity Doctrines and Remedies* (4th edn), ch 5.

[34] *English v Dedham Vale Properties Ltd* [1978] 1 WLR 93, 110 (Slade J); *Hospital Products Ltd v United States Surgical Corp* (1984) 156 CLR 41, 96. See also *Gummow, Meagher & Lehane's Equity Doctrines and Remedies* (4th edn), 157.

[35] [1911] 1 Ch 723.

another where the one is wholly in the hands of the other because of his infinite trust in him. All these are cases of fiduciary relations, and the Courts have again and again, in cases where there has been a fiduciary relation, interfered and set aside acts which, between persons in a wholly independent position, would have been perfectly valid. Thereupon in some minds there arises the idea that if there is any fiduciary relation whatever any of these types of interference is warranted by it. They conclude that every kind of fiduciary relation justifies every kind of interference. Of course that is absurd.[36]

8.31   The nature of the fiduciary duties will depend not just on the nature of the relationship but will also be affected by the terms of any contractual arrangement reached between the parties. Indeed, in the context of commercial fraud litigation, it is very likely that the relevant fiduciary relationship will be affected, to some extent, by the terms of a contract.

8.32   All that can be done in this section is to highlight the more common types of fiduciary duties which typically arise in most cases. More detailed accounts can be left to the specialist texts.

8.33   In *Bristol and West Building Society v Mothew*,[37] Millett LJ set out a list of what he understood the core duties of a fiduciary are:

> The principal is entitled to the single-minded loyalty of his fiduciary. The core liability has several facets. A fiduciary must act in good faith; he must not make a profit out of his trust; he must not place himself in a position where his duty and his interest may conflict; he may not act for his own benefit or the benefit of a third person without the informed consent of his principal. This is not intended to be an exhaustive list, but it is sufficient to indicate the nature of fiduciary obligations. They are the defining characteristics of the fiduciary.[38]

(a) No conflict of interest—No personal profit—Two duties not one

8.34   It would be very easy to form the conclusion that there is no need for both the no conflict of interest rule and the no personal profit rule. On first reading, the two rules appear to overlap, but they are in fact aimed at two differing evils. One places an embargo on making profits out of the party's position as a fiduciary. This can operate harshly so that it may result in depriving a fiduciary of profits which the principal could never have made. In those circumstances, there may not be any real risk of conflict of interest—because the principal has or had no intention or possibly even ability of securing that transaction and yet the fiduciary will still not be permitted to retain the profits. The second seeks to prevent the fiduciary from being influenced by his own interests in any manner at all or even running the risk of being so influenced. It matters not whether such influence is predicated upon obtaining personal profit or on other reasons.

---

36   728–9.
37   [1998] Ch 1.
38   ibid, 18.

The inter-relationship between these two duties is well illustrated by Deane J in **8.35**
Chan v Zacharia:[39]

> The variations between more precise formulations of the principle governing the
> liability to account are largely the result of the fact that what is conveniently regarded
> as the one 'fundamental rule' embodies two themes. The first is that which appropri-
> ates for the benefit of the person to whom the fiduciary duty is owed any benefit or
> gain obtained or received by the fiduciary in circumstances where there existed a con-
> flict of personal interest and fiduciary duty or a significant possibility of such conflict;
> the objective is to preclude the fiduciary from being swayed by considerations of per-
> sonal interest. The second is that which requires the fiduciary to account for any bene-
> fit or gain obtained or received by reason of or by use of his fiduciary position or of
> opportunity or knowledge resulting from it: the objective is to preclude the fiduciary
> from actually misusing his position for his personal advantage. Notwithstanding
> authoritative statements to the effect that the 'use of fiduciary position' doctrine is
> but an illustration or part of a wider 'conflict of interest and duty' doctrine . . . the two
> themes, while overlapping, are distinct. Neither theme fully comprehends the other
> and a formulation of the principle by reference to one only of them will be incom-
> plete. Stated comprehensively in terms of the liability to account, the principle of
> equity is that a person who is under a fiduciary obligation must account to the person
> to whom the obligation is owed for any benefit or gain (i) which has been obtained
> or received in circumstances where a conflict or significant possibility of conflict
> existed between his fiduciary duty and his personal interest in the pursuit or possible
> receipt of such a benefit or gain or (ii) which was obtained or received by use or by
> reason of his fiduciary position or of opportunity or knowledge resulting from it.

The English courts have taken a strict approach to the application of the various **8.36**
duties. Far more so than is evident in Australia. A few examples from the authorities will suffice to illustrate the point.

In *Keech v Sandford*[40] the lease of a market was settled on trust for an infant. The **8.37**
trustee was unable to secure the lease renewal for and on behalf of the infant. To
protect the infant's interest, the trustee renewed the lease in his own name, intending to pass it on to the infant when able so to do. The Lord Chancellor, Lord King,
held that the lease was held on trust, despite the absence of any bad faith and
indeed an intention to assist the infant:

> This may seem hard, that the trustee is the only person of all mankind who might not
> have the lease: but it is very proper that rule should be strictly pursued, and not in the
> least relaxed; for it is very obvious what would be the consequence of letting trustees
> have the lease, on refusal to renew to cestui que use.[41]

---

[39] (1984) 154 CLR 178.
[40] (1726) 2 Eq Cas Abr 741. This case is discussed in detail in J Getzler, 'Rumford Market and
the Genesis of Fiduciary Obligations' in A Burrows and A Rodger (eds), *Mapping the Law: Essays In
Honour of Peter Birks* (Oxford University Press, 2006).
[41] For a recent application of the *Keech v Sandford* principle in a commercial setting see *Don King
Productions inc v Warren* [2000] Ch 291, 339–40.

8.38 To similar effect is Lord Cranworth LC in *Aberdeen Ry Co v Blaikie Bros*:[42]

> And it is a rule of universal application that no one having such duties to discharge shall be allowed to enter into engagements in which he has or can have a personal interest conflicting or which possibly may conflict with the interests of those whom he is bound to protect.

8.39 In *Bray v Ford*[43] Lord Herschell observed:

> It is an inflexible rule of a court of equity that a person in a fiduciary position . . . is not, unless otherwise expressly provided, entitled to make a profit; he is not allowed to put himself in a position where his interest and his duty conflict. It does not appear to me that this rule is as has been said, founded upon principles of morality. I regard it rather as based on the consideration that, human nature being what it is, there is danger, in such circumstances, of the person holding a fiduciary position being swayed by interest rather than by duty, and thus prejudicing those whom he was bound to protect. It has, therefore, been deemed expedient to lay down this positive rule.

It is evident, even in these earlier cases, that the emphasis for the basis of the rules is the practical effect the absence of such rules might have on the conduct of the trustees and their ability to carry out their obligations and not because of some moral turpitude to be attached to a breach of trust allegation. As we shall see later, the honesty and good faith of the breaching fiduciary are irrelevant considerations.

8.40 The strictness of equity's application of the duties not to make unauthorized gains and/or place oneself in a position of potential conflict of interest is most evident in the House of Lords' decision, *Boardman v Phipps*.[44] In summary:

- The appellants were the solicitor ('Boardman') to a trust fund made up of the estate of the late C W Phipps and one of its beneficiaries.

- By virtue of their involvement with the trust, they obtained information about the value of shares in a company in which the trust had invested.

- They were concerned about the trust's return on this investment and believed this to be due to poor management on the company's part.

- Boardman sought to persuade the beneficiary to purchase shares in the company, independent of the trust, so as to have greater influence with the board.

- The beneficiary would only do so if Boardman would do likewise.

- The trustee of the trust fund was well aware of all of these events and gave his approval. The daughter of the deceased also approved. The third trustee was senile.

---

42 (1854) 2 Eq Rep 1281.
43 [1896] AC 44, 51.
44 [1967] 2 AC 46.

- The plan was only partially a success as they failed to obtain all the shares they wanted.

- They thereafter entered into a period of negotiations, with Boardman acting on behalf of the trust.

- During the course of those negotiations, the beneficiary and Boardman obtained further information they would not otherwise have been able to obtain and armed with that further information, they made a further bid for the outstanding shares.

- Before bidding, Boardman wrote to the remaining beneficiaries and obtained their consent. The widow was not consulted before she died.

- The bid was successful and ultimately it proved possible to distribute the company's assets amongst the solicitor, the trust and the beneficiary. Each party made a substantial profit.

- Wilberforce J held that the shares and profits obtained by Boardman and the beneficiary were to be held on constructive trust. This was affirmed in the Court of Appeal and by majority in the House of Lords.

- The majority considered Boardman to be in a fiduciary position, as sometime solicitor to the trustees and that the disclosure made to obtain the beneficiaries' consent was not adequate.[45]

- All agreed that Boardman and the beneficiary had acted in good faith. Indeed, it was the absence of bad faith on his part which led, in part, to Vicount Dilhorne and Lord Upjohn dissenting.

- Their Lordships appear to have been agreed on the relevant general principle applicable on the facts, namely that a fiduciary must not place himself in a position of conflict of interest.[46] Lord Cohen remarked that 'an agent is, in my opinion, liable to account for profits which he makes out of the trust property if there is a possibility of conflict between his interest and his duty to his principal.'[47]

- As an alternative, Lords Hodson and Guest considered that Boardman may have misused trust property—the relevant property being the confidential information he obtained as to the company during the negotiations.[48]

---

45 One oddity about the decision is the basis upon which the House of Lords concluded that the beneficiary owed fiduciary duties to other beneficiaries. Normally that would not be the case e.g. *Featherstonhaugh v Fenwick* (1810) 17 Ves 298; *Kennedy v De Trafford* [1897] AC 180, 186–90. Lord Cohen observed it would be a strange result if the solicitor were liable but the beneficiary was not.
46 See also *Bhullar v Bhullar* [2003] 2 BCLC 241, [27] (Parker LJ).
47 [1967] 2 AC 46 at 103.
48 Lord Cohen did not consider the information to be 'property in the strict sense' [103] and Lord Upjohn did not consider the information fell within the definition of 'trust assets' [127–8]. A similar point was conceded in *Crown Dilmum plc v Sutton* [2004] 1 BCLC 468 The fiduciary duty

8.41   The decision in *Boardman v Phipps* raised a question as to just how likely must the conflict of interest be in order to bring the rule into play. In that case, it was invoked merely because the solicitor had previously acted as a solicitor to the trustees and *may* have been asked to provide advice on further purchases of the shares. The majority of their Lordships considered that sufficient to create the relevant conflict of interest.[49] But it is odd that none of their Lordships gave any thought to the practical issue that had the trustees subsequently approached Boardman to seek his legal advice he could very properly have declined to act on the grounds of conflict of interest. The conflict of interest would surely only have arisen had Boardman agreed to act and that would arise only after he had been asked to act. We did not even get to first base on the facts. Nevertheless, this was considered by the majority to be sufficient to establish a real sensible possibility of conflict of interest.[50]

8.42   Just standing back and considering the outcome in *Boardman v Phipps*, it is a perfect illustration of the severity of equity's application of these rules and duties on fiduciaries. Boardman was held liable even though he acted honestly throughout, he used his own considerable skill and care to generate the profit, he acted in the best interests of the trust, he, at least, tried to and thought he had obtained all necessary consents from the beneficiaries, and the trust financially benefited from his actions in a manner which would not otherwise have been possible. The decision is an important wake-up call to anyone contemplating committing a fraud via their position as a fiduciary.

D. Remedies for Breach of Fiduciary Duty

8.43   A breach of fiduciary duty may lead to both personal and proprietary remedies. Our focus is, of course, on the imposition of a constructive trust but it is as well to be aware of the availability of personal remedies.

---

lasts only so long as the confidential information remains confidential: *A-G v Blake* [1998] 1 All ER 833, 842 (Lord Woolf MR); [2000] 4 All ER 385 (HL).

49   In *Boardman v Phipps* [1967] 2 AC 46, 124, Lord Upjohn said the phrase 'possibly may conflict' means: 'that the reasonable man looking at the relevant facts and circumstances of the particular case would think that there was a real sensible possibility of conflict; not that you could imagine some situation arising which might, in some conceivable possibility in events not contemplated as real sensible possibilities by any reasonable person, result in a conflict.'

50   In *Industrial Development Consultants v Cooley* [1972] 1 WLR 443, a director of a company was approached by the Gas Board and offered a contract in his personal capacity and not in the name of the company. The director feigned illness, left the company's employment and entered into the contract. The director was found to hold the contract on constructive trust. Roskill J estimated that there existed only a 10% chance [454F] of persuading the Gas Board to deal direct with the company and that sufficed.

(a) Personal remedy

There are, in effect, two main reasons why a claimant may pursue a personal rem-   **8.44**
edy instead of a proprietary remedy.

First, so long as the defendant remains solvent, there is no need to consider the   **8.45**
imposition of a proprietary remedy since the equitable duty to account to the principal will ensure that the breaching fiduciary is stripped of all benefits and profits
obtained as a result of the breach. So, in the leading case of *Boardman v Phipps*,[51] a
constructive trust was not imposed because, since Boardman was solvent, it was not
necessary. A personal claim based upon the equitable duty to account sufficed.[52]

Secondly, even if the fiduciary is solvent, there is no point claiming only a propri-   **8.46**
etary remedy in circumstances where it is clear that some or all of the profits
obtained no longer exist and there are no traceable proceeds left in the hands of
the fiduciary. In such an event, it is preferable to assert a personal claim for the full
amount, so long as the fiduciary is solvent. Similarly, if the value of the property
obtained as a profit of the breach has declined in value since the date it was received
by the fiduciary, the fiduciary is obliged to pay for the difference between the
present value of the asset and the value of the asset when received by the fiduciary.[53]

(b) An account of profits

This is a personal remedy[54] for the breaching fiduciary to disclose and pay up all   **8.47**
the profits he has made as a result of his breach. As a personal remedy, it does not
provide any priority in the insolvency of the fiduciary.

In determining just how much a fiduciary must pay under his equitable duty to   **8.48**
account, the cases reveal that the following approaches can or may be adopted.

- The equitable duty to account relates to the actual or net profit obtained by the
  breaching fiduciary and not his gross receipts. The fiduciary can therefore
  recover his costs and expenses.[55]

---

[51] [1967] 2 AC 46. See Birks, *An Introduction to the Law of Restitution* (Oxford University Press, 1985), 388.

[52] It is possible to read Lord Guest as suggesting that a constructive trust was imposed over the shareholding: [1967] 2 AC 46, 117: 'I have no hesitation in coming to the conclusion that the appellants hold the Lester & Harris shares as constructive trustees . . .'. See *A-G for Hong Kong v Reid* [1994] 1 AC 324, 338. Some of the confusion may well stem from the use by Lord Guest in *Boardman* of the phrase 'constructive trustee'. We have earlier noted that this phrase was some-times used as a shorthand for the personal liability to account arising under liability for dishonest assistance—none of which requires the establishment of a constructive trust per se.

[53] *A-G for Hong Kong v Reid* [1994] 1 AC 324.

[54] In *Warman v Dwyer* (1995) 128 ALR 201, 208, the High Court of Australia held that an account 'gives rise to a liability, even in the case of fiduciary, which is personal'.

[55] *Regal Hastings Limited v Gulliver* [1967] 2 AC 134, 154 (Lord Wright); *Nottingham University v Fishel* [2000] ICR 1462, 1498–9; *JJ Harrison (Properties) Ltd v Harrison* [2002] 1 BCLC 162, [50]; *Stocking v Montila* [2005] EWHC 2210 (Ch) at [43].

- When assessing what profit or advantage has been obtained, it is necessary to look at the whole situation in the round (per Dunn LJ in *O'Sullivan v Management Agencies Ltd*)[56] before deciding what is practically just (per Fox LJ in *O'Sullivan v Management Agencies Ltd*).[57]

- In some cases, such as *Boardman v Phipps*, the court will give an allowance for the skill and effort of the fiduciary, in some they will not (*Guinness v Saunders*).[58]

- In some, such as *Re Badfinger Music v Evans*,[59] the fiduciary was able to recover any fees paid to third parties in order to create the profit (irrespective of whether such fees were flat-fee or percentage based) and even the fiduciary could be paid on a percentage fee basis (although not on facts); *Marshall v Holloway*[60] (prospective and retrospective allowance given to the trustee of will trusts to compensate him for time and effort expended on the trusts); *Foster v Spencer*[61] (trustees of cricket club land permitted an allowance for past services to sell club and obtain another site); *Redwood Music v Chappell & Co Ltd*[62] (liberal allowance for skill and labour granted to music publishers who had innocently infringed a song's copyright). See also the Australian case of *Warman v Dyer*,[63] where the fiduciary is allowed a share of the profits made.

- The above are all exceptions to the general rule that fiduciaries are not to be paid any remuneration or retain any profits unless expressly agreed otherwise. Remuneration and fees are to be paid only in exceptional circumstances since there is an obvious risk of undermining the general rule.[64]

- Lord Goff in *Guinness* said:

  Plainly it would be inconsistent with this long-established principle to award remuneration in such circumstances as of right on the basis of a quantum meruit claim. But the principle does not altogether exclude the possibility that an equitable allowance might be made in respect of services rendered. That such an allowance

---

56 [1985] QB 428, 458E–H.

57 ibid, 466.

58 [1990] 2 AC 663.

59 (2002) EMLR 2. The Court held that the claimant who had remastered a recording of a live concert in a fiduciary capacity for other members of the group was entitled to recover remuneration for his work, notwithstanding the general rule against a fiduciary making profits.

60 (1820) 2 Swans 432.

61 [1996] 2 All ER 672.

62 [1982] RPC 109.

63 [1995] 128 ALR 201.

64 See Lord Templeman in *Guinness plc v Saunders* [1990] 2 AC 663. At 690D–E: 'As a result of the rule that a trustee cannot make a profit from his trust, trustees and executors are generally entitled to no allowance for their care and trouble. This rule is so strict that even if a trustee or executor has sacrificed much time in carrying on a business as directed by the trust, he will usually be allowed nothing as compensation for his personal trouble or loss or time.' Lord Templeman accepted there existed exceptions to this general rule (at 694B–C).

may be made to a trustee for work performed by him for the benefit of the trust, even though he was not in the circumstances entitled to remuneration under the terms of the trust deed, is now well established. In *Phipps v Boardman* . . . the solicitor to a trust and one of the beneficiaries were held accountable to another beneficiary for a proportion of the profits made by them from the sale of shares bought by them with the aid of information gained by the solicitor when acting for the trust. Wilberforce J directed that, when accounting for such profits, not merely should a deduction be made for expenditure which was necessary to enable the profit to be realised, but also a liberal allowance or credit should be made for their work and skill. His reasoning was, at p.1018:

'Moreover, account must naturally be taken of the expenditure which was necessary to enable the profit to be realised. But, in addition to expenditure, should not the defendants be given an allowance or credit for their work and skill? This is a subject on which authority is scanty; but Cohen J in *Re MacAdam* [1946] Ch 73, 82 gave his support to an allowance of this kind to trustees for their services in acting as directors of a company. It seems to me that this transaction, ie the acquisition of a controlling interest in the company, was one of a special character calling for the exercise of a particular kind of professional skill. If Boardman had not assumed the role of seeing it through, the beneficiaries would have had to employ (and would, had they been well advised, have employed) an expert to do it for them. If the trustees had come to the court asking for liberty to employ such a person, they would in all probability have been authorised to do so, and to remunerate the person in question. It seems to me that it would be inequitable now for the beneficiaries to step in and take the profit without paying for the skill and labour which has produced it.'

Wilberforce J's decision, including his decision to make such an allowance was later to be affirmed by the House of Lords . . .

It will be observed that the decision to make the allowance was founded upon the simple proposition that 'it would be inequitable now for the beneficiaries to step in and take the profit without paying for the skill and labour which has produced it.' Ex hypothesi, such an allowance would not in the circumstances be authorised by the terms of the trust deed; furthermore it was held that there had not been full and proper disclosure by the two defendants to the successful plaintiff beneficiary.

The inequity was found in the simple proposition that the beneficiaries were taking the profit although, if Mr Boardman, the solicitor had not done the work, they would have had to employ an expert to do the work for them in order to earn their profit.

The decision has to be reconciled with the fundamental principle that a trustee is not entitled to remuneration for services rendered by him to the trust except as expressly provided in the trust deed. Strictly speaking, it is irreconcilable with the rule as so stated. It seems to me, therefore, that it can only be reconciled with it to the extent that the exercise of the equitable jurisdiction does not conflict with the policy underlying the rule. And, as I see it, such a conflict will only be avoided if the exercise of the jurisdiction is restricted to those cases where it cannot have the effect of encouraging trustees in anyway to put themselves in a position where their interests conflict with their duties as trustees.

In *Guinness* itself, the director, Mr Ward, had undertaken conduct which the House **8.49** of Lords found created a 'stark conflict' with his duties as a director. Their Lordships were not prepared to circumvent the express provision in the Articles of Association for the grant of special remuneration by awarding remuneration under the court's inherent jurisdiction.

8.50 In *Re Badfinger*,[65] the Court considered Lord Goff's speech from *Guinness* set out above and drew the following conclusions as to when a fiduciary may be awarded some form of remuneration:

- Although some of the authorities had emphasized the honesty of the relevant fiduciaries, and no doubt that was a relevant factor, it was not decisive of whether to grant an award.

- Also relevant was whether the transaction was 'of a special character calling for the exercise of a particular kind of professional skill' (per Wilberforce J in *Phipps v Boardman*).

- Also relevant was whether the services can only realistically be supplied by the fiduciary: see *Bainbrigge v Blair*,[66] *Re Worthington*[67] and *Marshall v Holloway*.[68]

(c) Proprietary remedies

8.51 There is no doubt that where appropriate the court will grant a proprietary remedy by way of the imposition of a constructive trust over the profits obtained by a fiduciary in breach of his duties.

8.52 In *Keech v Sandford*[69] the renewed lease must have been held on a trust for the trust, since the court ordered that it be transferred to the infant beneficiary (i.e. the infant beneficiary must have had a proprietary interest in the renewed lease) and the breaching fiduciary was required to account for his profits.

8.53 In *Cook v Deeks*,[70] the Privy Council was dealing with a contract entered into by directors personally in breach of their fiduciary duties owed to the company. The Privy Council held that the relevant contract was held by the directors on trust for the company and was an asset of the company.

8.54 *Bhullar v Bhullar*[71] is a good illustration of the courts' approach. The case involved two families operating an investment company. Relations broke down and it was agreed that until things were sorted out the company should not invest in any further property. A property next door to one of its existing properties came onto the market and one of the directors purchased it. Thereafter there was a s 459 petition

---

65 (2002) EMLR 2.
66 (1845) 8B–Beav 588, 596.
67 [1954] 1 All ER 677.
68 1820) 2 Swans 432.
69 (1726) Sel Cas Ch 61.
70 [1916] 1 AC 554.
71 [2003] EWCA Civ 424, [2003] 2 BCLC 241 CA.

which ultimately failed but during it the court held that the property was held on constructive trust for the company. The matter was appealed.

On appeal, reference was made to Millett LJ's analysis of constructive trusteeship **8.55** in *Paragon Finance plc v DB Thakerar & Co*[72] where his Lordship indicated the need to distinguish between the constructive trusteeship which arises from a wrongful act, where there is no pre-existing fiduciary relationship, and a case (such as is being dealt with in this chapter) where the fiduciary relationship pre-exists the wrongful act.

It was argued, on appeal, that in the second category of case, the wrongful conduct **8.56** had to involve some form of improper dealing with property belonging to the *cestui que* trust. Since the property purchased next door to the existing property was not something then owned by the cestui que trust, there could be no breach of fiduciary duty.

This argument was rightly rejected by Jonathan Parker LJ.[73] His Lordship reiter- **8.57** ated the rule laid down in *Aberdeen Rly Co v Blaikie Bros*,[74] endorsed as 'inflexible' in *Bray v Ford*,[75] that no fiduciary:

> shall be allowed to enter into engagements in which he has, or can have, a personal interest conflicting, or which may possibly conflict,[76] with the interests of whose whom he is bound to protect.

To restrict the rule to interference where the *cestui que* trust has a beneficial interest in the corporate opportunity or property would be 'too formalistic and restrictive an approach'.[77]

One instance where it may be inaccurate to talk of the imposition of a constructive **8.58** trust is where a trustee acquires a substituted asset with misappropriated trust monies. In such a situation, it is said, correctly, that the substituted asset is simply the traceable proceeds of the monies which were already held on express trust.[78]

---

[72] [1999] 1 All ER 400, 408.
[73] *Bhullar v Bhullar* [2003] 2 BCLC 241 CA, [27]–[32].
[74] (1854) 1 Macq 461, 471.
[75] [1896] AC 44, 51.
[76] Jonathan Parker LJ, following Lord Upjohn in *Boardman v Phipps* [1967] 2 AC 46, 124, agreed that the phrase 'possibly may conflict' means where there was a 'real sensible possibility of conflict' [2003] 2 BCLC 241, [30].
[77] ibid, [28].
[78] This is precisely what Birks called 'the persistence of fiction'. For Birks, the reason why the newly acquired property is held on trust is not because the beneficiaries owned the monies used to purchase that property but because otherwise the breaching trustee would be unjustly enriched. This view was firmly rejected in *Foskett v McKeown* [2001] 1 AC 102; see also Lord Millett, 'Proprietary Restitution' in Degeling and Edelman (eds), *Equity in Commercial Law* (Law Book Co of Australasia, 2005), ch 12; D Fox, 'Overreaching' in Birks and Pretto (eds), *Breach of Trust* (Hart Publishing, 2002), ch 4.

8.59 Accordingly, rather than hold the substituted asset under a constructive trust, it is in fact held under the original trust, there being no need to resort to the imposition of a constructive trust.[79] Such reasoning has no application to those fiduciaries who do not hold assets on express trusts. So, for example, a company director does not hold the company's assets on trust although he is clearly in a fiduciary relationship with the company. For such fiduciaries, the imposition of the constructive trust will follow any unauthorized gains.

---

[79] *Foskett v McKeown* [2001] 1 AC 102, 130. Discussed in Underhill and Hayton, *Law of Trusts and Trustees* (17th edn), paras [33.4]–[33.6].

PART V

STATUTORY LIABILITY

9

OVERVIEW OF INSOLVENCY-RELATED CLAIMS

Chapters 10 to 13 are concerned with statutory claims which are available to pro- **9.01**
tect genuine creditors in circumstances where steps are taken by an individual to
place his own assets, alternatively the assets of a company, effectively out of the
reach of creditors. As will be seen, commercial fraud litigators must have a sound
grasp of the general principles of insolvency and company law and particular
knowledge of the claims which are discussed in these chapters. Those engaged in
commercial wrongdoing or fraud will often try to circumvent the usual rules of
insolvency so that assets which should go to their own or their company's genuine
creditors are in fact transferred to the wrongdoers or their connected associates.

Chapter 10 focuses on the claims based upon transactions entered into at an under- **9.02**
value. For companies, the relevant provision is s 238 of the Insolvency Act 1986
whereas for individuals, it is s 339 of the Insolvency Act 1986. This is a claim which
can only be brought by the relevant office-holder. It is not a claim which the victim
of such a transaction (i.e. another creditor) can properly bring himself or itself.

Chapter 11 focuses on transactions amounting to a preference pursuant to s 239 **9.03**
of the Insolvency Act 1986 (in respect of companies) and to s 340 of the Insolvency
Act 1986 (in respect of individuals). Again, only the appropriate office-holder has
the *locus standi* to bring the statutory claims.

Chapter 12 is concerned with transactions defrauding creditors contrary to s 423 **9.04**
of the Insolvency Act 1986. Unlike both transactions entered into at an undervalue and transactions amounting to a preference, claims under s 423 can be
brought by anyone who is a 'victim' of such a transaction, i.e. anyone who is capable of being prejudiced by it. The relevant company need not be insolvent or in
administration and/or the individual need not be in bankruptcy before any claim
under s 423 is made.

Chapter 13 briefly examines a miscellaneous category of claims which may be **9.05**
relevant to a commercial fraud litigator. The chapter includes consideration of

(i) transfers entered into after the commencement of a winding up, sometimes known as the fraudster's last throw of the dice to get assets beyond the reach of genuine creditors or victims of his or its fraudulent activities; (ii) charges which have not been registered but need to be. Again, this may be an attempt by the fraudster to place certain assets beyond creditors by favouring other creditors with invalid charges, thereby giving them priority in any distribution; (iii) floating charges for past value which are used to provide certain creditors with secured status notwithstanding they have not lent any additional funds; (iv) the final category of claim is slightly different from the rest, being concerned with extortionate credit transactions.

9.06 Although the provisions which will be examined in Chapters 10 to 13 generally apply both to individuals as well as companies, it is an obvious fact that commercial fraud often involves the use of corporate identities both to carry out the fraud and ultimately to hide its proceeds. Fraudsters like companies. They can be created at will and provide the cover of anonymity those undertaking fraudulent conduct crave and require. A company, taken off the shelf, has a brand new identity, able to enter the commercial world without the stigma of any previous wrongdoing associated with those ultimately owning the new company or pulling the strings behind it.

9.07 When the company's financial standing collapses, as it does whenever one discovers the underlying fraud, those standing behind the company are often content to allow it to collapse, having undertaken steps to move assets out of the company and therefore away from the normal reach of its creditors, the victims of the fraud.

9.08 Chapters 10 to 13 are concerned with just that sort of behaviour. They will focus on those provisions specifically dealing with companies but, where possible, cross-reference will be made to the analogous provisions for individuals, which do not differ greatly.

9.09 One significant feature about these statutory claims is that in many cases the victim of the fraud will not himself be able to bring any claim under the relevant statutory provision. Rather, some of the claims are expressly to be brought, if at all, by the office-holder, being either the liquidator, administrator or trustee in bankruptcy. Thus, a claimant will not have the same sort of control over some of these claims as it would have in respect of typical private law claim. Further, in some instances, any claim will be brought, if at all, on behalf of a class of victims, and not just one individual victim.

9.10 Unlike many of the areas this book has looked at, where the claims are in their infancy and/or are still in development, this is an area where matters of construction and interpretation at least have the benefit of the wording of the relevant statute and a statutory structure to provide the context for that interpretation.

10

TRANSACTIONS AT AN UNDERVALUE: INSOLVENCY ACT 1986, SECTION 238[1]

A. Overview of Claim

10.01 A claim for a transaction at an undervalue under s 238 of the Insolvency Act 1986[2] requires the following conditions to be satisfied. The company:

- must be in liquidation or administration;
- have entered into a transaction;
- at the relevant time;[3]
- for an undervalue; and
- was unable to pay its debts at that time or as a consequence of that transaction.

10.02 The relevant application can only be made by the 'office-holder' being either the liquidator or the administrator (in the case of corporate insolvency)[4] or the trustee in bankruptcy (in the case of personal insolvency).[5] The transaction at an undervalue must have been entered into at the relevant time. In the case of a corporation, that means it must have been entered into within two years prior to

---

[1] See John Armour, 'Transactions at an Undervalue' in J Armour and H Bennett (eds), *Vulnerable Transactions in Corporate Insolvency* (Hart Publishing, 2003), 37.
[2] All section references in the chapter are to the Insolvency Act 1986, unless otherwise stated.
[3] Insolvency Act 1986, s 240.
[4] Insolvency Act 1986, s 238(1) and (2).
[5] Insolvency Act 1986, s 339(1).

the successful petition for administration or winding up and, at the time, been insolvent or became so because of the transaction. In the case of an individual, the relevant period is five years prior to bankruptcy and again a requirement that at the time the transaction was entered into the individual was insolvent or became so as a consequence of the transaction.[6]

10.03 Even if all of the above is established, no order will be made if the company entered into the transaction in good faith and for the purposes of carrying on its business and at the relevant time there existed reasonable grounds for believing that the transaction would benefit the company.[7]

10.04 If the claim is established, the court may make such order as it sees fit for restoring the position to what it would have been if the company had not entered into the transaction.[8]

10.05 The requirements of a claim to set aside a transaction as being at an undervalue under s 238 have been set out above. The company (i) must be in liquidation or administration and (ii) must have entered into a transaction at an undervalue and (iii) was unable to pay its debts at that time or as a consequence of that transaction.

10.06 The victim of the commercial fraud conduct will need to persuade the office-holder, whether it be the administrator or liquidator, depending on the status of the company, to bring these proceedings. The fraud victim himself cannot bring these proceedings. In deciding whether or not it is worth persuading the office-holder, no doubt the victim will take into account the fact that should proceedings be commenced by the office-holder they will not be on behalf of the victim claimant alone but will be on behalf of all genuine unsecured creditors of the company. That will clearly have a bearing on the value to be attached to any such proceedings by the victim claimant.

B. Unable to Pay its Debts at the Time or as a Consequence[9]

10.07 Section 123 contains various tests to check on the solvency of a company, the two most important being inability to pay debts as they fall due and the 'balance sheet' test, i.e. that the company's liabilities exceed its assets. The burden of proof of this

---

6 ibid, s 341.

7 ibid, s 238(5).

8 ibid, s 238(3). Without prejudice to the generality of s 238(3), and subject to s 241(2), the court may make one of the orders set out in s 241(1).

9 See Armour, 'Transactions at an Undervalue' in Armour and Bennett (eds), *Vulnerable Transactions in Corporate Insolvency*, paras 2.33–2.49.

issue vests with the liquidator or administrator unless the relevant transaction was entered into with a 'connected' party under s 240(2) or with an 'associate' of a bankrupt individual under s 341(2), (3). If so, the relevant financial condition will be presumed.

C. What is the Relevant Time for the Transaction?

Where the relevant transaction involves a company, the transaction must have **10.08** been entered into during the two years ending with the onset of insolvency[10] *and* at the time of entering into the transaction the company was unable to pay its debts within s 123 or it became unable to do so as a result of entering into the transaction. In the case of individuals, the relevant period is five years.[11]

D. What is a Relevant 'Transaction'?

A relevant 'transaction' for the purposes of s 238 can take many different forms. **10.09** It is to be given a wide interpretation, so as to embrace gifts and obviously covers contractual arrangements but is not necessarily limited to just one contract.[12]

Although gifts are included they would appear to be an exception to the general **10.10** requirement that there must exist some form of *dealing* between the parties.[13] This is likely to have an important impact on the role that might be played by these provisions in a commercial fraud where the defaulting directors are simply using the company to move monies around. In *Re Taylor Sinclair (Capital) Ltd*,[14] Robert Englehart QC (sitting as Deputy High Court Judge) emphasized that there must be some form of dealing between the parties, even if it fell short of a contractual arrangement, to fall within s 238. On that basis the mere transmission by two cheques of £200,000 from the company to another entity, without more, was not

---

[10] Insolvency Act 1986, s 240.
[11] ibid, s 341(1)(a).
[12] *Department for Environment Food and Rural Affairs v Feakins* [2006] BPIR 895, para 78.
[13] See *Re Taylor Sinclair (Capital) Ltd v Jones* [2002] 1 BLCL 5. Professor Goode supports this interpretation: see *The Principles of Corporate Insolvency Law* (3rd edn, Thomson/Sweet and Maxwell, 2005), para 11-19. Not all commentators agree: Janet Ulph, *Commercial Fraud, Civil Liability, Human Rights and Money Laundering* (Oxford University Press, 2006), 314–15. On this issue, and for the reasons set out in the pages identified in *Commercial Fraud*, Professor Ulph's view is to be preferred as it gives greater room to manoeuvre in making use of this section as a weapon against commercial fraud.
[14] [2001] 2 BCLC 179.

a 'transaction' for the purposes of s 238. There was no 'dealing' between the entities. This is a very restrictive view of the legislation.

10.11 The definition of 'transaction' extends to linked contracts which go to make up the overall transaction into which the relevant parties entered.

10.12 A good illustration of the flexible interpretation to be attached to 'transaction' for present purposes is the House of Lords decision in *Phillips v Brewin Dolphin Bell Lawrie Ltd*.[15] This decision has been generally welcomed for its approach to identifying the relevant 'transaction' but has proved more controversial in its apparent advocation of hindsight valuation. The facts can be summarized as follows.

- The claimant company entered into an agreement with B Ltd to sell its stock-broking business for £1.25m.
- The relevant part of the business including goodwill was transferred to a wholly-owned subsidiary of the claimant.
- For tax and regulatory reasons, the sale was effected by two agreements:
  - One agreement sold the subsidiary's share capital to B Ltd for £1.
  - One agreement sublet computer equipment used in the business to B Ltd's parent company (P Ltd) for four years' annual rent of £312,500, contrary to the terms of the headlease.
- B Ltd made a loan of £312,500 to the claimant, to be set off against first rental payment.
- B Ltd had decided not to use the computer equipment to run the business.
- The owners of the computer equipment terminated the lease for non-payment.
- P Ltd claimed discharge from the computer sub-let.
- The claimant company was wound up.
- The judge held that payments under the sub-lease were not part of the consideration and so it was a transaction at an undervalue.
- The Court of Appeal dismissed the appeal on the basis that the share sale agreement alone was the relevant transaction and this was at an undervalue.

10.13 On appeal to the House of Lords, Lord Scott held:

> One must obviously start with the share sale agreement. That was the agreement under which [the claimant] agreed to divest itself of its allegedly valuable asset, namely the shares in [the business]. It is worth repeating the language of section 238(4)(b): 'the company [AJB] enters into a transaction [the share sale agreement] with that person [Brewer Dolphin] for a consideration the value of which . . .' etc. The subsection does not stipulate by what person or persons the consideration is to be provided. It simply directs attention to the consideration for which the company

---

[15] [2001] UKHL 2, [2001] 1 WLR 143.

has entered into the transaction. It may also involve an issue of law, for example, as to the construction of some document. But if a company agrees to sell an asset to A on terms that B agrees to enter into some collateral agreement with the company, the consideration for the asset will, in my opinion, be the combination of the consideration, if any, expressed in the agreement with A and the value of the agreement with B. In short, the issue in the present case is not, in my opinion, to identify the section 238(4) 'transaction'; the issue is to identify the section 238(4) 'consideration'.

10.14 Accordingly, the relevant consideration was not only the share sale agreement price but also the sub-lease agreement.

10.15 Having determined that both the share sale agreement and the sub-lease agreement had to be considered for the purposes of 'consideration' and 'transaction', the House of Lords then went on to determine the best method of calculating the value to be attached to this transaction.

E. Role of Hindsight in Valuation

10.16 Lord Scott's approach to assessing the value to be attributed to the transaction can be summarized as follows.

(a) Given the headlease contained an express prohibition on sub-letting and that any such sub-letting would amount to a breach entitling immediate termination of the headlease and with it the sub-lease (and recovery of computer equipment), Lord Scott considered the sub-lease to be precarious and speculative.

(b) He dismissed counsel's submission that the court should not take into account the *ex post facto* events of a failure to pay under the sub-lease in January 1990, a claim for return of the computer equipment by the headlessors, a letter from the parent company accepting the headlessors' alleged repudiatory conduct, and that the claimant company had gone into compulsory winding up. As Lord Scott concluded: 'These events would inevitably have led the head lessors to terminate the head leases and recover their equipment, if they had not done so previously, thereby bringing the sublease to an end.'[16]

> In valuing the covenant as at that date, the critical uncertainty is whether the sublease would survive for the four years necessary to enable all the four £312,500 payments to fall due, or would survive long enough to enable some of them to fall due, or would come to an end before any had fallen due. Where the events, or some of them, on which the uncertainties depend have actually happened, it seems to me unsatisfactory and unnecessary for the court to wear blinkers and pretend that it does not know what has happened . . . For the purposes of s238(4) however, and the

---

[16] [2001] 1 WLR 143, [26].

> valuation of the consideration for which a company has entered into a transaction, reality should, in my opinion, be given precedence over speculation. I would hold, taking account of the events that took place in the early months of 1990, that the value of the parent company's covenant to pay in the sublease of 10 November 1989 was nil.[17]

10.17 Whilst some have suggested that Lord Scott was thereby applying an approach based upon hindsight,[18] others, such as Professor Goode, consider the matter is more complex than that:

> Lord Scott's speech has generated much debate on the use of hindsight to determine a value at the time of the transaction. But it seems clear that Lord Scott was not in truth applying a hindsight test; rather he was relying on evidence of subsequent events to show that from the outset the covenant under the sub-lease was so precarious and its value so speculative that even at the time it was entered into a bank or finance house with knowledge of the surrounding circumstances would not have attributed any value to the sub-lease covenant. In this connection it is helpful to recall the distinction drawn by the accountancy profession between adjusting and non-adjusting events in determining whether a balance sheet value should be corrected by reference to subsequent facts. In the present context an adjusting event is one which helps to establish the value of consideration at the transaction date, while a non-adjusting event is one which simply reduces or increases such value at the time the event occurs. It is obvious that a mere decline in the value of consideration by reason of an event after the transaction date is of no relevance whatsoever in determining whether the transaction was at an undervalue. But *Brewer Dolphin* did not concern a non-adjusting event; Lord Scott relied on the post-transaction termination of the sub-lease as validating what would anyway have been the perception at the time of the sub-lease of the nil value of the sub-lessee's covenant. In accountancy terms the termination was an adjusting event.[19]

10.18 There is no doubt that Lord Scott considered the sub-lease to be precarious and speculative at the outset and such a view was *not* based on what in fact happened but rather on the fact that there was an absolute bar on any sub-letting. 'So the head leases became terminable at any time by the head lessors and the equipment comprised in the sublease could at any time have been repossessed by the head lessors.'[20] There is no doubt, Lord Scott then went on to consider what in fact happened and concluded that gave the sub-lease a nil valuation.

10.19 Professor Goode's analysis is what one would hope Lord Scott had adopted, but the problem is that some of the language used by Lord Scott is not obviously in

---

[17] ibid, [26].
[18] E.g. Ulph, *Commercial Fraud*, 313.
[19] Goode, *The Principles of Corporate Insolvency Law* (3rd edn), para 11-31.
[20] *Phillips v Brewin Dolphin* [2001] 1 WLR 143, 152 [22].

support of such an interpretation. See, for example, the very next sentence from Lord Scott:

> After all, if, following the signing of the sub-lease, [the claimant] had taken the sub-lease to a bank or finance house and had tried to raise money on the security of the covenant, I do not believe that the bank or finance house, with knowledge about the circumstances surrounding the sub-lease, would have attributed any value at all to the sub-lease covenant.[21]

10.20 What is meant by 'knowledge about the circumstances surrounding the sub-lease'? If this is intended to include knowledge of the factors which occurred in early 1990, as set out above, then it does look like he is taking into account subsequent events. If, however, this phrase is a reference to the matters which were generally known as at the time of the transaction which rendered the transaction speculative and precarious, then it would appear to be support for an approach based on what a willing buyer, properly informed of events, would be prepared to pay for the transaction.

10.21 In *Re Thoars*[22] the Vice-Chancellor stated that he took the ratio of *Phillips v Brewer* to be:

> (1) the value of the consideration in money or money's worth is to be assessed as at the date of the transaction, (2) if at that date value is dependent on the occurrence or non-occurrence of some event and that event occurs before the assessment of value has been completed then the valuer may have regard to it, but (3) the valuer is entitled, indeed bound, to take account of all other matters relevant to the determination of value as at the date of the transaction.

10.22 The emphasis of approach on the part of the Vice-Chancellor is the need to value as at the date of the transaction, but the valuer being entitled to take later events into account in carrying out that valuation. However, it is clear, from the example of the lottery ticket, that the Vice-Chancellor is not advocating an approach where hindsight plays a major role. The fact that the lottery ticket ultimately won is something that the valuer may rely upon but it is not likely to carry much weight, if any, on the valuation exercise which will be based on whether anyone would pay more than the stake price for that ticket before the draw has been carried out. The problem with this approach is that on the lottery ticket example the valuation must properly take place without regard to whether it is in fact a winning ticket. For if it was a winning ticket, and this was something that was known, with hindsight, the reality is that yes, people would pay a lot more than the stake price for that ticket. It would have been preferable if it had been said that one must value the ticket as at the date of the transaction or purchase, attaching a value based upon its likely chances of being the winning ticket. There is little point in saying the fact

---

[21] [2001] 1 WLR 143.
[22] [2003] 1 BCLC 499, 504G–H.

it is a winning ticket is something that can be considered, although ultimately the valuer should accord it little weight. That would appear to be a most complicated manner of approaching this issue.

F. Ascribing a Precise Valuation

10.23 Whilst the court will always be encouraged, wherever possible, to ascribe precise valuations to the consideration received and given in respect of relevant transactions,[23] the Court of Appeal in *Re Thoars sub-nom Reid v Ramlort Ltd*[24] held that it was not necessary to identify the precise valuations of either consideration in order for s 339(3)(c) to apply. Having determined that s 238(4)(b) and s 339(3)(c) operate in the same way, Jonathan Parker LJ continued:

> 102. . . . For present purposes, the critical words in each of those paragraphs are the words 'significantly less'. For there to be a transaction by an 'individual' (whom I will call 'the debtor') at an undervalue within the meaning of those paragraphs, the value in money or money's worth, from the debtor's point of view, of the consideration for which he enters into the transaction (I will call it 'the incoming value') must be '*significantly less*' than the value in money or money's worth, again from the debtor's point of view, of the '*consideration provided*' by the debtor – that is to say, the value in money or money's worth of the totality of whatever it is that the debtor is parting with under the transaction (I will call it 'the outgoing value.').

> 103. Thus, there is nothing in the express provisions of paragraph (c) of section 339(3) which requires the court to ascribe a precise figure either to the outgoing value or to the incoming value. On the face of the paragraph, it will apply whenever the court is satisfied that, whatever the precise values may be, the incoming value is on any view '*significantly less*' than the outgoing value. *Woodward*[25] was just such a case.

> 104. Nor, in my judgment, is there any need to imply into paragraph (c) any further requirement in relation to the determination of the incoming value or the outgoing value. In particular, I can see no reason why the court, if it considers it appropriate to do so, should not address the issue of undervalue by taking from a range of possible values those which are the most favourable to the party seeking to uphold the transaction. If, even on that basis, the incoming value is '*significantly less*' than the outgoing value, paragraph (c) will apply. Thus I can see nothing in paragraph (c) to prevent the court from proceeding on the basis of a finding as to the maximum value for the incoming value, and/or a finding as to the minimum value for the outgoing value.

10.24 This view of the Court of Appeal appears to be at odds with that of Mummery LJ in *National Westminster Bank plc v Jones*.[26] In that case, Mummery LJ insisted that

---

[23] *Reid v Ramlort Ltd* [2004] EWCA Civ 800; [2005] 1 BCLC 331 (CA) [105].

[24] [2004] EWCA Civ 800, [2005] 1 BCLC 331 (CA).

[25] This is a reference to *Agricultural Mortgage Corporation plc v Woodward & Anor* [1995] 1 BCLC 1—a s 423 case.

[26] [2002] 1BCLC 55 (a s 423 case).

s 423 of the Insolvency Act 1986 required a comparison to be made between two figures where the court arrives at a conclusion based upon actual values. Even if a range is disclosed on the evidence, Mummery LJ insisted that the court determine the actual value against which the consideration for the transaction was to be measured. In *Reid*, the Court of Appeal said that Mummery LJ's comments were to be considered in their context of an allegation that the court should approach the issue of undervalue the same as it does negligent valuations. Jonathan Parker LJ remarked:

> . . . that contention involves the proposition that, notwithstanding a finding by the court that the incoming value is significantly less than the outgoing value, nevertheless the transaction is not be characterized as a transaction at an undervalue if the amount of the shortfall lies within some 'acceptable' range of values. In rejecting that contention I do not understand Mummery LJ to be saying that, in making its findings as to value, the court may not take from a range of possible values those values which are most favourable to the party seeking to uphold the transaction and make findings to that effect, whether as to the maximum figure for the incoming value or (as in the instant case) as to the minimum figure for the outgoing value.[27]

The views of Jonathan Parker LJ must also be set against those of Millett J in *Re* **10.25**
MC Bacon,[28] when discussing the correct approach to s 238(4)(b):

> To come within [section 238(4)(b)] the transaction must be:
>
> (1) entered into by the company;
> (2) for a consideration;
> (3) the value of which measured in money or money's worth;
> (4) is significantly less than the value;
> (5) also measured in money or money's worth;
> (6) of the consideration provided by the company.
>
> It requires a comparison to be made between the value obtained by the company for the transaction and the value of the consideration provided by the company. Both values must be measurable in money or money's worth and both must be considered from the company's point of view.

Millett J's views are very much premised upon the need to examine each transac- **10.26**
tion individually and consider the relative value of consideration flowing in either direction. Indeed, it is impossible to see how the section can be properly applied without a detailed examination of each individual transaction and the weighing up of the relative consideration for each. Although it is difficult to be precise as to

---

27 [2005] 1 BCLC 331, [106].
28 [1990] BCC 78, 92, aff'd in *National Bank of Kuwait v Menzies Ltd* [1994] 2 BCLC 306, 319; *Agricultural Mortgage Corp v Woodward* [1995] 1 BCLC 1, 9; *Phillips v Brewin Dolphin Bell Lawrie* [2001] UKHL 2, [21]; [2001] 1 WLR 143, 151.

what will amount to a 'significant' difference, it has been suggested,[29] based upon *National Westminster Bank plc v Jones*[30] that a difference of 15% or more may well be considered 'significant' for these purposes. Certainly, in other contexts, a 7% difference from expert valuation has not been considered 'substantial'.[31]

G. No Order if Company Acted in Good Faith and Reasonably

10.27 The fact that the court determines that a particular transaction is at an undervalue does not mean that it will automatically be set aside. Pursuant to s 238(5), the court 'shall' not make an order under s 238 if it is satisfied that such a transaction was entered into by the company in good faith and for the purpose of carrying on its business and at the time it did so there were reasonable grounds for believing that the transaction would benefit the company.[32]

H. Protection of Third Party Interests

10.28 Once the court determines a particular transaction to be one at an undervalue there is a risk that any order to restore the *status quo ante* is likely to have some form of impact on the interests of any third party who has purchased the asset from the entity who was a party to the transaction at an undervalue. In such circumstances s 241(2)(a) provides statutory protection by ensuring that any order under s 238 does not prejudice any interest in property which was acquired by a third party in good faith and for value.

10.29 In addition, a person who received a benefit from the transaction or the preference in good faith and for value shall not be required to pay a sum to the office-holder except where that person was a party to the transaction or the payment is to be in respect of a preference given to that person at a time when he was a creditor of the company.[33]

---

[29] J Armour, 'Transactions at an Undervalue' in Armour and Bennett (eds), *Vulnerable Transactions in Corporate Insolvency*, 68.

[30] [2001] 1 BCLC 98, 129; aff'd [2001] EWCA Civ 1541, [2002] 1 BCLC 55.

[31] *Re London Local Residential (No 2)* [2005] BPIR 163, [17].

[32] See *Re Barton Manufacturing Co Ltd* [1999] 1 BCLC 740 (Harman J: defence under s 238(5) failed). As recognized by Harman J, this defence would require a high volume of evidence to support it: see also D Staphos, [2001] 1 Journal of Corporate Law Studies 333, 353.

[33] Insolvency Act 1986, s 241(2)(b).

Section 241(2A) provides some guidance as to when a third party will be treated **10.30** as not acting in good faith. Such a third party will be deemed not to be acting in good faith if:

(a) he had notice of the relevant surrounding circumstances and of the relevant proceedings;[34] or
(b) he was connected with, or was an associate of, either the company in question or the person with whom that company entered into the transaction or to whom the company gave a preference.

I. Orders Available to the Court

In the event that the court does determine a particular transaction to be at an **10.31** undervalue and none of the defences to making an order arise on the facts, then the court has a wide ambit of potential orders it can impose to restore the position.

Without prejudice to that wide ambit, s 241(1) identifies certain specific orders **10.32** available to the court as follows:

(a) require any property transferred as part of the transaction, or in connection with the giving of the preference, to be vested in the company;
(b) require any property to be so vested if it represents in any person's hands the application either of the proceeds of sale of property so transferred or of money so transferred;
(c) release or discharge (in whole or in part) any security given by the company;
(d) require any person to pay, in respect of benefits received by him from the company, such sums to the office-holder as the court may direct;
(e) provide for any surety or guarantor whose obligations to any person were released or discharged (in whole or in part) under the transaction, or by the giving of the preference, to be under such new or revived obligations to that person as the court thinks appropriate;
(f) provide for security to be provided for the discharge of any obligation imposed by or arising under the order, for such an obligation to be charged on any property and for the security or charge to have the same priority as a security or charge released or discharged (in whole or in part) under the transaction or by the giving of the preference; and

---

[34] The Insolvency Act 1986, s 241(3) defines surrounding circumstances as being the fact the company has entered into a transaction at an undervalue or the circumstances amounted to a preference. S 241(3A), (3B) and (3C) set out the facts that need to be known by the third party so to have knowledge of the relevant proceedings.

(g) provide for the extent to which any person whose property is vested by the order in the company, or on whom obligations are imposed by the order, is to be able to prove in the winding up of the company for debts or other liabilities which arose from, or were released or discharged (in whole or in part) under or by, the transaction or the giving of the preference.

11

PREFERENCES: INSOLVENCY ACT 1986, SECTION 239

A. Overview of Claim

A claim that a transaction amounts to a preference for the purposes of s 239 of the **11.01** Insolvency Act 1986 must satisfy the following conditions.[1] The company must:

- be in liquidation or administration;
- have given a preference to a creditor, surety or guarantor by doing something or suffering something to be done;
- within the relevant time;
- have been influenced by a desire to improve the position of the preferred person;
- have been unable to pay its debts within s 123 of the Insolvency Act 1986 either at the time of or in consequence of entering into the transaction.

Only the office-holder (being either the liquidator or the administrator) can bring **11.02** a claim under s 238. In the case of an individual, it is the trustee in bankruptcy who decides whether to bring these proceedings under s 340.

---

[1] The equivalent claim in respect of an individual is under the Insolvency Act 1986, s 340. (Please note that all section references in this chapter are to the Insolvency Act 1986, unless otherwise stated.)

11.03 If the claim is established the court may make such order as it thinks fit for restoring the position to what it would have been if the company had not given that preference.[2]

B. Introduction[3]

11.04 A preference is a payment to a creditor to settle an existing debt at a time when the company is facing insolvency and when that payment undermines the *pari passu* principle of distribution by ensuring that the creditor obtains a greater share of the limited assets of the insolvent company than would be the case on a proper distribution. If the preference is made to an unconnected person, it must be shown that the company was influenced by a desire to prefer the creditor, surety or guarantor. If a preference is made to a connected person, it is presumed that the company was influenced by a desire to prefer the connected person. The burden to prove to the contrary is placed on the connected person.

Under s 239(4), a company gives a preference to a person if:

(a) that person is one of the company's creditors or a surety or guarantor for any of the company's debts or other liabilities; and

(b) the company does anything or suffers anything to be done which has the effect of putting that person into a position which, in the event of the company going into insolvent liquidation, will be better than the position he would have been in if that thing had not been done.

11.05 At the heart of a preference is the improvement of the position of one creditor at the expense of other creditors.[4] A preference claim can only be made against a creditor, surety or guarantor, since they are the only parties allowed to prove in a winding up of the claimant.

11.06 There is no authority directly on point as to what is meant by 'suffers anything to be done'. It has been suggested, admittedly in another context, that this might incorporate the company failing to take steps to prevent X in circumstances where it would be reasonable for the company to take such steps.[5] Logically, the phrase

---

[2] Insolvency Act 1986, s 239(3). Without prejudice to the generality of s 239(3), and subject to s 241(2), the court may make one of the orders set out in s 241(1). See s 342 for the range of orders in the case of an individual.

[3] See Adrian Walters, 'Preferences' in J Armour and H Bennett (eds), *Vulnerable Transactions in Corporate Insolvency* (Hart Publishing, 2003), 123.

[4] See Insolvency Act 1986, s 239(4)(b). Putting a creditor in a better position in the event of insolvent liquidation can only take place at the expense of the true interests of creditors.

[5] Walters, 'Preferences' in Armour and Bennett (eds), *Vulnerable Transactions in Corporate Insolvency* at [4.38] citing *Berton v Alliance Economic Investment Co* [1922] 1 KB 742.

'suffering anything to be done' must at the very least relate to an activity which the company was in a position to prevent.

No claim for a preference can be made unless it is shown that the company **11.07** giving the preference did so influenced by a desire to produce the effect in (b) in that person.[6] If that person receiving the preference is connected to the company (other than as employee) then it will be assumed the preference was so influenced.[7]

Authorities arising under the old statutory regime are of no assistance in interpret- **11.08** ing this section and should not be cited.[8]

C. Examples of Preference

A preference can take many different forms so long as it improves the position of **11.09** a creditor, surety or guarantor over other creditors.

Typical examples[9] include a payment to a creditor or at the creditor's instruction; **11.10** granting security or additional security to a creditor for past advances and the transfer of debts to reduce the company's liability. Also included would be the situation where a company decides only to carry out its contractual performance in favour of some creditors but not others. That necessarily implies a decision to favour some creditors over others. A transaction may also amount to a preference notwithstanding it has been performed under the cloak of a court order. So, collusion to obtain favourable judgments for certain creditors is likely to amount to a preference: see s 239(7). However, if the judgment or court order has been obtained after lengthy or hard-fought litigation, it is unlikely that the necessary desire to prefer could be established.

D. Desire

English law still firmly believes in an approach premised upon establishing a motive **11.11** on the part of the company—a desire that one creditor be preferred over another.

---

[6] Insolvency Act 1986, s 239(5).

[7] ibid, s 239(6). See *Mills v Edict Ltd* [1999] BPIR 391 where the party preferred was the sole shareholder of the company.

[8] *Re MC Bacon Ltd* [1990] BCLC 324, 335c–d per Millett J: 'Section 44(1) has been replaced and its language has been entirely recast. Every single word of significance, whether in the form of statutory definition or in its judicial exposition, has been jettisoned. "View", "dominant", "intention" and even "to prefer" have all been discarded. These are replaced by "influenced", "desire" and "to produce in relation to that person the effect mentioned in sub s(4)(b)". I therefore emphatically protest against the citation of cases decided under the old law. They cannot be of any assistance when the language of the statute has been so completely and deliberately changed…'

[9] See E Goode, *The Principles of Corporate Insolvency Law* (3rd edn, Sweet and Maxwell, 2005), para 11-76.

11.12   In *Re MC Bacon Ltd*,[10] Millett J expounded on the differences between the old and new law in a section of his judgment which merits being quoted fully:

> This is a completely different test. It involves at least two radical departures from the old law. It is no longer necessary to establish a *dominant* intention to prefer. It is sufficient that the decision was *influenced* by the requisite desire. That is the first change. The second is that it is no longer sufficient to establish an *intention* to prefer. There must be a *desire* to produce the effect mentioned in the subsection.
>
> This second change is made necessary by the first, for without it it would be virtually impossible to uphold the validity of a security taken in exchange for the injection of fresh funds into a company in financial difficulties. A man is taken to intend the necessary consequences of his actions, so that an intention to grant a security to a creditor necessarily involves an intention to prefer that creditor in the event of insolvency. The need to establish that such intention was dominant was essential under the old law to prevent perfectly proper transactions from being struck down. With the abolition of that requirement intention could not remain the relevant test. Desire has been substituted. That is a very different matter. Intention is objective, desire is subjective. A man can choose the lesser of two evils without desiring either.
>
> It is not, however, sufficient to establish a desire to make the payment or grant the security which it is sought to avoid. There must have been a desire to produce the effect mentioned in the subsection, that is to say to improve the creditor's position in the event of an insolvent liquidation. A man is not to be taken as *desiring* all the necessary consequences of his actions. Some consequences may be of advantage to him and be desired by him; others may not affect him and be matters of indifference to him; while still others may be positively disadvantageous to him and not be desired by him, but be regarded by him as the unavoidable price of obtaining the desired advantages. It will still be possible to provide assistance to a company in financial difficulties provided the company is actuated only by proper commercial considerations. Under the new regime a transaction will not be set aside as a voidable preference unless the company positively wished to improve the creditor's position in the event of its own insolvent liquidation.[11]

11.13   His Lordship went on to hold that the presence of the relevant desire can be inferred from the circumstances of the case.[12] It must, however, be shown that the desired influenced the decision to enter into the transaction. That is not the same as saying it must have been the decisive factor or that without such desire, the company would not have entered the transaction. That would place too high a test on desire. It suffices if it was one of the factors which operated on the minds of those who made the decision.

---

[10]   [1990] BCLC 324.

[11]   ibid, 335–6.

[12]   See also *Rooney v Das* [1999] BPIR 404, 406. Although see *Re Beacon Leisure* [1992] BCLC 565 (R Wright QC as Deputy High Court Judge) where the court considered the circumstances did not suffice for the drawing of the inference.

It is important to be precise as to what must be desired. The test is not whether the **11.14** company desired to enter into the transaction which amounts to a preference. It is whether the company entered into the transaction with the desire that that transaction improve the position of the particular creditor vis-à-vis other creditors in a normal *pari passu* distribution.

The old test of intention was an objective one. The new test of desire is subject- **11.15** ive.[13] The office-holder must prove what the subjective motivation of the company was in agreeing to enter into a particular transaction. That is no easy task in the absence of direct evidence such as notes or minutes of meetings, which may be rarely available on such issues. It is also likely to be subject to direct denials from the relevant individuals.[14]

Applying such an approach, Millett J dismissed the application to have the deben- **11.16** ture set aside under s 238 or s 239 of the Insolvency Act 1986. The company had little choice but to agree to granting the bank security in order to continue trading and avoid potential liquidation. It was not possible in those circumstances to infer any desire to benefit one creditor over another.[15]

Millett J's reasoning in *Re MC Bacon* has generally been approved and followed in **11.17** subsequent cases. So, for example, in *Re Living Images Ltd*,[16] Laddie J was dealing with a director's disqualification application and the question of whether a prefer- ential payment had been made arose. Laddie J was content simply to adopt Millett J's reasoning:

> From that decision it appears to me that a preference exists if (a) in undertaking the transaction of which complaint is made the company had a desire or wish to improve the creditor's position in the event of an insolvent liquidation and (b) in deciding to make the alleged preference the company was influenced by that desire. However, a mere realisation that the creditor's position will be improved without wishing that to happen is not enough. On the other hand there is no need to show that the desire 'tipped the scales' in favour of the transaction, it being sufficient if it was one of the factors which operated on the minds of those who made the decision. It need not have been the decisive factor.[17]

---

[13] *Re Beacon Leisure* [1992] BCLC 565, 568 although the judge went on to say he considered 'the distinction in many cases may be small'.

[14] The court in *Re Beacon Leisure* was persuaded by the direct denials by the relevant individuals.

[15] Millett J also dismissed the claim the debenture was a transaction at an undervalue. The debenture did not fall within s 238(4)(a) as it was neither a gift nor a transaction without consideration. It also fell outside s 238(4)(b) as the creation of security per se did not deplete the company's assets.

[16] [1996] 1 BCLC 348, 356–7 (Laddie J)

[17] See also *Wills v Corfe Joinery Ltd (In Liquidation)* [1996] 2 BCLC 75 (relevant time for assess- ing whether company influenced by desire was not when they agreed not to repay the loans but the date the payment was made (i.e. cheques drawn up). Even if they had made an earlier decision, this would have had to be reviewed again later prior to actual payment; *Re MC Bacon* has been inter- preted as favouring the date of agreement. On this point, see also *Re Brian Pierson (Contractors) Ltd*

11.18 It makes no difference that at the time of making the preference there was a genuine belief on the part of the individual or company that it was not insolvent.[18]

E. Relevant Time for Making a Preference

11.19 This is governed by s 240. It is six months ending with the onset of insolvency or, in the case of a connected person, two years. So, if a preference is given outside the six-month period but within the two-year period, it will be essential to establish it was with a connected person.[19] The same time limits apply in the case of an individual bankruptcy: s 342.

F. Orders Available to the Court

11.20 The court has the same wide discretion on choosing a suitable order under s 239 as it does under s 238. See also the particular examples given in s 241 of the Insolvency Act 1986 (summarized above).

[1999] BPIR 18. Other cases generally following the Millet J approach include *Re Lewis's of Leicester Ltd* [1995] 1 BCLC 428; *Re Agriplant Services Ltd* [1997] 2 BCLC 598 (Jonathan Parker J)—see in particular how it was not enough to establish a desire to make the payment. It was necessary also to show a desire to improve the creditor's position on an insolvent liquidation of the company [610c–d].

18 *Re Exchange Travel (Holdings) Ltd (in Liquidation) (No 3)* [1997] 2 BCLC 579, 593g.

19 *Re Thirty-Eight Building Ltd* [1999] 1 BCLC 416, where the court found that trustees of a company's pension scheme were not 'associates' for the purposes of s 435 of the Insolvency Act 1986.

12

TRANSACTIONS DEFRAUDING CREDITORS: INSOLVENCY ACT 1986, SECTION 423[1]

A. Overview of Claim

A claim may be brought under the Insolvency Act 1986, s 423 if the following **12.01** conditions are satisfied.

- A person enters into a transaction at an undervalue by doing one of the following:
  - he makes a gift to another person or enters into a transaction on terms that provide for him to receive no consideration;
  - he enters into a transaction with another in consideration of marriage or civil partnership;
  - he enters into a transaction with another for a consideration the value of which, in money or money's worth, is significantly less than the value in money or money's worth of the consideration provided by himself.
- That person entered into that transaction for the purpose:
  - of putting his assets beyond the reach of a person who is making, or may at some time make, a claim against him; or
  - of otherwise prejudicing the interests of such a person in relation to the claim which he is making or may make.

---

[1] J Armour, 'Transactions at an Undervalue' in J Armour and H Bennett (eds) *Vulnerable Transactions in Corporate Insolvency* (Hart Publishing, 2003), ch 3.

- A claim may be brought by anyone who is the 'victim' of such a transaction (i.e. capable of being prejudiced by it) and any such application is to be treated as made on behalf of all victims of the transaction.

- There is no need for the individual to be in bankruptcy or the company to be insolvent or in administration before this claim can be brought.

- If the claim is established, the court may make such order as it thinks fit for restoring the position to what it would have been if the transaction had not been entered into, and protecting the interests of persons who are victims of the transaction.[2]

12.02 Sections 423–425 of the Insolvency Act 1986 provide a discrete set of provisions designed to deal with transactions intending to defraud creditors. It should be immediately pointed out that the words 'transactions defrauding creditors' appears only in the title to this set of provisions and nowhere within the relevant wording of these statutory provisions themselves. They represent a throw-back to the previous statutory wording under s 172 of the Law of Property Act 1925.[3]

B. Two Requirements for Claim

12.03 Section 423 lays down two specific requirements in order to bring a claim that a transaction is intended to defraud creditors:

- that the transaction entered into was at an undervalue: s 423(1); and
- that the person entering into that transaction did so with the purpose (a) of putting assets beyond the reach of a person who is making, or may at some time make, a claim against him, or (b) of otherwise prejudicing the interests of such a person in relation to the claim which he is making or may make.

C. Transaction at an Undervalue

12.04 A person enters into a transaction at an undervalue with another person if:

(a) he makes a gift to the other person or he otherwise enters into a transaction with the other on terms that provide for him to receive no consideration;

---

2 Insolvency Act 1986, s 423(2). Without prejudice to the generality of s 423(2), and subject to s 425(2), the court may make one of the orders set out in s 425(1).

3 Law of Property Act 1925, s 172: 'every conveyance of property made . . . with intent to defraud creditors, shall be voidable, at the instance of any person thereby prejudiced.' This provision was repealed by the enactment of s 423 of the Insolvency Act 1986 (29 December 1986) but still applies to all transactions entered into before that date.

(b) he enters into a transaction with the other in consideration of marriage or civil partnership;

(c) he enters into a transaction with the other for a consideration the value of which in money or money's worth, is significantly less than the value, in money or money's worth, of the consideration provided by himself.

These provisions mirror those relating to a transaction at an undervalue under   **12.05**
s 238 (discussed in Chapter 10). The reader is referred to that chapter for a more detailed discussion of what amounts to a transaction at an undervalue.

D. Purpose

In entering into the transaction, the person must have the purpose of putting   **12.06**
assets beyond the reach of a person who is making or may at some time make a claim against him *or* of otherwise prejudicing the interests of such a person in relation to the claim which he is making or may make.

It is no longer necessary to show that the person (the debtor) who entered into the   **12.07**
relevant transaction did so with a dishonest intention.[4] In *Arbuthnot Leasing v Havelet Leasing (No 2)*, Scott J accepted that there was no dishonest intent on the part of the debtor company but nevertheless found the relevant statutory purpose established. The debtor company had received and acted upon legal advice that it was appropriate to carry out the particular transaction. Further, the judge accepted that in carrying out the relevant transaction, the debtor company was in fact motivated by a desire to protect the position of creditors generally. None of this saved the transaction.

Having discounted any need to show a dishonest intention, the next issue is what   **12.08**
level of purpose will suffice. Some of the obvious candidates are: (i) only or sole purpose, (ii) predominant purpose, (iii) dominant purpose, or (iv) substantial purpose. It is important to bear in mind at all times that the court is searching for a 'purpose': the result of a transaction is not to be equated with the purpose for which that transaction was entered into.[5]

Before examining each candidate, it would be sensible to recall the guidance provided   **12.09**
by Mr Evans-Lombe QC, sitting as a judge of the High Court in *Chohan v Saggar*:[6]

As Lord Oliver in the well-known case of *Brady v Brady* [1989] AC 755 acknowledged, the word 'purpose' is a word of wide content. But he went on to say that it

---

[4] *Arbuthnot Leasing v Havelet Leasing (No 2)* [1990] BCC 636, 644; *Re Brabon, Treharne v Brabon* [2001] 1 BCLC 11, 44.
[5] *Royscott Spa Leasing Ltd v Lovett* [1995] BCC 502.
[6] [1992] BCC 306. This view was endorsed by the Court of Appeal in *Royscott Spa Leasing v Lovett* [1995] BCC 502, 507 and in *Barclays Bank v Eustice* [1995] BCC 978, 985.

must be construed bearing in mind the mischief against which the section in which that word appears is aimed. Here the purpose or mischief against which the section is aimed, namely s423, is the removal of assets by their owner, in anticipation of claims being made or contemplated, out of the reach of such claimants if those claims ultimately prove to be successful. It would defeat that purpose if it were possible successfully to contend that if the owner was able to point to another purpose, such as the benefit of his family friends or the advantage of business associated, the section could not be applied.

12.10 Candidate (i) can be immediately rejected. If the Act required that the debtor company's only or sole purpose in entering into the transaction was to place assets beyond the reach of creditors, it would be a fraudster's charter since it would be very simple for the debtor company to show that he had some other minimal purpose also in mind. It would rob s 423 of all practical effect.[7]

12.11 It is difficult to tell whether there is or is intended to be any real difference between candidate (ii) 'predominant purpose' and candidate (iii) 'dominant purpose'. The Concise Oxford English Dictionary defines 'predominant' as meaning 'the strongest or main element'; 'having or exerting the greatest control or power' and yet defines 'dominant' as 'most important, powerful or influential'. It is for seeking to draw such fine distinctions, if distinction there be between these definitions, that lawyers have gained such a bad reputation.

12.12 Mervyn Davies J in *Moon v Franklin*[8] opted for 'predominant purpose' but he appears to be the only one to do so. He has not, so far, been followed and was doubted by Sir Christopher Slade in *Royscott Spa Leasing Ltd v Lovett*.[9]

12.13 'Dominant purpose' was the favoured choice of Mr Evans-Lombe QC (sitting as Deputy High Court Judge) in *Chohan v Saggar*[10] and Evans-Lombe J in *Jyske Bank (Gibraltar) Ltd v Spjeldnaes*.[11]

12.14 But in *Pinewood Joinery v Starelm Properties*[12] Judge Moseley QC (sitting as judge of the High Court), not having had the benefit of full submissions on the point, doubted the 'dominant purpose' test could be the correct one:

> I have not read judgments in *Lloyds Bank v Marcan* before delivering this judgment, and have been referred to parts only of *Chohan v Saggar*. I have expressed the view

---

[7] See Mr Evans-Lombe QC (sitting as Deputy High Court Judge) in *Chohan v Saggar* [1992] BCC 306, 321.

[8] [1996] BPIR 196 (judgment in fact delivered in June 1990).

[9] [1995] BCC 502, 507.

[10] [1992] BCC 306, 323. The court there saw no reason to depart from the approach adopted under the old law of s 172 of the Law of Property Act 1925 and which, according to the Court of Appeal in *Lloyds Bank v Marcan* [1973] 1 WLR 1387, required a plaintiff to demonstrate a dominant purpose to remove assets from the reach of actual or potential creditors.

[11] [1999] 2 BCLC 101.

[12] *Pinewood Joinery v Starelm Properties* [1994] 2 BCLC 412, 418.

during the course of argument doubting the proposition that a dominant purpose must be established, but I reach no view on that issue given the fact that I have not read either of the two cases in detail. I merely state, subject to those observations, that it seems to me odd that if a transferor has two purposes which are equally paramount in his mind he fails altogether because he does not have a dominant purpose satisfying s.423(3).

The judge went on to find it did not matter on the facts because the dominant purpose was to obtain a tax advantage negotiated with the Inland Revenue and not to place the hotel property beyond the reach of creditors.

To the extent that there is a difference between 'dominant' and 'substantial', the **12.15** court in *Re Brabon, Treharne v Brabon*[13] was willing to proceed on the basis that 'substantial' represented the appropriate test. Jonathan Parker J made it clear that he did so on the same basis that the Court of Appeal did in *Royscott Spa Leasing v Lovett,*[14] namely that if the trustee was unable to meet this lower test, he would never have met the stricter test.

E. Who can Apply for an Order?

Proceedings under this section can be brought by a number of people, including **12.16** liquidators, the creditors of an insolvent company and persons who are litigants in proceedings against the insolvent, as a 'victim of the transaction' entered into by the insolvent company (s 24). A victim of the transaction is a person who is, or is capable of being, prejudiced by it (s 423(5)).

F. What Orders are Available?

Under s 423(2), upon the requirements being established, the court may make **12.17** such order as it thinks fit for restoring the position to what it would have been if the transaction had not been entered into. More specifically, although without prejudice to the generality of s 423(2), the court may make an order:

(a) requiring any property transferred as part of the transaction to be vested in any person, either absolutely or for the benefit of all the persons on whose behalf the application for the order is treated as made;

---

[13] [2001] 1 BCLC 11, 44.
[14] [1995] BCC 502 (CA).

(b) requiring any property to be so vested if it represents, in any person's hands, the application either of the proceeds of sale of property so transferred or of money so transferred;

(c) releasing or discharging (in whole or in part) any security given by the debtor;

(d) requiring any person to pay to any other person in respect of benefits received from the debtor such sums as the court may direct;

(e) providing for any surety or guarantor whose obligations to any person were released or discharged (in whole or in part) under the transaction to be under such new or revived obligations as the court thinks appropriate;

(f) providing for security to be provided for the discharge of any obligation imposed by or arising under the order, for such an obligation to be charged on any property and for such security or charge to have the same priority as a security or charge released or discharged (in whole or in part) under the transaction.

G. Protection of Third Party Interests

12.18 Section 425(2) provides that an order under s 423 may affect the property of, or impose any obligation on any person, whether or not he is the person with whom the debtor entered into the transaction.[15]

12.19 However, no order shall be made against a third party who acquired an interest in property from a person other than the debtor so long as that party acted in good faith, for value and without notice of the relevant circumstances.[16]

12.20 Further, no order for payment of any sum can be made against any person who received a benefit from the transaction but was not himself a party thereto and who acted in good faith, for value and without notice of the relevant circumstances.[17]

12.21 Accordingly, a party who was not a party to the transaction itself will be protected so long as they acted in good faith, for value and without notice of the relevant circumstances.

---

[15] Insolvency Act 1986, s 425.
[16] ibid, s 425(2)(a).
[17] ibid, s 425(2)(b).

13

MISCELLANEOUS

The purpose of this chapter is simply to bring to the reader's attention the exist- **13.01** ence of several miscellaneous categories of claim available under statute law which may prove useful in a commercial fraud setting. To the extent that any potential claim would appear to be suitable, resort can be had to the specialist insolvency texts for further guidance.

A. Transfers after Commencement of Winding Up

The Insolvency Act 1986, s 127[1] renders all dispositions of company property, or **13.02** transfer of shares, taking place after the commencement of the winding up as void unless a court orders otherwise.[2]

This is a general all-embracing embargo. It includes any disposition even if made **13.03** pursuant to a court order from a court other than that which is dealing with the company's winding up. This is intended to exclude collusion between parties such that certain debts are paid whilst others are left unpaid.

Careful consideration needs to be given to what constitutes a 'disposition' in the **13.04** context of payments into and out of bank accounts. It might seem odd, to a layman,

---

[1] Insolvency Act 1986, s 127 re-enacted in the same terms as s 522 of the Companies Act 1985.
[2] See also Insolvency Act 1986, s 284 for a comparable provision in respect of individual bankruptcy.

to say that to deposit money in cash into the company's bank account amounts to a disposition of the company's property but that, in reality, is the true legal position.[3] It is justified on the basis that one has exchanged the cash or property in the company's hand for a chose of action, being the debt owed by the bank to the company valued in the amount of cash deposited. So long as the bank remains solvent, in practical terms, it may not matter greatly but legally if the bank is insolvent it makes a great deal of difference. This point remains true, whether the bank account is in credit or overdrawn. As Buckley LJ remarked in *Gray's Inn Construction Co Ltd*:[4]

> In the present case the company's account with the bank was overdrawn, so that I need not consider what the position would have been if any cheque had been paid in when the account was in credit, but I doubt whether even in those circumstances it could properly be said that the payment in did not constitute a disposition of the amount of the cheque in favour of the bank.

13.05 Section 127 provides no guidance on the nature and type of remedy which may be available in the event that the court determines any particular transaction void. In the case of payments into bank accounts by cheque, it would appear, notwithstanding the analysis above, as though the *remedy* is limited to one against the payee and not the bank: see the Court of Appeal in *Hollicourt (Contracts) Ltd v Bank of Ireland*.[5]

13.06 A relevant transaction will be void unless the court orders otherwise. Some guidance on this issue has been given by the Court of Appeal in *Re Gray's Inn Construction Co Ltd*[6] which has been helpfully summarized into various principles by the Court of Appeal in *Denney v John Hudson & Co*[7] as follows:

(1) The discretion vested in the court . . . is entirely at large, subject to the general principles which apply to any kind of discretion, and subject also to limitation that the discretion must be exercised in the context of the liquidation provisions of the statute.

(2) The basic principle of law governing the liquidation of insolvent estates, whether in bankruptcy or under the companies' legislation, is that the assets of the insolvent at the time of the commencement of the liquidation will be distributed pari passu among the insolvent's unsecured creditors as at the date of the bankruptcy.

---

[3] It is unfortunate that the same rigorous legal analysis is not applied in the context of claims against banks for receipt of monies. Similarly, few would contend that the payment of cash into a bank account constituted a dissipation of assets under a freezing order.

[4] [1980] 1 All ER 814, 818.

[5] [2001] Ch 555.

[6] [1980] 1 All ER 814, 819–21.

[7] [1992] BCLC 901, 904–5. See also *Re S&D Wright Ltd* [1992] BCC 503.

(3) There are occasions, however, when it may be beneficial not only for the company but also for the unsecured creditors, that the company should be able to dispose of some of its property during the period after the petition has been presented, but before the winding-up order has been made. Thus, it may sometimes be beneficial to the company and its creditors that the company should be able to continue the business in its ordinary course.

(4) In considering whether to make a validating order, the court must always do its best to ensure that the interests of the unsecured creditors will not be prejudiced.

(5) The desirability of the company being enabled to carry on its business was often speculative. In each case the court must carry out a balancing exercise.

(6) The court should not validate any transaction or series of transactions which might result in one or more pre-liquidation creditors being paid in full at the expense of other creditors, who will only receive a dividend, in the absence of special circumstances making such a course desirable in the interest of the creditors generally. If, for example, it were in the interests of the creditors generally that the company's business should be carried on, and this could only be achieved by paying for goods already supplied to the company when the petition is presented (but not yet paid for) the court might exercise its discretion to validate payments for those goods.

(7) A disposition carried out in good faith in the ordinary course of business at a time when the parties were unaware that a petition had been presented would usually be validated by the court unless there is ground for thinking that the transaction may involve an attempt to prefer the disponee—in which case the transaction would not be validated.

(8) Despite the strength of the principle of securing pari passu distribution, the principle has no application to post-liquidation creditors; for example, the sale of an asset at full market value after the presentation of the petition. That is because such a transaction involves no dissipation of the company's assets for its does not reduce the value of its assets.

B. Unregistered but Registrable Charges[8]

Any potential creditor, particularly one looking for security for any financial **13.07** assistance, should be able to determine the value to attach to such security by being able to see the full range of security the company has already provided for its existing indebtedness. It is only against that knowledge that a creditor can make a fully and properly informed decision to lend.

---

[8] See the excellent discussion in Howard Bennett, 'Registration of Company Charges' in Armour and Bennett (eds), *Vulnerable Transactions in Corporate Insolvency* (Hart Publishing, 2003).

13.08 Section 395(1) of the Companies Act 1985 is intended to achieve that aim by laying down a regime for the registration of company charges, with such charges that fail to adhere to that regime being void as against third parties. It is by no means considered a complete success.[9]

13.09 Section 395(1) provides:

> Subject to the provisions of this Chapter, a charge created by a company registered in England and Wales and being a charge to which this section applies is, so far as any security on the company's property or undertaking is conferred by the charge, void against the liquidator or administrator and any creditor of the company, unless the prescribed particulars of the charge together with the instrument (if any) by which the charge is created or evidenced, are delivered to or received by the registrar of companies for registration in the manner required by this Chapter within 21 days after the date of the charge's creation.

13.10 Accordingly, any charge created by the company and falling within s 395 and 396 of the Companies Act 1985 must be registered within 21 days after creation,[10] otherwise it will be void as against a liquidator, administrator and creditor.

13.11 Importantly, the registration procedure is the means by which one notifies third parties of the existence of such a charge. As such, it does not invalidate the position as between the charge holder and the company, so long as the loan is fully paid off before the commencement of any liquidation or administration process.

C. Floating Charges for Past Value: Insolvency Act 1986, section 245[11]

13.12 Section 245 is intended to deal with the situation where, within a stipulated time prior to the commencement of insolvency or administration, a floating charge is created over the company's assets but without any new value or loan monies being provided. One can readily see that it is aimed at preventing those in control of the company from wrongfully seeking to favour a creditor at the expense of the company's other creditors by granting the creditor the protection of a floating charge.

---

[9] ibid, 219: 'In reality, the registration system under the Companies' Act produces a picture of a company's secured indebtedness that may be incomplete and unreliable.'

[10] Subject to the possibility of applying for an extension under s 404 of the Companies Act 1985.

[11] See generally Bennett, 'Late Floating Charges' in Armour and Bennett (eds), *Vulnerable Transactions in Corporate Insolvency*; R Goode, *The Principles of Corporate Insolvency* (3rd edn, Sweet and Maxwell, 2005), paras 11-10–11-119.

If the company is in liquidation or administration and a floating charge falls **13.13** within s 245 of the Insolvency Act 1986, it will be void.

(1) What is the relevant time?

If the floating charge is granted in favour of a person *connected* with the company, **13.14** it is two years[12] ending with the onset of insolvency.[13]

If the floating charge is granted in favour of any other person, it is 12 months[14] **13.15** ending with the onset of insolvency under s 245(5).

Irrespective of whether the floating charge is in favour of a connected person or **13.16** any other person, s 245 will catch all floating charges for past value granted between the presentation of filing of notice to appoint an administrator and the making of that appointment.

(2) Qualifying floating charges

A floating charge which is created at the relevant time will be invalid except to the **13.17** extent it can be shown that any new value was given for that charge. Section 245(2) defines new value as:

> . . . the aggregate of—
>
> (a) the value of so much of the consideration for the creation of the charge as consists of money paid, or goods and services supplied, to the company at the same time as, or after the creation of the charge,
>
> (b) the value of so much of the consideration as consists of the discharge or reduction, at the same time as, or after, the creation of the charge, of any debt of the company, and
>
> (c) the amount of such interest (if any) as is payable on the amount falling within paragraph (a) or (b) in pursuance of any agreement under which the money was so paid, the goods or services were so supplied or the debt was so discharged or reduced.

---

12 Insolvency Act 1986, s 245(3)(a).
13 ibid, s 245(5).
14 ibid, s 245(3)(b).

D. Extortionate Credit Transactions

13.18   An extortionate credit transaction is one in which a party (the company) agrees to borrow finance from a third party creditor but on ridiculously high credit terms. This places that creditor in a favoured position should the company end up in liquidation since that creditor will be able to prove in the insolvency for the inflated amount, thereby proportionately reducing the share available to the other creditors of the company.

13.19   From the perspective of commercial fraud litigation, one might readily view the provisions relating to extortionate credit transactions as being concerned to prevent those controlling the companies entering into sham arrangements with third parties as a means of channelling monies out of the company and away from genuine creditors. As one commentator put it:

> The aim of section 244 is, it appears, to ensure that the rights of unsecured creditors are not prejudiced by reason of the company having entered into a loan arrangement for which the consideration is excessive. The aim is not to attack loans which turn out to be bad bargains, but to allow for the impugning of those loans which are grossly unfair, *ie*, loans which no reasonable company in normal circumstances would enter into save where there was some underlying rationale such as where there is a sham agreement designed to confer an undue benefit on the lender.[15]

13.20   Another way of looking at this legislation is to note its close analogy with s 138 of the Consumer Credit Act. Looking at it from the consumer legislation point of view, one might consider the provisions relating to these sort of transactions are intended to protect the company from being forced to accept extortionate terms because, say, of its bad trading position. If this latter approach is adopted, one can see why commentators such as Professor Goode have sought to introduce some element of oppression or unequal bargaining power into the definition of extortionate. Whereas if one examines it from the first perspective, it is difficult to see why the provision needs to have such matters read into it.

13.21   Section 244 of the Insolvency Act 1986 provides:

> (1) This section applies as does section 238, and where the company is, or has been, a party to a transaction for, or involving, the provision of credit to the company.

> (2) The court may, on an application of the office-holder, make an order with respect to the transaction if the transaction is or was extortionate and was entered into in the period of 3 years ending with the day on which the company entered administration or went into liquidation.

---

[15] A Keay, *McPherson's Law of Company Liquidation* (Sweet and Maxwell, 2001), para 11-89.

(3) For the purposes of this section a transaction is extortionate if, having regard to the risk accepted by the person providing the credit—

(a) the terms of it are or were such as to require grossly exorbitant payments to be made (whether unconditionally or in certain contingencies) in respect of the provision of the credit, or

(b) it otherwise grossly contravened ordinary principles of fair dealing;

and it shall be presumed, unless the contrary is proved, that a transaction with respect to which an application is made under this section is or, as the case may be, was extortionate.

Ultimately, it will be a question of fact, to be decided on a case by case basis, whether, applying the principles set out in s 244(3), a particular transaction is considered to be extortionate. The office-holder at least has the benefit that upon any application being made under this section, there is a rebuttable presumption the transaction is extortionate. **13.22**

There is presently a difference of opinion as to whether the terms of s 244 require that the transaction not only to be unfair but also oppressive. Professor Goode has remarked: **13.23**

> What has to be demonstrated is that they were extortionate within the statutory defin-ition and this implies that they must be not merely unfair but oppressive, reflecting an imbalance in bargaining power of which the other party took improper advantage.[16]

Mr Edward Nugee QC (sitting as Deputy High Court Judge) in *Davies v Direct Loans Ltd*,[17] whilst dealing with the issue of an extortionate credit bargain under the similarly worded s 138 of the Consumer Credit Act, has rejected Professor Goode's opinion. He expressly rejected the notion that 'extortionate' included 'harsh and unconscionable'. He said it was wrong to look outside the terms of the Act in order to ascertain its meaning. The test is not whether the creditor has acted in a morally reprehensible manner but whether one or other of the conditions in s 138(1) of the Consumer Credit Act (or s 244 of the Insolvency Act 1986) is satis-fied. Even though one might conclude that if the conditions are satisfied, there is something morally reprehensible about the creditor's conduct, the starting and ending point in determining whether it is extortionate is the actual wording used. **13.24**

Unless and until s 244 of the Insolvency Act 1986 comes before the court, it remains unclear which of these views will prevail. The outcome may well turn on how one characterizes this provision—out to prevent sham arrangements to preju-dice creditors' interests or adopting a more protective approach to companies, **13.25**

---

[16] Goode, *The Principles of Corporate Insolvency* (3rd edn), para 11-106 citing, in support, *Wills v Wood* [1984] CCLR 7.
[17] [1986] 1 WLR 823, 831.

analogous to the consumer credit legislation. It is suggested that there is little to be gained by introducing additional concepts, such as unequal bargaining power or 'harsh and unconscionable', into s 244 via the definition of 'extortionate'.

(1) Available orders

13.26 In the event that the transaction does fall within s 244 of the Insolvency Act 1986, the court has a wide discretion to make the following orders or combination of orders:

(a) provision setting aside the whole or part of any obligation created by the transaction;

(b) provision otherwise varying the terms of the transaction or varying the terms on which any security for the purposes of the transaction is held;

(c) provision requiring any person who is or was a party to the transaction to pay to the office-holder any sums paid to that person, by virtue of the transaction, by the company;

(d) provision requiring any person to surrender to the office-holder any property held by him as security for the purposes of the transaction;

(e) provision directing accounts to be taken between any persons.

Part VI

MULTI-PARTY LIABILITY

14

CONSPIRACY[1]

A. Summary of Requirements

Conspiracy gives rise to two distinct tortious claims as examined below. For the **14.01** purposes of analysis, the first, and that which is likely to be of more relevance to a commercial fraud litigator, is usually called an unlawful means conspiracy. The second is called a simple conspiracy.

(1) Unlawful means conspiracy

The elements of this claim are as follows: **14.02**

- a combination or understanding between two or more people;
- aimed at or directed towards an individual or separate legal entity;
- concerted action, consequent upon the combination or understanding;

---

[1] See *Clerk & Lindsell* (19th edn), paras 25-116–25-137; Hazel Carty, *An Analysis of the Economic Torts* (Oxford University Press, 2001), ch 2.

- use of unlawful means as part of concerted action;
- resulting in damage being caused the target of the conspiracy.

(2) Simple conspiracy[2]

14.03 The elements of this claim are as follows:

- a combination or understanding between two or more people;
- to do acts which are themselves lawful;
- with the sole or predominant purpose or intention to cause injury to an individual or separate legal entity;
- resulting in damage being caused to the target of the conspiracy.

14.04 It is worth remarking at the outset that although a summary of the requirements for each type of tort of conspiracy has been outlined above, controversy and uncertainty surrounds several of the requirements. In the case of unlawful means conspiracy, for example, the case law is somewhat uncertain as to whether and to what extent equitable obligations may fall within the type of 'unlawful means' sufficient to give rise to such a conspiracy. Further, doubt surrounds whether the 'unlawful means', whatever they be, must be actionable at the instance of the claimant. It remains to be seen whether the narrow definition adopted by the majority of the House of Lords in *OBG Ltd v Allan*[3] in the context of the tort of interference with trade by unlawful means will be applied to claims arising under conspiracy, thereby limiting 'unlawful means' to those claims actionable at the instance of the claimant.

B. Introduction

(1) Advantages of pleading conspiracy

14.05 A complex commercial fraud will typically involve more than one defendant and thus potentially gives rise to the existence of a conspiracy. Whether in fact there exists the basis for a claim in conspiracy is dependent upon the circumstances of each case but if the facts support the allegation, there are distinct advantages in bringing such a claim.

- It enables the claimant to cast its net of potential defendants much wider than might otherwise be the case. More than one defendant may be liable for the same tort.

---

[2] Sometimes known as the *Quinn v Leatham*-type conspiracy or, as per W Rogers, *Winfield & Jolowicz on Tort* (17th edn, Sweet and Maxwell, 2006), 812–17, 'the Crofter-type' after the House of Lords decision in *Crofter Hand Woven Harris Tweed Co Ltd v Veitch* [1942] AC 435.
[3] [2007] UKHL 21, [50].

- A claim in conspiracy may be brought against individuals who could not in fact be held liable for any underlying wrongful act.[4]

- A conspiracy claim may catch individuals who, whilst not the central characters in the fraud, nevertheless play important roles in its success. If these characters have deep pockets, there is all the more reason to pursue them.[5]

- Evidence in respect of the 'acts and admissions by one in pursuance of the conspiracy are admissible against the other',[6] where this would not be permitted in the absence of any conspiracy allegation.

- So long as *some* loss is shown to flow from the conspiracy, damages are not limited to the precise level of provable loss.[7]

(2) Potential disadvantages of pleading conspiracy

Careful thought needs to be given whether or not to plead conspiracy. On the one hand, there are the potential advantages set out above. But these should be set against potential disadvantages, including:　**14.06**

- The courts will always keep a careful eye on any allegation of conspiracy and what precisely is being alleged. This can result in the claimant being placed under a significant burden to prove its case clearly in respect of each defendant.

- The inclusion of a conspiracy claim is always likely to increase the time and costs incurred in litigating any dispute.

- Necessarily it results in the claimant lining itself up against several defendants and not simply one defendant. Practically, this can add considerably to the claimant's burden.

(3) Two types of conspiracy

As Lord Devlin remarked in *Rookes v Barnard*,[8] English law recognizes two distinct forms of conspiracy:　**14.07**

> the *Quinn v Leathem* type which employs only lawful means but aims at an unlawful end, and the type which employs unlawful means.

---

[4] *Michaels v Taylor Woodrow Developments* [2001] Ch 493, para 65. This would be because their own conduct did not give rise to an actionable claim in itself by the claimant against that individual.

[5] This point should not be over-stated. Deep-pocketed defendants are typically financial or banking institutions which may have had some peripheral involvement in the underlying conspiracy. However, the court will not readily infer that such individuals or institutions have signed up to a conspiracy and so the evidence against that individual or institution should be carefully scrutinized before the decision is taken to add them as a defendant.

[6] *Derby & Co v Weldon (No 5)* [1989] 1 WLR 1244, 1254. See also *Phipson on Evidence* (16th edn, Sweet and Maxwell, 2005), para 37-12.

[7] Dillon LJ in *Lonrho v Fayed (No 5)* [1993] 1 WLR 1489, 1494B; *McGregor On Damages* (17th edn, Sweet and Maxwell, 2003), para 40-008. Damages are at large.

[8] [1964] AC 1129, 1204.

14.08   While several of the requirements for each of these types of conspiracy are the same, there are two essential distinguishing factors. The first is that in the case of the simple or *Quinn v Leatham* conspiracy, it must be shown that the conspirators' sole or predominant intention is to injure the target of the conspiracy, whereas unlawful means conspiracy requires only that the conspiracy be aimed or directed at the target. Secondly, the simple conspiracy does not require the use of unlawful means, whereas the unlawful means conspiracy obviously does.

14.09   The distinction between these two types of conspiracy has been blurred in the past due, in part, to the Court of Appeal's judgment in *Metall und Rohstoff AG v Donaldson Lufkin & Jenrette Inc*[9] which interpreted Lord Diplock's speech in *Lonrho Limited v Shell Petroleum Limited (No 2)*[10] as requiring a sole or predominant intention to injure for both types of conspiracy. This created a decade of uncertainty as to the distinction between these two types of conspiracy until order was restored when the House of Lords in *Lonrho Ltd v Fayed*[11] overruled *Metall und Rohstoff* on this point.

14.10   Although the two types of conspiracy are distinct in nature, they share the generally accepted common characteristic of economic torts, namely that the basis for liability is the intentional infliction of economic harm.[12] As we shall see, this rules out liability in circumstances where the harm to a third party is merely the foreseeable consequence of the conspiracy.[13]

(4) Distinction between civil and criminal conspiracy

14.11   In short, the distinction between civil and criminal liability for conspiracy lies in the fact that for civil liability, it is necessary to show damage having been caused by conduct pursuant to the agreement or combination. For criminal liability, proof of having reached an agreement or combination with others will suffice.

14.12   In the *History of English Law* (vol VIII, 2nd edn, 1937), Sir William Holdsworth observed:

> The fact that the conspiracy is the essence of the crime, while the damage is the essence of the tort, must make a great deal of difference in the rules applicable . . . The crime consists in the conspiracy; but the damage is the gist of the action by the party

---

[9]   [1990] 1 QB 391.

[10]   [1982] AC 173. For an excellent critique of the Court of Appeal's decision in *Metall und Rohstoff* see P Sales, 'The Tort of Conspiracy and Civil Secondary Liability' [1990] CLJ 491.

[11]   [1992] 1 AC 448.

[12]   *Douglas v Hello! Ltd (No 3)* [2005] 3 WLR 881, para 221.

[13]   Woolf LJ in *Lonrho plc v Fayed* [1990] 2 QB 479 had suggested that foresight by a defendant of harm to a claimant was sufficient to satisfy the mental element in the tort of unlawful interference even though there was no desire to bring about that consequence in order to achieve what he regarded as his ultimate end. This view was rejected, among others, by the CA in *Douglas v Hello! Ltd (No 3)* [2005] 3 WLR 881, para 218.

injured by the conspiracy – the damage, that is, flowing from the unlawful acts done by each and all of the conspirators in pursuance of their joint design. What we must look at, therefore, in order to establish a cause of action, is not so much the conspiracy, as the quality of the acts and the damage flowing therefrom.[14]

The cases are to similar effect. In *Marrinan v Vibart*,[15] Salmon J stated: **14.13**

> . . . the gist of the tort of conspiracy is not the conspiratorial agreement alone, but that agreement plus the overt act causing damage. It is true that the crime of conspiracy is the very agreement of two or more persons to effect an unlawful purpose, and any overt acts done in pursuance of the agreement are merely evidence to prove the fact of the agreement. The tort of conspiracy, however, is complete only if the agreement is carried into effect so as to damage the plaintiff. Accordingly, the acts done in pursuance of the agreement are an integral part of the tort: *Crofter Hand Woven Harris Tweed Co. Ltd v Veitch* [1942] AC 435.

So for the tort of conspiracy, it is necessary to look beyond the establishment **14.14** of some form of combination or understanding and to establish conduct by parties pursuant to this combination or understanding. Unlike criminal liability, that conduct is seen as an integral part of the commission of the tort and not simply as a means of evidencing the existence of the prior combination or understanding.

(5) Relationship with dishonest assistance

The similarities and differences between the equitable claim for dishonest **14.15** assistance and the tort of conspiracy are dealt with in Chapter 16 on dishonest assistance.[16]

C. Unlawful Means Conspiracy

In *Kuwait Oil Tanker Co SAK v Al Bader*[17] the Court of Appeal provided the fol- **14.16** lowing general guidance on the requirements for this type of conspiracy:

> A conspiracy to injure by unlawful means is actionable where the claimant proves that he has suffered loss or damage as a result of unlawful action taken pursuant to a combination or agreement between the defendant and another person or persons to injure him by unlawful means, whether or not it is the predominant purpose of the defendant to do so.[18]

---

14 393–4.
15 [1963] 1 QB 234, 238–9.
16 See Ch 16 at para 16.20.
17 [2000] 2 All ER (Comm) 271.
18 ibid, para 106.

14.17 To facilitate a better understanding of this type of conspiracy, the following issues will be examined in detail:

- who can be a party to a conspiracy?
- what type of combination/understanding and concerted action is required?
- what is the required intention?
- what qualifies as 'unlawful means'?

The first two of these questions will be answered the same irrespective of whether one is dealing with unlawful means or simply conspiracy. The third question will be answered differently as between these two types of conspiracy. The fourth question is relevant only to the unlawful means conspiracy.

(1) Who can be a party to a conspiracy?

14.18 Whatever the form of conspiracy, it requires a coming together of two or more persons. Ordinarily, the status of the individuals will not affect their ability to combine in a conspiracy. There are, however, three classes of relationship which call for some consideration:

- husband and wife;
- employer and employee;
- director and company.

(a) Husband and wife

14.19 It remains clear law that no criminal conspiracy can arise where the only alleged conspirators are husband and wife.[19] A marriage, entered into subsequent to the commencement of a conspiracy, will not, however, prevent criminal liability for conspiracy arising as between two individuals who happen to have become husband and wife.[20] Similarly, where those involved in the conspiracy were not limited to just the husband and wife, criminal liability could still arise.[21]

14.20 In *Midland Bank v Green (No 3)*,[22] Oliver J considered whether tortious liability for conspiracy could arise as between husband and wife or whether the same policy considerations justified placing an embargo on any such liability arising in tort as in criminal law. He examined what Professor Maitland had described as the 'impossible dogma' of treating husband and wife as one entity, which prevented a

---

[19] Criminal Law Act 1977, s 2(2)(a). The position under criminal law was discussed by Oliver J in *Midland Bank Trust Co Ltd v Green (No 3)* [1979] 1 Ch 496, 510, where it was noted that there had been no specific English law decision on point. The issue had arisen in several cases, only for it to be assumed or conceded that no conspiracy could arise as between husband and wife.

[20] *Rex v Robinson and Taylor* (1746) 1 Leach 37.

[21] *Midland Bank Trust Co Ltd v Green (No 3)* [1979] 1 Ch 496, 521.

[22] [1979] 1 Ch 496, aff'd [1982] Ch 529 at 538 (Lord Denning MR), at 541 (Fox LJ).

conspiracy arising in criminal law since one cannot agree with oneself.[23] He found that there was a shift from this original policy justification to one based upon masculine predominance in the marriage and a court-based desire to avoid interfering in marital affairs. Oliver J remarked:

> It looks therefore rather as if the strictly biblical notion of husband and wife as one flesh and thus one person had by this time become confused with, if not overtaken by, the equally fictitious concept of a predominating masculine will.[24]

By 1953, Denning LJ in *Broom v Morgan*[25] was prepared to say that the theory **14.21** that husband and wife are one 'has no longer any place in our law'. Having surveyed such case law, Oliver J concluded that:

> the continued existence of the rule, in relation to the crime of conspiracy rests, as the more modern cases suggest, not upon a supposed inability to agree as a result of some fictional unity, but upon a public policy which, for the preservation of the sanctity of marriage, accords an immunity from prosecution to spouses who have done no more than agree between themselves in circumstances which would lay them open, if unmarried, to a charge of conspiracy.[26]

Having not been persuaded by the merits of the fictional and/or public policy **14.22** basis for the embargo on liability for a husband and wife in criminal conspiracy, Oliver J refused to apply the same embargo in respect of the tort:

> In my judgment there is no good logical or historical reason for slavishly applying in the law of tort, simply because the tort is called the 'tort of conspiracy', the primitive and inaccurate maxim that spouses are one person, so as to confer upon them an immunity from civil liability not accorded to the unmarried. Indeed, to do so would be to apply it beyond the confines in which it was applied in the criminal law, for to found liability at all the matter must have proceeded beyond mere agreement to executive action . . . Unless, therefore, the applicant can point to some convincing reason in public policy why the law either did previously or should now apply the maxim so as to exclude civil liability in tort in the case of concerted and injurious action by spouses, I must reject the present motion.[27]

Oliver J's rejection of the old doctrine of unity as between husband and wife was **14.23** confirmed on appeal by the Court of Appeal.[28]

Accordingly, it is clear that the fact that the alleged co-conspirators are husband **14.24** and wife is no bar to the existence of liability for the tort of conspiracy.

---

23 See, e.g. *Blackstone Commentaries* (17th edn, 1830), vol 1, 442.
24 [1979] 1 Ch 496, 514G.
25 [1953] 1 QB 597, 609.
26 [1979] 1 Ch 496, 521C–D.
27 ibid, 525.
28 [1982] Ch 529.

(b) Employer and employee

14.25 In *Crofter Hand Woven Harris Tweed Co v Veitch*,[29] Lord Wright stated that ordinarily an employee is not taken to be 'in combination' with his or her employer. Lord Wright did not go on to explain precisely the grounds for his view. It is presumably based upon an understanding that an employee's actions may and ordinarily or typically can be explained by reference to his obligations owed to his employer and not because such actions have been taken pursuant to an antecedent combination or understanding.

14.26 In other words, in determining whether an employee is in combination with his employer it is necessary to establish that the employee is not simply carrying out his employment obligations. It will be necessary to show that the employee's actions or conduct are to be understood as being undertaken in compliance with a prior understanding with others and not because that is what that individual is employed to do.

(c) Director and company

14.27 In principle, it is entirely possible for a company, being a separate legal entity, to conspire with its directors. This is true both of criminal conspiracy[30] as well as tortious liability.[31] Whether a company is treated as a party to the conspiracy will depend on whether it can be established that the company had the requisite knowledge to have entered into the combination and carried out acts pursuant thereto.

14.28 Typically, the knowledge of a company is to be located in that of the director who is responsible, on the company's behalf, for the particular transaction or series of transactions in question. Such a director is sometimes described as the *alter ego* or directing mind of the company.[32]

14.29 The knowledge of an individual holding the position of a director of a company will not necessarily be imputed to that company.[33] If a director has obtained knowledge in a personal capacity, and not whilst acting as a director, this may not be imputed to the company.[34] Similarly, if the individual is director of two companies, his knowledge is not automatically to be imputed to both companies.

---

[29] [1942] AC 435, 468 (Lord Wright).

[30] *R v ICR Haulage Ltd* [1944] 1 All ER 691.

[31] E.g. *Belmont Finance Corpn v Williams Furniture Ltd (No 2)* [1980] 1 All ER 393 (CA).

[32] *El Ajou v Dollar Land Holdings plc* [1994] 2 All ER 685, CA; *Meridian Global Funds Ltd v Securities Commission* [1995] 2 AC 500, HL; *Clerk & Lindsell* (19th edn), para 25-119.

[33] *In Re Marseilles Extensions Ry Co* LR 7 Ch 161 (personal knowledge of an individual holding the position of director in two companies will not necessarily be imputed to those two companies).

[34] *Lagunas Nitrate Co v Lagunas Syndicate* [1899] 2 Ch 392, 431: 'To impute to the . . . company the knowledge which the directors had acquired in another capacity and, which knowledge they did not disclose to any one, is neither law or sense' per Lindley MR.

In *Re Hampshire Land Company*,[35] Vaughan Williams J held that the relevant test was:

> ... that the knowledge which has been acquired by the officer of one company will not be imputed to the other company, unless the common officer had some duty imposed upon him to communicate that knowledge to the other company, and had some duty imposed on him by the company which is alleged to be affected by the notice to receive the notice.

The issue of imputing knowledge to the company should not be allowed to become entangled with an entirely distinct and separate question of when might a director be under a duty to disclose his own wrongdoing to the company and therefore be under a liability to his principal/company for any failure so to do. The latter issue is properly categorized as being concerned with the liability of a fiduciary to his principal. The present issue is, however, categorized as a rule of law in agency concerning the attribution of knowledge.[36] **14.30**

In *Belmont Finance Corpn v Williams Furniture Ltd (No 2)*,[37] the court was concerned with a conspiracy to provide company funds to finance the purchase of company shares contrary to s 54 of the Companies Act 1948. The court held that the knowledge of Mr James, who was a director in two of the relevant companies, as to the overall scheme, was to be imputed to those companies.[38] Buckley LJ stated: **14.31**

> Their knowledge must, in my opinion, be imputed to the companies of which they were directors and secretary, for an officer of a company must surely be under a duty, if he is aware that a transaction into which his company or a wholly-owned subsidiary is about to enter is illegal or tainted with illegality, to inform the board of that company of the fact. Where an officer is under a duty to make disclosure to his company, his knowledge is imputed to the company (*Re David Payne & Co Ltd, Re Fenwick, Stobart & Co Ltd*).[39]

Buckley LJ should not be interpreted as circumventing the fraud exception to the general rule, which Vaughan Williams J stated in the following terms: **14.32**

> ... if Wills had been guilty of a fraud, the personal knowledge of Wills of the fraud that he had committed upon the company would not have been knowledge of the society of the facts constituting that fraud; because common sense at once leads one to the conclusion that it would be impossible to infer that the duty, either of giving or receiving notice, will be fulfilled where the common agent is himself guilty of fraud. It seems to me that if you assume here that Mr Wills was guilty of irregularity – a breach

---

35 [1896] 2 Ch 743, 748 (Vaughan Williams J).
36 *Item Software (UK) Ltd v Fassihi* [2004] EWCA 1244; [2005] 2 BCLC 91, 104h–i (Arden LJ). The distinction between these issues can be blurred by the fact that some of the discussion as to when information will be imputed to a company is phrased in the language of duties owed to inform the company.
37 [1980] 1 All ER 393 (CA).
38 ibid, 404 (Buckley LJ).
39 ibid (Buckley LJ).

of duty in respect of these transactions – the same inference is to be drawn as if he had been guilty of fraud.[40]

14.33   Applying this reasoning to the facts of *In Re Hampshire Land Company*, Vaughan Williams J refused to impute the knowledge of Mr Wills, as a director of the borrowing company, that proper authorization for taking out the loan had not been obtained, to the lending society, of which Mr Wills was also a director. All this was well known to Buckley LJ when he wrote the comments set out above. Indeed, in the earlier case of *Belmont Finance v Williams Furniture*,[41] his Lordship was clear that knowledge of wrongdoing would not be imputed to a company who can properly be viewed as the victim of that wrongdoing.[42]

14.34   The difficulty surrounding the case law in this area is that whilst some authorities have expressly recognized the distinction to be drawn between imputation of knowledge and the duty on a director to disclose his own wrongdoing to the company, others have expressly relied upon the ambit of the duty to disclose as determining when it is right and proper to impute knowledge. This latter approach, if followed, would circumvent the principle in *In Re Hampshire Land Company* of the fraud exception given the ambit of the duty to disclose as set out in *Item Software (UK) Ltd v Fassihi*.[43]

14.35   What can perhaps be said is this. Where it is clear that a company is the victim of the wrongdoing of one of its directors, it is unlikely that the court will impute the director's knowledge of that wrongdoing to that company. The core issue here is not so much the wrongdoing of the director but the fact that the company is the victim of that wrongdoing. Such reasoning can be gleamed from the House of Lords decision in *Houghton v Nothard Lowe and Wills*[44] where Viscount Dunedin stated:

> But what if the knowledge of the director is the knowledge of a director who is himself *particeps criminis*, that is, if the knowledge of an infringement of the right of the company is only brought home to the man who himself was the artificer of such infringement? Common sense suggests the answer, but authority is not wanting.[45]

The authority to which Viscount Dunedin refers is *In Re Hampshire* and *Lacey v Hill*.[46] Viscount Dunedin went on to find on the facts that the only manner in which knowledge could be imputed to the company was through individuals who 'were all parties to the arrangement, which was a fraud on the true interests of the company'.[47]

---

40 [1896] 2 Ch 743, 749 (Vaughan Williams J). This dicta was expressly approved by the House of Lords in *Houghton v Nothard Lowe and Wills* [1928] AC 1, 14–15 (Viscount Dunedin).
41 [1979] Ch 250.
42 ibid, 261 H.
43 [2005] 2 BCLC 91.
44 [1928] AC 1.
45 ibid, 14.
46 (1876) 4 Ch D 537.
47 [1928] AC 1, 15.

Similar reasoning, invoking the status of the company as a victim of the conspir-   **14.36**
acy as a bar to the imputation of knowledge, can be seen in *Belmont Finance v
Williams Furniture*:[48]

> But in my view such knowledge should not be imputed to the company, for the
> essence of the arrangement was to deprive the company improperly of a large part of
> its assets. I think it would be irrational to treat the directors, who were allegedly par-
> ties to the conspiracy, notionally as having transmitted this knowledge to the com-
> pany; and indeed it is a well-recognised exception from the general rule that a
> principal is affected by notice received by his agent that, if the agent is acting in fraud
> of his principal and the matter of which he has notice is relevant to the fraud, that
> knowledge is not to be imputed to the principal.

The common-sense basis of this approach should not disguise the difficulty of its   **14.37**
application. In particular, when is a company to be viewed as a victim of the direct-
or's wrongdoing for the purposes of barring any imputation of knowledge? If the
company's assets are being stripped by the arrangement, that would amount to a
clear case of its being a victim. But what about where the director simply involves
the company in some form of illegal activity, which may expose it to criminal
sanctions and/or potential civil liability? Is the company then considered a victim?[49] Does it suffice merely to show that the target of the wrongdoing was another
entity, and not the company, to displace the bar on imputation of this knowledge?
It is unfortunate that practitioners are left in the dark on many of these issues.

(2) Combination or understanding

The starting position is that unlike its criminal counterpart, the tort of conspiracy   **14.38**
is not complete by establishing the existence of an agreement, combination or
understanding between two or more persons:

> . . . the gist of the tort of conspiracy is not the conspiratorial agreement alone, but
> that agreement plus the overt act causing damage. It is true that the crime of conspir-
> acy is the very agreement of two or more persons to effect an unlawful purpose, and
> any overt acts done in pursuance of the agreement are merely evidence to prove the
> fact of the agreement. The tort of conspiracy, however, is complete only if the agree-
> ment is carried into effect so as to damage the plaintiff. Accordingly, the acts done in
> pursuance of the agreement are an integral part of the tort: *Crofter Hand Woven
> Harris Tweed Co Ltd v Veitch* [1942] AC 435 (per Salmon J in *Marrinan v Vibart*).[50]

---

[48] [1979] Ch 250, 261–2. On the facts, the court found the aim of the conspiracy was to remove
some £400,000 of assets from the company.

[49] It would appear that the company would not be considered a victim in these circumstances and
therefore the knowledge of the wrongdoing directors could be imputed to it: see *Belmont Finance v
Williams Furniture (No 2)* [1980] 1 All ER 393, where the knowledge of the conspiracy of Mr James
as director and chairman of both the first defendant and second defendant companies was imputed
to these companies in circumstances where a third related company, Belmont, was the actual target
of the illegal conduct.

[50] [1963] 1 QB 234, 238–9.

14.39 Given this distinction, it may be more appropriate to focus energies on establishing the existence of combined activities or actions in concert rather than simply looking for some form of an agreement on its own.[51] In any event, very rarely will it be possible, at the date of pleading the claim, to provide full and accurate details of the alleged agreement or understanding reached between the parties to carry out a conspiracy. The reality is that usually this has to be inferred from the relevant facts as known at that stage, which rather brings one back to identifying the appropriate activities which evidence the existence of some form of understanding between the parties, as well as being essential factors for the purposes of establishing liability for conspiracy.

14.40 Various terms have been used by the courts to describe this requirement, ranging from an 'agreement' or 'understanding' right through to a 'combination'. The latter is perhaps preferable because it is devoid of any connotation of legally binding arrangements.[52] That said, it must be recognized that many authorities still refer to the arrangement as an 'agreement' without thereby intending to imply any need to satisfy contractual requirements.

14.41 The practical reality is that it is unlikely that there will be much by way of direct evidence of the existence of any relevant understanding and it will be necessary to ask the court to draw inferences from the combined activities of the alleged conspirators. The potential range and ambit of such relevant activities is vast and can vary just as the individual participation in a conspiracy can vary. In one case, *Kuwait Oil Tanker Co SAK v Al Bader*,[53] the Court of Appeal was willing to draw an inference of a combination or understanding from the simple fact that the defendant failed to take any steps to prevent or stop the unlawful activities.

14.42 It is not essential that all conspirators join the combination at the same time, but they should be in possession of all relevant facts and have a similar[54] aim in mind. In *Huntley v Thornton*[55] Harman J said:

> no doubt it is not necessary that all the conspirators should join at the same time, but it is . . . necessary that they should know all the facts and entertain the same object.

---

[51] As Lord Diplock remarked in *Lonrho Ltd v Shell Petroleum (No 2)* [1982] AC 173, 188, '. . . the tort, unlike the crime, consists not of agreement but of concerted action taken pursuant to agreement'.

[52] Buckley LJ favoured 'combination' with common intention for this very reason: *Belmont Finance v Williams Furniture* [1980] 1 All ER 393, 404. His Lordship also drew support from the speeches in *Crofter Hand Woven Harris Tweed Co Ltd v Veitch* [1942] AC 435 to similar effect.

[53] [2000] 2 All ER (Comm) 271.

[54] Harman J in *Huntley v Thornton* [1957] 1 WLR 321, 343 uses the language of all conspirators having the 'same' aim whereas *Clerk & Lindsell* (19th edn) at para 25-120 states that the conspirators 'nor need they have exactly the same aim mind'.

[55] [1957] 1 WLR 321, 343.

(3) Concerted action

The thrust of tortious liability for conspiracy is concerted action taken pursuant **14.43**
to the combination or understanding reached, expressly or impliedly, between the
conspirators. Action leading to actual damage rather than simple words lies behind
this head of claim.

There must be active participation—not mere facilitation. What must be shown **14.44**
is conduct which has been undertaken in order to implement or assist or carry out
the combination or understanding reached between the conspirators. The fact
that an individual's actions may be viewed as facilitating a particular conspiracy
will not, without more, suffice to establish that that individual is a member of a
conspiracy. The position is the same for both joint tortfeasance in procuring a
wrong by reason of a common design and for conspiracy.[56] As has been observed:
'Facilitating the doing of an act is obviously different from procuring the doing of
the act.'[57]

So, for example, the bank clerk who negligently fails properly to check the creden- **14.45**
tials and identity of those opening up a new bank account and thereby enables
them to open up an account in another's name no doubt provides tremendous
assistance to the conspiracy, but will not be a member of the relevant conspiracy
unless it can be shown that the negligent conduct was undertaken in order to carry
out that conspiracy.[58] But the man who opens and maintains a false bank account
in order to assist a forger to cash forged cheques and thereby defraud the bank goes
beyond mere facilitation and would be liable as a joint tortfeasor as well as
co-conspirator.[59]

In *CBS Songs Ltd v Amstrad Plc*,[60] Amstrad was not liable for procuring the breach **14.46**
of copyright by selling machines capable of making unlawful copies of the record-
ings. Lord Templeman observed:

> . . . I accept that a defendant who procures a breach of copyright is liable jointly and
> severally with the infringer for the damages suffered by the plaintiff as a result of the
> infringement. The defendant is a joint infringer; he intends and procures and shares
> a common design that infringement shall take place. A defendant may procure an
> infringement by inducement, incitement or persuasion. But in the present case

---

[56] *Clerk & Lindsell* (19th edn), para 24-120 citing several authorities including *CBS Songs Ltd v Amstrad* [1988] AC 1013 in support of this proposition. See also Carty, *An Analysis of the Economic Torts*, 24–6.

[57] Buckley LJ in *Belegging-en Exploitatiemaatschappij Lavender BV v Witten Industrial Diamonds Ltd* [1979] FSR 59, 65.

[58] But then the conduct would hardly be negligent— it would be deliberate in order to assist the conspiracy.

[59] See *Credit Lyonnais Bank Nederland NV v Export Credit Guarantee Department* [1998] 1 Lloyd's Law Rep 19, 44 col 1 per Stuart-Smith LJ commenting on *Thambiah v R* [1966] AC 37.

[60] [1988] 1 AC 1013.

Amstrad do not procure infringement by offering for sale a machine which may be used for lawful or unlawful copying and they do not procure infringement by advertising the attractions of their machine to any purchaser who may decide to copy unlawfully.[61]

14.47   In *Credit Lyonnais v ECGD*, Hobhouse LJ cited, with apparent approval, the summary of the relevant authorities undertaken by Mr Justice Aldous in *PLG Research Ltd v Ardon International Ltd*[62] as follows:

> ... the law distinguishes between facilitating and procuring a tort. A person who only facilitates a tort is not liable as a joint tortfeasor whereas a person who procures the tort is liable. (See *CBS Songs v Amstrad* [1988] RPC 567 and *B E Lavender v Witten Industrial Diamonds* [1979] FSR 9.) What amounts to facilitating tort will vary in case to case, but as Mellish LJ said in *Townsend v Haworth* (1879) 48 LJ CH 770 at 773:
>
> > 'Selling materials for the purpose of infringing a patent to the man who is going to infringe it even though the party who sells it knows that he is going to infringe it and indemnifies him, does not by itself, make the person who so sells an infringer. He must be party with the man who so infringes and actually infringe.'

(4) What intention suffices?

14.48   The present position can be succinctly stated. In the case of unlawful means conspiracy, the conspirators must have an intention to injure the target of the conspiracy, but it does not have to be the sole or predominant intention.[63]

14.49   Unlike the situation involving the simple conspiracy, it is not open to alleged conspirators to plead acting in their self-interest as a defence to a claim of having taken part in an unlawful means conspiracy.

14.50   In reaching this position, the House of Lords in *Lonrho v Fayed* emphatically rejected the attempt by the Court of Appeal in *Metall und Rohstoff AG v Donaldson, Lufkin & Jenrette Inc* to (re) interpret Lord Diplock in *Lonrho Ltd v Shell Petroleum*[64] as requiring any higher threshold of intention such as to equate that required for unlawful means conspiracy with that required for the simple conspiracy.

14.51   Lord Bridge, giving the main speech in *Lonrho v Fayed*, cited with approval Lord Denning in *Lonrho Limited v Shell Petroleum (No 2)*[65] whose observations merit full quoting:

> Is an agreement to do an unlawful act actionable at the suit of anyone who suffers damage from it which is reasonably foreseeable? Even though the agreement is not

---

[61] ibid, 1058E. See also the review of authorities undertaken by Mustill LJ in *Unilever Plc v Gillette (UK) Ltd* [1989] RPC 583.

[62] [1993] FSR 197, 238–9 (a patent infringement action, considering a director's personal liability).

[63] *Lonrho plc v Fayed* [1992] 1 AC 448, 466, 468.

[64] [1982] AC 173.

[65] Unreported CA (Civil Division) Transcript No 51 of 1981.

directed at him, nor done with intent to injure him? In discussing this point of law I put aside the many modern cases on conspiracy – in which there is an agreement by two or more to do a *lawful* act. It is now settled by the House of Lords that such an agreement is actionable if it is done with the predominant motive of injuring the plaintiff and does in fact injure him: see *Crofter Hand Woven Harris Tweed Co Ltd v Veitch* [1942] AC 435, where Lord Simon LC said, at p.445: 'Liability must depend on ascertaining the predominant purpose. If that predominant purpose is to damage another person and damage results, that is tortious conspiracy.' Here we are concerned with a different problem altogether. It is an agreement by two or more to do an *unlawful* act – when there is no intent to injure the plaintiff and it is not aimed or directed at him – is not actionable, even though he is damaged thereby. But if there is an intent to injure him then it is actionable. The intent to injure may not be the predominant motive. It may be mixed with other motives. In this context, when the agreement is to do an *unlawful* act, we do not get into the 'quagmire of mixed motives' as Lord Simon LC described them in the *Crofters* case at p.445. It is sufficient if the conspiracy is aimed or directed at the plaintiff, and it can reasonably be foreseen that it may injure him, and does in fact injure him.[66]

14.52 The necessary intent may be inferred, and often will need to be inferred, from the surrounding facts. In *Kuwait Oil Tanker Co SAK v Al Bader*[67] Nourse LJ, delivering the judgment of the Court of Appeal, said at paragraphs 120–1:

> [I]n the case of most conspiracies to injure by tortious means it will be clear from the acts of the conspirators that they must have intended to injure the claimant . . . An example of such an inference being drawn in a similar field is in *Bourgoin SA v Ministry of Agriculture, Fisheries and Food* [1986] QB 716 at 777 [where] Oliver LJ said . . . :
>
> > 'If an act is done deliberately and with knowledge of its consequences, we do not think that the actor can sensibly say that he did not "intend" the consequences or that the act was not "aimed" at the person who, it is known, will suffer them.'

14.53 The approach of the Court of Appeal in *Kuwait Oil Tanker* should not be misinterpreted as evidencing a willingness readily to infer intention from such surrounding circumstances. To do so would undermine any requirement for intention in the first place and ignore that this tort is very much concerned with 'directed harm'.[68]

14.54 This point was made in the subsequent Court of Appeal decision in *Douglas v Hello! Ltd (No 3)*[69] where the Court expressly disavowed any attempt to read the

---

[66] See also Neuberger LJ, delivering the judgment of the CA, in *IS Innovative Software Ltd v Howes* [2004] EWCA Civ 275, para 42.

[67] [2000] 2 All ER (Comm) 271.

[68] Carty, *An Analysis of the Economic Torts*, 17 cited with approval by the Court of Appeal in *Douglas v Hello! Ltd (No 3)*, para 224.

[69] [2005] EWCA Civ 595, [2005] 3 WLR 881.

above extract from the *Kuwait Oil Tanker* judgment as suggesting that foresight of consequences must always be equated with intention to cause them.[70]

14.55 On the facts, the Court of Appeal in *Douglas v Hello! Ltd (No 3)* rejected *OK!* magazine's assertion that *Hello!* had intended to cause *OK!* financial harm by publishing photographs of the wedding of Michael Douglas and Catherine Zeta-Jones, for which *OK!* had agreed an exclusive deal. In rejecting this claim, the Court of Appeal emphasized that the gist of the tort of unlawful interference is the intentional infliction of economic harm i.e. 'it must be shown that the object or purpose of the defendant is to inflict harm on the claimant, either as an end in itself, or as a means to another end. If foresight of probable consequences or subjective recklessness sufficed as the mental element of the tort, this would transform the nature of the tort.'[71]

14.56 Justifying the decision to impose liability in the *Kuwait Oil Tanker* case, the Court of Appeal in *Douglas v Hello! Ltd (No 3)* held that on the facts there 'the very act of diverting the money to the defendants required and involved (as opposed to merely resulted in) diverting the money away from the claimant. Indeed, it may be said that the wrongful act of diverting the money from the claimant in a sense preceded the ulterior motive, namely the receipt of the money by the defendant. However, in some situations an unlawful act will have adverse financial consequences to third parties, which are foreseeable and foreseen, but which are not consequences that the defendant desires or has any interest in bringing about.'[72]

14.57 In other words, the Court of Appeal in *Douglas* considered that *Hello!* was not trying to reduce the circulation of its rival paper *OK!* but rather trying to boost its own circulation and that it could not be assumed that by boosting its own circulation (by publishing these photographs), *Hello!* would thereby be reducing the circulation of *OK!* The House of Lords in *Douglas* took a different approach. The House of Lords held that the Court of Appeal had erred in holding that the defendants had no intention to cause loss to the claimant and had only intended to maintain their own sales. Their Lordships found that causing loss to the claimant was the means whereby the defendants intended to obtain their end and so they had the necessary intention. However, there had been no interference by unlawful means.

14.58 In *Meretz Investments NV v ACP Ltd,*[73] the Court of Appeal, in the first case to consider *OBG v Allan*, held that the relevant intention for conspiracy to injure by unlawful means was not established in circumstances where the defendants acted

---

[70] [2005] EWCA Civ 595; [2005] 3 WLR 881, para 217.
[71] ibid, para 223.
[72] ibid, para 217.
[73] [2007] EWCA Civ 1303.

not only to protect their own interests but also in the belief, based on legal advice, that they had the right to act as they did, notwithstanding that the loss or detriment to the claimant was an intended consequence of their action.

In the *Kuwait Oil Tanker* case, the receipt of monies properly belonging to the **14.59** claimant necessarily reduces the money in the possession of the claimant. It was thus necessary to inflict harm on the claimant in the *Kuwait Oil Tanker* case as a means to an end, i.e. enabling the defendants to receive the fraud proceeds.

(5) What qualifies as unlawful means?

There is little consistent judicial guidance on what amounts to unlawful means for **14.60** the purposes of this conspiracy and the Court of Appeal has recognized the difficulty of attempting to identify or formulate any principle of general application, given the state of the decided case law.[74] That said, the Court of Appeal did indicate that it would not favour an approach which limited what was meant by 'unlawful means' unless this was done clearly and distinctly. Anything else would simply contribute to the anomalous standing of the economic torts.[75] Similarly, Lord Bridge's speech in *Lonrho v Fayed*,[76] and its general references to 'unlawful means' cannot be interpreted as favouring artificial restrictions on what constitutes 'unlawful means'.

A useful starting point is the assertion by the editors of *Clerk & Lindsell* (para **14.61** 25-121) that there is no good reason for 'unlawful means' to have a different meaning in a conspiracy context than when used in respect of the other economic torts. The practitioner should at least be entitled to expect internal consistency within the economic torts on this issue.[77] On this basis, the House of Lords decision in *OBG Ltd v Allan* (in the context of the tort of causing loss by unlawful means) might well be seen to be influential in the context of conspiracy by unlawful means.

In *Crofter*, Lord Wright stated that whenever an individual act was itself tortious, **14.62** an agreement or combination to carry out that act would itself amount to a tortious conspiracy.[78] This would include the usual economic torts such as conduct amounting to procurement of a breach of contract,[79] fraud,[80] intimidatory threats

---

[74] *Douglas v Hello! Ltd (No 3)* [2005] 3 WLR 881, para 229.
[75] ibid, para 228.
[76] [1992] 1 AC 448, 463–6.
[77] *Michaels v Taylor Woodrow Developments Ltd* [2001] Ch 493, 502–3, Laddie J; see also Mance LJ (sitting at first instance) in *Grupo Torras SA v Al-Sabah* [1999] CLC 1469, 1649.
[78] [1942] 1 AC 435, 462.
[79] *Stratford v Lindley* [1965] AC 269; *Pritchard v Briggs* [1980] Ch 338.
[80] *Sorrell v Smith* [1925] AC 700, at 714 per Viscount Cave LC cited with approval by Lord Bridge in *Lonrho v Fayed* [1992] 1 AC 448, 464–5.

to break a contract, as well as other torts such as nuisance and trespass. It would appear that a conspiracy to break a contract would constitute 'unlawful means' although the matter is not entirely free from doubt.[81]

14.63   In *Douglas v Hello! Ltd (No 3)*, the Court of Appeal indicated that breach of confidence would amount to 'unlawful means' for these purposes. This was so even though the confidence breached was owed to the Douglases and not to the claimant, *OK!* As the Court of Appeal stated:

> We recognize that, having regard to the conclusions reached earlier as to OK!'s claim for breach of confidence, there was no breach of a duty of confidence owed to OK!, but it cannot be necessary for the unlawful means to amount to an actionable infringement of the claimant's own rights. Otherwise the tort would be largely ineffective: see *Associated British Ports v Transport and General Workers' Union* [1989] 1 WLR 939, especially per Stuart-Smith LJ, at p 965.[82]

The Court had concluded that *OK!* had no right to claim confidence in the photographs taken by *Hello! OK!*'s right to claim confidence was limited to those photographs taken by it to be published as part of its contractual arrangement with the Douglases. The right to claim breach of confidence in respect of any other photographs remained vested in the Douglases. The Court held this sufficed for the purposes of the claim for conspiracy.

14.64   *Douglas v Hello!* went on appeal to the House of Lords *sub-nom OBG Ltd v Allan* where the House of Lords rejected the Court of Appeal's finding that *Hello!* had used unlawful means in publishing the photographs.

14.65   Greater uncertainty surrounds the question whether equitable wrongs constitute 'unlawful means'. It is known, from the Court of Appeal's comments in *Douglas v Hello! Ltd (No 3)*, that it opposes any restriction on what may amount to 'unlawful means' unless such restriction can be clearly and distinctly justified. Similarly, Lord Nicholls in the House of Lords in *OBG Ltd v Allan*[83] suggested a wide test for 'unlawful means' conspiracy, embracing all acts a defendant is not permitted to do, whether by the civil law or the criminal law. In doing so, Lord Nicholls

---

[81] In *Kuwait Oil Tanker Co SAK v Al Bader (No 3)* [2000] 2 All ER (Comm) 271, Nourse LJ impliedly suggested that a breach of contract would suffice. In *Rookes v Barnard* [1964] AC 1129, the House of Lords held that a threat to break a contract may amount to an unlawful threat for the purposes of the tort of intimidation. However, Lord Devlin was at pains to express that he was not thereby deciding what amounted to unlawful means for the purposes of conspiracy: 'I have not been considering what amounts to unlawful means in the tort of conspiracy. I am not saying that a conspiracy to commit a breach of contract amounts to the tort of conspiracy; that point remains to be decided. I am saying that in the tort of intimidation a threat to break a contract would be a threat of an illegal act. It follows from that that a combination to intimidate by means of a threat of a breach of contract would be an unlawful conspiracy; but it does not necessarily follow that a combination to commit a breach of contract simpliciter would be an unlawful conspiracy' [1209–10].
[82] [2005] 3 WLR 881, [234].
[83] [2008] 1 AC 1, [162].

expressly adopted the approaches of both Lord Reid and Lord Devlin in *Rookes v Barnard*.[84] On this approach, one might expect that all equitable wrongs would fall within the definition, but apparently not.

It has been suggested that not all equitable wrongs qualify but that a court may be persuaded that a 'serious contravention' of an equitable wrong amounts to 'unlawful means'.[85] The learned editors of *Clerk & Lindsell* cite the case of *Belmont Finance Corpn v Williams Furniture Ltd (No 2)*[86] in support of this proposition. First, as a matter of principle, the introduction of a definition of 'unlawful means' which is dependent upon some view of the serious nature of the actual conduct, as opposed to objective categorization thereof, is a recipe for uncertainty and increased litigation costs. It is an approach to which this present author would have to be dragged kicking and screaming. Secondly, does *Belmont* require such a conclusion? With respect, the answer is no. There is not a word within this judgment of the Court of Appeal of the need to take into account the serious nature of any alleged misconduct to determine whether it amounts to 'unlawful means'. Indeed, none of their Lordships had any difficulty in accepting that breach of s 54 of the Companies Act 1948 would amount to illegal activity/unlawful means for the purposes of finding liability for conspiracy.

14.66

Buckley LJ stated (p 404):

14.67

> To obtain in civil proceedings a remedy for conspiracy, the plaintiff must establish (a) a combination of the defendants, (b) to effect an unlawful purpose, resulting in damage to the plaintiff . . .
>
> The unlawful purpose in this case was the provision of financial assistance in contravention of s.54 of the 1948 Act . . .

Goff LJ stated (p 407):

14.68

> . . . I shall proceed to consider the case in conspiracy. To succeed on this issue Belmont must establish that the agreement of 3 October 1963 was a breach of s.54 of the 1948 Act and, therefore, illegal and that the value of the Maximum shares was significantly less than £500,000, since otherwise Belmont suffered no damage which is not too remote.

Waller LJ stated (p 414):

14.69

> The next question is whether or not the defendants were guilty of conspiracy. A conspiracy is an agreement between two or more persons to effect an unlawful purpose which results in damage to somebody else. . . . A person is a party to a conspiracy if he knows the essential facts to constitute that conspiracy even though he does not know that they constitute an offence . . . Since there was a breach of s.54 and the

---

84 '[1964] AC 1129, 1168–9 (Lord Reid) and 1206–7 (Lord Devlin).
85 *Clerk & Lindsell* (19th edn), para 25-121.
86 [1980] 1 All ER 393.

defendants through their directors made all the arrangements and knew all the facts constituting the breach, it would follow that they conspired together to contravene s 54, the object of their conspiracy being Belmont, and if Belmont suffered damage they are liable.

14.70 Any attempt to define 'unlawful means' by reference to an ambiguous sliding scale of serious misconduct is directly at odds with the general approach advocated by the Court of Appeal in *Douglas v Hello! Ltd (No 3)*, namely that any restrictions on the type of conduct qualifying for 'unlawful means' be clearly defined and justified.

14.71 Uncertainty surrounds whether a breach of contract would amount to 'unlawful means' for the purposes of a claim in conspiracy.[87] The House of Lords in *Rookes v Barnard*[88] appeared to favour such an approach although it is noted that Lord Devlin expressly left the point open.

14.72 Not only is there difficulty in identifying a general principle outlining the type of wrongful conduct which would amount to 'unlawful means', there was, at least prior to the House of Lords decision in *OGD*, also a marked divergence of judicial views as to whether those means must be actionable at the instance of the claimant.

14.73 Stuart-Smith LJ in *Credit Lyonnais v ECGD*[89] considered actionability at the instance of the claimant to be essential[90] although in his prior decision in *Associated British Ports v TGWU*[91] he considered there was no need for a breach of statutory duty to be actionable in tort at the suit of the claimant, at least for the purposes of interference with trade or business.[92] It is perhaps worth noting that Stuart-Smith LJ's dicta in *Credit Lyonnais* was made on the back of counsel's concession on this issue.

14.74 Some judicial support for the view that it is 'eminently arguable' that there is no such requirement can be found in Waller LJ's judgment in *Surzur Overseas Ltd v Koros*.[93] Waller LJ noted that the present uncertainty derived from Lord Bridge in

---

87 See *Clerk & Lindsell* (19th edn), para 25-128.

88 [1964] AC 1129.

89 [1998] 1 Lloyd's Law Rep 19.

90 ibid, 32.

91 [1989] 1 WLR 939, 965.

92 How these dicta are interpreted will no doubt depend on whether one adopts the view of Hazel Carty, *An Analysis of Economic Torts*, that these are separate and distinct torts which do not share 'the same framework of liability'. If the view is taken that there is little merit in adopting a different view of 'unlawful means' depending on which economic tort is being considered, Stuart-Smith LJ's two dicta would have the air of inconsistency.

93 [1999] 2 Lloyd's Law Rep 611, 617. Waller LJ was speaking with the agreement of the Court of Appeal.

Lonrho v Fayed[94] adopting the dictum of Lord Devlin in *Rookes v Barnard*[95] where Lord Devlin, speaking of unlawful means conspiracy, commented:

> In the latter type . . . the element of conspiracy is usually only of secondary import-ance since the unlawful means are actionable by themselves.

Waller LJ noted the use of the word 'usually' in this dictum and stated that Lord Bridge, in adopting Lord Devlin's views, could not have been intending to lay down some definitive rule in respect of unlawful means conspiracy. This latter point is expressly supported by the comments of Lord Templeman in *Lonrho v Fayed* in agreeing with Lord Bridge and recognizing the need for the 'ambit and ingredients' of this tort to be reconsidered by the courts.[96]

In *Watson v Dutton Forshaw Motor Group Ltd*,[97] Waller LJ expressed similar reser- **14.75** vations on this issue, and in particular about the dictum of Stuart-Smith LJ in *Credit Lyonnais v ECGD* which was subsequently adopted by Toulson J in *Yukong Line Ltd v Rendsburg*:[98]

> I would simply like to put a marker down that in my view the point is by no means clear in the light of the House of Lords decision in *Lonrho v Fayed* [1992] 1 AC 448, and I am at present unconvinced by the reasoning of Toulson J in relation to that decision.

Although Waller LJ's comments, in both the *Watson* and *Surzur* cases, were in the **14.76** context of interlocutory applications, it is worthy of note that in the *Watson* case, his comments were agreed to by Butler-Sloss and Chadwick LJJ, and in the *Surzur* case, by Hirst and Aldous LJJ. This represents a formidable line-up of Court of Appeal judges who have serious concerns with the suggestion that the unlawful means must give rise to civil actionability.

Waller LJ's dicta in *Surzur* was followed by Nourse LJ in *Kuwait Oil Tanker Co* **14.77** *SAK v Al Bader (No 3)*.[99] Similarly, in *Bank Geselleschaft Berlin International SA v RaifZihnali*,[100] Colman J considered that Stuart-Smith LJ's dicta in *Credit Lyonnais* appeared to 'introduce a requirement which is conceptionally irrelevant'.[101] Without wishing to express a final view on the matter, Colman J did comment that the 'requirement of double actionability appears to be quite unsustainable'.[102]

---

94 [1992] 1 AC 448, 464C-D.
95 [1964] AC 1129, 1204.
96 [1992] 1 AC 448, 471.
97 Unreported CA (Civ Div) 22 July 1998.
98 [1998] 1 WLR 294.
99 [2000] 2 All ER (Comm) 271; see also J Ulph, in J Glister and M Tugendhat, *Commercial Fraud* (Oxford University Press, 2006), 410. Hazel Carty explains Nourse LJ's view on the basis that he considers there to be a symmetry between unlawful means conspiracy and the tort of unlawful inter-ference with trade. In *An Analysis of the Economic Torts*, 21, n 46, Carty rejects any such symmetry.
100 Unreported QBD (Com Ct) 16 July 2001, Colman J.
101 Transcript, para 32.
102 ibid.

14.78   More recently still, in *Douglas v Hello! (No 3)*,[103] the Court of Appeal did not consider it a bar to a finding of conspiracy to use unlawful means that *Hello!* owed the duty of confidentiality to the Douglases and not to the claimant, *OK!* Lord Phillips MR, giving the judgment of the Court of Appeal, stated:

> We recognize that, having regard to the conclusions reached earlier as to OK!'s claim for breach of confidence, there was no breach of a duty of confidence owed to OK!, but it cannot be necessary for the unlawful means to amount to an actionable infringement of the claimant's own rights. Otherwise the tort would be largely ineffective: see *Associated British Ports v Transport and General Workers' Union* [1989] 1 WLR 939, especially per Stuart-Smith LJ, at p.965.[104]

14.79   Against this background of a maze of conflicting dicta on the issue whether the 'unlawful means' must be actionable at the instance of the claimant, is to be placed the decision of the House of Lords in *OBG Ltd v Allan*[105] where it was stated clearly that the tort of causing loss by unlawful means and acts against a third party counted as unlawful means only if they were actionable by that third party if he had suffered loss. On the facts, the House of Lords held that the conduct of *Hello!* no doubt reduced the value to be attached to the contract as between the Douglases and *OK!*, but that conduct did not prevent or interfere with the Douglases' ability to deal with *OK!* or perform their contract with *OK!* Further, the Court of Appeal had erred in finding that *Hello!* did not intend to cause loss to *OK!*—causing loss to *OK!* was in fact *Hello!*'s means to an end. However, none of this would render *Hello!* liable in tort since the magazine had not in fact employed unlawful means.

14.80   On the basis that there is little disagreement that 'unlawful means' should have the same meaning for the tort of causing loss by unlawful means as it does for conspiracy to cause loss by unlawful means, the approach advocated by the House of Lords in *ODG* is likely to be utilized in the context of the conspiracy claims.

D. Simple Conspiracy

(1) Introduction

14.81   The simple conspiracy or the *Quinn v Leatham* conspiracy is now considered to be a somewhat 'anomalous' tort[106] because it operates as an exception to the well-known principle that acts which are not themselves unlawful do not become so simply because a group of individuals chose to come together to perform those acts.

---

[103] [2005] 3 WLR 881.
[104] ibid, para 234.
[105] [2008] 1 AC1 (*Douglas v Hello!* on appeal).
[106] Per Lord Diplock in *Lonrho Ltd v Shell Petroleum Co Ltd (No 2)* [1982] AC 173, 188–99.

For the purposes of a practitioner's book on commercial fraud, there is little need **14.82** to dwell on this tort. As will be seen, whilst there is no need to establish the use of unlawful means, this requirement is replaced by the imposition of a substantial hurdle in proving a sole or predominant intention to injure. This intention will not readily be proven and, it would appear, can be displaced if the defendant can show that he was acting for his own interests and not with the *sole or predominant* intention to injure the claimant.

If all other elements of a conspiracy are satisfied, it is hard to imagine too many **14.83** situations in which a commercial fraud would be carried out without the employment of some form of unlawful means, such as to enable the claimant to plead unlawful means conspiracy and thereby circumvent having to prove the difficult level of intention for a simple conspiracy.

There is little prospect of this tort being extended or expanded to meet modern **14.84** commercial frauds. Lord Diplock in *Lonrho v Shell Petroleum Ltd* expressly refused to extend the tort 'beyond those narrow limits that are all that common sense and the application of the legal logic of the decided cases require'.[107] No doubt one of the factors limiting any attempt to widen the ambit of this type of conspiracy is the inability to identify the true rationale for this tort in the first place.

Various justifications have been offered for the existence of this tort, many of **14.85** which are based upon the view that a 'combination may make oppressive or dangerous that which if it proceeded only from a single person would be otherwise'.[108] These do not find much favour in the modern case law.[109] Indeed, in a commercial world where one entity, such as a large supermarket chain, is able to exert far more influence than a combination of hundreds of small shopkeepers, the suggested rationale of the dangerous nature of group over single influence appears misplaced.

(2) Elements of simple conspiracy

The focus of the simple conspiracy is not the engagement in unlawful means **14.86** (as is the case in the unlawful means conspiracy) but rather the intention to injure through the combination of individuals to perform what would otherwise be lawful

---

107 [1982] AC 173.

108 *Mogul Steamship Co Ltd v McGregor, Gow & Co* (1889) 23 QBD 598, 616 (Bowen LJ).

109 *Lonrho v Shell Petroleum Co Ltd (No 2)* [1982] AC 173, 189A-B (Lord Diplock): '. . . to suggest today that acts done by one street-corner grocer in concert with a second are more oppressive and dangerous to a competitor than the same acts done by a string of supermarkets under a single ownership or that a multinational conglomerate such as Lonrho or oil company such as Shell or BP does not exercise greater economic power than any combination of small businesses, is to shut one's eyes to what has been happening in the business and industrial world since the turn of the century and, in particular, since the end of World War II.'

activities. In *Kuwait Oil Tanker Co SAK v Al Bader (No 3)*,[110] the Court of Appeal provided the following definition:

> A conspiracy to injure by lawful means is actionable where the claimant proves that he has suffered loss or damage as a result of action taken pursuant to a combination or agreement between the defendant and another person or persons to injure him, where the predominant purpose of the defendant is to injure the claimant.[111]

14.87   The issues of a combination or agreement and the need for concerted action pursuant thereto have already been dealt with in the context of an unlawful means conspiracy. The same points made there apply to a simple conspiracy.

14.88   The central issue in a simple conspiracy is the intention to injure. In *Crofter Hand Woven Harris Tweed Co v Veitch*,[112] Lord Wright observed that the important distinction was 'between the case where the object is the legitimate benefit of the combiners and the case where the object is deliberate damage without any . . . just cause'.

14.89   The fact that some damage may inevitably ensue does not in itself satisfy the need for a sole or predominant intention to injure. Similarly, if the combiners are able to establish a legitimate object for their conduct (their own commercial interests, for example) then this will negate any sole or predominant intention to injure for the purposes of simple conspiracy. Importantly, this is assessed on a subjective basis and not from an objective assessment of whether the combiners are, in fact, pursuing a legitimate object.

14.90   The House of Lords decision in *Lonrho v Fayed* re-asserted the importance of the intention to injure for this tort as a distinguishing factor from the unlawful means conspiracy. It will be recalled that the Court of Appeal had somewhat muddied the waters on this distinction by interpreting Lord Diplock in *Lonrho v Shell Petroleum* as indicating that it was necessary to establish a sole or predominant intention to injure for both types of conspiracy. The House of Lords in *Lonrho v Fayed* re-asserted the traditional stance that it was only in the case of the simple conspiracy that it was necessary to show a sole or predominant intention to injure.

14.91   Of course, given the existence of a combination of several individuals, it may be possible that there exists more than one intention. The Lord Chancellor, Lord Simon, provided some guidance on this issue in *Crofter v Veitch*:

> . . . liability must depend on ascertaining the predominant purpose. If that predominant purpose is to damage another person and damage results that is tortious conspiracy.

---

[110]   [2000] 2 All ER (Comm) 271.
[111]   ibid, para 106.
[112]   [1942] AC 435.

If the predominant purpose is the lawful protection or promotion of any lawful interests of the combiners (no illegal means being employed) it is not a tortious conspiracy even though it causes damage to another person.[113]

In circumstances where the case law is unable to identify a strong underlying **14.92** rationale for this tort, where that rationale which is offered appears misplaced in the modern business world, where the difficulties of proving the relevant intention are obvious and where the ability to raise a subjective defence of justification so easy, it is hardly surprising that this tort has limited practical importance.

E. Damages[114]

Unless the conduct complained of has in fact caused some form of loss or damage **14.93** to the claimant, no claim in conspiracy, whether of unlawful means conspiracy or simple conspiracy, can be brought. In this way, the torts of conspiracy differ from their criminal counterpart, where the agreement itself can give rise to criminal liability and sanction even if it remains unexecuted.

Damages are considered at large. The significance of this is that whilst the claim- **14.94** ant must establish and prove the existence of some loss to justify the claim, the amount of damages to be awarded is not limited to the level of provable loss caused by the tort.[115]

In *Quinn v Leatham*,[116] the trial judge's notes on evidence state: **14.95**

> I told the jury that pecuniary loss, directly caused by the conduct of the defendants, must be proved in order to establish a cause of action, and I advised them to require to be satisfied that such loss to a substantial amount had been proved by the plaintiff. I declined to tell them that if actual and substantial pecuniary loss was proved to have been directly caused to the plaintiff by the wrongful acts of the defendants, they were bound to limit the amount of damages to the precise sum so proved.[117]

These notes were cited with approval by Lord Halsbury LC in *Quinn v Leatham*.[118]

Although damages are considered at large, it is not good practice simply to plead **14.96** 'by reason of the matters set out above the plaintiffs have suffered loss, damage and

---

[113] [1942] AC 435, 445.
[114] *McGregor on Damages* (17th edn, Thomson/Sweet and Maxwell, 2003), paras 40-007–40-011 for a detailed assessment of the question of damages for conspiracy.
[115] *Lonrho v Fayed (No 5)* [1993] 1 WLR 1489, 1494 per Dillon LJ.
[116] [1901] AC 495.
[117] ibid, 498.
[118] ibid, 508.

injury' and provide no additional evidence or indication of loss suffered.[119] Such a pleading has been described as 'grossly inadequate'.[120]

14.97 Conspiracy claims can give rise to recovery for loss of profits and expenses incurred investigating the extent and nature of the conspiracy. Some doubt remains as to whether non-pecuniary loss (e.g. for injury to feelings) is recoverable. The Court of Appeal in *Joyce v Sengupta*[121] held they were, but a subsequent Court of Appeal in *Lonrho v Fayed (No 5)*[122] suggested otherwise. The better view, according to *McGregor on Damages*,[123] is that such damages should, in principle, be recoverable.[124]

F. Pleading Practice

14.98 A common defect in pleading a conspiracy claim is a failure properly and clearly to distinguish between the two types of conspiracy. Often they are pleaded together as alternatives but if this approach is to be adopted, the differing nature of each claim should be properly reflected in the pleading. A failure to get these basic elements correct from the outset will greatly hinder the litigator's ability to identify relevant evidence and marshal it for the purposes of the trial.

14.99 Any conspiracy claim in the context of a commercial fraud is going to be tantamount to pleading fraud. As such, it is incumbent upon the pleader to ensure that he has before him sufficient evidence upon which to base such a claim. Mere assertion from the client, without more, is unlikely to suffice.

14.100 Care should also be taken as to whether it is necessary or beneficial to add a claim in conspiracy to the other claims. There is little point in adding an additional claim if practically it does not assist any greater level of recovery or imposes additional evidential hurdles to overcome, thus rendering a trial more complicated, longer-lasting and therefore more expensive than it would otherwise be.

---

[119] As had occurred in *Lonrho v Shell Petroleum Co Ltd (No 2)* [1982] AC 173.
[120] *Lonrho v Fayed (No 5)* [1993] 1 WLR 1489, 1494 per Dillon LJ.
[121] [1993] 1 WLR 337 CA.
[122] [1993] 1 WLR 1489 CA.
[123] (17th edn), paras 40-010–40-011.
[124] *Clerk & Lindsell* (19th edn), para 25-137 takes a slightly different line. The learned editor suggests that the law is clearly against the granting of non-pecuniary damages at least in circumstances where no pecuniary loss has been established and this can be justified by the fact that otherwise one would be permitting a circumvention of the rules governing claims in defamation. But, with respect, the establishment of a pecuniary loss is the gist of a claim in conspiracy, without which no claim for conspiracy can be brought, and so to say that one could not claim for non-pecuniary loss where no pecuniary loss has been established says no more than to repeat the requirement for pecuniary loss to establish a claim in conspiracy.

As explained above, there are, however, significant benefits to be attached to a **14.101** conspiracy claim. For example, if it is known that the defendants all acted in concert but it is difficult to say who did what particular act, or there are some defendants who do not appear to have taken any steps to incur personal liability for the unlawful means employed, then a conspiracy plea will enable the claimant to impose liability on all defendants for all the acts, without needing to establish separate individual liability for any one act.

In order to assist in showing the subtle pleading differences as between the two **14.102** types of conspiracy, two very basic precedent forms are provided below.

(1) Unlawful means conspiracy precedent

On or about [   ], the Defendants entered into a combination or understanding **14.103** with each other with an intention to injure or cause financial loss to the Claimant by use of unlawful means and/or reached an understanding to embark upon concerted action with an intention to use unlawful means to injure or cause financial loss to the claimant and as a consequence such loss and damage was in fact caused to the Claimant.

Particulars of Unlawful Means

[set out each unlawful means employed e.g.]

(1) To procure the inducement of Mr [   ] breaking his contract with the claimant;

(2) To bribe Mr [   ], an employee or officer of the Claimant, to provide confidential information of the Claimant's business affairs/accept a tender on a contract etc.

(3) etc.

Particular of Loss and Damage

By virtue of the above conspiracy, the Claimant has been caused loss and damage including:

(1) £X being loss of profits arising from Mr A's breach of contract;

(2) £Y, being the amount of bribe paid over to the Claimant's officer.

(2) Simple conspiracy precedent

On or about [   ], the Defendants entered into a combination and/or reached an **14.104** understanding deliberately and without justification to injure or cause financial loss to the Claimant by way of concerted action.

Particulars of Concerted Action

(1) Most days the Defendants would congregate outside the Claimant's shop and behave in a rude and offensive manner to customers or potential customers of the Claimants;

(2) The Defendants would tell delivery men that the shop was closed and they would go away without delivering their goods;

(3) The Defendants would shout abuse to staff coming to and going from work at the Claimant's shop.

Particulars of Loss and Damage

(1) . . .

(2) . . .

15

INDUCING A BREACH OF CONTRACT

A. Overview

A party, X, commits the tort of inducing a breach of contract if he, X, (i) having **15.01** knowledge of the existence of a contract as between A and B, (ii) intentionally induces or procures that A breach his contract with B, (iii) and this, in fact, causes A to breach his contract with B; (iv) thereby causing loss to B; and (v) X has no justification for his actions.[2]

Damage is the gist of the action but there is no requirement of proof of special **15.02** damage since 'damages are at large'.[3] That said, it is not possible to give an accurate definition of all losses or damages which are recoverable by this tort claim. The court will readily infer loss of profits and these need not be limited to losses generated by the relevant breach of contract. They may extend to losses caused by A's inability to enter into other contracts as well as certain expenses, such as the cost of investigating the true cost of the conduct of X on B's business.

This claim is a true case of secondary or accessory liability. No liability can arise **15.03** under this tort unless and until there has been a breach of contract between A and B.

---

[1] [2008] 1 AC 1.

[2] *OBG Ltd v Allan* [2007] UKHL 21; [2008] 1 AC 1, [39]–[44] (per Lord Hoffmann); [191]–[193] (per Lord Nicholls); [264] per Lord Walker.

[3] *Exchange Telegraph Co v Gregory* [1896] QB 147 (CA), 153 per Esher MR.

The primary wrongful act is the breach of contract by A. Without that breach, X cannot be held liable for this tort.[4]

15.04 The law in this area has benefited from recent clarification from the House of Lords decision in *OBG Ltd v Allan* in four principal ways:

- Liability for inducing a breach of contract is secondary or accessory in nature. Accordingly, it follows that an actual breach of contract is an essential pre-requisite for liability under this tort.

- The distinction between direct and indirect inducement or interference, introduced by the Court of Appeal in *DC Thomson & Co Ltd v Deakin*,[5] has been abolished.

- Clarification has been given as to what kind of intention is necessary.

- A clear distinction has been drawn between the tort of inducing a breach of contract and the tort of causing loss by unlawful means.

B. Introduction

15.05 It is not unusual in complex commercial frauds for the fraud to be perpetrated by or with the assistance of employees and officers of the claimant company.[6] It is these individuals who have appropriate access to the company's bank accounts and other financial information. They literally, in some cases, have the key to the safe. But they rarely act alone and often the driving force for committing the fraud may come from someone outside the company. It is precisely in such a scenario that it may be possible to claim in tort for inducing a breach of contract.

15.06 Prior to the recent decision of the House of Lords in *OBG Ltd v Allan*,[7] the law in this area was in something of a mess. Confusion abounded as to whether there was one tort for inducing a breach of contract or two (direct and indirect), whether there was a distinction with the tort of causing loss by unlawful means, and what

---

⁴ *OBG Ltd v Allan* [2008] 1 AC 1, [44] (per Lord Hoffmann). There had been suggestions that the tort could be committed by simple interference with the contract not amounting to a breach of contract: see *Torquay Hotel Co Ltd v Cousins* [1969] 2 Ch 106, 138; *Merkur Island Shipping Corpn v Laughton* [1983] 2 AC 570, 607–8 (Lord Diplock).

⁵ [1952] Ch 646.

⁶ Some notable examples are from the criminal world: in 1975, £8m was stolen from the Mayfair branch of Bank of America. Stuart Buckley, an electrician employed to work at the bank, gave the robbers the various codes to the vaults. In 1983, Anthony Black, a security guard working at Heathrow, gave assistance to the robbers. In October 1997, vault supervisor, David Scott Ghantt, assisted in the US$17.3m robbery of the Loomis Fargo depot. In February 2006, the Securitas cash depot robbery took place with Ermir Hysenaj, a Securitas employee, assisting the robbery because he was being paid only £5.50 per hour and would have his lunchtime deducted by his employers.

⁷ [2008] 1 AC 1.

kind of intention was necessary for each of these torts, assuming they were in fact separate torts. None of this did the law any credit. Fortunately, given *OBG v Allan*, the practitioner can be spared a detailed historical account of the development of the tort of inducing a breach of contract.[8] The law is as clearly stated in *OBG v Allan*.

(1) *OBG Ltd v Allan*[9]

In *OBG Ltd v Allan*, there were three appeals being heard together. The relevant **15.07** facts, stated shortly, for each of the appeals are:

- *OBG Ltd v Allan* concerned the appointment of receivers under an invalid floating charge. Although the receivers at all times acted in good faith, they took control of the company's assets. It was argued that the receivers' conduct amounted to trespass to land, conversion and the tort of causing loss by unlawful means. The House of Lords dismissed the appeal: the receivers had acted in good faith and did not have any intention to cause loss or employ unlawful means. There could be no claim in conversion in respect of a chose in action and to extend the law in that direction would be too drastic a step to take.

- *Douglas v Hello! Ltd* concerned the publication by a rival magazine of photographs of the wedding of Michael Douglas and Catherine Zeta-Jones. *Hello!* magazine knew that all photography was banned on the basis that *OK!* had exclusive rights to the wedding pictures. It was argued that *Hello!* had committed the tort of causing loss by unlawful means and also a breach of confidentiality in respect of wedding photographs. The House of Lords allowed the appeal. The claim in breach of confidentiality succeeded. Whilst the defendants had the necessary intention to cause loss to the third claimant (since that was the means by which they intended to achieve their ends) the publication of pictures did not interfere with the claimants' ability to deal with the magazine.

- *Mainstream Properties Ltd v Young* concerned a diversion of a corporate opportunity by two employees to another company which they operated. The defendant financially assisted the employees in carrying out the transaction; he was assured by the employees that they were not acting in breach of their contracts with Mainstream. The issue was whether the defendant was liable to the employer company for tort of inducing a breach of contract. The House of Lords dismissed the appeal. The first and second defendants did not believe that the joint venture would result in any breach of contract and so they lacked the relevant intention for procuring a breach of contract or causing loss by unlawful means.

---

  [8] For a more detailed account of the problems in the law pre-*OBG v Allan* see the excellent Hazel Carty, *An Analysis of the Economic Torts* (Oxford University Press, 2001), ch 3; *Clerk & Lindsell* (19th edn), paras 25-15–25.64.
  [9] [2008] 1 AC 1.

15.08 In reaching its decision on each of these appeals, the House of Lords set out important principles governing this area of the law as discussed below.

C. Unified Theory Abandoned

15.09 The torts of inducing a breach of contract and causing loss by unlawful means were two distinct torts, each with their own conditions of liability.

15.10 It was the adoption by the Court of Appeal in *DC Thomson & Co Ltd v Deakin*[10] (particularly Jenkins LJ) of Lord Lindley's theory in *Quinn v Leatham*[11] that led to the principle that *Lumley v Gye* extended to all interference with contractual relations by unlawful means. In this way, the tort of inducing a breach of contract was treated as simply one type of a more general tort of actionable interference with contractual rights.

15.11 Lord Hoffmann considered the article by Philip Sales and Daniel Stilitz, 'Intentional Infliction of Harm by Unlawful Means'[12] in which it is said that the *Lumley v Gye* tort was founded on a different principle to that of unlawful means. The former is aimed at protecting contractual rights whereas the latter is concerned only with intention and wrongfulness and is not the slightest bit concerned as to the nature of the interest being interfered with. As Lord Hoffmann observed:

> 38. In my opinion, therefore, the distinction between direct and indirect interference is unsatisfactory and it is time for the unnatural union between the *Lumley v Gye* tort and the tort of causing loss by unlawful means to be dissolved. They should be restored to the independence which they enjoyed at the time of *Allen v Flood*.[13]

15.12 A further point of real distinction between these two claims is that the tort of inducing a breach of contract is a tort of accessory liability, whereas the tort of causing loss by unlawful means is a tort of primary liability.[14]

D. Elements Examined

(1) Knowledge of contract

15.13 On the issue of knowledge, the House of Lords was influenced by *Emerald Construction Co Ltd v Lowthian*.[15] A union sought to pressurize a contractor to

---

[10] [1952] Ch 646.
[11] [1901] AC 495.
[12] (1999) 115 LQR 411.
[13] ibid, [38] per Lord Hoffmann.
[14] ibid, [8] per Lord Hoffmann.
[15] [1966] 1 WLR 691.

terminate a sub-contract with the threat of a strike. It was found they knew about the existence but not the terms of the contract and in particular the union was unaware of any terms dictating how swiftly the contract could be terminated. Lord Denning MR stated:

> Even if they did not know the actual terms of the contract, but had the means of knowledge—which they deliberately disregarded—that would be enough. Like the man who turns a blind eye. So here, if the officers deliberately sought to get this contract terminated, heedless of its terms, regardless whether it was terminated by breach or not, they would do wrong. For it is unlawful for a third person to procure a breach of contract knowingly, or recklessly, indifferent whether it is a breach of not.[16]

15.14 Lord Hoffmann went on to say that a conscious decision not to inquire into the existence of a fact is in many cases treated as equivalent to knowledge of that fact: *Manifest Shipping Co Ltd v Uni-Polaris Insurance Co Ltd* [2003] 1 AC 469.

(2) Intention to induce or procure

15.15 The relevant intention for inducing a breach of contract is to cause a breach of contract, not to cause harm to the contracting party.

15.16 If someone knowingly causes a breach of contract, it does not normally matter that it is the means by which he intends to achieve some further end or even that he would rather have been able to achieve that end without causing a breach. But if the breach of contract is neither an end in itself nor a means to an end, but merely a foreseeable consequence then it cannot, for these purposes, be said to have been intended.

15.17 It was for this reason that the majority of the Court of Appeal was wrong to have allowed the claim to continue in *Millar v Bassey*.[17] Shirley Bassey breached her contract to perform and it was no doubt a foreseeable consequence that the record company would need to break contracts with the session musicians but it could not be said that was the end intended by Shirley Bassey, nor was it a means of achieving that end.

15.18 Similarly, Lord Nicholls stated:

> The defendant is made responsible for the third party's breach because of his intentional causative participation in that breach. Causative participation is not enough. A stranger to a contract may know nothing of the contract. Quite unknowingly and unintentionally he may procure a breach of the contract by offering an inconsistent deal to a contracting party which persuades the latter to default on his contractual obligations. The stranger is not liable in such a case. Nor is he liable if he acts carelessly.

---

[16] ibid, 700–1, endorsed by Lord Hoffmann in *OBG v Allan* [41].
[17] [1994] EMLR 44.

He owes no duty of care to the victim of the breach of contract. Negligent interference is not actionable.

> 192. . . . [The defendant] is liable if he intended to persuade the contracting party to breach the contract. Intentional interference presupposes knowledge of the contract. With that knowledge the defendant proceeded to induce the other contracting party to act in a way the defendant knew was a breach of that party's obligations under the contract. If the defendant deliberately turned a blind eye and proceeded regardless he may be treated as having intended the consequence he brought about. A desire to injure the claimant is not an essential ingredient of this tort.[18]

15.19   In summary, the relevant intention is not established simply because something is the foreseeable consequence of an action; it must be the end in itself or the means to an end. A deliberate decision to induce a breach of contract as a means to an end qualifies as the necessary intention, even if the aim was to obtain a financial benefit for the defendant. But a breach of contract which is neither an end in itself nor a means to an end but simply a foreseeable consequence of the acts does not qualify.

In *Meretz Investments NV v ACP Ltd*,[19] the Court of Appeal held that the relevant intention for inducing a breach of contract was not established in circumstances where the defendants acted not only to protect their own interests but also in the belief, based on legal advice, that they had the right to act as they did, notwithstanding that the loss or detriment to the claimant was an intended consequence of their action.

(3) Actual breach

15.20   As an accessory tort, inducing a breach of contract requires, as a pre-requisite of liability, an actual breach of contract. Mere interference not amounting to a breach would not suffice. To those not familiar with this area of law, this point may sound obvious but the law had got itself to a stage where interference, short of actual breach, would suffice. Lord Hoffmann stated:

> In *Torquay Hotel & Co Ltd v Cousins* [1969] 2 Ch 106, 138 Lord Denning said that there could be liability for preventing or hindering performance of the contract on the same principle as liability for procuring a breach. This dictum was approved by Lord Diplock in *Merkur Island Shipping Corpn v Laughton* [1983] 2 AC 570, 607-608. One could therefore have liability for interference with contractual relations even though the contracting party committed no breach. But these remarks were made in the context of the unified theory which treated procuring a breach as part of the same tort as causing loss by unlawful means. If the torts are to be separated, then I think that one cannot be liable for inducing a breach unless there has been a breach. No secondary liability without primary liability. Cases in which interference with contractual relations has been treated as coming within the *Lumley v Gye* tort

---

[18] *OBG Ltd v Allan* [2008] 1 AC 1, [191]–[192].
[19] [2007] EWCA Civ 1303.

(like *Dimbleby & Sons Ltd v National Union of Journalists* [1984] 1 WLR 67 and [1984] 1 WLR 427) are really cases of causing loss by unlawful means.[20]

(4) No lawful justification

A defendant may raise in his defence the fact he interfered with another's contract **15.21** in order to protect an equal or superior right of his own: see Lord Nicholls at [193] citing *Edwin Hill & Partners v First National Finance Corpn plc*.[21]

In *Edwin Hill*, Stuart-Smith LJ identified two instances where an equal or super- **15.22** ior right had been shown to exist:

- a moral duty to intervene: *Brimelow v Casson*;[22]
- the contract interfered with is inconsistent with a previous contract with the interferer: per Buckley LJ in *Smithies* case.[23]

Stuart-Smith LJ also identified several matters that will not amount to an equal or **15.23** superior right:

- absence of malice or ill-will or intention to injure the person whose contract is broken;
- the commercial or other best interests of the interferer or the contract breaker;
- the fact that A has broken his contract with X does not of itself justify X in revenge procuring a breach of an independent contract between A and B.

On the facts of *Edwin Hill* itself, the Court of Appeal dismissed the appeal and **15.24** found that the defendants' interference with the claimants' contract was justified by reference to the defendants' superior right under the legal charge to be repaid their loan plus interest.

E. Damages

McGregor on Damages[24] warns that little exact detail can be given as to the measure **15.25** of damages since they are considered to be at large: *Exchange Telegraph Co v Gregory*.[25] In *Goldsoll v Goldman*[26] Neville J held:

> The damage may be inferred, that is to say, that if the breach which has been pro-cured by the defendant has been such as must in the ordinary course of business

---

[20] ibid, [44] per Lord Hoffmann.
[21] [1989] 1 WLR 225.
[22] [1924] 1 Ch 302.
[23] [1909] 1 KB 310.
[24] (17th edn, Thomson/Sweet and Maxwell, 2003), para 40-003.
[25] [1896] 1 QB 147 (CA).
[26] [1914] 2 Ch 603.

inflict damage upon the plaintiff, then the plaintiff may succeed without proof of any particular damage which has been occasioned him.[27]

15.26 Certainly, the claimant can recover loss of profits on the contract which has been breached, as well as expenses incurred: see *British Motor Trade Association v Salvadori*.[28] The claimant may also recover any losses which are either not too remote[29] or can be shown to have been intended by the defendant.[30]

---

[27] ibid, 615.
[28] [1949] Ch 556.
[29] *British Motor Trade Association v Salvadori* [1949] Ch 556, 568–9.
[30] See *Lumley v Gye* (1853) 2 E & B 216, 233–4; *Quinn v Leatham* [1901] AC 495, 537.

16

DISHONEST ASSISTANCE

A. Introduction

Liability for dishonest assistance is a significant weapon in the armoury of the **16.01** commercial fraud litigator. If the elements of the claim are satisfied, it enables the victim of a commercial fraud to recover not just from those who financially bene-fited by way of the receipt of the proceeds of the fraud but also from those individuals (and institutions) who are often viewed as deep-pocketed defendants who have provided assistance to the fraudsters carrying out the commercial fraud. Such deep-pocketed defendants typically include banks, financial institutions and accountants. Their liability arises not from the *beneficial* receipt of fraud proceeds but from their dishonest participation in the underlying fraud. Through their participation, these defendants assisted the commission of the fraud. Their liability is based upon their wrongful conduct.

The decision of the Privy Council in *Royal Brunei Airlines v Tan*[1] has done much **16.02** to clarify some of the issues surrounding this claim but, as recent decisions have

---

[1] [1995] 2 AC 378 (PC).

indicated, there remains much work to be done. So, for example, whilst *Tan* removed the complications derived from applying the *Baden Delvaux* five levels of knowledge, these now appear to have been replaced by an equally difficult debate as to whether the relevant test for dishonesty is subjective, objective or some combination of the two. The House of Lords in *Twinsectra Ltd v Yardley*[2] has sought to re-interpret *Tan* as favouring a subjective approach whereas more recently the Privy Council in *Barlow Clowes International Ltd (In Liquidation) v Eurotrust Internatoinal Ltd*[3] has favoured the original objective interpretation of the test for dishonesty as laid down in *Tan*.

16.03 One of the important contributions of Lord Nicholls' speech in *Tan* was the clear divide it placed between the claims for knowing receipt and those now called dishonest assistance. Prior to this decision, these two claims were often treated together with the result that the juridical basis for either failed to be properly examined in any detail. With the increased and better understanding of the law of unjust enrichment, there were many calls for knowing receipt to be viewed as a claim based entirely upon unjust enrichment and therefore one which did not require any element of impropriety at all on the part of the recipient. At the same time, others were calling for the recognition of the similarity between dishonest assistance and its common law counterparts such as conspiracy to defraud. As examined below, much work has been done in both directions, although it is fair to say that not all juridical issues have to date been resolved. So, to take but one example, Professor Birks, who was the leading proponent of a strict liability unjust enrichment-based approach to knowing receipt, appeared to accept, just before his untimely death, that there may well be room for a wrong-based approach to this claim, or at least he was willing to accept the separate status of the knowing receipt head of liability. This is examined briefly below and in more detail in Chapter 5 on knowing receipt. If correct, this would suggest that wrongful conduct may well be the common thread between dishonest assistance and knowing receipt.

B. Problems of Language

16.04 Before embarking upon a detailed study of this cause of action, it is important that any uncertainty caused by the use of ambiguous language is removed. In the context of dishonest assistance claims, the most notorious example of this is the use of the phrase, 'liable as a constructive trustee', to describe the liability of a defendant who has dishonestly assisted in a breach of trust. Given that liability under this

---

[2] [2002] UKHL 12, [2002] 2 AC 164.
[3] [2005] UKPC 37, [2006] 1 WLR 1476 (PC).

heading does not require the receipt of any identifiable trust property, the use of such language is misleading and best forgotten.

It is of course true that in *Westdeutsche Landesbank Girozentrale v Islington LBC*[4]   **16.05**
Lord Browne-Wilkinson talked of a constructive trust being imposed upon a defendant found liable for dishonest assistance. His Lordship went on to describe this as 'an apparent exception' to the principle that there must be trust property in order to establish a trust. With respect, it makes no sense at all to recognize this use of the language as an exception since it is a fundamental requirement for the existence of a trust that there be identifiable trust property held thereunder.[5] In the absence of such property, there can be no trust.[6] To suggest otherwise only leads to undermining the core requirements of a trust and creates unnecessary confusion.

A further difficulty is that the mistaken assumption that the dishonest assistant   **16.06**
was indeed a proper constructive trustee has no doubt had a bearing on the court's treatment of the issue whether the breach of trust or fiduciary duty must involve the misapplication of trust property. One can readily see that where the starting point is that a dishonest assistant is to be treated as a constructive trustee, the courts are more likely to consider that any relevant breach must involve the misapplication of actual trust property. This issue is addressed at some length below. It suffices to say that when one properly removes the ambiguity created by the unnecessary use of the terminology of the constructive trust it is clear that there is no principled reason why it would be necessary to limit the ambit of the liability of dishonest assistants to the actual misappropriation of trust property. There can be many other ways in which a trust or fiduciary relationship can be breached which do not involve the misappropriation of trust property and insofar as a third party has dishonestly assisted in that breach there is no basis for denying a beneficiary the opportunity to claim against him.

The use of the language of the constructive trust has also contributed to other dif-   **16.07**
ficulties or developments in this area of the law. So, for example, it no doubt led Turner J (sitting in the CA) in *Dubai Aluminium v Salaam*[7] to the conclusion that the issue of the vicarious liability of partners for the dishonest assistance provided by another partner fell within s 13 rather than s 10 of the Partnership Act 1890.

But if a dishonest assistant is not a constructive trustee, what is the explanation for   **16.08**
the use of this language to describe him as one? The answer appears to be that this

---

[4] [1996] AC 669, 705F.
[5] *Re Barney* [1892] 2 Ch 265.
[6] Certainty of subject matter of a trust is one of the 'three certainties' essential to the creation of a valid trust arrangement: see generally, G Thomas and A Hudson, *The Law of Trusts* (Oxford University Press, 2004), ch 3, 'Certainty of Subject Matter'.
[7] [2001] QB 113, 144–50.

was considered a convenient shorthand to describe the nature of the personal liability to account attaching to a defendant who has dishonestly assisted in a breach of trust.[8] A dishonest assistant has the same type of personal liability to account as would be imposed on a trustee. The assistant is treated *as if* he were a constructive trustee even though the dishonest assistant is not, in fact, a properly constituted trustee.[9]

16.09 Whatever may have been the dubious merits in first using this terminology, it is now best abandoned in favour of a proper and unambiguous description of the nature of the personal liability to which a claim for dishonest assistance may give rise. This avoids the forlorn attempts by some judges and commentators to shoe-horn this head of liability into the scheme of (constructive) trusts generally and ensures that the discussion can focus on the nature and extent of liability.

C. Juridical Basis for Liability

16.10 Liability for dishonest assistance derives from the defendant's participation in a fraud on the beneficiary. This is evident even in the speech of Lord Selborne LC in *Barnes v Addy*[10] which, prior to the decision in *Royal Brunei v Tan*, was for many years treated as the starting point for any discussion of this head of liability. His Lordship stated:

> . . . strangers are not to be made constructive trustees merely because they act as the agents of trustees in transactions within their legal powers, transactions, perhaps, of which a Court of Equity may disapprove, unless . . . they assist with knowledge in a dishonest and fraudulent design on the part of the trustee.

---

[8] *Twinsectra Ltd v Yardley* [1999] Lloyd's Rep Bank 438, 467. See also *Selangor United Rubber Estates Ltd v Craddock (No 3)* [1968] 1 WLR 1555, 1582; *Agip (Africa) Ltd v Jackson* [1990] Ch 265, 292. This explanation is also supported in academic writing: P Birks, 'Trusts in the Recovery of Misapplied Assets' in E McKendrick (ed), *Commercial Aspects of Trusts and Fiduciary Obligations* (Clarendon Press, 1992) 149, 154. Sir P Millett, 'Restitution and Constructive Trusts' in Cornish, Nolan, O'Sullivan and Virgo (eds), *Restitution: Past, Present & Future* (Hart Publishing, 1998) 199, 200 and 'The Law of Restitution: Taking Stock' (1999) 14 Amicus Curiae 4, 6–7; C Mitchell, 'Assistance' in Birks and Pretto (eds), *Breach of Trust* (Hart Publishing, 2002), ch 6, 147.

[9] See *Bank of Scotland v A Ltd* [2001] 1 WLR 751 (CA). In this case, the bank sought to justify the costs of interpleading on the grounds that it was concerned that should it pay out monies held in one of its customer's accounts, it might be liable for dishonest assistance. The bank argued it was entitled to interplead on the grounds that it was acting as a potential constructive trustee seeking guidance from the court. The court rejected this argument, holding the bank should first have consulted the Serious Fraud Office but in any event held that the jurisdiction of the court to provide appropriate directions and guidance was not limited to circumstances where the applicant was or might otherwise become a (constructive) trustee. In reaching this conclusion, the Court of Appeal accepted that any liability on the bank's part as dishonest assistant would not render the bank a properly constituted constructive trustee.

[10] (1874) 9 Ch App 244, 251–2.

As is examined below, the law has moved on since *Barnes v Addy* and it is no longer necessary that the trustee be fraudulent so long as the third party himself is acting in a dishonest manner. Nevertheless, it is clear, whether one adopts Lord Selborne LC's statement or the modern interpretation of the law that the basis for equity's intervention in either case is fraudulent or dishonest conduct.

It is the defendant's wrongful conduct which gives rise to the liability and not his **16.11** receipt of trust property. It is a form of accessory liability as it is dependent upon there having been some form of breach of trust or fiduciary duty. For a long period, it was treated simply as the sister-claim to that for knowing receipt. The relationship between these two claims is examined below. In addition, commentators have suggested similarities between a claim for dishonest assistance and the common law claims of conspiracy and conversion. Examination of these suggestions will assist in understanding the juridical basis of liability for dishonest assistance.

(1) The relationship between dishonest assistance and knowing receipt claims

As stated above, historically, the courts and commentators tended to consider **16.12** together liability for knowing assistance (as it was then known) and that for knowing receipt. This had the consequence that the independent basis for imposing liability in either situation was not the subject of proper scrutiny leading to requirements of one claim being treated as requirements for the other. A good illustration of this was the tendency of courts to apply the same reasoning on the question of level of knowledge for both claims.[11]

It was not until the express recognition by the House of Lords in *Lipkin Gorman* **16.13** *v Karpnale Ltd*[12] of free-standing claims in the law of unjust enrichment, that proper focus began to be placed on our understanding of the relationship between these two claims. This immediately led to the conclusion that liability for dishonest assistance derived from the defendant's wrongful conduct in assisting a breach of trust or fiduciary duty whereas the liability for knowing receipt arose from the receipt of trust monies. What was not entirely clear to the commentators was why liability for knowing receipt required the receipt to have been made knowingly whereas liability at common law for unjust enrichment was strict. Indeed, the law of unjust enrichment typically focuses on the quality of the transferor's intention and not on the *mala fides* of the recipient. In this regard, to borrow the language of the restitution lawyer, it is often considered to be plaintiff- or claimant-sided.

This led various commentators, most notably Professor Birks, to argue that there **16.14** was no justification for the separate existence of the knowing receipt head of claim

---

11 C Harpum, 'The Stranger As Constructive Trustee' (1986) 102 LQR 114, 162.
12 [1991] 2 AC 548.

and that it should be subsumed within the strict liability approach of the law of unjust enrichment.[13] He sought to explain (or perhaps more accurately re-interpret) the series of cases which established the level of knowledge required for knowing receipt claims as being cases where the issue of knowledge was in fact being directed towards the availability or otherwise of a defence and not to the issue of liability.[14] Ultimately, however, Birks' approach represented more of an attempt to re-invent the reasoning adopted in these cases rather than simply interpreting the judicial reasoning in fact applied. On the latter approach, it remains clear that the question of bad faith arose in these authorities as a question relating to primary liability and not, as Birks would have us believe, simply in relation to the defence of bona fide purchaser for value without notice.

16.15   But Professor Birks was not alone. Lord Nicholls, writing extra-judicially, set out a sustained argument in favour of this approach concluding with these observations:

> In this respect equity should now follow the law. Restitutionary liability, applicable regardless of fault but subject to a defence of change of position, would be a better-tailored response to the underlying mischief of misapplied property than personal liability which is exclusively fault-based. Personal liability would flow from having received the property of another, from having been unjustly enriched at the expense of another. It would be triggered by the mere fact of receipt, thus recognising the endurance of property rights. But fairness would be ensured by the need to identify a gain, and by making change of position available as a defence in suitable cases when, for instance, the recipient had changed his position in reliance on the receipt.[15]

16.16   To a similar end, Lord Millett, influenced by the strict liability approach of the law of unjust enrichment, held, in a series of cases, that constructive notice rather than actual knowledge sufficed for the purposes of a knowing receipt claim.[16]

16.17   As can readily be seen, the more the restitutionary lawyers argued in favour of strict liability, the greater became the distinction between the knowing receipt and dishonest assistance claims. This was further enhanced when commentators began to focus their attention on the assistance claim which, given it did not depend upon receipt of trust money, was not viewed as a restitutionary claim. This focus

---

[13] Birks, *Restitution—The Future* (Federation Press of Australia, 1992), 26–42; see also 'Misdirected Funds: Restitution from the Recipient' [1989] LMCLQ 296; 'Persistent Problems in Misdirected Money: A Quintet' [1993] LMCLQ 218. Not all restitutionary lawyers were arguing for a strict liability approach to the knowing receipt claims: see N McBride and P A McGrath, 'The Nature of Restitution' (1995) 15 OJLS 33.

[14] Birks, 'Misdirected Funds: Restitution from the Recipient' [1989] LMCLQ 296; 'Persistent Problems in Misdirected Money: A Quintet' [1993] LMCLQ 218.

[15] 'Knowing Receipt: The Need for a New Landmark' in Cornish et al (eds), *Restitution: Past Presnt & Future*, 231.

[16] It is likely that Lord Millett's approach was tempered by the realization that authority constrained him from adopting the strict liability approach advocated by the commentators.

resulted in a greater appreciation that liability was based upon the wrongful nature of the assistant's conduct. The issue then became one of what type of wrongful conduct would suffice for the purposes of imposing liability. It also raised the question whether this liability was in fact founded on an equitable tort. Unlike with the knowing receipt claim, there was no theoretical basis to contend for strict liability and in any event there would be no justification for permitting the beneficiaries to pursue a claim against a third party (as opposed to their trustee) on a non-fault basis. But it remained unclear whether something short of dishonesty would suffice and no clear guidance could be determined from the case law.

As will be seen below, Lord Nicholls in *Tan* undertook an extensive analysis of the various levels of knowledge for the imposition of liability for dishonest assistance. He ultimately came down firmly in favour of dishonesty, believing this better expressed the reason for the imposition of liability than any test based purely on knowledge and contending that the five-level *Baden Delvaux* test had best be forgotten in this context. **16.18**

The debate generated by the better understanding of the law of unjust enrichment has undoubtedly served to sever any belief that the level of knowledge between these two claims should be the same. For all their argument, the restitutionary lawyers have to date failed to achieve recognition by the courts of a strict liability approach to knowing receipt. Indeed, their arguments have resulted in no more than a lower threshold of knowledge being required for receipt of trust property than for assisting in a breach of trust or fiduciary duty. It remains to be seen whether and to what extent the courts might fully embrace the restitutionary lawyers' arguments in favour of strict liability, but some force has perhaps been taken out of their arguments by Professor Birks' late recognition that there may indeed be a role or justification for a separate claim based upon the wrongful receipt of trust property: **16.19**

> Although I have myself strenuously argued that 'knowing receipt' should be regarded as a claim in unjust enrichment, and should therefore discard the incongruous requirement of fault implicit in the word 'knowing', the courts appear to have set their face against that view. It now seems right to abandon that analysis once and for all. It was a mistake to insist that 'knowing receipt' was simply a species of unjust enrichment which had been slow to understand itself and, in particular, slow to understand that liability in unjust enrichment is strict though subject to defences.
>
> The better way of proceeding is to accept that the ambiguities and uncertainties in the case law of knowing receipt arise from its having failed to distinguish between two very different kinds of liability, one wrong-based and the other based on unjust enrichment. The task is then, not to force 'knowing receipt' into one or other category, but to demonstrate that both kinds of liability are necessary and that neither renders the other redundant. Within the law of obligations the recipient of trust

property can, on appropriate facts, be made liable for the wrong of misappropriation or he can be compelled to make restitution of his unjust enrichment.[17]

(2) The relationship between dishonest assistance and conspiracy

16.20   In most commercial frauds, if the facts exist to justify a claim for dishonest assistance they are likely also to justify a claim in conspiracy between the breaching trustee and the dishonest assistant. It is of course accepted that the requirements of these two heads of claim are not exactly the same and so in theory it remains possible for one to exist without the other but with one exception, the same factual basis will usually justify both claims being brought.

16.21   The one exception is the situation where the breach of trust is entirely innocent on the part of the trustee who has been deliberately misled by the third party adviser as to his entitlement so to act. In these circumstances, it would be wrong to conclude that the innocent trustee had reached an understanding or formed a combination with the dishonest third party adviser to defraud the beneficiaries. In the absence of such a common understanding or combination, there is no conspiracy between the trustee and the dishonest adviser and yet it is known that post-*Royal Brunei v Tan*, the adviser may still be liable for dishonest assistance.

16.22   Where, however, both the third party and the trustee are aware that what is proposed would amount to a breach of trust or fiduciary duty and each conducts themselves with a view to cause that breach of trust or fiduciary duty, that conduct has the makings of a clear conspiracy claim. Careful consideration would need to be given as to whether it would add anything to the client's ability to recover to bring both claims.

16.23   The similarity between these two heads of claim helps to illustrate that liability for dishonest assistance is very much derived from the third party's participation in a fraud. That fraud might be of the third party's own making and indeed might not be known to the innocent trustee in breach. Alternatively, it may well be the trustee who is the mastermind and driving force behind the fraud and the third party's liability is based upon the fact that he happened to provide some assistance at a time when he was considered to be acting dishonestly. The third party does not need to gain financially from his participation in order to be rendered liable. Loss caused to the beneficiary will suffice, even if that loss corresponds to benefits received by the breaching trustee.

---

[17] Birks, 'Receipt' in Birks and Pretto (eds), *Breach of Trust* (Hart Publishing, 2002), 223–4. Some will disagree with the position taken in the text and will no doubt contend that Birks' revised position in fact frees up the possibility of arguing in favour of strict liability whilst at the same time giving some recognition to the established authorities requiring a fault-based approach. It remains to be seen whether this proves to be correct. What is true is the tragic misfortune that Birks will not be the one pushing for the adoption of such an approach.

The similarity between knowing or dishonest assistance and the tortious claims of **16.24** fraud and inducing breach of contract has been pointed out by Lord Hoffmann, writing extra-judicially, where he noted that the development of the claim for knowing assistance had taken place at a time when at common law there was little scope for recovery of economic loss outside a breach of contract claim. Lord Hoffmann's conclusions are:

> The conclusion I would draw is that the action for knowing assistance in a breach of trust should be abolished. If the defendant has knowingly assisted in a fraudulent design, he should be answerable in fraud. If he was negligent in a situation in which he owed a duty of care, he should be answerable for negligence. If he has intentionally interfered with the plaintiff's rights in law or equity, he should be liable on the principles of *Lumley v Gye* with whatever adaptation is required by the nature of the particular equitable right.[18]

Such a drastic step has not yet taken place and there appears little prospect of it **16.25** occurring within the near future. Nevertheless, what Lord Hoffmann's observations do show clearly is the potential overlap between claims in equity and in tort when dealing with commercial fraud. Although the claims may overlap in criteria, different limitation periods may apply as may different considerations when dealing with questions of choice of law and jurisdiction. All this must be well known to the commercial fraud litigator.

That said, it is equally important for the litigator to be aware of the differences **16.26** between these two claims. Such differences may well be swept away should it be determined these two claims can be assimilated, but at present they represent quite subtle but important differences between the claims and how they are pleaded.

- One of the most important distinctions lies in the fact that conspiracy is considered very much a joint exercise between two or more individuals whereas dishonest assistance need involve the dishonest conduct of no one but the assister. Whereas in the conspiracy one would need to show an understanding reached between the parties and concerted action towards implementing that understanding, there need not be any such understanding in a dishonest assistance claim. The trustee could very well be entirely innocent, save for breach of his fiduciary duties, which is a matter of strict liability.

- To that end, the pleading of parties' intentions and conduct will be different for a conspiracy claim than for a dishonest assistance claim. In a conspiracy claim, the intention is presumably to implement the common aim and, depending on the type of conspiracy, intending to cause some harm to the object of the conspiracy. In a dishonest assistance claim, the intention of the assister will be focused on persuading the trustee to breach his fiduciary duties.

---

[18] 'The Redundancy of Knowing Assistance' in Birks (ed), *The Frontiers of Liability Vol 1* (Oxford University Press, 1994), 29.

- It is really only when the trustee is himself acting dishonestly that the close relationship between the two claims becomes much clearer.

D. Overview of Elements of Claim for Dishonest Assistance

16.27   The following elements are required to be satisfied in order to establish a claim for dishonest assistance:

- there must be a trust or fiduciary relationship;
- that trust or fiduciary relationship must have been breached;
- the trustee or fiduciary need not have been dishonest;
- the third party must have induced or assisted in the breach;
- the third party must have acted dishonestly in providing the inducement or assistance.

(1)   There must be a trust or fiduciary relationship

16.28   There is no requirement that the relevant trust be an express formal trust. To hold otherwise would have been a severe limitation on the scope of this head of liability, particularly when many of the more recent cases have arisen in the context of commercial fraud litigation rather than any formal trust dispute.

16.29   It suffices if it can be shown that one party owes fiduciary obligations to another in respect of that other's property. In commercial settings, obvious examples include a director and his company,[19] solicitor and client,[20] and accountant and client.[21] As is well known, the category of relationships which might give rise to fiduciary obligations is not closed.[22]

16.30   In the absence of any requirement that the trust be an express formal trust, it is clear that a dishonest assistance claim may well arise in the context of a constructive or resulting trust.[23] It is irrelevant that the trust imposed is no more than a bare trust simply to hold and restore to the rightful owner the property taken by

---

[19] *Selangor United Rubber Estates Ltd v Craddock (No 3)* [1968] 1 WLR 1555; *Karak Rubber Co Ltd v Burden (No 2)* [1972] 1 WLR 602; *Belmont Finance Corporation Ltd v Williams Furniture Ltd* [1980] 1 All ER 393; *Cowan de Groot Properties Ltd v Eagle Trust plc* [1992] 4 All ER 700; *Heinl v Jyske Bank (Gibraltar) Ltd* [1999] Lloyd's Rep Bank 511.

[20] *Twinsectra Ltd v Yardley* [2002] UKHL 12, [2002] AC 164.

[21] *Agip (Africa) Ltd v Jackson* [1990] Ch 265, [1991] Ch 547.

[22] *Hospital Products Ltd v United States Surgical Corp* (1984) 156 CLR 41, 96 (Mason J). See also *Lac Minerals Ltd v International Corona Resources Ltd* [1989] 2 SCR 574, 597. This issue is discussed in detail in *Meagher, Gummow & Lehane's Equity Doctrines & Remedies* (4th edn, LexisNexis Butterworths, 2002), ch 5.

[23] *Bank Terjerat v Hong Kong and Shanghai Banking Corpn (CI) Ltd* [1995] 1 Lloyd's Rep 239; *Bankgesellschaft Berlin AG v Makris* (unreported, 5 April 2000); *Heinl v Jyske Bank (Gibraltar) Ltd* [1999] Lloyd's Rep Bank 511.

theft, fraud or mistake. If the third party provides assistance to the trustee result-ing in the trustee failing to restore the property to its rightful owner, then so long as the third party was acting dishonestly, a claim for dishonest assistance is made out.[24]

This conclusion provides some support for those commentators who maintain that liability for dishonest assistance does not require breach of fiduciary duties and that breach of an equitable duty will suffice. It is said that a resulting or con-structive trustee owes no fiduciary duties to the beneficiary as such but is subject only to an equitable duty to transfer over the relevant asset or assets.[25] Whatever the merits of the contention that resulting or constructive trustees owe no fidu-ciary duties at all but are simply subject to an equitable duty, what is clear is that a party can be liable for dishonestly assisting in a breach of a resulting or construc-tive trust. **16.31**

(2) There must have been a breach of trust or fiduciary duty

This section covers two issues: **16.32**

• what type of breach of trust or fiduciary duty will suffice?
• what is the relevance (if any) of a trustee's exemption clause?

(a)   What type of breach of trust or fiduciary duty will suffice?

Liability for dishonest assistance is a form of accessory liability. It is dependent upon the trustee having breached his duties under the trust or fiduciary relation-ship. There can be no claim for dishonest assistance if there is no breach of trust or fiduciary duty.[26] So much is clear and straightforward. **16.33**

The difficult question in this area is what type of breach will suffice for the pur-poses of a claim for dishonest assistance. In particular, is it necessary that the breach involves a misappropriation or misapplication of property held under the trust or will a breach, not involving trust property, suffice? **16.34**

---

[24] It is said, by some commentators (e.g. Mowbray et al, *Lewin on Trusts* (18th edn, Thomson/ Sweet and Maxwell, 2008), [40-17], that there is no fiduciary relationship at all or at least in any meaningful sense in circumstances where the trust is imposed because of e.g. fraud, since the only obligation is to restore the property to its owner.

[25] L Smith, 'Constructive Fiduciaries?' in P Birks (ed), *Privacy and Loyalty* (Clarendon Press, 1997), 249, 267. See also C Mitchell, 'Assistance' in Birks and Pretto (eds), *Breach of Trust* 166.

[26] *Royal Brunei v Tan* [1995] 2 AC 378, 382 (Lord Nicholls). There may, however, be a claim against a dishonest third party in circumstances where the trustee is not in breach but such a claim, if available, would have to be in contract or possibly tort. It would not be a claim for dishonest assistance as such: see *Lewin on Trusts* at [43-01], [43-05]. See the suggestion that no breach of trust should be required for dishonest assistance considered in S Gardner, 'Knowing Assistance and Knowing Receipt: Taking Stock' (1996) 112 LQR 56, 68.

16.35   The authorities do not provide clear guidance on this issue. Those in favour of limiting claims for dishonest assistance to a claim involving the transfer of trust property include *Cowan de Groot Properties Ltd v Eagle Trust plc*,[27] *Bankgesellschaft Berlin AG v Makris*,[28] *Satnam Investmens Ltd v Dunlop Heywood & Co Ltd*[29] and *Petrotrade Inc v Smith*.[30]

16.36   At first instance, Rimer J held in *Goose v Wilson & Sandford*[31] that there could be no claim for dishonest assistance in the absence of a fiduciary relationship existing between Mr Bray and Mr Wilson arising out of the venture to purchase land in France. In reaching that conclusion, Rimer J stated that a claim for dishonest assistance required a misapplication of trust property. On appeal,[32] the Court of Appeal held that no relevant fiduciary relationship arose until the charge on the land was executed.[33] Prior to that, no fiduciary relationship existed and accordingly no claim for dishonest assistance could be made. The Court of Appeal did expressly leave open the issue of the requirement of a misapplication of trust property, with Morritt LJ stating that the Court was not prepared to accept Nourse LJ's statement in *Satnam* that trust property must exist, and noting that there was nothing in *Royal Brunei* which required such an approach.[34]

16.37   Other cases in which the point was left open include *Brown v Bennett*,[35] *Fyffes Group Ltd v Templeman*,[36] and *Gencor ACP Ltd v Dalby*.[37] *Gencor* was a further

---

[27] [1991] BCLC 1045, 1103 (the point appears to have been accepted by the parties).

[28] (Unreported, 5 April 2000) (there appears to have been no argument that it was necessary to establish that the mistaken payment gave rise to equitable proprietary interests before a dishonest assistance claim could be made in relation to assistance given to the recipients of the mistaken payments).

[29] [1999] 1 BCLC 385, 404. Nourse LJ held that claims for both knowing receipt and knowing assistance require the existence of trust property or the traceable proceeds thereof.

[30] [2000] 1 Lloyd's Rep 486, 491–2. David Steel J held that bribing a fiduciary would not amount to dishonest assistance in the absence of the misappropriation or misapplication of trust property.

[31] *The Times*, 19 February 1998. The Court of Appeal decision is reported at [2001] 1 Lloyd's Rep PN 189

[32] ibid.

[33] ibid, [84].

[34] ibid, at [88].

[35] [1999] 1 BCLC 649, 657–9 where Morritt LJ refused to accept Rattee J's view at first instance that dealings with trust property was a necessary condition of a claim for dishonest assistance. The claim concerned breach of fiduciary duty by directors relating to the management of company affairs (without affecting company property as such). Although Morritt LJ could see some merit in the wider approach, it was not necessary for him to reach any firm conclusion on it because he agreed with the judge's second reason for dismissing the claim, namely that Oasis had not in fact provided any relevant assistance in respect of the breaches of trust or fiduciary duty.

[36] [2000] 2 Lloyd's Rep 643 (a case involving the payment of commission by way of bribes to a fiduciary to secure a contract). The point as to whether or not a claim for dishonest assistance was limited to unauthorized transfers of trust property appears not to have been argued (see 660, col 1 where Toulson J remarked: 'This head of claim gives rise to no dispute about the law but a sharp dispute about the facts.').

[37] [2000] 2 BCLC 734, 757.

decision of Rimer J who, having considered the authorities on this issue, concluded (contrary to his decision in *Goose v Wilson*) that whether or not there was any requirement for the involvement of trust property in a dishonest assistance claim was 'something of an open question'.

In principle, there is no good reason to limit the claim for dishonest assistance to **16.38** instances where the breach of trust or fiduciary duty involves a misapplication of trust property. This head of claim is concerned at providing protection to a beneficiary who has been caused harm or loss by virtue of a third party dishonestly assisting in or procuring a breach of trust by the trustee. There is no reason at all for limiting such a claim to loss caused only by the misapplication of trust property. If loss is caused by some other form of breach of trust or fiduciary duty, the interest of the beneficiary is equally entitled to protection by way of a claim against the dishonest assistant.

It may be that historically the reticence of the courts expressly to endorse the wider **16.39** approach is explicable by reference to the confusion caused by the (mis)use of the language of the constructive trustee when applied to describe the liability of a dishonest assistant. This may well have created the impression that the assistance must be in relation to trust property. Whatever the true explanation, there is no justification now for maintaining this narrower approach to this head of claim.

The difficulties in determining the appropriate breach of trust or breach of fidu- **16.40** ciary duty for the purposes of a dishonest assistance claim do not end with the issue of the misapplication of trust property. To what extent is it possible, for example, to bring a dishonest assistance claim in relation to a breach of confidence? In *Thomas v Pearce*[38] Buxton LJ held that in principle a claim for dishonest assistance in respect of confidential information was available, although on the facts the claim failed as dishonesty could not be proven.[39] In so holding, Buxton LJ approved the following statement:

> Where the third party receives information knowing that it has been disclosed by his informant in breach of confidence, he will himself owe a duty of confidence to the confider. This principle is derived from the doctrine that it is equitable fraud in a third party knowingly to assist in a breach of trust, confidence, or contract by another.[40]

The facts of *Thomas v Pearce* concerned an Elizabeth Pearce leaving the employment of Susan Thomas in a letting and management agency and taking with her

---

[38] (2000) FSR 718 (CA: Buxton LJ, Gage J).

[39] It might be questioned whether the CA would adopt the same rather subjective approach to determining the assistor's alleged dishonesty post-*Barlow Clowes International Ltd (In Liquidation) v Eurotrust International Ltd* [2006] 1 WLR 1476.

[40] R Toulson and C Phipps, *Confidentiality* (Sweet and Maxwell, 1996), 92. The suggestion of a dishonest assistance claim in respect of assistance in the breach of a contract may be doubted.

a substantial list of clients. Mrs Pearce presented the list to a Mrs Price, who worked for her new employers, Darlows Ltd (the second defendant) and Mrs Price immediately instructed her staff to send out a letter to all the listed clients informing them of Mrs Pearce's change of employment. Mrs Pearce was found to have breached her duty of confidence to Susan Thomas in handing over the list of clients. At first instance, the court rejected the claim against Darlows Ltd on the grounds that it had not acted dishonestly. On appeal, the Court of Appeal upheld the first instance decision, contending that dishonesty under *Royal Brunei v Tan* was not an objective test. For present purposes, the more interesting aspect was that the Court had no apparent difficulty in accepting that there could, in principle, be a claim for dishonest assistance in respect of a breach of confidence. Buxton LJ remarked that: 'the same broad principles apply whether the question is wrongful knowledge on the part of a third party in respect of a breach of confidence. . . . or, on the other hand, knowing assistance in a breach of trust'. It would appear, although the point is not free from doubt, that the Court was acting on the basis that these were distinct heads of claim albeit governed by similar principles.

(b) What is the relevance (if any) of any trustee exemption clause?

16.41 The point can be taken shortly although there is no clear authority on it. It is submitted that, as a matter of principle, the answer lies in the nature of the relevant clause and, in particular, whether it simply serves to identify the proper ambit of the trustee's duties or whether it provides protection from personal liability for the trustee in the event of a breach of trust. If the trustee's conduct falls within the ambit of a clause of the former type, it will not amount to a breach of trust at all and therefore there could be no liability for dishonest assistance on the part of the third party. If the clause is of the latter type, which protects the breaching trustee from any personal liability, it is suggested that a breach of trust does in fact occur and that, assuming all the other requirements are established, a claim for dishonest assistance could still be brought. This conclusion is supported by Lord Nicholls' analysis above as to the nature of liability for dishonest assistance. The fact that the trustee is able to protect himself from any personal liability for the breach of trust by virtue of the relevant clause is irrelevant to the entitlement of the beneficiary to pursue a remedy against a dishonest third party who chose to interfere with the fiduciary duties owed to the beneficiary and has therefore caused the beneficiary a loss.

(3) Does the breach of trust or fiduciary duty need to be dishonest?

16.42 Prior to the Privy Council decision in *Royal Brunei v Tan*,[41] it had been believed that a claim for dishonest assistance (or knowing assistance as it was then known)

---

[41] [1995] 2 AC 378.

did require that the trustee's conduct be dishonest and fraudulent. This derived from the famous statement of Lord Selborne LC in *Barnes v Addy*[42] that third parties could not be liable for assistance unless: 'they assist with knowledge in a dishonest and fraudulent design on the part of the trustees'.

In delivering his unreserved judgment, it does not appear as though Lord Selborne LC had the benefit of several earlier decisions in which it had been held that there was no such requirement.[43]   **16.43**

This issue came before the Privy Council in *Royal Brunei v Tan*. In short the salient facts were that the claimant airline ('Royal Brunei') had appointed Borneo Leisure Travel ('BLT') as its travel agent for certain areas with a responsibility for collecting in and accounting to Royal Brunei for passenger payments. It was accepted that the monies so received by BLT were held on trust for Royal Brunei. Mr Philip Tan Kok Ming ('Mr Tan') was managing director and principal shareholder in BLT (the other director and shareholder being his wife). Monies which should have been paid to Royal Brunei were used to pay BLT's general operation costs. The trial judge found Mr Tan liable for dishonest assistance without finding that BLT was involved in a fraudulent and dishonest design. In the Court of Appeal of Brunei, the Court held that BLT was guilty of breaking promises and general mismanagement but was not in fact involved in a fraudulent and dishonest design. As Faud P in the Brunei Court of Appeal held: **16.44**

> As long standing and high authority shows, conduct which may amount to a breach of trust, however morally reprehensible, will not render a person who has knowingly assisted in the breach of trust liable as a constructive trustee if that conduct falls short of dishonesty.[44]

In rejecting this requirement, Lord Nicholls adopted a two-stage approach. He first examined some practical difficulties which arise as a consequence of requiring that the breach of trust itself be dishonest. Thereafter, he examined the three possibilities: namely (i) no liability, (ii) strict liability or (iii) fault-based liability on the part of the third party.   **16.45**

---

[42] (1874) 9 Ch App 244, 252. See also *Belmont Finance Corpn Ltd v Williams* [1979] Ch 250, 267 where Buckley LJ refused to depart from the established principles laid down by Lord Selborne LC that dishonesty and not simply some 'unethical conduct' was required on the part of the trustee. At 274, Goff LJ similarly held that it would be dangerous and wrong to depart from 'the safe path of the principle as stated by Lord Selborne LC to the unchartered sea of something not innocent. . .but still short of dishonesty'.

[43] *Fyler v Fyler* (1841) 3 Beav 550; *A-G v Corpn of Leicester* (1844) 7 Beav 176; *Eaves v Hickson* (1861) 30 Beav 136. Lord Langdale MR gave the leading judgment in the first two of these cases and it is clear that he was only concerned with whether the assister in fact knew that he was inducing or assisting in a breach. If so, he or she would be liable. See C Harpum's discussion in 'The Basis of Equitable Liability' in Birks (ed), *The Frontiers of Liability, Vol 1* at p 11.

[44] Quoted in *Royal Brunei v Tan* at 383–4.

(a) Practical problems associated with Lord Selborne LC's requirement of a dishonest breach of trust

16.46   In a section worth quoting in full, Lord Nicholls stated:

> Take the simple example of an honest trustee and a dishonest third party. Take a case where a dishonest solicitor persuades a trustee to apply trust property in a way the trustee honestly believes is permissible but which the solicitor knows full well is a clear breach of trust. The solicitor deliberately conceals this from the trustee. In consequence, the beneficiaries suffer a substantial loss. It cannot be right that in such a case the accessory liability principle would be inapplicable because of the innocence of the trustee. In ordinary parlance, the beneficiaries have been defrauded by the solicitor. If there is to be an accessory liability principle at all, whereby in appropriate circumstances beneficiaries may have direct recourse against a third party, the principle must surely be applicable in such a case, just as much as in a case where both the trustee and the third party have been dishonest. Indeed, if anything, the case for liability of the dishonest third party seems stronger where the trustee is innocent, because in such a case the third party alone was dishonest and that was the cause of the subsequent misapplication of the trust property.

> The position would be the same if, instead of *procuring* the breach, the third party dishonestly *assisted* in the breach. . . .

> These examples suggest that what matters is the state of mind of the third party sought to be made liable, not the state of mind of the trustee. The trustee will be liable in any event for the breach of trust, even if he acted innocently, unless excused by an exemption clause in the trust instrument or relieved by the court. But *his* state of mind is essentially irrelevant to the question whether the *third party* should be made liable to the beneficiaries for the breach of trust. If the liability of the third party is fault-based, what matters is the nature of his fault, not that of the trustee. In this regard dishonesty on the part of the third party would seem to be a sufficient basis for his liability, irrespective of the state of mind of the trustee who is in breach of trust. It is difficult to see why, if the third party dishonestly assisted in a breach, there should be a further prerequisite to his liability, namely that the trustee also must have been acting dishonestly. The alternative view would mean that a dishonest third party is liable if the trustee is dishonest, but if the trustee did not act dishonestly that of itself would excuse a dishonest third party from liability. That would make no sense.[45]

16.47   Lord Nicholls went on to consider some of the pre-*Barnes v Addy* case law and concluded that there was authority against there needing to be any form of fraud or dishonesty on the part of the trustees before being entitled to bring proceedings against the dishonest third party.[46] His Lordship considered that the law took a

---

45   [1995] 2 AC 378, 384–5.

46   *Fyler v Fyler* (1841) 3 Beav 550 (trustees making what they considered to be a genuine investment in interests of beneficiaries assisted by solicitors who knowingly procured that to be done for their own benefit); *A-G v Corpn of Leicester* (1844) 7 Beav 176 (Lord Langdale MR at 179: 'it cannot be disputed that, if the agent of a trustee . . . knowing that a breach of trust is being committed, interferes and assists in that breach of trust, he is personally answerable . . .'); *Eaves v Hickson* (1861)

wrong turn following *Selangor v Craddock (No 3)*[47] after which Lord Selborne LC's statement in *Barnes v Addy* was treated and interpreted rather like a statute.

In order to reach a conclusion on whether the breach of trust needed to be dishonest, it was necessary, according to Lord Nicholls, to examine the whole issue of accessory liability including the level of knowledge required on the part of the third party. This examination led Lord Nicholls to conclude that dishonesty was the key factor: so long as the third party had acted dishonestly that would justify the imposition of accessory liability without having any requirement that the trustee itself be dishonest or fraudulent.[48]   **16.48**

He determined that a fault-based approach was the only sensible answer and that, after a thorough analysis of the relevant case law, he concluded that dishonesty was a sufficient basis to render the third party liable without also having to conclude that the trustees were themselves also behaving dishonestly.[49]   **16.49**

Lord Nicholls' conclusion is hardly surprising and must be welcomed. Once it is established that a third party has dishonestly interfered with a trustee's obligations to the beneficiary, it cannot be relevant to enquire into the level of culpability on the part of the trustee to determine whether or not the beneficiary might have a claim directly against the dishonest third party for any loss caused or gain obtained. The only relevance of any inquiry into the conduct of the trustees is to determine there has been a breach of trust or fiduciary duty and no more. That is a necessary inquiry due to the accessory nature of the third party's liability. But it makes no sense at all to absolve the dishonest third party from any liability whatsoever to the beneficiary on the basis that the trustee was acting innocently when he breached the trust or fiduciary duties.   **16.50**

(4) The third party must have induced or assisted in the breach

Although this head of liability has become known as dishonest assistance it covers both the inducement of a breach of trust as well as assistance in causing the breach.[50] It is of course a factual question whether there has been inducement of or assistance in the breach. The former will require evidence of activity undertaken   **16.51**

---

30 Beav 136 (innocent trustees duped by forged marriage certificate to distribute funds to children of third party forger). See also *Powell v Thompson* [1991] 1 NZLR 597, 610–15 where Thomas J rejected the suggestion that the liability of the third party depended on the degree of impropriety in the trustee's conduct.

[47] [1968] 1 WLR 1555.

[48] Lord Nicholls' examination of the whole area of accessory liability is considered below in para 16.68 *et seq.*

[49] The issue of dishonesty and the vexed question of what Lord Nicholls meant by its use is examined in the relevant section below: para 16.68 *et seq.*

[50] The earlier authorities drew no distinction between liability based upon assistance or inducement: see e.g. *Fyler v Fyler* (1841) 3 Beav 550 and *A-G v Corpn of Leicester* (1844) 7 Beav 176.

prior to the breach with an intention to persuade or encourage the trustee to carry out the activities which constitute the breach of trust. So, for example, where the trustee was provided with a forged marriage certificate to persuade him to distribute trust funds to children who were not properly beneficiaries of the trust, the provider of the forged document was found liable of having induced a breach of trust.[51] But for the forged document, there was no suggestion that the trustee would have breached his duties. In such a situation, the dishonest assistant is considered to be the driving force behind the breaching of the trust.

16.52   Where it is not said that the third party has induced the breach but has provided assistance, it is necessary to show that the relevant assistance played more than a minimal role in the breach being carried out.[52] It is not necessary, however, to show that the assistance provided would inevitably have resulted in the beneficiary suffering a loss.[53] Nor is it an answer to a claim for dishonest assistance to show that the breach of trust would have occurred in any event, regardless of whether the assistance was provided.[54] If, however, the breach has been completed prior to the assistance being provided, it is likely that the court will conclude that there was no assistance as such with the breach.[55]

16.53   However, one can readily see a situation where the assistance provided is by way of the laundering of the traceable proceeds of the breach of trust. Such assistance is necessarily provided after the completion of the breach of trust. It would be remarkable if the court were to conclude that such assistance could not amount to dishonest assistance. To overcome this obvious difficulty, the court has indicated that in the case of misappropriation of trust funds, the breach is not complete until the monies have been spirited away by way of money laundering and so any third party who dishonestly assists by way of the provision of money laundering services can be liable for dishonest assistance.[56] The court's conclusion on this issue is to be welcomed but it might be questioned whether it really is necessary to reach it by expanding the concept of when a breach of trust comes to an end.

---

[51] *Eaves v Hickson* (1861) 30 Beav 136.

[52] *Baden v Societe General pour Favoriser le Development du Commerce et de l'Industrie en France SA* [1983] 1 WLR 509, 574.

[53] ibid, 574–5.

[54] *Balfron Trustees Ltd v Peterson* [2001] IRLR 768 (Laddie J).

[55] *Brown v Bennett* [1998] 2 BCLC 97, 105 (Rattee J). The case went to appeal [1991] 1 BCLC 649 and Rattee J was affirmed on this point.

[56] *Agip (Africa) Ltd v Jackson* [1990] Ch 265, 293, [1991] Ch 547 (CA); *Heinl v Jyske Bank (Gibraltar) Ltd* [1999] Lloyd's Rep Bank 511, 523. See, however, the decision of Rimer J in *Brinks Ltd v Abu-Saleh (No 3) The Times,* 23 October 1995, (1996) CLC 133 where his Lordship held that a wife who accompanied her husband on trips to Switzerland carrying cash to be laundered from the Brinks gold bullion robbery was not liable for dishonest assistance. This, with respect, appears to have been a rather generous interpretation of her involvement, particularly since her presence expressly supported the cover story provided by her husband as to why the trips were being made in the first place.

The relevant issue should be whether material assistance has been provided dishonestly in respect of any breach of trust. The laundering of proceeds of fraud is seen as an important part of any such fraud and so assistance provided in this regard would clearly be material, irrespective of whether it was concluded that the breach of trust took place earlier.

Against the approach of the courts explored above must be placed the decision of Mance LJ (sitting at first instance) in *Grupo Torras SA v Al Saba (No 5)*[57] in which he held that a company director was not liable for dishonest assistance by providing misleading information to the auditors and shareholders, thereby assisting in the cover-up of the misappropriation of company funds.[58] It is submitted assistance provided with the aim of ensuring that the breach of trust is not discovered plays just as important a role in the breach of trust as assistance provided by way of money laundering services. Both are aimed at hindering the beneficiaries' opportunity to discover the true position and recover their losses and both types of conduct should be capable of giving rise to dishonest assistance. **16.54**

One additional issue to be resolved is whether and to what extent a third party may be liable for assistance provided by way of omissions rather than active conduct. There is no doubt that in *Royal Brunei v Tan*, Lord Nicholls stressed his view that dishonesty was 'mostly concerned with advertent conduct, not inadvertent conduct. Carelessness is not dishonesty. Thus, for the most part, dishonesty is to be equated with conscious impropriety.'[59] **16.55**

It is of course accepted that it can be very difficult to attach the connotation of dishonesty to a failure to act rather than to a positive act. However, the proper approach should be, whilst recognizing these obvious difficulties, whether it can be shown that the omission, whatever it was, played some form of causative role in the carrying out of the breach of trust. If so, that should suffice for dishonest assistance. **16.56**

(5) The third party must have acted dishonestly in providing the assistance

There is no doubt that the law as it presently stands requires that the third party has acted 'dishonestly' in providing the assistance in order to be liable for dishonest assistance. What is not as clear as it might have been, and no doubt was intended **16.57**

---

[57] (1999) CLC 1469. Mance LJ's views on this issue were not considered when the matter went to appeal: [2001] Lloyd's Rep Bank 36.

[58] Mance J stated: '. . . reprehensible though Mr Soler's conduct was, I do not consider that it attracts accessory liability as a constructive trustee. I do not consider that dishonest accounting intended to cover up a transaction believed to have been in a company's interest can or should axiomatically render a defendant liable if in reality the transaction involved a fraud on the company under which monies were misappropriated at an earlier stage' (at p 239 of transcript).

[59] [1995] 2 AC 378, 389D–E.

to be by Lord Nicholls when he laid this test down in *Royal Brunei v Tan*, is precisely what is meant and understood by the term 'dishonesty' in this context. Examination of the case law below will reveal marked differences in approach and whilst the latest decision of the Privy Council has sought to re-establish the orthodox understanding of Lord Nicholls' speech in *Royal Brunei v Tan*, it remains to be seen how this will be worked out in the English courts when faced with the conflicting views expressed in the House of Lords in *Twinsectra v Yardley*.

16.58 Whilst an examination of the historical position as to the appropriate level of knowledge for an assistance claim would not normally be appropriate in a practitioner's text, given the state of the present authorities, an understanding of all the relevant case law will hopefully assist in identifying the correct future approach of the courts.

16.59 There are effectively four distinct stages to the relevant case law:

- the conflicting state of the authorities pre-*Royal Brunei v Tan*;
- the decision in *Royal Brunei v Tan*;
- the (re-)interpretation of *Royal Brunei v Tan* in the House of Lords decision of *Twinsectra v Yardley*;
- the reinstatement in *Barlow Clowes International Ltd (in Liquidation) v Eurotrust International Ltd*[60] of the original interpretation of *Twinsectra v Yardley*.

(a) The conflicting state of the authorities pre-Royal Brunei v Tan

16.60 An understanding of some of the more important decisions pre-*Royal Brunei* is necessary for the practitioner since they often appear in the discussion of this area of the law and therefore the practitioner must be aware of them. There is, however, little point dwelling too heavily on them since, in most instances, the law has very much moved on. They can be thought of as useful stepping-stones on the path to the present state of the law.

16.61 There is no doubt that much of the confusion in the pre-*Royal Brunei* authorities derived from a failure properly to differentiate the assistance claim from the receipt claim. This, in turn, led to a failure to consider the differing basis for liability under both heads of claim which, in turn, has a bearing on the level of knowledge and/or dishonesty required for the claims.

16.62 Prior to the *Selangor United Rubber Estates Ltd v Craddock (No 3)*[61] decision, the traditionally accepted view was that the third party had to be dishonest in order to be liable for assistance in a breach of trust. *Selangor* represented the first modern

---

[60] [2005] UKPC 37, [2006] 1 All ER (Comm) (PC). See T M Yeo, 'Dishonest Assistance: A Restatement from the Privy Council' (2006) 122 LQR 1.
[61] [1968] 1 WLR 1555, 1590 (Ungoed-Thomas J).

decision which suggested a lower threshold of liability based upon knowledge of circumstances which would have indicated to 'an honest, reasonable man' that the breach in question was being committed or would put him on inquiry.

The same view was reached in *Karak Rubber Co Ltd v Burden (No 2)*[62] by Brightman J   **16.63** and by Peter Gibson J in *Baden v Societe Generale pour Favoriser le Development du Commerce et de l'Industrie en France SA.*[63] In reaching his conclusion, Peter Gibson J adopted counsel's five-point scale of knowledge which soon became the starting point for any discussion of knowledge in this area of the law for over a decade:

(1) actual knowledge;
(2) wilfully shutting one's eye to the obvious;
(3) wilfully and recklessly failing to make such inquiries as an honest and reason-able man would make;
(4) knowledge of circumstances which would indicate the facts to an honest and reasonable man; and
(5) knowledge of circumstances which would put an honest and reasonable man on inquiry.[64]

This view that liability could be imposed on the assister for less than dishonesty   **16.64** did not sustain support for long. Doubts emerged as to this threshold test in *Belmont Finance v Williams Furniture*[65] which had previously been raised by the High Court of Australia.[66]

Millett J in *Agip (Africa) Ltd v Jackson* also disavowed any approach to knowing   **16.65** assistance claims based upon constructive notice alone. He said:

> Tracing claims and cases of 'knowing receipt' are both concerned with rights of priority in relation to property taken by a legal owner for his own benefit; cases of 'knowing assistance' are concerned with the furtherance of fraud. In *Belmont Finance Corporation Ltd. v. Williams Furniture Ltd.* [1979] Ch. 250, the Court of Appeal insisted that to hold a stranger liable for "knowing assistance" the breach of trust in question must be a fraudulent and dishonest one. In my judgment it necessarily follows that constructive notice of the fraud is not enough to make him liable. There is no sense in requiring dishonesty on the part of the principal while accepting negligence as sufficient for his assistant. Dishonest furtherance of the dishonest scheme of another is an understandable basis for liability; negligent but honest failure to appreciate that someone else's scheme is dishonest is not.

---

[62] [1972] 1 WLR 602. Like *Selangor*, this case is a further example where no real distinction is drawn between knowing receipt and knowing assistance heads of liability. See also *Rowlandson v National Westminster Bank* [1978] 3 All ER 370.

[63] [1993] 1 WLR 509 (Note). The case was actually decided in 1982 and not published until 1993.

[64] (1982) [1993] 1 WLR 509, 575–6.

[65] [1979] Ch 250, 267 (Buckley LJ) and 270 (Goff LJ).

[66] *Consul Development Pty Ltd v D P C Estates Pty Ltd* (1975) 132 CLR 373, 376, 398, 412.

In *In re Montagu's Settlement Trusts* [1987] Ch. 264, 285, Sir Robert Megarry V.-C. doubted whether constructive notice is sufficient even in cases of 'knowing receipt'. Whether the doubt is well founded or not (as to which I express no opinion), 'knowing assistance' is an a fortiori case.

Knowledge may be provided affirmatively or inferred from circumstances. The various mental states which may be involved were analysed by Peter Gibson J. in *Baden's* case [1983] B.C.L.C. 325 as comprising: (i) actual knowledge; (ii) wilfully shutting one's eyes to the obvious; (iii) wilfully and recklessly failing to make such inquiries as an honest and reasonable man would make; (iv) knowledge of circumstances which would indicate the facts to an honest and reasonable man; and (v) knowledge of circumstances which would put an honest and reasonable man on inquiry.

According to Peter Gibson J., a person in category (ii) or (iii) will be taken to have actual knowledge, while a person in categories (iv) or (v) has constructive notice only. I gratefully adopt the classification but would warn against over refinement or a too ready assumption that categories (iv) or (v) are necessarily cases of constructive notice only. The true distinction is between honesty and dishonesty. It is essentially a jury question. If a man does not draw the obvious inferences or make the obvious inquiries, the question is: why not? If it is because, however foolishly, he did not suspect wrongdoing or, having suspected it, had his suspicions allayed, however unreasonably, that is one thing. But if he did suspect wrongdoing yet failed to make inquiries because 'he did not want to know' (category (ii)) or because he regarded it as 'none of his business' (category (iii)), that is quite another. Such conduct is dishonest, and those who are guilty of it cannot complain if, for the purpose of civil liability, they are treated as if they had actual knowledge.

16.66 Although it is evident that Millett J's reasoning was, to some extent, influenced by the requirement, emphasized by the Court of Appeal in *Belmont,* that the underlying breach of trust had to be fraudulent and dishonest, there is no doubt that he considered concepts such as constructive notice and negligence as inappropriate bases for asserting liability upon a third party assister.

16.67 Similar reasoning is to be found in Vinelott J's judgment in *Eagle Trust Plc v SBC Securities Ltd*[67] where he considered that the Court of Appeal in *Agip* should be taken to have endorsed Millett J's approach to the need for dishonesty. Vinelott J's reasoning, in turn, was supported by the Court of Appeal in *Polly Peck International Plc v Nadir (No 2)*.[68]

(b) The decision in Royal Brunei v Tan

16.68 The Privy Council's decision in *Royal Brunei v Tan* is generally considered to be the benchmark for the future development of the knowing or dishonest assistance head of liability. The reasoning of Lord Nicholls (who gave the speech) has already been examined in the context of whether there existed a requirement that the

---

[67] [1993] 1 WLR 484, 495.
[68] [1992] 4 All ER 769, 777 per Scott LJ.

trustee himself be dishonest and fraudulent before any liability can be imposed on an interfering third party. That was the actual issue before the Privy Council on appeal. Lord Nicholls rejected any such requirement, stating that the only relevant state of mind was that of the third party and not that of the trustee. In so doing, his Lordship examined this whole area of law and it is his conclusion on the level of knowledge required on the part of the third party which is examined below.

The salient facts were that the claimant airline ('Royal Brunei') had appointed **16.69** Borneo Leisure Travel ('BLT') as its travel agent for certain geographical areas of responsibility for collecting in and accounting to Royal Brunei for passenger payments. It was accepted that the monies so received by BLT were held on trust for Royal Brunei. Mr Philip Tan Kok Ming ('Mr Tan') was managing director and principal shareholder in BLT (the other director and shareholder being his wife). Monies which should have been paid to Royal Brunei were used to pay BLT's general operation costs. The trial judge found Mr Tan liable for dishonest assistance without finding that BLT was involved in a fraudulent and dishonest design. In the Court of Appeal of Brunei, the Court held that BLT was guilty of breaking promises and general mismanagement but was not in fact involved in a fraudulent and dishonest design.

On appeal to the Privy Council, Lord Nicholls held that there was no requirement **16.70** for the trustee to have acted dishonestly or fraudulently before liability could be imposed on the third party. In so doing, Lord Nicholls declined to follow Lord Selborne LC's celebrated statement to this effect in *Barnes v Addy*. At the heart of Lord Nicholls' rejection of this approach was the fact that the only relevant fault was that of the third party and it was necessary to establish an appropriate level of fault to justify the imposition of such liability.[69]

In this regard, his Lordship examined three extreme positions: (i) no liability, **16.71** (ii) strict liability and (iii) fault-based.

He 'dismissed summarily' the no-liability approach as the beneficiary was entitled **16.72** to look to an interfering third party for any loss caused by that interference. Lord Nicholls stated:

> . . . a trust is a relationship which exists when one person holds property on behalf of another. If, for his own purposes, a third party deliberately interferes in that relationship by assisting the trustee in depriving the beneficiary of the property held for him by the trustee, the beneficiary should be able to look for recompense to the third party as well as the trustee. Affording the beneficiary a remedy against the third party serves the dual purpose of making good the beneficiary's loss should the trustee lack

---

[69] 'A conclusion cannot be reached on the nature of the breach of trust which may trigger accessory liability without at the same time considering the other ingredients including, in particular, the state of mind of the third party' per Lord Nicholls [1995] 2 AC 378, 386E–F.

financial means and imposing a liability which will discourage others from behaving in a similar fashion.[70]

16.73 He also rejected the strict liability suggestion on the basis that this would render a third party liable to a beneficiary even when he unknowingly interfered with the trust. In the absence of receipt of trust property, there could be no justification for such liability being imposed:

> But ordinary, everyday business would become impossible if third parties were to be held liable for *unknowingly* interfering in the due performance of such personal obligations. Beneficiaries could not reasonably expect that third parties should deal with trustees at their peril, to the extent that they should become liable to the beneficiaries even when they received no trust property and even when they were unaware and had no reason to suppose that they were dealing with trustees. [71]

16.74 Having rejected the two extreme positions of no liability and strict liability, Lord Nicholls concluded that some form of fault-based liability was appropriate. He examined the various and conflicting decisions identified above and concluded that authority and academic writing supported a test of dishonesty.

16.75 In the light of subsequent doubts as to the proper interpretation of what Lord Nicholls meant by 'dishonesty' in this context, it will assist to set out in full the relevant definition:

> Whatever may be the position in some criminal or other contexts (see, for instance, *Reg v Ghosh* [1982] QB 1053), in the context of the accessory liability acting dishonestly, or with a lack of probity, which is synonymous, means simply not acting as an honest person would in the circumstances This is an objective standard. At first sight this may seem surprising. Honesty has a connotation of subjectivity, as distinct from the objectivity of negligence. Honesty, indeed, does have a strong subjective element in that it is a description of a type of conduct assessed in the light of what a person actually knew at the time, as distinct from what a reasonable person would have known or appreciated. Further, honesty and its counterpart dishonesty are mostly concerned with advertent conduct, not inadvertent conduct. Carelessness is not dishonesty. Thus for the most part dishonesty is to be equated with conscious impropriety. However, these subjective characteristics of honesty do not mean that individuals are free to set their own standards of honesty in particular circumstances. The standard of what constitutes honest conduct is not subjective. Honesty is not an optional scale, with higher or lower values according to the moral standards of each individual. If a person knowingly appropriates another's property, he will not escape a finding of dishonesty simply because he sees nothing wrong in such behaviour.
>
> In most situations there is little difficulty in identifying how an honest person would behave. Honest people do not intentionally deceive others to their detriment. Honest people do not knowingly take others' property. Unless there is a very good and compelling reason, an honest person does not participate in a transaction if he knows it

---

[70] [1995] 2 AC 378, 386–7.
[71] ibid, 387.

involves a misapplication of trust assets to the detriment of the beneficiaries. Nor does an honest person in such a case deliberately close his eyes and ears, or deliberately not ask questions, lest he learn something he would rather not know, and then proceed regardless.

Lord Nicholls went on to consider the application of the test of dishonesty in more difficult situations where the answers were not so obvious. He considered the following: **16.76**

- an authorized but imprudent investment;
- an unauthorized investment;
- an investment where there was doubt as to whether it was authorized or not.

(i) An authorized but imprudent investment   Lord Nicholls held that 'imprudence is not dishonesty'[72] and so an imprudent but otherwise authorized investment would not lead to questions about the honesty of any third party assisting in the making of those investments. This situation was, however, to be distinguished from that where the trustee knows the investment is unauthorized but believes that it is likely to result in a benefit to the beneficiary. This is not the type of risk the trustee is permitted to take and if the third party knows this, he can be accountable as a dishonest assistant. **16.77**

(ii) An unauthorized investment   The trustee may well be undertaking this type of investment for the best intentions, believing that it will substantially benefit the beneficiaries. However well intentioned, the trustee is not authorized to make this investment. This is not a case of imprudent investment as in the previous category, but rather unauthorized investment. As Peter Gibson J remarked in *Baden*,[73] involvement in this type of investment could amount to fraud since fraud includes taking 'a risk to the prejudice of another's rights, which risk is known to be one which there is no right to take'. Any third party assisting in the carrying out of this type of investment runs the risk of being held accountable as a dishonest assistant. **16.78**

(iii) An investment where there is doubt as to whether it is authorized   The first two situations gave rise to clear answers as to the availability of a dishonest assistance claim. This third category is far more difficult. It provides no clear answers. Of course, the liability of the trustee remains clear. If the investment is found to be unauthorized, he will be strictly liable. The real issue is how one determines whether a third party who assisted in that investment should be accountable to the beneficiary. If the accessory knows there is a doubt as to the validity of the transaction, **16.79**

---

72 [1995] 2 AC 378, 389H.

73 *Baden v Societe General pour Favoriser le Development du Commerce et de l'Industrie en France SA* [1983] 1 WLR 509, 574.

what is that accessory to do, consistent with acting honestly? Lord Nicholls provided the following guidance:

> The only answer to these questions lies in keeping in mind that honesty is an objective standard. The individual is expected to attain the standard which would be observed by an honest person placed in those circumstances. It is impossible to be more specific. Knox J captured the flavour of this, in a case with a commercial setting, when he referred to a person who is 'guilty of commercially unacceptable conduct in the particular context involved': see *Cowan de Groot Properties Ltd v Eagle Trust Plc* [1992] 4 All ER 700,761. Acting in reckless disregard of others' rights or possible rights can be a tell-tale sign of dishonesty. An honest person would have regard to the circumstances known to him, including the nature and importance of the proposed transaction, the nature and importance of his role, the ordinary course of business, the degree of doubt, the practicability of the trustee or the third party proceeding otherwise and the seriousness of the adverse consequences to the beneficiaries. The circumstances will dictate which one or more of the possible courses should be taken by an honest person. He might, for instance, flatly decline to become involved. He might ask further questions. He might seek advice, or insist on further advice being obtained. He might advise the trustee of the risks but then proceed with his role in the transaction. He might do many things. Ultimately, in most cases, an honest person should have little difficulty in knowing whether a proposed transaction, or his participation in it, would offend the normally accepted standards of honest conduct.[74]

16.80 Similarly, in assessing whether a third party, faced with this situation, has acted honestly, the court will look at all the circumstances known to the third party at the time and will also have regard 'to personal attributes of the third party, such as his experience and intelligence, and the reason why he acted as he did'.[75]

16.81 Although Lord Nicholls was at pains to emphasize his view that dishonesty was an objective standard, it is quite clear from the court's ability to take into account the personal attributes of the third party, that it is an objective standard which must be applied in the context of these attributes. So, for example, in determining the honesty of a solicitor who has assisted in an unauthorized transaction, one takes into account the knowledge and experience of the particular solicitor and ask the objective question whether a solicitor, with that degree of knowledge and experience, acting honestly, would have participated in the transaction. The fact that the particular solicitor genuinely believes he was entitled so to do is irrelevant if, objectively assessed, other solicitors with that degree of experience, would not have.

16.82 In favouring a test based upon dishonesty, Lord Nicholls declined to apply the *Baden* five-level test of knowledge which he considered was 'best forgotten'.[76]

---

[74] [1995] 2 AC 378, 390–1.
[75] ibid, 391.
[76] ibid, 392G–H.

An inquiry into the honesty of a third party was a far more meaningful inquiry than one based upon the levels of knowledge of the third party which quickly descended into the complex and unhelpful issue of the sort of knowledge required for liability. Lord Nicholls similarly rejected the potentially broader and more vague test of unconscionable conduct as favoured by Thomas J in the New Zealand case of *Powell v Thompson*.[77]

There is no doubt that the Privy Council decision in *Royal Brunei v Tan* was welcomed by the courts and commentators alike for its clarity and clear guidance as to the criteria necessary for what became known as the dishonest assistance claim. **16.83**

C. The (re-)interpretation of Royal Brunei v Tan in the House of Lords decision of Twinsectra v Yardley

It is perhaps fair to say that this was not the House of Lords' finest hour. We can take shortly the issue of what in fact *Twinsectra* decided on the question of what is meant by dishonesty since we are told, by Lord Hoffmann in *Barlow Clowes International Ltd v Eurotrust International Ltd*,[78] that *Twinsectra* did not in fact say what most thought it did. We will begin with what *Twinsectra* at least *seemed* to be saying about the test for dishonesty. **16.84**

The House of Lords in *Twinsectra* had to decide whether Lord Nicholls in *Tan* was intending to lay down a test of dishonesty which incorporated not only the fact that the acts are considered dishonest by right-thinking individuals but that the defendant is aware of this fact. **16.85**

Lord Hutton identified three concepts of dishonesty.[79] **16.86**

First, there is the purely subjective standard 'whereby a person is only regarded as dishonest if he transgresses his own standard of honesty, even if that standard is contrary to that of reasonable and honest people'. This standard, often termed the 'Robin Hood test' has been decisively rejected by the courts.[80] **16.87**

Secondly, there is the purely objective standard 'whereby a person acts dishonestly if his conduct is dishonest by the ordinary standards of reasonable and honest people, even if he does not realise this'. This is what Lord Millett, dissenting, considered Lord Nicholls to be saying in *Tan*. **16.88**

---

[77] [1991] 1 NZLR 597, 612–13, 615. It is interesting to note that although Lord Nicholls considered the concept of unconscionability as too wide and unmanageable for the purposes of determining liability for dishonest assistance, the Court of Appeal in *BCCI (Overseas) Ltd v Akindele* [2001] Ch 437 was happy to embrace it as the general test for the purposes of knowing receipt. It has also surfaced as the benchmark for the availability of the defence of change of position.

[78] [2005] UKPC 37, [2006] 1 WLR 1476.

[79] [2002] UKHL 12; [2002] 2 AC 164, [27].

[80] See *Walker v Stones* [2001] QB 902, 939.

16.89　Thirdly, there is what is known as the combined test 'which requires that before there can be a finding of dishonesty it must be established that the defendant's conduct was dishonest by the ordinary standards of reasonable and honest people and that he himself realised that by those standards his conduct was dishonest'.

16.90　Lord Hutton favoured the third test, the combined test:

> dishonesty requires knowledge by the defendant that what he was doing would be regarded as dishonest by honest people, although he should not escape a finding of dishonesty because he sets his own standards of honesty and does not regard as dishonest what he knows would offend the normally accepted standards of honest conduct.[81]

16.91　Similarly, Lord Hoffmann concluded that dishonesty, for these purposes, requires 'more than knowledge of the facts which make the conduct wrongful' and a 'consciousness that one is transgressing ordinary standards of honest behaviour'.[82]

16.92　Applying this combined test, the majority of the House of Lords concluded that Mr Leach, a solicitor, was not dishonest in releasing monies to his client absolutely, notwithstanding that he knew that another solicitor had given an undertaking that his client would hold those monies on trust. As Lord Hoffmann put the matter:

> Mr Leach believed that the money was at the disposal of Mr Yardley. He thought that whether Mr Yardley's use of the money would be contrary to the assurance he had given Mr Sims or put Mr Sims in breach of his undertaking was a matter between those two gentlemen. Such a state of mind may have been wrong. It may have been, as the judge said, misguided. But if he honestly believed, as the judge found, that the money was at Mr Yardley's disposal, he was not dishonest.[83]

16.93　Lord Millett delivered a powerful and compelling dissent against the adoption of the combined test of dishonesty maintaining it was inconsistent with what Lord Nicholls had in fact said in *Tan*. As far as Lord Millett was concerned, the combined test introduces an element of subjectivity which has more in common with the criminal understanding of dishonesty, such as set out in *R v Ghosh*,[84] than it does to the general understanding of civil liability.

16.94　Lord Millett's dissent was not based simply upon an analysis of what Lord Nicholls did or did not say in *Tan*. It ranged over a much broader examination of this area of the law and his conclusions were based upon the following grounds:

> (1) Consciousness of wrongdoing is an aspect of mens rea and an appropriate condition of criminal liability: it is not an appropriate condition of civil liability. This generally results from negligent or intentional conduct. For the purpose of civil liability, it should not be necessary that the defendant realised that his

---

[81] [2002] UKHL 12; [2002] 2 AC 164, 194–202.
[82] ibid, [20].
[83] ibid, [23].
[84] [1982] QB 1053.

conduct was dishonest; it should be sufficient that it constituted intentional wrongdoing.

(2) The objective test is in accordance with Lord Selborne's statement in *Barnes v Addy* LR 9 CH App 244 and traditional doctrine. This taught that a person who knowingly participates in the misdirection of money is liable to compensate the injured party. While negligence is not a sufficient condition of liability, intentional wrongdoing is. Such conduct is culpable and falls below the objective standards of honesty adopted by ordinary people.

(3) The claim for 'knowing assistance' is the equitable counterpart of the economic torts. These are intentional torts; negligence is not sufficient and dishonesty is not necessary. Liability depends on knowledge. A requirement of subjective dishonesty introduces an unnecessary and unjustified distinction between the elements of the equitable claim and those of the tort of wrongful interference with the performance of a contract.[85]

Applying this approach, Lord Millett concluded that Mr Leach knew all that he **16.95** needed to know to be liable for dishonest assistance.[86] This was not a case of wilful blindness or refusal to ask obvious questions for fear of getting answers not wanted. Mr Leach knew that Twinsectra had entrusted the money to Mr Sims with restricted authority to dispose of it; that Twinsectra trusted Mr Sims to ensure that the money was not used save for the acquisition of property; that Mr Sims had betrayed the confidence placed in him by paying the money to Mr Leach without ensuring that it was to be applied only for the acquisition of property; and that by putting the money at Mr Yardley's unfettered disposal, Mr Leach took the risk that the money would be applied for an unauthorized purpose and place Mr Sims in breach of his undertaking. Such knowledge was sufficient to render Mr Leach liable for dishonest assistance.

The reasoning of the majority of the House of Lords in *Twinsectra* on this issue came **16.96** as something of a surprise to most commentators. Lord Walker commented, extrajudicially, that he doubted 'whether the law as stated in *Royal Brunei* [was] clearer after *Twinsectra*'.[87] Underhill and Hayton[88] considered the majority's interpretation of Lord Nicholls to be 'strained', preferring the approach adopted in his dissent by Lord Millett. Some commentators considered it left the law 'in a confused state' and it remained uncertain precisely which Law Lord agreed with what aspect of Lord Hutton's and Lord Hoffmann's judgments.[89] Others considered it left the law in a state of 'ambiguity and uncertainty'.[90] It was, fortunately, not to last long.

---

85 [2002] UKHL 12; [2002] 2 AC 164, [127].

86 ibid, [143–4].

87 Lord Walker, 'Dishonesty and Unconscionable Conduct in Commercial Life' (2005) 27 Sydney LR 187, 197; C Rickett, 'Knowing What Is Dishonesty' (2002) 118 LQR 502.

88 Underhill and Hayton, *The Law of Trusts and Trustees* (17th edn, Lexis Nexis, 2006), at [100.56].

89 Thomas and Hudson, *The Law of Trusts* (Oxford University Press, 2004), para 30.34.

90 Pearce and Stevens, *The Law of Trusts and Equitable Obligations* (Oxford University Press, 2006), 833.

(d) Orthodoxy restored—Barlow Clowes International Ltd (in Liquidation) v Eurotrust International Ltd [91]

16.97 In *Barlow Clowes v Eurotrust*, a strong Privy Council (made up of Lord Hoffmann delivering the speech, and including Lords Nicholls and Walker) set about the task of trying to reconcile *Twinsectra* with *Royal Brunei* and remove any suggestion that *Twinsectra* intended to mark a departure from the reasoning of Lord Nicholls in *Royal Brunei*.

16.98 The issue in *Barlow Clowes* was whether or not Mr Henwood, the defendant director, was entitled to rely upon the second limb of the combined test in *Twinsectra*, namely that he did not himself know that his actions transgressed acceptable conduct, in his defence to a claim that, as financial adviser, he dishonestly assisted Peter Clowes and others to misappropriate funds which had been provided to Barlow Clowes for investment purposes. It was found as a fact by the Acting Deemster that Mr Henwood 'strongly suspected that the funds passing through his hands were moneys which Barlow Clowes had received from members of the public who thought that they were subscribing to a scheme of investment in gilt-edged securities . . . But Mr Henwood consciously decided not to make inquiries because he preferred in his own interest not to run the risk of discovering the truth'. The Acting Deemster went on to find that Mr Henwood had an:

> exaggerated notion of dutiful service to clients, which produced a warped moral approach that it was not improper to treat carrying out clients' instructions as being all important.[92]

16.99 Having failed to make such inquiries, the Acting Deemster found Mr Henwood liable for dishonest assistance. Mr Henwood successfully appealed to the Staff of Government of the High Court of the Isle of Man.

16.100 The issue which came before the Privy Council was whether Mr Henwood could be found to be dishonest in circumstances where he did not consider his actions contravened acceptable standards. Counsel for Mr Henwood relied upon the reasoning in *Twinsectra* to support his submission Mr Henwood could not, on this basis, be dishonest.

16.101 Lord Hoffmann, delivering the Privy Council speech, began by attempting to clear up any ambiguities created by the reasoning adopted in *Twinsectra*. Having set

---

[91] [2005] UKPC 37, [2006] 1 WLR 1476. See T M Yeo, 'Dishonest Assistance: A Restatement from the Privy Council' (2006) 122 LQR 1.

[92] Quoted by Lord Hoffmann in *Barlow Clowes Ltd v Eurotrust Ltd* [2006] 1 WLR 1476, 1480, para 12.

out the relevant extracts from *Twinsectra*,[93] in a section worth quoting in full, he said:

> 15 Their Lordships accept that there is an element of ambiguity in these remarks which may have encouraged a belief, expressed in some academic writing, that the *Twinsectra* case had departed from the law as previously understood and invited inquiry not merely into the defendant's mental state about the nature of the transaction in which he was participating but also into his views about generally acceptable standards of honesty. But they do not consider that this is what Lord Hutton meant. The reference to 'what he knows would offend normally accepted standards of honest conduct' meant only that his knowledge of the transaction had to be such as to render his participation contrary to normally acceptable standards of honest conduct. It did not require that he should have had reflections about what those normally acceptable standards were.

> 16 Similarly in the speech of Lord Hoffmann, the statement (in para 20) that a dishonest state of mind meant 'consciousness that one is transgressing ordinary standards of honest behaviour' was in their Lordships' view intended to require consciousness of those elements of the transaction which make participation transgress ordinary standards of honest behaviour. It did not also require him to have thought about what those standards were.[94]

But, if this is the true explanation of the reasoning in *Twinsectra*, what was the justification for not finding Mr Leach, the solicitor, dishonest? Lord Hoffmann said that *Twinsectra* had not involved any inquiry at all as to what Mr Leach's views were and how they equated with ordinary standards of honest behaviour. Although Mr Leach knew his client had received money from another solicitor who had given an undertaking that the client would only use that money to acquire property, that other solicitor had not in fact required Mr Leach to provide any similar undertaking when paying over the money to him. Thus, Mr Leach considered he was bound upon instructions to transfer the monies to his client unconditionally. As Lord Hoffmann indicated: 'The majority in the House of Lords considered that a solicitor who held this view of the law, even though he knew all the facts, was not by normal standards dishonest.'[95] **16.102**

Applying this approach to the facts of Mr Henwood's conduct, the Privy Council allowed the appeal and restored the decision of the Acting Deemster that there was sufficient evidence to find that Mr Henwood had consciously decided not to make inquiries through fear of discovering the truth and therefore that he had acted dishonestly in assisting in the fraud. **16.103**

The Staff of Government Division had considered it important that Mr Henwood knew nothing about the precise details of how the relevant business was conducted. **16.104**

---

93 [2002] 2 AC 164, 174 paras 35–6.
94 *Barlow Clowes Ltd v Eurotrust Ltd* [2006] 1 WLR 1476, 1481.
95 ibid, para 17.

The Privy Council held this contained two errors of law. First, it was not necessary that Mr Henwood should have concluded that the disposals were of monies held in trust. It was sufficient that 'he should have entertained a clear suspicion that this was the case'. Secondly, it was unrealistic to require Mr Henwood to know all the details of the underlying transactions before he had grounds to suspect that Mr Clowes and others were misappropriating the money of their investors:

> The money in Barlow Clowes was either held on trust for the investors or else belonged to the company and was subject to fiduciary duties on the part of the directors. In either case, Mr Clowes and Mr Cramer could not have been entitled to make free with it as they pleased. In *Brinks Ltd v Abu-Saleh* [1996] CLC 133, 151 Rimer J expressed the opinion that a person cannot be liable for dishonest assistance in a breach of trust unless he knows of the existence of the trust or at least the facts giving rise to the trust. But their Lordships do not agree. Someone can know, and can certainly suspect, that he is assisting in a misappropriation of money without knowing that the money is held on trust or what a trust means: see the *Twinsectra* case [2002] 2 AC 164, para. 19 (Lord Hoffmann) and para. 135 (Lord Millett). And it was not necessary to know the 'precise involvement' of Mr Cramer in the group's affairs in order to suspect that neither he nor anyone else had the right to use Barlow Clowes money for speculative investments of their own.[96]

16.105 Lord Hoffmann's attempt to restore the orthodox position in *Barlow Clowes* is to be welcomed, although it comes at the cost of a somewhat strained interpretation of *Twinsectra*. It can surely be questioned whether it is indeed permitted for one solicitor to deal with property in a manner inconsistent with the terms of an undertaking given by another solicitor and of which the first solicitor is aware.

16.106 The difficulty facing the practitioner is one of precedent. *Twinsectra*, as a House of Lords decision, is of course binding, whereas *Royal Brunei v Tan* and *Barlow Clowes* are only persuasive decisions of the Privy Council. To date, there has been a marked tendency to follow Lord Hoffmann in *Barlow Clowes* and favour the orthodox interpretation of *Royal Brunei v Tan*.

16.107 In *Fresh 'N' Clean Wales Ltd v Miah*,[97] the Court held that dishonesty:

> . . . simply means not acting as an honest person would – an objective standard which is assessed in light of what an alleged accessory actually knew at the relevant time, as distinct from what a reasonable person would have known or appreciated, taking into account any personal attributes of the alleged accessory such as his intelligence and experience, and the reason why he acted as he did; see *Royal Brunei v Tan* [1995] 2 AC 378, 389, 391. Hence, if judged by ordinary standards, an alleged accessory's mental state would, against this background, be characterised as dishonest, it is irrelevant that the alleged accessory judges his conduct by different standards. It is enough that his state of mind consists either in knowledge that the transaction is one in which he cannot honestly participate or in suspicion combined with a conscious

---

[96] [2005] UKPC 37; [2002] 2 AC 1476, 1483–4, para 28.
[97] [2006] EWHC 903 (Ch) (Martin Mann QC sitting as Deputy High Court Judge).

decision not to make inquiries which would have resulted in such knowledge; see *Barlow Clowes International Ltd v Eurotrust International Ltd* [2005] UKPC 37, paras.10,15.[98]

Abouh-Rahmah v Abacha[99] was the first Court of Appeal case to consider the effect **16.108** of *Barlow Clowes* on *Twinsectra*. The case concerned an appeal against a decision that a Nigerian bank had not dishonestly assisted a fraud notwithstanding it had general suspicions as to possible money laundering. Arden LJ favoured the Privy Council reasoning in *Barlow Clowes* on the grounds that:[100] (i) this did not involve any ignoring of precedent because *Barlow Clowes* simply attempted to explain the reasoning in *Twinsectra*; (ii) it did not say the case was wrong or should not be followed; (iii) the Privy Council in *Barlow Clowes* was made up of two judges who had sat on *Twinsectra*; (iv) there was no overriding reason why the civil liability test of dishonesty should require an inquiry into the defendant's views as to the morality of his actions.

In Arden LJ's view, the Court could not disturb the judge's finding that the general **16.109** suspicions of the Nigerian bank did not suffice to ground a finding of dishonesty in respect of the particular transactions which occurred, about which the bank had no particular suspicions.

Both Rix and Pill LJJ concluded that on the facts there was no need to resolve the **16.110** question of the impact of *Barlow Clowes* upon *Twinsectra*. Pill LJ did, however, agree with Arden LJ that the judge's finding of general suspicions in themselves did not give rise to dishonesty in relation to the particular transactions which were the subject matter of the claim. Rix LJ expressed some concerns that a bank, holding such general suspicions, is not considered dishonest in dealing with particular transactions. However, he did not consider it appropriate to disturb the judge's findings of fact on this issue and so concluded no dishonesty was found.

More recently, Peter Smith J has subjected this debate to typical forthright analysis **16.111** in *Attorney-General of Zambia v Meer Care & Desai (A Firm)*.[101] In his view, this area is a 'nightmare' for first instance judges borne out of over-elaboration and a general unwillingness to describe professional men as dishonest rather than attempting to identify some less offensive description. Peter Smith J gratefully adopted the extra-judicial observations of Lord Clarke MR:[102]

> . . . the simple fact of it seems to be that those who thought that the majority in Twinsectra interpreted the test for dishonesty as a combined test, had misunderstood the majority's decision. It might equally be said that the majority and minority in

---

[98] [2006] EWHC 903, [18].
[99] [2006] EWCA Civ 1492, [2006] 1 All ER (Comm) 247.
[100] ibid, paras 59a, 66–9.
[101] [2007] EWHC 952 (Ch).
[102] 'Claims Against Professionals: Negligence, Dishonesty and Fraud' [2006] 22 Professional Negligence [70/85].

Twinsectra had also misunderstood what each other meant:- Lord Hutton and Lord Hoffmann misunderstood what Lord Millett held and vice versa. Everyone agreed that the test was an objective one i.e. the test did not require any inquiry into the Defendant's subjective assessment of standards of honesty.

16.112 Peter Smith J went on to say he agreed with Lord Clarke's analysis and thought this was entirely consistent with the approach adopted by Kitchin J in *Barnes v Tomlinson*[103] where the judge identified two relevant points:

(1) It is for the court to determine what are the normally acceptable standards of honest conduct.

(2) The fact that a defendant genuinely believes that he has not fallen below the normally acceptable standards of honest conduct is irrelevant.

(e) Conclusions on present law

16.113 The road has been tortuous but the destination now appears clear. A person is dishonest if he fails to act as an honest person, having that person's attributes and experience, would in the circumstances. There is no requirement that the person should also be aware that his conduct falls below the generally accepted standards.

16.114 There is no need to prove that the defendant was aware of the details of the underlying fraud, that there existed a trust and/or that he knew the facts which give rise to the trust. If the defendant had such knowledge, it is likely a claim in conspiracy or joint tortious liability might be brought against him. It suffices if he simply knows that he is assisting the main fraudster to do something he is not entitled to do.[104] Although there was initial confusion on this issue, sensibly it will be no answer for the defendant to maintain he thought he was involved in a different dishonest transaction from the one he is actually involved in.[105] The intervention of equity cannot depend on such fine distinctions and there is no substantive difference between an individual who mistakenly believes he is assisting a fraud on X when in fact he is taking part in a fraud on Y and one who correctly believes he is helping to launder the proceeds of a theft. Both merit equity's intervention.

16.115 If he does not have that level of knowledge then the defendant can only be liable for dishonest assistance if it can be shown that, notwithstanding entertaining

---

[103] [2006] EWHC 3115.

[104] Per Lewison J in *Ultraframe (UK) Ltd v Fielding* [2005] EWHC 1638 (Ch), para 1504.

[105] *Agip (Africa) Ltd v Jackson* [1990] Ch 265, 295 (Millett J); aff'd [1991] Ch 547, 569; *Ultraframe (UK) Ltd v Fielding* [2005] EWHC 1638, para 1500; *Abou-Rahmah v Abacha* [2006] EWCA Civ 1492, para 39. A contrary view had been expressed by Rimer J in *Brinks Ltd v Abu-Saleh (No 3)* [1996] CLC 133, and endorsed by Mance LJ at first instance in *Grupo Torras SA v Al-Sabah (No 5)* unrep, 24 June 1999. However, the matter appears to have been resolved in favour of Millett J's view (as he then was) by Lord Hoffmann in *Barlow Clowes Ltd v Eurotrust Ltd* [2005] UKPC 37; [2006] 1 WLR 1476, para 28.

suspicions about the relevant transaction, the defendant decided against asking any questions through fear of being told the truth.

E. Remedies

Liability for dishonest assistance gives rise to a personal liability to account. Such personal liability has previously been clouded in the inappropriate language of constructive trusteeship which has now, hopefully, been abandoned.[106]   **16.116**

The assister's liability is not limited to the loss caused by his assistance but extends to the loss which flows from the breach of fiduciary duties.[107] This has been justified on the basis that this is secondary liability which 'derives from and duplicates the liability of the trustee or fiduciary whose breach has been assisted'.[108] On this basis, it is said that the remedies available against the assistant are identical to those available against the trustee.   **16.117**

As discussed in Chapter 17 on bribery,[109] there is a respectable argument in favour of permitting an account of profits to be recovered from the assister, consistent with the court's general approach in cases such as breach of confidentiality: see Toulson J in *Fyffes Group Ltd v Templeman*.[110]   **16.118**

It would appear, however, that the court is unlikely to render the assister personally liable for any profit that the trustee may have made as a result of the breach: see Lewison J in *Ultraframe (UK) Ltd v Fielding* [2005] EWHC 1638 (Ch) at [1589]–[1601].   **16.119**

F. Vicarious Liability

It is clear following the House of Lords decision in *Dubai Aluminium Co Ltd v Salaam*[111] that a firm can be vicariously liable for the dishonest assistance of one of its partners, acting in the ordinary course of business of the firm or with his co-partners' authority, under s 10 of the Partnership Act 1890 and individual partners are liable under s 9 of the Act. The same reasoning, although not the statutory basis, applies rendering an employer vicariously liable for the dishonest assistance   **16.120**

---

[106] See e.g. Millett LJ in *Paragon Finance plc v DB Thakerar and Co* [1999] 1 All ER 400, 408.

[107] See *Grupo Torras SA v Al Sabah* [1999] CLC 1469, 1666; *Lewin On Trusts* (18th edn, Thomson/Sweet and Maxwell, 2008), [40-40].

[108] Underhill and Hayton, *The Law of Trusts and Trustees* (17th edn), [100.43].

[109] See para 17.59.

[110] [2000] 2 Lloyd's Rep 643. See also Underhill and Hayton, *The Law of Trusts and Trustees* (17th edn), [100.45].

[111] [2002] UKHL 48, [2003] 2 AC 366.

of an employee so long as there is an adequate connection between the assistance provided and the employment and between the employer and the claimant: see *Balfron Trustees Ltd v Petersen*.[112]

G. Limitation Period

16.121 While the point cannot be said to have been finally resolved, the decision in *Cattley v Pollard*[113] favours a six-year limitation period for claims in dishonest assistance from the date of accrual. Accrual takes place when the cause of action is complete, namely when assistance is provided and the fiduciary duty has been breached. *Lewin on Trusts* (18th edn, 2008)[114] considers this decision is probably correct. However, the alternative view, that an accessory's liability is based on fraud and therefore has no limitation period under s 21(1)(a), has the support of Evans–Lombe J in *Statek Corporation v David Alford*.[115]

---

[112] [2002] WTLR 157; *Lewin On Trusts* (18th edn), [40-44].
[113] [2006] EWHC 3130 (Ch) (Richard Sheldon QC).
[114] At [44-56]–[44-58].
[115] [2008] EWHC 32 (Ch).

17

BRIBERY[1]

A. Overview of Claims

In its most simple terms, a claim based upon bribery is established in the event that **17.01** a third party (the briber) is shown to have paid a commission to the agent (the bribee) of a principal in circumstances where that principal is unaware of the payment.

It is not necessary to establish that the secret commission was paid with a corrupt **17.02** motive or intention to persuade or influence the agent. That will be presumed in the event of the payment of a secret commission to an agent in circumstances where the principal is not informed.[2]

---

[1] See 'Bribes and Secret Commissions' [1993] RLR 1, where Sir Peter Millett suggests the use of 'secret commissions' to describe those payments to an agent which are not intended to have a corrupt purpose but nevertheless represent a breach of the agent's fiduciary duty not to make a profit. In *Daraydan Holdings Ltd v Solland International Ltd* [2004] EWHC 622 (Ch), [2005] 1 Ch 119, Lawrence Collins J used the term 'secret commission' without indicating any substantive difference between them. Given there is in fact no need to embark upon a separate enquiry into whether or not a bribe was paid with a corrupt motive, since this will always be presumed, there seems little practical benefit to be derived from drawing a distinction between these two types of payment.

[2] *Tesco Stores Ltd v Pook* [2003] EWHC 823 (Ch), paras 39–45 citing and explaining Romer LJ in *Hovenden and Sons v Millhoff* (1900) 83 LT 41.

17.03 It is also not necessary to establish on the evidence that the bribee was in fact influenced by the payment of the secret commission. Receipt of the bribe gives rise to an irrebutable presumption of inducement.[3] It is perhaps more accurate to say that in every case there exists a risk of the bribee being induced and that risk is all that is necessary to justify intervention to protect the principal.[4]

17.04 It is similarly not necessary to establish that the principal in fact suffered a loss as a result of its agent having been bribed.[5] In other words, whilst recognizing that a loss might be incurred in the event that the agent is held liable to account to the principal, it is not necessary to show that the relevant transaction was disadvantageous to the principal in respect of its terms or pricing. That said, the bribe payment is always deemed to form part of the purchase price.[6]

17.05 This is therefore an odd factual scenario from which various causes of action arise since many of the 'evils' which might surround the payment of a bribe justifying the courts' intervention are presumed and need not actually be proven. So the payment of a secret commission is, in itself, sufficient (i) to infer a corrupt motive or intention on the part of the briber; (ii) to infer it had an influence on the agent or at least there was a risk it would have; and (iii) to establish the level of loss (if loss needs to be proven), which is presumed at the level of bribe payment unless it can be established and proven at a higher level.

17.06 There are a variety of potential remedies available to the principal upon discovery of a bribe having been paid:

- *As against the bribed agent:* the principal can recover the bribe payment from the agent on the grounds of money had and received; alternatively personal liability to account for profits in equity; alternatively as money held under a constructive trust. Further, should the principal believe he has suffered losses greater in amount than the level of the bribe payment, he will be entitled to claim them as damages for fraud.

- *As against the briber:* the principal is entitled to rescind the underlying transaction (so long as *restitutio in integrum* is still possible) and if he does so, there is

---

[3] *Hovenden & Sons v Millhoff* (1900) 83 LT 41, 43 per Romer LJ.

[4] Sir Peter Millett, 'Bribes and Secret Commissions' [1993] 1 RLR 1 at 13, n 42.

[5] *Parker v McKenna* (1874) 10 Ch App 96. As the Court of Appeal recognized in *Re North Australian Territory Company* [1892] 1 Ch 322, 337 ultimately this issue depends on the way it is examined. On one level the company in *Re North* lost nothing having issued the shares and received the par value for them. On another level, if it is accepted that the director is liable to account to the company for the monies received as part of his arrangement with the promoter to buy-back those shares at par value, then the company has lost something. *Reading v Att-Gen* [1951] AC 507 (HL). All this ultimately depends on the nature of the remedy sought. If a claim is founded on breach of fiduciary duty and a restitutionary/disgorgement remedy is sought, then the claim is based upon the defendant's gain and is not concerned at all with any loss suffered by the claimant.

[6] *Hovenden & Sons v Millhoff* (1900) 83 LT 41.

no requirement on his part to give any credit for the amount of the bribe, even if recovered from the bribed agent.[7] The principal may also bring a claim in tort for the amount of the bribe (on the basis this is presumed to be equal to the principal's loss unless proven otherwise). In addition, the briber is jointly and severally liable in damages (with the bribed agent) for fraud in respect of any losses proved greater in amount than the bribe. Additionally, the briber may also be liable in tort for inducing the agent's breach of contract and/or in equity for dishonestly assisting in the agent's breach of fiduciary duty.

B. Introduction

Whilst it might be considered that Lord Templeman was somewhat exaggerating the position when he described bribery as 'an evil practice which threatens the foundations of any civilized society',[8] nevertheless, it is true to say that bribery more often than not has a role to play in many of the complex commercial frauds faced by litigators. **17.07**

But what amounts to a bribe? It consists of no more and no less than the payment of a secret[9] commission to an agent.[10] In *Petrotrade Inc v Smith*[11] David Steel J provided the following simple and clear guidance: **17.08**

> For the purposes of the civil law a bribe means the payment of a secret commission, which only means (i) that the person making the payment makes it to the agent of the other person with whom he is dealing (ii) that he makes it to that person knowing that that person is acting as the agent of the other person with whom he is dealing; and (iii) that he fails to disclose to the other person with whom he is dealing that he has made that payment to the person whom he knows to be the other person's agent.

In *Anangel Atlas Cia v Naviera SA v Ishikawajima-Harima Heavy Industries Ltd*,[12] Leggott LJ, to similar effect, stated: **17.09**

> More succinctly it may be said that a bribe consists in a commission or other inducement which is given by the third party to an agent as such, and which is secret from the principal.

---

[7] *Logicrose Ltd v Southend United Football Club Ltd* [1988] 1 WLR 1256 (Millett J).

[8] *Att-Gen for Hong Kong v Reid* [1994] 1 AC 324, 330–1. Quoted with approval by Lawrence Collins J in *Daraydan Holdings Ltd v Solland International Ltd* [2004] EWHC 622; [2005] Ch 119 at [1] where the judge added: 'It corrupts not only the recipient but the giver of the bribe.' For equally strong language, see *Parker v McKenna* (1874) 10 Ch App 96, 124–5 where James LJ describes it as a matter of the 'safety of man' that a bribed agent not be permitted to deny liability on the ground that such profits were not otherwise available to the principal.

[9] The commission is 'secret' because the principal is deliberately left uninformed of the payment.

[10] *Industries and General Manager Co Ltd v Lewis* [1949] 2 All ER 573, 575 per Slade J.

[11] [2000] 1 Lloyd's Rep 486, para 16.

[12] [1990] 1 Lloyd's Rep 167 at 171 per Leggatt LJ.

17.10   Lawrence Collins J in *Daraydan Holdings Ltd v Solland International* has given a more detailed description of the relevant principles to be distilled from the cases:

> 52. An agent should not put himself in a position where his duty and interest may conflict, and if bribes are taken by an agent, the principal is deprived of the disinterested advice of the agent, to which the principal is entitled. Any surreptitious dealing between one principal to a transaction and the agent of the other is a fraud on the other principal. For this purpose sub-agents owe the same duty not to take bribes as agents, despite the absence of privity of contract between them and the principal: . . .

> 53. In proceedings against the payer of the bribe there is no need for the principal to prove (a) that the payer of the bribe acted with a corrupt motive; (b) that the agent's mind was actually affected by the bribe; (c) that the payer knew or suspected that the agent would conceal the payment from the principal; (d) that the principal suffered any loss or that the transaction was in some way unfair; the law is intended to operate as a deterrent against the giving of bribes, and it will be assumed that the true price of any goods bought by the principal was increased by at least the amount of the bribe, but any loss beyond the amount of the bribe itself must be proved; (e) that the bribe was given specifically in connection with a particular contract, since a bribe may also be given to an agent to influence his mind in favour of the payer generally (e.g. in connection with the granting of future contracts.)

> 54. The agent and the third party are jointly and severally liable to account for the bribe, and each may also be liable in damages to the principal for fraud or deceit or conspiracy to injury by unlawful means. Consequently, the agent and the maker of the payment are jointly and severally liable to the principal (1) to account for the amount of the bribe as money had and received and (2) for damages for any actual loss. But the principal must now elect between the two remedies prior to final judgment being entered: *Mahesan s/o Thambiah v Malaysia Government Officers' Co-Operative Housing Society Ltd* [1979] AC 374, 383. The third party may also be liable on the basis of accessory liability in respect of breach of fiduciary duty: *Bowstead & Reynolds on Agency*, para.8-221. The principal is also able to rescind the contract with the payer of the bribe.

17.11   As stated above, many of the reasons for court intervention in the payment of a bribe are in fact presumed or inferred from the very act of payment itself without needing to be proven before establishing the claim. So there is no need for the claimant to become embroiled in the difficult task of showing that the agent was in fact influenced by the payment. It suffices, and rightly so, that there exists a real risk of his being influenced after receipt of the secret commission. The principal is entitled to have the advice and assistance of the agent free from any influence or the risk of any influence from a third party.

17.12   Similarly, it would impose a difficult burden on the claimant principal to have to show that the third party was making the payment in order to induce the agent. The sanctity of the relationship between principal and agent in commercial relationships is upheld by simply barring any commission paid to an agent by a third party without the knowledge of the principal.

It is clear that a bribe is not limited to the payment of money alone. Other forms of **17.13** inducement, such as the promise of employment,[13] will suffice to amount to a bribe.

But what is the 'evil' inherent in a case of bribery? Is it simply the receipt of money **17.14** by an agent of which the principal was unaware? In the case of a fiduciary agent, such money would of course represent a secret profit obtained in breach of the agent's fiduciary duty and would be recoverable by the principal. But the obtaining of a secret profit is not, in itself, the answer: it is because such payments create the potential for a conflict of interest as between the agent and the principal that the court will not allow an agent to retain such sums.

The receipt of the bribe creates a conflict of interest which means that the princi- **17.15** pal can no longer be confident, as it is entitled to be, that it is the recipient of disinterested advice from its agent. Once tainted with the bribe, there exists a real risk (and that is all that is required) that the agent will not provide disinterested advice to its principal.

The fact that the briber knows and is the cause of the agent no longer being able **17.16** to provide disinterested advice is the very reason why the principal is able to claim against the briber.[14]

It will become readily apparent that one of the aims of this chapter, and the reason **17.17** why bribery is being accorded separate treatment, is to illustrate the importance of understanding all the potential claims which may arise from a bribe. Such claims range from a claim in tort for damages for fraud, to unjust enrichment or in breach of fiduciary duty for restitution/disgorgement. Bribery can and often does give rise to a myriad of such claims and it will be fact-dependent which one is appropriate to be pursued in any given case. So, for that reason, it was decided to give bribery its own chapter in which all the potential claims can properly be identified in one place.

(1) Bribery and deceit

In *Salford v Lever*,[15] the claim for bribery was characterized as one in fraud[16] and **17.18** there have been attempts to shoe-horn it into the traditional criteria for a claim in deceit.[17]

---

[13] *Amalgamated Industrials Ltd v Johnson & Firth Brown, The Times*, 15 April 1981.
[14] See *Logicrose Ltd v Southend United FC* [1988] 1 WLR 1256, 1261 D–H (Millett J).
[15] [1891] 1 QB 168.
[16] See also A Tettenborn, 'Bribery, Corruption and Restitution—the Strange Case of Mr Mahesan' (1979) 95 LQR 68.
[17] Hazel Carty, *An Analysis of the Economic Torts* (Oxford University Press, 2001), 133–6. Under the editorship of Prof Carty, this appeared in the 18th edition of *Clerk & Lindsell*, para 15-04. It is noted that the discussion is removed in the 19th edition (R Simpson (ed)), *Clerk & Lindsell*, ch 18.

17.19 At the heart of a claim in deceit is some form of misrepresentation which has been relied upon by the claimant. That is not something which is evident in the act of bribery and attempts to infer such a misrepresentation are only likely to stretch the concept beyond credulity. When the real harm behind bribery is understood (see above), it is instantly recognized that it does not readily fall within the traditional understanding of a claim in deceit[18] particularly because it must be an agent who is bribed.

17.20 The preferable approach is to recognize it as a 'hybrid form of legal wrong'[19] which stands as a distinct tort. This will give rise to a claim in damages which may prove far more profitable than simply the recovery of the bribe, in circumstances where the principal can establish that but for the bribe he would have been able to enter into a far more advantageous transaction.

(2) Bribery and fiduciary relationships

17.21 Bribes involve agents and the relationship between agent and principal invariably, if not always, gives rise to fiduciary duties on the agent's part. It follows, of course, that the payment of a bribe will always involve an agent in breach of its fiduciary duties.

17.22 The equitable treatment of bribery in the texts tends to be the more detailed because it is in the context of the equitable claims arising from a bribe that the most controversial decision, and perhaps the most practically useful from a commercial fraud litigator's perspective, arises, namely the availability of a proprietary claim in respect of the bribe monies.[20] This will be examined in some detail below.

17.23 Equity has an important role to play in any case of bribery. If it applies, it gives rise to potential claims for an account of profits and, if appropriate, a proprietary claim based upon the bribe being held on constructive trust for the principal. Whilst it remains theoretically possible for a particular agent not to owe fiduciary duties to its principal,[21] the reality is that the tendency of the courts is in favour of

---

[18] It would be necessary to characterize the failure by the agent to disclose the existence of the payment of the bribe as a misrepresentation, by conduct, that the agent was able to provide disinterested advice to the principal. There is nothing to be gained by such strained reasoning.

[19] *Arab Monetary Fund v Hashim* [1993] 1 Lloyd's Rep 543, 564 per Evans J.

[20] *Att-Gen for Hong Kong v Reid* [1994] 1 AC 324 in which the Privy Council held that the Court of Appeal's decision in *Lister & Co v Stubbs* (1890) 45 Ch D 1 to restrict the remedy to a personal liability to account on the agent's part was wrong.

[21] *Goff & Jones* at para 33-021, n 49 cites a series of cases said to involve 'non-fiduciary' agents. (It is not at all clear that these authorities all support a characterization of the agent as non-fiduciary. See, for example, the headnote to *Erskine, Oxenford & Co v Sachs* [1901] 2 KB 504: 'Held that, the brokers having acted in a fiduciary capacity in the sale of the shares, and having, by reason of that sale and the repurchase being effected as one transaction, obtained a profit for themselves, they were

finding fiduciary relationships arising out of the principal–agency relationship and so it is likely to be a rare agent who is not capable of being characterized as being a fiduciary for these purposes.[22]

Indeed, the accepted characteristics of the fiduciary relationship are the reasons **17.24** why a bribe might be paid to an agent. So, for example, in *Reading v The King*[23] Asquith LJ held that there existed a fiduciary relationship whenever the claimant entrusts a job to be performed, e.g. the negotiation of a contract, and relies on the agent to get the best terms available.[24] It is precisely because the agent is in that position of trust and confidence that a third party thinks it is worth paying the bribe. The bribe wins over the agent which in turn secures the contract because of the principal's trust and confidence in the agent. A non-fiduciary agent would not have his principal's trust and confidence at all or to that extent and/or would not be given such authority over the business affairs of the principal. The point holds good for other well-known definitions or descriptions of the fiduciary relationship.[25]

(3) Bribery and unjust enrichment

In addition to potential claims arising in tort (for damages), and in equity (account **17.25** of profits/constructive trust), a claim based upon bribery may also give rise to a claim at common law for money had and received (in old language) or unjust enrichment (in modern parlance). The amount of any such claim is the amount of the bribe.

---

bound to account for that profit to their principals, the clients.' See also *Kimber v Barber* (1872) 8 Ch App 56 where Barber told Kimber he could acquire certain shares at £3 each. Kimber agreed to proceed and having purchased the shares subsequently discovered that Barber had in fact purchased the shares himself for £2 and was making an additional £1 per share profit. It appears from p 59 of the report that the Court concluded that there did exist a fiduciary relationship arising from the agency relationship between Kimber and Barber. As regards *Powell & Thomas v Evans Jones & Co* [1905] 1 KB 11, Asquith LJ in *Reading v Att-Gen* [1949] 2 KB 232 at p 236 re-interpreted the case as one involving a fiduciary relationship. It is worth noting that *Bowstead & Reynolds* [6-036] accept that their general rule (Articles 1 and 43) presuppose that all agents are fiduciaries, although they concede that the range of fiduciary duties will vary from agent to agent.)

[22] See *Goff & Jones* at para 33-021 citing the leading case of *Reading v Att-Gen* [1951] AC 507.

[23] [1949] 2 KB 232, 236.

[24] Asquith LJ's description of the fiduciary relationship was approved by Lord Porter in *Reading v Attorney-General* [1951] AC 507, 516. It was also cited with apparent approval by Lawrence Collins J in *Daraydan Holdings Ltd v Solland International Ltd* [2005] Ch 119, [56].

[25] E.g. Millett LJ in *Bristol and West Building Society v Mothew* [1998] Ch 1, 18: 'A fiduciary is someone who has undertaken to act for or on behalf of another in a particular matter in circumstances which give rise to a relationship of trust and confidence. The distinguishing obligation of a fiduciary is the obligation of loyalty. The principal is entitled to the single-minded loyalty of his fiduciary . . .'. That loyalty is exactly what the briber purchases with the bribe.

17.26　As will be seen, such a claim potentially lies against both third party briber and agent bribee, notwithstanding the obvious fact that only the agent bribee actually *received* any commission. Indeed, it is nothing short of anomalous that a claim in money had and received can lie against the briber who, by definition, has paid out and not received any payment. It simply does not fit our present understanding of such a claim and attempts to characterize such a claim consistent with that understanding border on the ridiculous. How can the payor be enriched to the extent he paid out to the payee? We have to stretch our understanding of receiving an enrichment beyond credibility to make any sense of this claim. An attempt to explain the position is made later in the chapter. It is not convincing.

C. Claims against Briber

17.27　Upon discovery of the bribe payment, the principal has the following potential claims against a briber:

- transaction void *ab initio*;
- rescission;
- damages;
- money had and received;
- liability to account for dishonest assistance.

(1) Transaction void *ab initio*

17.28　When discussing potential relief available to the principal of a bribed agent, it can often be overlooked that the transaction entered into as a result of the agent being bribed may well be considered void at common law in circumstances where the briber, as the other party to the transaction, is on notice that the principal's agent is acting beyond its actual authority in agreeing to enter into the transaction on the principal's behalf which is contrary to the principal's interests.[26] The generally perceived view is that the contract is voidable.[27]

17.29　*Bowstead & Reynolds*, Article 23 provides:

> Unless otherwise agreed, authority to act as agent only includes authority to act for the benefit of the principal.

---

[26] See *Bowstead & Reynolds*, para 8-218. This point, arising from agency law, appears not to have been cited to Blackburne J in *Tajik Aluminium Plant v Abdukadir Ermatov & Ors* [2006] EWHC 7 at para 21. See also *Bowstead & Reynolds*, Article 73: 'No Unauthorised Act Binding with Respect to Persons with Notice'. See also *Albright & Wilson UK Ltd v Biachem Ltd* [2001] EWCA 537; [2001] 2 All ER (Comm) 537 at para 16; on appeal [2002] UKHL 37, [2002] 2 All ER (Comm) 753.

[27] *Re a Debtor* [1927] 2 Ch 367 (CA); *Logicrose Ltd v Southend United Football Club Ltd* [1988] 1 WLR 1256; *Tajik Aluminium Plant v Ermatov (No 3)* [2006] EWHC 7 (Ch), [21]–[22].

In discussing the situation where a third party bribes an agent to secure its principal's business, *Bowstead & Reynolds* goes on to say:

> ... there is in such situations considerable scope for use of the basic agency reasoning that the agent is simply not authorized to act contrary to his principal's interests: and hence that an act contrary to those interests is outside his actual authority. On this basis the transaction is actually void unless the third party can rely on the doctrine of apparent authority: and in the situations ... where the third party is actually involved in the agent's breach of duty, there can usually *ex hypothesi* be no apparent authority.[28]

This view is supported by the Court of Appeal in *Heinl v Jyske Bank*[29] where one of the defendants was a bank manager who had agreed to enter into loan transactions on behalf of the bank for certain business ventures in which he and others had vested interests. **17.30**

Having considered the observations of Slade LJ and Browne-Wilkinson LJ in *Rolled Steel Products (Holdings) Ltd v British Steel Corporation*,[30] Nourse LJ stated: **17.31**

> Those observations all come to the same thing. Where an agent is known by the other party to a purported contract to have no authority to bind his principal, no contract comes into existence. The agent does not purport to contract on his own behalf and the knowledge of the other party unclothes him of ostensible authority to contract on behalf of the principal. Whether or not such a transaction is accurately described as a void contract, it is plainly not voidable. If no contract comes into existence, there is nothing to avoid or rescind, nor can any property pass under it ...[31]

The criteria that the briber be acting beyond its actual authority and the third party have notice thereof will be readily established in a typical case of bribery. **17.32**

Given the fiduciary status of the agent, the fact that the transaction is void, rather than voidable, will not prevent any arguments based upon equitable proprietary remedies.[32] **17.33**

(2) Rescission

The typical purpose for which a bribe is paid is to exert influence over an agent to persuade its principal to enter into some form of transaction with the briber. There is no doubt that, subject to any argument that the transaction is in fact void (see above) a principal is entitled to have a transaction rescinded if it is discovered **17.34**

---

[28] *Bowstead & Reynolds*, para 8-218.
[29] *Heinl v Jyske Bank (Gibraltar) Ltd* [1999] Lloyd's Rep Bank 511, 521 (Nourse LJ).
[30] [1986] Ch 246.
[31] [1999] Lloyd's Rep Bank 511, 521. This proposition appears now to be accepted by the editors of *Chitty on Contractss*, vol 2, para 31-073.
[32] *Heinl v Jyske Bank (Gibraltar) Ltd* [1999] Lloyd's Rep Bank 511, 521. See also *Matthews v Gibbs* (1860) 30 LJQB 55, (1860) 3 El & El 282; *Bowstead & Reynolds*, para 8-219; O'Sullivan, Elliot and Zakrzewski, *The Law of Rescission* (Oxford University Press, 2007), [1.78]–[1.80].

that a bribe has been paid to the principal's agent. There is no requirement to show a corrupt motive or purpose on the part of the payor/briber; such is presumed from the payment of a secret commission to the agent.

17.35 In *Panama and South Pacific Telegraph Company v India Rubber*,[33] James LJ stated:

> According to my view of the law of this court, I take it to be clear that any surreptitious dealing between one principal and the agent of the other principal is a fraud on such other principal, recognizable in this Court. That I take to be a clear proposition, and I take it . . . to be equally clear that the defrauded principal, if he comes in time, is entitled, at his option, to have the contract rescinded, or, if he elects not to have it rescinded, to have such other adequate relief as the Court may think right to give him.[34]

17.36 Upon discovery of a bribe having been paid, the first issue to be considered by the principal is whether or not to continue with the transaction.

17.37 This issue will require the principal to undertake an assessment of the merits of the transaction. Is the principal otherwise happy or content with the terms of the transaction? Does the principal believe that a better deal could have been obtained elsewhere? Would rescinding the transaction in fact cause more difficulties for the principal's business than simply continuing with it? These and no doubt a host of other commercial questions will need to be considered by the principal, and without delay, so as to determine whether to exercise the option to rescind the transaction.

17.38 The principal will be entitled to rescind the transaction unless it can be shown that either he has affirmed it, with full knowledge of the bribe, or alternatively that he is unable to make *restitutio in integrum*. If the transaction has been ongoing for some time and involves third parties, it may well be that the principal will not be in a position to offer full *restitutio in integrum*.

17.39 If the transaction is rescinded, there is no requirement for the principal to give credit for any bribe monies that may have been recovered from the agent.[35]

(3) Damages

17.40 A briber is also liable to the principal in damages for fraud for the loss suffered as a result of the principal having entered into the relevant transaction.

---

[33] (1875) LR 10 Ch App 515.
[34] ibid, 526. See also *Chandler v Bradley* [1897] 1 Ch 315; *Re A Debtor* [1927] 2 Ch 367; *Taylor v Walker* [1958] 1 Lloyd's Rep 490; *Amragas Ltd v Mundogas SA (The Ocean Frost)* [1986] AC 717, 742h–743B (Robert Goff LJ).
[35] *Logicrose Ltd v Southend United Football Club Ltd* [1988] 1 WLR 1256 (Millett J).

It has already been discussed that such a claim does not satisfy the typical require- **17.41**
ments of the tort of deceit (e.g. no need for intention, no obvious representation and no need for reliance on the part of the principal). There has been
some suggestion that this is a *sui generis* tort, in which loss is presumed to be the
same as the amount of the bribe unless the principal can prove actual additional
loss.[36]

Whatever the proper characterization, there is no doubting that such a claim exists **17.42**
and is available as against the briber for the amount of loss actually sustained.

The issue of election between the various remedies available will be discussed **17.43**
separately.

(4) Money had and received—unjust enrichment

Curiously, the principal is also entitled to recover from the briber the amount of **17.44**
the bribe on the grounds of money had and received.[37]

That this is the present state of the law is undoubtedly clear.[38] What remains less **17.45**
obvious is the theoretical justification for such a claim in circumstances where the
briber himself does not in fact receive the bribe—he pays it out. On this basis, it
is difficult to comprehend how it could be said that he has been in any way enriched
in the amount of the bribe.

It might be said, without much conviction, that the briber is unjustly enriched in **17.46**
at least the amount of the bribe. The argument would go as follows: (i) the true
purchase price is assumed to be at least purchase price plus bribe; (ii) the briber
only paid the principal the purchase price but not the bribe, which went to someone else; (iii) therefore, as between briber and principal, the briber has obtained
the contract for less than its true purchase price. The fact that the briber paid a bribe
to someone other than the principal cannot be brought into the equation. All that
matters is what was paid to the principal. On this basis, it might be said, without
much conviction, that the briber has been unjustly enriched (in his obtaining the
contract) and that enrichment is measured by the amount of the bribe.

It would be preferable to abandon all notion of a claim in unjust enrichment as **17.47**
against the briber. This will not leave any lacuna in the law or ensure that the principal is left without any effective remedies against the briber.

---

[36] *Mahesan v Malaysian Government Officers' Co-Operative Housing Society Ltd* [1979] AC
374, 383.
[37] ibid, per Lord Diplock.
[38] *Bowstead & Reynolds*, [8-010].

17.48 This difficulty is compounded in circumstances where the briber may be liable to the principal for a promised but not in fact paid bribe.[39]

17.49 The existence of a claim against the briber for money had and received has not received universal acceptance in the authorities. In *Grant v Gold Exploration and Development Syndicate Ltd*[40] the Court of Appeal was split on the issue. Collins LJ (p 249) favoured the existence of such a claim whereas both Smith LJ (pp 244–5) and Vaughan Williams LJ (p 256) doubted the availability of such a claim and preferred to express themselves in terms of damages for fraud where the amount of the bribe proves at least loss to that sum for the purposes of assessing damages.

17.50 Subsequently, Smith and Vaughan Williams LJJ, this time sitting with Romer LJ in the Court of Appeal in *Hovenden and Sons v Millhoff*,[41] decided, or have at least been interpreted by the Privy Council in *Mahesan v Malaysia Housing Society*, as having decided there exists two causes of action, one for money had and received and the second for damages for tort. Having considered the various rules put forward by Romer LJ in *Hovenden*, the Privy Council stated:

> These rules refer to three of the elements in the tort of fraud, the motive, the inducement, and the loss occasioned to the plaintiff, but go on to say that the existence of the first two elements and of the third up to the amount of the bribe are to be irrebuttably presumed. This is merely another way of saying that they form no part of the definition of bribery as a legal wrong. To the extent that it is said that there is an irrebuttable presumption of loss or damage to the amount of the value of the bribe this is another way of saying that, unlike in the tort of fraud, actual loss or damage is *not* the gist of the action. But then to go on to say that actual loss in excess of the amount of the bribe can be recovered only if it is proved, is to produce a hybrid form of legal wrong of which actual damage *is* the gist of part only of a single cause of action.
>
> Upon analysis, what these rules really describe is the right of a plaintiff who has alternative remedies against the briber (1) to recover from him the amount of the bribe as money had and received, or (2) to recover, as damages for tort, the actual loss which he has sustained as a result of entering into the transaction in respect of which the bribe was given; but in accordance with the decision of the House of Lords in *United Australia Ltd v Barclays Bank Ltd* [1941] AC 1 he need not elect between these alternatives before the time has come for judgment to be entered in his favour in one or other of them.[42]

---

[39] *Grant v Gold Exploration and Development Syndicate* [1900] 1 QB 233. It is also to be noted that Millett J in the extract quoted in the text from *Logicrose* used the phrase 'or promised to the agent' indicating that actual payment may not be necessary.

[40] [1900] 1 QB 233.

[41] (1900) 83 LT 41.

[42] *Mahesan v Malaysia Housing Society Ltd* [1979] AC 374, 383.

The Privy Council in *Mahesan* fully recognized the conceptual difficulties of a **17.51** claim in money had and received but maintained that it was now too well established a principle from which to depart.[43]

One potential explanation offered by Millett J in *Logicrose Ltd v Southend United* **17.52** *FC*[44] for the existence of a claim in money had and received is that the principal 'is entitled to treat the benefit obtained by *or promised to the agent* as part of the consideration which should have been received by the principal (if he is a vendor) or as excess consideration provided by the principal (if he is a purchaser)'.[45]

Notwithstanding valiant attempts to characterize the claim as one in unjust **17.53** enrichment, it cannot be denied that the claim does not exhibit the typical features of such a claim (most notably since it involves the defendant being the payor and the payee of an enrichment). And there being nothing obvious for the briber to restore or to disgorge. *Goff & Jones* states that the briber's restitutionary liability in the amount of the bribe is based upon the 'irrebuttable presumption' that this is the amount the principal has lost.[46]

One possibly better explanation lies in the law on accessory liability and not unjust **17.54** enrichment.[47] This would justify a claim for recovery of the bribe amount on the basis of equitable compensation due for the briber's assistance in a breach of fiduciary duty by the agent. On this basis, the whole analysis of bribes would move into equity and abandon the common law of money had and received and the tort of deceit, with which it does not neatly fit.

It is unlikely any such major shift in our understanding of the law of bribery will **17.55** be achieved any time soon. It is more likely that this new approach will become an additional rather than substituted means of explaining the various heads of liability arising from a bribe case. Only time will tell whether it is greeted with such support that it eventually becomes the accepted explanation. Until such a time, practitioners are advised to be aware of the analysis of bribery under each of unjust enrichment, tort and equity (breach of fiduciary duty).

(5) Liability to account for dishonest assistance

The agent owes fiduciary duties to his principal. The payment of a bribe by the **17.56** briber to the agent will result in a breach of those fiduciary duties. Whether or not

---

[43] ibid, 383G–H.
[44] [1988] 1 WLR 1256.
[45] ibid, 1263 (emphasis added).
[46] *Goff & Jones*, para 33-032; *Petrotrade Inc v Smith* [2000] 1 Lloyd's Rep 486, para 18; *Fyffes Group Ltd v Templeman* [2000] 2 Lloyd's Rep 643, 668–9 (Toulson J).
[47] *Bowstead & Reynolds*, para 8-221.

the briber will be liable to account for *dishonest* assistance will depend on whether he was acting *dishonestly* in making the payment.

17.57 Exactly what amounts to dishonesty for these purposes has been subjected to detailed scrutiny in Chapter 16 on dishonest assistance.[48] It is likely that most scenarios in which a bribe payment is made will equate to dishonest conduct.[49] There may well be odd situations where the briber is able to persuade the court that the payment of the commission was simply in line with custom and practice in the particular jurisdiction in which the payment was made.

17.58 Assuming liability can be established, the briber will be personally liable to account for any loss caused to the principal by the breach of fiduciary duty.[50] It is to be noted that the briber's liability will be loss flowing from the breach of fiduciary duty and not from his assistance.[51]

17.59 It remains somewhat unclear whether a briber could be made liable to account for the profits obtained by him in giving the assistance. The issue arose for determination in *Fyffes v Templeman*.[52] The facts were that Mr Templeman acted as Fyffes' agent and he received a secret commission from Seatrade, in return for assisting Seatrade to win a service agreement from Fyffes where Toulson J said that there was no direct English authority on the point, that the textbooks were generally against it, and that whilst *Lister & Co v Stubbs* was generally considered good law, there could be no such remedy against the briber.[53]

17.60 Toulson J recognized that just because such a remedy was available against the bribed agent did not necessarily imply it would be a good thing it should be available also against the bribing party. One of the reasons is that there were good policy grounds based in deterrence for ensuring that fiduciaries were not allowed to retain any profits obtained by their wrongdoing. The question was whether the same sort of policy arguments extended to the briber.

17.61 In *Consul Development Pty Ltd v DPC Estates Pty Ltd*,[54] Gibbs J said:

> The strict rule of equity that forbids a person in a fiduciary position to profit from his position appears to be designed to deter persons holding such a position from being

---

48 Chapter 16, para 16.68 *et seq.*
49 Particularly if one thinks of the guidance provided by Knox J in *Cowan de Groot Properties v Eagle Trust* [1992] 4 All ER 700, and approved of by Lord Nicholls in *Royal Brunei v Tan*, namely 'commercially unacceptable conduct'. It is of course accepted that there is no need to establish motive or intention to influence in order to succeed in a claim for a bribe but it is submitted that the act of paying over in secret monies to an agent will be considered by most people as 'dodgy' conduct.
50 *Twinsectra Ltd v Yardley* [2002] UKHL 12, [2002] 2 AC 164.
51 See para 16.68 *et seq.*
52 [2000] 2 Lloyd's Rep 643 (Toulson J).
53 ibid, 668, col 2.
54 [1975] 132 CLR 373.

swayed by interest rather than by duty (see *Bray v Ford* [1896] AC 44, 51); it is 'A rule to protect directors, trustees, and others against the fallibility of human nature' *Costa Rica Railway Co Ltd v Forwood* [1901] 1 Ch 746, 761. If the maintenance of a very high standard of conduct on the part of fiduciaries is the purpose of the rule it would seem equally necessary to deter other persons from knowingly assisting those in a fiduciary position to violate their duties. If, on the other hand, the rule is to be explained simply because it would be contrary to equitable principles to allow a person to retain a benefit that he had gained from a breach of his fiduciary duty, it would appear equally inequitable that one who knowingly took part in the breach should retain a benefit that resulted therefrom. I therefore conclude, on principle, that a person who knowingly participates in a breach of fiduciary duty is liable to account to the person to whom the duty was owed for any benefit he has received as a result of such participation.[55]

Toulson J noted that this principle had been applied by the High Court of Australia in *Warman International Ltd v Dwyer*[56] where the Court awarded an account of profits as against two companies found liable for dishonest assistance. His Lordship also took into account analogous cases in the law of confidentiality where newspapers knowingly assisting individuals to breach their obligations of confidentiality have been made liable to account for their profits: see *Attorney-General v Guardian Newspapers (No 2)*;[57] *Peter Pan Manufacturing Corporation v Corsets Silhouette Ltd.*[58] **17.62**

Toulson J concluded: **17.63**

> I would conclude that there are cogent grounds, in principle and in practical justice, for following the approach of Gibbs J and holding that the briber of an agent may be required to account to the principal for benefits obtained from the corruption of the agent. In *Attorney-General for Hong Kong v Reid* Lord Templeman described bribery (p.330) as 'an evil practice which threatens the foundations of any civilized society.' The law should not assist a party to retain the profits of such a vice.[59]

Having agreed in principle with the availability of an account of profits against the briber, Toulson J held there was no basis for such an award on the facts of *Fyffes* and in particular the finding that Fyffes (the principal) would have entered into a service agreement with Seatrade (the briber) even if Mr Templeman (the agent) had not been dishonest. The court found that any ordinary profits obtained from the service agreement by Seatrade were not obtained by the bribery since they would have been obtained even if there was no bribery at all. Insofar as it could be shown that Fyffes had suffered any damage for the amount it had paid under the service agreement, that could be recovered by an award of damages.

---

[55] ibid, 397.
[56] (1995) 128 ALR 201.
[57] [1990] 1 AC 109.
[58] [1969] 1 WLR 96.
[59] [2000] 2 Lloyd's Rep 643, 672.

17.64 In principle, it is difficult to see why such an award of an account of profits cannot be made. It will, no doubt, not be the normal measure of recovery, but it should be available in the court's amoury to ensure that where a wrongdoer has profited by his activities, there is a means of depriving him of that profit.[60]

D. Claims against Bribed Agent

17.65 In addition to any employment contract remedies, the principal has the following claims against a bribed agent:

- a claim in damages for fraud;
- unjust enrichment/breach of fiduciary duty, for the bribe;
- constructive trust over the bribe monies.

(1) Damages for fraud

17.66 Whether or not the tort fits the traditional category of deceit or is to be treated as some form of 'hybrid legal wrong' or *sui generis* tort, it is clear that a principal has a claim in tort for the damages caused to the principal as a result of the payment of the bribe.[61]

17.67 It is presumed that the bribe has caused the principal loss at least in the amount of the bribe paid over or alternatively promised to be paid to the agent. If the principal wishes to claim any additional sums by way of damages, it is necessary to prove such additional losses in the usual manner.[62]

(2) Recovery of the bribe—a claim in unjust enrichment or restitution for wrongs?

17.68 Whilst the conceptual difficulties which arise in respect of a claim in unjust enrichment by the principal against the briber do not arise in respect of any such claim against the briber, nevertheless the claim in unjust enrichment against the bribed agent is not itself free from all conceptual difficulties.

---

[60] See G Virgo, *The Principles of the Law of Restitution* (2nd edn, Oxford University Press, 2006), 535–6; Elliott and Mitchell, 'Remedies for Dishonest Assistance' (2004) 67 MLR 16.

[61] *Mahesan v Malaysia Housing Society Ltd* [1979] AC 374; *Goff & Jones*, para 33-024. *Bowstead & Reynolds*, Article 96(2) provides: '(2) Where an agent is induced by bribery to depart from his duty to his principal, the third party who bribed or promised the bribe to the agent is liable at common law jointly and severally with the agent to the principal (a) in restitution, for the bribe; or (b) in tort, for any loss sustained by the principal from entering into the transaction in respect of which the bribe was given.'

[62] *Hovenden & Sons v Millhoff* (1900) 83 LT 41; *Industries & General Manager Co v Lewis* [1949] 2 All ER 573; *Grant v Gold Exploration and Development Syndicate Ltd* [1900] 1 QB 233.

There is no doubt that the authorities establish that the principal is entitled to **17.69** claim, from the bribed agent the amount of the bribe payment.[63] The issue is whether it is correct to treat such recovery as an instance of a claim in unjust enrichment or whether, in fact, it represents an instance of restitution for wrongdoing based upon the agent's breach of fiduciary duty. The difficulty any analysis of this sort of issue faces is the fact that the older cases are not as clear in distinguishing unjust enrichment by way of subtraction from restitution for wrongdoing.

(a) Argument in favour of unjust enrichment

The starting point is that whilst the agent has been enriched, can it be said to be **17.70** by way of subtraction from the principal? The principal was not entitled to the bribe monies and would not have received them had they not been paid to the bribed agent. Certainly, the agent was under a duty to account for such sums to the principal but is that enough to establish the agent's receipt of those funds amounts to enrichment by subtraction?

One possible way of viewing the situation is to recognize that the bribe is treated **17.71** as part of the purchase price. On that basis, the bribe does constitute monies which should have been paid to the principal and to which the principal has an entitlement. That is one way of explaining the 'at the expense of' requirement for unjust enrichment claims. That money went to the agent and not the principal and so the agent is clearly enriched.

But there is also the need to identify the relevant unjust factor at play in such **17.72** claims. The most obvious candidate is ignorance.[64] Part of the purchase price (represented by the bribe) has been diverted away from the principal without the principal being aware this was being done.

It is accepted that some will dislike the *deeming* aspect of the explanation in favour **17.73** of 'at the expense of' and others will not accept ignorance as an unjust factor, but the above represents an entirely reasonable explanation of the claim against the bribed agent arising in unjust enrichment.

A claim to recover the value of the bribe in unjust enrichment is a personal claim. **17.74** In the event that the agent is insolvent, the principal will need to take *pari passu* with the agent's other creditors unless he brings a proprietary claim (see below).

---

[63] *Reading v A-G* [1951] AC 507; *Bowstead & Reynolds*, Article 96(2).
[64] It is noted that ignorance is not universally accepted as part of the list of unjust factors. However, the reasoning put forward by Professor Birks and others for its inclusion is compelling and persuasive. It appears to be no more than a logical extension to the principles underlying the acceptance of mistake as an unjust factor.

(b) Argument in favour of restitution for wrongdoing[65]

17.75   The argument in favour of restitution for wrongdoing proceeds as follows.

- The agent is in a fiduciary relationship with the principal and owes the principal duties typically associated with such a relationship.

- That relationship is one of trust and confidence giving rise to a main duty of ultimate loyalty to the principal from which flows more specific duties such as not to place oneself in a position of conflict of interest or potential conflict of interest, not receiving and retaining secret profits, and no self-dealing.

- The receipt by the agent of a bribe represents a clear breach of his fiduciary duties. He has thereby placed himself in a position of conflict of interest, obtained a secret profit and there is a real risk he will no longer provide disinterested advice to the principal.

- This gives rise to various potential claims including an account of profits. This is a personal remedy which certainly includes the value of the bribe and may, per Burrows,[66] include any profits obtained by having received the bribe, e.g. the land purchased with the bribe in *A-G for Hong Kong v Reid*.[67] There is no need to turn such a claim into a proprietary one: the breaching fiduciary simply has to pay the value of the land and not transfer the land itself. This gives the principal no priority in any insolvency.[68]

(3) Constructive trust

17.76   There is no doubt that this section is the most controversial aspect of any claim relating to a bribed agent. The short answer for the practitioner is that although the Court of Appeal in *Lister & Co v Stubbs*[69] had held that the agent was only under a personal liability to account for the bribe monies, the subsequent Privy Council decision in *Att-Gen of Hong Kong v Reid*[70] held that the bribe monies were in fact held on constructive trust for the principal, thus providing the principal with the benefit of a proprietary claim. In so doing, the Court of Appeal were, correctly, aligning the position of a defaulting agent with that of any other fiduciary who receives a secret profit.

17.77   The starting point for our discussion is the decision in *Lister & Co v Stubbs*.[71] The Court of Appeal in this case was concerned with a claim for injunctive relief to

---

65   See generally, Virgo, *The Principles of the Law of Restitution* (2nd edn), ch 18.
66   Burrows, *The Law of Restitution* (2nd edn, Butterworths, 2002), 500–1.
67   [1994] 1 AC 324, 330 (Lord Templeman).
68   This is effectively the position as existed under *Lister and Co v Stubbs* (1890) 45 Ch D 1.
69   ibid.
70   [1994] 1 AC 324.
71   (1890) 45 Ch D 1.

prevent an agent from dealing with certain investments into which secret commissions had been paid. The Court of Appeal refused to grant the relief on the grounds that the agent was only under a personal liability to account to the principal. On this basis, the agent owed only a personal obligation to the principal to repay the money. As Lindley LJ remarked: 'ownership should not be confused with obligation'.[72]

The principal itself did not have any proprietary interest in the bribe monies and therefore had no basis to claim injunctive relief over the investments into which such monies had been paid. **17.78**

It was unfortunate that the Court of Appeal in *Lister v Stubbs* did not have the benefit of submissions based on some earlier Court of Appeal authorities, such as *In re Morvah Consols Tin Mining Co (McKay's Case)*[73] or *In re Caerphilly Colliery Co (Pearson's Case)*[74] which clearly held in favour of the existence of a proprietary claim in respect of the receipt of a bribe. **17.79**

It is fair to say that *Lister & Co v Stubbs* was the subject of much criticism.[75] Much of this centred on the fact that it appeared to run counter to the usual equitable treatment of fiduciaries who make a secret profit and are found to hold that secret profit on trust for the beneficiary. **17.80**

If a director such as in *Phipps v Boardman*,[76] who honestly believes that his company is not able to take advantage of a corporate opportunity, diverts that opportunity to himself and is found to hold any profits obtained thereby on trust for the beneficiary, on the ground that a fiduciary cannot be permitted to make a secret profit, then it is illogical that an agent who knowingly receives a bribe is only subject to a personal liability to account. **17.81**

The reasoning of *Lister v Stubbs* was clearly at odds with the clear and more recent views expressed by the House of Lords in *Phipps v Boardman* where their Lordships had adopted a particularly strict attitude towards the principle preventing fiduciaries obtaining secret profits. Against such reasoning, the treatment of the bribed agent in *Lister v Stubbs* appeared an unjustifiable anomaly. **17.82**

---

72 ibid, 15.

73 (1875) 2 Ch D 1 (CA).

74 (1877) 5 Ch D 336 (Jessel MR). As Lord Templeman in *Att-Gen of Hong Kong v Reid* remarked: 'This is an emphatic pronouncement by the most distinguished equity judge of his generation that the recipient of a bribe holds the bribe and the property representing the bribe in trust for the injured person' [1994] 1 AC 324, 334F.

75 Sir Peter Millett, 'The Error in *Lister v Stubbs*' in P Birks (ed), *The Frontiers of Liability*, vol 1 (Oxford University Press, 1994), 56; Sir Peter Millett, 'Bribes and Secret Commissions' [1993] RLR 7; Meagher, Gummow and Lehane, *Equity Doctrines and Remedies* (4th edn, Butterworths, 2002), [5-220]; Sir Anthony Mason, *Essays in Equity* (LBC, 1985), 246; Needham (1979) 95 LQR 536; Braithwaite [1980] Conv 200.

76 [1967] 2 AC 46.

17.83   However, not everyone considers *Lister v Stubbs* to be wrongly decided. Some consider that it was correct to take into account the interests of the agent's creditors and deny any proprietary claim for the recovery of the bribe in circumstances where those monies never belonged to the principal. Such a view necessarily required treating the defaulting agent differently from the defaulting fiduciary and the present writer for one cannot see any justification for such an approach.

17.84   Amongst those who support the decision is Professor Goode[77] who defended the decision on the following lines:

> . . . despite the criticism to which it has been subjected the decision of the Court of Appeal in *Lister v Stubbs* refusing to recognize P's proprietary right to a bribe received by D, and restricting P to the amount of the bribe itself, is clearly correct, for the bribe was not a form of benefit which it was D's duty to obtain for P; it resulted from conduct in which D ought not to have engaged at all. The distinction is between a benefit which P would never have obtained if D had fulfilled his duty and a benefit which would never have been conferred at all if D had observed that duty. Hence P was properly restricted to a personal order for payment, and to a sum limited to the bribe and not extended in a property-like fashion to assets acquired with the bribe moneys.

17.85   Similarly, Professor Birks has defended *Lister & Stubbs* on the ground that there was no pre-existing proprietary base justifying the grant of a proprietary claim.[78] On this analysis, if the claimant did not have an initial proprietary interest in the subject matter of the claim, the court should not grant him one and thereby ride roughshod over the agent's creditors.

17.86   They were the battle lines when the matter came before the Privy Council in *Att-Gen of Hong Kong v Reid*.[79] Lord Templeman, delivering the Opinion of the Privy Council, held that *Lister v Stubbs* had been wrongly decided and indeed had been decided against the weight of earlier authorities.

17.87   Lord Templeman's reasoning merits being set out in full:

> When a bribe is offered and accepted in money or in kind, the money or property constituting the bribe belongs in law to the recipient. Money paid to the false fiduciary

---

[77] Goode, 'Ownership and Obligation in Commercial Transactions' (1987) 103 LQR 433, 441–5; Goode, 'Property and Unjust Enrichment' in Burrows (ed), *Essays on the Law of Restitution* (Clarendon Press, 1991), 215, 231, 237–44 where Professor Goode points out that the reasoning of *Lister & Co v Stubbs* had been applied in *Attorney-General's Reference (No 1 of 1985)* [1986] QB 491; *Daly v Sydney Stock Exchange Ltd* (1986) 160 CLR 371; *Islamic Republic of Iran Shipping Inc v Denby* [1987] 1 Lloyd's Rep 367; see also Goode, 'Proprietary Restitutionary Claims' in Cornish et al (eds), *Restitution: Past Present and Future*, 63, 69 and 72.

[78] Birks, *An Introduction to the Law of Restitution* (Clarendon Press, 1985), 388–9. He does, however, appear to recognize the inconsistency between this decision and that in *Boardman v Phipps* [1967] 2 AC 46, where equally there was no obvious pre-existing proprietary base to justify the granting of proprietary relief in that case. Most recently, in *Unjust Enrichment* (2nd edn, Clarendon Press, 2006) at 34, Birks categorizes the decision of *Att-Gen of Hong Kong v Reid* [1994] 1 AC 324 as a rare example of the acquisition of a proprietary claim by a wrong done.

[79] [1994] 1 AC 324.

belongs to him. The legal estate in freehold property conveyed to the false fiduciary by way of bribe vests in him. Equity, however which acts in personam, insists that it is unconscionable for a fiduciary to obtain and retain a benefit in breach of duty. The provider of a bribe cannot recover it because he committed a criminal offence when he paid the bribe. The false fiduciary who received the bribe in breach of duty must pay and account for the bribe to the person to whom that duty was owed. In the present case, as soon as the first respondent received a bribe in breach of the duties he owed to the Government of Hong Kong, he became a debtor in equity to the Crown for the amount of that bribe. So much is admitted. But if the bribe consists of property which increases in value or if a cash bribe is invested advantageously, the false fiduciary will receive a benefit from his breach of duty unless he is accountable not only for the original amount or value of the bribe but also for the increased value of the property representing the bribe. As soon as the bribe was received it should have been paid or transferred instanter to the person who suffered from the breach of duty. Equity considers as done that which ought to have been done. As soon as the bribe was received, whether in cash or in kind, the false fiduciary held the bribe on a constructive trust for the person injured.[80]

Lord Templeman went on to identify two potential objections to this analysis: **17.88**

Two objections have been raised to this analysis. First it is said that if the fiduciary is in equity a debtor to the person injured, he cannot also be a trustee of the bribe. But there is no reason why equity should not provide two remedies, so long as they do not result in double recovery. If the property representing the bribe exceeds the original bribe in value, the fiduciary cannot retain the benefit of the increase in value which he obtained solely as a result of his breach of duty. Secondly, it is said that if the false fiduciary holds property representing the bribe in trust for the person injured, and if the false fiduciary is or becomes insolvent, the unsecured creditors of the false fiduciary will be deprived of their right to share in the proceeds of that property. But the unsecured creditors cannot be in a better position than their debtor. The authorities show that property acquired by a trustee innocently but in breach of trust and the property from time to time representing the same belong in equity to the cestui que trust and not to the trustee personally whether he is solvent or insolvent. Property acquired by a trustee as a result of a criminal breach of trust and the property from time to time representing the same must also belong in equity to his cestui que trust and not to the trustee whether he is solvent or insolvent.[81]

Having dealt with these two potential objections, Lord Templeman was able to   **17.89** reach his conclusions:

When a bribe is accepted by a fiduciary in breach of his duty then he holds that bribe in trust for the person to whom the duty was owed. If the property representing the bribe decreases in value the fiduciary must pay the difference between that value and the initial amount of the bribe because he should not have accepted the bribe or incurred the risk of loss. If the property increases in value, the fiduciary is not entitled

---

[80] ibid, 331B–E.
[81] ibid, 331E–H.

to any surplus in excess of the initial value of the bribe because he is not allowed by any means to make a profit out of a breach of duty.[82]

17.90   If a criticism is to be made of Lord Templeman's reasoning it may lie in his reliance upon the maxim that equity treats that as done which ought to be done to treat the personal obligation to transfer the bribe to the principal as having been deemed to have occurred, thus treating the principal as owner of the bribe paid over. That is not the most persuasive of reasons for his decision.[83] As set out above, all that is required is to recognize the fiduciary status of the agent, and ensure that the defaulting agent, who has placed himself in a position of conflict of interest, is treated in exactly the same manner as would any defaulting fiduciary. In this regard, it matters not that the bribe was never intended as a payment to the principal to justify the imposition of a constructive trust.[84] The position can be readily equated with those situations which arise all the time with directors diverting corporate opportunities from one company to another, in circumstances where the first company could never and perhaps would never have taken up the corporate opportunity had it been offered.

17.91   For the reasons expressed above, the Privy Council's decision is to be welcomed as restoring a consistency in the court's approach to the receipt of bribes and secret commissions by defaulting fiduciaries. Whatever the merit of insisting that defaulting fiduciaries hold the secret profits on trust for the beneficiaries, there can be no merit at all in seeking to draw artificial distinctions between bribes and secret commissions especially where the stronger (proprietary) relief is to be available in the latter but not in the former scenario.

17.92   The obvious difficulty for the practitioner is that *Att-Gen of Hong Kong v Reid* is a decision of the Privy Council and strictly, according to the rules on precedent, that will not undermine the binding nature of the Court of Appeal's decision in *Lister v Stubbs*.[85] There have already been two Court of Appeal decisions, post-*Reid*, which have maintained that *Lister v Stubbs* remains a binding authority.[86]

---

[82] ibid, 331H–332A.

[83] For criticism see Virgo, *The Principles of the Law of Restitution* (2nd edn), 523–4; Crilley, 'A Case of Proprietary Overkill' [1994] RLR 57, 65–6.

[84] Lord Millett (extra-judicially) has suggested that the bribe payment be *deemed* to be a payment for the principal to justify the imposition of a constructive trust: [1993] RLR 7. For the reasons set out above, it is suggested this is unnecessary. See also *Goff & Jones*, para 33-025 and n 83.

[85] This situation is not unique. See the Privy Council's decision in *Barlow Clowes International Ltd (In Liquidation) v Eurotrust International Ltd* [2006] 1 WLR 1476 re-asserting Lord Nicholl's objective approach to the issue of dishonesty in *Royal Brunei v Tan* contrary to the attempt by the House of Lords in *Twinsectra v Yardley* [2002] 2 AC 164 to impose a re-interpretation of Lord Nicholls based upon a combination of subjective and objective factors. See also the attitude of the Court of Appeal in *Abou-Ramah v Abacha* [2006] EWCA Civ 1492, [2006] 1 All ER (Comm) 247.

[86] *Attorney-General v Blake* [1997] Ch 84, 96 (Sir Richard Scott V-C); *Halifax Building Society v Thomas* [1996] Ch 217, 229. Neither case involved a bribe payment to an agent.

It is evident, however, that the English courts have so far shown a willingness **17.93**
to embrace the reasoning of Lord Templeman in place of that of the Court of
Appeal in *Lister v Stubbs*. In *Daraydan Holdings Ltd v Solland International Ltd*[87]
Lawrence Collins J remarked that it would be an 'unfavourable' day for the precedent system if it was necessary for a litigant to have to take an appeal all the way to the
House of Lords simply to confirm the Privy Council decision, especially where that
Privy Council decision 'is recent, where it was a decision on the English common law,
where the Board consisted mainly of serving Law Lords,[88] and where the decision had
been made after full argument on the correctness of the earlier decision'.[89]

In the end, however, Lawrence Collins J was able to distinguish *Lister v Stubbs* on **17.94**
two grounds. The facts can be summarized as follows:

- The claimants consisted of a high-ranking Qatar government official and various corporate vehicles through which the official held properties in England.
- The claimants contended that a former employee, the fifth defendant, received
  10% commission payments amounting to £1.8m when arranging refurbish-
  ment of the claimant's properties by the first to fourth defendants.
- It was alleged that the commission payments were bribes and were held on trust
  for the claimants.

Lawrence Collins J held that in receiving the 10% commission payments, the fifth **17.95**
defendant was thereby in breach of his fiduciary duty owed to the claimants. The
10% commission was held on trust for the claimants. He distinguished *Lister v
Stubbs* on the following grounds.

First, the evidence in *Daraydan* shows that the purchase price was in fact inflated **17.96**
by the amount of the bribe and 'where the bribe was paid out of the money paid
by the claimants for what they thought was the price. These factors make the
claim one for the restitution of money extracted from the claimants'.[90] On this
basis, the commission represents part of the purchase price and not simply deemed
to be part of it.

Secondly, Lawrence Collins J relied on the fact that the portion of the purchase **17.97**
price which represented the bribe monies had been paid as a result of a fraudulent misrepresentation to which both the briber and bribee was each a party.[91]

---

[87] [2004] EWHC 622 (Ch), [2005] Ch 119.
[88] The Board in *Att-Gen of Hong Kong v Reid* consisted of Lord Templeman, Lord Goff, Lord
Lowry, Lord Lloyd and Sir Thomas Eichelbaum.
[89] [2005] Ch 119, 139, para 85.
[90] ibid, 140, para 87.
[91] ibid, para 88.

Those monies were received by Mr Khalid, the fiduciary agent and therefore held on trust for the principal.[92]

17.98 Further support for *Att-Gen of Hong Kong v Reid* at first instance court level has come from Laddie J in *Ocular Sciences Ltd v Aspect Vision Care Ltd*[93] and (obiter) from Toulson J in *Fyffes Group Ltd v Templeman*.[94]

17.99 *Reid* has also been briefly cited and referred to in the Court of Appeal decision in *Tribe v Tribe*[95] without any disapproval.

17.100 It is therefore more likely than not that the English courts will follow the approach advocated by the Privy Council in *Att-Gen of Hong Kong v Reid* in future cases concerning the availability of proprietary relief for bribes.

E. Election

17.101 Given the myriad of potential claims available to a principal whose agent has been bribed, the courts must be astute to avoid problems of double-recovery as well as ensuring that the principal does not enter judgment on alternative and inconsistent remedies.

17.102 It is now clear that the principal can pursue the alternative causes of action (e.g. restitution or damages for fraud) but must elect between the causes of action. The final time for making such an election is immediately prior to entering judgment.[96]

---

[92] In reaching this conclusion, Lawrence Collins J distinguished the Court of Appeal decision in *Halifax Building Society v Thomas* [1996] Ch 217 on the grounds that the fraudster in that case was not considered to be a fiduciary: (para 88) and the building society had affirmed the mortgage and so was only a secured creditor.

[93] [1997] RPC 289, 412–13. This is a breach of confidence case.

[94] [2000] 2 Lloyd's Rep 643.

[95] *Tribe v Tribe* [1996] 1 Ch 107, 133 (Millett LJ).

[96] *Mahesan v Malaysia Government Officers' Co-Operative Housing Society Ltd* [1979] AC 374 applying *United Australia Ltd v Barclays Bank Ltd* [1941] AC 1; *Chitty on Contracts,* vol 2, para 31-071.

PART VII

CONFLICT OF LAWS

18

THE CONFLICT OF LAWS—OVERVIEW

A. Introduction

The conflict of laws can be a complex and bewildering area of law.[1] It is also a very **18.01** important area of law for any commercial litigator. It is, therefore, all the more unfortunate that it is rarely studied in depth at undergraduate level, where students focus on categories of substantive law such as contract and tort but do not often get exposed to the problems of which forum has jurisdiction to hear a case or what law should apply. The result is, that for some, their first contact with the topic will come during their practice when faced with a real case. The learning curve then is necessarily steep and error-prone.

---

[1] Judge Cardozo once remarked: 'The average judge, when confronted by a problem in the conflict of laws, feels almost completely lost, and, like a drowning man, will grasp at a straw.' Cited in Cook, *Logical and Legal Bases of the Conflict of Laws* (1942). Fortunately, the judges of the High Court have a better understanding of the topic.

B. What is the Conflict of Laws?

18.02   The conflict of laws is that system of rules devised by all legal systems to deal with cases involving some foreign element. If the facts of the case concern only English parties, carrying out activities in England and there is no connection at all with any other legal system, then the claim does not give rise to any issue of the conflict of laws. It will be dealt with by English domestic law. But if the facts are tweaked slightly so that the defendant has a French and not an English domicile, or the activities leading to the personal injury took place in Spain, then English law must have a system of rules in place to determine whether such contact with a foreign system of law should be taken into account in resolving the dispute. Should the claim be sent off to France or Spain? Should it remain in England but be dealt with in accordance with French or Spanish law? These are the issues dealt with by the conflict of laws.

18.03   Principally, the conflict of laws is concerned with answering two main issues:

- the jurisdiction issue—where can or should the case be brought?
- the choice of law issue—what law in fact governs the substantive issues?

18.04   As Lord Nicholls of Birkenhead remarked in *Kuwait Airways Corpn v Iraqi Airways Co (Nos 4 and 5)*:[2]

> Conflict of laws jurisprudence is concerned essentially with the just disposal of proceedings having a foreign element. The jurisprudence is founded on the recognition that in proceedings having connections with more than one country an issue brought before a court in one country may be more appropriately decided by reference to the laws of another country even though those laws are different from the law of the forum court.

18.05   The decision *where* to litigate does not in itself resolve the issue of *what law* is to govern the resolution of the substantive issues. The Commercial Court in London is full of examples of claims brought within this jurisdiction but governed by a foreign law.

18.06   Even if the conclusion is reached, applying the English conflict of laws rules identified below, that it is appropriate to apply a foreign legal system to a particular dispute, it will still be necessary to decide what issues in the dispute are to be governed by the foreign legal system and what remain to be determined by English law as the *lex fori*. The short answer is: matters of substance are governed by the *lex causae* (even if foreign) and matters of procedure are governed by the *lex fori* or English law.

---

[2] [2002] UKHL 19; [2002] 2 AC 883 at [15].

So, whatever law is said to apply to the substantive issues, the usual Civil Procedure **18.07**
Rules (CPR) apply to determine the appropriate procedure to resolve that dispute. So much is clear. Difficulties start to emerge when it is appreciated that some
but not all aspects of the law of evidence are considered to be procedural in nature
(and therefore governed by the *lex fori*).[3] Other examples of difficulty include
whether an estoppel is considered procedural or substantive and therefore governed by the *lex fori* or the *lex causae* respectively. This is entirely dependent on the
precise nature of the estoppel.[4] The detail of these matters are for the specialist
texts on the conflict of laws but it is important that those commercial fraud litigators faced with dealing with an issue in the conflict of laws for the first time at least
know a potential difficulty exists.

Determining the distinction between substance and procedure is just one way the **18.08**
conflict of laws seeks to identify the appropriate law to apply to a particular dispute. Other techniques include characterization, the incidental question, renvoi
and the time factor.

Putting aside characterization (since this is focused on below), a very brief over- **18.09**
view of each of these techniques is as follows:

- *The incidental question.* The problem stated: assuming English conflict of laws
  rules identify a foreign law as applicable to a dispute and assuming that during
  the course of dealing with that dispute a further discrete issue arises which, if
  English conflict of laws rules were applied, would be decided by a different foreign law, should English conflict of laws rules be applied to that discrete question or should it be the conflict of laws rules of the foreign law already identified
  as relevant to the main issue?

---

[3] In *Bain v Whitehaven and Furness Junction Ry* (1850) 3 HLC 1, 19: 'The law of evidence is the
lex fori which governs the courts. Whether a witness is competent or not; whether a certain matter
requires to be proved by writing or not; whether certain evidence proves a certain fact or not; that
is to be determined by the law of the country where the question arises, where the remedy is sought
to be enforced and where the court sits to enforce it.' But the *lex causae* generally determines what
facts are in issue and may stipulate how they are to be proved, although this is typically a matter for
the *lex fori*: see *Dicey, Morris & Collins* (14th edn), para 7-015 and see the more specific examples
set out at paras 7-017–7-030 dealing with difficult issues such as admissibility, burden of proof and
presumptions.

[4] T M Yeo, *Choice of Law for Equitable Doctrines* (Oxford University Press, 2004), para 4.104:
'In domestic law, estoppels may be procedural or substantive depending on the context. Its choice
of law characterization also depends on the context in which it arises. Estoppel by record raises an
issue of procedure or public policy. . . . The following types of estoppels have been assumed (correctly, it is suggested) to be substantive for choice of law purposes: estoppel by convention [*The
Amazonia* [1990] 1 Lloyd's Rep 236 (CA), 247]; estoppels on the issue of title [*Colonial Bank v Cady
& Williams* (1890) 15 App Cas 267]; and estoppels in the context of ostensible authority of an agent
to bind a principal [*Presentaciones Musicales SA v Secunda* [1994] Ch 271 (CA) 283]. Estoppel arising in the context of a claim in contract is arguably substantive [*Libyan Arab Foreign Bank v Bankers
Trust Co* [1989] QB 728, 773]. Waiver operates like an estoppel, and may be substantive for the
same reasons.'

It is generally accepted that three conditions must be satisfied in order for a true incidental question to arise.[5] First, English conflict of laws must identify a foreign law as applicable to govern the main issue. Secondly, the main issue must give rise to a subsidiary issue, which is capable of arising in its own right, and it has its own conflict of laws rule. Thirdly, the English conflicts rule must point to a different foreign law to govern the subsidiary issue than the conflict of laws rules of the foreign legal system which governs the main issue.

Whilst the weight of authorities (such as they are, including Commonwealth) appears to favour the application of the conflict of laws rules of the foreign legal system identified to govern the main issue, academics remain divided.[6]

The most recent approach to find favour with *Dicey, Morris & Collins* is to forgo intellectual attempts at identifying one single principled approach which will answer all scenarios, in return for closely examining each situation as it arises, determining the answer that 'provides the best results in that situation . . . Instead of trying to solve the problem on the basis of general theory, one should consider the practical consequences in each situation.'[7] *Dicey, Morris & Collins* applies such an approach to three distinct areas, none of which relate to commercial fraud. It remains to be seen whether the pragmatic approach advocated by *Dicey, Morris & Collins* will be adopted by the courts, notwithstanding that the absence of a general theory or principle may hamper clear guidance being given to litigators.

- *Renvoi*. In its simplest form, renvoi involves the situation where English conflict of laws rules point to a foreign law to apply to a particular issue and that foreign law has its own conflict of laws rules for such an issue which, if applied, would point to another foreign law or indeed back to English law. The issue therefore is when the English conflict of laws rules point to a foreign law, does that mean its domestic law only or does it include its conflict of laws rules as well?

This is another topic that has generated immense academic discussion. Fortunately, for present purposes, renvoi has no role to play in contractual[8] or tortious[9] disputes,

---

[5] *Dicey, Morris & Collins* (14th edn), para 2-047; McLean and Beevers, *Morris, The Conflict of Laws* (6th edn, Thomson/Sweet and Maxwell, 2005), paras 20-011–20-015.

[6] ibid, para 20-014.

[7] *Dicey, Morris & Collins* (14th edn), para 2-049.

[8] Rome Convention, Art 15, incorporated into English law by the Contracts (Applicable Laws) Act 1990, provides: 'The application of the law of any country specified by this Convention means the application of the rules of law in force in that country other than its rules of private international law.' For contractual matters outside the Rome Convention, the common law position also excluded reference to renvoi: see *Amin Rasheed Shipping Corp v Kuwait Insurance Co* [1984] AC 50, 61–2; *Re United Railways of Havana and Regla Warehouses Ltd* [1960] Ch 52, 96–7, 115.

[9] Private International Law (Miscellaneous Provisions) Act 1995, s 9(5). In respect of matters falling outside of the Act, there is no direct English authority.

which will form a major part of the likely claims arising in a commercial fraud scenario.

There are two areas in which there is a strong argument that renvoi will apply and which are likely to be of interest to commercial fraud litigators: title to land situated abroad and title to movables situated abroad. Such questions may well arise as a consequence of the use of the proceeds of fraud to purchase property abroad.

As regards title to land situated abroad, the English court typically would have no jurisdiction to deal with such a claim.[10] One exception to this rule, which is important to commercial fraud litigators, is where the claim is based on a contract or equity between the parties.[11] Assuming the English court has jurisdiction to hear the case whether an individual has acquired a proprietary interest in land situated abroad, it will apply the *lex situs* principally because there would be little point in deciding the case differently to the local law since any such decision would need to be enforced locally. That, in turn, means there is no point deciding the issue other than as the local court would do and that includes availing oneself of renvoi as well.[12]

The same principle applies to the situation where the claim relates to the title to movables situated abroad although it is weakened by the obvious transient nature of the connection between the tangible movable and the situs as compared to land and the situs.[13]

To sum up renvoi in the modern-day conflict of laws, one could do worse than quote from Millett J in *Macmillan Inc v Bishopsgate Investment Trust plc* who stated:

> It is probably right to describe it as largely discredited. It owes its origin to a laudable endeavour to ensure that like cases should be decided alike wherever they are decided, but it should now be recognized that this cannot be achieved by judicial mental gymnastics but only international conventions.[14]

That said, it is only likely to have minimal impact on the work of commercial fraud litigators being limited to questions arising about title to land or movables situated abroad.

- *The time factor.*[15] For our purposes, this can be taken shortly. The main issue is how the courts are to react to changes in the *lex causae* over time. If English

---

[10] *Dicey, Morris & Collins* (14th edn), Rule 122.

[11] *R Griggs Group Ltd v Evans* [2004] EWHC 1088 (Ch), [2005] Ch 153.

[12] *Dicey, Morris & Collins* (14th edn), para 4-024.

[13] *Winkworth v Christie, Manson & Woods Ltd* [1980] Ch 496, 514; *Dicey, Morris & Collins* (14th edn), para 4-025.

[14] Noted by MooreBick J in *Glencore International AG v Metro Trading International Inc* [2001] 1 Lloyd's Rep 284 but who proceeded to apply the doctrine in any event.

[15] Discussed in detail in *Dicey, Morris & Collins* (14th edn), ch 3.

conflict of laws rules point to a foreign law as the *lex causae*, does that mean the *lex causae* as frozen at the time the contract was concluded or the *lex causae* as has been amended subsequently?

Subject to one dissenting authority,[16] the general consensus appears to be that the *lex causae* should be applied in its entirety, including its transitional rules.[17]

C. Understanding Characterization

18.10   It has been shown that the conflict of laws rules aim to answer two main questions: where should the dispute be heard and what law should govern the determination of the substantive issues in dispute?

18.11   It has further been shown that various techniques are employed to identify precisely what aspect of the foreign law is applied to what issue or issues arise. For the purposes of commercial fraud litigation, one of the most important of those techniques is the process of characterization. It particularly features when trying to pigeon-hole equitable and restitutionary claims into the overall scheme of English conflict of laws. This is not surprising. Some such claims have only recently been fully recognized by English domestic law, whilst others have been the subject of tremendous academic and court scrutiny in the last decade or so, resulting in a better understanding of their nature but one which has yet to be worked out in terms of applicable rules of the conflict of laws. It would not be inappropriate to say that English conflict of laws rules have yet to be fully developed for some equitable and restitutionary claims.[18]

18.12   The problem of characterization has been accurately described as follows:

> The conflict of laws exists because there are different systems of domestic law. But systems of the conflict of laws also differ. Yet all systems have at least one thing in common. They are expressed in terms of juridical concepts or categories, and localizing elements or connecting factors . . . In the majority of cases it is obvious that the facts must be subsumed under a particular legal category, that a particular conflict rule is available, and the connecting factor indicated by that conflict rule is unambiguous. But sometimes it is not obvious. Even if the forum and the foreign country have the same conflict rule and interpret the connecting factor in the same way, they may still reach different results because they characterize the question in different

---

[16]   *Lynch v Provisional Government of Paraguay* (1871) LR 2 P & D 268.

[17]   *Dicey, Morris & Collins* (14th edn), para 3-012.

[18]   A Briggs, 'Restitution Meets the Conflict of Laws' [1995] RLR 94, 97, commenting on Millett J's judgment in *Macmillan Inc v Bishopsgate Investment Trust (No 3)* [1995] 1 WLR 978: 'It is a commonplace that conceptual divisions in domestic law do not necessarily translate into the conflict of laws . . . To take a distinction which is struggling to define itself within the domestic law of restitution and then project this into the realm of choice of law may be unwise'; see also Auld LJ in *Macmillan v Bishopsgate Investment Trust (No 3)* [1996] 1 WLR 387, 407 (CA).

ways. For instance, the forum may regard the question as one of succession, while the foreign law may regard the same question as one of matrimonial property. This is the problem of characterization.[19]

As with the other techniques, the process of characterization has managed to cre-   **18.13**
ate voluminous literature from leading academics, much of which has failed to have any direct impact on the approach adopted in the courts. In *Dicey, Morris & Collins* (14th edn), the learned editors remark:

> The problem of characterization has given rise to a voluminous literature, much of it highly theoretical. The consequence is that there are almost as many theories as writers and the theories are for the most part so abstract that, when applied to a given case, they can produce almost any result. They appear to have had almost no influence on the practice of the courts in England.

As evident in their approach to the issue of incidental question, *Dicey, Morris &*   **18.14**
Collins clearly prefer 'commonsense solutions based on practical considerations'[20]
rather than abstract theories. Their suggested approach to this issue is:

> The way the court should proceed is to consider the rationale of the English conflict rule and the purpose of the rule of substantive law to be characterized. On this basis, it can decide whether the conflict rule should be regarded as covering the rule of substantive law. In some cases, the court might conclude that the rule of substantive law should not be regarded as falling within either of the two potentially applicable conflict rules. In this situation, a new conflict rule should be created.[21]

A good illustration of the process of characterization in action is the decision of   **18.15**
the Court of Appeal in *Macmillan Inc v Bishopsgate Investment Trust plc (No 3)*.[22]
The facts of the case concern the activities that led to the downfall of Robert Maxwell. Maxwell was the owner and controller of Macmillan, a Delaware Corporation, which in turn, held shares in Berlitz International Inc ('Berlitz'), a company incorporated in New York. Upon the instruction of Maxwell, but without Macmillan's knowledge, Macmillan's shares in Berlitz were transferred into the name of Bishopsgate Investment Trust plc ('Bishopsgate') to be held by it as nominee for Macmillan. Thereafter, some of the shares were used, without Macmillan's knowledge, as security to raise loans for other companies within the Maxwell Group. In March 1991, 76m of the shares were deposited with the central depository system of the Depository Trust Co ('DTC') in New York and from that point

---

[19] Morris, *The Conflict of Laws* (6th edn), para 20-003.
[20] *Dicey, Morris & Collins* (14th edn), para 2-045.
[21] ibid, para 2-037. Such an approach appears to have been adopted by the learned editor sitting as High Court Judge in *Konamaneni v Rolls Royce (India) Ltd* [2002] 1 WLR 1269, [45]–[50]. In this case, Lawrence Collins J held that whilst the English court could entertain a derivative action by minority shareholders in respect of a foreign company, on a consideration of the relevant factors, India, being the place of incorporation, was the most appropriate or natural forum in which to determine these issues.
[22] [1996] 1 WLR 387.

on the shares ceased to be registered in the name of Bishopsgate and were registered in the name of Morgan Stanley Trust Co, acting as Maxwell's DTC agent. Macmillan sought to recover the shares.

18.16 Macmillan sought to characterize the relevant issue as essentially being a claim in equity for restitution and on that basis asserted that English law applied as the place where the enrichment took place. The defendants contended (for differing reasons) that New York law applied to the question of who had better title to the shares.

18.17 The Court of Appeal held that characterization required analysing the particular *issue or issues* in dispute and not simply the cause of action relied upon in the pleading. The relevant disputed issue was whether the defendants could take advantage of the defence of bona fide purchaser for value without notice and thus obtain title to the shares. The availability of the defence was the means of determining which party had a better claim to title in the shares. The Court of Appeal held that questions of title to shares should be treated in the same way as title to tangible movables and be governed by the *lex situs*, which was the place where the company was incorporated, unless the shares were negotiable instruments. This, therefore, led to New York law applying.

18.18 In considering the problem of characterization, Auld LJ observed:

> Subject to what I shall say in a moment, characterization or classification is governed by the *lex fori*. But characterization or classification of what? It follows from what I have said that the proper approach is to look beyond the formulation of the claim and to identify according to the *lex fori* the true issue or issues thrown up by the claim and defence. This requires a parallel exercise in classification of the relevant rule of law. However, classification of an issue and rule of law for this purpose, the underlying principle of which is to strive for comity between competing legal systems, should not be constrained by particular notions or distinctions of the domestic law of the *lex fori*, or that of the competing system of law, which may have no counterpart in the other's system Nor should the issue be defined too narrowly so that it attracts a particular domestic rule under the *lex fori* which may not be applicable under the other system . . .[23]

18.19 Staughton LJ laid down a helpful three-stage test for determining whether a foreign law applied to any particular dispute.

- *First, the relevant issue must be characterized.*

Staughton LJ characterized the relevant issue as being concerned with whether the defendants were purchasers for value in good faith without notice, so as to obtain good title to the shares.

---

[23] [1996] 1 WLR 387, 407B–D.

- *Secondly, select the rule of conflict of laws which lays down a connecting factor for the issue in question.*

The judge started from the proposition that the general rule is that rights to property are determined by the *lex situs* of the property. After examining the case law, he concluded that the issue as to title to shares in a company, excluding negotiable instruments, should be decided by the law of the place where the shares are situated (*lex situs*).

- *Thirdly, the system of law which is tied by the connecting factor found in stage 2 to the issue characterized in stage 1 should be identified.*

On the facts, this was New York law.

This three-stage approach, helpful though it undoubtedly is, should not be rigidly **18.20** applied. As Mance LJ observed in *Raiffeisen Zentralbank v Five Star Trading LLC*:[24]

> **[27].** While it is convenient to identify this three-stage process, it does not follow that courts, at the first stage, can or should ignore the effect at the second stage of characterizing an issue in a particular way. The overall aim is to identify the most *appropriate* law to govern a particular issue. The classes or categories of issue which the law recognizes at the first stage are man-made, not natural. They have no inherent value, beyond their purpose in assisting to select the most appropriate law. A mechanistic application, without regard to the consequences, would conflict with the purpose for which they were conceived. They may require redefinition or modification, or new categories may have to be recognized accompanied by new rules at stage 2, if this is necessary to achieve the overall aim of identifying the most appropriate law. . . .
>
> **[29].** There is in effect an element of interplay or even circularity in the three-stage process identified by Staughton LJ. But the conflict of laws does not depend (like a game or even an election) upon the application of rigid rules, but upon a search for appropriate principles to meet particular situations.

Applying that flexible approach to the facts of the case before it, the Court of **18.21** Appeal in *Raiffeisen Zentralbank v Five Star* held that the relevant issue, being whether the insurer as assignee or the vessel owner as assignor, had to pay the proceeds of the insurance to the bank after the assignment of the benefit of the insurance policy, was a contractual and not a proprietary issue and therefore was governed by Article 12 of the Rome Convention.

Overall, it is evident that the courts are encouraging parties to adopt a flexible **18.22** approach to the issue of characterization and to bear in mind this is not an exact science but is rather a search for appropriate principles to meet particular situations. It will be seen that a fair amount of flexibility may be necessary when it

---

[24] [2001] QB 825, [26]–[29].

comes to characterizing equitable claims for jurisdictional or choice of law purposes.

D. Commercial Fraud and the Conflict of Laws

18.23 Fraud carried out on a commercial scale typically involves an international element. This may be due to the fact that the transaction or purported transaction which is the vehicle for the fraud was itself international in nature (e.g. sale of goods from one country to another). Or it may be due, in no small part, to the fact that fraudsters see the use of more than one jurisdiction as one of the better ways of laundering the proceeds of their fraud and ultimately to defeat or at least render more difficult any attempts by the victim to trace into the proceeds of the fraud and claim them.

18.24 Whatever the reason, commercial fraud litigators must have a sound grasp of the English rules on the conflict of laws. It will be evident from what has been discussed so far in this overview chapter that the conflict of laws raises some complex issues, of which a litigator must be aware if he wishes properly to practise in this area.

18.25 Some of the more important issues having an international element about which a litigator will need to give advice to the client at a very early stage in fraud investigation include:

- Can the fraudster be sued here? Does the client have a choice? If so, where? What factors come into play in making that choice? Are only *some* of the possible claims justiciable in this jurisdiction?

- If a foreign law is more attractive from a remedies point of view, can the claim be brought here under that law? Or can it be brought in that foreign legal system?

- If the claim can be brought in the foreign legal system, is there anything that the English court can do to protect the client's position e.g. s 25 of the Civil Jurisdiction and Judgments Act 1982 relief?

- Where has the money gone? Is it still within the jurisdiction or is it now outside the jurisdiction? Is it possible to obtain interim relief abroad in aid of proceedings in this jurisdiction?

18.26 These questions are clearly not intended to be exhaustive. Each case will turn up its own set of relevant questions but the point is that the client will rightly expect speedy answers to what may appear to be rather daunting issues and the litigator must be on top of these issues. From this, it can readily be seen that the commercial fraud litigator must be armed with a detailed understanding of all aspects of the conflict of laws. Time does not generally permit a familiarization process being undertaken at the same time the client is keen to recover its monies.

E. Overview of Regimes—Jurisdiction

It is not the aim of this book to provide a detailed treatment of the English rules **18.27**
on the conflict of laws. The practitioner is fortunate to have the benefit of several
excellent texts which give such a treatment.[25] The aim of this book is more limited
and more focused on those particular rules which impact on the types of claim
which typically arise in a commercial fraud setting. The overview is provided simply to make that more focused examination more intelligible.

There are several different regimes within the English conflict of laws dealing with **18.28**
the question of the allocation jurisdiction. Putting aside the question of allocation
of jurisdiction within parts of the United Kingdom and focusing just on allocation between England and Wales, on the one part, and another state outside of the
United Kingdom, those regimes are as follows.

(1) The Brussels Convention

In 1968, the original six members of the European Economic Community[26] **18.29**
agreed the terms of the Brussels Convention in order to create the circumstances
to permit the free movement of judgments within the European Community.
Agreement on free movement required a general consensus on the grounds which
justify a forum taking jurisdiction in the first place.

In summary, the Convention provides for a basic principle that jurisdiction is **18.30**
to be based upon the domicile of the defendant subject to specific heads of jurisdiction based upon clear connecting factors arising out of tort, contract and other
particular causes of action. The Convention also provides for exclusive jurisdiction in respect of jurisdiction agreements and certain claims in respect of title
to land.

There have been four Accessions to the 1968 Convention, which have, to varying **18.31**
extents, amended its terms. The details of these Accessions are not for this book:

    (a) The UK, Danish and Irish Accession of 1978.
    (b) The Greek Accession of 1982.

---

[25] The leading text is *Dicey, Morris & Collins on the Conflict of Laws* (14th edn, Thomson/Sweet
and Maxwell, 2006). For jurisdiction and enforcement of judgments, see the excellent Briggs and
Rees, *Civil Jurisdiction and Judgments* (4th edn, LLP, 2005). As an introduction to the topic, see
Briggs, *The Conflict of Laws* (2nd edn, Clarendon Press, 2008). For a detailed treatment of jurisdic-
tion and choice of law agreements, see Briggs, *Agreements on Jurisdiction and Choice of Law* (Oxford
University Press, 2008). For the application of the conflict of laws rules in the context of inter-
national sale of goods, see Fawcett, Harris and Bridge, *International Sale of Goods in the Conflict of
Laws* (Oxford University Press, 2005).

[26] Belgium, (W) Germany, France, Italy, Luxembourg and the Netherlands.

(c) The Spanish and Portuguese Accession of 1989 (the San Sebastian Convention).

(d) The Austrian, Finnish and Swedish Accession of 1996.

18.32 The Brussels Convention was enacted into English law by the Civil Jurisdiction and Judgments Act 1982 (CJJA 1982), which came into force on 1 January 1987.

(2) The Lugano Convention

18.33 The Lugano Convention was agreed between the EFTA states[27] in an effort to assist the process of co-operation as between the EC and EFTA. As far as typical commercial fraud claims are concerned, there is very little difference in how the claims are treated as between the Brussels and Lugano Conventions and so no separate treatment will be accorded the Lugano Convention in this book.

18.34 It suffices to state when the Lugano Convention will apply. It will apply whenever a defendant is domiciled in an EFTA contracting state. Since EC member states are contracting states to both the Brussels and Lugano Conventions, Article 54B of the Lugano Convention provides that the Brussels Convention will apply if the defendant is domiciled in an EC contracting state and the Lugano Convention will apply if the defendant is domiciled in an EFTA contracting state.

18.35 Further, the Lugano Convention will apply if the exclusive articles relating to title to land or exclusive jurisdiction agreements give jurisdiction to an EFTA contracting state. The Lugano Convention will also apply if there is an issue of *lis alibi pendens* as between an EC contracting state and an EFTA contracting state.

18.36 The Lugano Convention was enacted into English law by the CJJA 1991 (amending the CJJA 1982) and came into force on 1 May 1992.

(3) The Judgments Regulation: Council Regulation (EC 44/2001)[28]

18.37 The Judgments Regulation took effect in all member states (excluding Denmark) on 1 March 2002. As from May 2004, the Judgments Regulation has applied to the ten newest member states (Czech Republic, Cyprus, Estonia, Hungary, Latvia, Lithuania, Malta, Poland, Slovakia and Slovenia). In December 2005, Denmark negotiated a separate agreement with the European Community which was ratified in 2007.[29]

18.38 Iceland, Norway and Switzerland remain parties to the Lugano Convention only. However, they have agreed to bring the Lugano Convention into line with the

---

[27] Originally this included Iceland, Norway, Switzerland, Austria, Finland and Sweden. Austria, Finland and Sweden are not members of the EC and so the jurisdictional requirements of these states are determined by reference to the Brussels Convention.

[28] Sometimes also referred to as the 'Brussels I Regulation'.

[29] SI 2007/1655.

Judgments Regulation during 2008. Once that is done, there will be just one text, the Judgments Regulation, which will govern all 27 states.

There have been certain minor amendments and corrections to the Judgments **18.39** Regulation.[30] With the addition of ten new member states to the EU,[31] minor formal amendments were made to the Regulation by way of an Act of Accession.[32]

For our present purposes, all discussion of Articles of a Convention or Regulation **18.40** will relate to the Judgments Regulation is which is now by far the most important to govern questions of jurisdiction and enforcement of judgments.

(4) Common law rules

The traditional rules on jurisdiction have developed through a combination of **18.41** the rules of court (formerly Rules of the Supreme Court (RSC), now known as the Civil Procedure Rules (CPR)), and case law. These rules operate as a residual category of jurisdiction, applicable only when the various Regulations and Conventions are not.

The common law rules divide into two parts. One is concerned with the ability to **18.42** serve on a defendant *as of right* i.e. without having to seek the court's permission. Such a right arises simply because of the defendant's presence within the jurisdiction, however fleeting or temporary in nature. Secondly, if the claimant cannot serve as of right, he must ask the court for permission to serve out on the defendant. As set out below, such an application is based on showing that the claim falls within a head of jurisdiction which has a factual connection with England and which, in part, mirrors the rules existing under the various Conventions.

The major difference in approach is that the doctrine of *forum conveniens* plays a **18.43** significant role in the application of the traditional rules of English conflict of laws.

- If a defendant has been served as of right in the jurisdiction e.g. he just happens to be visiting London and is served with papers, then the English court has jurisdiction as of right over that individual. So much is uncontestable. But the basis for taking jurisdiction does not establish any significant connection between the defendant and England. What the defendant can argue is that the English court should not *exercise* the jurisdiction it undoubtedly has. The main ground for so arguing would be to say that there exists another forum which is more appropriate to determine the case, which has a greater connection with

---

[30] See 2001 OJ L307/28 and 2002 OJ L225/13.
[31] Cyprus, the Czech Republic, Estonia, Hungary, Latvia, Lithuania, Malta, Poland, Slovakia, and Slovenia.
[32] 2004 OJ L236/33.

the relevant factors, where the witnesses are present and which can generally deal with the case better than if it were brought in England. So here the defendant makes use of the doctrine of *forum conveniens* to displace English jurisdiction.[33]

- If the applicant has to ask the English court for permission to serve the defendant out of the jurisdiction under CPR r 6.21 then he must satisfy the following procedure:[34]

  - He must show there is a good arguable case that the court has jurisdiction within one of the heads of service out identified in CPR, r 6.20.
  - He must show there are reasonable prospects of succeeding on that claim.
  - He must show the case is a proper one for service out of the jurisdiction i.e. *forum conveniens*. Here, the doctrine of *forum conveniens* is employed to persuade the English court to *exercise* jurisdiction it would not otherwise have.

(5) When does each regime apply?[35]

18.44 The Judgments Regulation will apply to all claims which come before the English court unless the following occurs, which results in the common law rules applying:

- the subject matter of the dispute is not within the ambit of the Regulation (e.g. not a civil or commercial matter); or

- another Convention gives jurisdiction to the English courts;[36] or

- none of the exclusive[37] or other heads of jurisdiction, dealing with submission,[38] insurance claims,[39] employment contracts,[40] consumer contracts[41] or choice of court clauses[42] apply.[43]

---

[33] See *Spiliada Maritime Corp v Cansulex Ltd* [1987] AC 460 (HL).

[34] See generally, *Seaconsar Far East Ltd v Bank Markazi Jomhouri Islami Iran* [1994] 1 AC 438 (HL).

[35] The best diagrammatic illustration of the applicability of each regime is to be found in Briggs and Rees, *Civil Jurisdiction and Judgments* (4th edn), Appendix VI, Figure 1: 'The Jurisdiction of an English Court under the Council Regulaton and Common Law.' The author was fortunate enough to be taught conflict of laws by Professor Briggs.

[36] Article 71.

[37] Article 22.

[38] Article 24.

[39] Articles 8–14.

[40] Articles 18–21.

[41] Articles 15–17.

[42] Article 23.

[43] It is to be noted that the special heads of jurisdiction contained within Articles 5–7, dealing with claims such as contract and tort depend on at least the defendant being domiciled in a member state.

F. Overview of Regimes—Choice of Law

There are two relevant regimes for choice of law: **18.45**

- In relation to contract, there is the Rome Convention as enacted into English law under the Contracts (Applicable Laws) Act 1990.
- In relation to torts, there is the Private International Law (Miscellaneous Provisions) Act 1995, soon to be replaced by the Rome II Regulation.

(1) Contract: The Rome Convention

The Rome Convention applies to all 'contractual obligations in any situation **18.46** involving a choice between the laws of different countries'.[44] Given the passage of time since its enactment and coming into force, it is unlikely that the litigator will need to resort to the traditional common law rules unless one of the express exclusions apply.

The most relevant exclusions include: **18.47**

- obligations arising under bills of exchange, cheques and promissory notes and other negotiable instruments;
- arbitration agreements and agreements on the choice of court;
- matters relating to the internal organization, capacity, winding up of companies, lifting the corporate veil;
- whether an agent is able to bind its principal;
- insurance (but not re-insurance) contracts covering member states.

When the Convention identifies a law as applicable it means the domestic law and **18.48** not its conflict of laws rules. In other words, *renvoi* is excluded.[45]

The provisions of the Convention will be examined in some detail in Chapter 20. **18.49** At this overview stage, it suffices to say that the Convention operates on the principle of party autonomy:

- Article 3: It will look to see what law the parties have expressly or impliedly chosen to govern their relationships.
- Article 4: It is only if that fails to identify a particular legal system, that the search moves on to identify the legal system having the closest connection with the contract. In making that determination, there is a presumption in favour of the country where the party who is to effect the performance which is characteristic

---

44 Article 1(1).
45 Article 15.

of the contract has his habitual residence or central administration. This pre-sumption can be disregarded if no characteristic performance can be identified or if from the circumstances as a whole the contract is more closely connected with another country.

- Certain provisions exist for the application of mandatory rules of the forum.

(2) Tort: Private International Law (Miscellaneous Provisions) Act 1995

18.50 Fortunately, the modern-day practitioner need not have a detailed understanding of the development of the common law rules which have been abolished by the Tort: Private International Law (Miscellaneous Provisions) Act 1995.[46]

18.51 Under the Act, the general principle is that a tort should be governed by the law of the country in which the events (or at least the most significant events) making up the tort took place.[47] If this consists of damage to property, it will be the law of the country where the property was when damaged. In all other cases, it is the law of the country in which the most significant elements of the events occurred.

18.52 The general principle can be displaced by another law if it would be substantially more appropriate to apply that other law.[48]

18.53 The Act applies equally to torts taking place within this jurisdiction as without.

(3) Rome II: Regulation on Choice of Law for Non-Contractual Obligations

18.54 On 11 January 2009, the Regulation on choice of law for non-contractual obliga-tions comes into force. It will apply to all events occurring on or after this date leading to non-contractual obligations.

18.55 Although this Regulation will supersede the 1995 Act, as its name implies, it extends beyond tortious claims and includes express provision for claims in 'unjust enrichment'.[49]

18.56 The general rule for tortious claims is that the law of the place of the damage (not the event giving rise to the damage) will govern, with the possibility that the par-ties can enter into choice of law agreements for such claims.

---

[46] The Tort: Private International Law (Miscellaneous Provisions) Act 1995, s 10 abolishes the rules of the common law insofar as (i) they require actionability under both the law of the forum and the law of another country for the purposes of establishing a tort (double-actionability rule as per *Boys v Chaplin* [1971] AC 356) or (ii), as an exception to (i), allow the law of a single country to apply to determine the issues.

[47] ibid, s 11.

[48] ibid, s 12.

[49] 'Unjust enrichment' is to be given an autonomous meaning.

The general rule for unjust enrichment is that the law of any prior relationship **18.57** between the parties shall govern the claim, failing which, the law of any joint habitual residence, failing which, the place of unjust enrichment (not enrichment alone). In one fell swoop, out of the window go all the intellectual arguments which have been raging for the last decade or so as to the appropriate choice of law rule for unjust enrichment claims. The complexity of the arguments have been replaced by a factually simple and presumably easy to apply regime, which will give *an* answer, however intellectually unsatisfying it may be to some.

19

JURISDICTION

A. Introduction

This chapter focuses on those rules of the English conflict of laws which establish **19.01** whether the English court has jurisdiction in respect of a dispute. Such jurisdiction may take two forms.

The first, and most commonly understood sense of jurisdiction, is jurisdiction to **19.02** hear the substantive dispute. Such jurisdiction arises because of connecting factors either between the defendant and the English jurisdiction or between the relevant events and the English jurisdiction. It is important to note at the outset that a claimant's connection with the jurisdiction, without more, has little relevance for the purposes of taking jurisdiction.[1]

(1) Non-claim-based jurisdiction

The first section of this chapter will deal with those instances where jurisdiction is **19.03** taken based upon (i) the relationship between the defendant and the forum, e.g. the defendant is domiciled or present within the forum at the relevant time or has

---

[1] English conflict of laws typically examines the appropriate nature of a jurisdiction from the perspective of the relationship of the forum with the defendant or with the underlying events. The fact that the claimant may well be domiciled in that forum is not, without more, a good reason for that jurisdiction to determine the case.

otherwise submitted to that forum's jurisdiction; (ii) the defendant has agreed that any such dispute be dealt with in the forum; and (iii) the defendant has taken steps to submit to this forum's jurisdiction.

19.04 It will immediately be apparent that these grounds for taking jurisdiction have nothing whatsoever to do with the nature of the claim brought and so do not give rise to issues of particular interest or importance to a commercial fraud litigator. They are well covered in the major texts and we shall therefore tread lightly over the issues they raise.

(2) Claim-based jurisdiction

19.05 The second section of this chapter is concerned with those grounds for taking jurisdiction which are specifically associated with the nature of the claim being brought. As we shall see, some areas are clear and relatively straightforward. These include the well-known rules which apply to simple contract or tort claims. For some claims, the difficulty that arises is based upon identifying the appropriate category or rule which is applicable to the claim.

19.06 So, for example, doubt surrounds the proper treatment of claims in dishonest assistance. As a matter of English domestic law such claims are equitable claims. That, however, is no answer to how such a claim is properly to be characterized for the purposes of English conflict of laws where a broader approach is adopted to characterization of claims. One might conclude there is no specific category for such a claim and it therefore falls to be treated under the general domicile rule. Alternatively, one might see such similarities in this head of claim with those brought under the tortious head of jurisdiction as to equate dishonest assistance with a tortious claim for the purposes of characterization in the conflict of laws.

19.07 The typical approach to claim-based jurisdiction is that the relevant convention or case law at common law have identified specific connecting factors establishing a clear relationship between that claim and English jurisdiction.

(3) Jurisdiction in respect of pre-emptive remedies

19.08 The second sense of jurisdiction concerns, and is limited to, the jurisdiction to grant pre-emptive relief. Examples of such relief include freezing injunctions, search orders, seizure orders, etc. Here, the English court recognizes that another jurisdiction will be dealing with the substantive dispute but that assistance can be provided by the English court granting interim orders, for example, by freezing any relevant assets, such as the proceeds of the fraud, which may be located within the English jurisdiction.

19.09 The jurisdiction to grant such relief is statutory-based, under s 25 of the Civil Jurisdiction and Judgments Act 1982 (CJJA 1982), as amended by Order in Council in 1997.

As to when the English court has jurisdiction in the second more limited sense, a **19.10** series of cases, including Millett J's judgment in *Credit Suisse Fides Trust SA v Cuoghi*[2] and *Motorola Credit Corp v Uzan*,[3] have developed a list of relevant criteria which will be examined in some detail below.

B. Jurisdiction Irrespective of Nature of Claim

This section does not give rise to any issues peculiarly related to commercial fraud **19.11** litigation. That said, it is nevertheless an important section since it sets out some of the common methods for taking jurisdiction that are not dependent upon the nature of the claim as a commercial fraud. Domicile, presence, agreement or submission may well represent the easiest means of obtaining English jurisdiction over a commercial fraud claim.

It should not be forgotten that just as the client's best claim may well not involve **19.12** alleging fraud at all, the best opportunity of having the case heard in one's chosen jurisdiction may also not depend upon the fraudulent nature of the allegations underpinning the substantive claims. Just because fraud may have taken place does not mean one needs to prove fraud to make a successful recovery for the client. As practitioners, we are always looking for the simplest, cheapest routes to recovery as befits the client's best interests.

(1) Domicile

In circumstances where any of the Judgments Regulation, the Brussels Conven- **19.13** tion or alternatively the Lugano Convention applies to determine jurisdiction, the general principle is that a defendant can always be sued in his, her or its own domicile. This principle is encapsulated in Article 2[4] of the Judgments Regulation which provides:

> Article 2
>
> 1. Subject to this Regulation, persons domiciled in a Member State shall, whatever their nationality, be sued in the courts of that Member State.

The justification for this approach is obvious. No one can seriously complain **19.14** about being sued in their own territory where, at least in theory, they will be familiar with the laws which are applied to determine the claims.

---

[2] [1998] QB 818.
[3] [2003] EWCA Civ 752, [2004] 1 WLR 1113.
[4] All references to articles are to the Judgments Regulation unless expressly stated otherwise.

19.15   The Conventions do not provide or adopt a uniform approach as to what is meant by 'domicile'—that is a matter left to each contracting state. Article 59 of the Judgments Regulation provides:

1.   In order to determine whether a party is domiciled in the Member State whose courts are seized of a matter, the court shall apply its internal law.

2.   If a party is not domiciled in the Member State whose courts are seized of the matter, then, in order to determine whether the party is domiciled in another Member State, the court shall apply the law of that Member State.

19.16   Where the Brussels and/or Lugano Conventions apply, the CJJA 1982, s 41 provides the relevant English law definition of 'domicile'. This definition should not be confused with the traditional English law concepts of domicile of origin and domicile of choice, which have no application at all under the Conventions or Regulation. Where the claim falls within the Judgments Regulation, the definition of 'domicile' is to be found in the Civil Jurisdiction and Judgments Order 2001, Schedule 1.[5]

19.17   *For an individual:* Domicile within the UK is established where the individual is (i) resident in the UK and (ii) the nature and circumstances of that residence indicates a substantial connection with the UK.[6] A substantial connection will be presumed (unless proved otherwise) by a residence within the UK for the last three months or so.[7]

19.18   Career fraudsters often have homes in several major jurisdictions and live their lives switching between homes as it suits them. It is entirely possible under the Conventions and Judgments Regulation for a defendant to have a domicile in more than one member state. In other words, the fact that the defendant is able to show he lives a life in, say, France will be no answer to the English court's jurisdiction over him if the requirements of domicile under the CJJA 1982 are satisfied.

19.19   *For a company:* Domicile within the UK is established by showing that the company has its 'statutory seat' or 'central administration' or 'principal place of business' in the UK.[8] Article 60(2) provides that '[f]or the purposes of the United Kingdom. . . . "statutory seat" means the registered office or, where there is no such office anywhere, the place of incorporation or, where there is no such place anywhere, the place under the law of which the formation took place.'

19.20   This marks a departure from the position adopted under the Brussels or Lugano Conventions since there each member state was left to apply its own definition

---

⁵ SI 2000/3929. The main difference between the CJJA 1982 and SI 2000/3929 lies in the definition given to the 'seat' of a company.
⁶ Para 9 of Sched 1; CJJA 1982, s 41(2).
⁷ Para 9 of Sched 1; CJJA 1982, s 41(6).
⁸ Judgments Regulation, Art 60.

of 'seat'. Under the Judgments Regulation, Article 60 lays down a common code as to a company's domicile.

Finally, the definition of domicile employed under Article 60 of the Judgments **19.21** Regulation should not be confused with the concept of domicile for the purposes of establishing exclusive jurisdiction under Article 22(2) of the Judgments Regulation.[9]

(2) Presence within jurisdiction

This head of jurisdiction is only available in circumstances where the Judgments **19.22** Regulation and/or any of the Conventions do not apply. So one cannot establish English jurisdiction over a French domiciliary who happens to be passing through London. But these rules would result in a Brazilian domiciliary passing through London being susceptible to this head of jurisdiction.

Realistically, in a fraud case, this head of jurisdiction may only be available in the **19.23** very early stages of discovering the fraud before the fraudster is even aware his conduct has been uncovered and so has not yet had the opportunity to flee the country. Thereafter, this head of jurisdiction would require a great deal of luck and a fair amount of stupidity on the part of the fraudster to be successful.

For an individual: Jurisdiction is established by virtue of the individual's actual **19.24** presence within the jurisdiction. It matters not how transient or temporary such presence may in fact be.

For a company: A company is considered present within the United Kingdom under **19.25** the Companies Act 1985 insofar as it is registered within the UK jurisdiction.

Given the limited factual connection presence gives a jurisdiction over a particular **19.26** claim, any exercise of jurisdiction based upon presence is subject to a *forum conveniens* argument, i.e. that there exists another jurisdiction which has a better connection to the dispute and in which the dispute can be tried better in the interests of justice.[10]

(3) Submission to jurisdiction/entering an appearance

This is not a head of jurisdiction often invoked in fraud cases since a defendant, **19.27** rightly or wrongly facing such serious allegations, is unlikely to want to take a step in proceedings which assists the claimant to pursue its claim.

---

[9] Article 22(2) gives exclusive jurisdiction to the following courts, irrespective of domicile 'in proceedings which have as their object the validity of the constitution, the nullity or the dissolution of companies or other legal persons or associations of natural or legal persons, or of the validity of the decisions of their organs, the courts of the Member State in which the company, legal person or association has its seat. In order to determine that seat, the court shall apply its rules of private international law.'

[10] *Spiliada Maritime Corp v Cansulex Ltd* [1987] AC 460 (HL).

19.28 This head of jurisdiction is dealt with by Article 24 of the Judgments Regulation which provides that:

> Apart from jurisdiction derived from other provisions of this Regulation, a court of a Member State before which a defendant enters an appearance shall have jurisdiction. This rule shall not apply where appearance was entered to contest the jurisdiction, or where another court has exclusive jurisdiction by virtue of Article 22.

19.29 Article 24 is strictly only concerned with one aspect of, and one means of achieving, a submission to jurisdiction, namely by way of entering an appearance before the courts.[11] There are other ways of achieving a submission to jurisdiction, such as by a contractual choice of court clause or by agreeing to accept service of process. However, Article 24 does not appear to embrace these other methods.

19.30 Article 24 is not limited to those defendants who are domiciled within a member state but extends to all defendants, wherever domiciled, who choose to enter an appearance before the courts of a member state.

19.31 So long as the defendant has made it clear that he wishes to challenge jurisdiction at the earliest opportunity, he will not be taken to have entered an appearance for the purposes of Article 24.[12] This Article clarifies those situations, particularly in Europe, where it is often advisable that a party submit a case on the merits at the same time as it contests jurisdiction.

(4) Jurisdiction agreements[13]

19.32 The English conflict of laws recognizes and gives effect to party autonomy to choose the jurisdiction in which any dispute is to be resolved. This principle is also enshrined in the Judgments Regulation.

19.33 Article 23 of the Judgments Regulation provides:

> 1. If the parties, one or more of whom is domiciled in a Member State, have agreed that a court or the courts of a Member State are to have jurisdiction to settle any disputes which have arisen or which may arise in connection with a particular legal relationship, that court or those courts shall have jurisdiction. Such jurisdiction shall be exclusive unless the parties have agreed otherwise. Such an agreement conferring jurisdiction shall be either:
>   (a) in writing or evidenced in writing; or

---

[11] Briggs and Rees, *Civil Jurisdiction and Judgments* (4th edn, LLP, 2005), para 2.66.

[12] E.g. Case 150/80 *Elefanten Schuh GmbH v Jacqmain* [1981] ECR 1671 (challenge came too late); Case 27/81 *Rohr SA v Ossberger* [1981] ECR 2431. As a matter of caution, all formal documents and important inter-solicitor correspondence should be expressly headed as reserving rights to challenge jurisdiction so there can be no misunderstanding. If that is understood, it would be difficult for it thereafter to be said that the party had entered an appearance for the purposes of Art 24.

[13] Briggs, *Agreements on Jurisdiction and Choice of Law* (Oxford University Press, 2008).

(b) in a form which accords with practices which the parties have established between themselves; or

(c) in international trade or commerce, in a form which accords with a usage of which the parties are or ought to have been aware and which in such trade or commerce is widely known to, and regularly observed by, parties to contracts of this type involved in the particular trade or commerce concerned.

2. Any communication by electronic means which provides a durable record of the agreement shall be equivalent to 'writing'.

3. Where such an agreement is concluded by the parties, none of whom is domiciled in a Member State, the courts of other Member States shall have no jurisdiction over their disputes unless the court or courts chosen have declined jurisdiction.

4. . . . .

5. . . . .

Assuming one party to be domiciled in a member state, Article 23 provides that **19.34** any agreement in writing or evidenced in writing for the choice of a member state jurisdiction shall be valid and binding. Discretionary considerations arising from *forum conveniens* have no application unless neither party to the agreement was domiciled in a member state. If the choice of jurisdiction is outside of the member states, Article 23 has no application since the Judgments Regulation cannot presume to bind a third party jurisdiction to accept jurisdiction over a dispute whilst that third party jurisdiction is not otherwise bound as a signatory to the Judgments Regulation.

It will also be evident that Article 23 seeks to lay down guidance on the formalities **19.35** which need to be complied with in order to ensure a valid and binding choice of court clause. These are pretty wide and should not ordinarily cause any real difficulties.

The principal role for jurisdiction agreements in founding jurisdiction in com- **19.36** mercial fraud cases is likely to be where the parties have entered into some form of a contractual arrangement based upon the fraudulent misrepresentations of one of the parties. The issue that the claimant will need to consider carefully is whether to seek to rely upon the jurisdiction agreement and run the risk of being taken to affirm the contract, thereby preventing the claimant from rescinding the contract and pursuing a proprietary claim.

(5) Jurisdiction over co-defendants

(a) *Under the Judgments Regulation and Conventions*

Article 6(1) of the Judgments Regulation provides: **19.37**

A person domiciled in a Member State may also be sued where he is one of a number of defendants, in the courts for the place where any one of them is domiciled provided the claims are so closely connected that it is expedient to hear and determine them together to avoid the risk of irreconcilable judgments resulting from separate proceedings.

19.38 The aim behind Article 6(1) is clear and laudable—the avoidance of irreconcilable judgments being obtained in different member states in respect of related claims. There are two main conditions which must be satisfied before this article can be called into play.

19.39 The first condition is that Article 6(1) requires that the claim proceed in the forum in which at least one of the defendants is domiciled. So long as the claim is proceeding in the jurisdiction where one of the parties happens to be domiciled, there is little basis for the other party to complain if jurisdiction is exerted over him as well, given this is perhaps the most logical solution to cases which have connections with several jurisdictions.

19.40 The relevant time for that defendant to be domiciled in this jurisdiction for the purposes of the first condition of Article 6(1) is at the date of issue of the proceedings against him.[14]

19.41 One important consequence of this first condition is that it will not suffice, for the purposes of Article 6(1), for the English courts to have asserted jurisdiction over the original defendant based upon, say, a contract or tort claim head of jurisdiction.

19.42 The second condition is that the claims being brought against each defendant must be 'closely related' so as to make it 'expedient' to have them heard together. This requirement, which derives from *Kalfelis v Bankhaus Schroder Munchmeyer Hengst & Co*,[15] is entirely consistent with the aim of reducing the possibility of irreconcilable judgments whilst at the same time creates a threshold so as to prevent Article 6(1) being abused through the inclusion of straw men defendants who happen to be domiciled in the UK.

19.43 One unresolved issue is whether to be 'closely related' the claims against each defendant need to be both contractual or both tortious. In *Reunion Europeene SA v Spliethoff's Bevrachtingskantoor BV*,[16] the European Court of Justice (ECJ) held that a claim arising in respect of a contract cannot be 'so closely related' or 'connected' with a claim arising in tort for the purposes of Article 6(1). This rather narrow view has, however, been doubted by the Court of Appeal in *Watson v First Choice Holidays and Flights Ltd*.[17]

---

[14] *Canada Trust Co v Stolzenberg (No 2)* [2002] 1 AC 1.
[15] Case 189/87, [1988] ECR 5565.
[16] Case C-51/97 [1998] ECR I-6511.
[17] [2001] 2 Lloyd's Rep 339.

(b) At common law

19.44

CPR r 6.20(3) provides:

> a claim is made against someone on whom the claim form has been or will be served
> and—
> a. There is between the claimant and that person a real issue which it is reasonable
>   for the court to try; and
> b. The claimant wishes to serve the claim form on another person who is a necessary
>   or proper party to that claim.

19.45 It is not a requirement of this rule that service must have taken place on the original defendant ('D1') in order to invoke this head of jurisdiction.

19.46 It is immediately noticeable that CPR r 6.20(3) is wider in scope than its counterpart under the Judgments Regulation in that the conditions for bringing the additional defendant into the proceedings are that: (i) some form of jurisdiction has been taken over the first defendant ('D1'). Unlike Article 6(1), jurisdiction over D1 is not limited to domicile and may include any of the heads of jurisdiction; (ii) there exists a real issue to be tried between the claimant and D1. This was introduced to curb any abuse of this head of jurisdiction. This would exclude claims against D1 where the law or facts are uncontradicted and it is clear that the claimant could not succeed against D1;[18] and (iii) the additional defendant ('D2') must be a 'necessary' or 'proper' party to the claim. D2 does not need to be both necessary and proper in order to be brought in.

19.47 Compliance with the requirements for joinder of parties will suffice to render D2 a proper party under CPR r 6.20(3).[19] It has been said that CPR r 6.20(3) is no less wide than the court's powers to add or substitute a party under CPR r19.1(2).[20]

C. Jurisdiction Based on Nature of Claim

19.48 This section focuses on those examples where the English court has jurisdiction over a dispute because and only because of a connection between the facts of the dispute and the English forum.

19.49 To assist the practitioner, this book will examine each of the potentially relevant heads of jurisdiction in turn, identify the relevant factors which justify English jurisdiction and consider, to the extent necessary, whether other claims might fall within each head of jurisdiction. As always, the focus of any discussion will be on those issues which have particular relevance to commercial fraud litigators.

---

[18] *Tyne Improvement Commissioners v Arnement Anversois SA (The Brabo)* [1949] AC 326; *Multinational Gas and Petrochemical Co v Multinational Gas and Petrochemical Services Ltd* [1983] 2 All ER 563; *The Berge Star* [2001] 1 Lloyd's Rep 663 HL.

[19] *Massey v Heynes* [1881] 21 QBD 330 (CA).

[20] *United Film Distribution Ltd v Chhabria, The Times*, 5 April 2001 (CA).

(1) Contract

19.50 Just because fraudulent conduct has occurred it does not necessarily follow that a client's interests are best served by abandoning the contract and seeking tortious or equitable relief for such conduct. It may well be preferable to seek one's remedies within the law of contract.

19.51 It should be noted that any decision to bring a claim in contract is highly likely to mean that the claimant has abandoned any attempts to bring proprietary claims other than any security claims contained within the terms of the contract. It should always be borne in mind that exercising any contractual rights, such as security under a contract, will almost always amount to affirming the contract after the discovery of a fraud, thereby negating any possibility of rescission and the commencement of a tracing exercise. As mentioned at the outset, these are the very issues the litigator needs to give advice on without delay so that the legal team knows which route it is to go down.

19.52 Further, jurisdictional issues arise when the issue in dispute is the validity of the contract in the first place. English law has always turned its face against any suggestion that fraud renders a contract void as opposed to voidable. Fortunately, as will be seen, the greater difficulties arise when dealing with void as opposed to voidable contracts and so whilst noticing the issue it is unlikely in practice to cause substantial difficulty in commercial fraud cases.

19.53 In addition to the difficult issue of whether a contract void *ab initio* should be subject to the same jurisdictional rule as a valid contract, it is necessary to bear in mind that a broader approach is adopted as to what amounts to a contract or a contractual dispute for the purposes of the conflict of laws than would apply in domestic law. This approach reflects the differing views, particularly amongst civilian jurisdictions, as to what amounts to a contract. The typical example given is the treatment of a negligent misstatement case as a contractual case rather than a tort case. Under English contract law, the lack of any consideration would prevent the obligation arising as a result of the misstatement from being a contractual one and yet such a case neatly falls within the *Handte*[21] definition of a contractual obligation as being one voluntarily undertaken by one person to another.

(a) Under the Judgments Regulation

19.54 The Judgments Regulation's special head of jurisdiction dealing with contract claims will only apply in circumstances where the defendant is domiciled in a member state other than the English forum.[22]

---

[21] Case C-26/91 *Handte GmbH v Soc Traitements* [1992] ECR I-3967.
[22] Of course, if the defendant was already domiciled within the UK, the claimant could rely upon the domicile principle deriving from Art 2 to obtain English jurisdiction.

Article 5(1) provides as follows: **19.55**

> A person domiciled in a Member State, may, in another Member State, be sued—
>
> '. . . (a) in matters relating to a contract, in the courts for the place of performance of
> the obligation in question; (b) for the purpose of this provision and unless otherwise
> agreed, the place of performance shall be: in the case of the sale of goods, the place in
> a Member State where, under the contract, the goods were delivered or should have
> been delivered, in the case of the provision of services, the place in a Member State
> where, under the contract, the services were provided or should have been provided;
> (c) if subparagraph (b) does not apply then subparagraph (a) applies.'

(i) Matters relating to contract In most scenarios, this phrase will pose no diffi- **19.56**
culties at all. It will generally include claims for non-payment, non-delivery and
non-performance of a contract.

Such arguments form the paradigm example of contractual disputes and clearly **19.57**
fall within Article 5(1). Difficulties arise in two principal areas:

(a) Where there exists some doubt as to whether the contract is void *ab initio*;
(b) Where the nature of the claim is such that there exist good arguments to
     include it within a broader concept of contract even if that broader concept
     would fall outwith the traditional English law definition of contract.

Contracts void ab initio: Where an arrangement thought or considered to be a **19.58**
contract is subsequently discovered to be void *ab initio*, that means, as a matter of
law, it is not and never was a valid contract. On that basis, one might not unreasonably conclude that the jurisdictional rules designed for dealing with contractual disputes should have no application. After all, no contract exists or ever existed
and therefore why should any dispute arising therefrom be subject to the contractual rules on jurisdiction? The problem with such a view, which has a superficial
attraction, is that one is left with an approach where the correct jurisdictional rule
to apply will be determined by reference to the outcome of the dispute between
the parties. Jurisdictional rules are designed by reference to the nature of the dispute and not by reference to the outcome of that dispute. The relevant case law
fails to provide a uniform approach to this issue.

No dispute as to validity: In *Kleinwort Benson Ltd v Glasgow City Council*,[23] the **19.59**
House of Lords, by a bare majority, held that the phrase 'matters relating to a contract' as defined in Schedule 4 to the CJJA 1982, did not include a claim where
both parties accepted that the contracts were void on the ground that the local
authority had no authority to enter into such a contract. If there was no contract,
there could be no contractual obligation in question.

---

[23] [1999] 1 AC 153.

19.60 This decision was heavily criticized at the time for ignoring that the parties at least intended to enter into a contract and as such would not have been in any position to complain if the rule of the putative contract had been allowed to apply. It also has the unhappy consequence of drawing a distinction between the situation where both parties accept the contract is void and where there is a dispute between the parties as to whether the contract was void *ab initio*. It is difficult to see any justification for a different jurisdictional approach to these two types of dispute.

19.61 *Disputed validity*: If there exists a dispute between the parties as to the existence or validity of the contract, that will still amount to a matter relating to a contract. In *Effer SpS v Kantner*[24] the ECJ held:

> in article 5(1) of the Convention, the national court's jurisdiction to determine questions relating to a contract includes the power to consider the existence of the constituent parts of the contract itself, since that is indispensable in order to enable the national court in which proceedings are brought to examine whether it has jurisdiction under the Convention. If that were not the case, article 5(1) of the Convention would be in danger of being deprived of its legal effect, since it would be accepted that, in order to defeat the rule contained in that provision it is sufficient for one of the parties to claim that the contract does not exist.[25]

19.62 The House of Lords, by a majority, in *Agnew v Lansforsakringsbolagens AB*[26] held that a claim to avoid a contract of re-insurance on the grounds of material non-disclosure was a 'matter relating to a contract' within Article 5(1), particularly where one party pleaded its validity and existence. Their Lordships accepted that pre-contractual duties of good faith and fair and proper presentation of risk fell within Article 5(1).

19.63 Lord Cooke described an action to avoid a contract as 'patently' a 'matter relating to a contract' and took support from the fact that all other English judges to consider the issue from first instance up to the House of Lords had taken a similar view. The difficulty lay in whether the words 'the place of performance of the obligation in question' are satisfied by such a claim. In agreeing with the majority that they were satisfied, Lord Cooke noted:

> The obligation in question may be variously described as an obligation to make a fair presentation of the risk, an obligation not to misrepresent the risk, or an obligation to disclose facts material to the risk which the reinsured knows or ought to know. However described, it is an obligation falling on the reinsured for breach of which a remedy, namely the setting aside of the contract, is available against the reinsured. Cases where an apparent contract is void *ab initio*—for such causes as failure to

---

[24] Case 38/81 [1982] ECR 825.
[25] ibid, 834, para 7.
[26] [2001] 1 AC 223—a case based upon the Lugano Convention. There is no reference to the ECJ under the Lugano Convention.

comply with a statutory requirement as to form, lack of contractual power in one party, or uncertainty, - are distinguishable.[27]

So what appears to have been of some significance, at least to Lord Cooke, is the **19.64** distinction between a contract which is void *ab initio* because, say, it failed to satisfy a statutory requirement and a contract which is and remains valid and binding unless and until one party exercises its remedy to have the contract set aside on the ground of non-disclosure. Such a remedy—to set aside a contract—must be a matter relating to a contract and thus fall within Article 5(1).

This view is, with respect, to be preferred to that held in *Alfred Dunhill Ltd v* **19.65** *Diffusion Internationale de Maroquinerie de Prestige Sarl*[28] where it was held that a claim in damages for a misrepresentation leading to entering into a contract was a tortious claim and not one relating to a contract.[29]

The problem left for the practitioner is how these authorities are to be interpreted **19.66** in a consistent manner. Is it really the case that if there is no dispute as to the validity of a contract void *ab initio* one jurisdictional rule applies but if there is a dispute another (contractual) one applies?

Further difficulties start to arise when one moves away from the core concept of a **19.67** contract, as understood by English domestic law, to a much broader concept of a contract being an obligation freely entered into by one person with another: see *Jakob Handte & Co GmbH v Soc Traitements Mecano-Chimiques des Surfaces.*[30] This broader concept is more apt to include what might traditionally be characterized in a matter of English domestic law as a tortious claim for negligent misstatement.[31]

(b) Under the common law

In the event that the defendant is not domiciled in a member state (of the **19.68** Judgments Regulation, or, in the case of the remaining EFTA states, until the proposed move to the Regulation due in 2008, the Lugano Convention) such that there is no application of the Judgments Regulation, the Brussels Convention and/or the Lugano Convention, the claimant will need to resort to the traditional jurisdictional rules at common law for contractual claims.

---

[27] [2001] 1 AC 223, 246.

[28] [2001] CLC 949.

[29] It is a matter of much debate in English law whether such duties comprise contractual duties, based upon the nature of the contract as one of insurance, or equitable duties, imposed by equity given the nature of the contract. In any event, this decision is to be contrasted with that of the ECJ in Case C-334/00 *Fonderie Officine Meccaniche SpA v HWS GmbH* [2002] ECR I-7357 where the Court held in an Italian claim, that a failure to negotiate in good faith was a matter relating to a tort.

[30] Case C-26/91, [1992] ECR I-3967.

[31] See the discussion in Briggs and Rees, *Civil Jurisdiction and Judgments* (4th edn), paras 2.125–2.127.

19.69 The grounds for taking jurisdiction at common law are now set out and to be found in the CPR or White Book as it is more colloquially described.

19.70 One general point to be made about CPR r 6.20(5) is that it has been held that the phrase 'in respect of a contract' does not require the relevant claim for which English jurisdiction is sought to arise under the contract itself. As Lightman J in *Albon v Naza Motor Trading Sdn Bhd*[32] held, 'it requires only that the claim relates to or is connected with the contract'. In that case, the claim was said to lie in restitution, being a claim for the recovery of overpayments made under a contract.

19.71 Under CPR r 6.20(5)–(7), the English court has jurisdiction to determine a 'contractual' dispute in the following events:

(a) if the contract was made within the jurisdiction[33]

In respect of instantaneous communications such as fax, telephone or email, a contract is deemed to be made where the acceptance is communicated. So in *Entores Ld v Miles Far East Corporation*[34] the acceptance was sent by the defendant's agents based in Holland by telex received in England. The English court had jurisdiction as the contract was made in England.

(b) if the contract was made by or through an agent trading or residing within the jurisdiction on behalf of a principal trading or residing out of the jurisdiction[35]

This head of jurisdiction is not limited to contracts concluded by agents having the authority to conclude contracts on behalf of their principal. It extends to agents who simply assist in the negotiations notwithstanding the absence of any authority actually to conclude such a contract.

This head of jurisdiction cannot be invoked by a claimant: *Union International Co Ltd v Jubilee Insurance Co Ltd*[36] where Phillips J accepted that the underlying principle behind this head of jurisdiction was correctly identified by Atkin LJ in *National Mortgage and Agency Co of New Zealand Ltd v Gosselin* as follows:

> Formerly, proceedings for service of writs abroad would not be granted unless the breach complained of had occurred within the jurisdiction, but a new principle had now been adopted, as it was considered that if foreigners chose to carry on business here by means of agents it would only be right and proper to serve them although they were out of the jurisdiction. In order to carry out that principle it was thought

---

[32] [2007] 1 WLR (Ch D 2489).
[33] CPR r 6.20(5)(a).
[34] [1955] 2 QB 327 CA.
[35] CPR r 6.20(5)(b).
[36] [1991] 1 WLR 415; *Dicey, Morris & Collins* (14th edn), para 11-187.

necessary to include cases in which a foreigner who carried on his business abroad had an agent in this country whose duty it was to obtain orders, although he had no authority to accept them. It was to cover a case like that, that in his opinion the words 'by or through' has been inserted in the rule.[37]

(c) the contract is governed by English law[38]

The applicable law of a contract is determined by reference to the Rome Convention on the Law Applicable to Contractual Obligations enacted in the UK by the Contracts (Applicable Law) Act 1990.

It should be noted that the House of Lords has considered this head of jurisdiction to be somewhat exorbitant[39] and therefore a claimant would be well advised to marshal as many facts as possible which render the English forum the *forum conveniens* to justify the English court exercising its discretion in favour of taking jurisdiction over the dispute.

(d) the contract contains an English jurisdiction clause[40]

This head of jurisdiction will only apply to give the English courts jurisdiction in circumstances where Article 23 of the Judgments Regulation or Article 17 of the Conventions does not apply.

Unlike its Regulation or Convention counterpart, the common law does not stipulate any particular formal requirements for a valid jurisdiction clause.

(e) the relevant breach of contract was committed within the jurisdiction[41]

This head of jurisdiction differs from that offered in the Judgments Regulation due to the absence of any reference to the place of performance of the obligation in question. This is significant since it is possible, under English law, to breach a contract other than where it was intended to be performed. Clearly, such instances would be the typical example of breach under this head of jurisdiction so that, e.g. X fails to deliver sugar to Y in England as required under the terms of the contract. The failure would result in a breach of contract being committed within the jurisdiction because that is where it was stipulated that performance was to take place.

There are, however, breaches which can be committed without reference to the place of performance. So, to take an obvious example, X may expressly repudiate the contract by stating his intention not to perform its terms. If this is done in

---

[37] (1922) 38 TLR 832, 833.
[38] CPR r 6.20(5)(c).
[39] *Amin Rasheed Shipping Corp v Kuwait Insurance Co* [1984] AC 50, 65 (Lord Diplock).
[40] CPR r 6.20(5)(d); e.g. *The Chaparral* [1968] 2 Lloyd's Rep 158.
[41] CPR r 6.20(6).

England, there is a relevant breach of contract in London, irrespective of the fact that the contract did not require any performance in London.[42]

(f) **the claim is made for a declaration that no contract exists where, if the contract was found to exist, it would comply with the conditions contained within sub-paragraphs (a) to (d) but not (e) above**[43]

The jurisdictional difficulties which arise when it is alleged by one party or the other that the relevant contract is void have already been discussed in the context of the Judgments Regulation and Conventions above. This head of jurisdiction removes any significance to be attached to whether it is the claimant or the defendant who is alleging that the contract is void. It is no longer relevant who is alleging that the contract is void—the matter will still be treated as a contractual dispute for jurisdictional purposes so long as the requirements of this head of jurisdiction are otherwise satisfied. To this extent, the position under the English common law is to be preferred to that which presently prevails under the Judgments Regulation.

(2) Tort

19.72 As previously discussed, the English law has eschewed all attempts at identifying a single tort claim to cover fraud. Instead, there are a myriad of claims to cover the various guises in which a fraud may be committed. So, we have the typical claims of deceit, conspiracy, bribery and inducing a breach of contract. All such claims will be dealt with, for jurisdictional purposes, under the tort head of jurisdiction. It remains to be seen how many other claims, such as dishonest assistance, may be characterized as tortious for jurisdictional purposes notwithstanding their characterization as equitable claims in domestic English law.

(a) Under the Judgments Regulation

19.73 The Judgments Regulation applies to any tortious claims whenever the putative defendant is domiciled in a member state other than that of the forum (in our case, other than the UK). So long as this condition is satisfied, the Judgments Regulation provides for a special head of jurisdiction whereby a court, other than that of the individual's domicile, may take jurisdiction over tortious claims.

19.74 The special head of jurisdiction dealing with tortious claims is contained within Article 5(3) which provides that:

> in matters relating to tort, delict or quasi-delict, in the courts for the place where the harmful event occurred or may occur.

---

[42] See e.g. *Cooper v Knight* (1901) 17 TLR 299 (CA) (contract to marry in England—letter calling off marriage sent from Belgium and received and read in England).
[43] CPR r 6.20(7).

(i) Matters relating to tort   In order to ensure some form of unanimity in   **19.75**
approach across member states, 'matters relating to a tort' has been given an
autonomous meaning. It should not be interpreted in line with domestic English
law concepts of a tort.

The most important attempt at defining 'matters relating to a tort' came in the   **19.76**
ECJ's decision in *Kalfelis v Bankhaus Schroder Munchmeyer Hengst & Co.*[44] The
ECJ held (i) that Article 5(3) was to be given an autonomous definition and was
not to be interpreted solely by reference to concepts of national law; (ii) the fact
that the English court might have jurisdiction over a tortious claim under Article
5(3), it does not, for that reason alone, have jurisdiction over other claims; and
(iii) it included 'all actions which seek to establish the liability of a defendant and
which are not related to a contract within the meaning of Article 5(1)'.

Put more simply, *Kelfelis* has been interpreted by some as holding that any claim   **19.77**
which gives rise to 'liability' which falls outside of Article 5(1) would fall within
Article 5(3). This reasoning has the attraction of simplicity, reducing Article 5(3)
to a residual category into which all claims for liability that do not come within
Article 5(1) must be placed. This would include claims such as those arising under
unjust enrichment.

However, the approach adopted in *Kalfelis* or, perhaps more accurately, this sug-   **19.78**
gested interpretation of the approach adopted in *Kalfelis* has not received universal
approval. In particular, the House of Lords in *Kleinwort Benson Ltd v Glasgow City
Council*[45] considered that it was a simple misreading of the *Kalfelis* judgment to
suggest that the ECJ, when referring to 'liability' meant to refer to any liability as
opposed to liability arising under tort, delict or quasi-delict.

To assess this approach it is necessary first to see what questions the ECJ was asked   **19.79**
to answer and how they answered them in the *Kalfelis* judgment. The ECJ was
asked the following question (being question 2):

> (a) Must the term 'tort' in article 5(3) of the EEC Convention be construed inde-
> pendently of the Convention or must it be construed according to the law applic-
> able in the individual case (lex causae), which is determined by the private
> international law of the court applied to? (b) Does article 5(3) of the Convention
> confer, in respect of an action based on claims in tort and contract and for unjust
> enrichment, accessory jurisdiction on account of factual connection even in
> respect of the claims not based on tort.[46]

The ECJ answered these questions in the following manner: **19.80**

> (a) The term 'matters relating to tort, delict or quasi-delict' used in article 5(3) of the
> Convention must be regarded as an independent concept covering all actions which

---

[44] Case 189/87 [1988] ECR 5565.
[45] [1999] AC 153.
[46] Case 189/87 [1988] ECR 5565, 5569.

seek to establish the liability of a defendant and which are not related to a 'contract' within the meaning of article 5(1); (b) A court which has jurisdiction under article 5(3) over an action in so far as it is based on tort or delict does not have jurisdiction over that action in so far as it is not so based.[47]

19.81 The crucial issue is the proper interpretation of answer (a) and in particular whether the reference to 'liability of a defendant' is to be construed as referring to *any* form of liability so long as it is not related to a contract or whether it is to be interpreted more restrictively as meaning liability within the scope of Article 5(3) i.e. liability in tort, delict or quasi-delict.

19.82 The House of Lords in *Kleinwort Benson* held that the latter more restrictive interpretation was to be preferred. Lord Hutton remarked: 'the court in its answer to question 2(b) is stating that a court which has jurisdiction under article 5(3) over an action in so far as it is based on tort or delict does not have jurisdiction over an action in so far as it is not based on tort or delict but is based on unjust enrichment'.[48]

19.83 It has been suggested that the House of Lords in *Kleinwort Benson* was seeking to limit Article 5(3) to 'claims which are in the nature of what an English court would recognize as a tort'.[49] Briggs and Rees, whilst recognizing inherent difficulties and drawbacks, go on to put forward an alternative restricted interpretation of 'liability' so as to limit it to 'the obligation to compensate for wrongdoing'.[50] This is based upon the view that the original linguistic versions of the relevant words in *Kalfelis* more readily give rise to such a meaning as the English term 'liability'.

19.84 But, with respect, when one examines the reasoning given by each of the Law Lords in *Kleinwort Benson* for rejecting the wide interpretation of Article 5(3) none would appear to have been based upon a desire to impose a domestic concept of tort on this Article. What the Law Lords were deciding was that the reference to 'liability' was to be understood as meaning 'liability in tort, delict or quasi-delict' *whatever the autonomous definition given to these concepts.*

19.85 Exactly how *Kalfelis* is to be interpreted has not yet worked itself out in the case law. Until that happens, doubt and uncertainty will surround its true meaning. It is submitted that unless the ECJ holds otherwise, the reasoning of the House of Lords in *Kleinwort Benson*, that it is 'liability based on tort, delict or quasi-delict'

---

[47] Case 189/87 [1988] ECR 5565, 5587.

[48] *Kleinwort Benson Ltd v Glasgow City Council* [1999] AC 153, 196. The other Law Lords were dismissive of any suggestion that 'liability' should be given a wider meaning: see Lord Goff at 172B–D ('a misreading which is plainly inconsistent with paragraph 2(b) of the same ruling . . . no substance in the point . . .'); Lord Mustill at 172H; Lord Nicholls at 177F; Lord Clyde at 185C–E.

[49] Briggs and Rees, *Civil Jurisdiction and Judgments* (4th edn), para 2.146.

[50] ibid.

provides the most persuasive interpretation of the *Kalfelis* judgment. It thus excludes any claim arising in unjust enrichment.[51]

Place where the harmful event occurred: The European Court in *Bier v Mines de Potasse D'Alsace*[52] has held that this phrase must be given an autonomous meaning and that it includes both (i) the place where the damage occurs and (ii) the place where the event which caused that damage takes place. The oft-cited example is that of pollution being poured into a river in country X only to flow down the river into country Y and damage crops growing in an adjacent field. Under *Bier*, Article 5(3) would give jurisdiction to country X, as being the place where the event which caused the harm occurred (i.e. pollution of river) and also to country Y, as being the place where the harmful event occurred.   **19.86**

It is important to be clear about what *Bier* decided, in particular in relation to (i) above. The place where the damage occurs does not mean the place where the damage is suffered, although in practice, the two may in fact be the same. As Langley J pointed out in *Sunderland Marine Mutual Insurance Co Ltd v Francis Wiseman & Ors*,[53] if it did, this would be tantamount to making the claimant's domicile a sufficient basis for jurisdiction.   **19.87**

Bier may provide useful guidance where the damage caused is physical.[54] The same cannot be said where in a commercial fraud the concern is with the financial or economic loss caused by the deceit or conspiracy. It is not possible to rely upon this decision to justify an argument jurisdiction should be given to the place of a claimant's business because that is where it suffered its economic damage. This point was made clear in *Dumez France v Hessische Landesbank*.[55]   **19.88**

In *Dumez France v Hessische Landesbank* French companies suffered losses in France as a consequence of the alleged negligence of German banks handling the accounts of German subsidiaries of the French companies. Allegedly as a result of the German banks' negligence, the German subsidiaries became insolvent. The French parent companies could not sue the German banks in France based on the fact that they had suffered economic loss in France.[56] Based on *Dumez*, jurisdiction based upon economic loss having been incurred will be limited to such loss   **19.89**

---

[51] This is also the conclusion reached in *Dicey, Morris & Collins* (14th edn), para 11.299. The decision in Case C-261/90 *Reichert v Dresdner Bank (No 2)* [1992] ECR I-2149 also makes it clear that Art 5(3) does not include claims to set aside transactions entered into as a fraud on creditors.

[52] Case 21/76 [1976] ECR 1735, [1978] QB 708.

[53] [2007] EWHC 1460 (Comm), [26].

[54] See also *Henderson v Jaouen* [2002] EWCA Civ 75, [2002] 1 WLR 2971 (CA) where the fact that an injury originally sustained in a road accident in France subsequently deteriorated in England did not give England jurisdiction under Art 5(3).

[55] Case C-220/88 [1990] ECR I-49; Case C-168/02 *Kronhofer v Maier* [2004] ECR I-6009.

[56] See also Case C-364/93 *Marinari v Lloyds Bank Plc* [1995] ECR I-2719, [1996] QB 217 (an Italian arrested in England due to alleged wrongful conduct of employees of Lloyds Bank in England

as incurred by the immediate victim and not by any parent company. Any other conclusion would result in the claimant's main place of business becoming a ground for jurisdiction, something which is alien to the overall scheme of the Judgments Regulation. The judgment of the ECJ in *Dumez* is instructive on this conclusion.

19.90   Having made the point that Article 5(3) is an exception to the general domicile rule and is justified by giving rise to connecting factors which create a very close connection between the tort and a particular jurisdiction, such as to justify it being an exception to the general principle, and having identified the sound administration of justice and the efficacious conduct of proceedings as being an objective in jurisdictional matters, the ECJ went on:

> 18. In order to meet that objective, which is of fundamental importance in a convention which has essentially to promote the recognition and enforcement of judgments in States other than those in which they were delivered, it is necessary to avoid the multiplication of courts of competent jurisdiction which would heighten the risk of irreconcilable decisions ...
>
> 19. Furthermore, that objective militates against any interpretation of the Convention which, otherwise than in the cases expressly provided for, might lead to recognition of the jurisdiction of the courts of the plaintiff's domicile and would enable a plaintiff to determine the competent court by his choice of domicile.
>
> 20. It follows from the foregoing considerations that although, by virtue of a previous judgment of the court [*Bier*], the expression 'place where the harmful event occurred' contained in Article 5(3) of the Convention may refer to the place where the damage occurred, the latter concept can be understood only as indicating the place where the event giving rise to the damage, and entailing tortious, delictual or quasi-delictual liability, directly produced its harmful effects upon the person who is the immediate victim of that event.

19.91   *Dishonest assistance*: In *Cronos Containers NV v Palatin*[57] the defendant wrongfully obtained payment of money by a third party from a bank account held abroad into the defendant's own account held in the UK. It was held that there existed English jurisdiction under Article 5(3) because the dishonest assistance had taken place in England or the defendant converted the property to their own use in England.

19.92   *Negligent misstatement*: It has been held in *Domicrest Ltd v Swiss Bank Corp*[58] that under Article 5(3) the place where the harmful event giving rise to damage occurs is considered to be where the statement originated from and the place where the misstatement is received and relied upon.

---

could not bring claim in Italy based upon damage to reputation and additional economic loss suffered in that jurisdiction).

[57] [2002] EWHC 2819 (Comm).
[58] [1999] QB 548; see also *Dicey, Morris & Collins* (14th edn), para 11-303 n 69.

(b) Under the common law

Pursuant to CPR 6, r 20(8) a claim is made in tort where—   **19.93**

   (a) damage was sustained within the jurisdiction; or
   (b) the damage sustained resulted from an act committed within the
        jurisdiction.

The amendment to the old head of jurisdiction was very much based upon   **19.94**
Article 5(3) of the Brussels Convention.

Deceit and negligent misstatement: In the case of a claim based upon a negligent   **19.95**
misstatement, it has been held by Rix J in *Domicrest Ltd v Swiss Bank Corp*[59] that
the place where the harmful event giving rise to the damage occurred is where the
misstatement originated or was made and not the place where it is received and
relied upon.[60] Rix J went on to hold that typically the place where the misstatement was received and relied upon would usually be where the damage occurs.
However, on the facts, although the negligent misstatement was received in
England, it was thereafter acted upon by releasing goods in Switzerland without
first obtaining payment, thus giving alternative jurisdiction to Switzerland and
not to England.

This approach is to be contrasted with, and not to be confused with, the well   **19.96**
established English law proposition that the tort of fraudulent misrepresentation
is committed in the place where the misrepresentation was received and acted
upon and not the place from where it was sent.[61] Under earlier versions of the
heads of jurisdiction for permission to serve out, one relevant ground was that a
tort had been committed within the jurisdiction. That is no longer the case and
any authorities dealing with that head of jurisdiction should be treated with
caution.

Rix J's approach was approved *obiter* by the Court of Appeal in *ABCI v BFT*.[62] In   **19.97**
doing so, the Court of Appeal indicated their preference for the reasoning of
Rix J, to that of Steyn J in *Minster Investment Ltd v Hyundai Precision & Industry Co
Ltd*.[63] In dealing with Article 5(3), Steyn J had adopted an approach based upon

---

   59 [1999] QB 548.
   60 ibid.
   61 *Diamond v Bank of England* [1979] 1 Lloyd's Rep 335.
   62 [2003] EWCA Civ 205, [41]: '[Rix J] concluded that the mere receipt here of negligent
assurances conveyed by telephone from abroad, on which the recipient acted by releasing goods
abroad, did not constitute the commission by the person giving the assurances of an act here which
could ground jurisdiction in respect of the damage suffered abroad.' See also Kenneth Rokison QC,
sitting as a Deputy Judge of the Commercial Court, in *Alfred Dunhill v Diffusion Internationale
Moroquinerie De Prestige Sarl* [2002] 1 All ER (Comm) 950.
   63 [1988] Lloyd's Rep 621. Steyn J had advocated an approach to Art 5(3) based upon inquiry into
where 'in substance the cause of action arises, or with what place the tort is most closely connected'.

where in substance does the cause of action arise or with what place does the tort have the closest connections.

19.98   In *Newsat Holdings Ltd & Ors v Charles Zani*,[64] David Steel J was asked to proceed on the basis that *Domicrest* was wrongly decided. Having carefully surveyed the relevant authorities of this area, David Steel J was not prepared to find that *Domicrest* was wrongly decided.

19.99   There is no logical reason why a different approach should be adopted for a claim in deceit.

19.100   *Conspiracy*: A claim in conspiracy to commit a serious commercial fraud will involve the conduct of more than one person potentially taking place in more than one jurisdiction. The court must be wary of adopting a position in which jurisdiction is conditional upon *all* relevant events having taken place within the jurisdiction.[65] But, equally, it cannot adopt too liberal an approach for fear it runs the risk of accepting jurisdiction where there are no or no substantial factual connections with this jurisdiction.

19.101   In *Metall und Rostoff AG v Donaldson Lufkin & Jenrette Inc*,[66] the Court of Appeal was faced with *inter alia* a conspiracy claim in which some elements involved this jurisdiction and others did not. The question of permission to serve out was governed by the old service out procedure (i.e. the common law rules) and not under any of the Regulations or Conventions.[67] The Court of Appeal adopted the following (correct) approach:

> As the rule now stands it is plain that jurisdiction may be assumed only where (a) the claim is founded on a tort and either (b) the damage was sustained within the jurisdiction or (c) the damage resulted from an act committed within the jurisdiction. ... Condition (b) raises the question: what damage is referred to. It was argued for ACLI that since the draftsman had used the definite article and not simply referred to 'damage', it is necessary that all the damage should have been sustained within the jurisdiction. No authority was cited to support the suggestion that this is the correct construction of the Convention to which the rule gives effect and it could lead to an absurd result if there were no one place in which all the plaintiff's damage had been suffered. The judge rejected this argument and so do we. It is enough if some significant damage has been sustained in England. Condition (c) prompts the inquiry: what if damage has resulted from acts committed partly within and partly without the jurisdiction? This will often be the case where a series of acts, regarded by English law as tortious, are committed in an international context. It would not, we think, make sense to require all the acts to have been committed within the jurisdiction,

---

[64]   [2006] EWHC 342 (Comm).
[65]   This would be to take too narrow a position on jurisdiction.
[66]   [1990] 1 QB 391.
[67]   The provisions for permission to serve out were amended to mirror the wording in Art 5(3). Hence the Court of Appeal's views are instructive when examining the position under the Convention.

because again there might be no single jurisdiction where that would be so. But it would certainly contravene the spirit, and also we think the letter, of the rule if jurisdiction were assumed on the strength of some relatively minor or insignificant act having been committed here, perhaps fortuitously. In our view condition (c) requires the court to look at the tort alleged in a common sense way and ask whether damage has resulted from substantial and efficacious acts committed within the jurisdiction (whether or not other substantial and efficacious acts have been committed elsewhere): if the answer is yes, leave may (but of course need not) be given. But the defendants are, we think, right to insist that the acts to be considered must be those of the putative defendant, because the question at issue is whether the links between him and the English forum are such as to justify his being brought here to answer the plaintiffs' claim.[68]

(3) Unjust enrichment

This section will deal with the jurisdictional rules which apply to claims arising in unjust enrichment. There is a marked divergence in approach as between the Judgments Regulation and the common law in that the latter has now made specific provision for claims in restitution (which will include unjust enrichment) whereas the Regulation has not. **19.102**

(a) Under the Judgments Regulation

Claims in unjust enrichment are not expressly catered for in the Judgments Regulation or any of the Conventions. That leaves just three options open. **19.103**

- *Option (1).* The first is to recognize that, for whatever reason, claims in unjust enrichment are not considered to give rise to special connecting factors such as would justify a departure from the normal jurisdictional rule that a defendant is sued in his domicile (Article 2). That would be a perfectly sensible conclusion to reach. It may leave unjust enrichment lawyers smarting that unjust enrichment, unlike contract and tort, has not been given a special head of jurisdiction. But we can live with that.

- *Option (2).* The second option is to recognize the separate category claims that fall under the umbrella of unjust enrichment as a single group of claims and try to locate all such claims in one of the heads of special jurisdiction under Article 5.

- *Option (3).* The third and final option is to recognize that if the second option was viable, there would be no logical reason why this was not done expressly at least by the time the Judgments Regulation was drafted. This option seeks to make the best of a bad deal. It tries to squeeze *some* claims in unjust enrichment into one or other of the existing special heads of jurisdiction, recognizing that others simply will not go and may have to be dealt with in accordance with the first option.

It is probably fair to say that the present state of the law reflects option (3). **19.104**

---

[68] [1990] 1 WLR 391, 437B–G (Slade LJ).

19.105   (i) **Article 5(1)**   Article 5(1) has been examined above in the context of jurisdiction for contracts. It was seen then that it is far from clear which claims in unjust enrichment fall within Article 5(1). For the following summary, some of the propositions are supported by case law and others by first principles alone.

(a)   If the unjust enrichment claim arises out of a void contract, and both parties to that void contract accept it is void, the claim does not appear to fall within Article 5(1): see *Kleinwort Benson v Glasgow City Council*.[69] The majority of the House of Lords could not see how the relevant obligation in question could be said to be contractual in nature:

> Where . . . the claim is for money paid under a supposed contract which in law never existed, it seems impossible to say that the claim for the recovery of the money is based upon a particular contractual obligation.[70]

(b)   If there is a dispute between the parties as to whether the contract is void, the claim appears to remain one within Article 5(1): see *Agnew v Lansforsakringsbolagens AB*.[71]

(c)   If negotiations for the conclusion of a contract break down prior to any agreement having been reached, some applicable laws afford the injured party a right to recover losses by the other party's unjustifiable withdrawal. The ECJ has held that such a claim did not fall within Article 5(1): *Fonderie Officine Mecchaniche Tacconi SpA v Heinrich Wagner Sinto Maschinenfabrik GmbH*.[72]

(d)   It has been suggested that claims (i) for monies due under a frustrated contract and (ii) for recovery of purchase price for goods not delivered, are likely to be viewed as within Article 5(1).[73]

(e)   If the claim in unjust enrichment has no connection whatsoever to a real or supposed contract, Article 5(1) is unlikely to apply.

19.106   (ii) **Article 5(3)**   Article 5(3) has been examined in some detail above. It was there argued that Article 5(3) was not the fall-back head of jurisdiction for all claims which did not fall within Article 5(1). Such a view was based on a mis-reading of the *Kalfelis* judgment and was, in any event, at odds with the whole structure of the Judgments Regulation and the various Conventions which gave a primary role

---

[69]   [1999] 1 AC 153.

[70]   ibid, 167 per Lord Goff.

[71]   [2001] 1 AC 223 (HL). See also *Boss Group Ltd v Boss France SA* [1996] 4 All ER 970.

[72]   Case C-334/00 [2002] ECR I-7357. It is questionable whether *Agnew* is consistent with *Fonderie*. If the ratio of *Fonderie* is taken to be that pre-contractual obligations imposed by the general law are not within Art 5(1), then it is difficult to see how the House of Lords decision in *Agnew* can stand: see J Hill, *International Commercial Disputes in English Courts* (3rd edn, Hart Publishing, 2005), [5.6.18]–[5.6.20]. One possible distinguishing feature, as Hill recognizes, is that in *Agnew* ultimately a contract was formed whereas that is not the case with *Fonderie*.

[73]   Briggs and Rees, *Civil Jurisdiction and Judgments* (4th edn), para 2.130.

to the defendant's domicile and limited exceptions to be permitted when factually proven to provide clear connecting factors as between the claim and the jurisdiction.

It is suggested that insofar as any claims in unjust enrichment fall outside Article 5(1), **19.107** they will be dealt with under the general domicile rule. It is difficult to see any basis for a claim in unjust enrichment, a matter of strict liability, being treated as a 'wrong' in order to get under Article 5(3). That does not close the door to that other category of claims known as restitution for wrongs.

(b) At common law

In 2000, the Civil Procedure Rules were amended[74] and new heads of jurisdic- **19.108** tion were introduced. The one which is most obviously relevant to taking jurisdiction in respect of an unjust enrichment claim is CPR r 6.20(1)(15) which provides:

> (15) a claim is made for restitution where the defendant's alleged liability arises out of acts committed within the jurisdiction.

CPR Rule 6.20(15) is drafted in terms of 'restitution' which is generally consid- **19.109** ered to be wider in scope than unjust enrichment since it incorporates acts of wrongdoing as well.[75] There can be little doubt that in future, claims in unjust enrichment should be dealt with in accordance with this head of jurisdiction. One issue which remains a little uncertain, although the trend does appear to be in one direction, is the extent of the acts which need to take place within the jurisdiction in order to give rise to liability.

The phrase 'alleged liability arises out of acts committed within the jurisdiction' **19.110** had previously appeared in the earlier version of the Rules and had been subject to interpretation by Millett J in *ISC Technologies Ltd v Guerin*.[76] Millett J placed a very restrictive interpretation on this phrase, maintaining it requires that all acts necessary to impose liability take place within the jurisdiction. It is fair to say that this narrow interpretation did not receive universal approval.[77]

---

74 The Civil Procedure (Amendment) Rules 2000 (SI 2000/221).

75 Strictly, 'restitution' is the remedy which is available for claims in unjust enrichment or, on occasion, for wrongdoing.

76 Unreported, 7 December 1990, discussed in *ISC v Guerin* [1992] 2 Lloyd's Rep 430.

77 See ibid, 433 where Hoffmann J said that Millett J's interpretation was too narrow. Hoffmann J went on to say that the old RSC Order 11, rule 1(1)(t) was primarily designed for the case of a foreign entity which had not participated in the fraud but had been used as a receptacle for the proceeds. On this basis, he did not consider it a requirement that every act necessary to create liability should have been committed within the jurisdiction. Similarly, Knox J in *Polly Peck International plc v Nadir*, *The Independent*, 2 September 1992; G Panagopoulos, *Restitution in Private International Law* (Hart Publishing, 2000), 35–239; Briggs and Rees, *Civil Jurisdiction and Judgments* (4th edn), paras 4.50–4.51.

19.111 In *Nabb Brothers Ltd v Lloyds Bank International (Guernsey) Ltd,* Lawrence Collins J accepted that there must be some link between the acts committed within the jurisdiction and the defendant. He went on to say:

> In my judgment, if the principal fraudster gives instructions for money in London to be paid abroad to a knowing recipient, it is not necessary for jurisdictional purposes that the recipient should have done anything in London for CPR Rule 6.20(14)[78] to apply. In most cases the principal fraudster will be subject to the jurisdiction under another head, and there will be jurisdiction over the accessory party under the necessary and proper party provision of CPR Rule 6.20(3). The jurisdiction is not exorbitant, because in each case the claimant will have to show as against the foreign defendant that England is clearly the appropriate forum.

(4) Equity

19.112 In this section, the purpose is to examine the jurisdictional rules which potentially apply to the varying types of equitable claim. Included in this section are claims relating to (i) knowing receipt, (ii) constructive trusts, (iii) dishonest assistance, and (iv) equitable proprietary interests. Once again, it will become clear that the English common law rules more specifically cater for these claims than the Judgments Regulation.

19.113 Finally, the approach adopted below is very much influenced by the desire of the House of Lords, as expressed in *The Spiliada* that jurisdictional issues should not be unduly complicated. To that end, we perhaps need not spend an inordinate amount of time trying to determine whether a knowing receipt properly falls within either CPR r 6.20(14) or (15), particularly where the same connecting factors appear to be relied upon.

(a) Under the Judgments Regulation[79]

19.114 There are no express clauses in the Judgments Regulation which deal with the jurisdictional issues arising from claims in equity. Nor have we had a case which greatly assists in suggesting a way forward. Much of what is said below, therefore, is based upon principle and is necessarily a little tentative.

19.115 If the claim in equity arises out of a pre-existing fiduciary relationship, where one party has voluntarily assumed obligations to another, then there is an obvious and powerful analogy with contractual claims (as defined by *Handte*) under Article 5(1). Such claims would include a director–company relationship (which features highly in commercial fraud work), principal–agent, and solicitor–client.[80] Included

---

[78] CPR r 6.20(14) contains the same phrase 'liability arises out of acts committed within the jurisdiction'.

[79] T M Yeo, 'Constructive Trustees and the Brussels Convention' (2001) 117 LQR 560–5.

[80] Briggs and Rees, *Civil Jurisdiction and Judgments* (4th edn), para 2.152.

in this category would be Class 1 constructive trusts as defined by Millett LJ in *Paragon Finance plc v DB Thakerar*.[81] To assist the court's process in determining how best to deal with equitable claims, it may be necessary to identify better the core elements of the particular claim—in other words, strip away the title of the claim and look underneath. This is what the Court of Appeal appeared to demand in *Grupo Torras SA v Al Sabah*[82] where it took a constructive trust claim and broke it down to see whether its underlying issues were based upon vindication of property rights, unjust enrichment or wrongdoing. That is an approach which should be employed more and more, particularly in the conflicts of laws area.

If the claim in equity arises out of an event which is entirely independent of any **19.116** relationship based upon voluntarily assumed obligations, such a claim is more likely to be characterized as tortious for the purposes of Article 5(3). So, claims included in this category are likely to be the knowing recipient, the dishonest assistant, and Millett LJ's Class 2 constructive trustees.

The Court of Appeal's approach in *Casio Computer Co Ltd v Eugen Kaiser*[83] is **19.117** illustrative of the problems of language in this area[84] but is nevertheless instructive generally of the approach to adopt. The facts can be summarized as follows:

- Claimant C employed S as its manager, who was entrusted by C to invest some US$30m.
- T, one of S's accomplices, obtained control over the funds by forged powers of attorney.
- T transferred the monies through several US accounts and eventually into a London account held in the name of C but having S and T as its signatories.
- T transferred US$25m to an account under his (T's) sole control and from there to an account held in an Isle of Man company name, O, in London pursuant to an investment agreement. K was the President and controlling mind of O.
- The monies were transferred from O's London account to its Isle of Man account from where it was dissipated via several countries.
- Anthony Mann QC, sitting as Deputy High Court Judge, held that a constructive trust claim based upon dishonest assistance was a matter 'relating to tort, delict or quasi-delict' for the purposes of Article 5(3) and that the harmful event alleged against K, a Spanish domiciliary, occurred in England.
- The issue for the appeal was: is a constructive trust claim based on dishonest assistance a matter 'relating to tort. . . .' for the purposes of Article 5(3)?

---

81 [1999] 1 All ER 400.
82 [2001] Lloyd's Rep Bank 36, 62.
83 [2001] EWCA Civ 661.
84 I.e. the reference to a constructive trust claim for dishonest assistance liability.

19.118 Tuckey LJ, delivering the lead judgment, agreed with Anthony Mann QC's judgment that a constructive trust claim based on dishonest assistance was a matter which could fall within Article 5(3). In reaching this conclusion, Tuckey LJ was influenced by the CA's reasoning in *Grupo Torras* and in particular its willingness to recognize dishonest assistance as equitable wrongdoing akin to tortious wrongdoing.

19.119 In *Dexter Ltd (In Administrative Receivership) v Edwina Harley*[85] the facts can be summarized as follows:

- Claimant D alleged he had suffered substantial loss as a result of breaches of fiduciary duty by a former director, H's son.

- D claimed money wrongfully misappropriated from it had passed through a Guernsey account in the name of H, such as to make her a constructive trustee for knowing receipt or dishonest assistance (more accurately—such as to make her liable to account for knowing receipt or dishonest assistance).

- At all times, H was domiciled in Spain—none of the acts alleged against her took place in this jurisdiction.

- Counsel conceded that a constructive trust-type claim, with its connotation of wrongdoing, would fall within Article 5(3) even though the House of Lords in *Kleinwort Benson v Glasgow City Council* had held that a claim in unjust enrichment would not. Lloyd J agreed with the concession made.

- The judge then went on to consider whether the facts showed that the harmful event took place inside the jurisdiction. He found they did not. Having considered matters such as the removal of monies within the jurisdiction, Lloyd J went on:

  > Although those matters are clearly part of the chain of events which has to be pleaded and proved in order to establish liability against the Defendant, I cannot accept that it is sufficient, for the purposes of article 5(3), to point to acts within the jurisdiction which have nothing to do with the Defendant, and the proof of which, by themselves, would not establish liability on the part of the Defendant. In principle it seems to me that, in applying the concept of the harmful event to a constructive trust claim based on knowing receipt or dishonest assistance, it is not relevant to show that the original breach of trust or fiduciary duty by someone other than the Defendant took place in the jurisdiction if nothing which involved the Defendant occurred within the jurisdiction. The harmful event must, in my judgment, be a harmful event on the part of the Defendant, whether it is the act or omission of the Defendant from which the harm results, or the direct result of such an act or omission through its impact on the Claimant.[86]

- His Lordship concluded that the only relevant acts of the defendant took place in Alderney and so there was no jurisdiction under Article 5(3).

---

[85] *The Times*, 2 April 2001 (Ch D); transcript at [19].
[86] *Dexter Ltd (In Administrative Receivership) v Edwina Harley* (2001) unrep, at [19].

- It would appear as though Lloyd J was content to have the knowing receipt claims dealt with as falling within Article 5(3). There was no real separate examination on this issue. It falls foul of the attempts at English common law to characterize the claim as arising in unjust enrichment. It is unlikely to be the last word on this issue.

(b) At common law

The following heads of jurisdiction are the most likely to apply to equitable claims of the sort identified above: **19.120**

- CPR r 6.20(14): 'A claim is made for a remedy against the defendant as constructive trustee where the defendant's alleged liability arises out of acts committed within the jurisdiction.'
- CPR r 6.20(15): 'A claim is made for restitution where the defendant's alleged liability arises out of acts committed within the jurisdiction.'

(i) Knowing receipt claims   Chapter 5 on knowing receipt has set out the various arguments as to the nature of this claim. It will be recalled there is a groundswell of academic opinion that such a claim is based upon unjust enrichment whereas recent case law appears to be resiling from that position, emphasizing the wrongful nature of the receipt. It will also be recalled that traditionally, but wrongly, a defendant liable for knowing receipt is often described as a constructive trustee. Lord Millett has convincingly argued against the use of such terminology.   **19.121**

Each of these matters is mentioned here because, in the context of the conflict of laws, where it is important to be willing to adopt a more flexible approach to the issue of characterization, these matters may push this claim into one or other of the heads of jurisdiction.   **19.122**

Under the old head of jurisdiction for liability as a constructive trustee (RSC Order 11 r 1(1)(t)), the initial view was taken by the courts that all the acts relevant to the defendant's liability had to take place within the jurisdiction: see Millett J in *ISC Technologies Ltd v Guerin*.[87] There was a danger such a restrictive view would exclude a knowing receipt claim where the receipt of monies happens to have taken place outside of the jurisdiction. The courts came to the view that this was too restrictive an interpretation. It sufficed if only a substantial part of the acts took place inside the jurisdiction, even if other substantial acts took place outside it: *ISC Technologies Ltd v Guerin*.[88]   **19.123**

---

[87] Unreported, 7 December 1990.
[88] [1992] 2 Lloyd's Rep 430 (not to be confused with the earlier unreported decision of the same name); *Polly Peck International Plc v Nadir* unreported, 17 March 1993 (CA).

19.124 More recently, in *Nabb Brothers Ltd v Lloyds Bank International (Guernsey) Ltd*,[89] it was alleged that a managing director of company X had misappropriated assets from company X, transferred them into his personal account in London and then on to a Guernsey trust held by a professional trustee, L. Company X sought a declaration that L held certain funds on trust for it. L applied to set aside the master's order for service out.

19.125 Lawrence Collins J held that the Guernsey trust was subject to Guernsey law and jurisdiction and that the company had not shown that England was the natural forum. He went on to say, obiter, that the company's claim fell within CPR r 6.20(14) and (15) and that if a principal fraudster gave instructions for money in London to be transferred abroad to a knowing recipient, it was not necessary for jurisdictional purposes for the recipient to have done anything in London for CPR r 6.20(14) to apply.

19.126 Briggs, writing about the old rule (RSC Ord 11 r 1(1)(t)) and prior to the decision in *Nabb* came to a pretty similar conclusion:

> Where the liability is based on receipt with the necessary mens rea, it is likely to be sufficient that receipt took place in England. Where receipt by the defendant took place out of the jurisdiction, but the breach of trust took place by means of acts done at least partially within the jurisdiction, this may still be sufficient.[90]

19.127 In the premises, it is clear that a knowing receipt will fall within CPR r 6.20(14) and, it is submitted, CPR r 6.20(15). It is unlikely to make any practical difference under which head the claim proceeds.

19.128 **(ii) Constructive trusts**   CPR r 6.20(14) is the obvious starting point for a claim against a defendant as a constructive trustee. There is unlikely to be any real distinction, for jurisdictional purposes, between constructive trust claims and claims based upon knowing receipt. It is accepted, of course, that the latter is only a claim in personam but equally if the assets are retained then the claimant can call for their return, as would be the case under a constructive trust.

19.129 It is also likely to fall under CPR 6.20(15) being a claim for restitution by wrongs, although this is unlikely to lead to a conclusion on jurisdiction different from that arising under CPR r 6.20(14).

19.130 **(iii) Dishonest assistance**   Such a claim will also fall to be governed by CPR r 6.20(14) and (15). Whilst it is accepted that the language of constructive trusteeship is inappropriate when applied to a claim in dishonest assistance, there is no doubting that a defendant liable for such a claim is often called a constructive

---

[89] [2005] EWHC 405 (Ch) (Lawrence Collins J).
[90] Briggs, 'Jurisdiction under the Traditional Rules' in F Rose (ed), *Restitution and Conflict of Laws* (Mansfield Press, 1995), 62.

trustee. Further, there is much force in the argument that dishonest assistance should be characterized as a restitution for a wrongdoing claim. On that basis, CPR r 6.20(15) would be a suitable head of jurisdiction. The approach to be adopted can be gained by recalling Briggs' observations when dealing with the old RSC Ord 11 r 1(1)(t):

> Where the dishonest assistance in a breach of trust took place by means of acts done at least partially in England, the case should also fall within [RSC Ord 11 rule 1(1)(t)]. Once again, it will be necessary to identify with some care the acts of the defendant (and of the defaulting fiduciary, if the liability of the defendant is based upon such acts); and if these are substantially located within England, the case will fall within the sub-rule.[91]

(iv) Equitable proprietary claims Such claims arise where an existing trustee has **19.131** misappropriated trust assets and transferred them to a third party who does not have the knowledge of the underlying events to be personally liable for knowing receipt. Such a claim arose on the facts of *Nabb Brothers v Lloyds Bank* (see above).

Lawrence Collins J stated, obiter, that such claims are often described as being **19.132** claims for constructive trusts and so fell within CPR r 6.20(14). [92]

His Lordship then went on to consider whether such a claim also fell within CPR **19.133** r 6.20(15) as a restitutionary claim. He noted this might depend on how one understood 'restitution' and whether it was limited to unjust enrichment claims or extended beyond that.[93] He analysed the conclusions reached in *Foskett v McKeown*, to the effect that unjust enrichment has nothing to do with proprietary claims and noted the conclusions drawn from this case by notable commentators, such as Goff and Jones, *The Law of Restitution*, Burrows, 'Quadrating Restitution and Unjust Enrichment: A Matter of Principle'[94] and Burrows, *The Law of Restitution*.[95] Lawrence Collins J:

> But there is a powerful view that, although restitutionary claims are normally based on unjust enrichment, that does [not][96] exclude from the scope of the law of

---

91 Briggs, 'Jurisdiction under Traditional Rules' in Rose (ed), *Restitution and the Conflict of Laws*, 62.

92 Lawrence Collins J in *Nabb Brothers Ltd v Lloyds Bank International* [2005] EWHC 405 (Ch) [72]–[73] was influenced by Sir Peter Millett's observations in 'Restitution and Constructive Trusts' in Cornish, Nolan, O'Sullivan and Virgo (eds), *Restitution: Past, Present & Future: Essays in Honour of Gareth Jones* (Art Publishing, 1998), 199 at 200: '[W]e use [the expression 'constructive trust'] not only to describe the trust itself but also to describe a particular proprietary remedy, and even as shorthand for saying that proprietary relief is available in equity.'

93 It is submitted that no one seriously argues that restitution is limited to unjust enrichment alone. What is said is that 'restitution' is simply the remedy for unjust enrichment but it is accepted by most unjust enrichment lawyers, including Professor Birks, that the remedy of restitution may be available other than for unjust enrichment claims.

94 [2000] RLR 257, 268.

95 (2nd edn, Butterworths, 2002).

96 The text in the official transcript makes no sense without the addition of 'not' in this sentence.

restitution proprietary equitable claims: Birks, *Misnomer* in *Restitution, Past, Present & Future*[97] ... Birks, *Unjust Enrichment* (2003), p.55. See also Virgo, *Principles of the Law of Restitution*[98] ... *Macmillan Inc v Bishopsgate Investment Trust plc* [1996] 1 WLR 387 (CA) involved an equitable proprietary claim to shares. The Court of Appeal did not disagree with the submission that the claim was restitutionary in nature, but it did not follow that the conflict of laws rules relating to restitution were applicable to the issue in the case, namely who had the better title to the shares in question.

Having recognized the issue did not arise for final determination, the judge expressed his tentative view that an equitable proprietary claim of the type in *Nabbs* was likely to come within the ambit of CPR r 6.20(15) as well.

---

[97] Cornish et al (eds), *Restitution: Past, Present and Future* 1, 22 where Birks refers to *Macmillan Inc v Bishopsgate Investment Trust plc* [1996] 1 All ER 585, [1996] BCC 453, CA and says: 'What matters here is only that the case illustrates a claim which is indeed restitutionary but which not only does not arise from unjust enrichment but does on analysis arise from an event in the fourth category, namely the receipt of a *res* which belongs in equity to another.'

[98] (1st edn), 13; Virgo has updated this section in his second edition (11–17) to record the House of Lords' acceptance of the argument that unjust enrichment is not relevant to proprietary claims.

20

CHOICE OF LAW

A. Introduction

This chapter is concerned with the question of what law applies to the substantive **20.01** issues in a dispute. The fact that the English court may have taken jurisdiction over the substantive law should not be misinterpreted as implying that English law must be the applicable law. In many cases, it will not be.

As with the previous chapter on jurisdiction, it is not the function of this chapter **20.02** to give a detailed account of all aspects of the English conflict of laws rules with regard to choice of law. Resort must be made to the specialist texts for a complete account of the law.[1] Instead, this chapter will focus on those particular issues which are of greater concern to a commercial fraud litigator, whilst ensuring an understanding of how those issues fit in the larger picture.

20.03 This chapter will provide a broad examination of the three relevant codes, being the Rome Convention concerned with the law of contracts, the Private International (Miscellaneous Provisions) Act 1995, concerned with the law of torts, and the Regulation 'Rome II' which supersedes the 1995 Act from 11 January 2009. Whilst these codes may contain certain provisions which are controversial, and in the case of Rome II, still to be worked out and understood, it will be seen that, in general, they provide a reasonably clear road-map to determining the relevant applicable law for claims in contract and tort.

20.04 The same cannot be said, however, when it comes to identifying the relevant choice of law rules for claims in equity and unjust enrichment. Immediately, the same difficulties start to emerge as can be seen in Chapter 19 on jurisdiction. It is here where resort to the doctrine of characterization really starts to become important as many issues need to be resolved as a matter of first principles.

B. Choice of Law for Contractual Claims: The Rome Convention

(1) Preliminary issues

(a) Introduction

20.05 In 1969, the European Community began work on the Rome Convention on the Law Applicable to Contractual Obligations. This was very much in the wake of the success of the Brussels Convention on matters of jurisdiction and the recognition and enforcement of judgments from contracting states. The aim was to try and produce uniform rules governing the question of choice of law for contractual obligations.

20.06 The Rome Convention was concluded on 19 June 1980[2] and initially applied to the then ten member states.[3] It was extended to Spain and Portugal in 1992[4] and to Austria, Finland and Sweden in 1996.[5]

---

[1] *Dicey, Morris & Collins, The Conflict of Laws* (14th edn, Thomson/Sweet and Maxwell, 2006); J Hill, *International Commercial Disputes in English Courts* (3rd edn, Hart Publishing, 2005); Fawcett, Harris and Bridge, *International Sale of Goods in the Conflict of* Laws (Oxford University Press, 2005); Rose (ed), *Restitution and the Conflict of Laws* (Mansfield Press, 1995); T M Yeo, *Choice of Law for Equitable Doctrines* (Oxford University Press, 2004). For an excellent summary of the law on choice of law issues, see A Briggs, *The Conflict of Laws* (2nd edn, Clarendon Press, 2008).

[2] [1980] OJ L266/1.

[3] Belgium, Denmark, France, Germany, Greece, Ireland, Italy, Luxembourg, Netherlands and the United Kingdom.

[4] The Funchal Convention [1992] OJ L333/1.

[5] The Convention on the Accession of Austria, Finland and Sweden 1996.

The intention is that all new member states will sign up for the Rome Convention **20.07** and it would appear likely that the Rome Convention will in the near future become a Regulation.[6]

(b) Enacted into English law by the Contracts (Applicable Law) Act 1990

The Rome Convention on the Law Applicable to Contractual Obligations (the **20.08** Rome Convention) was enacted into English law by the Contracts (Applicable Law) Act 1990.

English law gave effect to the later accessions of Spain and Portugal and subse- **20.09** quently Austria, Finland and Sweden by the Contracts (Applicable Law) Act 1990 (Amendment) Orders 1994 and 2000.[7]

(c) Matters of interpretation

The courts can look to the *Report on the Law Applicable to Contractual Obligations* **20.10** by Giuliano and Lagarde[8] for guidance on interpreting provisions of the Convention.

As from 2004, the ECJ has had jurisdiction to give rulings on matters of **20.11** interpretation.[9]

In order to ensure as far as possible a uniform approach to the question of inter- **20.12** pretation, Article 18 of the Convention provides:

> In the interpretation and application of the preceding uniform rules, regard shall be had to their international character and to the desirability of achieving uniformity in their interpretation and application.

This is simply a codified form of the approach to be expected in all aspects of choice of law. There is no room for peculiar domestic concepts or requirements preventing a more internationalist approach, where such an internationalist approach might assist in minimizing the differences of approach between nations on matters such as what amounts to a contract.

(d) Applies to all contracts after 1 April 1991

The Act applies to all contracts made after 1 April 1991 and, save for some minor **20.13** exceptions, effectively abolishes the English common law rules on choice of law for contracts. The common law rules, as laudable an achievement as they may have

---

⁶ See the European Commission's Green Paper: COM/2002/0654 final. As a Regulation, it will thus have legal effect in member states without the need for a local Act to be passed.
⁷ SI 1994/1900 and 2000/1825.
⁸ [1980] OJ C282/1 (hereinafter 'the Giuliano and Lagarde Report').
⁹ There is a protocol, called the Brussels Protocol, which would give a discretionary right to the English appellate courts to seek a ruling from the ECJ: [1989] OJ L48/17.

been and as lamentable as their replacement might be viewed,[10] will not be examined in this book.[11]

20.14 The application of the Rome Convention by the English courts is not limited by concepts such as domicile, residence or place of performance. Any party appearing before the English court with a qualifying contractual dispute will be dealt with in accordance with the provisions of the Rome Convention.

20.15 The English court will also apply the Rome Convention irrespective of whether the parties have chosen the law of a contracting state or a non-contracting state.[12]

20.16 Although the highly respected Dr F A Mann suggested it might be possible to contract out of the Rome Convention,[13] the better view is that this is not possible.[14] It has been considered whether, following on from this conclusion, the Rome Convention may well represent an exception to the usual English law position that foreign law must be expressly pleaded and proved as a fact for an English court to take notice of it.[15] It is suggested not, given the Rome Convention expressly excludes matters of evidence and procedure.[16] But even if the judge were permitted to insist on the matter being dealt with under the Rome Convention, it remains to be seen whether the court will insist on the parties adducing foreign

---

[10] F A Mann (1991) 107 LQR 353: 'The Act replaces one of the great achievements of the English judiciary during the last 140 years or so, an achievement which produced an effective private international law of contracts, was recognised and followed in practically the whole world and has not at any time or anywhere led to dissatisfaction or to demand for reform.'

[11] For a detailed treatment of the English common law rules on choice of law for contracts, it is necessary to revert to *Dicey & Morris on the Conflict of Laws* (11th edn, Stevens & Sons, 1987), ch 32. The most recent edition of the text does not carry a detailed commentary on the common law.

[12] Article 2: 'Any law specified by this Convention shall be applied whether or not it is the law of a Contracting State.'

[13] Mann (1991) 107 LQR 353.

[14] See *Dicey, Morris & Collins* (14th edn), para 32-044; Hogan (1992) 108 LQR 12; North, *Essays in Private International Law* (Clarendon Press, 1993), 171.

[15] For the general rule, see *Dicey, Morris & Collins* (14th edn), Rule 18; R Fentiman, *Foreign Law in English Courts* (Oxford University Press, 1998). Both *Cheshire and North on Private International Law* (13th edn, Oxford University Press, 1999), 545 and Fawcett, Harris and Bridge, *International Sale of Goods in the Conflict of Laws*, [13.19]–[13.20] suggest that an English judge could insist on the application of foreign law in a contractual matter without the parties having raised it themselves in their pleading. The reality is, of course, that nothing quite so dramatic will ensue. A judge may well have the power under the Act to raise the foreign law issue with the parties—perhaps during a case management conference prior to trial. If the judge wishes to pursue the matter, he will simply give directions for the service of foreign law evidence, either by both parties or by a court-appointed expert, and give the parties the opportunity to reflect their stance on the foreign law issues in their pleadings ahead of trial. That way, the mandatory aspect of the Convention is adhered to and matters of evidence and procedure remain, as they should, the domain of the English court.

[16] Rome Convention, Art 1(2)(h). See *Dicey, Morris & Collins* (14th edn), para 9-011 for a more detailed discussion; C Morse, 'Conflict of Laws' in *Benjamin's Sale of Goods*, ch 25, esp [25-029].

law evidence or whether it will simply adopt the assumption that foreign law is the same as English law unless and until proved otherwise.

(2) What is included in the Convention?

Article 1(1) provides: **20.17**

> The rules of this Convention shall apply to contractual obligations in any situation involving a choice between the laws of different countries.

(a) Contractual obligations

There is little or no point seeking to obtain guidance on what amounts to 'con- **20.18** tractual obligations' under the Rome Convention by reference to the Judgments Regulation and/or various jurisdiction conventions.

First, Article 5(1) of the Judgments Regulation is concerned with matters 'relat- **20.19** ing to a contract' and not 'contractual obligations'. The decision of the ECJ in *Jakob Handte GmbH v Traitements*[17] was thus concerned with entirely different wording.

Secondly, there is no actual requirement that there be uniformity in approach to **20.20** the characterization of an issue as contractual as between the jurisdiction and choice of law conventions. This point was made by Advocate General Jacobs in *Jakob Handte*:

> It is above all important to stress that the jurisdiction rules of the Convention deal solely with the issue of jurisdiction. They do not affect the classification of the action for such purposes as determining the applicable principles of liability or deciding what limitation period applies. A court that acquires jurisdiction under Article 5(1) is not prevented by the Convention from proceeding with the action on the basis that it is delictual and a court that acquires jurisdiction under Article 5(3) is not prevented by the Convention from proceeding with the action on the basis that it is contractual.[18]

This is another good illustration of the flexible approach to characterization of issues and claims, which may well differ for jurisdictional and choice of law purposes.

What is clear is that the reference to 'contractual obligations' must be interpreted **20.21** such as to include the consequences of contracts being found to be void. Article 10(1)(e) expressly provides that the Rome Convention is to govern 'the consequences of nullity of the contract'. Although the UK chose not to sign up to this particular provision, it must be questionable whether this can have any impact on the definition of 'contractual obligations', as opposed to making it clear that should the issue which has arisen relate to the consequences of a contract being a

---

[17] Case C-26/91, [1992] ECR I-3967.
[18] ibid, para 24 of Opinion.

nullity that is not something the English court determines by reference to the Rome Convention.

20.22 Given the need to apply an autonomous meaning to this phrase, it may well be that claims for negligent misstatement, which would traditionally be categorized as tortious in English domestic law would be considered contractual for the purposes of the Rome Convention.[19]

20.23 A further possibility, to be discussed in greater detail in para 20.172 below, is whether equitable duties arising out of a contractual relationship may well qualify as falling within this phrase.[20]

(b) 'Choice'

20.24 This is satisfied if any element of the contract contains a foreign element, is located in a foreign jurisdiction or governed by a foreign law.[21] So, if one party is resident abroad, or the place of performance was to take place abroad or simply that two parties, from the same jurisdiction, have chosen to subject their contractual relationship to the laws of the foreign state, that will generally suffice for the purposes of establishing a 'choice'.

20.25 Any concerns that parties may deliberately subject their contractual relationship to a foreign law that has no objective connection with the contract, in order to circumvent mandatory rules of another country with which the contract does have objective connections, will be dealt with under the appropriate provisions dealing with restrictions or limitations on the freedom of choice.[22]

(3) What is excluded from the Convention?

20.26 Article 1(2) sets out those matters which are expressly excluded from the ambit of the Convention. The more relevant or important exclusions for present purposes include:

- bills of exchange, cheques, promissory notes or other negotiable instruments;[23]
- governance issues arising out of company law including the personal liability of officers and members for the corporate obligations;

---

[19] Fawcett, Harris and Bridge, *International Sale of Goods in the Conflict of Laws,* [13.15].

[20] It will be seen that the generally accepted choice of law rule for claims in unjust enrichment or equity which arise out of or are closely associated with a pre-existing relationship is the law governing that relationship. If the relationship is contractual, then this will mean such law as determined by the Rome Convention.

[21] The Giuliano and Lagarde Report, 10.

[22] See Rome Convention, Art 3(3).

[23] It is for the *lex fori* to decide whether any given instrument is a negotiable instrument and if it is whether the relevant obligation with which the dispute is concerned is derives from the negotiable status of the instrument. If so, it is excluded: see the Giuliano and Lagarde Report, 11.

- questions of authority as between principal and agent[24] and as between entity and a company;
- formal constitution of trusts and the relationship between settlors, trustees and beneficiaries;
- subject to Article 14, evidence and procedure.

Article 1(3) expressly excludes contracts of insurance (but not re-insurance)[25] cov- **20.27** ering risks situated within a member state of the EEC.[26]

(4) Freedom of choice: Article 3

Party autonomy to choose the law governing the contractual relationship is at the **20.28** heart of the Rome Convention. Article 3, which is headed 'Freedom of Choice', provides as follows:

1. A contract shall be governed by the law chosen by the parties. The choice must be expressed or demonstrated with reasonable certainty by the terms of the contract or the circumstances of the case. By their choice the parties can select the law applicable to the whole or a part only of the contract.

2. The parties may at any time agree to subject the contract to a law other than that which previously governed it, whether as a result of an earlier choice under this Article or of other provisions of this Convention. Any variation by the parties of the law to be applied made after the conclusion of the contract shall not prejudice its formal validity under Article 9 or adversely affect the rights of third parties.

3. The fact that the parties have chosen a foreign law, whether or not accompanied by the choice of a foreign tribunal, shall not, where all the other elements relevant to the situation at the time of the choice are connected with one country only, prejudice the application of rules of the law of that country which cannot be derogated from by contract, hereinafter called 'mandatory rules'.[27]

4. The existence and validity of the consent of the parties as to the choice of the applicable law shall be determined in accordance with the provisions of Articles 8, 9 and 11.

---

[24] The exclusion is limited to questions of authority only.

[25] Art 1(4).

[26] It is worth noting that Art 1(3) talks in terms of member states and not contracting states.

[27] For an understanding as to what amounts to a 'mandatory rule': see Tillman, 'The Relationship between Party Autonomy and the Mandatory Rules in the Rome Convention' [2002] JBL 45; McLean and Beevers, *Morris, The Conflict of Laws* (6th edn, Thomson/Sweet and Maxwell, 2005), para 13-016: 'Mandatory rules may serve many purposes. They may relate to the socio-economic policies of states, for example, in the field of competition or "anti-trust" law; exchange control designed to protect the national economy or its currency; laws designed to protect the environment. Or they may seek to regulate the contents of private contracts, requiring the inclusion of certain types of term, or prohibiting exclusion or exemption clauses or the imposition of unreasonable sanctions in penalty clauses. They may be designed to protect the interests of those seen as economically weak, such as workers (with rules as to health and safety at work and to safeguards from unfair dismissal) or consumers (with rules designed to help them in disputes with suppliers of goods and services). Or they may serve more general interests such as the proper administration of justice or the uniform regulation of an international industry such as aviation.'

(a) *Express choice*

20.29   Given the prominence accorded to party autonomy, under Article 3(1) the parties are free expressly to choose a law to govern their contractual relationship.[28]

20.30   Whether or not there has been an express choice of law is unlikely, in most circumstances, to give rise to much debate. However, it has been suggested that where the matter is in doubt, there is some uncertainty as to the appropriate law to apply to resolve that doubt.[29] Having rejected the putative applicable law approach, *Dicey, Morris & Collins* suggests[30] that a 'broad Convention-based approach' be adopted which is not dependent on satisfying any particular legal system's rules on implied terms.

(b) *Implied choice of law*

20.31   In the event that the parties have not expressly chosen a law, Article 3(1) provides for the courts to determine whether there has been an implied choice of law 'demonstrated with reasonable certainty by the terms of the contract or the circumstances of the case'.

20.32   Given there are other provisions from which a court might form an objective view of a law having a close connection with the contract without having to form the view that the parties must have chosen that law, it is important that the search for an implied choice of law remains exactly that—a search for an actual choice of law by the parties to be implied from the circumstances. That is not the same as simply identifying a law that has a close connection with the contract.[31]

20.33   Fortunately, the Giuliano and Lagarde Report[32] provides some guidance as to the type of factors the court can take into account in assessing whether there has been an implied choice of law. These include:

- the use of terminology or a standard form related to a particular law;
- a choice of law clause in a previous course of dealing or in a related transaction between the parties;[33]

---

[28] *Renvoi* is excluded: Art 15. A brief summary of what is meant by *renvoi* is given in Chapter 18, The Conflict of Laws: An Overview. The choice therefore is of the domestic law of the chosen legal system. See A Briggs, 'On Drafting Agreements on Choice of Law' [2003] LMCLQ 389 and A Briggs, *Agreements on Jurisdiction and Choice of Law* (Oxford University Press, 2008).

[29] The Giuliano and Lagarde Report provides no guidance on the issue. See Fawcett, Harris and Bridge, *International Sale of Goods in the Conflict of Laws*, [10.28]–[10.35].

[30] *Dicey, Morris & Collins* (14th edn), para 32-080.

[31] See J Hill, 'Choice of Law in Contract under the Rome Convention: the Approach of the UK Courts' (2004) 53 ICLQ 325.

[32] The Giuliano and Lagarde Report, 17.

[33] See *Kloeckner & Co AG v Gatoil Overseas Inc* [1990] 1 Lloyd's Rep 177 (a common law case).

- an arbitration[34] or choice of court clause.[35]

20.34 So the use of a standard Lloyd's policy for a re-insurance contract in *Tiernan v Magen Insurance*[36] was sufficient for Longmore J to imply a choice of English law.[37]

20.35 In *Tryg Baltica International (UK) Ltd v Boston Compania de Seguros SA*[38] Cooke J stated:

> The only possible rival contender for applicable law is Argentina, because of the connection with the underlying policies but it appears to me that the most obvious inference from all the circumstances in which the Reinsurances were written is that the parties must have intended English law to apply. The reinsurance contracts were . . . made in England, in the London market. The presentations were made to Tryg in London, the slips were scratched in London and the wordings were agreed in London on London market forms. The certificates of reinsurance were issued in London by HSBC, operating under the facility agreement and superseded the off-slips which had been scratched by Tryg. All the contractual and relevant pre-contractual documentation is expressed in English. In my judgment Tryg are correct in saying that the reinsurance contracts are governed by English law under the terms of Article 3(1) of the Rome Convention (implied choice of English law) or under Article 4(2) of the same Convention on the basis of Tryg's central administration being in this country.

20.36 In *Aeolian Shipping SA v ISS Machinery Services Ltd*[39] the claimants had supplied a turbo-charger to be installed on the defendant's vessel. That contract was expressly governed by Japanese law. The turbo-charger failed and the claimants sought replacement parts. A dispute arose between the parties as to who would pay for the parts and the cost and expenses of surveying the turbo-charger. In order to persuade the claimants to supply the spare parts, the defendants' P&I Club gave an undertaking in the following terms:

> In consideration of your refraining from arresting the Ship . . . we hereby undertake to pay to you forthwith upon your first demand such sums as may be adjudged to be due to you in respect of the Claim,[40] interest thereon and costs from [the defendants]

---

[34] *Egon Oldendorff v Libera Corp (No 1)* [1995] 2 Lloyd's Rep 64 (incorporation of English arbitration clause led to English law applying); *Egon Oldendorff v Libera Corp (No 2)* [1996] 1 Lloyd's Rep 380.

[35] *Egon Oldendorff v Libera Corp (No 1)* [1995] 2 Lloyd's Rep 64; *Egon Oldendorff v Libera Corp (No 2)* [1996] 1 Lloyd's Rep 380.

[36] [2000] IL Pr 517, 522–3.

[37] See also, pre-1990 Act, *Amin Rasheed Shipping Corp v Kuwait Insurance* [1984] AC 50; *King v Brandywise Reinsurance Co Ltd* [2004] EWHC 1033 (Comm).

[38] [2004] EWHC 1186 (Comm).

[39] [2001] EWCA Civ 1162, [2001] 2 Lloyd's Rep 641 (CA).

[40] The 'Claim' was defined as the claim for payment for goods and materials supplied to the ship for her use referred to in the claimant's invoice dated 27 October 1999.

by a final judgment of the English High Court of Justice or by judgment on appeal therefrom . . .

And for the consideration aforesaid:

1 . . .
2 We confirm that . . . [the defendants] . . . agree that the Claim shall be determined by reference to English law and shall be submitted to the exclusive jurisdiction of the English High Court of Justice. We hereby undertake to instruct English solicitors, within fourteen days of your written request to do so, to accept service of claim form or other initiating process on behalf of . . . [the defendants] . . . and to require the said Solicitors to confirm to you that they are authorized to accept service on behalf of . . . [the defendants].

20.37   The claimants commenced an action for the cost of the spare parts. The defendants counterclaimed based upon the turbo-charger having failed and argued that the undertaking contained an implied choice of English law. It was argued that this represented a variation of the Japanese choice of law clause in the turbo-charger contract. Morison J and the Court of Appeal rejected that argument:

> 16. The circumstances which may be taken into account when deciding whether or not the parties have made an implied choice of law under art.3 of the Rome Convention (whether by initial choice or subsequent change) range more widely in certain respects than the considerations ordinarily applicable to the implication of a term into a written agreement, in particular by reason of the reference in art.3(1) to the circumstances of the case. As stated in the Giuliano-Lagarde Report at p.17 the provision 'recognizes the possibility that the Court may, in the light of all the facts, find that the parties have made a real choice of law although this is not expressly stated in the contract', but that it 'does not permit the court to infer a choice of law that the parties might have made where they had no clear intention of making a choice'; see also the general discussion in Dicey & Morris: The Conflict of Laws (13 ed), pars.32-089 to 32-097.[41] In my view, none of the authorities there cited assists the defendants in the circumstances of this case. In this respect I would add that it does not seem to me that the express provision for the exclusive jurisdiction of the English Courts over the claim as defined in the undertaking can give rise to any inference that English Law should govern the cross-claim. It begs the question raised rather than providing the answer.[42]

(c) Depecage and altering the applicable law after contract created

20.38   If the parties wish to, they can even have different laws applying to different parts of the contract[43] and can, subject to maintaining formal validity of the contract, alter the governing law during the currency of the agreement.

---

[41] Now *Dicey, Morris & Collins* (14th edn), paras 32-091–32-099.
[42] [2001] 2 Lloyd's Rep 641, 645 [16].
[43] This is known as depecage and is permitted by the last sentence of Art 3(1).

(d) No requirement to choose a law having a connection with the contract

There is no requirement that the chosen law has any connection with the contract.[44] **20.39**
The parties are free to choose whatever law they wish to apply to their contract.
There is no fetter on the parties' ability to make an express choice of law. However,
any risk of abuse of the freedom of choice so as to circumvent mandatory laws is
dealt with by Article 3(3) of the Rome Convention. This does not bar the choice
made by the parties but simply applies the mandatory provisions of another law
to which all connecting factors point. The choice made by the parties is effective
outside the ambit of the relevant mandatory provisions.

(e) Article 3(3)

It has been seen that Article 3(1) does not require the parties to choose a law with **20.40**
which the transaction has any factual connection. That said, if all other elements[45]
relevant to the situation point to the law of one country applying (country X), and
the parties choose another law, Article 3(3) permits the relevant choice of law but
it takes effect subject to the terms of any mandatory laws of country X. As stated
in *European Contracts Convention*,[46] Article 3(3) is 'designed to prevent parties
from circumventing the mandatory rules in a country in a wholly domestic situation by the simple expedient of selecting as an applicable law some legal system
which fails to contain those rules'.[47]

In *Caterpillar Financial Services Corporation v SNC Passion*,[48] Caterpillar, a US **20.41**
company, agreed to provide financial assistance to SNC, a company incorporated
under French Law in Guadelope, pursuant to a Loan Agreement which was
expressly subject to English law. Some of the loan monies were to be employed
towards the cost of building a vessel in Singapore. It was common ground that
SNC defaulted on its repayments. It sought to invoke Article 3(3) and contend
that the Loan Agreement was invalid since all lenders had to be authorized under
French law and Caterpillar was not so authorized. Cooke J rejected that argument, finding that there were significant elements of the situation which were
connected with territories other than France and Guadelope. Caterpillar was a US
company, the offer and commitment letters had been sent from the UK, the loan
repayments were to be made into a UK bank account and the vessel was built in
Singapore.

---

[44] *Dicey, Morris & Collins* (14th edn), paras 32-065–32-068.
[45] A high hurdle to overcome.
[46] Plender and Wilderspin (2nd edn, Sweet and Maxwell, 2001), 105.
[47] See also *Dicey, Morris & Collins* (14th edn), para 32-071.
[48] [2004] EWHC 569 (Comm), [2004] 2 Lloyd's Rep 99 (Cooke J)

20.42   Further, Cooke J considered that the domicile of the lending banker, being different to that of the other contracting party, was a significant factor. His Lordship
observed:

> For a bank in one country making a loan to a borrower in another, in respect of
> a transaction to be performed in a yet further country, both choice of law and
> jurisdiction are highly significant. In *NM Rothschild Ltd v Equitable Life Assurance
> Society* [2002] EWHC 1021 (QB) I held that the domicile of a lending bank was
> plainly a relevant element for the purposes of Article 3.3 and although, in that case,
> the bank's choice of law corresponded with its domicile, the point remains the
> same in so far as the nationality of the lender is clearly a crucial point for it in deciding
> what law it would like to see applied, whether that of its own or that of a 'neutral'
> jurisdiction.[49]

20.43   So it would appear likely that the courts will adopt a reasonably strict approach to
the application of Article 3(3). This is entirely in line with the general approach
and structure of the Rome Convention where party autonomy is given prece-
dence. Any relaxing of the requirements set out in Article 3(3) would undermine
that approach.

20.44   Articles 8, 9 and 11, and their effect on the existence and validity of the parties'
consent as regards choice of law, will be dealt with below.

(5) Applicable law in the absence of choice: Article 4

20.45   If the parties have not made a choice of the applicable law under Article 3, then
Article 4(1) provides that:

> . . . the contract shall be governed by the law of the country with which it is most
> closely connected. Nevertheless, a separable part of the contract which has a closer
> connection with another country may by way of exception be governed by the law of
> that other country.

20.46   So in the absence of any choice, express or implied, the court falls back on applying the law of the country which has the closest connection with the contract. This
is determined by reference to exclusive objective factors.[50] However, to avoid this
exercise becoming too uncertain and vague—something that should not be tolerated in international commercial agreements—the Convention provides for the
application of a presumption based upon the party performing the characteristic
performance.

---

[49] ibid, [29].
[50] *Credit Lyonnais v New Hampshire Insurance Co* [1997] 2 Lloyd's Rep 1, 7 per Hobhouse J. In
this judgment, Hobhouse J distinguishes the common law approach from that advocated under the
Convention.

(a) *Characteristic performance presumption*

The use of a presumption based upon the party performing the characteristic **20.47** performance of the contract is the most controversial aspect of the Rome Convention.[51]

Pursuant to Article 4(2), the law of closest connection will be presumed to be the **20.48** law of the place:

> . . . where the party who is to effect the performance which is characteristic of the contract has, at the time of conclusion of the contract, his habitual residence,[52] or, in the case of a body corporate or unincorporated, its central administration.

Whilst there is nothing in principle wrong with an approach based upon the **20.49** country having closest factual connection with the contract, there are some obvious oddities with the Convention's approach to identifying that law.

To identify the relevant law, we first must identify the party performing the char- **20.50** acteristic obligation of the contract. The 'characteristic obligation' is said to be the main obligation for which payment of money is made. The Giuliano and Lagarde Report provides the following guidance:[53]

> The submission of the contract, in the absence of a choice by the parties, to the law appropriate to the characteristic performance defines the connecting factor of the contract from the inside, and not from the outside by elements unrelated to the essence of the obligation such as the nationality of the contracting parties or the place where the contract was concluded. In addition it is possible to relate the concept of characteristic performance to an even more general idea, namely the idea that his performance refers to the function which the legal relationship involved fulfils in the economic and social life of any country. The concept of characteristic performance essentially links the contract to the social and economic environment of which it will form a part.

It is difficult to know where to start with this justification for the use of characteristic performance. It beggars belief why the habitual residence of the party performing the characteristic performance should be considered an 'inside' connecting factor whereas that party's national law or the law of the place where the contract was concluded should be considered unrelated.

It is the law of the habitual residence of the party performing the characteristic performance, not the law of the place of performance of that characteristic obligation, which is relevant. So in what way, precisely, does such a presumption link the

---

[51] F A Mann, 'The Proper Law of the Contract—An Obituary' (1991) 107 LQR 353, 354 describes this aspect of the Convention as 'almost bizarre'.

[52] The Rome Convention does not define what is meant by 'habitual residence'. This is unfortunate and will not aid the Convention being interpreted and applied uniformly across different jurisdictions.

[53] The Giuliano and Lagarde Report, 20.

contract 'to the social and economic environment of which it will form a part'? There are obvious difficulties applying such a notion to, say, a joint venture, where each party contributes to the overall aims of the contract or a typical loan agreement.[54] This is not the place to examine in detail the concept of characteristic performance. For detailed discussion the reader is referred to: J Hill, *International Commercial Disputes in English Courts* (3rd edn), [14.2.41]–[14.2.82]; *Dicey, Morris & Collins* (14th edn), paras 32-113–32-123.

20.51　The presumption has no application to contracts relating to immovables, which are to be governed by the law where the land is situated, or to contracts for the carriage of goods, which are subject to separate rules.[55]

(b) Disregarding the presumption

20.52　Pursuant to Article 4(5), the presumption shall not apply if it appears from the circumstances as a whole that the contract is more closely connected with another country.

20.53　In *Definitely Maybe (Touring) Ltd v Marek Lieberberg Konzertagentur GmbH*[56] the English-based claimants contracted with the German-based defendants for Oasis to play two concerts in Germany. Oasis played the two concerts but without Noel Gallagher and the defendants refused to pay the full price. The claimants brought an action in England claiming the difference. A jurisdictional battle thereafter ensued which was entirely dependent upon whether the governing law was English or German. The Master concluded that the matter appeared more closely connected to Germany and therefore under Article 4(5) disregarded the presumption.

20.54　On appeal, Morison J held, in dismissing the appeal, that it was for the defendants to establish that the presumption should be disregarded. This was more readily achievable where the place of performance is different from the place of the performer's business. That 'due weight' had to be attached to the presumption in

---

[54] As regards loans, applying the Swiss approach, which underlies the concept of characteristic performance, it is the lender who performs the characteristic performance because he or it takes the greater risk: see J Hill, *International Commercial Disputes in English Courts* (3rd edn, Hart Publishing, 2005), [14.2.6] citing Oliveira, '"Characteristic Obligation" in the Draft EEC Obligation Convention' (1977) 25 Am J Comp L 303, 314. For basic-type contracts it is not satisfactory that the practitioner does not find the necessary guidance within the Convention itself.
[55] Article 4(4): 'A contract for the carriage of goods shall not be subject to the presumption in paragraph 2. In such a contract if the country in which, at the time the contract is concluded, the carrier has his principal place of business is also the country in which the place of loading or the place of discharge or the principal place of business of the consignor is situated, it shall be presumed that the contract is most connected with that country. In applying this paragraph single voyage charterparties and other contracts the main purpose of which is the carriage of goods shall be treated as contracts for the carriage of goods.'
[56] [2001] 1 WLR 1745 (Morison J).

this process. However, he concluded that 'Germany has more attachment to or connection with the contract than England. Aside from any other consideration, the centre of gravity of the dispute is in Germany, which will provide the more convenient forum for deciding to what extent Oasis without Noel Gallagher was worth anything, and, if so, how much.' Accordingly, the presumption was to be disregarded in favour of Article 4(5).

In *Samcrete Egypt Engineers and Contractors SAE v Land Rover Exports Ltd*,[57]   **20.55**
Samcrete agreed to act as guarantor of Technotrade SAE, which was Land Rover's appointed distributor in Egypt. The guarantee was signed by Samcrete after the English choice of law and court clause had been deleted by them. The distribution agreement had an English law and choice of court clause. A dispute arose between Technotrade and Land Rover and a demand for monies due was made under the guarantee.

At first instance, the judge rejected the argument that there was an implied choice   **20.56**
of law under Article 3 of the Rome Convention since the choice of court and law clauses had been deleted. The Court of Appeal agreed with this conclusion, citing Clarke J in *Egon Oldendorff v Libera Corporation* that it was necessary to adopt a purposive approach to construction:

> It is sufficient to say that the party relying upon art.3 must demonstrate with reasonable certainty that the parties have chosen a particular law as the governing or applicable law. I accept the submission that, as the Giulano-Lagarde Report says, it must be a real choice which the parties had a clear intention to make. In *Redfern & Hunter on International Commercial Arbitration* (2nd ed at p.123) the authors say that in the absence of an expressed choice the tribunal must look for a tacit choice of law which they say may be known as an implied inferred or implicit choice. They add that art 3 makes it clear that a tacit choice must only be found where it is reasonably clear that it is a genuine choice by the parties. I accept that approach. See to the same effect *Jaffey* in (1984) 33 ICLQ 545.[58]

On this basis the Court of Appeal held that the judge was correct to reject the submissions based upon Article 3.

Applying the presumption in Article 4, Egyptian law should have been applied as   **20.57**
the law governing the guarantee since that is the place of principal business of Samcrete who was the party providing the characteristic performance of the guarantee. However, the judge and the Court of Appeal discharged the presumption of Egyptian law in favour of English law, for different reasons.

Potter LJ held that the judge should not have considered the use of the English   **20.58**
choice of law and court clause in the distributorship agreement as being 'largely

---

[57] [2001] EWCA Civ 2019.
[58] [1996] 1 Lloyd's Rep 380, 387.

determinative under Article 4'. In reaching this conclusion, Potter LJ relied upon Hobhouse LJ's approach in *Credit Lyonnais v New Hampshire Insurance Company*:[59]

> . . . the question of choice and absence of choice becomes irrelevant to the question of ascertaining with what State the contract is most closely connected. Similarly, to refer to contemplation by one party or another that certain local laws may or may not be relevant is to be influenced by considerations of inferred choice and connection with the legal system and not with questions of performance and the location of the performing parties.

Potter LJ also rejected, as factors having little significance on the issue, the fact that the guarantee was written in English (it is a 'language of international commerce'), that Land Rover, one of the parties to the guarantee, was situated in England.[60] His Lordship was more influenced by (i) the obligation to pay under the guarantee was to be performed in England and therefore any breach in failing to pay would take place in England[61] and (ii) consideration for the guarantee included Land Rover continuing to supply products to Samcrete 'delivery ex UK works' and payable in sterling. Accordingly, 'the centre of gravity of the guarantee was located squarely in England'.[62]

20.59 The approach adopted by the English courts as to the displacement of the presumption in Article 4(2) is not mirrored by that adopted elsewhere in Europe. The most obvious example is the Dutch decision of *Societe Nouvelle des Papeteries de L'Aa v BV Maschinefabrieke BOA*.[63] On the facts of the case, the presumption led to Dutch law applying, yet the delivery of the machinery was to take place in France to a French company and to be paid in French francs. And, for good measure, the contract was negotiated in France. The Dutch court refused to disapply the law identified by the presumption unless it could be shown to have 'no real value as a connecting factor'. This would appear to be a much stricter approach than that adopted by the English courts.

(6) Scope of the applicable law

(a) Material validity: Article 8

20.60 Article 8 provides:

> 1. The existence and validity of a contract, or of any term of a contract, shall be determined by the law which would govern it under this Convention if the contract or term were valid.

---

[59] [1997] 2 Lloyd's Rep 1, 5.
[60] [2001] EWCA Civ 2019, [46].
[61] ibid, [47].
[62] ibid, [48].
[63] 25 September 1992; discussed in Struycken [1996] LMCLQ 18.

2. Nevertheless a party may rely upon the law of the country in which he has his habitual residence to establish that he did not consent if it appears from the circumstances that it would not be reasonable to determine the effect of his conduct in accordance with the law specified in the preceding paragraph.

20.61 The material validity of a contract is governed by the applicable law or the putative applicable law. This includes matters such as the requirement for offer and acceptance, consideration, whether there exists the necessary legal intention, whether there exists any factors vitiating consent such as mistake, duress, etc. These latter points are of course of particular interest in a commercial fraud setting, where there is every likelihood that a claimant may wish to set aside a contract he has been deceived into entering.

(a) Formal validity: Article 9

20.62 Article 9 provides as follows:

1. A contract concluded between persons who are in the same country is formally valid if it satisfies the formal requirements of the law which governs it under this Convention or of the law of the country where it is concluded.
2. A contract concluded between persons who are in different countries is formally valid if it satisfies the formal requirements of the law which governs it under this Convention or of the law of one of those countries.
3. Where a contract is concluded by an agent, the country in which the agent acts is the relevant country for the purposes of paragraphs 1 and 2.
4. An act intended to have legal effect relating to an existing or contemplated contract is formally valid if it satisfies the formal requirements of the law which under this Convention governs or would govern the contract or of the law of the country where the act was done.
5. The provisions of the preceding paragraphs shall not apply to a contract to which Article 5 applies, concluded in the circumstances described in paragraph 2 of Article 5. The formal validity of such a contract is governed by the law of the country in which the consumer has his habitual residence.
6. Notwithstanding paragraphs 1 to 4 of this Article, a contract the subject matter of which is a right in immovable property or a right to use immovable property shall be subject to the mandatory requirements of form of the law of the country where the property is situated if by that law those requirements are imposed irrespective of the country where the contract is concluded and irrespective of the law governing the contract.[64]

20.63 With the various options open to render a contract formally valid, it is clear that the general aim is to try and validate a contract rather than render it invalid due to some technicality, such as the absence of writing. Included within the question of formal validity is the English law requirement for certain contracts in relation to

---

[64] See the Giuliano and Lagarde Report, 29.

land to be in writing.[65] Hill has queried whether the Statute of Frauds 1677, which was considered procedural in *Leroux v Brown*,[66] would fall within or without Article 9. He ultimately concludes that s 4 of the Statute of Frauds 1677 should be interpreted as establishing formal requirements within Article 9.[67]

(b) Scope of applicable law: Article 10

20.64 Article 10 provides:

1. The law applicable to a contract by virtue of Articles 3 to 6 and 12 of this Convention shall govern in particular:
   (a) interpretation;
   (b) performance;
   (c) within the limits the powers conferred on the court by its procedural law, the consequences of breach, including the assessment of damages in so far as it is governed by rules of law;
   (d) the various ways of extinguishing obligations, and prescription and limitation of actions;
   (e) the consequences of nullity of the contract.
2. In relation to the manner of performance and the steps to be taken in the event of defective performance regard shall be had to the law of the country in which performance takes place.

20.65 Article 10(1)(e) has not been enacted into English law.[68] The consequences of nullity are considered part of the law of unjust enrichment or restitution rather than the law of contract. However, where a benefit has been transferred pursuant to a contractual arrangement which turns out to be void, it is generally accepted that English conflict of laws principles would dictate that it is the law of the supposed contract which will be the law governing any question of restitution.[69]

20.66 The other matters set out in Article 10 are self-explanatory and hardly controversial. In order to ensure a uniform approach to contracts, the applicable law has been given a very wide scope of application.

(c) Mandatory rules: Article 7

20.67 Article 7 provides:

1. When applying under this Convention the law of a country, effect may be given to the mandatory rules of the law of another country with which the situation has a close connection, if and in so far as, under the law of the latter country, those

---

[65] The Law of Property (Miscellaneous Provisions) Act 1989, s 2.
[66] (1852) 12 CB 801.
[67] Hill, *International Commercial Disputes in English Courts* (3rd edn), [14.4.14].
[68] Contracts (Applicable Law) Act 1990, s 2(2).
[69] See *Dicey, Morris & Collins* (14th edn), Rule 230.

    rules must be applied whatever the law applicable to the contract. In considering whether to give effect to these mandatory rules, regard shall be had to their nature and purpose and to the consequences of their application or non-application.

2. Nothing in this Convention shall restrict the application of the rules of the law of the forum in a situation where they are mandatory irrespective of the law otherwise applicable to the contract.

20.68 We can pass over Article 7(1) quickly. The UK did not enact this provision into English law: Contracts (Applicable Law) Act 1990, s 2(2). There were concerns as to the likely uncertainty such a provision may cause.[70]

20.69 Article 7(2) is concerned with those laws which are considered so important that they apply to all disputes being determined within the forum irrespective of whether English law applies. Obvious examples in English law are the Unfair Contracts Terms Act 1977 and the Carriage of Goods By Sea Act 1971. Article 7(2) prevents parties from attempting to circumvent these laws by ensuring their application irrespective of the law chosen by the parties. The choice of law remains effective in all other areas.

In conclusion, the Rome Convention, overall, has proved a success. It no doubt has its problems, most notably with the introduction of the concept of characteristic performance, but the structure and clarity it has imposed in other areas of determining the choice of law for contractual disputes outweighs the problems associated with characteristic performance. Finally, a new Regulation, Rome I, is to be introduced during 2008 and is intended ultimately to replace the Rome Convention for contracts entered into after late 2009. However, the UK has exercised its option not yet to be bound and so the details of this Regulation are not dealt with in this book.

C. Private International Law (Miscellaneous Provisions) Act 1995—Tort Claims

(1) Applicable regimes

20.70 Until 11 January 2009, the English conflict of laws choice of law rules for torts are contained in the Private International Law (Miscellaneous Provisions) Act 1995 (the 1995 Act). For any events taking place on or after 11 January 2009, a new EC Regulation comes into effect to deal with the law applicable to non-contractual obligations.

---

[70] See L Collins, 'Contractual Obligations—the EEC Preliminary Draft Convention on Private International Law' (1976) 25 ICLQ 35, 49–51 for more detailed criticism of this provision.

20.71   As its name implies, the ambit of the new Regulation (to be known as 'Rome II') extends beyond just tort claims. In addition to the changes it makes in respect of tortious claims, of most interest to commercial fraud litigators is the introduction, for the first time, of a codified approach to the choice of law rules for unjust enrichment. Many issues will remain unanswered for the time being and others have been given an answer that some might find surprising or at least difficult to equate with a detailed analysis of an unjust enrichment claim.

20.72   Since Rome II will not take effect until 11 January 2009 and given that it will take some time for cases under the new regime to filter through to litigators thereafter, it is still essential to have an understanding of the provisions of the 1995 Act.

20.73   Accordingly, this section will deal with the 1995 Act. The provisions of Rome II, which extend beyond that of tortious claims, will be dealt with at the end of this chapter.

(2) Private International Law (Miscellaneous Provisions) Act 1995

(a) Brief overview of law pre-1995 Act

20.74   Prior to the 1995 Act, the English choice of law rule for tort claims was known as the double-actionability rule. This required establishing that the conduct complained of gave rise to civil actionability under the law of the foreign legal system where the events took place *and* would, if that conduct had occurred in this jurisdiction, have constituted an English tort. This general rule was subject to an exception whereby the law of another country could apply if that country has the most significant relationship with the occurrence and parties: see *Boys v Chaplin*.[71]

(b) Introduction to 1995 Act

20.75   The 1995 Act came into force for torts committed on or after 1 May 1996. Rome II will take effect in the courts from 11 January 2009 but will apply, retrospectively, to events which took place on or after 20 August 2007.

20.76   The main aim of the 1995 Act was to abolish the traditional common law rules (double-actionability under the House of Lords decision in *Boys v Chaplin*) and its proper law of a tort exception.

20.77   The Act provides no definition of what is meant by 'tort' and in particular whether it is to be limited to English law concept of tort claims. It is suggested that the Act is not so limited. Section 9(4) of the Act says that it is the applicable law which shall determine whether an actionable tort had occurred. This strongly suggests that it was not intended to limit 'tort' to the English law concept. Whilst characterization

---

[71]   [1971] AC 356.

is a matter for the forum (s 9(2)), we have already seen that a flexible approach must generally be adopted to that process in the conflict of laws. Finally, *Dicey, Morris & Collins* has pointed out that it is 'axiomatic' that claims will fall within the 1995 Act even if they do not give rise to a cause of action known to English law, thus paving the way for the adoption of a flexible approach to what amounts to a tort.[72]

(c) The general rule: section 11

The general rule of the Act is to be found in s 11 which provides as follows: **20.78**

> (1) The general rule is that the applicable law is the law of the country in which the events constituting the tort or delict in question occur.

Thus, the double-actionability rule is replaced by the simple law of the place of the wrong rule.

The assumption in s 11(1) is that the relevant events all took place in one country. **20.79**
If they did not, and often they do not, regard is to be had to s 11(2) which provides:

> (2) Where elements of those events occur in different countries the applicable law under the general rule is to be taken as being—
> (a) For a cause of action in respect of personal injury caused to an individual or death resulting from personal injury, the law of the country where the individual was when he sustained the injury;
> (b) For a cause of action in respect of damage to property, the law of the country where the property was when it was damaged; and
> (c) In any other case, the law of the country in which the most significant element or elements of those events occurred.

It is noted that in a commercial fraud, the Act does not seek to identify any one **20.80**
connecting factor as being decisive, as it is willing to do in respect of personal injury or damage to property. Instead, the Act provides an extremely flexible test of place where the 'most significant element or elements of those events' occurred.

That is a new test and it differs from the approach based upon asking where 'in **20.81**
substance' did the tort take place. Indeed, it is clear that reliance on the old authorities is misplaced. In *Protea Leasing Ltd v Royal Air Cambodge Co Ltd*[73] Moore-Bick J commented:

> The 1995 Act establishes a new set of principles which make it unnecessary for the court to identify a single country in which the tort was 'in substance' committed. Section 11(2)(c) only requires the court to identify the country in which the most significant element of the events constituting the tort occurred. That seems to me to

---

72 *Dicey, Morris & Collins* (14th edn), para 35-024.
73 [2002] EWHC 2731 (Comm).

be a much more flexible principle and one which might yield different answers in different cases even in relation to the same tort.[74]

20.82 That assistance in interpreting the 1995 Act will not be found in the older authorities is confirmed by the Court of Appeal in *Morin v Bonhams & Brooks Ltd.*[75] This case concerned the purchase of a Ferrari at auction in Monaco. The purchaser was first informed of the auction by the London office of BBL, a subsidiary of BBM. He requested and obtained a brochure from BBL in London. That contained a certain description of the car including mileage. The purchaser flew out to Monaco, looked over the car but was not allowed to drive it. Ultimately he bid for and won the car, had it brought back to England only to discover it was in poor mechanical shape and the mileage on the clock was inaccurate.

20.83 Mance LJ held that s 11(2)(c) 'required . . . an analysis of all the elements constituting the tort as a matter of law, and a value judgment regarding their "significance", in order to identify the country in which there is either one element or several elements, which taken alone or together, outweighs or outweigh in significance any element or elements to be found in any other country. The governing law under s.11(2)(c) will be the law of that country.' His Lordship disavowed the usefulness of looking at earlier authorities on the old law or seeking to draw analogies from the various Conventions. Mance LJ went on to say, whether or not the two schemes (i.e. common law and the 1995 Act) amounted to pretty much the same approach:

> . . . it is inappropriate for disputes under a new statutory wording to become clogged with an overlay of arguments about whether and how far this was true, based on authorities on different and now irrelevant wording. It seems to me even less fruitful to try to refer for inspiration . . . to other schemes, such as that under the Brussels Convention or Regulation 44/2001.

20.84 Applying this approach to the facts of the case, Mance LJ concluded:

> In the present case, elements constituting the alleged tort occurred both in England and in Monaco. But I agree with the Judge that the most significant elements occurred in Monaco. The making by BBM through its catalogue in England of a negligent misstatement is of course one essential element. But the element of reliance was present in the form of a continuum of activity, starting in England, but having by far its most significant aspect in the form of Mr Morin's presence and successful bidding in Monaco. By the same token although some loss was caused in England, the successful bid involved Mr Morin entering into a contract in Monaco, under which he bought and received the car there and became liable to pay there the price and auction premium, which he met by the remittance from the Bahamas. It is his decision on the spot when making his successful bid, and his resulting commitment to buy the car and pay that price and premium, which represent by far the major element of

---

74 ibid, [78].
75 [2003] EWCA Civ 1802, [2004] 1 Lloyd's Rep 702.

his reliance and of the loss caused and claimed in this case. The entering into of an adverse contractual commitment involves on its face an actionable loss, even prior to any actual financial expenditure pursuant to it (see e.g *Forster v Outred* [1982] 1 WLR 86, 97b-c).

(d) The exception: section 12

Ordinarily, the application of the provisions of s 11 will have resulted in identify- **20.85** ing the relevant law to govern the particular tortious claim. If not, the 1995 Act provides for an exception to s 11. Section 12 provides:

(1) If it appears, in all the circumstances from a comparison of—
  (a) The significance of the factors which connect a tort or delict with the country whose law would be the applicable law under the general rule; and
  (b) The significance of any factors connecting the tort or delict with another country, that it is substantially more appropriate for the applicable law for determining the issues arising in the case, or any of those issues to be the law of the other country, the general rule is displaced and the applicable law for determining those issues or that issue (as the case may be) is the law of that other country.
(2) The factors that may be taken into account as connecting a tort or delict with a country for the purposes of this section include, in particular, factors relating to the parties, to any of the events which constitute the tort or delict in question or to any of the circumstances or consequences of those events.

By virtue of s 12, the general rule can be displaced entirely or simply in respect of **20.86** one issue arising in the claim. So if the claim was one in conspiracy, and most of the events took place in France but the conspirators and the victim of the conspiracy were all English, s 12 might displace s 11 with English law. As can be seen, this exception is potentially wide in scope.

D. Rome II—The Law Applicable to Non-Contractual Obligations

(1) Introduction

On 11 July 2007, Regulation (EC) No 864/2007 On the Law Applicable **20.87** to Non-Contractual Obligations, known more conveniently as 'Rome II'[76] was published. The aim behind the Regulation is to try and achieve greater certainty and uniformity of approach to the question of choice of law for non-contractual obligations.

---

[76] 'Rome I' being, of course, a reference to the new Regulation intended eventually to replace the Rome Convention on the applicable law of contract.

20.88 The Regulation will no doubt be subject to close scrutiny and criticism over the years and we will not properly know its true ambit and perhaps its true pitfalls until some of its provisions have been tested in court. That said, for anyone who has had the misfortune to have to spend the number of days researching issues such as choice of law for unjust enrichment or equitable wrongdoing, the Regulation is refreshing in its adoption of some rather simplistic answers to issues which have generated lengthy intellectual debate. In particular, one might readily criticize from an intellectual perspective the use of joint habitual residence to answer some of the choice of law rules but it is at least clear and easily applied and most importantly, clients will not be spending a great deal on what they perceive to be esoteric issues such as the characterization of a claim in unjust enrichment.

20.89 The main provisions of the Regulation will apply in court from 11 January 2009[77] and the Regulation will apply to events taking place after 20 August 2007.[78] Necessarily, at the time of writing, there is no guidance from the courts as to the meaning of certain phrases. There is a limit, therefore, as to what can be said at this stage.

20.90 Rome II will obviously replace the 1995 Act in respect of the choice of law for torts and will also impose a whole new and much simplified regime for claims in unjust enrichment, however such phrase comes to be defined. The grey area relates to its application to equitable claims. On one level, such claims fall within 'non-contractual obligations' but we are told (Preamble (11) to Rome II) this is to be given an autonomous meaning. Whether that includes equitable obligations is unclear. Further, the structure of Rome II is to separate out certain known categories of 'non-contractual obligations'. Although there is a similarity between the rules, there is not, as such, a rule dealing with 'non-contractual obligations' generally. This may well mean that if equitable obligations are to fall within Rome II they will need to be dealt with under a specific category, perhaps tort (for equitable wrongdoing) and unjust enrichment for all other examples. Curiously, Article 2(2) provides that '[t]his Regulation shall apply also to non-contractual obligations that are likely to arise'. Again, no guidance is given as to what is meant by this. Insofar as equitable obligations are considered 'likely to arise', in what way will the Regulation *apply* to them?

20.91 For our present purposes we are interested in only some of the provisions.

20.92 Article 3 makes it clear that any law identified by the Regulation shall be applied, irrespective of whether it is a law of a member state.

---

[77] Art 32.
[78] Arts 31 and 32: see Briggs, *The Conflict of Laws* (2nd edn, Clarendon Press, 2008), 201.

(2) Matters excluded from the Regulation

Article 1(1) provides that the Regulation will apply, in situations involving a **20.93**
conflict of laws, to non-contractual obligations in civil and commercial matters,
excluding certain state-related matters such as revenue, customs or administrative
issues.

Article 1(2) mirrors the Rome Convention in listing certain non-contractual obli- **20.94**
gations which are excluded from the ambit of the Regulation. They include:

- non-contractual obligations arising under bills of exchange, cheques and promissory notes and other negotiable instruments to the extent that the obligations
  under such other negotiable instruments arise out of their negotiable
  character;
- non-contractual obligations arising out of the law of companies and other bodies corporate or unincorporated regarding matters such as the creation, by registration or otherwise, legal capacity, internal organization or winding up of
  companies and other bodies corporate or unincorporated, the personal liability
  of officers and members as such for the obligations of the company or body and
  the personal liability of auditors to a company or to its members in the statutory
  audits of accounting documents.

Article 1(3) excludes matters of evidence and procedure except as covered by **20.95**
Article 21 (Formal Validity)[79] and Article 22 (Burden of Proof).[80]

(3) General rule for torts: Article 4

The general choice of law rule for tort is the 'law of the country in which the dam- **20.96**
age occurs irrespective of the country in which the event giving rise to the damage
occurred and irrespective of the country or countries in which the indirect consequences of that event occur'.[81]

This rule is clearly attempting to avoid uncertainty by insisting the only relevant **20.97**
damage, for choice of law purposes, is the immediate directly incurred damage
and not any economic damage being felt by parent companies in other jurisdictions. The focus is on the damage being suffered and not on the event leading to
that damage.

---

[79] An act is considered to be formally valid if it is valid in accordance with either the law governing the non-contractual obligations or the law of the place where the act was performed.
[80] The law governing the non-contractual obligation will apply if it contains rules which raise
presumptions or determine burdens of proof. Acts may be proved by any permissible method under
the *lex fori* or by any of the laws under Art 21.
[81] Art 4(1).

20.98 If, however, when the damage occurred, the parties had the same habitual residence, it is the law of that residence which shall apply.[82] There is no obvious intellectual merit in opting for joint habitual residence—it is not a choice borne out of a detailed characterization of non-contractual obligations. It appears to be premised on nothing more than the not entirely unreasonable notion that it might be in the interests of both parties to have the matter determined by reference to the law of their joint habitual residence.

20.99 Finally, if it is 'clear from all the circumstances of the case that the tort/delict is manifestly more closely connected with a country other than' that indicated above, the law of that other country shall apply. In determining whether the law of another country is manifestly more closely connected regard may be had to any pre-existing relationship between the parties, such as contract, that is closely connected with the tort/delict in question.[83]

(4) General rules for unjust enrichment: Article 10

20.100 Article 10 makes provision for certain choice of law rules to apply to non-contractual obligations arising out of unjust enrichment. Although 'unjust enrichment' is to be given an autonomous meaning, no actual definition of 'unjust enrichment' is provided for in the Regulation. Until clarified in the courts, this will leave many doubts lingering as to what exactly is supposed to fall within the term, 'unjust enrichment'. Is it limited to unjust enrichment by subtraction or does it extend to restitution for wrongdoing? These issues remain unresolved at the moment.

20.101 Article 10(1) provides that the law of any existing (contractual or tortious) relationship between the parties, which is closely connected with the unjust enrichment, shall govern any non-contractual obligation arising out of that unjust enrichment. The similarities with *Dicey, Morris & Collins* Rule 230(2)(a) are obvious.

20.102 If Article 10(1) does not apply, and the parties have their habitual residence in the same country when the event giving rise to unjust enrichment occurs, the law of that country shall apply.[84] This is a marked departure from the position so far adopted in English conflict of laws. It has the attraction of simplicity and ease of application but can hardly be said to be based upon the obvious connecting factors arising in a claim in unjust enrichment, unless it is going to be said that if England is the place of habitual residence of both parties, it is likely to be (although there are no guarantees) the place where the mistake in transferring

---

82 Art 4(2). Habitual residence is to be determined in accordance with Art 23.
83 Art 4(3).
84 Art 10(2).

funds was made by the claimant and where the enrichment was received by the defendant.

If the law applicable cannot be determined by reference to Article 10(1) or (2), 'it **20.103** shall be the law of the country in which the unjust enrichment took place'. It is uncertain how this clause is to be interpreted. One reading is that it is the law of the place of enrichment with the addition of 'unjust' adding nothing. Indeed, the only place of enrichment which would be relevant for such a claim is where that enrichment is 'unjust'. If that is what was intended, it would be in line with *Dicey, Morris & Collins* Rule 230(2)(c) applying the law of the place of enrichment.[85] Again, it remains to be seen whether the addition of 'unjust' to 'enrichment' adds anything of substance to the test.[86] It is suggested that it is unlikely that it was intended thereby to introduce, into this test, any consideration of the unjust factors at play in such a claim.[87]

As with the general rule on tort, there is a proviso that if it is clear from all the cir- **20.104** cumstances that the non-contractual obligation arising out of unjust enrichment is manifestly more closely connected with a country other than that indicated in Article 10(1), (2), and (3), then the law of that other country shall apply.[88]

(5) Freedom of choice: Article 14

This Article applies to all non-contractual obligations falling within the **20.105** Regulation.

Article 14 provides an opportunity for the parties to subject their non-contractual **20.106** dispute to an agreed choice of law reached after the event giving rise to the damage occurred or if all the parties are pursuing a commercial activity, by an agreement freely negotiated before the relevant event occurred, so long as the agreement is clearly expressed and does not prejudice third parties.

It will thus be possible for commercial entities to agree choice of law clauses in **20.107** their respective contracts which cover both contractual and non-contractual disputes.

---

[85] Although a reading of Rule 230 suggests that Rule 230(2)(c) is a mop-up provision to cover all cases not dealing with land or contract. However, the commentary to that Rule suggests that whilst there was much to commend proceeding by way of categories of claim, it must always be possible to depart from a category if the overall factors justify doing so.

[86] It is noted that the Report of Diana Wells PEP on the Regulation expressly states that the Rapporteur disagreed with the original idea that it should be the law of the place of enrichment since the place where the enrichment takes place may be entirely fortuitous.

[87] For a discussion based upon such an approach, see G Panagopoulos, *Restitution in Private International Law* (Hart Publishing, 2000).

[88] Arts 10(4) and 11(4).

20.108 If all the elements relevant to the situation at the time when the event giving rise to the damage occurs are located in:

- A country other than the country whose law has been chosen, then the choice of law shall not prejudice the application of provisions of the law of that other country which cannot be derogated from by agreement.[89]

- One or more member states, the parties' choice of the law applicable other than that of a member state shall not prejudice the application of provisions of Community law, where appropriate as implemented in the member state of the forum, which cannot be derogated from by agreement.[90]

20.109 One can see where commercial entities, used to drawing up agreements with jurisdiction and choice of law clauses, may well see real advantages in being able to ensure, within the criteria of the Regulation, that a certain law will apply to any non-contractual obligations which may arise.

(6) Scope of applicable law: Article 15

20.110 The applicable law shall apply to all the following issues:

- the basis and extent of liability, including the determination of persons who may be held liable for acts performed by them;
- the grounds for exemption from liability, any limitation of liability and any division of liability;
- the existence, the nature and the assessment of damage or the remedy claimed;
- within the limits of powers conferred on the court by its procedural law, the measure which a court may take to prevent or terminate injury or damage or to ensure the provision of compensation;
- the question whether a right to claim damages or a remedy may be transferred, including by inheritance;
- persons entitled to compensation for damage sustained personally;
- liability for the acts of another person;
- the manner in which an obligation may be extinguished and rules of prescription and limitation, including rules relating to the commencement, interruption and suspension of a period of prescription or limitation.

(7) Overriding mandatory provisions: Article 16

20.111 Article 16 permits the *lex fori* to apply any provision of its law which is mandatory irrespective of the law otherwise applicable to the non-contractual obligation.

---

[89] Art 14(2). This is similar to Rome Convention, Art 3(3).
[90] Art 14(3).

(8) Direct action against the insurer of the person liable: Article 18

Article 18 provides that the claimant may bring his claim directly against the **20.112** wrongdoers' insurer if the law applicable to the non-contractual obligation or the law applicable to the insurance contract so provides.

(9) Subrogation: Article 19

Article 19 provides: **20.113**

> Where a person (the creditor) has a non-contractual claim upon another (the debtor), and a third person has a duty to satisfy the creditor, or has in fact satisfied the creditor in discharge of that duty, the law which governs the third person's duty to satisfy the creditor shall determine whether, and the extent to which, the third person is entitled to exercise against the debtor the rights which the creditor had against the debtor under the law governing their relationship.

(10) Multiple liability: Article 20

Article 20 provides: **20.114**

> If a creditor has a claim against several debtors who are liable for the same claim, and one of the debtors has already satisfied the claim in whole or in part, the question of that debtor's right to demand compensation from the other debtors shall be governed by the law applicable to that debtor's non-contractual obligation towards the creditor.

(11) Formal validity: Article 21

Article 21 provides that the formal validity of an act intended to have legal effect **20.115** will be determined by reference to the law governing the non-contractual obligation, alternatively the law of the country in which the act is performed.

(12) Burden and mode of proof: Article 22

Although Article 22 is expressly headed 'Burden of Proof' it deals with both bur- **20.116** den and mode of proof. The former, together with presumptions, is subject to the law governing the non-contractual obligation, whereas for the latter, acts may be proved by any mode of proof recognized by the *lex fori* or any of the laws under Article 21 under which the act is formally valid and such mode of proof can be administered by the forum.

E. Unjust Enrichment Claims

(1) Introduction

The examination of substantive claims for unjust enrichment, which has been **20.117** undertaken elsewhere in the book, reveals a topic very much in development.

Indeed, if *Lipkin Gorman*[91] can be viewed as the birth of this area of the law, or at least its formal recognition, then it might be said that unjust enrichment is presently in its troubling teenage years, eager to assert itself among the other claims such as contract and tort, but perhaps not yet achieving full adult status. Given this state of affairs on the domestic side of unjust enrichment, it can hardly come as a surprise to discover that little progress, and even less agreement, has been made on the development of choice of law rules for such claims.

20.118 Further, until *Lipkin Gorman*, unjust enrichment lawyers had to fight hard to have unjust enrichment accepted as a stand-alone cause of action, able to take its position next to contract, tort and trusts as opposed to the topic being considered some adjunct to the law of contract (i.e. quasi-contract). Having done the hard work in *Lipkin Gorman,* such lawyers are naturally reticent about openly adopting a flexible approach to the interpretation or characterization of the claim in unjust enrichment for the purposes of the conflict of laws. There is an understandable but mistaken concern that somehow agreeing to have the claim in unjust enrichment characterized as one governed by the same choice of law rules that apply to contractual claims might be taking a backward step. Such concerns are misplaced and should be put aside.

Of course, much of the detailed work that has started to be done in this area will be replaced with the introduction of Rome II in January 2009.[92] The details of these new provisions have been examined in paras 20.100–20.104 above. They have the benefit, in the main, of simplicity and clarity, which should assist in reducing litigation costs in this area and enable practitioners to provide clearer advice to clients on questions of choice of law. Inevitably, there remain some issues of uncertainty but it is hoped they will be clarified sooner rather than later. It is highly likely that should the publishers permit a further edition of this text, this chapter will look very different.

(2) Characterization

20.119 As we have seen,[93] characterization of an issue is an essential pre-requisite to determining what is the appropriate choice of law rule to apply to that issue.[94]

---

[91] *Lipkin Gorman v Karpnale Ltd* [1991] 2 AC 548 (HL).

[92] It would be wrong to think all such work would be redundant since Rome II still contains a fall-back of the law having the closest connection to the unjust enrichment. Inevitably such a rule will involve some of the thinking that has been exhibited in the case law and articles to date.

[93] See para 18.10 *et seq.*

[94] Although this section is dealing with unjust enrichment *claims*, the proper approach to choice of law rules is to search for the appropriate *issue* to be characterized. So the fact that the claim generally in *Macmillan v Bishopsgate* was described as restitutionary did not assist the identification of the relevant choice of law rule. The issue was identified as being the priority to shares and on the back of identifying that issue, the relevant choice of law rule was determined.

The process of characterization involves identifying connecting factors from which a relevant legal category or categories can be identified. Both the establishment of the facts and the relevant categories is a matter for English conflicts of laws and English domestic law. That said, categories which work as a matter of domestic law may not work on the international stage. The point is perfectly illustrated by the following extract from Auld LJ's judgment in *Macmillan Investment Inc v Bishopsgate*:[95]

> Subject to what I shall say in a moment, characterization or classification is governed by the *lex fori*. But characterization or classification of what? It follows from what I have said that the proper approach is to look beyond the formulation of the claim and to identify according to the *lex fori* the true issue or issues thrown up by the claim and defence. This requires a parallel exercise in classification of the relevant rule of law. However, classification of an issue and rule of law for this purpose, the underlying principle of which is to strive for comity between competing legal systems, should not be constrained by particular notions or distinctions of the domestic law of the *lex fori*, or that of the competing system of law, which may have no counterpart in the other's system. Nor should the issue be defined too narrowly so that it attracts a particular domestic rule under the *lex fori* which may not be applicable under the other system . . .
>
> The dispute about the nature of the issue in this case, whether it is about restitution, stemming from the developing notion of a 'receipt-based restitutionary claim' or about property, is a good example of the danger of looking at the problem through domestic eyes. There is a long and growing line of cases . . . indicating a right to restitution flowing from the circumstances of receipt regardless of the knowledge of or notice to the recipient . . .
>
> The 'receipt-based restitutionary claim' is a notion of English domestic law that may not have a counterpart in many other legal systems, and is one that it may not be appropriate to translate into the English law of conflict. In my view, it would be wrong to attempt to graft this equitable newcomer onto the class of cases where English courts will intervene to enforce an equity in respect of property abroad . . .

Auld LJ's warning is well made. This is all the more so in this area of the law where the heat of the domestic battle on the existence of unjust enrichment as a separate cause of action is still present and runs the risk of unduly influencing how one approaches the process of characterization.

20.120 Applying this approach to a claim in unjust enrichment, we can identify, from English domestic law that the defining characteristics of such a claim are an enrichment received by the defendant in circumstances rendering that enrichment unjust. According to the traditional categorization of claims in unjust enrichment, the factors which render such enrichment unjust are that it was made by

---

[95] [1996] 1 WLR 387, 407.

mistake, ignorance, paid under duress, etc.[96] Issues of loss caused to the claimant are not relevant, nor is the conduct of the defendant, save in the different context of raising a defence.

20.121 It is emphasized that this section is concerned solely with claims in unjust enrichment. It is not concerned with that category of claims put under the umbrella of restitution for wrongs. The characterization process we have just undergone for unjust enrichment claims highlights the importance of drawing a clear distinction between the two sets of claims.[97] Unfortunately, that has not always been the case.

(3) Possible candidates

20.122 There are several candidates for the role of the choice of law rule for claims in unjust enrichment, each having some form of support in the academic world or the cases but none appearing to command universal respect and approval. In the absence of a decisive rule, everything is up for grabs.

20.123 The candidates are:

(1) *lex fori;*
(2) *Dicey, Morris & Collins* Rule 200;
(3) the place of enrichment;
(4) the law determining the unjust nature of the enrichment.

(a) Lex fori

20.124 This is not a viable option. It is submitted that any serious conflict of laws lawyer would and should immediately reject the suggestion that the relevant choice of law rule for claims in unjust enrichment should be the law of the forum. The suggestion is premised upon the mistaken notion that unjust enrichment has something to do with justice and public policy and these are matters for the forum.[98]

20.125 Unjust enrichment is a stand-alone cause of action; it is not, as Ehrenzweig would call it, simply a remedial device.[99] It is no more interested in or associated with

---

[96] For present discussion, Birks' new suggestion of eliminating the individual unjust factors in favour of one category being 'absence of consideration' can be put to one side.

[97] Characterization of restitution for wrongs would put a far greater focus on the conduct of the defendant as the wrongdoer. Claims in unjust enrichment are considered claimant-sided—focusing on the quality of the intention to transfer, etc. rather than the conduct of the recipient defendant. Restitution for wrongdoing does what its name suggests: it focuses on the wrongdoing of the defendant, not the intention to transfer of the claimant. The relevant connecting factors are significantly different as between the two types of claim.

[98] See A Ehrenzweig, 'Restitution in the Conflict of Laws' (1961) 36 NYULR 1298.

[99] ibid, 1302, 1314.

notions of justice and public policy than the law of contract or the law of torts. As an independent cause of action, unjust enrichment merits its own choice of law rule (even if it turns out to share that rule with another cause of action) rather than being left to the whim of the *lex fori*. To treat it as a matter of procedure to be dealt with by the forum is to ignore its new-found status. That is not to say that unjust enrichment cannot be flexible in the international arena, merely that it should not be reduced to some form of procedure. The process of characterization cannot ignore the major elements of the claim and reduce it to a remedial device capable of being manipulated for the good of justice and public policy.

Finally, choice of law rules which are based on the *lex fori* tend to have one detrimental effect and that is they tend to promote or provide incentives for forum shopping—something which other rules within the conflict of laws rules are usually designed against. **20.126**

(b) Dicey, Morris & Collins *Rule 230*

Rule 230 of *Dicey, Morris & Collins* provides: **20.127**

> Rule 230 – (1) The obligation to restore the benefit of an enrichment obtained at another person's expense is governed by the proper law of the obligation.
> (2) The proper law of the obligation is (semble) determined as follows:
>> (a) If the obligation arises in connection with a contract, its proper law is the law applicable to the contract;
>> (b) If it arises in connection with a transaction concerning an immovable (land), its proper law is the law of the country where the immovable is situated (*lex situs*);
>> (c) If it arises in any other circumstances, its proper law is the law of the country where the enrichment occurs.

With respect to the learned editors, Rule 230 is not happily drafted. On its face, its meaning is unequivocal. We are told in Rule 230(1) that the obligation to restore the unjust enrichment is determined by reference to the proper law of the obligation. Rule 230(2)(a) to (c) then goes on to tell us how one determines the proper law of the obligation in certain circumstances concluding with the rule in sub-paragraph (c) that if none of the above circumstances apply, the general rule is that the proper law of the obligation is determined by reference to the law of the place of receipt of the enrichment. Putting aside any subsequent commentary or footnote explanations, that is how one interprets Rule 230 as drafted. **20.128**

The most important consequences of that approach are twofold. **20.129**

- The proper law of the obligation is not a flexible test based upon a consideration of the facts which may point to a particular law having the closest and most real connection with the underlying claim. Rather, the very wide general test is immediately cut down to various categories which, if applicable, lead to the determination of the relevant applicable law.

- The general rule is not the flexible test of closest and most real connection but rather fall-back (c), namely the law of the place of receipt of the enrichment. Or, to put it another way, the law of the place of receipt is considered to be the law having the closest and most real connection, unless the obligation to restore is associated with a contract or land.

20.130 But a close read of the commentary to Rule 230 reveals an entirely different approach. Gone is the rigidity of wording of Rule 230, i.e. if connected to a contract, the proper law of the obligation will be the law of the contract. If not connected with a contract or land, then the place of enrichment applies. The commentary exhibits a far more flexible and discretionary approach to determination of the proper law of the obligation and one that, with respect, is more likely to be correct:

> **34-018** To be useful in practice, this general principle needs to be broken down to reflect various types of claims to restitution which may come before the courts. Such restitutionary claims may arise (i) either in connection with an actual or a supposed contract between the parties or (ii) in connection with a transaction referring to land or (iii) without either connection. In order to determine the law with which the obligation is most closely connected, one must, it is submitted, classify it in terms of these three categories. If it belongs to the first category *it is likely to be most closely connected* with the law which governs the contract between the parties; if it belongs to the second category *it would seem that* its proper law is the *lex situs* of the land, and if it belongs to the third category the obligation of a person to restore the benefit obtained *may be most closely connected* with the law of the country in which he obtained the benefit.[100]

20.131 It is unfortunate that leading texts, one of which *Dicey, Morris & Collins* undoubtedly is, feel constrained to retain the old wording of various rules, even when it is clear that the present editors consider that that wording does not properly or accurately reflect the modern-day approach. That the wording of the Rule is out of date is hardly surprising given the wording was first introduced in 1949, some fifty years before unjust enrichment was in fact recognized by the House of Lords in *Lipkin Gorman* and at a time when quasi-contract was the accepted description of the claim. The reality is that if one were to adopt the approach of the editors commenting on Rule 230, the only conclusion one could sensibly draw is that the categories set out in Rule 230(2)(a) to (c) are no more than guides which can be departed from if other factual circumstances reveal another law to have the closest and most real connection with the claim. Rule 230 should be amended to reflect that approach.

20.132 The editors' departure from the rigid approach in Rule 230 is all the more evident when they come to discuss Rule 230(2)(c), which, on the wording of Rule 230,

---

100 *Dicey, Morris & Collins* (14th edn), para 34-018. Emphasis added.

applies when the claim is not connected to a contract or land. It will be seen below that the editors are willing to contemplate a much broader approach to the determination of the proper law in circumstances falling within Rule 230(2)(c).

None of this is to criticize the broader and more flexible approach adopted by the editors of *Dicey, Morris & Collins*. They are right to do so. The criticism is reserved for the maintenance of the rigid and inaccurate Rule from which the commentary clearly departs. The area is complex enough without having to worry about whether the Rules of *Dicey, Morris & Collins* match the commentaries to follow. **20.133**

Further difficulties emerge when one draws a distinction between the law of unjust enrichment and restitution for wrongs. Save where the wrong is a breach of contract, restitution for wrongs do not appear, expressly, to fall within any part of Rule 230—unless, taking it at face value, it is to be inferred that they are to be dealt with by the residual category Rule 230(2)(c), i.e. the law of the place of enrichment. The commentary, however, does discuss restitution for wrongs and says,[101] in the context of restitution after a commission of a tort, that the tortious choice of law rule should apply. That is a perfectly valid position to adopt and for many is entirely uncontroversial. The problem is that it bears no resemblance to Rule 230 and is buried in the text of the commentary. **20.134**

This whole area is in need of expert guidance. It is submitted, with the greatest respect to the learned editors of the next edition of *Dicey, Morris & Collins,* that serious consideration be given as to how best (i) to reflect the views in the commentary in the wording of Rule 230 and (ii) to have a distinct rule dealing with restitution for wrongs. Unless that is done, it will be difficult to get clarity in the case law since the courts are heavily influenced, and rightly so, by the views expressed in *Dicey, Morris & Collins*. **20.135**

(i) Rule 230(1): the proper law of the obligation   Assuming that the test is the flexible test as expounded in the commentary and not the rigid test assumed in the Rule itself, it is, necessarily, so vague and flexible that few will complain in principle that this is the correct approach.[102] On its own, it provides little practical guidance, although it has received some limited judicial endorsement. **20.136**

In *Arab Monetary Fund v Hashim*[103] the Court of Appeal applied Rule 201 of *Dicey & Morris* (equivalent to the present Rule 230(1)) and held that the law relating to the claim for bribery was Abu Dhabi. This authority is examined in some detail in para 20.212 *et seq* below. **20.137**

---

[101]   *Dicey, Morris & Collins* (14th edn), para 34-032.
[102]   Briggs, *The Conflict of Laws* (2nd edn), 213.
[103]   [1996] 1 Lloyd's Law Rep 589 (CA).

20.138   Some further, albeit limited, support for this Rule can also be found in the Court
of Appeal's decision in *Macmillan Inc v Bishopsgate Investment Trust plc (No 3)*.[104]
The facts of the case concern the activities that led to the downfall of Robert
Maxwell. Maxwell was the owner and controller of Macmillan, a Delaware
Corporation, which in turn, held shares in Berlitz International Inc ('Berlitz'), a
company incorporated in New York. Upon the instruction of Maxwell, but without Macmillan's knowledge, Macmillan's shares in Berlitz were transferred into
the name of Bishopsgate Investment Trust plc ('Bishopsgate') to be held by it as
nominee for Macmillan. Thereafter, some of the shares were used, without
Macmillan's knowledge, as security to raise loans for other companies within the
Maxwell Group. In March 1991, 76m of the shares were deposited with the central depository system of the Depository Trust Co ('DTC') in New York and from
that point on the shares ceased to be registered in the name of Bishopsgate and
were registered in the name of Morgan Stanley Trust Co, acting as Maxwell's DTC
agent. Macmillan sought to recover the shares.

20.139   Macmillan sought to characterize the relevant issue as essentially being a claim
in equity for restitution and on that basis asserted that English law applied as
the place where the enrichment took place. The defendants contended (for differing reasons) that New York law applied to the question of who had better title to
the shares.

20.140   The Court of Appeal held that characterization required analysing the particular
issue or issues in dispute and not simply the cause of action relied upon in the
pleading. The relevant disputed issue was whether the defendants could take
advantage of the defence of bona fide purchaser for value without notice and thus
obtain title to the shares. The availability of the defence was the means of determining which party had a better claim to title in the shares. The Court of Appeal
held that questions of title to shares should be treated in the same way as title to
tangible movables and be governed by the *lex situs*, which was the place where the
company was incorporated, unless the shares were negotiable instruments. This,
therefore, led to New York law applying.

20.141   In reaching this decision, Staughton LJ remarked:

> I am prepared to accept that Macmillan's claim is restitutionary in nature and
> I would accept without deciding that rule 201 of *Dicey & Morris, 12ᵗʰ ed.* determines
> what system of law governs such a claim. But the issue is not, or not any longer,
> whether Macmillan have a cause of action for restitution; it is whether the defend-
> ants have a defence on the ground that they were purchasers for value in good faith
> without notice of Macmillan's claim.

---

104   [1996] 1 WLR 387 (CA).

Auld LJ did not see a need to comment on the cases supporting the *Dicey, Morris & Collins* Rule.[105] Aldous LJ stated that the relevant Rule had no application on the facts[106] without casting any doubt on the Rule itself.

So what are we to make of a flexible proper law of the obligation approach? Briggs **20.142** is in general agreement with it, stating that it follows the best traditions of the conflict of laws in searching for the legal system which has the closest and most real connection to the claim. He sees such a flexible approach being particularly appropriate where the unjust enrichment claim does not arise in connection with a pre-existing legal relationship:

> In these cases, therefore, a flexible proper law rule is inevitable and correct, and the answer should be the law which has the closest and most real connection with the alleged obligation to make restitution, without embellishment. Any attempt to specify in advance what this means does not seem sensible.[107]

Jonathan Hill adopts a similar approach.[108] He appears to welcome the flexible **20.143** approach of the proper law of the obligation in circumstances where there is no pre-existing contractual relationship. In such circumstances, he does not believe a rigid adoption of the place of enrichment approach is suitable. He states:

> The logic of a proper law approach is to apply the law of the country with which the situation is most closely connected. If the country in which the money is received is not, on the facts of the case, the country with which the claim is most closely connected, the law of that country should not be the applicable law.

> Having said that, the task of identifying the most closely connected country is not always easy. It is tempting to treat the elements which are central to an unjust enrichment claim—the defendant's gain, the claimant's loss,[109] the unjust factor (such as fraud or mistake) and the territorial connections of the parties—as localizing elements within a general proper law doctrine. How these various factors might be weighted in a particular case is potentially unpredictable. Whereas in a simple tort case the place where the tort is committed has, prima facie, a direct and meaningful connection with the tort, the connection between an unjust enrichment claim and the place where the defendant's gain or the claimant's loss occurs is less obviously a strong one.[110]

---

105 ibid, 409.

106 ibid, 418G–H.

107 Briggs, *The Conflict of Laws* (2nd edn), 213.

108 Hill, *International Commercial Disputes in English Courts* (3rd edn), [15.5.17] *et seq.*

109 It is questionable whether the claimant's loss is in any way relevant or qualifies as a connecting factor for a claim in unjust enrichment. It is of course necessary to show that the benefit was received 'at the expense of' the plaintiff but the measurement of recovery is the gain received not the loss suffered. 'At the expense of' establishes the claimant's title to sue in any particular case: *Kleinwort Benson plc v Birmingham City Council* [1997] QB 380 CA. For a more detailed discussion, see Chapter 3, paras 3.33–3.45.

110 Hill, *International Commercial Disputes in English Courts* (3rd edn), 584.

It is indisputable that the approach to weighing up of these various factors is something that will need to be worked out on a case by case basis. But once the courts are presented with a consistent approach to determining the proper law of an unjust enrichment claim, it can be applied in the cases, thereby building up the sort of guidance this area of the law requires.

20.144   Joanna Bird's view is that a single choice of law rule may appear to cover all bases but will fail to provide any practical guidance in any individual case.[111] Further, she considers the rigid sub-rule approach, which is how she interprets *Dicey, Morris & Collins*' approach in Rule 230, to be too inflexible to capture all factual scenarios that may arise in an unjust enrichment claim. She advocates a half-way house where there are specific rules but there is also the flexibility to depart from those rules as and when it is evident another law is more closely connected with the claim. Her suggested choice of law rule is thus:

1. As a general rule actions in unjust enrichment are governed by:
   (a) The governing law of the contract, when there is or was a contractual relationship between the parties, or both parties were under the mistaken assumption that there was such a relationship between them, and the enrichment would not have occurred but for that real or supposed contract;
   (b) The law of the relationship, when there is or was a legal relationship between the parties, or the parties assumed that there was such a relationship between them, and the enrichment would not have occurred but for that real or supposed relationship;
   (c) The lex situs, where the enrichment arises from a transaction in relation to land; or
   (d) In the remaining cases, the law of the place of enrichment.
2. However,
   (a) if, in the circumstances of the particular case and in light of the purposes of the sub-rules in paragraph 1, another law is clearly more appropriate than that identified by reference to the sub-rules in paragraph 1, that other law should be applied; or,
   (b) if the law identified in paragraph 1(d) cannot be identified with precision, the law with which the obligation to make restitution is most closely connected should be applied.[112]

20.145   On close examination there would appear to be a marked degree of agreement as to the correct approach as between Joanna Bird and *Dicey, Morris & Collins*.

---

[111] This is inevitable since the single choice of law rule is trying to be all things to all men. It is important to remember of course that the Court of Appeal in *Macmillan v Bishopsgate* talked of characterizing the relevant issue not the claim. A claim in unjust enrichment may give rise to many issues: is the issue between the parties whether the defendant received anything? Or if he did, whether that amounts, in law, to an enrichment? Or is liability not really in issue but a defence of change of position is?

[112] J Bird, 'Choice of Law' in F Rose (ed), *Restitution and the Conflict of Laws* (Mansfield Press, 1995), 135.

In particular, Bird's suggested choice of law rule reads like one that might have been written by the editors of *Dicey, Morris & Collins* to reflect the more flexible approach exhibited in their commentary to Rule 230. The main difference is that Bird starts with the categories of unjust enrichment claims, rather than a general proper law of the obligation test, but accepts that another law might apply if other considerations dictate. It is not entirely clear whether and if so when such an approach might produce a different result from the approach advocated in the commentary to Rule 230.

(ii) Rule 230(2)(a): the law of the connected contract   There is pretty much **20.146** unanimity amongst most commentators. To the extent that the claim in unjust enrichment is connected to a contract or what was believed by the parties to be a valid contract, the prima facie rule is that the law of the contract should govern any unjust enrichment claim arising thereunder.

Such a view receives the support of *Dicey, Morris & Collins*,[113] Briggs,[114] Bird,[115] **20.147** and Hill.[116]

Stevens similarly supports such an approach,[117] identifying no less than eight rea- **20.148** sons, of varying weight and importance, why he considers this to make 'considerable sense':

(1) No claim in unjust enrichment can arise until the contract is no longer effective. It would be circular for the law of the contract to impose a duty to confer a benefit and the law of unjust enrichment to give a right to obtain the benefit back.
(2) It is usually sufficient for the claimant to establish that performance was made under an ineffective contract to establish a claim in unjust enrichment.
(3) A claim in unjust enrichment after the contract was declared ineffective would not conflict with the law on illegality or informality.

---

113 Rule 230(2)(a).
114 Briggs, *The Conflict of Laws*, 196. Briggs' view is expressed in general terms and is not limited to contract: 'Where there was a prior relationship between claimant and defendant, which has its own choice of law rule, and from or in connection with which the claim arose, the law governing the restitutionary obligation . . . to restore the benefit will be overshadowed, and will usually be governed, by the law which applied to this prior relationship. So if the restitutionary obligation arises upon the failure of a real or supposed contract, or from the commission of a tort, the law which governed the contract or the tort will have a strong claim also to govern the restitutionary claim [196–7].
115 Bird, 'Choice of Law' in Rose (ed), *Restitution and the Conflict of Laws*, 135.
116 Hill, *International Commercial Disputes in English Courts* (3rd edn), 582–4.
117 R Stevens, 'The Choice of Law Rules of Restitutionary Obligations' in Rose (ed), *Restitution and the Conflict of Laws*, 193–4.

(4) Insofar as the parties may have an expectation that their relationship is to be governed by a chosen law, they may also not unreasonably expect the restitutionary issues to be resolved by the same law.

(5) There is a marked reduction in characterization issues if the same law applies to both the contractual and the restitutionary issues.

(6) Problems with concurrent actions are also minimized.

(7) The uniform application of the Rome Convention 'avoids sterile disputes' as to the ambit of the Rome Convention.

(8) It will also assist uniformity of result with other signatories to the Rome Convention.

20.149 There was some concern whether this view was open to English law given the UK government's decision not to enact Article 10(1)(e) of the Rome Convention (applicable law deals with consequences of nullity): s 2(2) of the Contracts (Applicable Laws) Act 1990. Some maintain it is not, in the case of void contracts.[118] Others have explained that s 2(2) is simply an opt-out which leaves open whether the statutory rules apply: in itself it does not rule they should not apply.[119] Stevens adopts a more vigorous stance. He maintains that Article 10(1)(e) should be narrowly construed so as to be limited to void and not discharged contracts.[120] As Burrows remarks: 'On his interpretation, the reliance on the Rome Convention for determining the choice of law for restitution in respect of ineffective contracts is not merely possible but, in respect of restitution consequent on the discharge of a contract for breach or frustration, is dictated by the Rome Convention (because not within the opt-out).'[121]

20.150 The other potential concern about adopting this approach was the fear it may be misinterpreted as a throw-back to the days when unjust enrichment was not considered as an independent cause of action. Such fears are unjustified. This is no more than a reflection of the appropriate flexible attitude that needs to be adopted when considering choice of law rules. Categories, newly-established in domestic law, may need to be opened up in the conflict of laws when considering the appropriate choice of law rule. This is recognized by Briggs:

> This is not because the restitutionary obligation is itself contractual or tortious— it is plainly neither—but because it arises from and by reason of a prior relationship which is the *causa sine qua non* of the present claim, and because it is simply unreal to regard the consequential obligation as free-floating, independent of and uncoloured

---

[118] Hedley and Halliwell (eds), *The Law of Restitution* (Butterworths, 2002), [22.47]; *Cheshire and North's Private International Law* (13th edn, Oxford University Press, 1999), 673.

[119] Bird, 'Choice of Law' in Rose (ed), *Restitution and the Conflict of Laws,* 129.

[120] Stevens, 'The Choice of Law Rules of Restitutionary Obligations' in Rose (ed), *Restitution and the Conflict of Laws,* 194–5.

[121] A Burrows, *The Law of Restitution* (2nd edn, Butterworths, 2002), 620.

by its history. Quite apart from that, consistency of result may be enhanced by a choice of law rule according to which the laws applicable to history, claim, and remedy dovetail one with another.[122]

(iii) Rule 230(2)(b): proper law—*lex situs* Commercial fraud typically relates **20.151** to assets which can be quickly dissipated or at least swiftly transferred from one jurisdiction to another in an attempt to evade enforcement of any judgment the victim of the fraud may obtain. It is not often that Rule 230(2)(b) will be relied upon in this context and so we need not dwell upon it.

Its content is not surprising or controversial. Land holds a unique place in the **20.152** conflict of laws. Usually, both jurisdiction and choice of law will point to the situs of the land since any other approach would not guarantee that the outcome would be enforceable or have any effect at all on the relevant piece of land.

(iv) Rule 230(2)(c): law of the place of enrichment The main arguments for and **20.153** against this choice of law rule will be examined in the next section. For present purposes, it is important to understand what precisely *Dicey, Morris & Collins* is saying.

Taking Rule 230 and Rule 230(2)(c) at face value, it is quite clearly being said that **20.154** if the claim in enrichment does not relate to a contract (Rule 230(2)(a)) or to land (Rule 230(2)(b)), then it will be governed by the choice of law rule in Rule 230(2)(c), i.e. the law of the place of enrichment. In other words, the proper law of the obligation is the law of the place of enrichment unless the enrichment relates to a contract or land.

But a significantly different approach is revealed when one reads the commentary **20.155** to this rule by the present editors:

> **Clause 2(c) of the Rule.** Where money is paid to, or a benefit is conferred upon, another person with whom no prior contract, or supposed contract, exists, and it is alleged that the money or the value of the benefit is recoverable, eg because of a mistake of fact, the enrichment is likely to be most closely connected with the country in which it occurred, and the obligation to restore it to be governed by the law of that country. The rationale for the traditional formulation of clause 2(c) is that in the absence of a prior relationship between the parties to which reference may be made, or which may contribute to the identification of the proper law of the obligation to make restitution, the law of the place where the enrichment occurred may be expected to be that which has the best claim to be applied to any obligation to restore.[123]

The editors go on to point out that Clause 2(c) and the paragraph quoted above **20.156** have been judicially approved: see *Kuwait Oil Tanker Co SAK v Al Bader*.[124]

---

[122] Briggs, *The Conflict of Laws*, 197. Briggs is not a commentator known for his enthusiastic support of the unjust enrichment movement.

[123] *Dicey, Morris & Collins*, para 34-030.

[124] [2000] 2 All ER (Comm) 271 (CA). See also *Gulf International Bank BSC v Albaraka Islamic Bank BSC* [2004] EWCA Civ 416 (rule endorsed for purpose of dismissing summary judgment

20.157 But the following is then said, which appears to cut right through the whole approach previously adopted:

> But in view of the diversity of situations in which a restitutionary claim may arise, it may be that the place of the enrichment will not always give an answer which corresponds to the law which has the closest connection with the claim. In some cases there will be a pre-existing relationship between the parties which, though not contractual, may justify giving weight to the law which governed that relationship in the search for the law with which the obligation to make restitution has its closest connection; in other cases there may be no relationship prior to the event which gives rise to the claim for restitution.

The editors thereafter proceed to examine various examples of tortious and equitable wrongdoing.

20.158 The conclusion to be drawn from this commentary on Rule 230(2)(c) is that the editors believe that the law of the place of the enrichment is *generally* the appropriate means of determining the proper law of the obligation under an unjust enrichment claim which falls outside of Rule 230(2)(a) or (b). The editors consider that exceptions to this general rule are more likely to occur when dealing with restitution for wrongs as opposed to claims for unjust enrichment.[125]

20.159 The merits of the law of the place of enrichment, as the basis for the proper law of a claim in unjust enrichment, fall now to be examined.

(c) The law of the place of enrichment

20.160 There is no doubt that the law of the place of enrichment has received some support in the cases falling short of a clear endorsement as part of the *ratio* of a decision.[126]

- In *Chase Manhattan Bank NA v Israel-British Bank (London) Ltd*[127] the law of the place of enrichment had featured in counsel's submissions but ultimately the parties agreed that New York law applied on the substantive issues.

---

application). The editors recognize that Rule 2(c) has not been adopted as part of the *ratio* of any English decision: *Barros Mattos Jnr v MacDaniels Ltd* [2005] EWHC 1323 (Ch).

[125] See *Dicey, Morris & Collins*, para 34-052. It is to be inferred, from comments such as these, that Rule 230 is intended to cover both claims arising in unjust enrichment and restitution for wrongs—otherwise there would be no point in referring to exceptions to Rule 230(2)(c) being mainly derived from restitution for wrongs cases. There is no real justification nowadays for having one Rule govern both claims in unjust enrichment and for wrongs. One would not suggest one rule for contract and tort and the same reasoning applies here.

[126] See the excellent summary of the relevant case law in Lawrence Collins J's judgment in *Barros Mattos v MacDaniels Ltd* [2005] EWHC 1323 (Ch) at [84]–[105].

[127] [1981] Ch 105.

- In *Re Joggia (a Bankrupt)*[128] Sir Nicolas Browne-Wilkinson V-C agreed that Rule 230(2)(c) was sound in principle but held it was not necessary for him to come to any final view on the facts of the case before him.

- At first instance in *El Ajou v Dollar Land Holdings plc*[129] Millett J stated that a knowing receipt claim was equity's counterpart to the common law action for money had and received and that both could be classified as 'receipt-based restitutionary claims'. On this basis, he considered the governing law to be that of the country where the enrichment was received.

- In *Macmillan Inc v Bishopsgate Investment Trust plc (No 3)*[130] Staughton LJ was prepared to accept the correctness of Rule 230 generally but stated it had no application to the issue to be determined in this case. Auld LJ, after referring to Rule 230(2)(c), *Chase Manhattan Bank NA v Israel-British Bank (London) Ltd*, *Re Joggia (A Bankrupt)* and *El Ajou v Dollar Land Holdings* held that there was at best a *tendency to endorse* the approach in *Dicey, Morris & Collins* but no binding decision to that effect. He ultimately refrained from expressing a view on this issue.

- For the purposes of dismissing a summary judgment application, the Court of Appeal in *Gulf International Bank BSC v Albaraka Islamic Bank BSC*[131] was willing to accept Rule 230(2)(c).

- In *Arab Monetary Fund v Hashim*,[132] a case involving the receipt of bribe monies in return for acceptance of contract tenders, Evans J, at first instance, was unwilling to apply the place of enrichment test. He said:

  > . . . the 'place of enrichment' test described in sub-r2(c) makes obvious sense when the defendant to a restitutionary claim has received a sum of money in a foreign country where either he is resident or for some other reason he receives the benefit of enrichment there. But Dr Hashim had no connection with Switzerland apart from his interest in the JOJ bank account, and the money paid into that account was dispersed to a number of other jurisdictions, presumably on his instructions and for his enjoyment there. Switzerland was at best a temporary staging post for the money and was never its journey's end. A substantial part of it was used to purchase the English property which Dr Hashim intended to sell and has since made his home. None, or no significant amount, went to Abu Dhabi. This lends support to the plaintiff's alternative submission, which is that, even if the place of enrichment fact applies . . . the correct choice in the circumstances of the present case is English law.[133]

---

128 [1988] 1 WLR 484, 495–6.
129 [1993] 3 All ER 717 (rev'd on other grounds: [1994] 2 All ER 685).
130 [1995] 1 WLR 975 (Millett J), aff'd on appeal [1998] 1 WLR 387.
131 [2004] EWCA Civ 416.
132 [1993] 1 Lloyd's Rep 543 (Evans J), aff'd [1996] 1 Lloyd's Rep 589 (CA).
133 [1993] 1 Lloyd's Rep 543, 565–6.

Evans J was correct to reject the place of enrichment test for the bribery claim. It is not the correct choice of law rule for claims in bribery. The jurisdiction where a bribed agent receives the bribe may be entirely fortuitous, or it may be chosen deliberately to disguise his receipt—either way it should have no real bearing on what law to apply. A proper characterization of a bribe claim would look to the relationship between the bribed agent and his principal. Evans J did conclude the matter fell within Rule 230(2)(a) and not (c).

It is noted that Lawrence Collins J in *Barros Mattos* categorized both *Arab Monetary Fund* and *Kuwait Oil Tanker* as cases involving a pre-existing relationship and so falling within rule 230(2)(a).[134] With respect, he was right to do so.

20.161 Standing back from the cases, for a moment, what are the arguments for and against the law of the place of enrichment?

20.162 Various arguments have been put forward in favour of the law of the place of enrichment.

(1) The receipt of the enrichment is a central aspect of the liability for unjust enrichment, properly so characterized. On this basis, it might be said that it is appropriate to formulate a choice of law rule around the issue of receipt.

(2) Liability is being imposed on the defendant for his simple receipt of an enrichment. It makes sense that such liability be imposed by a law which has a close connection with that enrichment and which, in turn, is likely to be that which has some relationship with the defendant himself.

(3) Defences, such as change of position, are likely to involve conduct taking place at the location of receipt of enrichment and so it is appropriate to use that law for both issues of liability and defences.

(4) The enrichment or some of it may well still be located in the place of initial receipt of the enrichment. That law would be the only suitable law to permit proprietary relief for such claims.

(5) The place of enrichment has the same factual connotations as other connecting factors such as the place where the damage was incurred for tort. It is a factual issue and not a particularly difficult or complex one.

20.163 The problem is that the central element is the *fact* of receipt and not *where* it was received and in the modern age of CHAPS and BACS payments, it might be entirely fortuitous into which bank account in which jurisdiction the monies might be paid. Indeed, if the place of enrichment were to play such a high profile in the choice of law rule, it would create all the wrong incentives to choose some

---

[134] *Barros Mattos Jnr v MacDaniels Ltd* [2005] EWHC 1323 (Ch), [103].

form of off-shore tax haven where enforcement of any subsequent judgment may be difficult. If we can avoid creating choice of law rules which create such wrong incentives, it is suggested we should do so.

A second difficulty is determining the place of enrichment. Is that to be decided **20.164** simply by identifying the first bank account into which the monies were deposited? Commercial frauds of any sizeable amount are likely to involve the substantial moving around of monies, to launder the monies and avoid detection. When can we simply ignore the first receipt and consider the second and third? What criteria apply to determine which receipt is to be considered the material or relevant receipt? It is to be assumed that the place of enrichment is not to be pared down to a domicile/place of business test. Some of these difficulties were already encountered by Evans J in *Arab Monetary Fund v Hashim*.[135]

Panagopoulos argues that the place of enrichment theory derives from the fallacious **20.165** and now abandoned implied contract theory.[136] While there may well be some historical truth about this, it is questionable whether any modern-day advocate of the law of the place of enrichment is doing so on the basis of the implied contract theory.

Panagopoulos also suggests that it gives too much emphasis to just one element **20.166** of the claim for unjust enrichment.[137] The difficulty for Panagopoulos is that his overall theory relies entirely on the unjust factor establishing the relevant applicable law. Whilst it is certainly true, as he tells us, that receipt of enrichment is not all that is involved in a claim in unjust enrichment, the fact remains that it is closer to the heart of such a claim than simply to point to a mistake without enrichment. To focus solely on the unjust factor ignores the enrichment aspect entirely and with that, the heart of a claim in unjust enrichment.

(d) The law relating to the unjust nature of the receipt

In his thought-provoking book, *Restitution in Private International Law*[138] George **20.167** Panagopoulos puts forward an entirely different approach to the choice of law rule for unjust enrichment claims. He suggests that properly analysed the most crucial

---

[135] [1993] 1 Lloyd's Rep 543, 565–6. See also *Hong Kong and Shanghai Banking Corp Ltd v United Overseas Bank Ltd* [1992] Sing LR 495 (Sing HC) (supporting ultimate rather than initial receipt); *Thahir v Pertamina* [1994] 3 Sing LR 257 (CA). For a more detailed discussion as to the problems inherent in a place of enrichment test, see T W Bennett, 'Choice of Law and Unjust Enrichment' in (1990) 39 ICLQ 136.

[136] For a detailed account of this criticism, see G Panagopoulos, *Restitution in Private International Law* (Hart Publishing, 2000), 134–6.

[137] ibid, 137.

[138] (Hart Publishing, 2000).

element to a claim in unjust enrichment is not so much the enrichment but the unjust factor. Based on that theory, he advocates:

> ... the general choice of law rule, in terms of the proper law of the unjust factor, may be restated: restitutionary issues are governed by the law or the law of the place, with which the unjust factor has its closest and most real connection.[139]

20.168 There is no doubt that this approach has the attraction of being consistent with the general view that the law of unjust enrichment is claimant-sided, with the focus, for liability purposes, being on the quality of the intention to transfer rather than the conduct of the transferee.[140] On this approach, for a payment by mistake, the choice of law rule would be the law of the place where the mistake was made.

20.169 However, such a claimant-sided rule might sit a little uneasily in the conflict of laws which endeavours to generate rules which favour the defendant e.g. dominance afforded the law of the defendant's domicile for jurisdiction purposes. There must also be a danger that such a rule, in practice, turns into simply applying the law of the domicile or place of business of the claimant, since that is where they will often be when making such transfers which are in some way vitiated. In addition, the oddity of this approach is that it ignores entirely the issue of enrichment, which some might find is of at least equal importance to the claim in unjust enrichment as that of the unjust factor. It also has the consequence that the defendant's entitlement to rely upon security of its receipt of the enrichment will not be determined by the law of the place where that enrichment took place. In other words, a defendant may find the issue of whether it is entitled to retain the enrichment it has received in country X to be determined by reference to the law of country Y, which happens to be where the mistake was made. One might expect issues such as entitlement to rely upon security of receipt would be subject to or at least take into account the law of the place of receipt.

20.170 There is little sign, to date, that this theory has received any support in the case law. Unless and until it does, we need not dwell on it any longer.

(e) Concluding observations on choice of law for unjust enrichment

20.171 Practitioners looking for clear and simple answers will not find them in this area. That is unfortunate. The most likely candidates are:

(1) The overall test is a flexible one, based upon the proper law of the obligation, which is that law which has the closest connection to the obligation to restore.[141]

---

[139] ibid, 167. Although there is little to show that this view has any support in the case law, Panagopoulos's book and theory are important contributions to the debate.

[140] The law of the place of enrichment does not focus on the conduct of the defendant as opposed to the fact of receipt of the enrichment.

[141] *Cheshire & North's Private International Law* (13th edn, Oxford University Press, 1999), 687, citing in support, *Arab Monetary Fund v Hashim* [1996] 1 Lloyd's Rep 589, CA and *Baring Bros & Co Ltd v Cunninghame District Council* [1997] CLC 108 (Outer House of Court of Session).

(2) If the claim for unjust enrichment arises in connection with a contract (void or valid but terminated), *Dicey, Morris & Collins* suggests that the law governing the contract (or what would govern it if it were valid) applies to the unjust enrichment, subject to the possibility of applying (1) above: Rule 230(2)(a).[142] This view is also supported by Fawcett, Harris and Bridge.[143] The three cases cited in *Dicey, Morris & Collins* in the main text have been powerfully criticized by *Cheshire & North* (13th edn).[144] Lord Penrose in *Baring Bros & Co Ltd v Cunninghame District Council*,[145] after reviewing the relevant authorities, concluded 'that the sub-rule is wholly without judicial support'. If Rule 230(2)(a) is valid, the same principle is likely to apply to any claim for unjust enrichment arising out of any other pre-existing relationship such as a fiduciary relationship.

(3) If there is no pre-existing relationship, there is some limited judicial and academic support for the law of the place of enrichment (see above). It is recognized by *Dicey, Morris & Collins* that there is no actual *ratio* of a case which has endorsed Rule 230(2)(c). Indeed, Lawrence Collins J in *Barros Mattos Jnr v MacDaniels Ltd*[146] disagreed with Moore-Bick J's view in *Kuwait Oil Tanker Co SAK v Al Bader*[147] that the Court of Appeal in *Arab Monetary Fund v Hashim*[148] held approving the application of Rule 230(2)(c).[149] Lawrence Collins J concluded:

> The weight of dicta on the applicable law of receipt-based restitutionary claims is against the claimants. There is, however, no decision of the Court of Appeal in which approval of Rule[230(2)(c)], or the application of a similar principle,

---

It should be noted that although Evans J and the Court of Appeal treated *Arab Monetary Fund* as a case in unjust enrichment, it was in fact a case concerning a bribe, which would be more likely categorized as restitution for wrongdoing. *Baring Bros* was a void swaps case. Lord Penrose refused to apply Rule 230(2)(a) since the contract was void. He applied the flexible proper law approach. Lord Penrose did concede that this may lead to the same law as Rule 230(2)(a) in many cases. As set out in the main text, *Dicey, Morris & Collins*, in the commentary, differs only in that it sees a continued role for the sub-rules, even if they can be departed from. *Cheshire & North* does not.

[142] As set out above, the UK's decision not to enact the Rome Convention, Art 10(1)(e) into English law does not prevent the above conclusion or at least there is a reasonable argument to that effect. One is here applying the law of contract not on the basis of a provision in the Rome Convention but because the relevant choice of law rule for unjust enrichment points to the law of contract.

[143] *International Sale of Goods in the Conflict of Laws*, [19.10]–[19.34].

[144] *Fibrosa Spolka Akcyna v Fairbairn Lawson Combe Barbour Ltd* [1943] AC 32 (no discussion on point by House of Lords—no foreign law pleaded in any event); *Etler v Kertesz* (1960) 26 DLR (2d) 209, Ont CA (unclear why no unjust enrichment claim: one possible alternative explanation: *Baring Bros* [1997] CLC 108 at 121); *Dimskal Shipping Co SA v International Transport Workers' Federation* [1992] 2 AC 152 (parties agreed to apply English Law).

[145] [1997] CLC 108, 121.

[146] [2005] EWHC 1323 (Ch).

[147] Unreported, 16 November 1998.

[148] [1996] 1 Lloyd's Rep 589.

[149] [2005] EWHC 1323 (Ch) at [103].

is the ratio. Rule [230(2)(c)] is a tentative formulation of the application of the basic principle in Rule [230(1)] where the parties have no prior connection. There is no decision that Rule [230(2)(c)] must be treated as a free-standing rule mechanically applying the law of the place where bank accounts are kept irrespective of the factual circumstances and irrespective of the particular issue.[150]

(4) Although this section is dealing with claims of unjust enrichment, it is as well to record here that that category of claim called restitution for wrongs is most likely to be governed by the law of the wrong.

(5) Under Rome II, many of these erudite and intellectual issues will be swept away in favour of a simple factual regime. The starting point is that any pre-existing relationship between the parties will govern the recovery in unjust enrichment (Article 10(1)). This has the air of similarity to Rule 230 of *Dicey, Morris and Collins*. If, however, they have their habitual residence (as defined in Article 23) in the same jurisdiction, the law of that jurisdiction shall apply (Article 10(2)). This is a brand new approach to the issue of choice of law and has no comparison in the common law. If neither approach is available, it is the law of the place of unjust enrichment which will govern (Article 10(3)). This is one of the existing possibilities at common law although it is a little unclear whether 'unjust' adds much to 'place of enrichment'. Finally, if the unjust enrichment obligation is manifestly more closely connected with a country other than indicated under Article 10(1), (2) or (3), the law of that other country shall apply. This latter option has some similarities with a flexible proper law of the obligation approach which has been examined in the text above.

These rules will not, however, be universally applicable. Rome II excludes non-contractual obligations such as those arising from bills of exchange, cheques and other negotiable instruments to the extent the obligations arise out of the negotiable character of the instrument. Also excluded are such obligations arising out of the law of companies regarding creation, legal capacity, internal organization and winding up of companies. Although personal liability of officers is also excluded, this would appear to be limited to liability for company obligations as opposed to liability for breach of their own obligations.

Rome II also excludes matters relating to the voluntarily created trusts. Whilst it is true that a fair amount of commercial fraud concerns trusts imposed by law such as constructive trusts, off-shore trusts are very often used as the vehicle to hold substantial sums and are therefore just as likely to be the victim of a fraud by a breaching trustee as a company or other institution.

---

[150] ibid, [117].

What remains to be seen is the degree to which those claims which fall outside Rome II come to be treated in the same or a similar way to those claims within Rome II, on the basis that there exists no other dominant answer to the question of choice of law. Certainly it would be odd if a claim arising from a voluntarily created trust happened to be treated significantly differently to other similar claims not involving such a trust.

F. Equitable Claims/Restitution for Wrongs

The previous section was concerned with the choice of law rules for the strict **20.172** liability claims in unjust enrichment. In old parlance, such claims would fall into the common law category of money had and received. This present section is concerned with those equitable claims which may typically arise in a commercial fraud. Chief amongst our interest are knowing or unconscionable receipt claims, dishonest assistance claims and constructive trusts.

Before examining what little case law there is for each of these specific claims, it is **20.173** necessary to set the scene by examining the state of the relationship between equity and the conflict of laws, which, in turn, requires an understanding of the role of equity in domestic law. It will become obvious very quickly that this is an area which has suffered from very little attention by academics and very few airings before the court. Definitive answers are elusive.

(1) Understanding equity

The traditional role of equity is to fill in gaps and holes in the common law which, **20.174** left unfilled, would create undue hardship. To that extent, therefore, its role has always been as an accessory to the development of the common law. Whilst space does not permit a detailed examination of the role of equity in English law, it is hoped that a few specific quotations may help to make that role clear, which in turn may assist in determining how to approach the question of choice of law rules for equitable claims:

- *Snell's Equity* describes equity thus:

  Equity is thus a body of rules or principles which form an appendage to the general rules of law, or a gloss upon them. In origin at least, it represents the attempt of the English legal system to meet a problem which confronts all legal systems reaching a certain stage of development. In order to ensure that smooth running of society it is necessary to formulate general rules which work well enough in the majority of cases. Sooner or later, however, cases arise in which, in some unforeseen set of facts, the general rules produce substantial unfairness. When this occurs, justice requires either an amendment of the rule or, if (as in England some five or six centuries ago) the rule is not freely changeable, a further rule or body of rules to mitigate the severity of the rules of law. This new body of rules (or 'equity') is therefore distinguishable from the general body of law, not because it seeks to achieve a different end (for both aim at justice), nor because it relates necessarily to a different subject-matter, but merely because it appears at a later stage of legal development.[151]

- A further excellent description of the role of equity is found in *Lord Dudley and Ward v Lady Dudley*[152] by Sir Nathan Wright LK:

  Equity is no part of the law, but a moral virtue, which qualifies, moderates, and reforms the rigour, hardness and edge of the law, and is a universal truth; it does also assist the law where it is defective and weak in the constitution (which is the life of the law) and defends the law from crafty evasions, delusions, and new subtleties, invented and contrived to evade and delude the common law, whereby such as have undoubted right are made remediless; and this is the office of equity, to support and protect the common law from shifts and crafty contrivances against the justice of the law. Equity therefore does not destroy the law, nor create it, but assist it.

20.175 Immediately, such descriptions raise the following issues.

- The accessory role played by equity may not lend itself to choice of law rules separate and distinct from those employed by common law.
- In any event, the necessarily fluid nature of equity is likely to make any attempt to define specific rules for equity all that much harder.

(2) The options

20.176 Essentially, three main options present themselves[153] as the proper approach to the choice of law for equitable claims:

- no separate choice of law rule;
- equity is available whenever the English court has personal jurisdiction;
- equity is available whenever the English court has personal jurisdiction but tempered by reference to whether the law of the place where the wrongful conduct took place itself considers the conduct to be wrongful.

(a) *No separate choice of law rule*

20.177 Under this option, equitable claims would not have their own choice of law rules but rather would be accommodated within existing choice of law rules available for claims at common law. This approach is premised on the view that equity acts to mitigate the rigours of the operation of the common law and so does not require separate free-standing choice of law rules, since it can operate under the same choice of law rules applying for the common law claims.

---

[151] *Snell's Equity* (17th edn, Sweet and Maxwell, 2004), [1-03].
[152] (1705) Prec Ch 241. Described as a 'classic eighteenth-century statement' by ibid.
[153] See Briggs, *The Conflict of Laws* (2nd edn), 216–20.

Applying this approach: **20.178**

(i) Where the equitable claim is very much based upon the wrongdoing of the defendant, such as dishonest assistance in a breach of trust or fiduciary duty, that claim should be treated analogously to a claim in tort. Indeed, there is a reasonable argument that the definition of 'tort' in the Private International Law (Miscellaneous Provisions) Act 1995 is wider than the English domestic definition and able to accommodate this approach.

(ii) Where the equitable claim arises out of a pre-existing fiduciary duty,[154] or contractual relationship that claim will be governed by the law governing that pre-existing relationship.

(iii) Where the equitable claim is characterized as based upon unjust enrichment, such as, for some commentators, the knowing receipt claim, the choice of law rule for claims in unjust enrichment to apply.

It is tentatively suggested that there is much to be said in favour of option (i). **20.179** On its face, it would appear to fit most closely the role to be played by equity as outlined in the brief explanation set out above.

This is the option favoured by Jonathan Hill.[155] His concern is to avoid option **20.180** (ii) and the traditional view that all matters of equity are governed by the *lex fori*. In his view, option (i) is preferable because it enables equitable wrongs to be fitted within analogous legal categories without needing to formulate a specific choice of law rule.

Adrian Briggs, writing in *English Private Law*,[156] says it is 'strongly arguable' that **20.181** the distinction between common law and equity is a matter of domestic law only and should not be replicated in the conflict of laws. He goes on to say, however, that such an approach would create 'dissonance between domestic and private international law'. It is not entirely clear why such dissonance should be created and if so why it should justify adopting a different approach. Time and again we are told that we must be flexible in how we characterize certain legal concepts when it comes to the conflict of laws.

Given that *Kuwait Oil Tanker Co SAK v Al Bader* and *Grupo Torras SA v Al Sabah* **20.182** both pre-date the Private International Law (Miscellaneous Provisions) Act 1995, it still remains open to an English court to conclude that the definition of 'tort' in Part III of the Act is not limited to the English domestic law concept of tort and is wide enough to embrace equitable wrongdoing such as dishonest assistance.

---

[154] In other words, what Millett LJ called a Class 1 constructive trust in *Paragon Finance v Thakerar & Co* [1999] 1 All ER 400.

[155] Hill, *International Commercial Disputes in English Courts* (3rd edn), [15.5.5]–[15.5.8].

[156] Burrows (ed), *English Private Law* (2nd edn, Oxford University Press, 2007), ch 20, [20.186].

20.183   Yeo is not convinced that an English court, when faced with the appropriate facts, would be willing to characterize a dishonest assistance claim as a 'tort' for the purposes of the Act.[157] This is on the basis that there is no indication of any legislative intention to include equitable wrongs in this definition and there has already been some judicial opposition to characterizing the claim as being tortious: *Metall und Rohstoff v Donaldson Lufkin & Jenrette Inc*[158] and *Arab Monetary Fund v Hashim*.[159]

(b) Personal jurisdiction over the defendant

20.184   This option is premised upon the fact that equity has jurisdiction to act so long as the English court has personal jurisdiction over the defendant. If the court has that personal jurisdiction, equity can be invoked in exactly the same circumstances as would be the case in any domestic case. In other words, the personal jurisdiction over the defendant overrides and renders irrelevant any foreign law aspects which may exist in respect of the underlying claim. Equity applies as part of the *lex fori*.

20.185   There is some limited authority to support the proposition that equitable obligations of English domestic law will apply as part of the *lex fori* to anyone subject to the personal jurisdiction of the English court.[160]

20.186   There is little or no real support for option (ii) in the case law, i.e. the application of equity to an otherwise foreign law claim without any resort at all to the law of the place where the relevant activities took place. The few authorities in this area appear to require some resort to the foreign law to assist in determining the defendant's liability. That at least suggests option (iii).

(c) Modified personal jurisdiction over the defendant

20.187   The basis for this option is the same as in (ii). What is recognized in this option is the fact that the conduct of the defendant may take place in a different jurisdiction and so it is only right and proper to allow the law of that jurisdiction a say in whether or not the conduct was wrongful or dishonest. It would not be fair to render the conduct wrongful or dishonest if the local jurisdiction in which such conduct took place would see nothing wrong with it.

---

[157] T M Yeo, 'Choice of Law for Fiduciary Duties' (1999) 115 LQR 571.

[158] [1990] 1 QB 391 (CA).

[159] Unreported, Ch D 29 July 1994.

[160] Briggs, 'Private International Law' in Burrows (ed), *English Private Law*, [20.186] citing *National Commercial Bank v Wimborne* (1978) 5 Butterworths Property Reports 11958, NSW; *Paramasivam v Flynn* (1998) 160 ALR 203, 214–18 Aust Fed Ct. See also *United States Surgical Co v Hospital Products International Pty Ltd* [1982] 2 NSWLR 766, 796–9; *A-G (UK) v Heinemann Publishers Australia Pty Ltd* (1987) 75 ALR 353, 414–15.

As one commentator remarks: **20.188**

> On this view, notice will be taken of a foreign law if it has a significant connection to the case. But on this view, the maximum role of the foreign law will be to contribute data for the purpose of helping decide what English equity requires—if it requires proof of dishonesty, standards prevailing in the place where the defendant acted will shine a light by which to evaluate his conduct as honest or dishonest—or expects of a defendant in a given case. If this is correct, the availability to a claimant of English equitable doctrines would again depend not upon the prior application of choice of law rules, but only upon the existence of personal jurisdiction. So far as can be deduced from cases on dishonestly assisting in a breach of trust, in particular, this is approximately the basis of liability as it is currently understood: as long as the foreign law (usually in practice the place where the defendant acted) imposes a form of liability resembling the nature of the English action,[161] the claim will proceed on the basis of English law; were it to be shown that under the foreign law there was no ground for even arguing that there would be liability, this would be a weighty factor in denying that there was dishonesty for the purposes of the English claim. In other words, English equity would apply, without regard to choice of law, but with notice taken of foreign law. It is a possible answer but it is not the right answer.[162]

The cases referred to in this extract from Briggs are *Grupo Torras SA v Al Sabah*[163] **20.189** and *Kuwait Oil Tanker Co SAK v Al Bader*.[164] Both will be examined in some detail below.

Option (iii) appears to be in line with the decision in *Paramasivam v Flynn*[165] in **20.190** which the Australian Federal Court held that the *lex fori* applied as the applicable law to fiduciary duties. However, the Court went on to place this limitation on the application of the *lex fori*:

> . . . subject, perhaps, to this: that where the circumstances giving rise to the asserted duty or the impugned conduct (or some of it) occurred outside the jurisdiction, the attitude of the law of the place where the circumstances arose or the conduct was undertaken is likely to be an important aspect of the factual circumstances in which the Court determines whether a fiduciary relationship existed and, if so, the scope and content of the duties to which it gave rise.[166]

Applying this approach, Briggs says that 'the role of a potentially connected for- **20.191** eign law is to contribute data to what English equity requires or imposes in a given

---

161 In *Grupo Torras SA v Al Sabah* [2001] 1 CLC 221, the court stated that it was looking to the foreign law in order to see if there was anything in that law which rendered the imposition by the English court of liability for dishonest assistance 'inequitable', e.g. such as the existence of some form of defence under the relevant foreign law: see Chadwick J in *Arab Monetary Fund v Hashim* unrep. 29 July 1994 at p 45 of the transcript.

162 Briggs, *The Conflict of Laws* (2nd edn), 219.

163 [2001] CLC 221 (CA).

164 [2000] 2 All ER (Comm) 271.

165 (1998) 160 ALR 203. See T M Yeo, 'Choice of Law for Fiduciary Duties' (1999) 115 LQR 571.

166 (1998) 160 ALR 203, 217.

case in order to decide whether relief should be granted'. This is not so much a choice of law rule for the application of English equity but rather recognition that such an application is dependent upon jurisdiction. It is rejected as a viable option by Briggs on the basis that the whole of equity cannot simply be said to be a manifestation of English public policy.[167]

(3) Analysis of specific equitable claims

(a) *Knowing receipt claims*

20.192 The elements required for a knowing receipt claim have been examined in some detail in Chapter 5. For convenience, they will be summarized in this section.

- assets held under a trust or fiduciary duty;
- disposal of those assets in breach of that trust or fiduciary duty;
- beneficial receipt of those assets[168] by the defendant;
- the defendant having sufficient knowledge to render it unconscionable for it to retain the assets.[169]

20.193 There are certain obvious factors or characteristics that should be noted. Behind all claims for knowing receipt there is a pre-existing trust or fiduciary relationship pursuant to which the dissipated assets were previously held. That raises the possibility that Rule 230(2)(a) might apply. That said, the pre-existing relationship is not as between the defendant and claimant but as between the transferor and the claimant. It is thus one stage removed. Further, beneficial receipt and sufficient knowledge on the part of the recipient are core requirements which might suggest Rule 230(2)(c) or even the application of the closest and most real connection test. Exactly how these factors feature in the process of characterization is much dependent on English law's attitude towards their continued role in the law of knowing receipt.

20.194 As always, the process of characterization begins by understanding the domestic characterization of the claim and moving outwards, always being willing to be flexible and responsive to the fact that other jurisdictions may have similar but not identical claims.

20.195 As a matter of English domestic law, there has been a tremendous movement[170] on how to understand this equitable claim and place it in the hierarchy of other similar claims. In particular, there has been a groundswell of opinion that this

---

[167] Briggs, 'Private International Law' in Burrows (ed), *English Private Law,* [20.186].
[168] Or traceable proceeds thereof.
[169] Hoffmann LJ in *El Ajou v Dollar Land Holdings plc* [1994] 1 All ER 685, 700 CA.
[170] Although not necessarily agreement.

equitable claim is 'receipt-based' which properly forms part of the law of unjust enrichment and not restitution for wrongs.

- The driving force behind wishing to see knowing receipt claims characterized as being receipt-based and assimilated with the strict liability approach at common law was Professor Birks.[171] Much of his earlier work on this issue involved an attempt to re-interpret a whole series of knowing receipt authorities and in particular to suggest that the focus on fault in those cases was in fact directed at the availability of the defence of bona fide purchaser for value without notice and not, as would appear, at the question of primary liability. As already indicated in Chapter 5, whilst many will consider the argument, as a matter of principle, to be correct, the re-writing of the authorities to fit this approach most definitely was not.[172]

- In a seminal article, 'Knowing Receipt: The Need for A New Landmark',[173] Lord Nicholls took up the baton and argued along similar lines:

  > In this respect equity should now follow the law. Restitutionary liability, applicable regardless of fault but subject to a defence of change of position, would be a better-tailored response to the underlying mischief of misapplied property than personal liability which is exclusively fault-based. Personal liability would flow from having received the property of another, from having been unjustly enriched at the expense of another. It would be triggered by the mere fact of receipt, thus recognising the endurance of property rights. But fairness would be ensured by the need to identify a gain, and by making change of position available as a defence in suitable cases when, for instance, the recipient had changed his position in reliance on the receipt.

  One of the most important contributions made by Lord Nicholls in this article is the recognition that 'knowing receipt' may well involve two distinct claims: one based on wrongdoing and the other receipt-based.[174] Both Professor Birks and Lord Millett also favour this dual approach.

- In *Twinsectra Ltd v Yardley*,[175] Lord Millett added further support to the argument in favour of a strict liability approach based upon receipt of assets:

  > Liability for 'knowing receipt' is receipt-based. It does not depend on fault. The cause of action is restitutionary and is available only where the defendant received

---

[171] Birks, *An Introduction to the Law of Restitution,* 140–6; Birks, *Restitution—The Future* (Federation Press of Australasia, 1992), 26–42; Birks, 'Misdirected Funds: Restitution from the Recipient' [1989] LMCLQ 296; Birks, 'The English Recognition of Unjust Enrichment' [1991] LMCLQ 473; Birks, 'Trusts in the Recovery of Misapplied Assets: Tracing, Trusts and Restitution' in McKendrick (ed), *Commercial Aspects of Trusts and Fiduciary Obligations* (Clarendon Press, 1992), 149, 159–61; Birks, 'Persistent Problems in Misdirected Money: A Quintet' [1993] LMCLQ 218. For a different view see N McBride and P McGrath, 'The Nature of Restitution' (1995) 15 OJLS 33.

[172] *BCCI v Akindele* [2001] Ch 437 CA.

[173] Lord Nicholls, 'Knowing Receipt: The Need for a New Landmark' in Cornish et al (eds), *Restitution: Past, Present and Future* (Hart Publishing, 1998), 230–45. See also Lord Nicholls in *Royal Brunei v Tan* [1992] 2 AC 378, 382.

[174] Lord Nicholls, 'Knowing Receipt: The Need for a New Landmark' in Cornish et al (eds), *Restitution: Past, Present and Future*, 244.

[175] [2002] UKHL12, [2002] 2 AC 164.

or applied the money in breach of trust for his own use and benefit . . . There is no basis for requiring actual knowledge of the breach of trust, let alone dishonesty, as a condition of liability. Constructive notice is sufficient, and may not even be necessary. There is powerful academic support for the proposition that the liability of the recipient is the same as in other cases of restitution, that is to say strict but subject to a change of position defence.[176]

20.196 The thrust of these views, and the many other supporting examples that could be cited, is that there is no justification for treating knowing receipt claims differently from a strict liability claim at common law. Liability arises from the moment of receipt and fault is relevant only to the question of the availability of defences to the claim.

20.197 Of course, the authorities cited above are all considering this claim from a domestic law perspective only. However, it is difficult to see how such an approach would translate into anything other than the adoption of the choice of law rule for unjust enrichment claims for knowing receipt claims.

20.198 The one caveat to this approach of total assimilation of the knowing receipt and unjust enrichment claims, at least for conflict of laws purposes, is the degree to which the opinion that knowing receipt involves two distinct claims proves influential. We have already seen that Lord Nicholls put this view forward in his article cited above. It caused Professor Birks to re-think his position:

> Although I have myself strenuously argued that 'knowing receipt' should be regarded as a claim in unjust enrichment, and should therefore discard the incongruous requirement of fault implicit in the word 'knowing', the courts appear to have set their face against that view. It now seems right to abandon that analysis once and for all. It was a mistake to insist that 'knowing receipt' was simply a species of unjust enrichment which had been slow to understand itself and, in particular, slow to understand that liability in unjust enrichment is strict though subject to defences.
>
> The better way of proceeding is to accept that the ambiguities and uncertainties in the case law of knowing receipt arise from its having failed to distinguish between two very different kinds of liability, one wrong-based and the other based on unjust enrichment. The task is then, not to force 'knowing receipt' into one or other category, but to demonstrate that both kinds of liability are necessary and that neither renders the other redundant. Within the law of obligations the recipient of trust property can, on appropriate facts, be made liable for the wrong of misappropriation or he can be compelled to make restitution of his unjust enrichment.[177]

20.199 Such an approach appeared also to meet the approval of Lord Millett in *Dubai Aluminium Ltd v Salaam*.[178]

---

[176] ibid, 194. See also *Grupo Torras SA v Al Sabah (No 5)* [2001] Lloyd's Rep Bank 36, 62 where the Court of Appeal held that the knowing receipt claim may be either 'a vindication of persistent property rights or a personal restitutionary claim based upon unjust enrichment by subtraction'.

[177] Birks, 'Receipt' in Birks and Pretto (eds), *Breach of Trust* (Hart Publishing, 2002), 223–4.

[178] [2002] UKHL 48; [2003] 2 AC 366 at para 87.

One obstacle in the way of adopting either the strict liability approach or indeed **20.200** the dual-liability approach is the Court of Appeal decision in *BCCI (Overseas)Ltd v Akindele*.[179] In a section of the judgment of Nourse LJ (with whom Sedley and Ward LJJ agreed) headed, 'Knowing Receipt—a footnote', his Lordship referred to Lord Nicholls' article cited above and commented as follows:

> No argument before us was based on the suggestions made in Lord Nicholls' essay. Indeed, at this level of decision, it would have been a fruitless exercise. We must continue to do our best with the accepted formulation of the liability in knowing receipt, seeking to simplify and improve it where we may. While in general it may be possible to sympathize with a tendency to subsume a further part of our law of restitution under the principles of unjust enrichment, I beg leave to doubt whether strict liability coupled with a change of position defence would be preferable to fault-based liability in many commercial transactions, for example where, as here, the receipt is of a company's funds which have been misapplied by its directors. Without having heard argument, it is unwise to be dogmatic, but in such a case it would appear to be commercially unworkable and contrary to the spirit of the rule in *Royal British Bank v Turquand* (1856) 6 E & B 327 that, simply on proof of an internal misapplication of the company's funds, the burden should shift to the recipient to defend the receipt either by a change of position or perhaps some other way. Moreover, if the circumstances of the receipt are such as to make it unconscionable for the recipient to retain the benefit of it, there is an obvious difficulty in saying that it is equitable for a change of position to afford him a defence.[180]

The comments of the Court of Appeal should be placed in their proper context. **20.201** As their Lordships indicated, they had not had the benefit of any argument in favour of the strict liability approach and were also of the view that little could be done below the House of Lords.

So where does that leave the state of domestic authorities on the nature of liability **20.202** for knowing receipt?

- There are clear and unambiguous authorities which say fault of some form is required. They cannot be ignored or re-interpreted, notwithstanding the best efforts of Professor Birks.

- There are equally clear statements made in the House of Lords, and extra-judicially by Law Lords, of where the law *should* be going with this claim.[181] For practitioners, of course, the present state of the law is far more important, usually, than where it is proposed to develop the law.

---

[179] [2001] Ch 437.

[180] ibid, 456.

[181] In *Koorootang v ANZ Banking Group* [1998] 3 VR16, 100, Hansen J was considerably persuaded by the view that knowing receipt 'is most appropriately governed and explained by the law of restitution of unjust enrichment'.

- There is one authority, at Court of Appeal level, which has raised some concerns as to the merits of at least the strict liability approach to knowing receipt.

- The one interesting aspect that remains to be tested in the courts, and may well deal with some of the concerns of the Court of Appeal in *BCCI v Akindele* is the dual approach to liability. Such an approach would enable both sides of the debate to succeed, to an extent, although how such an approach might work in practice would need to be worked out.[182]

20.203 On this dual-liability basis, the precise nature of the claim being brought would need to be considered in order to know how best to characterize it. If it is based on receipt alone, then regard would be had to the unjust enrichment choice of law rule. If, in fact, the focus of the claim is the wrongdoing, then there is a greater argument in favour of applying the tortious choice of law rule under the 1995 Act and, after 11 January 2009, the provisions of Rome II.

(b) The conflict of laws authorities on knowing receipt claims

20.204 It is probably fair to say that the majority of decisions on knowing receipt claims have applied the *Dicey, Morris & Collins* Rule 230 as the choice of law rule for unjust enrichment claims and many of these have applied the law of the place of enrichment: *Chase Manhattan Bank NA v Israel-British Bank (London) Ltd*,[183] *El Ajou v Dollar Land Holdings plc*.[184]

20.205 In Singapore, two notable authorities deal with the question of proper law of a knowing receipt claim: *Hong Kong and Shanghai Banking Corp Ltd v United Overseas Bank Ltd*[185] and *Thahir v Pertamina*.[186]

- In *Hong Kong and Shanghai Banking Corp Ltd v United Overseas Bank Ltd*,[187] US$536,000, belonging to the claimants, was misappropriated by U, an employee of the claimant. It was transferred from Manila to New York and US$515,000 was thereafter transferred to Singapore. Michael Hwang JC had no apparent hesitation in applying what is presently Rule 230(2)(c). He considered whether 'enrichment' had to be immediate or whether ultimate enrichment survived. Applying the latter, he concluded the law of Singapore applied as the law of the place of ultimate enrichment.

---

182 Is there really any need for this dual approach? Would it not be more sensible to advocate the extension of the strict liability equitable claim based on *Re Diplock* [1948] Ch 465?

183 [1981] Ch 105 (Rule 230 used in counsel's submissions—the point was not disputed). This was not technically a knowing receipt claim.

184 [1993] 3 All ER 717, rev'd on other grounds (knowing receipt of proceeds of fraud).

185 [1992] 2 Sing LR 495 (knowing receipt claim).

186 [1994] 3 Sing LR 257 (CA).

187 [1992] 2 Sing LR 495 (knowing receipt claim).

- *Thahir v Pertamina*[188] concerned an agent receiving bribes. The Court held that it was unconscionable for the bribed agent to retain the bribe and that the obligation to restore the bribed monies did not arise in connection with the contract.

It appears likely that, unless the dual-liability approach is adopted, knowing receipt claims will be treated as claims in unjust enrichment and Rule 230 will be applied.[189] Further, it would appear that within Rule 230, Rule 230(2)(c)—the law of the place of enrichment—is the favoured approach. However, some flexibility is likely to be retained in the event that on the facts of a given case another legal system appears more closely connected to the claim. It is highly likely that knowing receipt claims will fall within Article 10 (dealing with unjust enrichment claims) of Rome II when it comes into force: see paras 20.100–20.104 for more details of the operation of this Article. **20.206**

To date, no case law has been found in which the knowing receipt claim has been characterized as analogous to a tortious wrong for the purposes of applying the tort choice of law rule.[190] It will be interesting to watch the development in this area as the comments in *BCCI v Akindele* filter through to knowing receipt claims requiring the application of conflict of laws principles. It may well be that Rome II is implemented before any such development takes place, leaving a knowing receipt claim to be governed by the choice of law rules set out in Article 10 of Rome II. **20.207**

(c) Dishonest assistance claims

The elements of this claim have been examined in detail in Chapter 16 on dishonest assistance and, for convenience, will only be summarized in this section. **20.208**

- there must be a trust or fiduciary relationship involving X, as trustee/fiduciary, and Y;
- X must have breached that trust or fiduciary relationship;
- Z must have induced or assisted in the breach by X;
- Z must have acted dishonestly in providing the inducement or assistance.

Although this claim includes a pre-existing fiduciary relationship, as between X and Y, and a breach of that relationship, it is quite clear that the core element is the dishonest inducement or assistance in that breach provided by Z. **20.209**

---

[188] [1994] 3 Sing LR 257 (CA).

[189] *Dicey, Morris & Collins* (17th edn): 'The conclusion to be drawn from these cases is that an equitable claim which is founded on an allegation of unlawful or knowing receipt, or any other equitable claim to disgorge an unjust enrichment, will fall within the scope of the present Rule [230]' para 34-041.

[190] Yeo, *Choice of Law for Equitable Doctrines* (Oxford University Press, 2004), ch 8 appears to favour knowing receipt claims being treated as a tort for conflict of laws purposes.

20.210 There is a marked degree of agreement amongst commentators that dishonest assistance claims should be treated akin to torts for conflict of laws purposes.[191] Hill has remarked:

> Where . . . there is no formal relationship between the alleged wrongdoer and the claimant an equitable wrong should be treated as a tort for the purposes of Part III of the Private International Law (Miscellaneous Provisions) Act 1995. So, Part III should apply both to cases where a duty of confidence arises otherwise than in the context of a contractual or analogous relationship and to cases where the claim is based on the defendant's knowing assistance in a breach of trust. The fact that English domestic law regards breach of confidence and knowing assistance in a breach of trust as equitable wrongs—rather than economic torts at common law—is more an accident of history than the articulation of an intelligible principle.[192]

20.211 The difficulty is that whilst this may appear to be a sensible proposal, it has not yet received clear approval in the authorities. So, it is often pointed out that the Court of Appeal in *Metall und Rohstoff AG v Donaldson Lufkin & Jenrette Inc*[193] rejected the argument that dishonest assistance could be regarded as a tort. However, in a comment which rather suggested they did not wholly agree with that conclusion, the Court of Appeal in *Grupo Torras SA v Al Sabah*[194] said 'that was in the limited domestic context of the old RSC, O.11, r.1(1)(f)'.[195]

20.212 In *Arab Monetary Fund v Hashim*,[196] a case concerning a large-scale fraud, Chadwick J was faced with the following argument:

- Money which had been misappropriated by Dr Hashim had been transferred to accounts at the Geneva branch of a bank ('the Bank').

- The present action consisted of contribution proceedings brought against Dr Hashim by FNBC which had paid US$13.45m in settlement of a claim for dishonest assistance made against it.

- It was argued before Chadwick J that the Bank's conduct was not actionable as a tort in England and any accessory liability for breach of trust would be actionable in England but not in Switzerland, which had no concept of proprietary rights arising under a trust.

- The issue before Chadwick J was therefore whether and to what extent an English court ought to recognize and enforce an equitable claim for monetary

---

191 R Stevens, 'The Choice of Law Rules of Restitution' in Rose (ed), *Restitution and the Conflict of Laws*, 189. One exception is Barnard, 'Choice of Law in Equitable Wrongs: A Comparative Analysis' [1992] CLJ 475.

192 Hill, *International Commercial Disputes in English Courts* (3rd edn), [15.5.7]. See also Clarkson and Hill, *The Conflict of Laws* (3rd edn, Oxford University Press, 2006), 246–7.

193 [1990] 1 QB 391, 474.

194 [2001] CLC 221

195 ibid, 256.

196 Unreported, 29 July 1994.

compensation based on fault where the fault alleged lies wholly in things done or not done in a foreign jurisdiction.

Chadwick J reasoned as follows.   **20.213**

- The fact that Switzerland did not recognize proprietary rights arising under a trust was irrelevant to a claim for dishonest assistance which is 'a claim for monetary compensation based on fault; it is not a claim to enforce a proprietary interest against a holder of a fund'.[197]

- His Lordship, relying upon Slade LJ in *Metall und Rohstoff*[198] expressly refused to equate dishonest assistance claims with claims in tort. Two points are worth making: (i) the only justification offered by Slade J for his view is that it is historical—hardly a ringing endorsement; (ii) Chadwick J questioned whether this reasoning could fully stand after the decision of the House of Lords in *Red Sea Insurance v Bouyges SA*.[199]

- Chadwick J reminded himself of what Selwyn LJ said in *The Halley*[200] as to why the English court inquires into and acts on the law of foreign country:

  in these and similar cases the English court admits the proof of the foreign law as part of the circumstances attending the execution of the contract, or as one of the facts upon which the existence of the tort, or the right to damages, may depend, and then it applies and enforces its own law so far as it is applicable to the case thus established.

- Chadwick J considered this approach was not limited to tort 'in the strict, common law sense'.

- Having concluded there existed a cause of action under English law, Chadwick J held:

  The second requirement, as it seems to me, was that the English court must have satisfied itself that was no rule of any relevant foreign law which—in the words of Lord Pearson in *Boys v Chaplin* ([1971] AC 356 at p.397)—would provide a defence to the AMF's cause of action; or—as it might, perhaps, be put in the context of a *Barnes v Addy* constructive trust claim—would make it inequitable to hold that an FNBC [the Bank] defendant should be treated as if it were a trustee. If, as the authorities show, the basis of such a claim is dishonesty or lack of probity on the part of the defendant, then it must be right to judge honesty or dishonesty in the light of all relevant circumstances; and those circumstances must include relevant provisions of the local law.

  It follows that I think the appropriate course, in the present case is to examine the evidence as to Swiss law not for the purpose of identifying any rule of that law which the English court would have been concerned to enforce, but rather for the

---

197 Transcript, p 42.
198 [1998] 1 QB 391, 474D–E.
199 [1995] 1 AC 19.
200 (1868) LR 2 PC 193, 203–4.

purpose of deciding whether, having regard to the legal framework within which the FNBC and its affiliates were conducting the operation of the numbered accounts at its Geneva branch, there was such dishonesty or lack of probity as would have made it equitable for the English court to treat those defendants as if they were trustees.

• Although Chadwick J decided the case based upon the need to establish civil liability in the place of the tort (Switzerland)—and this was satisfied on the facts—he nevertheless queried whether there was such a need. In particular, he doubted whether it was correct to say that the English court would afford no remedy in circumstances where the conduct of the defendant was found to be dishonest in the law of the place of the tort, albeit no claim could be established under the foreign law.[201] Given the facts, he did not need to decide this issue.

• Chadwick J concluded that the claimant would have succeeded in the English court in its claim against the bank and would have recovered not less than US$13.45m.

20.214   In the circumstances, the actual decision in *Arab Monetary Fund* was that the dishonest assistance claim was established by reference to the existence of civil liability under Swiss law. It may well have been that Chadwick J would have been prepared to find liability for dishonest assistance even if there was no civil liability under Swiss law, but that did not prove necessary.

20.215   In *Dubai Aluminium Co Ltd v Salaam*[202] Rix J adopted the approach taken by Chadwick J, and accepted that equitable wrongdoing, whilst not a tort in English law, nevertheless had marked similarities to it:

> It is true that liability in dishonest assistance is not a liability in tort: *Generale Bank Nederland NV v ECGD* [1998] 1 Ll Rep 19. Rather it is a liability in equity to pay damages based on fault: as Mr Justice Chadwick said in *Arab Monetary Fund v Hashim* (July 29 1994, unreported) at p.42B:
>
> '. . . the defendant is held liable in equity not because he is, or has been, a trustee of trust property; but because his conduct in relation to trust property has been such that he ought to be liable in damages for its loss as if he were a trustee who had disposed of the trust property in breach of trust. The claim is a claim for monetary compensation based on fault . . .'
>
> We of course know that dishonest assistance is not a tort in English law.[203] Our quest, however, is to suitably categorise these claims, not for the purpose of English domestic law, but for the purpose of the conflict of laws. That involves, as stated above, a bit of give and take on traditional categories. It is exactly the sort of marked similarities

---

[201]   Chadwick J contended that neither Lord Donovan nor Lord Pearson would have endorsed an approach that left no remedy under English law: *Boys v Chaplin* [1971] AC 356.

[202]   [1999] Lloyd's Law Rep 415 at 467.

[203]   Although see Lord Hoffmann's observations in 'Knowing Assistance and Knowing Receipt' in Birks (ed), *The Frontiers of Liability*, vol 1 (Oxford University Press, 1994).

highlighted by Rix J which make it suitable to treat dishonest assistance claims like tort claims for conflict of laws purposes.

Rix J in *Dubai Aluminium* was prepared to agree with Chadwick J that the custom **20.216** and practice in Dubai may be relevant, as a matter of English law, to the honesty or dishonesty of the parties before the Court [453]. But this would have no bearing on the parties' conduct outside of Dubai. In doing so, Rix J appears to be endorsing the approach which looks to the foreign law only to provide data for questions of honesty or dishonesty as opposed to requiring full double actionability.

Sitting at first instance, Mance LJ in *Grupo Torras v Al Sabah* was willing to adopt **20.217** the same approach as Chadwick J in *Arab Monetary Fund* and Rix J in *Dubai Aluminium*. Applying that approach, he found that Mr Folchi, the lawyer, should have realized that the instructions from his client were, on their face, improper. The lawyer's subsequent conduct in concealing what had occurred demonstrated his awareness of the wrongdoing. That sufficed to render Mr Folchi liable for dishonest assistance.

Mr Folchi appealed. In the Court of Appeal, it was argued that the restitutionary **20.218** choice of law rule (Rule 230) should have been applied. The Court of Appeal refused, maintaining that dishonest assistance is not a receipt-based liability amounting to unjust enrichment.

Mr Folchi also argued on appeal that Mance LJ should have applied the full double-actionability rule.[204] The Court of Appeal rejected this argument as being contrary to binding authority including the House of Lords in *Boys v Chaplin* and the Court of Appeal in *Kuwait Oil Tanker Co SAK v Al Bader*.[205] In *Kuwait Oil Tanker*, Nourse LJ explained: **20.219**

> The rationale of the rule that the act or omission of the defendant must be actionable abroad in civil proceedings between the same parties is by way of a safeguard against imposing liability upon a defendant in England as the lex fori for acts in respect of which there would be no liability in the lex loci delicti. However, it is not necessary for the act or omission to be characterised as a tort or delict under the foreign law, provided there is a right of recovery to a similar extent by way of civil action. The reasons of policy which dictate that the defendant should not be held liable in circumstances where, or to the extent that, he would not be held civilly liable in the country where the relevant acts or omissions took place, do not dictate that the legal basis of such liability should be the same. Indeed, the degree to which systems of civil law differ the world over, and the diversity of the conceptual routes by which they impose liability on a defendant to compensate or otherwise make restitution to a claimant in

---

204 The Court of Appeal understood this to mean that Mr Folchi could not be held liable in the English court for dishonest assistance if the evidence of Spanish law showed that it did not recognize a liability with essentially the same ingredients and basis of liability: *Grupo Torras v Al Sabah* [2001] CLC 221, at [141].

205 [2000] 2 All ER (Comm) 271.

respect of a civil wrong, militate against the requirement that the court of the lex fori should enmesh itself in an exercise of characterisation and fine distinction as between the remedies afforded by different jurisdictions to achieve a similar result.[206]

20.220 The Court of Appeal went on to examine the focus of Mr Folchi's conduct being in Spain and in particular examined the nature of his liability under Spanish law (breach of contract).[207] The Court of Appeal relied upon the findings of fact by Mance LJ at first instance that Mr Folchi would be held individually responsible for loss. He was described as the linchpin in giving dishonest assistance as he would have been had he been found liable as conspirator.

20.221 It would appear that the Court of Appeal in *Grupo Torras* applied English equity having regard to any foreign law which has a close connection with the facts of the claim for the nature and extent of any duties owed thereunder.[208]

20.222 The approach in *Grupo Torras* bears the hallmarks of option (iii) above, namely applying English law to determine the claim for dishonest assistance but taking into account the foreign law to ensure that it was not inequitable for liability to be imposed on the defendant.[209] *Dicey, Morris & Collins* says of this case:

> The court ruled that neither the choice of law rules for restitutionary claims, nor the common law choice of law rules for tort claims were applicable. It rejected the view that it was appropriate to apply a restitutionary choice of law rule to a claim which was for equitable compensation based on fault; and that there was a single choice of law rule for all claims in which the defendant was alleged to be personally liable as a constructive trustee. In the result the court freed itself from other constraints, applied Spanish law, semble as the law where the defendant had carried out those acts from which his liability was alleged to flow, to ascertain that his conduct gave rise to liability; and upon its being shown that it did, the liability which his conduct gave rise to under English law was confirmed and established. Hence a claim cannot fall within Rule 230 unless the measure of recovery is determined by the level of enrichment of the defendant. Claims for compensation for loss, or for expectation damages, will fall outside the rule.[210]

20.223 It remains to be seen whether the approach adopted in *Grupo Torras* will be maintained or whether, as many commentators would prefer, when faced with a set of facts falling within the 1995 Act, the court will be bold enough to interpret 'tort' widely enough under the Act to include dishonest assistance claims. After January 2009, it is likely that claims for dishonest assistance will be characterized as tortious for the purposes of Rome II and thus fall to be dealt with in accordance

---

206 ibid, [171]; see also Millett J in *El Ajou v Dollar Land Holdings* [1993] 3 All ER 717, 736
207 [2001] CLC 221 at [142]–[146].
208 See Yeo, *Choice of Law for Equitable Doctrines* for a discussion of this case: 278–82.
209 For a similar approach, see *Paramasivam v Flynn* (1998) 160 ALR 203; See Yeo, 'Choice of Law for Fiduciary Duties' (1999) 115 LQR 571.
210 *Dicey, Morris & Collins* (14th edn), para 34-035.

with Article 4: see paras 20.96–20.99 for an overview of the provisions of Article 4.

(d) Constructive trusts

It has already been seen that with claims such as knowing receipt and dishonest **20.224** assistance, the elements of which are firmly established as part of English law, that tremendous difficulties arise when trying to identify the appropriate choice of law rule or rules. Greater difficulties surround constructive trusts and issues of choice of law since English domestic law has not firmly and clearly established the criteria for such trusts. If the claim itself is not properly developed, no blame can attach to the conflict of laws for failing to sort out the issue of choice of law.

Against this background, it will come as no surprise that it is difficult at this stage **20.225** to be definitive as to the proper approach to choice of law issues arising in respect of constructive trusts. Such authority as there is can hardly be said to be setting out a principled basis for the approach.

Perhaps the best starting point is to remind oneself of certain incorrect usages of **20.226** the language of constructive trusteeship. These, at least, can be stripped away, to clear the decks. It will be recalled that this book adopts the modern approach and disavows any use of the language of constructive trusteeship to apply to a claim in dishonest assistance. It is a confusing short-hand for personal liability to account. This latter description of liability is more accurate. Such liability has nothing whatever to do with constructive trusts, as that phrase is properly used.

The Court of Appeal in *Grupo Torras v Al Sabah*[211] urged the need to go behind **20.227** the phrase constructive trust to discover whether the issues in dispute related to unjust enrichment, breach of fiduciary duty or vindication of property rights.

In addition, it is now necessary to factor into the equation the reasoning of the **20.228** House of Lords in *Foskett v McKeown,*[212] namely that proprietary claims, which includes claims for a constructive trust, have nothing to do with unjust enrichment and everything to do with the vindication of existing property rights. If that is how such claims are to be characterized as a matter of English law, then it is unlikely that an English forum would use the choice of law rule or rules for unjust enrichment claims if ultimately a constructive trust is claimed.

Some of the authorities dealing with choice of law for constructive trusts abide by **20.229** the distinction drawn between those cases where the constructive trust is imposed on an individual who has abused a *pre-existing* fiduciary relationship and those constructive trusts which have been imposed, in certain defined categories of case,

---

[211] [2001] CLC 221 at [122].
[212] [2001] 1 AC 102.

because of the unconscionable conduct on the part of the defendant. However, such distinctions are not always maintained in the case law. So, for example, a claim for bribery might in one case be dealt with as a claim in unjust enrichment and in another as a claim for wrongdoing.

20.230   In *Arab Monetary Fund v Hashim*[213] Chadwick J was concerned with that aspect of this massive fraud which related to Dr Hashim's misappropriation of monies away from the Fund of which he was President. Applying Rule 230(2)(a) of *Dicey, Morris & Collins* Chadwick J held that the law governing the pre-existing relationship as between Dr Hashim and the Fund was the *lex causae*. Chadwick J identified four relevant questions to be asked:

> I find nothing in the rule which is inconsistent with the view that, in cases involving a foreign element in which an English court is asked to treat a defendant as a constructive trustee of assets which he has acquired through misuse of his powers, the relevant questions are: (i) What is the proper law which governs the relationship between the defendant and the person for whose benefit those powers have been conferred, (ii) what, under that law, are the duties to which the defendant is subject in relation to those powers, (iii) is the nature of those duties such that they would be regarded by an English court as fiduciary duties and (iv) if so, is it unconscionable for the defendant to retain those assets.

20.231   It should be noted, however, that Chadwick J made it clear that he was treating the case as one giving rise to restitutionary obligations and was not making any ruling relating to property rights. Yeo says that had Chadwick J been trying to affect property rights he would have had to start from the *lex situs* and not from the restitutionary choice of law rule.[214]

20.232   In an earlier instalment of *AMF v Hashun*[215] the Court of Appeal was concerned with the payment of a secret commission or bribe into one of the defendant's accounts in Switzerland. The bribe was paid in respect of a building contract entered into by the parties which was governed by Abu Dhabi law. The basis for the claim in unjust enrichment was an allegation of breach of fiduciary duty.

20.233   Evans J held:

- the law of the employment contract could apply to the unjust enrichment claim;
- but he said he preferred to decide the case on the broader principle of the proper law of the obligation;
- the Court of Appeal affirmed the broader approach.

---

[213]   Unreported, 15 June 1994, Chadwick J. This case is not to be confused with the 29 July 1994 unreported decision of Chadwick J on another aspect of *AMF v Hashim*.
[214]   Yeo, *Choice of Law for Equitable Doctrines*, [5.51] and [9.09].
[215]   [1993] 1 Lloyd's Rep 543.

In *Kuwait Oil Tanker Co SAK v Al Bader (No 3)*, the claimants were various Kuwaiti **20.234**
companies and the defendants were senior officers of the first and second claimants. Pursuant to several scams, the defendants profited at the expense of the
claimants and misappropriated funds belonging to the claimants. The receipt of
the enrichment took place both in Kuwait and Switzerland—although only
Kuwaiti law was raised in argument. The claimants brought a claim against the
defendants in England for recovery of the monies.

Moore-Bick J held: **20.235**

- There were two claims, both of which were characterized as being restitutionary.

- In respect of the first claim, the place of enrichment (Kuwaiti law) applied to
  those claims where there was no pre-existing relationship between the parties.

- Under Kuwaiti law, the defendants would be under a duty to account for the
  property and that sufficed to render the defendants liable as constructive trustees in an English court.

- It is clear that Moore-Bick J's approach was to apply the restitutionary choice of
  law rule, being the place of enrichment in the absence of any pre-existing relationship. Under that law, being Kuwaiti law, there was a duty to account
  imposed on the defendants for their conduct. That was sufficiently similar to
  duties arising under a fiduciary duty for the judge to impose constructive trusts
  over them. Moore-Bick J stated there was:

  > . . . no reason why [Chadwick J's] principle should be limited to obligations which
  > arise under fiduciary relationships since what is ultimately important is the exist-
  > ence and nature of the underlying obligation. If the defendant incurs an obliga-
  > tion to the plaintiff under the *lex causae* which requires him to account for property
  > he has received, that in my judgment ought equally to provide a sufficient basis for
  > holding him liable as a constructive trustee in proceedings in this country.

- In the second type of claim, he held that the claimants and defendants were
  already in a pre-existing contractual relationship governed by Kuwaiti law and
  under Kuwaiti law the defendants owed the claimants the kind of duties that
  could be classed as fiduciary by an English court. Moore-Bick J thereafter
  applied the four questions identified by Chadwick J.

- The Court of Appeal[216] approved Chadwick J's reasoning. It did not proceed by
  way of the place of enrichment approach but was content to apply Chadwick J's
  four questions directly. The CA held: Kuwaiti law was the proper law of the
  relationship between the parties; under Kuwaiti law, the defendants were under
  a duty to account for the misappropriated monies; the nature of the duty to
  account would be classed as being fiduciary in nature by an English court; an

---

[216] [2000] 2 All ER (Comm) 271 (CA).

English court would regard the defendants as constructive trustees since it would be unconscionable for them to retain the funds.

It is difficult to be dogmatic as to how constructive trusts will be dealt with under Rome II since they arise in a myriad of different ways. Perhaps at this early stage, it suffices to say that constructive trusts typically arise on the wrongful receipt of payments which would strongly point to Article 10, dealing with unjust enrichment claims, being applicable.

(e) Breach of fiduciary duty

20.236 This section is concerned with those instances where an individual, who is in a fiduciary relationship with another and breaches his fiduciary duty in so doing. Obvious examples which arise in commercial fraud settings all the time include a director who misappropriates corporate assets or opportunities, or a solicitor who misappropriates his client's assets. These are all examples where there is a pre-existing fiduciary relationship. The unconscionable conduct does not itself both establish and prove the breach, as occurs where a stranger steals from another.

20.237 Accordingly, it is inconceivable that such claims would be subject to any choice of law rule except one based very much on the law governing the pre-existing relationship that establishes the fiduciary duties in the first place. The point is well made by reference to the Court of Appeal's decision in *Base Metal Trading Ltd v Shamurin*.[217] This case concerned three Russian individuals who set up a company in Guernsey to carry out trading outside of Russia. The defendant was made one of the directors of the company. Most business was in fact conducted in Russia for and on behalf of the company. The investments failed miserably and claims were brought against the defendant in tort for breach of duty of care and in equity for breach of fiduciary duty. At first instance, Tomlinson J held that the claims in duty of care and in equity were governed by Russian law being where, in substance, the cause of action had arisen.

20.238 On appeal, the Court of Appeal (i) upheld Russian law as being the law governing the tortious claim since that was where in substance that cause of action accrued, and (ii) held that Guernsey law applied to the breach of fiduciary duty claim since the relationship between the defendant director and the company was governed by the law of the place of incorporation of the company, being Guernsey.

20.239 It is unlikely that any different conclusion would have been reached on the choice of law for breach of fiduciary duty claim had the matter been governed by Rome II, since Article 10(1) provides for the court to take into account any pre-existing relationship between the parties which may be closely connected with the dispute.

---

[217] [2005] 1 WLR 1157.

PART VIII

TRACING, DISCLOSURE AND INJUNCTIONS

21

TRACING

A. Introduction

Complex commercial fraud and money laundering are bed-fellows. It is one thing **21.01** to deceive a company or individual out of a lot of money. It is quite another to ensure that the proceeds of that deception are not readily located. An intrinsic aspect of any complex commercial fraud is the issue of how best to launder the proceeds and thereby place as much distance between the fraudulent events and the present location of the proceeds of that fraud. It is here where the law of tracing plays a crucial role.

Tracing is one important means by which the claimant can link the fraud with **21.02** particular assets believed to be the proceeds of that fraud. It is tracing that provides or should provide the mechanism to combat and meet the demands created by modern day money laundering. Given money laundering techniques are constantly

473

evolving and taking advantage of improvements in technology, it is important that tracing is capable of evolving and adapting to meet such changes. A system of tracing which fails to adapt to modern money laundering techniques will very quickly render common law and equitable remedies for fraud impotent. Indeed, as shall be seen, the debate about the (in)ability of the common law rules to trace through a 'stream of electrons' is a frightening example of how the proper and continual development of this area of the law can be hampered by reasoning which refuses to permit the common law to evolve to meet the demands of money laundering.

21.03 The law of tracing has undergone a significant period of clarification and development over the last decade or so. This has principally been driven by the work of academics and academically minded judges which has shown clearly the distinction between tracing, on the one hand, and the concepts of following and claiming on the other. In divorcing tracing from any notion of claiming, this exercise has highlighted the need for a unified approach to tracing, rather than the maintenance of the dual system at common law and equity. Our better understanding of the distinction between tracing and following has helped to clarify when the court will impose proprietary relief. Not all agree with the outcome.

21.04 This chapter examines the nature of tracing and the modern approach to this topic. Thereafter, it analyses the two distinct sets of rules for tracing at common law and in equity. As will be seen in the last section, the calls for the unification of these two sets of rules may well be deafening but unless and until the House of Lords in fact removes the barriers to unification, it is necessary for practitioners to work within the two systems as they exist at the moment. It is for that reason that the two sets of rules must be examined separately.

B. Nature of Tracing

(1) Traditional view

21.05 The traditional view sought to treat the law of tracing as some ill-defined cause of action or (proprietary) remedy in itself. Parties would talk of having a 'tracing claim' or seeking a 'tracing injunction', where the word 'tracing' would be used to describe the nature of the claim or type of injunction. So a 'tracing claim' would be one in which the claimant is seeking to establish a proprietary claim to particular assets. Similarly, a 'tracing injunction' was the name given to an injunction in aid of such a proprietary claim, and was to be distinguished from the typical Mareva or freezing injunction by the fact that it sought to freeze a specific asset over which the claimant asserts ownership.

Likewise, the earlier academic work used the language of a 'right to trace' or a 'tra- **21.06**
cing remedy':

> The right to trace is recognised both at common law and in equity. It may be invoked
> for a number of reasons, for example, to claim a share in the profit if property has
> increased in value, or to avoid a limitation period. It is used much more frequently,
> though, on an insolvency or bankruptcy, for the *tracing remedy* gives priority over
> general creditors, the claimant recovering his property (or its value in full) before the
> other claims are satisfied.[1]

The use of this type of language was not the reserve of the academic and was **21.07**
known to appear in judgments, from time to time.[2] So, for example, in *El Ajou v
Dollar Land Holdings plc (No 2)*,[3] Robert Walker J talked of the 'proprietary remedy of tracing' and in *Agip (Africa) Ltd v Jackson*[4] Millett J stated that '[t]he tracing
claim in equity gives rise to a proprietary remedy'. Occasionally, in the confusion,
the 'tracing claim' was even pleaded independently of the claim for a constructive
trust.[5]

Even in his seminal article, 'Tracing the Proceeds of Fraud',[6] Sir Peter Millett drew **21.08**
a distinction between common law and equitable tracing as follows:

> Tracing at common law, unlike its counterpart in equity, is neither a cause of action
> nor a remedy but serves an evidential purpose. The cause of action is for money had
> and received. The remedy is an order for account and payment. Tracing at common
> law enables the defendant to be identified as the recipient of the plaintiff's money
> and the measure of his liability to be determined by the amount of the plaintiff's
> money he is shown to have received.[7]

While Sir Peter Millett's description of the role played by common law tracing
would find favour with modern thinking, the same cannot be said for his view that
tracing in equity represents a cause of action or a remedy in itself. Indeed, Sir Peter
Millett himself would not now endorse such a view.[8]

---

[1] Robert Pearce, 'A Tracing Paper' (1976) 40 Conv 277.
[2] It would be wrong to conclude that this inappropriate use of language to describe the tracing
process was confined only to the English judiciary. Australian and New Zealand judgments were not
immune from the language of the 'tracing claim' or the 'tracing remedy': see e.g. *Liggett v Kensington*
[1993] 1 NZLR 257 at 269 and 281; *Re Stephenson Nominees Pty Ltd v Official Receiver: ex parte
Roberts* (1987) 76 ALR 485 at 493.
[3] [1995] 2 All ER 213, 219.
[4] [1990] Ch 265, 290.
[5] See *Cowan de Groot Properties Ltd v Eagle Trust plc* [1992] 4 All ER 700, 767.
[6] (1991) 107 LQR 71. It is indicative of just how far the law of tracing has developed when one
compares Sir Peter Millett's views on tracing as stated in this article and those he sets out in subsequent judgments such as *Boscawen v Bajwa* [1996] 1 WLR 328.
[7] 'Tracing the Proceeds of Fraud' (1991) 107 LQR 71, 72.
[8] See Millett LJ in *Boscawen v Bajwa* [1996] 1 WLR 328, 334. This is just one example of the
manner and force in which Millett LJ has adopted the new thinking on the law of tracing.

21.09   The traditional view conflated the concepts of tracing and claiming with the consequence that tracing was simply seen as the descriptive element of the equitable proprietary claim and was never subjected to the type of sustained analysis which has incurred in recent times. By separating tracing from claiming, we are afforded a chance to examine the relationship between tracing and claiming, what types of claims require tracing and what role tracing plays in those claims. This analysis reveals that the role of tracing is not confined to equitable proprietary claims and extends to common law claims and to certain personal claims.

21.10   Further, the traditional view did not appear to draw any distinction between the physical act of 'following' one's assets and the metaphysical act of 'tracing'. This will be examined in more detail below and it will be evident that the distinction between 'following' and 'tracing' has helped to define the parameters of the debate as to when the English court will grant proprietary remedies.

(2) Modern view

21.11   The driving force behind the recent clarification in our thinking on the law of tracing has been the work of Lionel Smith and the late Professor Birks.[9] Their work, together with recent judicial pronouncements in this area, has identified and grappled with the following issues in the law of tracing:

- following and tracing;
- tracing assets or value;
- tracing and claiming;
- tracing and causation.

Each of these topics merits close analysis.

(a) *Following and tracing*[10]

21.12   (i) **The distinction established**   An asset is followed (but not traced) when, remaining in its identifiable form, it is passed through the hands of subsequent recipients without substitution or change in form. So if my pen is taken by X and transferred to Y, I can follow my pen into the hands of X and from there to Y. Following does not involve any exchange product or substitutions of the original asset. It is the physical act of identifying the location of the pen.[11]

---

⁹ See, e.g. Birks, 'Mixing and Tracing: Property and Restitution' (1992) 45 CLP 69; Birks, 'On Taking Seriously the Difference Between Tracing and Claiming' (1997) 11 Trust Law International 2; Lionel Smith, 'Tracing into the Payment of a Debt' [1995] CLJ 290; Smith, *The Law of Tracing* (Oxford University Press, 1997). See also earlier articles by Scott, 'The Right to "Trace" at Common Law' (1965–6) 7 W Aus LR 463; Professor Goode, 'The Right to Trace and its Impact on Commercial Transactions' (1976) 92 LQR 360, 528.

¹⁰ This distinction is examined in some detail by Smith, *The Law of Tracing*, ch 2.

¹¹ See ibid, 6.

The factual context of tracing is substitution.[12] The issue of tracing only arises **21.13** when the original object (the pen) is exchanged for another product (say a ruler). The process of tracing is not concerned with locating the original asset, the pen, but rather with its exchange product or substitute in which the value located within the original asset is now said to be present. So if, in our example, Y gives X a ruler in exchange for the pen, one can follow the pen into the hands of Y and trace into its exchange product, the ruler, now in the hands of X.

The distinction between following and tracing has now received judicial recogni- **21.14** tion and endorsement by the House of Lords in *Foskett v McKeown*[13] where Lord Millett stated:[14]

> The process of ascertaining what happened to the plaintiff's money involves both tracing and following. These are both exercises in locating assets which are or may be taken to represent an asset belonging to the plaintiffs and to which they assert ownership. The processes of following and tracing are, however distinct. Following is the process of following the same asset as it moves from hand to hand. Tracing is the process of identifying a new asset as the substitute for the old. Where one asset is exchanged for another, a claimant can elect whether to follow the original asset into the hands of the new owner or to trace its value into the new asset in the hands of the same owner. In practice his choice is often dictated by the circumstances.[15]

(ii) **The importance of the distinction**   The recognition of this distinction has **21.15** a significant bearing on our understanding of when the court will grant propri- etary remedies. This was examined in greater detail in Chapter 3 on unjust enrich- ment but it suffices to give an overview in this chapter.

In the case of following, it is relatively easy to appreciate that the reason why the **21.16** claimant can assert ownership over the pen is because it was his pen to start off with and it remains so. The claimant's ownership, which existed right at the begin- ning, is the reason why he can now claim ownership over the very same pen, albeit in different hands. The only answer to such a claim would be whether the present recipient can establish some form of defence (such as bona fide purchaser for value without notice). In this case, the proprietary claim is governed by the claimant's pre-existing ownership of the pen. Some commentators call this a 'pure propri- etary claim'.[16]

---

12 Birks, 'Mixing and Tracing: Property and Restitution' (1992) 45(2) CLP 69, 84.
13 *Foskett v McKeown* [2001] 1 AC 102.
14 ibid, 127.
15 This distinction appears also to be accepted by *Goff and Jones* (7th edn), 98, n 1.
16 Burrows, *The Law of Restitution* (2nd edn, Butterworths, 2002), 81. According to Burrows, a pure proprietary claim lies outside of the law of restitution (or at least outside the law of unjust enrichment). The existence or otherwise of the claim is dependent upon the law of property.

21.17 In the case of tracing, however, the claimant may wish to assert ownership over the ruler and not the pen. But the ruler was not the claimant's at the start of the story and so it is unclear upon what basis the claimant can assert ownership of it. This issue has given rise to a myriad of questions. Is it enough simply to point to the fact that the ruler is the substituted product of the pen and the pen was originally owned by the claimant for the claimant to assert ownership over the ruler? If so, why does the claimant's ownership of the pen mean he now owns the ruler? Does this imply he no longer owns the pen? If so, at what point did he lose ownership in the pen and gain it in the ruler? Or does he have a choice as to which he now wishes to own?

21.18 There are two schools of thought in respect of these questions: (i) the unjust enrichment school,[17] and (ii) the proprietary school.[18] The debate between these two schools of thought is no arid academic exercise.[19] It has fundamental practical consequences for the development of proprietary remedies under English law. The outcome to this debate has a direct bearing on the following issues: what criteria are necessary for a proprietary claim? Do the requirements for a claim in unjust enrichment have to be satisfied? If so, what are the relevant unjust factors which would justify a proprietary claim? What is the relevant limitation period, if any, for such a claim? Is the proprietary claim fault-based or strict liability? What defences are available to such a claim? These and other practical issues are premised upon a proper classification of proprietary remedies and an understanding of the basis for granting such remedies.

21.19 According to the unjust enrichment school, there are at least two main types of proprietary claim. There is what we have already labelled the pure proprietary claim where, to revert to our example, the claimant is seeking the return of his pen. That claim does not establish *new* proprietary rights but rather simply recognizes and gives effect to the existing ownership rights of the claimant in respect of the pen. Such a claim has nothing to do with the law of unjust enrichment: it is a claim arising out of the law of property. See Birks, *Unjust Enrichment* (2nd edn).

21.20 But where, in our example, the claimant wishes to assert ownership over the ruler, this school of thought rejects the notion that any such claim could reasonably be based upon the fact that the claimant was, at the start of the story, the owner

---

[17] The main advocates of this point of view are Birks, see e.g. 'Establishing a Proprietary Base' [1997] RLR 83, 91; 'On Taking Seriously the Difference between Tracing and Claiming' (1997) 11 Trust Law Int 2, 7–8; Burrows, 'Proprietary Restitution: Unmasking Unjust Enrichment' (2001) 117 LQR 412; *The Law of Restitution*, 60–4. *Goff and Jones* (para 2-005) no longer appears to draw this distinction post the decision of the House of Lords in *Foskett v McKeown* [2001] 1 AC 102.

[18] See the House of Lords in ibid.

[19] The practical consequences of the outcome of this debate were highlighted by Lord Millett in his speech in ibid, 129.

of the pen.[20] Ownership of the pen says nothing about ownership of the ruler.
The reason for the granting of ownership over the ruler is to prevent the unjust
enrichment of the recipient of that ruler:

> Without P's consent, D employs the value of P's asset to acquire a new store of value
> for himself. D is enriched from P, in the sense of from the use of P's property, and the
> law's response is to create a new right that carries the enrichment back to P . . .
> Proprietary interests contingent upon tracing, which is as much to say proprietary
> interests in traceable substitutes, for other assets in which the claimant undoubtedly
> did hold a proprietary interest, always arise from unjust enrichment.[21]

21.21 According to the proprietary school, the claimant obtains a property claim to the
exchange product (e.g. the ruler) because and only because the claimant had such
a claim to the original asset (the pen) and through the process of tracing it is now
established that the value which existed in the pen is to be located in its substitute,
the ruler. Unjust enrichment has no relevance to such a claim because it is 'the fact
of substitution [which] creates a proprietary interest in the new asset by operation
of law because the substitute represents the original asset'.[22]

21.22 This debate has, at least for the present, been resolved in favour of the proprietary
school by the House of Lords decision in *Foskett v McKeown*.[23] This case concerned a trustee who had misappropriated trust money belonging to the beneficiaries and used it to pay for the fourth and fifth premiums on his own life insurance
policy. The trustee committed suicide, giving rise to a payment under the policy
of £1m. The beneficiaries claimed a proportionate share of this £1m (£400,000,
in fact) on the basis that trust money had been used to pay two of the premiums
under the policy. The Court of Appeal limited the beneficiaries to a lien over
the trust funds for the recovery of the misappropriated funds. The House of Lords
(3–2) held that the beneficiaries were entitled to a proportionate share of the policy proceeds, being £400,000. In so doing, their Lordships emphatically rejected
the theory that any such claim was based upon unjust enrichment.

---

[20] In *The Law of Restitution*, Burrows argues at 81: '. . .it is misleading to regard tracing as being
concerned with 'the vindication of proprietary rights'. That is, it is fictional to say that a claimant is
given ownership of traced property because his or her ownership of the original property continues
through to the substitute property. The truth is that the claimant may be given a new title to the
traced property to reverse the defendant's unjust enrichment at the claimant's expense.'

[21] Birks, 'Property and Unjust Enrichment: Categorical Truths' [1997] New Zealand Law Rev
623, 661. See also Burrows, *The Law of Restitution*, at 62: 'The law of restitution, being concerned
with the principle against unjust enrichment, includes that part of the law of property in which
proprietary remedies respond to (or, as one might otherwise express it, proprietary rights are created
in response to) unjust enrichment.'

[22] Graham Virgo, 'Vindicating vindication: *Foskett v McKeown* reviewed' in Hudson (ed), *New
Perspectives on Property Law, Obligations and Restitution* (Routledge/Cavendish, 2003), ch 10. This chapter provides a detailed analysis of the reasoning of the House of Lords in *Foskett v McKeown*. The analysis
is developed in his *Principles of the Law of Restitution* (2nd edn, Oxford University Press, 2006).

[23] [2001] AC 102.

21.23   Lord Millett, giving the leading speech, said:

> The transmission of a claimant's property rights from one asset to its traceable pro-
> ceeds is part of our law of property, not of the law of unjust enrichment. There is no
> 'unjust factor' to justify restitution (unless 'want of title' be one, which makes the
> point). The claimant succeeds if at all by virtue of his own title, not to reverse unjust
> enrichment.[24]

21.24   He later went on to add:

> As I have already pointed out, the plaintiffs seek to vindicate their property rights,
> not to reverse unjust enrichment. . . . A plaintiff who brings an action in unjust
> enrichment must show that the defendant has been enriched at the plaintiff's
> expense, for he cannot have been unjustly enriched if he has not been enriched at all.
> But the plaintiff is not concerned to show that the defendant is in receipt of property
> belonging beneficially to the plaintiff or its traceable proceeds. The fact that the bene-
> ficial ownership of the property has passed to the defendant provides no defence;
> indeed it is usually the very fact which founds the claim. Conversely, a plaintiff who
> brings an action like the present must show that the defendant is in receipt of prop-
> erty which belongs beneficially to him or its traceable proceeds, but he need not show
> that the defendant has been enriched by its receipt. He may, for example, have paid
> full value for the property, but he is still required to disgorge it if he received it with
> notice of the plaintiff's interest.

21.25   To similar effect, Lord Browne-Wilkinson said:

> The contrary view appears to be based primarily on the ground that to give the pur-
> chasers a rateable share of the policy moneys is not to reverse an unjust enrichment
> but to give the purchasers a wholly unwarranted windfall . . . But this windfall is
> enjoyed because of the rights which the purchasers enjoy under the law of property.
> A man under whose land oil is discovered enjoys a very valuable windfall but no one
> suggests that he, as owner of the property, is not entitled to the windfall which goes
> with his property right. We are not dealing with a claim in unjust enrichment.[25]

21.26   Lord Hoffmann was equally decisive in rejecting the unjust enrichment theory.
Having agreed with the conclusion that Mr Murphy's (the trustee's) children and
the trust beneficiaries whose money Mr Murphy used were entitled to share in the
proceeds of the insurance policy in proportion to the value which they respectively contributed to the policy, Lord Hoffmann said:

> This is not based upon unjust enrichment except in the most trivial sense of that
> expression. It is . . . a vindication of proprietary right.[26]

21.27   Given the forcefulness with which the unjust enrichment approach was rejected
by the House it is difficult seeing any change in the House's attitude in the

---

[24] ibid, 127.
[25] ibid, 110.
[26] ibid, 115.

near future.[27] That said, those favouring the unjust enrichment school continue their debate and have raised powerful arguments against the reasoning in *Foskett v McKeown*. Birks has contended that:[28]

- It fails to give any relevance to the distinction between following and tracing.
- The fact the claimant had title to the original asset does not provide any explanation or justification for the claimant's entitlement to assert ownership in another asset, even after tracing. This is an assertion of a new proprietary right and not simply the original proprietary right.
- The only justification for permitting the creation of a new proprietary right is the unjust enrichment which would otherwise ensue if the claimant were denied a proprietary claim.

None of these arguments is new, however. They were known to, and rejected by, **21.28** the House of Lords in *Foskett v McKeown*. In any event, each may be countered.

(a) *It ignores the distinction between following and tracing*: The fact that the House of Lords rejected the notion that unjust enrichment was the relevant factor justifying a proprietary claim after tracing does not mean that the House ignored the distinction between following the original asset and tracing into its substitute. Indeed, the House of Lords was at pains to stress the distinction but saw that the justification for permitting a proprietary claim after tracing arising in the law of property and not in the law of unjust enrichment (and following clearly falls within the law of property). The court simply based its decision on a different factor, but that cannot be misunderstood as the court ignoring the distinction between following and tracing.

(b) *Assertion of a new proprietary right*: The proprietary right in the substitute asset may well be a new one (although this depends on how we define proprietary rights) but it is one which is explicable within the confines of the law of property. It is the law of property which provides that a party can assert a proprietary interest in the traceable substitute. The fact that the claimant never previously asserted title over the substitute asset does not mean that it is necessary to search outwith the law of property for a justification for the claimant being able so to do after a successful tracing exercise. For Birks, however, this approach represents the 'fiction of persistence' whereby, in our example, the claimant can assert ownership over the ruler simply because at some prior point the claimant had obtained ownership over the pen and

---

[27] Writing extra-judicially, Lord Millett has re-emphasized his thinking behind the decision in *Foskett v McKeown* in 'Proprietary Restitution' in S Degeling and J Edelman (eds), *Equity in Commercial Law* (Thomson Publishers, 2005), ch 12.

[28] Birks, 'Property, Unjust Enrichment and Tracing' (2001) 54 CLP 231. See also Burrows, 'Proprietary Restitution: Unmasking Unjust Enrichment' (2001) 117 LQR 412.

the process of tracing identifies the value inherent in the pen in the ruler.[29] Birks looks to the non-consensual substitution as the new event which triggers the claimant's entitlement to assert a proprietary right over the ruler.[30] Under the law of property analysis, one simply traces the value inherent in the pen into the ruler for which it has been substituted, enabling the claimant to assert ownership over the substituted asset.

(c) *Only justification for new proprietary right is avoidance of unjust enrichment:* This view has no support in the authorities.[31] Further, it is not every case of unjust enrichment which gives rise to a proprietary claim, some give rise only to claims in personam (e.g. only certain types of mistake). The problem for those who favour the unjust enrichment analysis is that there is an absence, within the law of unjust enrichment, of any clear guidance as to when a claimant would be entitled to a proprietary claim and when a claimant must settle for a personal claim. Views differ considerably amongst the commentators and unless and until a clear and compelling case is made out as to when unjust enrichment gives rise to a proprietary claim and when it gives rise only to a personal claim, it is unlikely to mount any serious challenge to the reasoning of the House of Lords in *Foskett v McKeown*. The law of property analysis is based on the complex law as to when property passes at law and in equity.[32]

21.29 In any event, whatever the ultimate merits of the unjust enrichment school's argument in respect of proprietary claims, for practitioners the law is as set out in *Foskett v McKeown*. Indeed, post this decision, *Goff and Jones* has declared:

> Foskett v McKeown leads to the firm conclusion that English law does not recognize a restitutionary proprietary claim.[33]

(b) Tracing assets or value

21.30 Although colloquially one still talks of tracing assets, the true position, as now recognized in the case law, is that tracing is all about locating value and not specific assets.

---

[29] For a detailed exposition of Birks' views see, *Unjust Enrichment* (2nd edn, Clarendon Press, 2005), 34–8.

[30] This explanation calls for the identification of the unjust factor.

[31] See Lord Millett in 'Proprietary Restitution' in Degeling and Edelman (eds), *Equity in Commercial Law*, ch 12, 313–14.

[32] See Virgo, *The Principles of the Law of Restitution* (2nd edn), ch 20.

[33] *Goff and Jones*, 86. The learned authors might have been more accurate to have talked about the English law not recognizing proprietary claims based upon the law of unjust enrichment since it is possible to describe a proprietary claim arising after a successful tracing exercise as being a *restitutionary* proprietary claim. Lord Millett still talks of 'proprietary restitution' post-*Foskett v McKeown* in 'Proprietary Restitution' in Degeling and Edelman (eds), *Equity in Commercial Law*, ch 12.

The value which is the object of the tracing exercise is that value which was present in the original asset and is now to be found in a substituted asset. So, using our example of the pen being exchanged for the ruler, the claimant's interest in the ruler lies in the fact that the value in the pen (originally owned by the claimant) is now vested in its substitute product, the ruler. The claimant traces that value from the pen to the ruler. This was recognized in *Foskett* itself.

This distinction between assets and value is reflected in the distinction between   **21.31**
following and tracing discussed above. The process of following is always concerned with locating the original asset, the pen, whereas, by contrast, tracing is concerned with identifying the present location of the value of the pen in legally relevant substitutions. One does not trace an asset as such; one traces value. As one commentator has put it:

> Tracing and following are, in one sense, opposites. The object of 'follow' is 'thing'. The object of 'trace' is 'value', because we cease to be concerned with a particular physical thing and instead focus on different physical manifestations of the value which was inherent in the original thing.[34]

This reasoning received the express support of Lord Millett in *Foskett v McKeown*   **21.32**
where he stated:

> Where one asset is exchanged for another, a claimant can elect whether to follow the original asset into the hands of the new owner or to trace its value into the new asset in the hands of the same owner . . . What [the claimant] traces . . . is not the physical asset itself but the value inherent in it.[35]

It is immediately apparent that the distinction between tracing assets and tracing   **21.33**
value highlights the need for a claimant to make an election as to where he or she sees the value previously located in the original asset, namely the pen. The concept of value is thus able to float over the various legally relevant substitutions unless and until the claimant makes the election Lord Millett has talked about. This process is one way to answer the problem of geometric progression which is discussed below.

Further, and on the basis that it is well established that one traces value as opposed   **21.34**
to assets, it is difficult to understand how the common law method of tracing has become caught up in a discussion (for historical reasons relating to the remedies available at law) based upon the unhelpful notion of 'a stream of electrons'. What is relevant in a tracing exercise is not a stream of electrons or paper on which a cheque is written but rather the value represented by the transfer order or the cheque. As between banks, that value is never lost in the clearing system or otherwise. If it is entirely possible to trace the value through the clearing system, it is not

---

[34] Smith, 'Tracing Into the Payment of a Debt' [1995] CLJ 290.
[35] *Foskett v McKeown* [2001] AC 102, 127–8.

clear why so much concern should be expressed as to streams of electrons or supposed mixing of funds in the clearing systems.

(c) Tracing and claiming distinguished[36]

21.35   As shown above, the traditional approach often used 'tracing' as little more than the adjective to describe the type of claim being brought. The modern approach seeks to distinguish the process of tracing from the process of claiming:

> ... there is no such thing as a right to trace, and tracing is not a remedy (if 'remedy' can be sensibly contrasted with 'right'). Tracing is no more than the means of finding out where at any relevant moment value is located. It is a preliminary or ancillary exercise. There are two quite separate questions. One is whether the value in question can be located. The other is whether, once it has been located, a right of some kind may be exigible in respect of it. Nor will the right ultimately exacted always be of the same kind.[37]

21.36   The rallying call was taken up by Millett LJ in *Boscawen v Bajwa* where he said:

> Equity lawyers habitually use the expressions 'the tracing claim' and 'the tracing remedy' to describe the proprietary claim and the proprietary remedy which equity makes available to the beneficial owner who seeks to recover his property in specie from those into whose hands it has come. Tracing properly so-called, however, is neither a claim nor a remedy but a process ... It is the process by which the plaintiff traces what has happened to his property, identifies the persons who have handled or received it, and justifies his claim that the money which they handled or received (and if necessary which they still retain) can properly be regarded as representing his property.[38]

21.37   More recently, in *Foskett v McKeown*, Lord Millett emphasized his thinking on this issue:

> Tracing is thus neither a claim nor a remedy. It is merely the process by which a claimant demonstrates what has happened to his property, identifies its proceeds and the persons who have handled or received them, and justifies his claim that the proceeds can properly be regarded as representing his property. Tracing is also distinct from claiming. It identifies the traceable proceeds of the claimant's property. It enables the claimant to substitute the traceable proceeds for the original asset as the subject matter of his claim ...[39]

21.38   Tracing can therefore be described as a process of identifying legally relevant substitute assets against which the claimant is able to assert whatever claim he had

---

[36] Birks, 'Mixing and Tracing: Property and Restitution' (1992) 45 CLP 69; Birks, 'On Taking Seriously the Difference Between Tracing and Claiming' (1997) 11 Trust Law Int 2; Smith, 'Tracing into the Payment of a Debt' [1995] CLJ 290.

[37] Birks, 'Mixing and Tracing: Property and Restitution' (1992) 45 CLP 69, 86, citing *Chase Manhattan N A Ltd v Israel-British Bank (London) Ltd* [1981] Ch 105 as a good illustration of this distinction.

[38] *Boscawen v Bajwa* [1996] 1 WLR 328, 334.

[39] *Foskett v McKeown* [2001] AC 102, 128.

against the original asset for which this new asset now stands substitute. Tracing enables whatever claim (if any) that may have existed in relation to the original asset (in our example, the pen) (so a prior proprietary base needs to be established) to be asserted against its substitute (the ruler). It does not determine the existence or nature of any such claim.

By distinguishing the process of tracing from claiming it becomes clear that the **21.39** completion of a successful tracing exercise may lead to differing claims, some proprietary and some merely personal. Lord Millett in *Foskett v McKeown* has indicated that, subject to any defences available by virtue of the intervening events, the claimant will be entitled to assert the same claim against the traceable proceeds as was available against the original asset. That claim may well be a proprietary one ('that ruler is mine because it represents the traceable proceeds of my pen'), or it may be a personal claim.[40] It may be a claim enforcing legal or equitable rights.[41] Accordingly, the language of the 'tracing claim' can now be ignored.

Whilst it is undoubtedly the case that there is a distinction between tracing and **21.40** claiming, it is equally clear that the manner in which a claimant is permitted to trace may be determined or influenced by the nature of the claim and/or the identity of the other party against whom the tracing exercise is being conducted.[42] In other words, the presumptions which are said to apply to tracing into and through mixed funds are influenced by factors such as whether the mixed fund is made up entirely of innocent parties' contributions or a combination of the fraudster and innocent parties. The presumptions, and therefore the tracing exercise, will always be applied in a manner which favours the interests of the victim of the fraud over those of the fraudster. In this regard, it is not entirely accurate to say that tracing is neutral of the claim being brought.

Finally, the distinction now drawn between the process of tracing and the process **21.41** of claiming has highlighted the illogical position of having two systems of tracing. If tracing is a process which can lead to legal or equitable claims (this being dependent on the nature of the proprietary base at the outset) then there is no need for two types of tracing rules.[43] The call for the abolition of the dual system is examined at the end of this chapter.

---

[40] See *El Ajou v Dollar Land Holdings plc* [1993] 3 All ER 717.

[41] *Trustees of the Property of FC Jones & Sons v Jones* [1997] Ch 159 is an example of the enforcement of a legal right by means of a personal remedy.

[42] This point does not appear to have been addressed by those who favour the view that tracing is entirely neutral as to the claims brought: see Birks 'Overview, Tracing, Claiming and Defences', in Birks (ed), *Laundering and Tracing* (Clarendon Press, 1995).

[43] Some commentators (e.g. Birks, *An Introduction to the Law of Restitution* (Clarendon Press, 1985), 361–2) have suggested that *Banque Belge pour l'Etranger v Hambrouck* [1921] 1 KB 321 is an example where the Court of Appeal (principally Scrutton and Atkin LJJ) was willing to employ

(d) Tracing and causation

21.42 The decision in *Foskett v McKeown* has also severed the connection between tracing and any need to establish causation on a 'but for' test. There is no need to prove that the substitute asset was only obtained because of the receipt of the original asset. Of course, in many cases, such causation will exist. In the pen/ruler example, the 'but for' test is readily satisfied. The ruler would not have been obtained but for its exchange for the pen. However, their Lordships in *Foskett v McKeown* held that there was no need to prove causation in order to trace from the pen to the value now inherent in the ruler.

21.43 On the facts of *Foskett v McKeown*, the policy would have paid out the £1m irrespective of whether the fourth and fifth premiums had been paid[44] (by virtue of the prior purchase of units which maintained the policy). These payments, using the misappropriated trust funds, were not causative of the £1m pay-out under the terms of the policy. According to their Lordships, all that was necessary to show was that the payment out of £1m was in consideration of all premiums paid and therefore it could be said that the £1m payment was attributable to the fourth and fifth premium payments. There was a 'transactional link'[45] between the payment of the fourth and fifth premium payments and the payment out of the £1m death benefit.

21.44 Freeing the process of tracing from the confines of a 'but for' causative approach has been welcomed by some commentators[46] on the basis that it is considered likely to render the whole tracing process easier to apply. However, one might well question whether the ambit of the concepts of 'attribution' and 'transactional links' remain to be worked out on a case by case basis with the attendant uncertainty that will inevitably bring.

C. Motives for Tracing

21.45 One of the myths exploded above is that tracing is only concerned with one type of claim, the (equitable) proprietary claim. There are in fact many different reasons why it is necessary for the claimant to show that the defendant received the traceable proceeds of property originally belonging to the claimant. A greater

---

equitable rules on tracing to assist in a common law claim. This interpretation of *Banque Belge* was rejected by the Court of Appeal in *Agip (Africa) Ltd v Jackson* [1991] Ch 547, 566.

[44] These premiums would have had a role to play in keeping the policy valid in the event that the assured had lived for a longer period.

[45] *Foskett v McKeown* [2001] AC 102, 128 (Lord Millett).

[46] See G Virgo, 'Vindicating vindication: *Foskett v McKeown* reviewed' in A Hudson (ed), *New Perspectives on Property Law, Obligations and Restitution* (Routledge Cavendish, 2003), ch 10, 206.

understanding can be obtained if the role played by tracing in various types of claim is examined: (1) proprietary claim;[47] (2) personal claim in equity; (3) personal claim at common law. Each of these claims must be considered against the background that the fraudster is likely to have invoked all the usual techniques of money laundering so as to place as much distance as possible between the fraud and its proceeds.

(1) Tracing and proprietary claims

The assertion of a proprietary claim is the most obvious reason why a claimant **21.46** may wish to invoke the rules on tracing. It is only by successfully using the tracing rules that a claimant is able to point to an asset (which he did not originally own) and assert a proprietary interest over it by virtue of it being the traceable proceeds of the asset which was originally owned by the claimant. Without tracing, proprietary claims in substitute assets would not be possible.

(2) Tracing and in personam claims in equity

Some in personam claims in equity require the claimant to establish, for example, **21.47** that the defendant did something in respect of the claimant's property before any personal liability will arise. It is in that context that a claimant often has to rely upon the rules of tracing to establish an in personam claim in equity.

A typical equitable in personam claim which may arise in a commercial fraud **21.48** context is liability for knowing receipt. The role of tracing is to identify whether or not any of the trust assets came into the possession of the defendant, irrespective of whether he retained them. It is only through tracing that we are able to establish the necessary receipt for the purposes of this claim.

As emphasized above, tracing is distinct from claiming. Tracing does not establish **21.49** the defendant's liability for knowing receipt: that will depend on other factors and is governed by the requirements for knowing receipt and not by the law on tracing.

Tracing is also essential to establish that the monies beneficially received by the **21.50** defendant are the traceable proceeds of a breach of fiduciary duty. If this is established, along with the other requirements for this claim, the claim for personal liability for knowing receipt will be made out.

---

[47] The majority of proprietary claims which will arise in a commercial fraud context will be equitable in nature. Common law proprietary claims (i.e. for delivery up) are rare.

(3) Tracing and common law in personam claims

21.51   Traditionally, the common law has provided protection to legal ownership via the granting of personal claims such as for conversion. However, to be able to bring such claims, it is often necessary to show that the defendant in fact received property belonging at law to the claimant. Here again reliance must be placed on the rules of tracing.

21.52   Tracing is also essential when the claimant wishes to bring a personal claim in unjust enrichment but the defendant has received the monies not directly from the claimant but via a third party. Take, for example, the leading case of *Lipkin Gorman v Karpnale Ltd*[48] where tracing was required to establish that the monies paid over by a third party (in that case the partner, Cass) were, at the time they were paid over to the gambling club, in fact owned by the solicitors, such that the solicitors had title to sue in unjust enrichment. Tracing was necessary to provide the link between the asset originally owned by the solicitors to the value transferred by Cass to the club. Of course, whether the solicitors still had legal title or indeed any interest in the asset paid over to the club by Cass was to be determined other than by reference to the rules on tracing.[49] Tracing at law was in fact conceded.

21.53   It is evident, therefore, that the rules on tracing have an importance which goes beyond simply establishing proprietary claims. It is for that reason that this is such an important area of law for a commercial fraud litigator.

D. Common Law Tracing[50]

21.54   As set out above, a claimant may be required to invoke the common law rules on tracing because he is seeking a common law proprietary claim (i.e. delivery up) or more typically because he is seeking a common law in personam claim and he needs to show that monies or assets received by the defendant legally belonged to him.[51]

---

[48] [1991] 2 AC 548.

[49] See *Equiticorp Industries Group Ltd (In Statutory Management) v The Crown (Judgment No 47)* [1998] 3 NZLR 481; *Nimmo v Westpac Banking Corporation* [1993] 3 NZLR 218 as two New Zealand examples where tracing was essential to the bringing of a personal claim.

[50] Thomas and Hudson, *The Law of Trusts* (Oxford University Press, 2004), paras 33.21–33.26; Smith, *The Law of Tracing* (Oxford University Press, 1997); Goode, 'The Right to Trace in Commercial Transactions' (1976) 92 LQR 360 and 528; Scott, 'Tracing at Common Law' (1965–6) 7 University of Western Australia Law Review 463.

[51] E.g. *Lipkin Gorman v Karpnale Ltd* [1991] 2 AC 548 (where the solicitors' firm had to establish that the monies withdrawn from the firm's client account by Cass, one of the partners, legally belonged in a relevant sense to the solicitors' firm when paid over to gambling casino).

Whatever the reason or motive for resorting to the rules, the claimant will quickly **21.55**
discover that there are serious limitations to the scope of common law tracing.
The scope of common law tracing can be summarized as follows.

At common law it is possible to trace: **21.56**

- the same asset that originally belonged to the claimant;[52] or
- a 'clean substitute' for the asset that originally belonged to the claimant;[53]
- profits obtained from the original asset or clean substitute.[54]

Common law tracing is unable, on traditional thinking, to trace through: **21.57**

- a mixed fund;[55]
- banks' clearing systems;[56]
- electronic bank payments.[57]

There is little doubt that common law tracing, in its accepted form, gives rise to a **21.58**
money launderer's charter. Unlike tracing in equity, it ceases to operate at the
slightest of difficulties, whether it be the mixing of funds or the common day use
of electronic means to transfer money. There has unfortunately been something
of a tendency to lament the failings of the common law rules on tracing and simply to look forward to the day when the dual system is abolished.[58] It is submitted
that, in the best traditions of the development of the common law, such an
approach must be rejected in favour of constantly challenging and striving to
improve and develop the common law rules. So long as we have such rules, it is
incumbent upon us to ensure that we make the best we can of them.

---

[52] This is strictly an example of following and not tracing. In our example, this would be *follow-ing* the pen from A to B.

[53] In our example of the pen and the ruler, this would be the ruler for which the pen has been exchanged without any other property or money being involved.

[54] *Jones v Jones* [1997] Ch 159.

[55] *Taylor v Plumer* (1815) 3 M&S 562. As discussed below, this case in fact concerned an equit-able and not a common law claim but per *Jones v Jones* [1997] Ch 159 its precedent value on this issue is not diminished.

[56] *Agip (Africa) Ltd v Jackson* [1991] Ch 547 (CA).

[57] *Agip (Africa) Ltd v Jackson* [1990] Ch 265, 285E (per Millett J); *El Ajou v Dollar Land Holdings Plc* [1993] 3 All ER 717; *Bank Terjarat v HSBC* [1995] 1 Lloyd's Rep 239. This view is also accepted in the New Zealand case of *Nimmo v Westpac Banking Corporation* [1993] 3 NZLR 218. It should, however, be noted that the views of Millett J at first instance were not endorsed by Fox LJ in the CA in *Agip* [1991] Ch 547, 565.

[58] A good example of this approach is Millett J's judgment in *Agip (Africa) Ltd v Jackson* [1990] Ch 265 where he stated that the common law was incapable of tracing through a 'stream of elec-trons'. If that really is the case, then the comment in the text that the common law rules give rise to a money launderer's charter rings true.

(1) Common law tracing and mixed funds

21.59 The generally accepted position is that the common law rules on tracing are not able to trace through a mixed fund.[59]

21.60 If X takes Y's £5,000 and uses it to buy a motorbike, Y can trace into the motorbike (a clean substitute) at common law. If, however, X mixes £5,000 of Y's money with £1,000 of his own money and then pays £5,000 out of this mixed fund to purchase the motorbike, it is not possible at common law to trace through the mixed fund into the motorbike.

21.61 It is to be noted that this limitation on common law tracing typically arises in a two-transfer situation. In the example above, X takes Y's £5,000 and deposits it in his account ('transfer 1'). So far, no problems for the common law. Y can claim at common law for the £5,000. It is the second transfer which causes the problems, namely that *from* the mixed fund to purchase the motorbike ('transfer 2'). Given the mixture of Y's £5,000 with X's own £1,000 in the account, the common law is unable to confirm that the motorbike has been purchased with Y's money alone.

21.62 The basis for this is said to be the judgment of Lord Ellenborough in *Taylor v Plumer*.[60] The reality, however, as has been pointed out by academics, such as Lionel Smith[61] and David Fox,[62] is that this case in fact involved equitable rules on tracing and not common law rules. In *Trustees of the Property of FC Jones v Jones*,[63] Millett LJ, whilst recognizing this fact, maintained that this does not alter the force of precedent which establishes that the common law cannot trace through a mixed fund.

21.63 Accordingly, whatever the rights or wrongs of the original decision in *Taylor v Plumer*, through the force of precedent, practitioners are now stuck with its consequences. That is unfortunate.

21.64 There is a variety of explanations offered for this limitation on common law tracing. One such explanation is that the common law, unlike equity, had not developed the concept of a general charge over a mixed fund for the payment of a debt. The problem with this explanation is that it equates tracing with claiming once again. If tracing is truly divorced from any notion of claiming, the availability or otherwise of remedies such as general charges would be irrelevant to the ambit of the rules on tracing, legal or equitable.

---

59 *Taylor v Plumer* (1815) 3 M&S 562.
60 ibid.
61 'Tracing in *Taylor v Plumer*: Equity in the Court of King's Bench' [1995] LMCLQ 240.
62 'Common Law Claims to Substituted Assets' [1999] RLR 55.
63 [1997] Ch 159.

There are some commentators, such as Professor Lionel Smith, who maintain that **21.65** this restriction on the ability to trace at common law is unjustified.[64] He comments that if the rule is limited to physical mixtures then it is in fact a rule about following and not tracing and is untenable since the common law has well developed rules for dealing with issues arising from physical mixtures.[65] He goes on to find that the rule is in fact one for mixtures of value and that it similarly cannot be justified.

In *Re Diplock*,[66] the Court of Appeal remarked: **21.66**

> The common law approached [tracing] in a strictly materialistic way. It could only appreciate what might almost be called the 'physical' identity of one thing with another. It could treat a person's money as identifiable so long as it had not become mixed with other money. It could treat as identifiable with the money other kinds of property acquired by means of it, so long as there was no admixture of other money.

It remains unclear how the common law's supposed fascination with all things physical equates with the prevalent view, endorsed by the House of Lords in *Foskett v McKeown*, that tracing is all about locating value not physical assets.

The Court of Appeal in *Re Diplock* went on to try to justify this inability to trace **21.67** through a mixed fund by reference to the availability of remedies in the common law. Whilst the court is empowered to order damages, or a particular sum, to be paid, it does not have the power, unlike equity, to subject an asset or mixed fund to a charge. Smith is not persuaded. First, as set out above, this argument ignores the distinction between tracing and claiming. If it is irrelevant what rights might be asserted to the conduct of a tracing exercise, it is similarly irrelevant what remedies might exist to protect any such rights. Secondly, if the claimant wishes to invoke common law tracing in order to bring an in personam claim for money, then the fact that the common law is limited to monetary claims is no answer as to why that claimant cannot trace through a mixed fund. Thirdly, even if the claimant wished to invoke common law tracing in order to bring a proprietary claim, the ability to bring such a claim is an entirely separate question from whether the claimant is able to trace at common law through a mixed fund.

Whatever the merits of Smith's contentions, as a matter of binding precedent, **21.68** practitioners must accept that it is not possible to trace at common law through a mixed fund. This conclusion seriously limits the range of personal claims available at common law after tracing. On this basis, it is not possible at common law to

---

[64] See Smith, *The Law of Tracing*, 162–83.
[65] The relevant common law rules on physical mixtures are examined in some detail by Birks, 'Mixing and Tracing: Property and Restitution' (1992) 45 CLP 69.
[66] [1948] Ch 465, 518.

bring any claim for unjust enrichment (i.e. the old money had and received claim) against a recipient of monies paid out of a mixed fund. Any such claim will need to be established in equity. None of the recent cases[67] have indicated any relaxation of this requirement and so we will need to await reform of the whole area of tracing to remove this obstacle to common law tracing.

(2) Common law tracing and bank accounts

21.69 In the case of commercial fraud, the ability of the common law to trace into and through bank accounts is central to its ability to confront the demands of the modern day money launderer. The following issues arise for discussion in this context:

- Bank accounts, cash and choses in action.
- Does the method by which payment is made matter?
- Clearing systems and the problem of mixed funds.
- Tracing unauthorized payments—who is the proper claimant?

(a) Bank accounts, cash and choses in action

21.70 As the law has developed in respect of tracing and restitutionary claims, the courts have shown a willingness to undertake careful examination of how to characterize the relevant assets which are the subject of the tracing exercise. Bank accounts are no longer thought of (if ever they were) as bags of coins; rather, they are contractual relationships which give rise to a debtor/creditor relationship in which one party has a chose in action (being the claim or debt) against the other. How the court characterizes the relevant asset (whether it be cash or a chose in action) has an important bearing on the outcome of a case.

21.71 This is seen most readily in the leading case of *Lipkin Gorman v Karpnale Ltd*. The facts are well known but can be briefly summarized as follows.

- Cass, a partner in a firm of solicitors, wrongly withdrew monies from the client accounts and gambled it away at a club. The solicitors brought a claim for money had and received against, inter alia, the club. The difficulty for the solicitors was to show that the monies that the club received *legally* belonged to the solicitors. If not, no common law claim could be maintained. The problem was that there was strong authority that Cass, as a partner in the solicitors, obtained good title to the monies upon their unauthorized withdrawal from the bank.
- The House of Lords refused to overrule the problematic authorities and instead held that whilst the monies were in the bank account, the solicitors had a chose in action against the bank in the relevant amount; when the monies were

---

[67] E.g. *Lipkin Gorman v Karpnale* [1991] 2 AC 548; *Jones v Jones* [1997] Ch 159.

wrongly withdrawn, Cass may have legally obtained good title to the cash, but nevertheless that cash represented the exchange-product for the solicitors' original chose in action against the bank.

- By adopting an analysis which draws a distinction between cash and choses in action, the House of Lords was able to provide a remedy to the solicitors where none might otherwise have existed had the focus been entirely on the cash.

- However, it is an approach which has opened the door to many further issues. It rather suggests that both the solicitors and the rogue partner held title to the cash withdrawn from the client accounts at one and the same time. This clearly could not be the case, but the true nature of the solicitors' interest in the cash remains unclear.

It would be fair to say that the courts have not truly worked out what type of proprietary interest it is said someone in the position of the solicitors has over cash as substitute for its chose in action. This is unfortunate since one has, on the one hand, clear authority that the cash belongs, in the circumstances, to Cass, and on the other, some form of power in rem enabling the solicitors to elect to assert a proprietary interest over that money. Much work clearly remains to be done in this area. **21.72**

(b) Does the method of payment matter?

Logically, the answer must be no. So long as it can be shown that a payment has been made, it should not matter whether that payment was made electronically, by cheque or postal order, or by cash. It would be an unjustified restriction on the ability of the common law rules to trace if those rules were capable of dealing with only certain methods of payment but not others. This point is illustrated by the following examples where X pays Y £500 by mistake: **21.73**

- X hands over £500 in cash to Y;
- X hands over £500 in a cheque to Y;
- X instructs his online bank to make a CHAPS payment of £500 to Y.

In each example, there is no factual uncertainty or ambiguity as to whether X paid Y £500. The fact of payment is established by the evidence of X and Y in the case of payments by cash and cheque and supported by the subsequent evidence of deposits in Y's account. Similarly, in the example of the CHAPS payment, it will be possible to establish that a credit in Y's bank account derives from a debit in X's account coupled with a clear bank instruction to transfer £500 between these two accounts. None of these methods of payment create any form of uncertainty that £500 has been paid by X to Y. There is, therefore, no logical reason why the common law tracing rules should treat one method of payment differently from the others. **21.74**

21.75 Whilst common sense dictates that the common law rules on tracing should not be blind to what is so obvious to the man on the Clapham omnibus, unfortunately, this is not the case. It is becoming increasingly evident that a distinction is drawn by the courts between transfers made by way of cheques and those made electronically. The chief proponent of this distinction is Lord Millett.

21.76 At first instance in *Agip*, Millett J held that one of the reasons why common law tracing was not possible was because one of the relevant transfers had been made by way of telegraphic transfer and the common law was not capable of tracing through what he called a 'stream of electrons' passing through the banks' clearing systems. Common law tracing, he said:

> . . . can only follow a physical asset, such as a cheque or its proceeds, from one person to another. It can follow money but not a chose in action.[68]

See also Sir Peter Millett's seminal article, 'Tracing the Proceeds of Fraud',[69] which sets out this theory in greater detail.

21.77 Millett J repeated this view at first instance in *El Ajou v Dollar Land Holdings Plc*[70] where he held that it was 'manifestly impossible' to trace where the funds had been paid by electronic means and through the clearing system.

21.78 A similar view was taken in *Bank Tejarat v HSBC*[71] where Tuckey J applied the same reasoning to deny common law tracing in respect of payments under letters of credit, holding that it made no difference whether the payment came from the original payee or from a third party.[72] This decision is a particularly worrying one as it applies this restrictive thinking to payments made directly between X and Y albeit through the banking system. If correctly decided, this severely limits the availability of claims in unjust enrichment based simply on the fortuity that X happened to choose to pay using his online banking facility rather than by cheque or in cash.

21.79 A common theme running through these case examples of *Agip*, *El Ajou* and *Bank Terjarat* is the importance attached by the court to the physical aspect of a tracing exercise at common law. It remains to be seen whether and in what form this thinking is sustained in the light of the modern view that tracing is concerned solely with locating relevant value as opposed to tracing physical assets as such. If, as is suggested, it is possible to identify the relevant value of a given transaction at any time in the banking system without having to trace any physical asset, there should be no problems for the common law to trace that value.

---

68 [1990] Ch 265, 285E.
69 (1991) 107 LQR 71, 73–4.
70 [1993] 3 All ER 717.
71 [1995] 1 Lloyd's Rep 239.
72 ibid, 245–6.

As part of his thinking on the inability of the common law to trace through a **21.80** 'stream of electrons', Lord Millett has emphasized that the difficulties caused thereby can be circumvented when payment has been made by way of cheque. In *Jones v Jones*, the Court of Appeal (including Millett LJ) allowed money to be traced from one account in a bank to another account at a different bank as the payments were made by way of cheques. Millett LJ remarked:

> The trustee does not need to follow money from one recipient to another or follow it through the clearing system: he can follow the cheques as they pass from hand to hand.[73]

It is submitted that this creates arbitrary distinctions between methods of pay- **21.81** ment, leaving the common law to trace so long as the modern fraudster uses his cheque book but not otherwise. On this basis, the marked decline in the use of cheques will see a corresponding diminution in the ability of the common law to meet the demands of modern day money laundering.

Lord Millett's views have not received universal approval in the courts. For exam- **21.82** ple, his views on this issue, expressed at first instance in *Agip*, were not approved by Fox LJ in the Court of Appeal in *Agip*:

> The inquiry which has to be made is whether the money paid . . . 'was the product of, or substitute for, the original thing'. In answering that question I do not think that it matters that the order was not a cheque. It was a direction by the account holder to the bank.[74]

This distinction between tracing 'electrons' and tracing through cheques has little **21.83** to recommend it.[75] It is certainly difficult to justify as a matter of precedent or principle and appears to be contrary to the desire of Lord Millett (expressed elsewhere) that the court be astute to make sure that the tracing rules can match modern day laundering.

Further, it is not at all clear that the simple use of a cheque circumvents any **21.84** requirement to involve the clearing system. It is still necessary to connect the cheque with the value with which it is to be paid and this will often involve some form of a clearing system which, as has been pointed out,[76] has not traditionally given rise to any difficulties.[77]

---

[73] [1996] AC 815, 834.
[74] [1991] Ch 547, 565.
[75] Birks [1989] LMCLQ 296, Birks (1989) 105 LQR 528, Birks (1995) 9 Tru LI 91; Burrows, *The Law of Restitution*, 89.
[76] *Ellinger's Modern Banking Law* (3rd edn, Oxford University Press, 2002), 279.
[77] *Marsh v Keating* (1834) 2 Cl & Fin 250; *Banque Belge pour l'Etranger v Hambrouck* [1921] 1 KB 321.

21.85 In any event, there would be no need to draw such an arbitrary distinction between payment mechanisms if, as suggested below, the clearing system ceased to present an insurmountable obstacle to common law tracing when viewed as a series of exchange products and substitutions. If that approach were to be adopted, the fact that a cheque had been used would become, as it should be, an irrelevant consideration to the question of whether any payment is traceable.

(c) Clearing systems and the problem of mixed funds

21.86 One might, not unreasonably, consider that the limitation on tracing through a mixed fund would automatically prevent common law tracing through the banks' clearing systems. In fact, while the general position is that the common law is unable to trace through the clearing systems, the case law has not been entirely consistent on this issue.

21.87 In *Banque Belge pour L'Etranger v Hambrouck*,[78] the fraudster forged a number of cheques and paid the proceeds into his own bank account, thereafter drawing from that account monies to be paid to his mistress, Mlle Spanoghe. When the claim was brought, Mlle Spanoghe's account stood at £315 in credit. The Court of Appeal permitted the claimant to trace into Mlle Spanoghe's account. It was emphasized that there had been no mixing of funds in either the fraudster's bank account or in Mlle Spanoghe's account[79] but of course the payments via the cheques would have had to go through the banks' clearing system.

21.88 There are two possible explanations for the decision in *Banque Belge*. The first is that the Court of Appeal recognized that the claimant was able to trace its original money into its exchange product, being the fraudster's chose in action against his own bank when he deposited the stolen monies into his own account. Thereafter, the claimant was able to trace from this chose in action into its exchange product, being the monies withdrawn from the fraudster's bank and subsequently into the new chose in action held by Mlle Spanoghe against her bank. This reasoning entirely by-passes the need to examine what became of the monies when in the banks' clearing systems. This is the interpretation which finds favour with Professor Burrows.[80]

---

[78] ibid.

[79] Curiously, Atkin LJ remarks: 'In substance no other funds were paid into the account than the proceeds of these forged cheques.' (ibid, 331). It is not known what is meant by 'In substance . . .'. Both Scrutton and Bankes LJJ are clear that no other funds were paid into the account.

[80] Burrows, *The Law of Restitution*, 86. It is noted that this justification depends on the common law tracing through choses in action; cf Millett J in *Agip* [1990] Ch 265, 285E (common law cannot trace through choses in action).

The second interpretation focuses on the comments made by Scrutton LJ   **21.89**
and Atkin LJ that if it was not possible to trace at common law, it was possible
to invoke equitable rules on tracing to assist the common law claim. Some view
this case as an example where the Court of Appeal was willing to invoke equitable
rules on tracing to assist in a common law claim.[81] Whilst there are dicta along
these lines, the case was not in fact decided on this basis and the Court of Appeal
in *Agip (Africa) Ltd v Jackson*[82] made it clear that this interpretation went
too far.[83]

In *Agip*, the common law claims for money had and received were defeated because   **21.90**
the Court held that the various transfers of monies had taken place through the
New York clearing system and therefore through a mixed fund. *Banque Belge* was
distinguished on the grounds that in *Agip* the Baker Oil account was credited
before being put in funds from the London Lloyds account. But there was no
examination in *Banque Belge* as to whether the fraudster was permitted to withdraw funds from his account and so it is not known whether this really is a point
of distinction between the cases. As one commentator has remarked: '. . . in *Banque
Belge* there was no enquiry as to whether Farrow's Bank had allowed Hambrouck
to draw against the cheques before they collected them. The matter was treated as
being irrelevant and, if it was irrelevant in *Banque Belge*, it is not at all clear why it
should be a relevant factor in *Agip*.'[84]

It is evident that, with these notable exceptions aside, in the event that it proves   **21.91**
necessary to trace at common law through a bank's clearing system, this will not
be possible at common law. Unless the court is able to by-pass the need to trace
through the clearing system,[85] the inability of common law to trace through a
mixed fund will prevent tracing through the clearing systems of banks.

(i) Any justification for an embargo on common law tracing through the clear-   **21.92**
ing system? It is perhaps all too easy simply to adopt the reasoning that the
clearing system is equivalent to a mixed fund and the identity of the particular funds
being traced is lost in that system. In addition to its unconvincing origin,[86] this
embargo ignores two further issues.

---

[81] Birks, *An Introduction to the Law of Restitution*, 361–2. For a contrary interpretation of *Banque Belge* see Burrows, *The Law of Restitution*, 87.

[82] [1991] Ch 547.

[83] ibid, 566.

[84] McKendrick, 'Tracing Misdirected Funds' [1991] LMCLQ 378, 384.

[85] Such as in *Jones v Jones* [1996] AC 815, where the Court of Appeal emphasized that there was no need to trace through the clearing systems given it was possible to follow the cheques from hand to hand.

[86] *Taylor v Plumer* (1815) 3 M&S 562, now generally recognized to be a case dealing with equit-able and not common law claims.

21.93   (ii) **Tracing value and not assets**   This reasoning is difficult to justify when it is accepted, as it now is, that one is not tracing any particular asset as such but rather the value inherent in the original asset located in a legally relevant substitute. Value itself does not go missing in the clearing systems. Each bank, at the end of the day, knows precisely what is owed to each other and how that figure has been calculated. Given that factual knowledge on the part of the banks, tracing value through the clearing systems at common law should be possible.

21.94   (iii) **Embargo based upon a misunderstanding of the operation of the clearing systems**   It is clear that the inability of the common law to trace through a clearing system is based upon an assumption that the mixing of funds in a clearing system and the subsequent loss of identity of any individual funds, is to be equated to a mixed fund from which monies cannot be traced at common law.

21.95   The first and obvious point to make is that there is no mixing of funds at all in the operation of a clearing system. There is a netting off of a series of individual credits and debits on the part of the banks signed up to the clearing system but no exchange of funds as such. The individual credits and debits retain their separate status unless and until the netting off process, which takes place at a stipulated time.

21.96   It has been convincingly argued that there is no need to trace each such credit or debit through the clearing system in order to enable the common law to trace payments made through the clearing systems. The process should properly be viewed as one of exchange products and substitutions.[87] Consider the following example where A wishes to transfer £500 to B. They use different banks:

- A deposits £500 into his account with Bank 1. By so doing, A exchanges the £500 for a chose in action being a debt owed by Bank 1 to A.

- A instructs Bank 1 to pay £500 to B at Bank 2. Given that A and B use different banks, a clearing system common to both banks will need to be used to effect this transaction.

- By virtue of the above instruction, Bank 1's liability to A for £500 has been exchanged for a liability owed by Bank 1 to Bank 2 in the same amount.

- Once Bank 2 is credited with the £500 under the clearing system, Bank 1's liability to Bank 2 is exchanged for a liability owed by Bank 2 to B (its customer) reflected in a credit of £500 in B's account with Bank 2.

---

[87] See Smith, *The Law of Tracing*, 252–5. This view is supported in Ellinger, Lomnicka and Hooley (eds), *Ellinger's Modern Banking Law* (Oxford University Press, 2003), 274–9. This approach mirrors Burrows' interpretation of *Banque Belge*, examined above.

- None of these steps required showing that the monies or credits received represented the actual traceable proceeds of the original £500 deposited by A into Bank 1.

- None of these steps required tracing through a mixed fund or the netting off process within the clearing system. The focus is entirely on the various exchange products or substitutions involved.

This whole process is no different, it is submitted, than that which occurs on a **21.97** simple cash deposit, such as A's deposit of £500 in cash with Bank 1. Having removed once and for all any notion that a bank account is akin to a bag of coins, we do not trouble ourselves with determining what in fact occurred to the actual £500 deposited by A in Bank 1. The reason we do not is because it is reflected in the credit in A's account with Bank 1 to the same amount, £500. So long as the Bank's books properly reflect the amounts credited and deposited into an account, no further enquiry is sought or necessary.

It is suggested that there is no requirement to approach matters differently simply **21.98** because it has been necessary to involve the clearing system due to another bank's role in the transaction. There is no doubt that this deposit comes from A's account in Bank 1. It was not a question that needed to be asked once A's account with Bank 1 was credited and it is submitted it is equally not relevant once B's account with Bank 2 is credited.

(iv) Unauthorized payments by the bank   This raises a discrete but important **21.99** issue. If a bank is fraudulently induced by Y to transfer money from X's account, who can invoke the rules of tracing, X or the bank? In theory, both X and Y could invoke the tracing rules (since these are divorced from any rules on claiming) but in reality only the party with an opportunity to make a claim in respect of the unauthorized payment is likely to want to incur the time and cost of invoking any tracing rules.

One would be forgiven for believing that the answer must be the bank since **21.100** a bank which wrongly pays out of a customer's account is treated as having paid out its own funds and not those of the customer.[88] However, Millett J in *Agip*, whilst noting the issue, maintained that he was engaged in a 'factual enquiry':

> The fact that a transaction is unauthorized does not mean that it has not taken place.[89]

---

[88] *Barclays Bank Ltd v WJ Simms & Cooke* [1980] QB 677.
[89] [1990] 1 Ch 265, 283F.

21.101 It would appear that if the bank has in fact debited the account, it may be possible for either the bank or the customer to undertake the exercise of tracing the missing funds. As has been pointed out,[90] this may well be a pragmatic solution but it ignores entirely the strict legal rights existing in the banker–customer relationship. Indeed, this approach lacks any of the rigorous analysis to be found in other areas of the law of tracing.

E. Tracing in Equity [91]

21.102 There are three main issues to be addressed in this section on equitable tracing:

- Who can invoke the equity rules on tracing?
- How are equity's presumptions applied in modern fraud contexts?
- What is 'backwards tracing' and does it have a role to play in equity's tracing rules?

21.103 The rules on tracing in equity do not, in the main, suffer from the same technical limitations which we have addressed at common law. There are no problems tracing through mixed funds or clearing systems and there is no suggestion that tracing requires some form of physical substitution. But it is nevertheless hampered by an historic if not principled requirement of the existence of a fiduciary relationship. As examined below, this requirement can often be fudged but it does lead to difficult issues of legal principle arising.

21.104 Given equity permits tracing through a mixed fund, it was inevitable that it would need to develop rules or presumptions to deal with payments made out of those mixed funds. Although well established, these presumptions are constantly coming under pressure as they are applied to the factual context of modern frauds. On occasion, as we shall see, the court simply concludes that an alternative approach is to be preferred. So long as the departures from these presumptions are principled and manifest an intention by the court to adapt to changing times, they are to be welcomed.

(1) Summary of the equitable rules on tracing

21.105 The main principles of equitable tracing may be summarized as follows.

- It would appear that there is still a need for the presence of a fiduciary in order to be able to invoke the rules on tracing.

---

90 Band, 'The Development of Tracing Rules in Commercial Cases' [1997] LMCLQ 65.

91 *Goff and Jones* (7th edn), [2-031]–[2-053]; Burrows, *The Law of Restitution* (2nd edn), 93–104; Underhill and Hayton, *Law of Trusts and Trustees* (16th edn, Butterworths, 2006), 993–1003; *Lewin on Trusts* (17th edn), ch 41; Hayton, 'Equity's Identification Rules' in Birks (ed), *Laundering and Tracing*, 1–21.

- The claimant who invokes equity's rules on tracing is seeking to identify the present location of his pre-existing equitable interest. Such an interest can arise under an express trust instrument, or under a resulting trust or under a constructive trust.

- Unlike its common law counterpart, equity will permit a party to trace into and through a mixed fund.

- If the mixed fund is made up of contributions from innocent parties then:
  - In the case of a current account, *Re Clayton's Case* is usually applied (first in, first out) unless this would cause injustice or is too impractical to apply.[92]
  - In the case of a deposit account, the parties share rateably in proportion to their contributions.

- If the fund is made up of a mixture of the innocent claimant's money and that of the wrongdoer, then initial withdrawals are deemed to be made with the wrongdoer's own funds (*Re Hallett's*)[93] unless those withdrawals have resulted in a lucrative investment which the innocent claimant wishes to claim (*Re Oatway*).[94]

- A claimant is unable to trace beyond the lowest balance of the mixed fund after the claimant's contribution has been made: *Roscoe v Winder*.[95]

- It remains uncertain whether equity will permit 'backwards tracing', namely the tracing into and through a payment of a debt and into the object purchased which created that debt.[96] There are good reasons to allow such tracing.

- Where a wrongdoer has purchased property using the mixed fund, the claimant is not limited to a lien[97] over the purchased property and can assert a rateable share of the purchased property in line with the level of the claimant's funds used to make the purchase: *Foskett v McKeown*.[98]

- Lord Templeman's swollen assets theory, set out in *Space Investments Ltd v Canadian Imperial Bank of Commerce*[99] permitting a claimant to trace into the general assets of a defendant rather than any specific fund or group of assets to which the claimant's own monies may have been added, has not generally been followed[100] and is unlikely to receive judicial support in the near future.

---

[92] See *Barlow Clowes International Ltd v Vaughan* [1992] 4 All ER 22.
[93] (1880) 13 Ch D 696.
[94] [1903] 2 Ch 356.
[95] [1915] 1 Ch 62.
[96] See, e.g. Smith, 'Tracing into the Payment of a Debt' [1995] CLJ 290.
[97] As had been suggested by Jessel MR in *Re Hallett's* (1880) 13 Ch D 696, 709.
[98] [2001] 1 AC 102. See also *Re Tilley's Will Trust* [1967] Ch 1179.
[99] [1986] 1 WLR 1072.
[100] It was distinguished in *Re Goldcorp Ltd* [1995] 1 AC 74. See also *Bishopsgate Investment Management Ltd v Homan* [1995] Ch 211.

(a) Who can invoke the equity rules on tracing?

21.106   The difficulty for equitable tracing is the starting principle that the claimant must be able to show that the relevant assets have passed through the hands of a fiduciary.

21.107   Greene MR in *Re Diplock*[101] remarked that the ability to trace in equity:

> depends on there having existed at some stage a fiduciary relationship of some kind . . . sufficient to give rise to the equitable right of property.[102]

That is to say, the money must have passed through the hands of a fiduciary.

The Court of Appeal's view in *Re Diplock* derives from their interpretation of the difficult judgments of the House of Lords in *Sinclair v Brougham*.[103] There is little point now trying to establish that the House of Lords laid down no such requirement in *Sinclair v Brougham*. Although the decision in *Sinclair v Brougham* was overruled in *Westdeutsche v Islington LB Council*,[104] the House of Lords in *Westdeustche* expressly stated that they were not thereby removing or undermining the fiduciary relationship requirement.

21.108   One might initially observe the oddity that, given the prevalent modern view that tracing and claiming are distinct exercises, the party seeking to invoke the equitable rules on tracing must show that the property has passed through the hands of a fiduciary such that his claim is one to enforce equitable rights. This is directly contrary to the modern approach to tracing, but it is consistent with the need to establish an equitable proprietary base.

21.109   Be that as it may, as practitioners, we are forced to work within the existing rules and so one asks: what type of fiduciary relationship suffices?

21.110   The paradigm example is a trustee misappropriating trust money. It is not necessary that there also exists a fiduciary relationship between the claimant and any subsequent recipient of the misappropriated property. This is because the initial relationship is sufficient to give rise to equitable claims.

21.111   If the claimant is the legal owner of the property and it is taken by an individual who owes the claimant a fiduciary duty, that again will suffice.[105] So if a solicitor misappropriates money belonging to his client that suffices to invoke the equitable rules on tracing.

---

[101] [1948] Ch 46.
[102] ibid, 240.
[103] [1914] AC 398.
[104] *Westdeutsche Landesbank Girozentrale v Islington LBC* [1996] AC 669.
[105] *Re Hallett* (1880) 13 Ch D 696.

The real difficulty lies when there is no pre-existing fiduciary relationship at all. **21.112**
There are varying examples.

(a) It is clear that the court will permit tracing in equity where there has been a
    fraudulently induced contract which is the subject of rescission: see e.g. *El
    Ajou v Dollar Land Holdings plc*.[106] The fiduciary relationship is found to exist
    notwithstanding the fact that, but for fraudulent misrepresentation, the rela-
    tionship was simply that of ordinary commercial men negotiating at arm's
    length.[107] The rescission of the fraudulently induced contract creates a con-
    structive trust.

(b) Although somewhat controversial, *Chase Manhattan Bank NA v Israel-British
    Bank (London) Ltd*[108] permits tracing in equity for a mistaken payment. It
    must be seriously questioned how long this authority can remain authoritative
    since it has been subject to revisionist interpretation[109] as well as having been
    the subject of general disapproval.[110] While it remains a scorned authority, its
    days must surely be numbered.

(c) More controversially still is the case of pure theft. For example, X simply
    comes along and steals £5,000 from the claimant and thereafter pays it into
    his own account which is already in credit. Subsequently, various purchases
    are made from this account. Given, on the present understanding of the com-
    mon law rules, it is not possible to trace at common law through the mixed
    bank account, can the claimant resort to equity's rules on tracing?

---

106 [1993] 3 All ER 717 (Millett J). See also *Lonrho v Fayed (No 2)* [1992] 1 WLR 1 (Millet J). The
obvious difficulty is that prior to exercising any right of rescission, the claimant has a mere equity
and no equitable interest as such. If property is transferred by the defendant prior to the claimant
rescinding the contract, it might not unreasonably be thought that the absence of any fiduciary
relationship at the relevant time would prevent the claimant tracing the monies into the hands of
the subsequent recipient. As he made clear in his judgment in *Bristol & West v Mothew* [1998] Ch 1,
Millett J permitted tracing in both *El Ajou* and *Lonrho* in order to circumvent the requirement for a
fiduciary relationship.

107 See also the Court of Appeal in *Halley v The Law Society* [2003] EWCA Civ 97 where the
Court held that the fiduciary relationship requirement was established where money had been paid
under a fictitious and fraudulent contract.

108 [1981] Ch 105.

109 In *Westdeutsche Landesbank Girozentrale v Islington LBC* [1996] AC 669, 714–15, Lord
Browne-Wilkinson re-interpreted *Chase Manhattan* on the basis that the recipient bank had the relevant knowledge of the mistake before they used the mistaken payment. It was the recipient's knowledge of the mistake which gave rise to the constructive trust as far as Lord Browne-Wilkinson was
concerned. None of this featured at all in Goulding J's analysis in *Chase Manhattan* itself.

110 See, e.g., Sir Peter Millett in 'Restitution and Constructive Trusts' in Cornish et al (eds),
Restitution: Past, Present & Future (Hart Publishing, 1998), 212: 'I agree with Lord Browne-
Wilkinson that *Chase Manhattan Bank N.A. v Israel-British Bank (London) Ltd* was wrongly decided,
but it was wrongly decided, not because the defendant had no notice of the plaintiff's claim before
it mixed the money with its own, but because the plaintiff had no proprietary interest for it to have
notice of. The plaintiff had intentionally though mistakenly parted with all beneficial interest in the
money.'

(d) Logically, the answer must be no. It is trite English law that a thief gains no title to the stolen goods. The original owner remains the true legal owner and he has not lost his title to the stolen item (but he will lose his title once the property cannot be traced at law). And yet it is precisely in this scenario that Lord Browne-Wilkinson suggested (albeit obiter) in *Westdeutsche* that the legal owner would be able to claim a constructive trust against the thief.[111] Such a view is also endorsed in *Goff and Jones*.[112] The support for this proposition does not derive from any understanding of the divergence of proprietary interests in a theft but rather from the clear view that the victim of a theft cannot be left with less remedies than a victim who has been defrauded by someone in whom they had placed trust and confidence. It has been further suggested that this stance can be justified on the basis that although the act of stealing does not in fact affect the legal owner's title, the fact that the stolen monies are then placed into and through a mixed fund, with the consequential inability to trace at common law, entitles the (legal) owner to pursue recovery of the monies in equity.[113]

21.113 Whilst one may applaud the common sense attitude underpinning a desire to permit equitable tracing in the case of a pure theft, it must be questioned how such an attitude is supposed to fit with the established legal principles as to theft and legal title. It would appear that the court is willing to ride rough-shod over such principles in order to overcome the obvious limitations on the court's ability to deal with modern fraud if the fiduciary relationship requirement was properly enforced. The conclusion is obvious: reform the rules on tracing and thereby avoid undermining established legal principle in an effort to overcome the shortcomings in those rules. The relevant legal principle which should be overridden is the requirement for a fiduciary relationship for equitable tracing and not the principle that a thief does not get any title to the stolen objects.

(b) Equity's presumptions

21.114 Given equity permits tracing into and through mixed funds, it was inevitable that it would need to generate some presumptions to assist in identifying the location of assets transferred out of a mixed fund. It is important to appreciate that these are merely presumptions and can be replaced if any other more suitable means of identifying the present location of such assets is determined.[114] Indeed, in modern

---

111 [1996] AC 669, 716.
112 *Goff and Jones*, para 2-033. See also *Black v Freeman and Co* (1910) 12 CLR 105 (Aus HCt).
113 Burrows, *The Law of Restitution*, para 4.22. See also W Swadling, 'Restitution for No Consideration' [1994] RLR 73, 81.
114 That the presumptions can be displaced by reference to the parties' contrary intention was accepted by Sir William Grant MR in *Devaynes v Noble, Clayton's Case* (1816), 1 Mer 529, 610, 35 ER 767, 793.

day fraud cases, the court is astute to ensure that these presumptions do not give rise to any money launderer's charter or apply unfairly as between innocent victims of a fraud.

(2) Treatment of monies in the mixed fund

There is some older authority which supports the proposition that if the trustee **21.115** mixes trust funds with his own funds such that it is no longer possible to identify which is which, the entire mixed fund belongs to the beneficiary.[115] This draconian approach was rejected in *Indian Oil Corpn v Greenstone Shipping Co*,[116] where the court held that because the quantities of each party's contribution could be determined, they were to be tenants in common in that proportion. More recently, Lord Millett in *Foskett v McKeown* stated that the law 'does not . . . exclude a pro rata division where this is appropriate as in the case of money and other fungibles like grain, oil or wine'.[117] A similar conclusion arises with monies mixed in a bank account. Here equity maintains that the contributors are tenants in common of the chose in action: *Re Tilley's Will Trusts*.[118]

(3) Transfers out of mixed fund made up of innocent parties' contributions

As stated above, equity has created certain presumptions to deal with the situation **21.116** where monies have been transferred into a mixed fund and thereafter some part thereof is paid out of that fund.

Equity applies different presumptions depending on whether the mixed fund is **21.117** contained within a current or deposit account. In *Clayton's Case*, Sir William Grant MR reasoned as follows:

> . . . this is the case of a banking account, where all the sums paid in form one blended fund, the parts of which have no longer any distinct existence. Neither banker nor customer ever thinks of saying, this draft is to be placed to the account of the £500 paid in on Monday, and this other to the account of the £500 on Tuesday. There is a fund of £1000 to draw upon, and that is enough. In such a case, there is no room for any other appropriation than that which arises from the order in which the receipts and payments take place, and are carried into the account. Presumably, it is the sum first paid in, that is first drawn out. It is the first item on the debit side of the account that is discharged or reduced by the first item on the credit side; the appropriation is made by the very act of setting the two items against each other . . .
>
> If appropriation be required, here is appropriation in the only way that the nature of the thing admits. Here are payments, so placed in opposition to debts, that, on the ordinary principles on which accounts are settled, this debt is extinguished.

---

[115] See e.g. *Lupton v White* (1808) 15 Ves 432.
[116] [1988] QB 345.
[117] [2001] 1 AC 102, 133C–D.
[118] [1967] Ch 1179.

> If the usual course of dealing was, for any reason, to be inverted, it was surely incumbent on the creditor to signify that such was his intention.[119]

21.118 A deposit account is treated as one common fund whereas in a current account, accounting rules have established certain principles to appropriate payments in with payments out. This has unfortunately led to a divergence between how the courts treat the distribution of funds in a deposit and current account. Two different rules have arisen.

(a) Innocent parties—deposit account

21.119 Where the monies in the mixed fund are made up of contributions from two or more innocent parties and the mixed fund is held in a deposit account (and not a current account), the parties share rateably in proportion to their contributions.[120]

(b) Innocent parties—current account—rule in Clayton's Case

21.120 If the mixed fund is held in a current account, then it is presumed, unless shown otherwise, that the *Clayton's Case* rule applies, namely the 'first in, first out' rule.

21.121 The application of *Clayton's Case* in such circumstances has been heavily criticized as being arbitrary as well as unfair.[121] Although the Court of Appeal in *Barlow Clowes International Ltd v Vaughan*[122] affirmed it as the general rule, the Court went on not to apply it. Lord Woolf there stated that:

> the use of the rule is a matter of convenience and if its application in particular circumstances would be impracticable or result in injustice between the investors it will not be applied if there is a preferable alternative.[123]

Applying this approach to the facts of the case, the Court of Appeal held that given the investors contributed to a common fund of investments, it would be contrary

---

[119] *Clayton's Case* at 1 Mer 608, 610; 35 ER 767, 793. This view was expressly endorsed by Lord Halsbury LC in *Cory Brothers and Co Ltd v The Owners of the Turkish Steamship 'MECCA'* [1897] AC 286, 290. See McConville, 'Tracing and the Rule in *Clayton's Case*' (1963) 79 LQR 388.

[120] *Sinclair v Brougham* [1914] AC 398; *Re Diplock* [1948] Ch 465; *Barlow Clowes International Ltd v Vaughan* [1992] 4 All ER 22.

[121] *Clayton's Case* does not apply in Canada or Australia to competing beneficial claims to a mingled trust funds where there have been withdrawals from the fund: see *Re Ontario Securities Commission and Greymac Credit Corporation*, (1986) 30 DLR (4th) 1 (Ont CA) app dismissed (1988) 52 DLR (4th) 767 (Sup Ct); *Re French Caledonia Travel Service Pty Ltd* (2003) NSWSC 1008, (2003) 204 ALR 353 (Campbell J).

[122] [1992] 4 All ER 22.

[123] ibid, 42. In this regard, Woolf LJ perhaps went further than Dillon and Leggatt LJJ. See also *Re Eastern Capital Futures* [1989] BCLC 371. These views are consistent with a line of older authority which expressly supports dispensing with the presumptions if the parties' contrary intention can be determined: e.g. *City Discount Co v McLean* LR 9 C P 692; *Henniker v Wigg* 4 QB 792; *Re Hallett's Case* (1880) 13 Ch D 728, 738. For academic support, see McConville, 'Tracing and the Rule in *Clayton's Case*' (1963) 79 LQR 388; Higgins, 'Re Diplock—A Reappraisal' (1965).

to their intentions to apply the 'first in, first out' rule.[124] Accordingly, the Court went on to hold the investment proceeds should be divided *pari passu* without regard either to the timing of investments or of any withdrawals. The only caveat was that this approach was subject to the 'lowest intermediate balance' rule as set out in *Roscoe v Winder*.[125]

Following on from *Barlow Clowes*, Mr Justice Lindsay in *Russell-Cooke Trust Co v Prentis*[126] remarked that it appeared from all three judgments in *Barlow Clowes* that *Clayton's Case* could readily be displaced by 'even a slight counterweight' and that '[i]n terms of its actual application between beneficiaries who have in any sense met a shared misfortune, it might be more accurate to refer to the exception that is, rather than the rule in, *Clayton's Case*'.[127]   **21.122**

Lindsay J went on to disapply the rule in *Clayton's Case* because, on the facts, investors to the relevant account were given no indication that their monies would be invested in any temporal sequence and indeed the suggestion was otherwise. As Lindsay J stated: **21.123**

> It is, as I see it, one thing to apply a 'first in, first out' rule where it *might* have been expected or intended by the investors to be applied and where nothing is known inconsistent with its being so expected or intended but quite another to presume it as an intention where both a reasonable contemplation of what was intended and the known facts can be seen to be inconsistent with it.[128]

Having rejected the rule in *Clayton's Case*, Lindsay J also rejected the possibility of applying the 'North American' method of distribution of funds, where a transfer from the mixed fund is considered in proportion to all parties' interests in the mixed fund at the time of the transfer.[129] This was a system described by Dillon LJ in *Barlow Clowes*[130] as one to be used to avoid a loss falling on the first depositor. Given *Clayton's Case* had been rejected by Lindsay J, the judge considered the basis for applying the 'North American' approach fell away. He also concluded that it would be complicated and expensive to apply. Ultimately, in line with the *Barlow Clowes* approach, his Lordship concluded that *pari passu* represented the 'least unfair' method of distributing the funds.   **21.124**

More recently, in *Commerzbank Aktiengesellschaft v IMB Morgan Plc*,[131] Lawrence Collins J also refused to apply the rule in *Clayton's Case* on the grounds that it   **21.125**

---

124 As a matter of reality, it must be seriously questioned whether any of the investors had any such intention at the time of investment. That said, the result in *Barlow Clowes* is to be welcomed.
125 [1915] 1 Ch 62.
126 [2003] 2 All ER 478, para 55.
127 ibid.
128 ibid, para 56.
129 ibid, para 57.
130 [1992] 4 All ER 22, 27–8.
131 [2005] 1 Lloyd's Law Rep 298.

would be extremely onerous and perhaps impossible to determine what sums had been paid away and it would apportion only a common misfortune through a test which he said bore no relation to the justice of the case.

21.126 The judge in *Commerzbank Aktiengesellschaft* was faced with a correspondent account which had received several payments as part of a Nigerian advance fee fraud. All monies received into a correspondent account were mingled. The account was frozen. It was found that the following parties had claims to part of the funds held in the correspondent account: (i) victims of a possible fraud; (ii) third parties; (iii) innocent IMB Morgan customers.

21.127 Lawrence Collins J examined the rule in *Clayton's Case* and stated:

> According to the rule in *Clayton's Case* payments out of an account are attributed to payments into the account in the order in which payments were made in. *Clayton's Case* was a case about appropriation of payments and not about tracing. The first payment out is attributed to the first payment in, and so on. But it can cause injustice when applied to tracing claims. The result can be 'capricious and arbitrary' (Goff & Jones on the Law of Restitution, 6ᵗʰ ed par.2-039). As *Lewin on Trusts*, 17ᵗʰ ed, par.41-53, points out, the effect of the rule, where withdrawals have been made and spent, is to establish a reverse order of priority. The later the payment into the account the greater the prospect of that payment not being attributed to payments out and hence still being represented in the remaining credit balance.

21.128 Lawrence Collins J considered the practical difficulties of trying to apply the rule in *Clayton's Case* to the operation of this correspondent bank account and concluded that 'it would be both impracticable and unjust to apply it. The only fair way to share the balances on each of the Accounts would be in proportion to the claims on the respective Accounts.'[132]

21.129 Practitioners are left with a situation where *Clayton's Case* remains applicable as a general rule but the courts have shown an increasing awareness of the unfair implications of applying it and of the need on occasion to apply the *pari passu* rule instead.

(4) Mixed fund made up of contributions from innocent party and wrongdoing trustee

(a) The rule in Re Hallett's *case*

21.130 In this situation, the court is concerned to ensure that the *Clayton's Case* rule does not result in the innocent victim of the fraud being prejudiced at the expense of the defrauding trustee who spends the victim's monies first whilst retaining his own funds.

---

132 [2005] 1 Lloyds' Law Rep 298, para 49.

To meet these concerns, the court initially applied what became known as the *Re* **21.131**
Hallett's presumption,[133] namely that the trustee is deemed to have intended to
spend his own money first and not that of the innocent victim. This is premised
on the legal principle that an individual cannot claim to have acted wrongfully in
order to defeat a legitimate claim. As Jessel MR stated:

> . . . nothing can be better settled in our own law . . . that where a man does an act
> which may be rightfully performed, he cannot say that that act was intentionally and
> in fact done wrongly . . . Wherever it can be done rightfully, he is not allowed to say,
> against the person entitled to the property or the right, that he has done it wrong-
> fully. That is universal law.[134]

So, if the mixed fund of £10,000 was made up of £3,000 of the fraudster's own **21.132**
monies and £7,000 of the innocent party's monies, and the fraudster spent £2,000
on a new motorbike, he will be deemed to have spent his own monies first. If the
motorbike cost £5,000 then he will be deemed to have spent the entirety of his
own £3,000 and £2,000 of the innocent party's monies.

(b) *The rule in* Re Oatway[135]

The rule in *Re Hallett's* left a lacuna, however, where the first withdrawal is invested **21.133**
well but the remaining monies in the fund are dissipated with no traceable proceeds. So, to take an example, consider that the fraudster decided to invest the
£3,000 in an investment fund rather than buying a motorbike and that fund
increased significantly in value such that it was now worth £10,000. In these circumstances, the innocent party will want to contend that it was its £3,000 that
was invested in the fund in order to claim the profits obtained thereby. A strict
application of *Re Hallett's* would give the fraudster the entire benefit of his shrewd
investment based on the fact that the investment was deemed to have been made
with the fraudster's own money.

Accordingly, the *Re Hallett's* presumption was modified in *Re Oatway*[136] such that **21.134**
the innocent victim can now trace into whatever was purchased with the first
withdrawals or the remaining monies, whichever is in their best interests.

(5) The lowest intermediate balance rule—*Roscoe v Winder*[137]

This rule is best explained by way of example. Consider a mixed fund which **21.135**
is made up of £3,000 of the fraudster's own money and £7,000 of the innocent

---

[133] *Re Hallett's Estate* (1880) 13 Ch D 696.
[134] ibid, 727.
[135] *Re Oatway* [1903] 2 Ch 356.
[136] ibid.
[137] *James Roscoe (Bolton) v Winder* [1951] 1 Ch 52. See also *Re Diplock* [1948] Ch 465, 521 (CA);
Re Goldcorp Exchange Ltd [1995] 1 AC 74; *Bishopsgate Investment Management Ltd (in liquidation)
v Homan* [1995] Ch 211.

victim's money, giving a total of £10,000. Various withdrawals are made from it, bringing it down to £5,000. Thereafter, the fraudster deposits further sums of his own into the mixed fund of, say, £5,000. By applying the lowest intermediate balance rule, the claimant is only entitled to make a claim to the mixed fund up to the value of £5,000. This is based upon the fact that it is indubitably correct that the mixed fund was depleted to this level, with the other funds having been dissipated in various spending.

21.136 This rule derives from the principle that one cannot trace that which no longer exists. Even though there have been subsequent deposits by the fraudster, ordinarily, these are not impressed with the same trust obligations owed to the claimant in respect of its monies originally deposited. Insofar as there have been payments out of the mixed fund using the claimant's monies, they are gone and are not to be replaced by these subsequent deposits by the fraudster.

21.137 The one limited exception to this rule is the circumstance where it can be shown that the subsequent deposits to the mixed fund were made with the intention to replace the monies transferred out of the mixed fund.[138] In practice, instances of proving such an intention are likely to be rare indeed.

21.138 One might be forgiven for wondering why it is that in this situation, equity requires proof of the actual intention on the part of the fraudster whereas in other situations, such as the *Re Hallett*'s rule, the fraudster is deemed to have a certain intention which favours the interest of the victim of the fraud. One suggested justification is that otherwise the victim of the fraud would be favoured ahead of other creditors of the fraudster:

> The real reason for allowing the claimant to reach the balance [of the mixed fund] is that he has an equitable interest in the mingled fund which the wrongdoer cannot destroy as long as any part of the fund remains; but there is no reason for subjecting other property of the wrongdoer to the claimant's claim any more than to the claims of other creditors merely because the money happens to be put in the same place where the claimant's money formerly was, unless the wrongdoer actually intended to make restitution to the claimant.[139]

21.139 It remains, however, questionable, whether this in fact justifies a difference in approach between the deemed intention scenario of *Re Hallett*'s and the need to establish an actual intention in the case of a subsequent deposit. The interests of other creditors of the fraudster are just as much in play in the *Re Hallett*'s scenario as in the case of a subsequent deposit. Indeed, one can quite readily imagine the genuine complaints of other creditors of the fraudster when the victim of the

---

[138] *Goff and Jones* (7th edn), para 2-038.
[139] *Scott on Trusts* (3rd edn, Aspen Publishers, 1998), §518.1 at 3638, cited with apparent approval in *Goff and Jones* (7th edn), para 2-038.

fraud uses the *Re Oatway* rule to claim the increased value of any investment made by the fraudster.

(6) Tracing into overdrawn accounts—swollen assets and backwards tracing

(a) The general rule—assets used to discharge liabilities cease to exist

If by applying the relevant tracing rules, the proceeds of a fraud are found to have **21.140** been paid into an account which is overdrawn in an amount equal to or in excess of the deposited fraud proceeds, the general principle is that the claimant is unable to trace any further and cannot assert a proprietary claim to those monies. The basis for this rule is that the fraud monies have been used to discharge a liability and are considered no longer to exist:

> The equitable remedies presuppose the continued existence of the money either as a separate fund or as part of a mixed fund or as latent in property acquired by means of such a fund. If, on the facts of any individual case, such continued existence is not established, equity is as helpless as the common law itself. [140]

(b) Lord Templeman's swollen assets theory

In *Space Investments Ltd v Canadian Imperial Bank of Commerce*,[141] Lord Temple- **21.141** man, delivering the advice of the Privy Council, stated, albeit by way of *obiter dicta*, that the beneficiaries of a trust could be granted a lien over the general assets of a bank in circumstances where the bank had agreed to hold trust assets separately but had failed so to do. His Lordship explained that the justification for this equitable charge was that the beneficiaries had not, whereas the bank's ordinary creditors had, taken the risk of the bank's potential insolvency. Lord Templeman reasoned thus:

> This priority is conferred because the customers and other unsecured creditors voluntarily accept the risk that the trustee bank might become insolvent and unable to discharge its obligations in full. On the other hand, the settlor of the trust and the beneficiaries interested under the trust never accept any risks involved in the possible insolvency of the trustee bank. On the contrary, the settlor could be certain that if the trusts were lawfully administered, the trustee bank could never make use of trust money for its own purposes and would always be obliged to segregate trust money and trust property in the manner authorised by law and by the trust instrument free from any risks involved in the possible insolvency of the trustee bank. It is therefore equitable that where the trustee bank has unlawfully misappropriated trust money by treating the trust money as though it belonged to the bank beneficially, merely acknowledging and recording the amount in a trust deposit account with the bank,

---

[140] [1948] Ch 465, 521. This principle was endorsed by the CA in *Bishopsgate Investment Management Ltd v Homan* [1995] Ch 211. See also *Style Financial Services Ltd v Bank of Scotland* [1995] BCC 785, 790; *Box v Barclays Bank plc* [1998] Lloyd's Rep Bank 185, 203, col 2; *Shalson v Russo* [2005] Ch 281.
[141] [1986] 1 WLR 1072 (PC).

then the claims of the beneficiaries should be paid in full out of the assets of the trustee bank in priority to the claims of customers and other unsecured creditors of the bank . . . Where a bank trustee is insolvent, trust money wrongfully treated as being on deposit with a bank must be repaid in full so far as may be out of the assets of the bank in priority to any payment of customers' deposits and other unsecured debts.

21.142   In *Re Goldcorp Ltd*,[142] the Privy Council distinguished *Space Investments* on the basis that there was no identifiable trust fund to start with in *Re Goldcorp*. Having established that the non-allocated claimants could not 'assert a proprietary interest over the purchase price and its fruits', the Privy Council (Lord Mustill) went on to remark:

> This makes it unnecessary to consider whether, if such an interest had existed, it would have been possible to trace from the subject matter of the interest into the company's present assets. . . . Their Lordships should, however, say that they find it difficult to understand how the judgment of the Board in *Space Investments Ltd v Canadian Imperial Bank of Commerce Trust Co. (Bahamas) Ltd* [1986] 1 WLR 1072 . . . would enable them to overcome the difficulty that the moneys said to be impressed with the trust were paid into an overdrawn account and thereupon ceased to exist: see, for example, *In re Diplock* [1948] Ch 465. The observations of the Board in the *Space Investments* case were concerned with a mixed, not a non-existent, fund.[143]

21.143   Similarly, the Court of Appeal in *Bishopsgate Investment* concluded that Lord Templeman could not have been contemplating applying this reasoning to trust monies paid into an overdrawn account as opposed to an insolvent bank since it would have created a 'fundamental change' in equitable tracing.[144]

21.144   In conclusion, Lord Templeman's novel swollen assets theory has received little support either in the case law or textbooks.[145] It represents a radical departure from established principles without those principles, and the case law in which they arise, having been subjected to any detailed examination in *Space Investments* itself. There is little likelihood that the swollen assets theory will be fully endorsed by an English court in the near future.

(c)   Tracing into the payment of a debt—backwards tracing[146]

21.145   'Backwards tracing' is best explained by way of examples.

- If Y transfers £50 out of his bank account, to place his account £50 in overdraft, and purchases a picture with that £50, and X subsequently pays £50 into the overdrawn account, to what extent if at all can X trace into the picture?

---

[142] [1995] 1 AC 74.

[143] *In re Goldcorp Ltd* [1995] 1 AC 74, 104–5.

[144] [1995] Ch 211, 217 per Dillon LJ.

[145] In Burrows, *The Law of Restitution* at para 4.39, it is suggested that no English court is likely to take up the idea.

[146] This whole area has been the subject of detailed examination by Professor Lionel Smith, 'Tracing into the Payment of a Debt' [1995] CLJ 290.

- What if Y purchases the picture with a loan from the bank of £50 and subsequently X pays off that loan? Can X trace into the picture now?

Whilst the weight of the prevailing case law may well favour a rejection of 'backwards tracing', it is fair to record that there is some case law and much academic support for this approach such that it would be premature to maintain that this issue is now closed. **21.146**

Professor Lionel Smith has been the driving force and main advocate in favour of 'backwards tracing'.[147] He persuasively contends that there is no logical bar to a claimant being entitled to trace into whatever was acquired for the incurring of the debt. So, to use his example, if a thief purchases a car on credit and the next day steals the claimant's money and pays off the debt, the claimant should be permitted to trace into the car which is the exchange product for the incurring of the debt which, in turn, has now been repaid with the claimant's stolen money. **21.147**

Given that the House of Lords in *Foskett v McKeown* rejected any notion that tracing was limited to the satisfaction of the 'but for' causation test, one might well question whether this adds support to those who favour backwards tracing. It will be recalled that in place of a causative test, Lord Millett talked in terms of 'attribution' or establishing a 'transactional link' such as to justify tracing. It is not at all easy to see a transactional link in the case of our example of the £50 overdraft. However, such a link may be found if it was established that X paid out using the £50 precisely because he knew that the second £50 was going to be paid into his account, thereby placing it back into credit. **21.148**

One of the most notable opponents of 'backwards tracing' is Leggatt LJ who stated in *Bishopsgate Investment Management v Homan*[148] that any payment of the claimant's monies into an overdrawn account would defeat tracing. He went on to say: **21.149**

> there can be no equitable remedy against an asset acquired before misappropriation of money takes place, since ex hypothesi it cannot be followed into something which existed and so had been acquired before the money was received and therefore without its aid.[149]

With respect, this reasoning contains a non-sequitur. It is entirely possible for the acquisition of an object to be aided by money anticipated to be, but not yet, received. Consider, for example, the willingness of banks to take into account the level of trade creditors in determining how much to loan a business.

---

[147] 'Tracing into the Payment of a Debt' [1995] CLJ 290; *The Law of Tracing*, 146–52, 353–6.
[148] [1995] Ch 211. See also *Re Diplock* [1948] 465.
[149] [1995] Ch 211, 221. Were the monies paid out under the policy in *Foskett v McKeown* *acquired* with the traceable proceeds of the beneficiaries' money?

21.150 Adopting a different approach, Dillon LJ in *Bishopsgate*, following the comments of Vinelott J at first instance, maintained that 'backwards tracing' should be possible where 'there was an inference that when the borrowing was incurred it was the intention that it should be repaid by misappropriations of [the claimant's] money.'[150]

21.151 Support for Dillon LJ's views can be found in Scott V-C in *Foskett v McKeown*[151] who stated:

> The availability of equitable remedies ought . . . to depend upon the substance of the transaction in question and not upon the strict order in which associated events happen.[152]

> . . . I do not regard the fact that an asset is paid for out of borrowed money with the borrowing subsequently repaid out of trust money as being necessarily fatal to an equitable tracing claim by the trust beneficiaries. If, in such a case, it can be shown that it was always the intention to use the trust money to acquire the asset, I do not see why the order in which the events happen should be regarded as critical to the claim. [153]

21.152 Perhaps the best that can be said at this stage is that given the increasing ingenuity adopted by money launderers seeking to hide the proceeds of their fraudulent activities, it would be wrong to close the door on the possibility of 'backwards' tracing even if the circumstances in which it is to operate remain to be worked out.[154]

F. Future for Tracing—Unified System of Tracing?[155]

21.153 There is no doubt that given the right case and the parties' desire to incur the not inconsiderable costs to take the matter to the House of Lords, the court will remove the distinction between legal and equitable tracing.[156] Indeed, once it is

---

[150] At 216.

[151] [1998] Ch 265. The other members of the CA in *Foskett* did not agree with Scott V-C's observations on this issue.

[152] ibid, 283.

[153] ibid, 283–4.

[154] See also *Goff and Jones* at para 2-046.

[155] The case law and literature calling for the unification of the tracing rules or one system of rules to apply to all claims, whether legal or equitable, is immense: e.g. *Foskett v McKeown* [2001] 1 AC 102, 113, 128–9; *Goff and Jones* (6th edn), paras 2-031–2-033; Birks, 'The Necessity of a Unitary Law of Tracing' in *Making Commercial Law: Essays in Honour of Roy Goode* (Oxford University Press, 1997), 239–58; Sir Peter Millett, 'Tracing the Proceeds of Fraud' (1991) 107 LQR 71, 85 where he advocated one system based upon the equitable rules. He urged that attempts to rationalize the common law rules should be abandoned. This may well explain his early judgments, such as in *Agip (Africa) Ltd v Jackson* [1990] Ch 265 where he restricted common law tracing to clean physical substitutions; Burrows, *The Law of Restitution* (2nd edn), 82.

[156] Some have wrongly interpreted the views of Lord Millett and Lord Steyn in *Foskett v McKeown* [2001] AC 102, 113, 128–9, as having already removed the distinction between the two systems

recognized that the process of tracing is independent of any claim to be brought, it is immediately apparent that there can be no justification for applying different rules depending on whether the claim is at common law or in equity. The House of Lords appears already to have recognized the force of this point.

In *Foskett v McKeown*,[157] Lord Millett (with whom Lords Browne-Wilkinson and Hoffmann agreed) stated: **21.154**

> Given its nature, there is nothing inherently legal or equitable about the tracing exercise. There is thus no sense in maintaining different rules for tracing at law and in equity. One set of tracing rules is enough . . . There is certainly no logical justification for allowing any distinction between them to produce capricious results in cases of mixed substitutions by insisting on the existence of a fiduciary relationship as a pre-condition for applying equity's tracing rules. The existence of such a relationship may be relevant to the nature of the claim which the plaintiff can maintain, whether personal or proprietary, but that is a different matter.[158]

While no doubt this is where the law is heading, it would be wrong to say that we have got there yet. *Foskett v McKeown*, while frowning on the historic accident leading to the dual rules in equity and at common law, did not in fact unify the tracing rules.[159] Practitioners are therefore left in the rather unhappy position of having to work within the existing dual system of rules, with all their shortcomings, whilst knowing that even the House of Lords believes that there should only be a unified system.   **21.155**

G. Concluding Observations

The law of tracing is in a state of flux. Practitioners are constantly told, by academics and House of Lords judges, that there should be only one system, and yet we have to work within the historical accident of the dual system. This creates tensions, particularly as these rules are now, more than ever, being forced to adapt to the modern methods of money laundering that follows any successful fraud.   **21.156**

In common law tracing, we have the disappointing insistence of some judges that tracing cannot take place through electronic transfers but can take place   **21.157**

(see Sir Robert Walker, 'Tracing after Foskett v McKeown' [2000] RLR 573 and *Bracken Partners v Gutteridge* [2003] BCLC 84, 90–1). Their Lordships' comments criticized the distinction but cannot be taken to have created one unified system of rules for tracing. That battle awaits.

[157] [2001] 1 AC 102.

[158] ibid, 128.

[159] The court (Peter Leaver QC) in *Bracken Partners v Gutteridge* [2003] BCLC 84 at 90–1 was of the view that if monies there were not held on trust, nevertheless that did not matter as there was no longer any requirement post-*Foskett v McKeown* for a fiduciary relationship to invoke equity's tracing rules. That is not correct.

through cheques.[160] It is thought by some that this restriction was an early attempt by Millett J (as he then was in *Agip*) to limit any further development of the common law, thus permitting the equitable rules to expand and take over. Unfortunately, this has not yet occurred, leaving the practitioner with comments suggesting that common law tracing is incapable of dealing with some of the most basic forms of money transfers now employed by banks. That is a far from satisfactory position. Having begun the task of understanding bank accounts in terms of choses in action, it is a pity that this analysis is not applied also to electronic money transfers. In a modern commercial world, common law tracing should be capable of applying to all modes of transfer of funds.

21.158 In equitable tracing, tremendous pressure is being brought to apply to the concept of a fiduciary simply and only to enable tracing in equity to take place. It is a sad day when the act of stealing is a determinative factor for the existence of fiduciary duties under English law. It is also disappointing that the existence of this fiduciary requirement is being allowed to ride roughshod over other basic principles of legal rights such as the trite point that a thief does not obtain any title to the stolen goods.

21.159 It is unlikely that we shall see much improvement in any of these areas unless and until the basic problem of the dual system is tackled and remedied in the House of Lords. Until then, the practitioner will probably find limited usefulness for common law tracing (and, therefore, common law claims in any complex fraud) and will constantly be required to resort to the rules in equity.

---

160 This insistence on corporeal substitutions for common law tracing is at odds with the House of Lords' willingness to permit tracing at common law through choses in action in *Lipkin Gorman v Karpnale* [1991] 2 AC 548, 574 where Lord Goff stated that a chose in action is to be treated in the same manner as any other property.

22

DISCLOSURE

A. Overview

(1) Pre-action disclosure

A claimant is entitled to pre-action disclosure in the following circumstances.   **22.01**

(a) As between future parties to litigation

Under CPR r 31.16, where it can be shown that both the applicant and the   **22.02**
respondent are likely to be parties to future litigation, the respondent is likely to
have in his possession, custody or power documentation relevant to the issues arising from such litigation and which would, if standard disclosure applied, be dis-
closable, and the applicant is able to show that such disclosure is desirable in order
(i) to dispose fairly of the anticipated proceedings; and/or (ii) to assist the dispute
to be resolved without proceedings; or to save costs.

(b) As between putative claimant and facilitator

Under the *Norwich Pharmacal* jurisdiction, the claimant is entitled to disclosure   **22.03**
of specified documents and information from a respondent who has become,
wittingly or unwittingly, mixed up in the wrongdoing of another. This jurisdiction has been considerably widened over the last decade to include attempts
not only to identify a wrongdoer but whether any wrongdoing had in fact taken
place at all.

(c) As between putative claimant and third party in possession of knowledge of missing assets

22.04   Under the *Bankers Trust* jurisdiction, the claimant is entitled to disclosure of specified documents and information from an individual in relation to the conduct of a tracing exercise where it can readily be shown that there is real merit in undertaking the tracing procedure.

(2) Post-action disclosure

22.05   After the commencement of litigation, it still remains open to a claimant to utilize either or both of the *Norwich Pharmacal* and *Bankers Trust* jurisdictions (where appropriate) to obtain relevant documentation and information.

(a) Disclosure against a non-party under CPR r 31.17

22.06   In addition, the claimant is entitled to seek disclosure against a non-party under CPR r 31.17, so long as it can be shown that such documents are likely to be in the possession of the non-party, are likely, if disclosed, to support or adversely affect one party's case and it is otherwise desirable to disclose the documents to fairly dispose of the claim and/or to save costs.

(b) Witness summons under CPR r 34.2

22.07   Under CPR r 34.2, a named individual may be required to attend trial to give oral evidence and/or to produce documentation. Unlike the old *subpoena duces tecum* procedure, there is no requirement that production of the documentation must take place at the trial itself. It will typically take place at a convenient date ahead of the trial so as to enable the parties to assimilate the new material ahead of the trial.

22.08   Each of these jurisdictions for obtaining disclosure and information will be examined in some detail below. Some are limited as to when an application can be made (pre- or post-action), others are limited as to the type of documentation recoverable (CPR r 34.2).

B. Introduction

22.09   This chapter is not concerned with the general rules on disclosure of documentation under the CPR. They are rules which should be familiar to any general practitioner and need not be considered in any detail in a book on commercial fraud litigation. What this chapter is concerned with is the various means open to a claimant to obtain documentation and information from the defendant or some other individual at the earliest possible opportunity including, most importantly, prior to the commencement of any litigation.[1]

---

[1] The principles relating to search orders are dealt with in Chapter 23.

A practitioner's ability to get hold of relevant documentation and/or information **22.10**
is crucial to the success of any commercial fraud investigation, since information:

- provides a better understanding of how the fraud was perpetrated;
- helps to identify all those individuals involved in the fraud;
- assists in identifying the present location of the fraud proceeds.

The more detailed knowledge a practitioner has in relation to each of these three **22.11**
areas, the better placed he will be to give focused advice to the client in the early
stages of the fraud investigation.

So, for example, knowing that the fraud was committed within a contractual con- **22.12**
text should immediately alert the practitioner to concerns to ensure that any steps
taken to protect the client's interest do not unwittingly amount to an affirmation
of the contract. Such an affirmation is likely to have an adverse impact on the ability of the claimant to pursue any proprietary relief arising out of the fraud.

If the suspected fraudsters are, or include, any of the claimant's employees or **22.13**
officers, then it is likely that they owe the claimant (and have breached their) fiduciary duties in carrying out the suspected fraud. Knowing this at the outset, will
make the initial formulation of any claim, and interim relief sought in support
thereof, a lot easier. If they are employees, the claimant should have details of their
bank accounts, which is always a useful starting point in any attempt to trace missing monies.

It is therefore essential that any practitioner in this area is well versed in the numer- **22.14**
ous avenues open to him from the court to obtain that documentation and
information.

C. Pre-action Disclosure

There is no doubt that the CPR has heralded a sea-change in the attitude of litiga- **22.15**
tors and the ability to obtain disclosure material prior to the commencement of
litigation. With the introduction of pre-action protocols,[2] and the duty to comply
(at risk of costs) with the spirit of such protocols in the event no specific protocol
covers the type of case being dealt with,[3] the CPR has forced litigators to exchange

---

[2] See the general discussion on pre-action protocols in *Zuckerman on Civil Procedure Principles
of Practice* (2nd edn, Thomson/Sweet and Maxwell, 2006), paras 1.04–1.112; C Hollander QC,
Documentary Evidence (9th edn, Thomson/Sweet and Maxwell, 2006).
[3] Practice Direction—Protocols, para 4: '4.1 In cases not covered by any approved protocol, the
court will expect the parties, in accordance with the overriding objective and the matters referred to
in CPR 1.1(2)(a), (b) and (c), to act reasonably in exchanging information and documents relevant
to the claim and generally in trying to avoid the necessity for the start of proceedings.'

far more information pre-action than had been the position under the old RSC regime. Under the CPR, cards on the table is the expected play in most cases.

22.16 This is all well and good, but when faced with a client who has been defrauded of several million dollars, talk of writing letters and seeking to comply with the spirit of pre-action protocols with potential defendants is unlikely to be heard favourably. Save in the very unusual circumstances where speed is of little importance to a claim in fraud, the need to move quickly will typically obviate the requirement to comply with such protocols.

22.17 Further, the dynamics of the dispute are substantially different in a commercial fraud context than say in a typical commercial contract dispute. In the latter situation, a healthy exchange of information and documentation may lead to a productive understanding of each side's respective position. This is not something required in a commercial fraud dispute, where speed is of the essence and any delay may simply hinder the ability to recover the proceeds of the fraud.

22.18 So, in a commercial fraud context, the interests of the client are likely to dictate that it may well be necessary to abandon the need to comply with the spirit of the pre-action protocols. What is required is the ability to obtain orders from the court against likely parties and non-parties as to documentation or information relevant to the underlying fraud. Voluntary exchange of correspondence is unlikely to achieve this and runs the risk of alerting the fraudster you are aware of the fraud and are seeking to recover the assets, while all the time delaying the litigator from taking the crucial steps to protect the interests of the client.

(1) CPR r 31.16

22.19 The statutory basis for the court's jurisdiction to obtain disclosure pre-action is derived from s 33(2) of the Supreme Court Act 1981[4] (SCA 1981) which provides:

> On the application, in accordance with rules of court, of a person who appears to the High Court to be likely to be a party to subsequent proceedings in that court the High Court shall, in such circumstances as may be specified in the rules, have power to order a person who appears to the court to be likely to be a party to the proceedings and to be likely to have or to have had in his possession, custody or power any documents which are relevant to an issue arising or likely to arise out of that claim—to disclose whether those documents are in his possession, custody or power; and to produce such of those documents as are in his possession, custody or power to the applicant or, on such conditions as may be specified in the order—to the applicant's legal advisers; or to the applicant's legal advisers and any medical or other professional adviser of the applicant; or if the applicant has no legal adviser, to any medical or other professional adviser of the applicant.

---

[4] As amended by the Civil Procedure (Modification of Enactments) Order 1998, art 5(a), pursuant to s 8 of the Civil Procedure Act 1997.

Pre-action disclosure against a likely defendant had, under the old RSC regime, **22.20** been limited to cases involving personal injury or death. CPR r 31.16 removed any such restrictions, such that the jurisdiction extends to all cases:

> **31.16**—(1) This rule applies where an application is made to the court under any Act for disclosure before proceedings have started.
>
> (2) The application must be supported by evidence.
>
> (3) The court may make an order under this rule only where—
>
> > (a) the respondent is likely to be a party to subsequent proceedings;
> >
> > (b) the applicant is also likely to be a party to those proceedings;
> >
> > (c) if proceedings had started, the respondent's duty by way of standard disclosure, set out in rule 31.6, would extend to the documents or classes of documents of which the applicant seeks disclosure, and
> >
> > (d) disclosure before proceedings have started is desirable in order to—
> >
> > > (i) dispose fairly of the anticipated proceedings;
> > >
> > > (ii) assist the dispute to be resolved without proceedings; or save costs.
>
> An order under this rule must specify the documents or the classes of documents which the respondent must disclose; and require him, when making disclosure, to specify any of those documents which are no longer in his control; or in respect of which he claims a right or duty to withhold inspection.

Such an order may require the respondent to indicate what has happened to any **22.21** documents which are no longer in his control; and specify the time and place for disclosure and inspection.

(a) The jurisdictional requirements

CPR r 31.16 essentially lays down three jurisdictional requirements which must **22.22** be met before consideration is given by the court as to the exercise of its discretion whether to grant pre-action disclosure. The three requirements are that: the applicant and respondent are likely to be parties to future proceedings; any disclosure sought would fall within the ambit of standard disclosure; such disclosure must be desirable in order (i) to dispose fairly of the proceedings; or (ii) to assist the dispute to be resolved without proceedings; or (iii) to save costs.

(i) Likely to be parties to future proceedings   In *Black v Sumitomo*,[5] Rix LJ **22.23** examined what precisely is meant by the phrase 'likely to be a party to subsequent proceedings'.

He first considered the meaning of s 31 of the Administration of Justice Act 1970, **22.24** the predecessor to s 33(2) of the SCA 1981, which read as follows (the italicized section being the additional wording no longer included in s 33(2) of the SCA 1981):

> On the application, in accordance with rules of court, of a person who appears to the High Court to be likely to be a party to subsequent proceedings in that court *in*

---

[5] [2002] 1 WLR 1562 CA.

which a claim in respect of personal injuries to a person or in respect of a person's death is likely to be made, the High Court shall . . .

22.25 Having carefully considered the Court of Appeal decision in *Dunning v United Liverpool Hospitals' Board of Governors*,[6] Rix LJ concluded that both Lord Denning MR and James LJ had agreed that the word 'likely' meant 'may' or 'may well' or 'reasonable prospect' if disclosure was granted. It did not mean 'more likely on the balance of probability than not'.

22.26 Rix LJ then turned to the wording of the present s 33(2) of the SCA 1981 which does not contain any wording that 'a claim . . . is likely to be made'. In these circumstances, Rix LJ construed the requirement as follows:

> 71. Of course, in one sense it might be said that a person is hardly likely to be a party to subsequent proceedings whether as a claimant or otherwise unless some form of proceedings is itself likely to be issued. Two questions, however, arise. One is whether the statute requires that it be likely that proceedings are issued, or only that the persons concerned are likely to be parties *if* subsequent proceedings are issued. The other is whether 'likely' means 'more probably than not' or 'may well'. As to the first question, in my judgment, the amended statute means no more than that the persons concerned are likely to be parties in proceedings if those proceedings are issued. That was what Lord Woolf had in mind when he wrote of the requirement that 'there is a likelihood that the respondent would indeed be a defendant if proceedings were initiated' (in Section III, para 50, of his final 'Access to Justice' report. . .). The omission of any language which expressly requires that the initiation of proceedings itself be likely, which could have been included in the amended section, appears to be to reflect the difficulties which the earlier authorities had explored in the sort of circumstances found in *Dunning v United Liverpool Hospitals' Board of Governors* [1973] 1 WLR 586. What the current language of the section appears to me to emphasise, as does the rule of court, is that the parties concerned in an application are parties who would be likely to be involved if proceedings ensued. The concern is that pre-action disclosure would be sought against a stranger to any possible proceedings, or by a party who would himself be unlikely to be involved. If the statute and the rule are understood in this sense, then all difficulties, which might arise where the issue of proceedings might depend crucially on the nature of the disclosure sought and where it is impossible at the time of making the application to say whether the disclosure would critically support or undermine the prospective claim, disappear.

> 72. As to the second question, it is not uncommon for 'likely' to mean something less than probable in its strict sense. It seems to me that if I am wrong about the first question, then it is plain that 'likely' must be given its more extended and open meaning (see Lord Denning MR in *Dunning's* case), because otherwise one of the fundamental purposes of the statute will have been undermined. If, however, I am right about the first question, the second question is of less moment. Even so, however, I am inclined to answer it by saying that 'likely' here means no more than 'may well'.[7]

---

6 [1973] 1 WLR 586 CA.
7 [2002] 1 WLR 1562, 1586 paras 71–2.

Accordingly, there is no requirement that it be shown that it is likely that proceed- **22.27**
ings will be commenced. All that must be shown is that *if* proceedings are commenced, the applicant and the respondent *may well* be parties to those proceedings.
Rix LJ considered that this jurisdictional hurdle would suffice to ensure that CPR
r 31.16 would not be used for pre-action disclosure against non-parties or by
an applicant who did not intend or was unlikely to bring any such proceedings
himself.[8]

It is submitted that Rix LJ's reasoning is to be welcomed. There is little point in **22.28**
asking the court to become embroiled in considering the likelihood of proceedings as part of the jurisdictional threshold for acceding to an application for pre-
action disclosure. Further, any higher threshold would place the applicant in a
difficult position. The more the applicant persuaded the court of the inevitability
of proceedings, the more likely the court might refuse the application on the
grounds that pre-action disclosure was not in fact necessary in order to advance
the dispute between the parties. The more difficult it is for the applicant to persuade the court of the likelihood of proceedings, the more likely the need of the
applicant for the disclosure but, on this basis, the greater the possibility that the
court will not be persuaded. On either example, too high a threshold on this issue
places the parties under all the wrong incentives.

(ii) Pre-action disclosure limited to standard disclosure The obvious diffi- **22.29**
culty with limiting the ambit of pre-action disclosure under CPR r 31.16 to that
available under standard disclosure is that typically standard disclosure takes place
after the close of pleadings/statements of case, when the issues have been fully
canvassed and identified as between the parties. It is against this background of
knowledge that the parties, and ultimately the court as final arbiter, can determine
whether a particular document will aid one party's case and/or be adverse to the
other party's case.

But, pre-action, the court will not have the benefit of any pleadings and so the **22.30**
applicant must do his best to identify what issues are likely to arise by way of claim
and defence in order to assist the court and show the relevance of the documents
sought.

If the applicant keeps shifting the nature of the claim to be brought, and fails **22.31**
properly to identify the relevant issues, by, say, producing a draft statement of case,
there is a real risk that the court will simply conclude that it is not possible to
determine whether these parties would be parties to any future litigation and if so

---

8 On the basis of *Black v Sumitomo* [2002] 1 WLR 1569, it is likely that *Burns v Shuttlehurst Ltd*
[1999] 1 WLR 1449 (needing to establish a reasonable basis for the intended claim) and *Rose v Lynx
Express Ltd* [2004] 1 BCLC 455 (needing to establish a substantive claim with a real prospect of
success) may be placing too high a threshold on the merit requirements of any application.

what issues might arise and accordingly dismiss the application for pre-action disclosure.[9]

22.32 So, for example, an application under CPR r 31.16 was dismissed where the applicant failed specifically to formulate the fraud claim to be pursued, and thus failed to identify the specific issues to which such claims would give rise.[10] The courts have not been slow to refuse applications under CPR r 31.16 on the grounds of the claims being speculative or badly formulated such that the real issues between the parties could not be identified.[11]

22.33 This was a point emphasized by Rix LJ in *Black v Sumitomo*.[12] Rix LJ also stated it would be a relevant consideration, for the purposes of exercising discretion, if there existed considerable doubt whether the proceedings would ever reach the disclosure stage.[13]

22.34 In *Bermuda International Securities Ltd v KPMG*,[14] Waller LJ said:

> The circumstances spelt out by the rule show that it will 'only' be ordered where the court can say that the documents asked for will be documents that will have to be produced at the standard disclosure stage. It follows from that, that the court must be clear what the issues in the litigation are likely to be i e what case the claimant is likely to be making and what defence is likely to be being run so as to make sure the documents being asked for are ones which will adversely affect the case of one side or the other, or support the case of one side or the other.

22.35 In *Hands v Morrison Construction Services Ltd*,[15] Jackson J, whilst recognizing that this requirement was, on its face, a strict test, accepted that typically it was complied with by an appropriate form of drafting which either included an express limitation of disclosure to the standard disclosure level alternatively a very precise formulation of the issue to which the documents must relate. Jackson J recognized that both techniques had been employed on the facts of *Hands* itself.

---

[9] As was the case in *Medisys Plc v Arthur Andersen (A Firm)* [2002] Lloyd's Rep PN 323 QB.

[10] *Cheshire Building Society v Dunlop Haywards (DHL) Ltd* [2007] EWHC 403 (Tugendhat J). The judge also held it was not desirable to grant similar fact evidence on a pre-action disclosure application when the court had not had the benefit of a statement of claim and defence from which it could assess the relevance and importance of such evidence to the conduct of the trial.

[11] *Cheshire Building Society v Dunlop Haywards (DHL) Ltd* [2007] EWHC 403; *Snowstar Shipping Company Ltd v Graig Shipping Plc & Ors* [2003] EWHC 1367 (Comm, Morison J)—claims speculative and disclosure sought too wide; *David Ruffle Architects v Potter Raper Partnership* [2002] EWHC 488 (TCC Judge Seymour QC)—applicant had failed properly to identify issues which would arise in any forthcoming litigation; *Medisys Plc v Arthur Andersen (A Firm)* [2002] Lloyd's Rep PN 323 (Cooke J)—changing case had made it impossible to know what the applicant's actual case was.

[12] [2002] 1 WLR 1562, 1585, para 76. In *Black v Sumitomo*, the parties agreed that any disclosure to be given was to be limited to standard disclosure.

[13] ibid, para 77.

[14] [2001] Lloyd's Rep PN 392, 297, para 26.

[15] [2006] All ER (D) 186 (Jun), Jackson J.

It is therefore critical for an applicant to take time to consider these matters **22.36** are properly and fully dealt with in his written evidence and submissions delivered to court as part of the application under CPR r 31.16. That said, the court must not allow itself to become involved in a mini-trial on complex legal or factual issues.[16]

(iii) **Disclosure should be desirable** This aspect has a dual role. It is both juris- **22.37** dictional as well as the framework in which to assess and exercise the discretion. Rix LJ in *Black v Sumitomo*[17] suggested that the two-stage approach be adopted as follows. The first stage, the jurisdictional stage, the court is only permitted to consider the granting of pre-action disclosure where there is a *real prospect in principle*[18] of such an order being fair to the parties if litigation is commenced, or of assisting the parties to avoid litigation, or of saving costs in any event. If the particular application passes this first stage, then the court should consider the matter as a question of discretion, which is to be considered based upon all the facts and not merely in principle but in detail.

Again, these hurdles, and in particular the avoiding of litigation and the saving of **22.38** costs, require the court to make value judgments on the impact of disclosure on the conduct of litigation yet to be commenced. This, in turn, places a burden on the applicant to ensure that the court is provided with the necessary information in order to make such assessments. If possible, applicants should seriously consider providing draft statements of case to assist the court.

(b) Discretion

It might be said that it is here that the court's work really is done. In *Black v* **22.39** *Sumitomo*, Rix LJ made it clear that the jurisdictional hurdles of CPR r 31.16 were not high and even if answered positively, were unable to assist any determination of the answer as a matter of discretion:

> The jurisdictional threshold is not . . . intended to be a high one. The real question is likely to be one of discretion, and answering the jurisdictional question in the affirmative is unlikely in itself to give the Judge much of a steer as to the correct exercise of his power.[19]

Rix LJ's views echoed those previously given by Waller LJ in *Bermuda International* **22.40** *Securities Ltd*, when Waller LJ indicated that notwithstanding having answered

---

16 *Total E&P Soudan SA v Edmonds & Ors* [2007] EWCA Civ 50 (Tuckey, Jacob and Moore-Bick LJJ) discussed in greater detail at para 22.43 below.

17 [2002] 1 WLR 1562, 1586, para 81.

18 This phrase, 'real prospect in principle' is taken up and applied by Jackson J in *Hands v Morrison Construction Services Ltd* [2006] All ER (D) 186 (Jun), para 27. This case concerns the application of Rix LJ's *Black v Sumitomo* approach in a construction case with voluminous documentation.

19 [2002] 1 WLR 1562, 1585 para 73.

the jurisdictional questions of CPR r 31.16, it was nevertheless open to the court to refuse to allow the application on some other ground.

22.41 In *Black v Sumitomo*, the Court of Appeal warned against an over-zealous employment of CPR r 31.16 whether as a means of determining whether one had a claim in the first place,[20] or simply as a means of getting early disclosure, when in fact there was little or no justification not to wait until the normal time for disclosure:

> . . . cannot be right to think that, wherever proceedings are likely between the parties to such an application and there is a real prospect of one of the purposes under sub-r (d) being met, an order for disclosure should be made of documents which would in due course fall within standard disclosure. Otherwise an order for pre-action disclosure should be made in almost every dispute of any seriousness, irrespective of its context and detail. Whereas outside obvious examples such as medical records or their equivalent (as indicated by pre-action protocols) in certain other kinds of disputes, by and large the concept of disclosure being ordered at other than the normal time is presented as something differing from the normal, at any rate where the parties at the pre-action stage have been acting reasonably.[21]

22.42 When the court moves away from the jurisdictional aspect towards applying its discretion it is required to take into account all relevant factors, and not simply those identified in CPR r 31.16(d). In this regard, the court will take into account, the nature of the claim,[22] the clarity with which the issues have been identified, the scope of the disclosure sought and the need for the pre-action disclosure in order to assist the case being properly pleaded.

22.43 The court must not, however, become embroiled in detailed argument of complex legal and factual issues in order to determine how to exercise its discretion under CPR r 31.16. In *Total E&P Soudan SA v Edmonds & Ors*,[23] Tuckey LJ, in a typically robust judgment, made it clear that the court was not to embark upon consideration of difficult legal issues such as justiciability or the mental element required for economic torts:

> Such applications are in the nature of case management decisions requiring the judge to take a 'big picture' view of the application in question. This obviously involves the judge taking a broad view of the merits of the potential claim, but should not necessitate an investigation of legally complex and debateable potential defences or grounds of stay. . . . Mr Greenwood conceded that the situation would be different if

---

[20] An application under the *Norwich Pharmacal* jurisdiction would be more appropriate in such a case.

[21] *Black v Sumitomo* [2002] 1 WLR 1562, para 85.

[22] A contrast might be drawn between personal injury claims, which are particularly suited to pre-action disclosure of specific documents and say a wide-ranging fraud claim, in which the categories of documents sought might be large and voluminous in content: see Rix LJ in *Black v Sumitomo* [2002] 1 WLR 1562, 1577 para 51 *et seq*.

[23] [2007] EWCA Civ 50.

a respondent could show beyond argument that the claim was hopeless or non-justiciable or if disclosure of the documents themselves raised non-justiciable issues such as sovereign confidentiality. I agree, but that is not this case.

In a similar vein, the Court of Appeal in *Rose v Lynx Express Ltd*[24] rejected the **22.44**
judge's approach of making a preliminary issue out of a central issue of construction which was at the heart of the dispute and would therefore have had a significant bearing on the outcome of the pre-action disclosure application. The Court of Appeal highlighted the dangers involved in trying to determine such issues on a preliminary basis without the benefit of seeing all the factual evidence and without the parties themselves having perhaps fully considered all the arguments they may wish to run. Assumptions would have to be made which may subsequently prove to be inaccurate. Peter Gibson LJ observed that:

> courts should be hesitant, in the context of an application for pre-action disclosure, about embarking upon any determination of substantive issues in the case. In our view it will normally be sufficient to found an application under CPR 31.16(3) for the substantive claim pursued in the proceedings to be properly arguable and to have a real prospect of success, and it will normally be appropriate to approach the conditions in CPR 31.16(3) on that basis.[25]

The Court of Appeal's concern that the courts do not become too involved in the **22.45**
detail of the underlying claims is to be welcomed. Any other approach would be inconsistent with the usually stated rule that English law does not typically like mini-trials conducted in an interlocutory setting—*a fortiori* when the application is made pre-action and without the benefit of pleadings.

Further, there is no need at all for the court to reach such definitive answers on **22.46**
such applications. The threshold has been identified above and the courts should work within it. In trying to do too much, the court runs the risk of making determinations on assumptions, which may or may not turn out to be true when the evidence is in fact assessed. There is no need to go out on such a limb. If the parties want an early neutral evaluation of their claim to aid settlement negotiations they can make the usual application to court.

Finally, the Court of Appeal's attitude in *Rose v Lynx Express* is entirely understand- **22.47**
able. Preliminary issues must be carefully considered before being pursued. Detailed consideration of the factual matrix is necessary and often has to be agreed between the parties to assist the preliminary issue determination. When this is not done properly, adopting a preliminary issue approach can lead to a substantial increase in the costs being incurred than if the matter had been allowed to proceed

---

[24] [2004] EWCA Civ 447, [2004] 1 BCLC 455.
[25] [2004] 1 BCLC 455, para 3.

as usual to a full trial. The risks and dangers are all the more so if decisions to proceed on a preliminary issue basis are being taken as early as pre-action.

22.48 Although in general it is correct to say that CPR r 31.16 is not available for what
litigators might call a 'fishing expedition', i.e. trying to determine whether a claim
in fact existed as opposed to trying to support an existing claim, Tugendhat J in
Baron Jay v Wilder Coe (A Firm)[26] made it clear that where an applicant has clearly
suffered some misfortune and the respondents declined to provide any answers to
the allegations, the court was willing to exercise its discretion to award pre-action
disclosure under CPR r 31.16.

22.49 Whilst the willingness of Tugendhat J to provide the would-be claimant with the
means of finding out more about its undoubted misfortune is to be welcomed, it
is suggested that it might have been preferable to allow such disclosure/informa-
tion to be sought under the *Norwich Pharmacal* jurisdiction rather than allow it
potentially to blur the lines of jurisdiction for CPR r 31.16.

22.50 An application under CPR 31.16 requires the issuing of an ordinary application
notice supported by evidence meeting the relevant criteria discussed above.

(c) Costs—CPR r 48.1

22.51 The general rule on costs for applications under CPR r 31.16 is that the applicant
must pay for obtaining pre-action disclosure. That is something that needs to be
borne carefully in mind in determining whether it is appropriate to pursue such
an application.

22.52 Although some commentators have justified this approach on the basis that it
ensures that applications under CPR r 31.16 are not lightly made and that 'it is
only natural that an applicant who puts another person to the trouble of providing
him with information should pay for that person's services'[27] it must surely be
questioned whether this approach is in fact the correct one.

22.53 First, the CPR encourages pre-action exchange of information between the parties as a means of fostering potential settlement without litigation or at an early
stage of litigation. CPR r 31.16 is one means available to parties to take up that
encouragement. If an application is inappropriately made it will (i) be rejected
and (ii) the applicant will, as is usual, pay for the costs incurred in that application.
It is odd, to say the least, that an applicant who has persuaded the court that it
meets all the criteria laid down in CPR r 31.16 for early disclosure is then penal-
ized by being hit with costs. This is all the more so where that pre-action disclosure

---

26 [2003] EWHC 1786 (QB).
27 *Zuckerman on Civil Procedure* (2nd edn, Thomson/Sweet and Maxwell, 2006), para 14.90.

leads to a settlement of the litigation or ensures that the litigation proceeds on a narrower and more focused basis.

Secondly, if the court was concerned that the disclosure resulted in no proceedings being commenced, and leaving the costs of the exercise on the shoulders of the respondent, it could simply have made appropriate provision for that in the order, i.e. costs in the case (in the event that proceedings are commenced) alternatively costs for the respondent (in the event no proceedings are issued within [X weeks] of the date of this order). **22.54**

Thirdly, there are many examples in interlocutory litigation where the question of costs is postponed until we know the outcome of the case. It is difficult to see why such an approach is not the norm for applications under CPR r 31.16. This would be preferable to the fact that the court can depart from CPR r 48.1(2) if the conduct of the respondent so justifies it.[28] **22.55**

The general rule on costs should be 'Costs in the Case' with the proviso in the event that no litigation was commenced at all, that applicant to pay the respondents' costs. Other considerations, such as abuse of the procedure, etc., should be taken care of by the courts properly applying the criteria and penalizing hopeless applications in costs. **22.56**

(2) The *Norwich Pharmacal* jurisdiction[29]

A commercial fraud litigator must have a detailed understanding of the parameters of the *Norwich Pharmacal* jurisdiction for obtaining disclosure and information. It is one of the most effective means of obtaining documentation and information at an early stage—typically pre-action—to get a better understanding of the details of the fraud to which the client has just fallen victim and/or the identity of those involved in that fraud. Likely respondents in a commercial fraud include banks, accountants and financial advisers. Anyone holding themselves out as a legal adviser to a victim of fraud should know the requirements of this jurisdiction inside out. **22.57**

Notwithstanding that CPR r 31.18 expressly left open the possibility for making use of common law or equitable remedies, it was expected by some that the *Norwich Pharmacal* head of jurisdiction would begin to wane in importance with **22.58**

---

[28] *Bermuda International Securities Ltd v KPMG* [2001] EWCA Civ 269, paras 30–3. The respondent had steadfastly opposed the application and so, notwithstanding CPR r 48.1, the court awarded costs to the applicant and the Court of Appeal held that order could not be disturbed.

[29] *Norwich Pharmacal Co v Customs and Excise Commissioners* [1974] AC 133 (HL). See C Hollander QC, *Documentary Evidence* (9th edn, Thomson/Sweet and Maxwell, 2006), ch 5; *Zuckerman on Civil Procedure* (2nd edn), paras 14.110–14.118; N Andrews, *English Civil Procedure* (Oxford University Press, 2006, 2003), [26.115]–[26.128].

the introduction of the ability to obtain pre-action disclosure such as under CPR r 31.16,[30] but this has not proved to be the case. Indeed, it is probably fair to say that there has been a willingness on the part of the courts to widen the circumstances in which it is possible to invoke this jurisdiction so as to meet the demands of modern day frauds and other forms of wrongdoing. That is as it should be.

(a) Norwich Pharmacal Co v Customs and Excise Commissioners—*analysis of the decision*

22.59   In this case, Norwich Pharmacal owned a chemical patent for immunizing poultry but believed that importers were infringing that patent. Norwich Pharmacal did not, however, know the identity of the relevant importers, but the Customs and Excise Commissioners did. Without such knowledge, Norwich Pharmacal was unable to commence any litigation and/or protect its patent.

22.60   The House of Lords, by reviving an old equity bill of discovery, allowed Norwich Pharmacal to obtain an order compelling the Customs and Excise Commissioners to disclose the identity of the wrongdoers. This was despite the absence of any cause of action as between Norwich Pharmacal and the Commissioners.

22.61   The relevant principle is set out by Lord Reid as follows:

> . . . that if through no fault of his own a person gets mixed up in the tortious acts of others so as to facilitate their wrongdoing he may incur no personal liability but he comes under a duty to assist the person who has been wronged by giving him full information and disclosing the identity of the wrongdoers. I do not think it matters whether he became so mixed up by voluntary action on his part or because it was his duty to do what he did. It may be that if this causes him expense the person seeking the information ought to reimburse him. But justice requires that he should co-operate in righting the wrong if he unwittingly facilitated its perpetration.[31]

22.62   The manner in which the Commissioners had unwittingly become mixed up in the wrongdoing of the importers was that the Commissioners allowed the importers to import their goods into the UK.

22.63   More recently, the requirements for *Norwich Pharmacal* relief have been summarized in *Mitsui & Co Ltd v Nexen Petroleum UK Ltd*:[32]

> (i) a wrong must have been carried out, or arguably carried out, by an ultimate wrongdoer, (ii) there must be the need for an order to enable action to be brought against the ultimate wrongdoer; and (iii) the person against whom the order is sought must: (a) be mixed up in so as to have facilitated the wrongdoing; and (b) be able or likely to be able to provide the information necessary to enable the ultimate wrongdoer to be sued.

---

[30]   See Andrews, *English Civil Procedure*, [26.101].
[31]   [1974] AC 133, 175.
[32]   [2005] EWHC 625, [2005] 3 All ER 511.

Care must be taken to avoid reading into this summary any requirement that the **22.64** relief is only available where legal proceedings are in contemplation and/or are necessary. The relief is available to assist any vindication of rights, whether it takes the form of self-help or litigation: *British Steel v Granada*.[33]

(b) Factors relevant to the granting of Norwich Pharmacal *relief*

In *Ashworth Hospital Authority v MGN Ltd*,[34] Lord Woolf CJ remarked: **22.65**

> 57 The *Norwich Pharmacal* jurisdiction is an exceptional one and one which is only exercised by the courts when they are satisfied that it is necessary that it should be exercised. New situations are inevitably going to arise where it will be appropriate for the jurisdiction to be exercised where it has not been exercised previously. The limits which applied to its use in its infancy should not be allowed to stultify its use now that is has become a valuable and mature remedy.

This head of jurisdiction, as set out above, is developing, and it is therefore unwise **22.66** to lay down a list of factors as being strict criteria which *must* be established before any such relief can be granted. There are certain issues or factors for which there appears to be a general consensus that they are required for this relief to be granted but others remain less certain, appearing in one case, only to be disavowed or ignored in a later case. It is for this reason that this section is focused on identifying all factors which are or have, in the authorities, been considered relevant to the granting of *Norwich Pharmacal* relief.

The authorities suggest that the following factors to varying degrees are relevant **22.67** to the court's determination of an application for this relief. Each is listed and thereafter subject to detailed examination.

- The respondent must have become mixed up in some form of wrongdoing or potential wrongdoing and his involvement must go beyond that of a mere witness.

- The applicant must require the information/documentation in order to vindicate some right or to take a step to protect itself arising out of some wrongdoing or potential wrongdoing. It is not a requirement of the *Norwich Pharmacal* jurisdiction that information is needed to start proceedings, although this will usually be the case.

- The wrongdoing or potential wrongdoing is not limited to tortious claims[35] and includes claims in equity, breach of contract,[36] breach of confidence,[37] equitable proprietary claims[38] and even crimes.

---

[33] [1981] AC 1096.

[34] [2002] 1 WLR 2033, [57].

[35] *Ashworth Hospital Authority v MGN Ltd* [2002] 1 WLR 2033 HL (breach of confidence/contract).

[36] *Carlton Film Distributors Ltd v VCI Plc* [2003] EWHC 616, [2003] FSR 47 (Ch).

[37] *British Steel Corporation v Granada Television Ltd* [1981] AC 1096 (HL).

[38] *Bankers Trust v Shapira* [1980] 1 WLR 1274 (CA).

- The information required is not limited to the identity of the individual who committed the wrongdoing but can extend to whether or not any such wrongdoing in fact took place.

- The respondent is required to give full information on the matters requested. It has been suggested this should be limited to that required to be produced under the old *subpoena duces tecum* procedure but such a restriction does not obviously sit with Lord Reid's views in *Norwich Pharmacal*.

- Under s 25(1)(5) of the CJJA 1982 (as amended), and the principles established in *Credit Suisse v Cuoghi*,[39] it is possible to obtain a *Norwich Pharmacal* order from the English court in respect of a respondent subject to English jurisdiction to assist proceedings taking place abroad.

- *Norwich Pharmacal* orders are not suitable means of obtaining information and discovery against respondents situated outside of the jurisdiction, even in aid of English proceedings. Letters rogatory are the appropriate means of obtaining such evidence.

- It has been suggested that *Norwich Pharmacal* applications should only be made in circumstances where none of the procedures under the CPR are available. While it is accepted that this head of jurisdiction should not be lightly invoked, it is denied that this jurisdiction is subject to any such sort of condition precedent.

22.68 Each of these factors merits closer examination.

22.69 **(i) The respondent must have become mixed up in some form of wrongdoing or potential wrongdoing and his involvement must go beyond that of a mere witness** The starting point is the guidance provided by Lord Reid in *Norwich Pharmacal* itself which, for convenience, is set out again below:

> ... that if through no fault of his own a person gets mixed up in the tortious acts of others so as to facilitate their wrongdoing he may incur no personal liability but he comes under a duty to assist the person who has been wronged by giving him full information and disclosing the identity of the wrongdoers. I do not think it matters whether he became so mixed up by voluntary action on his part or because it was his duty to do what he did. It may be that if this causes him expense the person seeking the information ought to reimburse him. But justice requires that he should co-operate in righting the wrong if he unwittingly facilitated its perpetration.[40]

22.70 It is clear from Lord Reid that the reason why someone has become mixed up in the wrongdoing of others is irrelevant. Whether they were acting voluntarily or alternatively simply acting in the line of their existing duty (as the Commissioners in *Norwich Pharmacal* were), does not matter. What is absolutely central to this

---

[39] [1998] QB 818.
[40] [1974] AC 133, 175.

head of jurisdiction is that the actions of the respondent take him beyond a mere witness to an incident. He must, somehow, have taken part, however unwittingly, in that incident or taken steps that can be viewed as facilitating such an incident taking place.

The reason a party is prevented from seeking to obtain evidence from a witness **22.71** pre-trial is because the witness could be compelled to provide the evidence at trial. Whether, in the light of the aims of the CPR and the desire for more open and informed litigation, this continues to justify the existence of this rule is another matter. What is clear is that the rule was not intended to operate so as to prevent litigation taking place in the first place. Lord Reid observed:

> I think that there has been a good deal of misunderstanding about this rule. It has been clear at least since the time of Lord Hardwicke that information cannot be obtained by discovery from a person who will in due course be compellable to give that information either by oral testimony as a witness or on a *subpoena duces tecum*. Whether the reasons justifying that rule are good or bad it is much too late to inquire: the rule is settled. But the foundation of the rule is the assumption that eventually the testimony will be available either in an action already in progress or in an action which will be brought later. It appears to me to have no application to a case like the present case. Here if the information in the possession of the respondents cannot be made available by discovery now, no action can ever be begun because the appellants do not know who are the wrongdoers who have infringed their patents. So the appellants can never get the information.
>
> To apply the mere witness rule to a case like this would be to divorce it entirely from its proper sphere. Its purpose is not to prevent but to postpone the recovery of the information sought . . .

The example often used to make this point, and to distinguish between mere wit- **22.72** ness and facilitator, is the person who happens to be standing by and witnesses a car accident. It is highly unlikely that any application for *Norwich Pharmacal* relief against the by-stander would be successful since it would be considered to be offending the mere witness rule. The fact that the by-stander might be in possession of information useful to the conduct of the case simply justifies calling him as a witness. It does not justify invoking this head of jurisdiction. As Lord Reid in *Norwich Pharmacal* made clear, *Norwich Pharmacal* relief:

> . . . is not available against a person who has no other connection with the wrong than that he was a spectator or has some document relating to it in his possession. But the respondents are in an intermediate position. Their conduct was entirely innocent; it was in excecution of their statutory duty. But without certain action on their part the infringements could never have been committed.[41]

---

41 *Norwich Pharmacal v Customs & Excise* [1974] 133, 174E–F.

22.73   By contrast, if the fraud has been committed and the proceeds misappropriated through a series of bank transfers (as is highly likely) then the relevant bank or banks will be viewed as appropriate respondents for *Norwich Pharmacal* relief. Indeed, in a typical fraud, obtaining information as to the movement of the funds from the banks is the starting point of a commercial fraud investigation. By providing banking assistance, however unwittingly, the bank or banks have become facilitators of the fraud or laundering of the proceeds of the fraud and so go beyond the 'mere witness' rule.

22.74   Other likely targets include accountants and financial advisers, insofar as it can be shown that they have had some involvement in the underlying transactions leading to the fraud. They may well have crucial information as to how the assets were to be handled or invested. If this was to be done via off-shore trusts, they may have the details of such trusts and be in possession of any other information which may assist any attempt to 'bust' the trusts and seize the proceeds of fraud held thereunder.

22.75   A good illustration of this factor at play is *Interbrew SA v Financial Times*.[42] This case concerned a potential share purchase in which a report was doctored and leaked to the press, making it appear as though Interbrew was being asked to pay in excess of the market price for the relevant shares. The false report was published and had a damaging effect on the value of Interbrew's shares. Both Lightman J[43] and the Court of Appeal[44] held that the conduct of the newspapers, in publishing the false document, took them beyond the 'mere witness' rule. Interbrew was entitled to *Norwich Pharmacal* relief.

22.76   It is readily apparent that the main justification for granting relief in *Interbrew* is that the newspapers in fact carried out the wishes and intentions of the wrongdoer in publishing the false report which, in turn, had the damaging impact on the value of Interbrew's shares. One might, therefore, reasonably conclude that should the newspapers have decided not to publish the piece, they may not have become subject to *Norwich Pharmacal* relief.

22.77   However, in *X Ltd v Morgan-Grampian Ltd*,[45] Lord Bridge indicated it made no difference to the question of entitlement to relief whether or not the article had been published. Lord Bridge drew a comparison where the Commissioner's liability to be subject to *Norwich Pharmacal* relief in the eponymous case commenced from the moment they received the infringing goods tortiously imported and

---

42   [2002] 1 Lloyd's Rep 542 (Lightman J).
43   [2002] 1 Lloyd's Rep 542.
44   [2002] EWCA Civ 274, [2002] 2 Lloyd's Rep 229.
45   [1991] 1 AC 1, 40.

similarly so did Mr Goodwin's liability derive from his receipt of 'confidential information tortiously disclosed'.[46]

One possible explanation for the difference in approach is that in *X Ltd v Morgan-* **22.78** *Grampian* the wrongdoing complained of related to the breach of confidence in divulging the information to the press whereas the focus in *Interbrew* was very much on the damage done to the value of the shares, which only came about as a result of the false report having been published.

Harrington v Polytechnic of North London[47] is one case where it might, initially, be **22.79** thought that the court contravened the 'mere witness' rule in ordering lecturers to examine certain photographs of a picket at the Polytechnic and to identify the students picketing the gates and preventing the applicant, a National Front Party member, from attending classes. After all, there was no suggestion of any involvement at all by any of the lecturers and indeed it was doubtful whether in fact they witnessed anything. All that was said is that they would know the identity of the students seen in the photographs.

The Court of Appeal dismissed the appeal and held that the court had jurisdiction **22.80** and should exercise that jurisdiction. The reasoning was that the applicant had previously obtained an order against the Polytechnic itself in order to divulge the identity of the students in the photographs and therefore the court had jurisdiction (see Lord Eldon in *Dummer v Chippenham Corporation*)[48] to order the servants to give discovery on behalf of the corporation. The court found it was no extension of this principle to include agents of the corporation as well. The disclosure order against the Polytechnic itself was not in breach of the 'mere witness' rule because there was a substantive claim for breach of contract brought by the applicant against the Polytechnic.

In *Douihech v Findlay*,[49] the vendor defendant sold what subsequently turned out **22.81** to be a very expensive but stolen cello to the claimant purchaser. It was thereafter recovered by the true owner P. The claimant purchaser wished to pursue a claim in damages based on the difference between price paid and market price of the cello. The true owner was joined by the master simply to obtain an order for inspection and photographs under the old RSC Order 29 r 2. In allowing the appeal from the master, the judge said that the true owner could not be compelled to give inspection or discovery under the *Norwich Pharmacal* jurisdiction as it would offend the 'mere witness' rule.

---

[46] [1991] 1 AC 1, 40C–D.
[47] [1984] 1 WLR 1293 CA.
[48] (1807) 14 Ves Jun 245.
[49] [1990] 1 WLR 269 (Judge Dobry QC sitting as High Court Judge).

22.82 In *Ricci v Chow*,[50] an article had appeared in an edition of the official journal of SNM (an unincorporated exiled Seychellois association) claiming that the claimant, in conjunction with the Seychelles' leader, had procured the assassination of SNM's President. Libel proceedings were commenced by the claimant against the defendant in his capacity as secretary general of SNM. On appeal from the master, the libel proceedings were struck out, but the court held the claimant was entitled to continue with two of its interrogatories, requiring disclosure of the publishers and printers of the relevant journal. On further appeal, the Court of Appeal held, *inter alia*, that since it could not be shown that the defendant was in any way mixed up with the printing or publishing of the relevant article, there was no jurisdiction under the *Norwich Pharmacal* head of relief.

22.83 It is interesting to note that the editors of *Commercial Litigation: Pre-Emptive Remedies*[51] cite various examples of what they consider to be occasions when the 'mere witness' rule is not breached. They include the need to identify the wrongdoer in order to bring any proceedings; the need for sufficient information to plead the case; the claims are trust property in danger of dissipation before proceedings. This equates with the stance adopted in this text, namely that if the information is needed to assert one's rights (in whatever form that might take) and the only person who has that information is X, then X will not be considered a 'mere witness'. Another way of looking at it is that the 'mere witness' rule applies where X can be compellable later in the proceedings.[52] But if no such proceedings can take place *until* X provides the information then X will not be considered a 'mere witness'.

22.84 One other aspect to the 'mere witness' rule is the apparent requirement that X's involvement be that of a facilitator and not a mere by-stander. The same points can be made against such a restriction as they were above in respect of the 'mere witness' rule generally. It is submitted that whilst it must be recognized that the authorities in general support this restriction, the preferable position is that the manner in which X obtained the necessary information should be irrelevant to the need to obtain disclosure from X.

22.85 This issue arose in *The Coca-Cola Company v British Telecommunications plc*[53] and it is submitted the flexible approach adopted by Neuberger J in respect of this requirement is to be welcomed. The case concerned allegations of trade-mark

---

50 [1987] 1 WLR 1658 (CA). See also *Axa v National Westminster Bank plc* [1998] PNLR 433 (CA).
51 (Int edn) (Thomson/Sweet and Maxwell, 2005), [A3-060].
52 *Mercantile Group (Europe) AG v Aiyela* [1994] QB 366, 374 per Hoffmann LJ: 'the order for discovery must not offend against the 'mere witness' rule, which prevents a party from obtaining discovery against a person *who will in due course be compellable to give that information* either by oral testimony as a witness or on a subpoena duces tecum' (emphasis added).
53 [1999] FSR 518.

infringements and passing-off. The defendant made reference to another individual who had been involved in the infringing activities but he only had his mobile telephone number. The issue was whether the claimant could obtain a *Norwich Pharmacal* order against BT to obtain the full address of this other individual.

Neuberger J held that such disclosure could be ordered. He concluded that the **22.86** 'mere witness' rule was not infringed since the relevant address of the other individual would not be the subject of witness statement evidence in the ongoing proceedings and so BT would not be compellable as a witness. He then had to overcome the requirement that BT was 'mixed up' or a facilitator as opposed to a by-stander. Neuberger J simply indicated he was willing to adopt a more flexible approach to this requirement. He held that the mobile phone was probably used in the business dealings between the defendant and this other individual and that sufficed.

In conclusion, it is evident that some of the earlier authorities did indeed devote **22.87** a fair amount of time discussing the 'mere witness' rule and how the *Norwich Pharmacal* jurisdiction is a justifiable exception to it. Whilst one cannot ignore what these authorities say, the reality of practice suggests that most applications for *Norwich Pharmacal* jurisdiction against banks, accountants or financial advisers are dealt with without much if any discussion of the ambit of the 'mere witness' rule.

Indeed, if one looks again at Lord Reid's comments about the 'mere witness' rule **22.88** not intending to prevent litigation from being commenced, it is difficult to accept that the court would refuse *Norwich Pharmacal* relief in the road traffic example against the so-called by-stander in circumstances where that by-stander is the only individual who can identify the car and its registration for the purposes of any litigation.[54] If the information cannot be gained pre-action from the by-stander because of the 'mere witness' rule that would prevent any litigation from proceeding, precisely the matter identified by Lord Reid in *Norwich Pharmacal* itself.

Finally, it is to be noted that this disclosure relief is equally available against the **22.89** wrongdoer as it is against an innocent third party: see *CHC Software Care v Hopkins & Wood*.[55]

(ii) The applicant must require the information/documentation in order to **22.90** **vindicate some right or to take a step to protect itself arising out of some wrong-doing or potential wrongdoing. It is not a requirement of the *Norwich Pharmacal* jurisdiction that information is needed to start proceedings, although this will usually be the case** The typical fact scenario of an application for *Norwich*

---

[54] Although that appears to be the view of Lord Woolf in *Ashworth Hospital v MGN Ltd* [2002] 1 WLR 2033.
[55] [1993] FSR 241 (Mummery J).

Pharmacal jurisdiction is the need for certain information without which it is not possible to commence any form of litigation. That was the driving force behind Lord Reid stating that what is now known as the *Norwich Pharmacal* jurisdiction did not infringe the 'mere witness' rule since the latter could not be expected to operate in a manner which prevents any form of litigation from in fact taking place. So it is no doubt sufficient to show that the information/documentation is required to commence litigation to justify obtaining this relief, all other requirements being satisfied.

22.91 The real issue is whether any need, short of commencing litigation, will suffice for these purposes as well. Following on from Lord Reid in *Norwich Pharmacal*, it is perhaps not surprising that earlier cases in this area did tend to suggest that the information was required to commence litigation.[56] But Lord Reid's comments must be viewed in the context that the applicant did intend to commence proceedings in that case. Further, careful reading of the other speeches does not suggest any such restriction. For example, Viscount Dilhorne, commenting on the 'mere witness' rule, observed:

> Someone involved in the transaction is not a mere witness. If he could be sued, *even though there be no intention of suing him*, he is not a mere witness.[57]

22.92 However, subsequent cases have suggested a wider basis for applying for this relief. Lord Denning MR rejected a restriction based on an intention to commence proceedings in the Court of Appeal in *British Steel Corpn v Granada Television Ltd.*[58] Lord Denning MR observed:

> Mr Irvine suggested this was limited to cases where the injured person desired to *sue* the wrongdoer. I see no reason why it should be so limited. The same procedure should be available when he desires to obtain redress against the wrongdoer—or to protect himself against further wrongdoing.

22.93 Similarly, Templeman LJ stated:

> In my judgment the principle of the *Norwich Pharmacal* case applies whether or not the victim intends to pursue action in the course against the wrongdoer provided that the existence of a cause of action is established and the victim cannot otherwise obtain justice. The remedy of discovery is intended in the final analysis to enable justice to be done. Justice can be achieved against an erring employee in a variety of ways and a plaintiff may obtain an order for discovery provided he shows that he is genuinely seeking lawful redress of a wrong and cannot otherwise obtain redress. In the present case BSC state that they will not finally determine whether to take legal proceedings or whether to dismiss the employee or whether to obtain redress in some

---

[56] E.g. *Handmade v Express Newspapers* [1986] FSR 463.
[57] [1974] AC 133, 188 and cited expressly with the same added emphasis on this point by Lord Woolf CJ in *Ashworth Hospital Authority v MGN Ltd* [2002] 1 WLR 2033, 2045.
[58] [1981] AC 1096, 1127.

other lawful manner until they have considered the identity, status and excuses of the employee. The disclosure of the identity of the disloyal employee will by itself protect BSC and their innocent employees now and for the future and is essential if BSC are to redress the wrong.[59]

In *X Ltd v Morgan-Grampian Ltd*,[60] it was argued that because they had already **22.94** managed to take the legal steps to restrain further publication, there was no need to grant any further relief. Lord Bridge however, disagreed: 'The plaintiffs here seek the identity of the source to enable them to take the necessary steps to protect themselves from other tortious dissemination of the confidential information which threatens to damage them so severely.'[61]

These authorities were examined and cited with approval by Lord Woolf CJ **22.95** in *Ashworth Hospital Authority v MGN Ltd*[62] and so it can be stated with reasonable certainty that there is no requirement on the part of an applicant for *Norwich Pharmacal* relief that the applicant have an intention to commence proceedings.[63]

(iii) The wrongdoing or potential wrongdoing is not limited to tortious claims **22.96** **and includes claims in equity, breach of contract, breach of confidence and even crimes** While one or two cases have cast some doubt on the accuracy of this statement, practitioners can now take it as the correct view of the ambit of the *Norwich Pharmacal* jurisdiction.

One of the main areas of dispute had been whether the jurisdiction extended **22.97** to criminal conduct. In *Interbrew SA v Financial Times*,[64] Sedley LJ stated that it was no function of the *Norwich Pharmacal* jurisdiction to identify would-be criminals since, in effect, that was now the function of specialist agencies of the government.[65]

---

[59] [1981] AC 1096, 1132. Lord Woolf CJ in *Ashworth* also noted that in the House of Lords in *BSC v Granada* at least Lord Wilberforce and Lord Fraser rejected any suggestion that intention to commence proceedings was necessary for *Norwich Pharmacal* relief. See *Ashworth Hospital Authority v MGN Ltd* [2002] 1 WLR 2033, 2046D–E.

[60] [1991] 1 AC 1.

[61] ibid, 40 per Lord Bridge.

[62] [2002] 1 WLR 2033.

[63] Although Judge McGonigal in *Aoot Kalmneft v Denton Wilde Sapte* [2002] 1 Lloyd's Rep 417 [17] might be read as suggesting that the *Norwich Pharmacal* jurisdiction is restricted to situations where a third party is under a duty to disclose information to enable the claimant to commence an action, a better reading is that this is simply one instance where this jurisdiction may be invoked. The other authorities make it plain that it is a not a pre-condition to entitlement to relief under this jurisdiction that one intends to commence litigation.

[64] [2002] EWCA Civ 274, [2002] 2 Lloyd's Rep 229.

[65] ibid, [20].

22.98 This view was forcefully rejected by Lord Woolf CJ in *Ashworth Hospital v MGN Ltd*:[66]

> In relation to crime, I would not accept the distinction that Sedley LJ makes. As Sedley LJ recognizes, it is likely that in the great majority of circumstances, if the wrongdoing constitutes a crime, it will also constitute a civil wrong so that the different treatment is unjustified. In addition the jurisdiction, as it has developed, enables an individual who has caused harm by wrongdoing, wrongdoing with which the defendant has become involved, to be identified. If the law has developed so as to enable, in the appropriate circumstances, the wrongdoer to be identified if he has committed a civil wrong I can find no justification for not requiring the wrongdoer to be identified if he has committed a criminal wrong. To draw a distinction between civil and criminal wrongs can only be justified if, contrary to the views I have already expressed, disclosure can only be ordered to enable civil proceedings to be brought against the wrongdoer. If the victim of the wrongdoing is content that the wrongdoer should be prosecuted by the appropriate prosecuting authority I cannot see any objection to his obtaining the identity of the wrongdoer to enable that to happen. The prosecution may achieve for the victim the remedy which the victim requires just as dismissal of an employee can do so.

22.99 So the House of Lords in *Ashworth Hospital v MGN Ltd* expressly rejected any suggestion that this jurisdiction could not be used in respect of criminal conduct. Further, the case itself was concerned with the equitable claim of breach of confidence and again the House of Lords saw no difficulty in the *Norwich Pharmacal* jurisdiction being invoked.

22.100 It is also now clear that even an ordinary breach of contract will suffice for the purposes of this head of jurisdiction. It therefore was capable of being invoked in *Carlton Film Distributors Ltd v VCI plc*[67] where Carlton had given VCI a licence in respect of the production of videos of certain films. VCI contracted with VDT to produce the videos. Carlton suspected that VCI had, in breach of its licence, produced too many videos. VCI refused to provide the information so discovery orders were made against VDT, the manufacturer of the videos.[68]

22.101 **(iv) The information required is not limited to the identity of the individual who committed the application, on the basis that the applicant was unable to identify any wrongdoing having been committed. Instead, in the best traditions of the Chancery Division, the Vice-Chancellor recognized the need for relief in the circumstances of the case and was content to extend the *Norwich Pharmacal* jurisdiction to cover the situation. He was right to do so**   The facts of *P v T* are these. The applicant was dismissed from his employment having been told that

---

66 [2002] 1 WLR 2033, 2048 [53].
67 [2003] EWHC 616 (Ch).
68 See also *P v T* [1997] 1 WLR 1309. The general proposition was agreed by Lightman J in *Mitsui v Nexen Petroleum* [2005] 3 All ER 511, 517.

serious allegations had been made against him, the details of which were not made known to him. Although his former employer was held to have unfairly dismissed him, this provided little comfort to the applicant when seeking alternative employment, not being in a position properly to deal with the unspecified allegations made against him which had led to his dismissal. Unlike the claimant in the *Norwich Pharmacal* case, the claimant in *P v T* was unable to establish that a tort or any form of wrongdoing had in fact taken place. That did not deter the court:

> The purpose of any order I make, as I suppose any order that a judge ever makes, is to try to enable justice to be done. It seems to me that in the circumstances of the present case justice demands that the plaintiff should be placed in a position to clear his name if the allegations made against him are without foundation. It seems to me intolerable that an individual in his position should be stained by serious allegations, the content of which he has no means of discovering and which he has no means of meeting otherwise than with the assistance of an order of discovery such as he seeks from me. It seems to me that the principles expressed in the *Norwich Pharmacal* case, although they have not previously been applied so far as I know to a case in which the question whether there has been a tort has not clearly been answered, ought to be applicable in a case such as the present.[69]

The decision in *P v T* has been approved by Rimer J in *Axa Equity & Law Life v National Westminster Bank*,[70] by Neuberger J in *Murphy v Murphy*,[71] and by Lord Woolf CJ in *Ashworth Hospital v MGN Ltd.*[72] **22.102**

In *Aoot Kalmneft v Denton Wilde Sapte*[73] Judge McGonigal rejected any suggestion that the information was to be limited to the identity of the wrongdoer, holding that: **22.103**

> . . . I see no reason why the principle is limited to disclosure of the identity of an unknown wrongdoer and does not extend to information showing that he has committed the wrong. [74]

It has even been said that the jurisdiction exists to provide disclosure where the applicant 'requires a missing piece of the jigsaw'.[75] A good example of this is *CHF Software Care Ltd v Hopkins and Wood*[76] where solicitors, who had challenged the applicant's copyright to certain products, were ordered to disclose the names and **22.104**

---

69 [1997] 1 WLR 1309, 1318D–F.

70 [1998] PNLR 433.

71 [1999] 1 WLR 282, 291 (disclosure ordered in favour of beneficiary relating to identity of trustee).

72 [2002] 1 WLR 2033 [57]: 'That new circumstances for its appropriate use will continue to arise is illustrated by the decision of Sir Richard Scott V-C in *P v T Ltd* [1997] 1 WLR 1309 where relief was granted because it was necessary in the interests of justice albeit that the claimant was not able to identify without discovery what would be the appropriate cause of action.'

73 [2002] 1 Lloyd's Rep 417 (Judge McGonigal).

74 ibid, [17].

75 *Mitsui v Nexen Petroleum* [2005] EWHC 625 (Ch); [2005] 3 All ER 511, [19].

76 [1993] FSR 241.

addresses of those to whom they had written the letters. The purpose behind granting the order was to enable the applicant to take its own steps to protect its own reputation by contacting the parties in order to put the record right. This case also therefore serves as a further example where the information was not required in order to commence proceedings but rather to take steps to protect one's own interest by putting the record straight.

22.105 **(v) The respondent is required to give full information on the matters requested. It has been suggested this should be limited to that required to be produced under the old subpoena duces tecum procedure but such a restriction does not obviously sit with Lord Reid's views in *Norwich Pharmacal*** In *Norwich Pharmacal* itself, Lord Reid was quite express about the need for the respondent to the application to provide 'full information' and 'full disclosure'.[77]

22.106 Others, such as Hoffmann J in *Arab Monetary Fund v Hashim (No 5)*[78] have suggested that the obligation to disclose is no greater than exists under a subpoena process. In other words, the applicant had to define the documents wanted with the same particularity as for a subpoena and all that was happening was the bringing forward of the date for the obligation to kick in. Hoffmann J remarked:

> The reference to 'full information' has sometimes led to an assumption that any person who has become 'mixed-up' in a tortious act can be required not merely to disclose the identity of the wrongdoer but to give general discovery and answer questions on all matters relevant to the cause of action. In my view this is wrong The principle upon which Lord Reid distinguished the 'mere witness' rule was that unless the plaintiff discovered the identity of the wrongdoer, he could not commence proceedings. The reasoning of the other members of the House is the same. The *Norwich Pharmacal* case is no authority for imposing upon 'mixed up third parties a general obligation to give discovery or information when the identity of the defendant is already known'.[79]

22.107 It is submitted that experience has shown that the courts have raised few difficulties in the path of orders demanding very detailed information and documentation from banks, financial advisers and accountants. It is to be remembered that it is the applicant who is paying for the privilege of the respondent identifying the relevant material and disclosing the same. The natural desire not to incur costs unnecessarily often ensures that a third party is not over-burdened with requests. Indeed, if one is wishing to move quickly, as part of a tracing exercise, to over-burden the third party is only likely to result in the whole process being slowed down and even brought to a halt because the third party cannot provide

---

[77] [1974] AC 133, 175B–D.
[78] [1992] 2 All ER 911.
[79] ibid, 914. See Hollander, *Documentary Evidence* (9th edn), paras 5-19–5-20 for criticism of Hoffmann J's approach as being inconsistent with that of Lord Reid in *Norwich Pharmacal* itself.

the requested disclosure in short order. Keep it short and to the point and if neces-sary go back for further information.

(vi) Under s 25(1)(5) of the CJJA 1982 (as amended), and the principles estab- **22.108**
lished in *Credit Suisse v Cuoghi*, it is possible to obtain a *Norwich Pharmacal*
order from the English court in respect of a respondent subject to English juris-
diction to assist proceedings taking place abroad The *Norwich Pharmacal*
jurisdiction is one of the established pre-emptive remedies available under English
civil procedure. Subject to one possible issue, there is, therefore, no reason in
principle, why this jurisdiction could not be invoked against persons subject to
the personal jurisdiction of the English court, to obtain information or documentation relevant to proceedings which have or are to be commenced in a foreign
jurisdiction.

Section 25 of the CJJA 1982 (as amended by the Civil Jurisdiction and Judgments **22.109**
Act 1982 (Interim Relief) Order 1997) permits an application to the English
court for interim relief in aid of foreign proceedings so long as the fact that the
English court does not have substantive jurisdiction over the main dispute does
not make it inexpedient for it to grant such interim relief.

The relevant principles for the exercise of the court's discretion under s 25 of the
CJJA 1982 were examined by the Court of Appeal (notably Millett LJ) in *Credit* **22.110**
Suisse Fides Trust SA v Cuoghi.[80] See also the Court of Appeal in *Motorola Credit*
Corp v Uzani.[81] Millett LJ emphasized that the interim relief available was not
limited by that which would otherwise be available from the court having substantive jurisdiction. Relevant factors included the fact that the respondent was
resident and domiciled in the UK and therefore subject to the personal jurisdiction of this court, and there was no danger of conflicting jurisdictions since the
foreign jurisdiction did not offer similar interim relief. On the facts, therefore, the
court granted a worldwide freezing order.

If the applicant is able to persuade the court that the relevant factors as discussed
in *Credit Suisse Fides Trust* are satisfied,[82] then a *Norwich Pharmacal* disclosure **22.111**
order could be made against an individual resident in the UK[83] in aid for foreign
proceedings.

---

[80] [1998] QB 818 CA.
[81] [2004] 1 WLR 1113.
[82] The requirements of s 25 of the CJJA 1982 (as amended) are dealt with in detail in
para 24.152.
[83] Worldwide freezing orders were obtained against non-UK residents in *Republic of Haiti v
Duvalier* [1990] 1 QB 202 in aid of French proceedings. This has been described as an extreme
decision: Collins, *Essays In International Litigation and the Conflict of Laws* (Clarendon Press, 1994),
207.

22.112 The stance adopted in this text is that *Norwich Pharmacal* relief is available in aid of foreign proceedings under s 25 of the CJJA 1982.[84] However, it is right to point out that this view is not universally accepted.[85] There is one school of thought that equates obtaining a disclosure order under this jurisdiction with collating *evidence* and that runs foul of s 25(7) of the CJJA 1982 which excludes evidence gathering from the range of potential interim remedies which can be granted in aid of foreign proceedings.

22.113 It is suggested that a distinction should be drawn between obtaining information which assists in deciding whether to bring proceedings, if so, against whom, what claims to be made, etc. on the one hand, and gathering evidence relating to issues already pleaded in a case. Further, no doubt one reason for s 25(7) of the CJJA 1982 is that the procedure for obtaining evidence is a matter peculiarly to be associated with the jurisdiction hearing the substantive proceedings. It has already been established that it forms no part of the conditions for obtaining *Norwich Pharmacal* relief that legal proceedings must be commenced. Finally, one need look no further than Lord Cross's pertinent observation in *Norwich Pharmacal* itself:

> This case has nothing to do with the collection of evidence.[86]

22.114 **(vi) *Norwich Pharmacal* orders are not suitable means of obtaining information and discovery against respondents situated outside of the jurisdiction, even in aid of English proceedings. Letters rogatory are the appropriate means of obtaining such evidence** It is possible to obtain *Norwich Pharmacal* relief against individuals abroad in aid of English proceedings.[87] Care should be taken, however, not to appear to circumscribe the agreed procedures for taking evidence abroad under the letters rogatory procedure.

22.115 **(vii) It has been suggested that *Norwich Pharmacal* applications should only be made in circumstances where none of the procedures under the CPR are available. Whilst it is accepted that this head of jurisdiction should not be lightly invoked, it is denied that this jurisdiction is subject to any such sort of condition precedent** In *Mitsui Ltd v Nexen Petroleum UK Ltd*,[88] Lightman J, in summarizing

---

[84] Hollander, *Documentary Evidence* (9th edn) cites a Gibraltar Court of Appeal decision, *Secilpar SL v Fiduciary Trust Ltd* (24 September 2004) in which the Gibraltar Court granted disclosure in aid of proceedings in Portugal.

[85] See Goldrein, Aird and Grantham (eds), *Commercial Pre-Emptive Remedies* (Sweet and Maxwell, 2005), [A3-071]. However, as pointed out by the editors, the court is empowered to grant *Norwich Pharmacal* relief and then release the usual restriction on its use in overseas proceedings. Indeed, experience suggests that the court prefers to do that than to get into an erudite debate as to whether disclosure under the *Norwich Pharmacal* order amounts to 'evidence' for the purposes of s 25(7) of the CJJA 1982. It also removes an appealable point.

[86] [1974] AC 133, 199.

[87] *Smith Kline and French Laboratories Ltd v Global Pharmaceutical Ltd* [1986] FSR 394; *Jade Engineering Ltd v Antiference Window Systems* [1996] FSR 461.

[88] [2005] EWHC 625, [2005] 3 All ER 511.

the requirements for *Norwich Pharmacal* relief, held that the applicant must show a need for an order to enable action to be brought against the ultimate wrongdoer.[89] From this, Lightman J concluded:

> The jurisdiction is only to be exercised if the innocent third parties are the only practicable source of information. The whole basis of the jurisdiction against them is that, unless and until they disclose what they know, there can be no litigation in which they can give evidence . . .

22.116 We have already seen, however, that this jurisdiction is not dependent on the disclosure of information necessary to commence proceedings. It extends to all manner of action which may be required to protect the interests of the applicant e.g. dismissing an employee, setting the record straight, etc. To that extent, therefore, it may be appropriate to criticize Lightman J's reasoning as applying too narrow a purpose to any application for *Norwich Pharmacal* disclosure.

22.117 It may well be that Lightman J was not intending to limit the circumstances where such relief can be obtained to that necessary for the commencement of proceedings. The focus of his comments may not have been intended to be the commencement of proceedings but the requirement that there exists a real need for the disclosure in order to commence proceedings or protect one's own interests or sack an employee, etc. In other words, the granting of an order for disclosure represented the only practical means by which the applicant would be able to achieve any one of these aims. If the applicant could achieve these aims easily and obviously by a route which did not involve making third parties subject to court orders, then the court should encourage the applicant to investigate that other route or routes.

22.118 That said, if the disclosure sought is readily and obviously available from another source, which does not require an order from the court against a non-party, Lightman J must be correct to say that the court, in exercising its discretion, is likely to tell the applicant to obtain the information from that other readily available source. Such an approach would be consistent with an aim of protecting innocent third parties from unnecessary disclosure orders.

22.119 Where perhaps Lightman J goes a little too far is to describe the remedy as one of 'last resort'. That has all the connotations of a remedy which is rarely invoked and seldom successful if invoked, which goes very much against the experience of commercial litigators dealing regularly with *Norwich Pharmacal* orders. Such a statement also appears at odds with the view of Lord Woolf CJ in *Ashworth Hospital v MGN Ltd* that this jurisdiction is a developing one and that nothing should be done to prevent it from adapting to new situations in the future.

---

[89] [2005] 3 All ER 511, [21].

(c) Costs

22.120 In principle, the third party respondent is entitled to be indemnified for the costs incurred in responding to a *Norwich Pharmacal* order. However, the third party is not relieved from a requirement to prove that the costs incurred have been reasonably incurred: *Westminster City Council v Porter*.[90] This will help to ensure that a third party does not incur substantial costs unnecessarily.

(d) Practice and procedure

22.121 An application for *Norwich Pharmacal* relief may be made either pre-commencement of proceedings, or at the same time as commencement of proceedings, or even during the course of proceedings. The application can be brought under Part 7 or Part 8 procedure. If necessary, it can be granted without notice (e.g. *Bankers Trust v Shapira*).[91]

22.122 The applicant should issue an application notice together with supporting witness statement and draft order. The applicant must be willing to give a cross-undertaking in damages. If at all possible, the hearing should take place on notice (to the respondent and not the intended defendant) but occasionally this presents difficulties by placing the respondent in an invidious position e.g. banks tend to believe they are under a duty to inform their customers about such an application and so it is usually preferable to proceed without notice in such circumstances and explain the position to the court.

22.123 For a useful practical guide as to the contents of the supporting witness statement, refer to *Commercial Pre-Emptive Remedies*.[92]

(3) The *Bankers Trust* jurisdiction

22.124 Applications under the *Bankers Trust* jurisdiction are concerned with obtaining information relating to the location of assets against which the claimant is asserting a proprietary claim. They are typically sought against third parties who become mixed up in the laundering of the proceeds of a fraud and are therefore in a position to provide information and documentation to assist the tracing exercise.

22.125 Although the *Bankers Trust* jurisdiction shares some common characteristics with the *Norwich Pharmacal* jurisdiction, it operates in a discrete factual context and it is therefore appropriate to examine the *Bankers Trust* orders separately.

22.126 Unlike *Norwich Pharmacal* orders, where the wrongdoing can take on a wide range of forms, *Bankers Trust* orders are only concerned with the tracing of assets

---

[90] [2003] EWHC 2373, [2005] 2 Costs LR 205.
[91] [1980] 1 WLR 1274 (CA).
[92] Goldrein et al (eds), (int edn), [A3-077].

as part of the assertion of a proprietary claim by the applicant. No other manner of wrongdoing can form the basis of an application for a *Bankers Trust* order.

Finally, instead of pursuing an application for *Bankers Trust* relief, it is open to the **22.127** claimant to consider making an application before a master under the Bankers' Books Evidence Act 1879. It is more limited in scope than a *Bankers Trust* order since 'bankers' books' has been held not to include cheques, paying in slips or even correspondence between the alleged fraudsters and the bank. The details of such a procedure are dealt with in the leading banking law texts.[93]

(a) Bankers Trust Co v Shapira[94]

This case concerned a fraud on the claimant bank which had honoured two forged **22.128** cheques presented for payment in New York by two individuals and drawn on a Saudi Arabian bank for a total of US$1m. Out of the US$1m, on instructions, the claimant bank transferred some US$708,203 to a London account at D Bank. Upon notification of the forgeries, the claimant bank re-credited the Saudi Arabian bank and commenced proceedings in the UK against the two individuals and D Bank.

In addition to being granted a Mareva injunction, the claimant bank sought a dis- **22.129** closure order against D Bank in respect of the operation of the relevant account. Mustill J refused the order, principally on the ground of concerns as to banker–customer confidentiality in circumstances where the two individuals had not been served with copies of the application.

On appeal, the Court of Appeal granted the orders sought. **22.130**

Lord Denning MR recognized the novelty of the application, and in particular, **22.131** based upon the width of the disclosure sought. It is therefore useful to set out the terms of the disclosure sought:

> For an order (1) Against the first, second and third defendants that each of them do disclose to the plaintiffs forthwith the sums or balances at present standing in any account in either of the names of the first or second defendants at the third defendants. (2) Against the third defendants '- that is, the bank-' that they do disclose to the plaintiffs forthwith and permit the plaintiffs to take copies of the following documents: - (i) all correspondence passing between the third defendants and the first and second defendants relating to any account at the third defendants in the names of either the first and/or second defendants from September 20, 1979, onwards: (ii) all cheques drawn on any account at the third defendants in the names of either the first and/or second defendants from September 20, 1979, onwards; (iii) all debit vouchers,

---

[93] M Hapgood (ed), *Paget's Law of Banking* (13th edn, LexisNexis Butterworths, 2007), 677–82; *Encyclopaedia of Banking Law* (LexisNexis Butterworths, Looseleaf), C(354); see also Hollander, *Documentary Evidence* (9th edn), paras 5-34–5-36.
[94] [1980] 1 WLR 1274 CA.

transfer applications and orders and internal memoranda relating to any account at the third defendants in the names of either the first and/or second defendants from September 20, 1979, onwards.

22.132   Three unreported cases were cited to the Court of Appeal, all of which involved the use of disclosure orders to trace the location of assets.

- In *London and Counties Securities (In Liquidation) v Caplan*,[95] Templeman J granted an order requiring the bank to disclose documents and accounts showing what had happened to the sum of £5m which Mr Caplan had allegedly embezzled.

- *Mediterranea Raffineria Siciliana Petroli Spa v Mabanaft GmbH*[96] was concerned with mistaken payments made to the wrong people. No fraud was involved. A freezing order was granted together with disclosure orders as to what had become of the payments. Templeman LJ emphasized the existence of equity's strongest powers to preserve trust funds.

- *A v C*[97] concerned a bank fraud and was similar to the facts of *Bankers Trust v Shapira* save that the alleged fraudsters had themselves been served. In that case, Robert Goff J granted a freezing order together with disclosure orders to determine what had become of the missing monies.

22.133   Drawing upon these three authorities, together with the *Norwich Pharmacal* jurisdiction, Lord Denning MR granted the disclosure orders sought:

> . . . here the Discount Bank incur no personal liability: but they got mixed up, through no fault of their own, in the tortious or wrongful acts of these two men: and they come under a duty to assist the Bankers Trust Co of New York by giving them and the court full information and disclosing the identity of the wrongdoers. In this case the particular point is 'full information'.
>
> This new jurisdiction must, of course, be carefully exercised. It is a strong thing to order a bank to disclose the state of its customer's account and the documents and correspondence relating to it. It should only be done when there is a good ground for thinking the money in the bank is the plaintiff's money—as, for instance, when the customer has got the money by fraud—or other wrongdoing—and paid it into his account at the bank. The plaintiff who has been defrauded has a right in equity to follow the money. He is entitled, in Lord Atkin's words, to lift the latch of the banker's door: see *Banque Belge pour L'Etranger v Hambrouck* [1921] 1 KB 321, 355. The customer, who has prima facie been guilty of fraud, cannot bolt the door against him. Owing to his fraud, he is disentitled from relying on the confidential relationship between him and the bank . . . If the plaintiff's equity is to be of any avail, he must be given access to the bank's books and documents—for that is the only way of tracing the money or of knowing what has happened to it . . . So the court, in order to give

---

[95] Unrep 26 May 1978.
[96] Unrep 1 December 1978, CA Civil transcript No 816 of 1978.
[97] Unrep, 18 March 1980.

effect to equity, will be prepared in a proper case to make an order on the bank for their discovery. The plaintiff must of course give an undertaking in damages to the bank and must pay all and any expenses to which the bank is put in making the discovery: and the documents, once seen, must be used solely for the purpose of following and tracing the money: and not for any other purpose. With these safeguards, I think the new jurisdiction—already exercised in the three unreported cases—should be affirmed by this court.[98]

Lord Denning MR in *Bankers Trust* considered that these orders derived in part **22.134** from the powers of equity to re-constitute and protect trust funds and in part from the *Norwich Pharmacal* jurisdiction. In *Murphy v Murphy*,[99] Neuberger J preferred to recognize the separate status of these two distinct jurisdictions, although he accepted that there was some overlap.[100]

The *Bankers Trust* jurisdiction was the subject of a review by Hoffmann J in *Arab* **22.135** *Monetary Fund v Hashim (No 5)*[101] where his Lordship laid down the following guidance:

> What are the limits of the *Bankers Trust* jurisdiction? They must, I think, be deduced from the reasoning upon which that jurisdiction, like the *Norwich Pharmacal* jurisdiction, is distinguished from the 'mere witness' rule. It rests upon the proposition that unless the assets in question can be located and secured, the ultimate determination of ownership of those assets may be frustrated by their removal or dissipation and there will be no point in calling on the third party at the trial to produce the required documents or give the requested information. In my judgment, therefore, the first principle of the *Bankers Trust* case is that the plaintiff must demonstrate a real prospect that the information may lead to the location or preservation of assets to which he is making a proprietary claim. This is a matter upon which opinions may differ. In the *Bankers Trust* case itself, Mustill J refused an order because the fraud had happened either months earlier and he thought that any money which was no longer in the account would long since have vanished. The Court of Appeal was more sanguine. Waller LJ said . . .

> '. . . where you have a fraud of this nature, although it may be late, and although much or perhaps all of the money may be now gone, the sooner that steps are taken to try and trace where it is the better. If steps are going to be taken, it is important that they should be taken at the earliest possible moment.'

Hoffmann J's first principle, that there must be a real prospect that the informa- **22.136** tion or documentation sought may lead to the location or preservation of the relevant assets, is entirely understandable. The *Bankers Trust* case is focused solely on the tracing of assets. If it is unlikely that such assets can, after the passage of time,

---

[98] [1980] 1 WLR 1274, 1282B–E.
[99] [1999] 1 WLR 282, 289.
[100] ibid, 290B.
[101] [1992] 2 All ER 911.

be found, then, with one possible exception, it must be questionable whether it is appropriate to invoke this equitable jurisdiction.

22.137 But what needs to be assessed with some care is whether this principle is simply a revised form of the old equitable maxim of the need not to delay if seeking equitable relief or whether it is truly focused on limiting the availability of this relief to those circumstances where, however understandable the reasons for the delay, there is a real prospect of actually locating the assets.

22.138 If it is the former, namely a principle to eradicate unnecessary delay, then the court must, and in practice does, recognize that there are often a whole host of very good reasons for delay in proceeding with claims, not least of which might be the need to have sufficient evidence upon which it becomes ethical to make the allegations required to support the proprietary claim. It would be harsh to penalize a claimant in such circumstances.

22.139 On this basis, the focus would be very much on the reasons for the delay and not the consequences of it.

22.140 If, as appears more likely from reading Hoffmann J's judgment, it is a principle based on the likelihood of recovery of assets, it is one that should be treated with some care.

22.141 If it is used to deny the claimant the opportunity to trace its assets that can only be on an assumption, reached by the court at an interlocutory stage, often without the benefit of detailed or any evidence to support it, that the assets are no longer capable of being found. Assumptions which might lead to a denial of equitable relief should not be lightly made.

22.142 If the relief is granted, and the assets prove to have gone, the third party may have been put to some limited inconvenience, at the claimant's expense, but no other harm ensues. On a balance of convenience, less harm appears to ensue in granting an order which fails to locate the assets than in denying the claimant the opportunity of any attempt at tracing its assets. Indeed, even if the assets are no longer in the identified account, the information obtained might assist as to where they have gone, it might assist identifying through whose hands the monies may have passed, and thus potentially identify other individuals who should be defendants to the action.

22.143 For these reasons, it is submitted that the court should require clear evidence that the tracing exercise is likely to be fruitless before it prevents a claimant from obtaining a *Bankers Trust* order on this ground alone.

22.144 On the facts of *Arab Monetary Fund v Hashim (No 5)*, Hoffmann J concluded that the first principle was not satisfied—some six or seven years having passed since the relevant transactions had taken place and there had been declarations by certain entities as to what precisely they hold by way of assets which, if true, would suggest the monies had gone.

Further, Dr Hashim had been subjected to previous orders for discovery, affida- **22.145** vits, cross-examination and years of the claimant's own inquiries, none of which had highlighted any other likely location for these assets.

Against that rather extreme background, Hoffmann J's decision to refuse the **22.146** *Bankers Trust* order on the facts was clearly justified. It is to be hoped when the evidence is not so straightforward that the applicant might be afforded the benefit of the doubt.

Hoffmann J's second limiting principle for *Bankers Trust* orders is that, whilst **22.147** these orders are not identical to the old *subpoena duces tecum*, the disclosure sought should not be drawn wider than would usually be available under that procedure. Hoffmann J specifically said that 'third party should be entitled to the same specificity in the documents he is asked to produce as he would be if served with a subpoena. Likewise, if he is asked for information, the questions should be directed with specificity to ascertaining the whereabouts of the assets in question.'[102]

These comments of Hoffmann J have already been considered and criticized in **22.148** the context of the *Norwich Pharmacal* jurisdiction. One notable commentator[103] has questioned whether Hoffmann J's dicta can truly represent the law on this issue, particularly given the development now in the availability of disclosure under the CPR from third parties, thus removing the rather traditional and narrow approach of the *subpoena duces tecum* procedure. It has also been pointed out that it is questionable whether such a narrow approach was ever intended by Lord Reid in *Norwich Pharmacal* itself.

So how is the practitioner to proceed? The starting point should be a recognition **22.149** as to why the old *subpoena duces tecum* procedure was as narrow and restrictive as it was. This was due to the fact that third parties could not be expected to give disclosure generally in a case where they were not parties and therefore had no direct knowledge of the issues to which such disclosure would typically be addressed. A *subpoena* was therefore supposed to be drafted in such a clear, express and unambiguous manner that the third party upon which it was served would be able to know precisely what information or documentation was being sought.

---

[102] [1992] 2 All ER 911, 919. In reaching this conclusion, Hoffmann J also relied upon his earlier decision in *MacKinnon v Donaldson Lufkin & Jenrette Securities Corp* [1986] Ch 482 where he had said that *Norwich Pharmacal* orders create: 'a general duty imposed on persons who become "mixed up" in tortious acts to produce evidence and documents *before trial* comparable with the general duty on all persons who have relevant knowledge or documents to give evidence *at the trial*' [498, original emphasis]

[103] Hollander, *Documentary Evidence* (9th edn), para 5-29.

The third party was not to be expected to exercise its own judgment as to the relevance of any documentation to the issues to be determined at trial.

22.150 With that in mind, drafters of orders for *Bankers Trust* relief or *Norwich Pharmacal* relief should ensure that their orders are clear and unambiguous. They must not assume knowledge of the issues of the case which may not be known to third parties. In effect, they should, so far as possible, be drafted as a complete code of what the third party needs to do in order to comply with it. Any uncertainty in its scope or width or meaning will be rightly considered a bar to the granting of such relief.

22.151 So long as drafters comply with this guidance, practitioners are advised to make the order as wide as they consider necessary for their purposes. Draft orders are constantly amended during the course of the hearing to meet any concerns of the court.

22.152 One way of limiting the ambit of the order is to make it clear to the court that the claimant is engaged in a tracing exercise. In the event that this present order results in further information, it may be necessary to resort to court for further orders consequential on that information. Such a 'stage-by-stage' approach has the advantages of ensuring that one only seeks disclosure based upon supporting evidence and that each time the order is narrowly drawn. The disadvantages are the increased costs of additional hearings (borne by the applicant) and a concern on the part of the court that repeated applications against the same individual may amount to harassment or abuse or at the very least amount to greater inconvenience than if everything had been sought in one order.

22.153 The practitioner must therefore undertake a careful balancing exercise as to which route is the most sensible on any given set of facts.

D. Post-action Disclosure

(1) Application against non-party under CPR r 31.17

22.154 CPR r 31.17 provides as follows:

> **31.17** – (1) This rule applies where an application is made to the court under any Act for disclosure by a person who is not a party to proceedings.
>
> (2) The application must be supported by evidence
>
> (3) The court may make an order under this rule only where—
>
>> (a) the documents of which disclosure is sought are likely to support the case of the applicant or adversely affect the case of one of the other parties to the proceedings and
>>
>> (b) disclosure is necessary in order to dispose fairly of the claim or to save costs.
>
> (4) An order under this rule must—
>
>> (a) specify the documents or the classes of documents which the respondent must disclose; and

(b) require the respondent, when making disclosure, to specify any of those documents—
    (i) which are no longer in his control; or
    (ii) in respect of which he claims a right or duty to withhold inspection.
(5) Such an order may—
    (a) require the respondent to indicate what has happened to any documents which are no longer in his control; and
    (b) specify the time and place for disclosure and inspection.

22.155 CPR r 31.17 has given rise to considerable difficulties in its short life since its introduction into the CPR and has been the subject of two detailed considerations by the Court of Appeal. The facts and decision of each Court of Appeal decision will be examined before going on to deal with some of the broader consequences for the operation of CPR r 31.17 of these and other decisions.

22.156 *American Home Products Corpn v Novartis Pharmaceuticals UK Limited*[104] concerned a patent action where a patent agent had visited a non-party to inspect certain documents relating to the patent. Having examined the documents, he placed them all into a box, including those he did not consider to be relevant. The claimant sought disclosure of the documents in the box under CPR r 31.17.

22.157 At first instance, Laddie J rejected the application on three grounds.

• Applying the reasoning of Pumfrey J in *In Re Howglen*,[105] the court had no jurisdiction to grant the order in circumstances where Dr Wright, the patent agent, had given evidence that the box contained both relevant and irrelevant documents.

• The judge was not persuaded that the documents were of anything other than secondary significance and therefore he was not convinced such wide-ranging disclosure could be considered necessary in order to dispose fairly of the claim or to save costs.

• The judge also rejected any suggestion that the documents might be relevant to the issue of novelty, which was central to the patent dispute.

22.158 The Court of Appeal allowed the appeal from Laddie J's decision for the following reasons.

• The Court accepted that it had no jurisdiction to order a non-party to disclose save where the 'documents . . . are relevant to an issue' (s 34 of the Supreme Court Act 1981).

---

[104] Unrep, 13 February 2001.
[105] [2001] 1 All ER 376, where Pumfrey J had remarked: 'If the order covers disclosure which, on any basis, includes material which is accepted to be irrelevant, then I do not think the court has the power to make the order' [382–3].

- The definition of 'relevance' for these purposes is 'documents . . . likely to support the case for the applicant or adversely affect the case of one of the other parties'. A document may be 'relevant' for these purposes yet turn out to be, in fact, as an individual document, to be irrelevant (in the different sense, that it contains no pertinent information at all). The distinction between the two approaches lies in the use of 'likely to support' which does not mean 'will definitely . . .' since the phrase 'likely to support' encompasses the possibility a document passing this threshold but not in fact providing any support for a case, etc. Unless and until the document is in fact reviewed, it would be unacceptable to place any higher threshold on the applicant.

22.159 However, the Court rejected the notion that Dr Wright's view of relevance was determinative of the issue relating to the documents within the box. This was all the more so given Dr Wright was considering this issue only from the perspective of individual documents as opposed to categories or classes of documents.

22.160 It was necessary to consider the documents in their context and not individually since otherwise a selection might paint a false picture.

22.161 The Court recognized that the documents within the box related to the question of collaboration between Fujisawa and Fisons which was relevant to the proceedings. Some documents in the box may turn out to be more relevant (in fact) than others and some individual documents may not be 'relevant' at all (in the sense that although they fell within a category 'likely to . . .' the particular document, in fact, did not provide any such support or did not in fact adversely affect the other party's case).

22.162 In *Three Rivers District Council v Bank of England (No 4)*[106] the claimant applied for an order for disclosure under CPR r 31.17 in respect of the documents (including witness statements and transcripts) generated as part of and leading up to the Bingham Report.

22.163 At first instance, Tomlinson J granted the application after having decided to apply the Court of Appeal's interpretation of the word 'likely' to mean 'may well' in the context of CPR r 31.16 application in *Black v Sumitomo*[107] to CPR r 31.17.

22.164 The Court of Appeal dismissed the appeal.

- The Court held it was necessary to have evidence before the Court to support any application for disclosure. The applicant did in fact file a witness statement although it did not attempt to describe the relevance of each category of document sought. However, the judge was very familiar with the facts of the case,

---

[106] [2002] EWCA Civ 1182, [2002] 4 All ER 881 CA.
[107] [2001] EWCA Civ 1819, [2002] 1 WLR 1562.

having been its assigned judge for some time. He had read the Bingham Report and had at least the opportunity of reading the various appendices. The Bingham Report was thus in evidence.

- The word 'likely' was to have the same meaning whenever used in the CPR, meaning 'may well' and not 'more probable than not'.

Under CPR r 31.17(3)(a) the Court needed to be satisfied that all documents **22.165** included within a class or category were 'likely' to support or to adversely affect one party's case. It did not matter if any document, having satisfied that threshold test of 'likely', did not in fact turn out to do either. The threshold test does not guarantee all documents so disclosed will be relevant either by supporting or adversely affecting one side's case.

The main issues which have arisen in these authorities for determination are: **22.166**

- the level of evidence required for disclosure applications;
- the test which the threshold condition requires;
- the proper treatment of classes of documents;
- limiting non-party disclosure to standard disclosure between parties.

(a) The level of evidence required for disclosure applications

This issue arose out of criticism by the Treasury in *Three Rivers* that Tomlinson J **22.167** had been prepared to grant the wide-ranging disclosure orders sought without detailed evidence in support. In particular, although Tomlinson J had the benefit of one witness statement from the applicant's solicitor, he did not have the benefit of any evidence which 'condescended to particulars', to borrow an old phrase, and set out why each category of documents was considered to satisfy the threshold condition.

The Court of Appeal in *Three Rivers* accepted that evidence was required for any **22.168** application under CPR r 31.17[108] and that the provision of the witness statement from Mr Grierson of Lovells solicitors meant that there had been at least formal compliance with that requirement.

The applicants had suggested that they might set out their position in respect **22.169** of each category in some detail but this would be time-consuming, costly and ultimately unnecessary. Tomlinson J accepted that proposition and, in the very unusual circumstances of this case, the Court of Appeal agreed with the judge's approach:

> [18] In our view, the judge was entitled to approach the matter on that basis. The judge had been concerned with this litigation for some time. He should be taken to have a comprehensive and detailed knowledge of the issues. We were told that the

---

[108] [2002] 4 All ER 881 [17].

judge had read the Bingham report; and that he read, or had the opportunity to read, the relevant appendices. It is, we think, fanciful to suggest that the Bingham report was not 'in evidence'; notwithstanding that it may not have been exhibited formally to a witness statement on this application. And, although the report is not evidence of the matters in issue in these proceedings, it is plainly, evidence of what material was before Bingham LJ and the conclusions which he drew from that material. The judge was entitled to accept the report and the appendices which he had read as evidence of what the scheduled material . . . was likely to contain.

22.170 So long as the test for the threshold condition was decided in favour of Tomlinson J's approach (as it was), the Court of Appeal was content that he had adopted a sensible approach to the level of evidence required for the purposes of an application under CPR r 31.17.

22.171 Practitioners will no doubt note the emphasis placed by the Court of Appeal on the 'very unusual circumstances' of the *Three Rivers* case including the background knowledge obtained by Tomlinson J as the assigned judge. More typically, applications under CPR r 31.17 should be approached from the perspective of needing to satisfy the threshold condition test for each category claimed and so, within reason, the court should be provided with reasonably detailed witness statement evidence in support.

(b) The test which the threshold condition requires

22.172 On appeal in *Three Rivers*, the Treasury argued that Tomlinson J had applied the wrong and lower meaning for the word 'likely' in CPR r 31.17, arguing that it should be interpreted as meaning 'more probable than not' and not merely 'may well be'.

22.173 The Court of Appeal rejected this ground of appeal, holding that the word 'likely' is to be interpreted to mean 'may well be'. The Court examined the use of the word 'likely' in CPR r 31.16 as well as r 31.17 and in other statutory provisions and concluded it was intended to have the same meaning in this context. Like Tomlinson J, the Court of Appeal found assistance in the decision of the Court of Appeal in *Black v Sumitomo*.[109] In that case, Rix LJ had stated: 'Temptations to gloss the statutory language should be resisted. The jurisdictional threshold is not, I think, intended to be a high one.'[110]

22.174 This approach not only justifies Tomlinson J's view on whether additional evidence was required but also has a significant impact on how the question of categories of documents are dealt with. In the absence of having the benefit of actually reviewing all the documents which go to make up the categories, it is impossible to conclude definitively as to the relevance of each individual document going to

---

[109] [2001] EWCA Civ 1819, [2002] 1 WLR 1562.
[110] [2002] 1 WLR 1562, [73].

make up a category of documents. All that can be said is that given the nature of the documents to be found in that category they are 'likely' (in the sense defined above) either to support one case or adversely affect the others.

The Court of Appeal was keen to stress that whilst the threshold test was lower **22.175** than 'more probable than not' it was not as low as the 'real prospect' test under, for example, CPR r 24.2 applications, i.e. realistic as opposed to fanciful.[111]

The Court of Appeal's reasoning on the threshold test is to be welcomed, as it **22.176** avoids the danger of placing an unrealistically high threshold test on an applicant in circumstances where that applicant is highly unlikely to be able to state with any confidence the contents of a box of documents held by third parties.

(c) The proper approach to a class or category of documents

The issue here is how the following two propositions can be consistent. **22.177**

- CPR r 31.17 does not permit disclosure of a category of documents in which it is known that some irrelevant documents are included ('the First Proposition').
- It is entirely right and proper to order disclosure of a category of documents even if it subsequently turns out that one or two of the documents within that category are irrelevant ('the Second Proposition').

The First Proposition derives from Pumfrey J in *Re Howlgen Ltd* and was applied **22.178** by Laddie J, at first instance, in *American Home Products* in refusing to grant the orders sought. Laddie J was persuaded by the evidence of Dr Wright that the document contained both relevant and irrelevant documents.

The Court of Appeal in *American Home Products* accepted the First Proposition, **22.179** as a matter of principle, but was not persuaded that Dr Wright's evidence alone was determinative of this issue. It was important to assess the relevance of the documents in their context and not simply as individual documents—something that Dr Wright had not done.

Some confusion has crept into understanding the reasoning of the Court of Appeal **22.180** because of its use of the word 'relevance' having two distinct meanings.

- The first meaning, as employed by Aldous LJ in *American Home Products*, paras [32] and [33], relates to the use of this word to describe documents falling within CPR r 31.17. In this context, 'relevance' is limited by the words used in CPR r 31.17, namely 'likely to support'. So if one concludes that a category of documents is relevant in this sense it means only that it is a category that is 'likely', i.e. may well be relevant to support or adversely affect. No one is here

---

[111] See e.g. *Swain v Hillman* [2001] 1 WLR 1311.

asserting or concluding that each and every document falling within that category will actually be able to support or adversely affect a party's position.

- The second meaning of 'relevance' employed by Aldous LJ in para [34][112] of *American Home Products* is whether each document in fact is relevant to supporting or adversely affecting one party's case. Aldous LJ accepted that one can conclude, at this stage, that a particular document was not in fact relevant without it being said that CPR r 31.17 disclosure was inappropriate in respect of that disclosure.

22.181 Chadwick LJ sought to explain the distinction in the Court of Appeal in *Three Rivers* thus:

> The distinction is between documents which are likely to support the case of the applicant or adversely affect the case of one of the other parties—which can be the subject of an order for disclosure—and documents which, in the event, turn out not to support the case for the applicant or adversely affect the case of one of the other parties—the presence of which within a class does not lead to the conclusion that the class ought not to have been the subject of an order for disclosure.[113]

(d) Limiting non-party disclosure to standard disclosure between parties

22.182 The Court of Appeal in *Three Rivers* is clear that CPR r 31.17 requires disclosure of documents within categories (a) and (b) of CPR r 31.16. As Chadwick LJ put the matter: 'The rule-making body has eschewed the wider test of relevance which is found in s34(2) of the 1981 Act.'[114]

22.183 The basis for this approach is a belief that a non-party should not typically be subjected to greater obligations of disclosure than would be the case between actual parties to the litigation.[115]

(e) Disclosure necessary in order to dispose fairly of the claim or to save costs:
   CPR r 31.17(3)(b)

22.184 If the other requirements are established, disclosure is not automatic. The court has a wide discretion to ensure that an order is only made where the above conditions are met. That is unlikely to be the case if there are other viable options available from which to obtain disclosure.[116]

---

[112] Aldous LJ indicates this second and different meaning through the use of quotation marks around relevance in para [34].

[113] *Three Rivers v Bank of England (No 4)* [2002] 4 All ER 881, 897 [37].

[114] ibid, 893 [28].

[115] *Zuckerman on Civil Procedure* (2nd edn), para 14-103.

[116] See *Frankson v Home Office* [2003] EWCA Civ 655, [2003] 1 WLR 1952; *Re Howglen Ltd* [2001] 1 All ER 376.

(f) Application for witness summons under CPR r 34.2

22.185 For completion, and at the risk of treading into the usual rules on disclosure which fall outside the ambit of this book, this section will deal briefly with applications under CPR r 34.2 for witness summons. More detailed treatment can be found in the White Book and in the leading texts.

22.186 CPR r 34.2 has replaced the old procedure for *subpoena ad testificandum* (directing a party to attend trial and give evidence) and *subpoena duces tecum* (directing a party to attend trial to produce documents). Although the old procedure had, in time, become modified to permit production of documents prior to the trial so that they could be examined by the respective legal teams,[117] it has now been entirely replaced by a new procedure.

22.187 As one might expect, orders directing witnesses to attend trial must follow the requirements laid down in CPR r 34 and the relevant practice direction carefully. The practitioner is directed towards the White Book for the details of this application.

22.188 The potential overlap between this procedure and that under CPR r 31.17 will be discussed below.

22.189 In *South Tyneside MBC v Wickes Building Supplies Ltd*[118] Gross J helpfully laid down some general guidance as to the relevant principles governing the grant of a witnesss summons:

(i) The object of a witness summons is to obtain production at trial of specified documents; accordingly, the witness summons must specifically identify the documents sought, it must not be used as an instrument to obtain disclosure and it must not be of a fishing or speculative nature.

(ii) The production of the documents must be necessary for the fair disposal of the matter or to save costs. The Court is entitled to take into account the question of whether the information can be obtained by some other means. It is to be remembered that, by its nature, a witness summons seeks to compel production from a non-party to the proceedings in question.

(iii) Plainly a witness summons will be set aside if the documents are not relevant to the proceedings; but the mere fact they are relevant is not by itself necessarily decisive in favour of the witness summons.

(iv) The fact that the documents of which production is sought are confidential or contain confidential information is not an absolute bar to the enforcement of their production by way of witness summons; however, in the exercise of its discretion, the Court is entitled to have regard to the fact that documents are confidential and that to order production would involve a breach of confidence. While the Court's paramount concern must be the fair disposal of the cause or matter, it is not unmindful

---

117 *Khanna v Lovell White Durrant (A firm)* [1995] 1 WLR 121.
118 [2004] EWHC 2428, [23].

of other legitimate interests and that to order production of a third party's confidential documents may be oppressive, intrusive or unfair. In this connection, when documents are confidential, the claim that their production is necessary for the fair resolution of proceedings may well be subjected to particularly close scrutiny.

(v) The Court has power to vary the terms of a witness summons but, at least ordinarily, the Court should not be asked to entertain or perform a redrafting exercise other than on the basis of a considered draft tendered by the party's advocate.

22.190 There has been some confusion as to the relationship, if any, as between CPR r 31.17 and CPR r 34.2. Moore-Bick LJ attempted to address this issue in *Tajik Aluminium Plant v Hydro Aluminium AS*.[119]

22.191 The Court rejected the submission, based upon the view expressed by C Hollander QC, in the 8th edition of *Documentary Evidence*, that CPR r 31.17 and CPR r 34.2 had similar aims and that it therefore sufficed for the documents to be broadly identified.

22.192 The Court preferred the views of *Phipson on Evidence*[120] that documents for a witness summons must be either individually identified, or identified by reference to a class of documents or things by which criterion the person to whom the summons is addressed can know what obligation the court imposes on him. This very much harks back to the view that the witness must not be expected to exercise any value judgment on the relevance of a document to a dispute to which it is not a party.

> Whatever may be the origin of the present rules, there are in my view clear distinctions to be drawn between an order for disclosure made against a third party and a witness summons to produce documents. An order for disclosure normally directs the person to whom it is addressed to carry out a reasonable search for documents falling within classes which are often broadly described and to list them for the information of the parties to the proceedings. Often the documents are described in terms which call for the exercise of a degree of judgment in determining whether a particular document does or does not fall within the scope of the order. Any order of that kind, being an order of the court, is one that must be strictly obeyed, but it would be extremely unusual for a penal sanction to be attached to it or for a failure to comply in some material respect to be treated as a contempt of court, save in the case of a contumacious refusal to obey. Moreover, although disclosure is usually a prelude to production for inspection, the person giving disclosure may resist production, if he has grounds for doing so, and in any event has no obligation to do more than make the documents available to the party who has obtained the order. A witness summons to produce documents, by contrast, involves the exercise of the court's coercive powers. The person to whom it is addressed is at risk of being in contempt of court if he fails to comply in any material respect, as the summons itself makes clear. He is obliged to bring the documents to which the summons refers to court, not simply to

---

[119] [2005] EWCA Civ 1218, [2006] 1 WLR 767 (Practice Note).
[120] (16th edn, Sweet and Maxwell, 2005), para 8-10.

list them or make them available for inspection. In substance a witness summons to produce documents is no different from a subpoena duces tecum and the differences between such a summons and an order for disclosure are reflected in the different procedures provided by rules 31.17 and 34.2.[121]

The Court agreed with Gross J in *South Tyneside Metropolitan Borough Council v* **22.193**
Wickes Building Supplies Ltd that, consistent with the earlier authorities on *sub-poena duces tecum*, the order needed to identify with particularity the documents being sought.

> A witness summons, unlike an order for disclosure, requires the person to whom it is addressed to attend court on a specified occasion and to produce to the court the documents to which it refers. It is a requirement reinforced with a penal sanction. Justice demands, therefore, that the person to whom it is addressed should be told clearly when and where he must attend and what he must bring with him. Anything less is unfair to the witness; it also makes supervision and enforcement by the court extremely difficult . . . For these reasons I consider that the view put forward in *Phipson* . . . is to be preferred. Ideally each document should be individually identified, but I do not think it is necessary to go that far in every case.

Applying this approach to the present witness summons before the Court of Appeal **22.194**
in *Tajik*, Moore-Bick LJ agreed with the judge in setting aside the witness summons on the grounds that the documents were described in broad terms, suitable for disclosure, but not for a witness summons. To assist the practitioner to appreciate the width of the order set aside by the Court, it is set out in part below:

> (1) Any documents relating to supplies of alumina, directly or indirectly, to the claimant by Hydro Aluminium AS ('Hydro');

> (2) Any documents relating to supplies of aluminium, directly or indirectly, by the claimant to Hydro.

> (3) Any documents passing between Ermatov and/or Shushko and/or Nazarov and/or Ashton and/or Ansol Ltd ('Ansol') and/or Hydro relating to the operation or performance of: (a) a barter agreement between the claimant and Hydro dated 21 July 2000; or (b) an aluminium agreement between Ansol and Hydro dated 21 July 20000; or (c) a barter agreement between the claimant and Hydro Ltd dated 25 September 2004; or (d) an alumimium agreement between Ansol and Hydro dated 25 September 2003. . . .

(g) Disclosure orders and the problem of tipping off

This chapter has focused on a claimant obtaining disclosure of documentation **22.195**
and information both pre- and post- the commencement of legal proceedings. That disclosure may come from an individual, who is likely to be a defendant to any proceedings, or from a third party who just became involved in the wrong-doing committed by others.

---

[121] *Tajik Aluminium Plant v Hydro Aluminium AS* [2006] 1 WLR 767, 772 [24] per Moore-Bick LJ.

22.196   The common theme has been the need for such disclosure in order to be able to pursue the proceedings or pursue a sensible tracing exercise arising as a result of the underlying fraud. The problem is that whilst the defrauded entity is taking steps to protect its position about recovering its assets, it may well be, and increasingly is the case that authorities such as the National Criminal Intelligence Service (NCIS) will also have become involved from a money laundering perspective. This does not simply become a rush to judgment or information but is rather more serious than that since the entity from whom disclosure is sought, say a bank, will be subject to criminal sanctions if they disclose or tip off the existence of the NCIS money laundering investigation.

22.197   Unfortunately, up to the Court of Appeal in *C v S*,[122] authorities such as NCIS had adopted a pretty unhelpful stance. They refused to assist banks who found themselves facing an order to disclose information and documentation about the bank accounts under the *Norwich Pharmacal* jurisdiction whilst at the same time being subject to the money laundering regulations and the need to ensure no tipping off.

22.198   Whilst lamenting the attitude of NCIS, Lord Woolf MR in *C v S* laid down certain guidelines for the future conduct of such a conflict.

(1)   As soon as a financial institution is aware that a party to legal proceedings intends to apply for or has obtained an order for discovery which might involve the institution having to give disclosure of information which could prejudice an investigation it should inform NCIS of the position and the material which it is required to disclose.

(2)   NCIS will then have the opportunity to identify the material which it does not wish to be disclosed and indicate any preference which it has as to how an application or order should be handled. In doing this it should be borne in mind that usually it will not be necessary to disclose any document or part of a document which refers to the fact of the investigation since this will not be relevant to the issues with which the applicant for the order is concerned. NCIS might be prepared to allow the applicant to be informed as to the existence of the investigation subject to an undertaking to keep the relevant information confidential.

(3)   If NCIS has no objection to partial disclosure the applicant may be satisfied by partial disclosure if it is explained that the alternative is for the matter to be considered by the court. Whether an explanation for the partial disclosure can be given will depend on the attitude of NCIS.

(4)   If the restricted disclosure is unacceptable to the applicant then the directions of the court will have to be sought. The degree to which the application can be informed of the reason for the issue being referred to the court will depend

---

122   [1999] 1 Lloyd's Rep Bank 26 (CA).

on the circumstances. The circumstances will also influence the way in which the matter is brought before the court. The application can be to set aside the order if it was made *ex parte*. Alternatively there can be an application for directions. If the order has not been made the problem can be brought to the attention of the court without the need for a separate application. The court will have to be warned in advance of the difficulties. Where a high degree of confidentiality is required a sealed letter can be written to the judge in charge of the relevant court setting out the circumstances and that judge can then put in place the necessary arrangements. This could be done by providing to the court alone a skeleton argument setting out the background facts and issues.

(5) On the issue being brought before the court the degree to which the applicant can be involved and the extent that it is possible for the issues to be resolved in open court again will depend on the circumstances, but the general approach must be to comply with the ordinary principles to the extent that this is possible. If it is necessary to exclude the applicant, transcripts should be obtained and made available to the applicant as soon as NCIS says this is possible.

In deciding what order should be made the court will have to decide what evidence it requires. In an obvious case a letter from NCIS will suffice. In other cases, their attendance will be required. If the court considers this is justified to achieve justice, NCIS can be made a party. **22.199**

It will be for NCIS (or other investigating authority) to persuade the court that, were disclosure to be made, there would be a real likelihood of the investigation being prejudiced. Were NCIS not to co-operate with the institution (and with any requirements of the court) in advancing such a case, the court could properly draw the inference that no such prejudice would be likely to occur and could accordingly make the disclosure order sought without offending the principle in *Rowell v Pratt* and without putting the institution at risk of prosecution. **22.200**

Especially when the applicant cannot be heard it is important that the court recognizes its responsibility to protect the applicant's interests. The court must have material on which to act if it is to deprive an applicant of his normal rights. The court should bear in mind that a partial order may be better than no order. It should also consider the desirability of adjourning the issue in whole or in part since the expiry of a relatively short period of time may remove any risk of the investigation being prejudiced. NCIS will no doubt wish to co-operate with the courts in achieving speedy progress as this will be the most productive way of avoiding prejudicing an investigation and protecting the interests of litigants. **22.201**

These guidelines were not met with universal endorsement. In particular, it was considered that they failed to take into account any issue of proportionality and/ **22.202** or the inability of the court properly and fully to protect the legitimate interests of those parties barred from attendance at hearings.

22.203 In *Bank of Scotland v A Ltd*,[123] the Court of Appeal took the opportunity to consider the issue once again.

- The Court made it clear that it disliked the growing practice of banks obtaining injunctions against themselves as a means of obtaining protection from any liability from either the customer or under the regulations.

- If a bank has any suspicions about financial wrongdoing, it should contact the Serious Fraud Office (SFO) and obtain their agreement as to what can be said to the customer.

- In the event that the bank and the SFO are unable to reach any agreement as to the level of information to be provided to the customer, the bank should make an application to court, seeking an interim declaration under CPR r 25.1(1)(b), naming the SFO as respondent.

- The bank and the SFO, but not the customer, would attend the hearing which would be in private.

- At the hearing, the Court would be entitled to make a declaration identifying what information could be disclosed.

- In the event that the customer decides to seek withdrawals or transfers in the interim period, and, upon the failure by the bank to comply with its customer's request, the customer commences proceedings, it may be necessary for the same judge who dealt with the bank/SFO declaration hearing to deal with this hearing.

22.204 Even this second attempt has not met with complete approval. One of the important criticisms has been the fact that it would be entirely inappropriate for the same judge that dealt with the bank/SFO hearing to deal with this one, without the information known by that judge being made known to the customer. Without such disgorging of information, it is impossible to see how the judge could act impartially or, which is equally important, appear so to do.[124]

22.205 Overall, it is difficult to see a perfect solution to these conflicting issues. The willingness of the Court of Appeal to keep the matters under review and to lay down guidelines in these two cases at least gives one hope that an informed judiciary will be overseeing the practical resolution of these conflicts as they occur application by application.

---

[123] [2001] 1 WLR 751 CA.
[124] *Zuckerman on Civil Procedure* (2nd edn), paras 2.178–2.179. Such a procedure would, according to Zuckerman, contravene a right to a fair trial.

23

SEARCH ORDERS

A. Overview of Search Orders

In order to obtain a search order or an Anton Piller order, as it was known pre- **23.01**
CPR, the following criteria must be established:

- There must be an extremely strong prima facie case on the merits of the underlying dispute.

- It must be shown that the defendant's conduct or activities result in very serious potential or actual harm to the claimant's interests.

- There must be clear evidence that the defendant has in his possession incriminating documents or materials.

- There must be a real possibility that such documents or materials may be destroyed before being able to issue an application on notice.[1]

- The harm likely to be caused by the execution of the Anton Piller order to the respondent and his business affairs must not be excessive or out of proportion to the legitimate object of the order.

23.02 Even if all these criteria are established on the facts, there is no guarantee that the court will grant a search order. It is, along with the Mareva injunction, considered to be one of the court's 'nuclear weapons'. As made clear in *Anton Piller v Manufacturing Process* itself, an order of this nature 'is at the extremity of this court's powers. Such orders, therefore, will rarely be made, and only when there is no alternative way for ensuring that justice is done to the plaintiff.'[2] So, if it is at all possible to obtain the necessary protection or documentation by way of a different route or procedure, that should be explored first.

23.03 It is no doubt this latter point, about the search order being one of 'last resort', coupled with the obvious attendant costs and expenses incurred in executing such an order (see below), that has had the sobering effect of limiting the number of applications. Indeed, an application for an Anton Piller order is considerably less popular than that for a Mareva order.

23.04 An application for a search order is made without notice and requires the usual form of cross-undertakings in damages (and likely fortification) and is subject to the duty to give full and frank disclosure. It also requires the employment of an independent firm of solicitors to execute the search order, thus ensuring that costs are high.

23.05 In the right hands, and carefully considered, an application for a search order can prove an extremely effective means of obtaining, at a very early stage, documents and information which would be crucial to the ultimate outcome of the case. If deployed early enough to catch the necessary documentation, it can have a devastating effect on the outcome of the litigation.

23.06 In the wrong hands, and applied for without proper care being given to matters of preparation and presentations, then the order can become an extremely costly affair without the clients' interests having been advanced. Indeed, an inappropriately obtained search order can quickly place the claimant on the back-foot in terms of control of the litigation and is something to avoid.

---

[1] The first four conditions derive from *Anton Piller KG v Manufacturing Processes* [1976] Ch 55, 62A–B per Ormrod LJ. The fifth condition comes from the Staughton Committee Report.

[2] ibid, 61H per Ormrod LJ.

B. Introduction

Contemporaneous documents tell the best story. This is as true in a commercial **23.07**
fraud case as it is in non-fraud litigation. The difference is that in the case of the
former, one might expect that those engaged in fraudulent activities would not
baulk at giving false oral evidence about their activities. It is for that reason that
the ability to present a case based upon contemporaneous documentation is so
important in the context of commercial fraud litigation.

The problem facing a litigator in commercial fraud is the simple fact that fraud- **23.08**
sters have no compunction about destroying or concealing incriminating evidence. The claimant would be placed at a distinct disadvantage should he have to
await disclosure in the normal course of events. It was therefore incumbent upon
the English High Court to devise a suitable procedure which carefully balanced
the interests of the claimant against those of the alleged fraudster.

The court was quick to dismiss the possibility of forced search warrants but saw **23.09**
the answer in consensual search warrants. In *Anton Piller*, Lord Denning MR
observed:[3]

> Let me say at once that no court in this land has any power to issue a search warrant
> to enter a man's house so as to see if there are papers or documents there which are of
> an incriminating nature, whether libels, or infringements of copyright or anything
> else of the kind. No constable or bailiff can knock at the door and demand entry so
> as to inspect papers or documents. The householder can shut the door in his face and
> say 'Get out.' That was established in the leading case of *Entick v Carrington* (1765) 2
> Wils.K.B. 275. None of us would wish to whittle down that principle in the slightest.
> But the order sought in this case is not a search warrant. It does not authorize the
> plaintiff's solicitors or anyone else to enter the defendant's premises against their will.
> It does not authorize the breaking down of any doors, nor the slipping in by a back
> door, nor getting in by an open door or window. It only authorizes entry and inspec-
> tion by the permission of the defendants. The plaintiffs must get the defendants' per-
> mission. But does do this: It actually orders them to give permission—with, I suppose,
> the result that if they do not give permission, they are guilty of contempt of court.

Although Lord Denning MR recognized that this reasoning simply led to 'search **23.10**
warrants in disguise' he found comfort in the fact that the House of Lords had
held such arrangements (in respect of the inspection of a warehouse) to be legitimate some 150 years earlier. In *United Company of Merchants of England, Trading
to East Indies, Kynaston*[4] Lord Redesdale remarked:

> The arguments urged for the appellants at the Bar are founded upon the supposition,
> that the court has directed a forcible inspection. This is an erroneous view of the case.

---

[3] ibid, 60B–E.
[4] (1821) 3 Bli OS 153.

The order is to permit; and if the East India Company should refuse to permit the inspection, they will be guilty of contempt of the court . . . It is an order operating on the person requiring the defendants to permit inspection, not giving authority of force, or to break open the doors of their warehouse.[5]

23.11 By the time the Anton Piller jurisdiction came to be examined in some detail by Scott J in *Columbia Picture Industries Inc v Robinson*[6] there was serious concern as to:

[a] procedure which, on a regular and institutional basis, is depriving citizens of their property and closing down their businesses by orders made ex parte, on applications of which they know nothing and at which they cannot be heard, by orders which they are forced, on pain of committal, to obey, even if wrongly made.[7]

23.12 Within 21 years, and as part of the overhaul of English civil procedure, the search order was placed on a statutory footing by s 7 of the Civil Procedure Act 1997 which provides in full as follows:

7. **Power of courts to make orders for preserving evidence, etc.**

(1) The court may make an order under this section for the purpose of securing, in the case of any existing or proposed proceedings in the court—the preservation of evidence which is or may be relevant, or the preservation of property which is or may be the subject-matter of the proceedings or as to which any question arises or may arise in the proceedings.

(2) A person who is, or appears to the court likely to be, a party to proceedings in the court may make an application for such an order.

(3) Such an order may direct any person described in the order, or secure that any person so described is permitted—to enter premises in England and Wales, and while on the premises, to take in accordance with the terms of the order any of the following steps.

(4) Those steps are—to carry out a search for or inspection of anything described in the order, and to make or obtain a copy, photograph, sample or other record of anything so described.

(5) The order may also direct the person concerned—to provide any person described in the order, or secure that any person so described is provided, with any information or article described in the Order, or secure that any person so described is allowed, to retain for safe keeping anything described in the order.

(6) An order under this section is to have effect subject to such conditions as are specified in the order.

(7) This section does not affect any right of a person to refuse to do anything on the ground that to do so might tend to expose him or his spouse to proceedings for an offence or for the recovery of a penalty.

(8) In this section—
'court' means the High Court, and 'premises' includes any vehicle;

---

5 ibid, 163–4.
6 [1987] Ch 38
7 ibid, 74B–C

And an order under this section may describe anything generally, whether by reference to a class or otherwise.

Anton Piller orders or search orders (as they are called post-CPR)[8] are one of the **23.13** established interim remedies listed in CPR r 25.1(1)(h). Not all commentators consider the names, Anton Piller and search orders, to be interchangeable. Steven Gee QC[9] maintains that the Anton Piller jurisdiction is wider than the search order under s 7 of the Civil Procedure Act 1997. The former arises under a combination of the court's inherent jurisdiction and s 37 of the Supreme Court Act 1981 and extends to materials held outside England and Wales. Section 7 of the Civil Procedure Act 1997 is an empowering section and was not intended to cut down in any way any existing inherent jurisdiction in this area.

C. Applicable Principles

Section A above set out, in overview, the relevant principles for an application for **23.14** a search order, being:

- there must be an extremely strong prima facie case on the merits of the underlying dispute;
- it must be shown that the defendant's conduct or activities result in very serious potential or actual harm to the claimant's interests;
- there must be clear evidence that the defendant has in his possession incriminating documents or materials;
- there must be a real possibility that such documents or materials may be destroyed before being able to issue an application on notice.

These criteria are the standard requirements for Anton Piller relief as set out by **23.15** Ormrod LJ in the eponymous case. In addition, however, the Staughton Committee Report[10] added a further requirement:

- the harm likely to be caused by the execution of the Anton Piller order to the respondent and his business affairs must not be excessive or out of proportion to the legitimate object of the order.

---

[8] Although the CPR intended to replace the Mareva and Anton Piller orders with freezing injunctions and search orders respectively, few would agree this has helped to clarify the law or make it any more accessible to the man on the Clapham omnibus. It will therefore not come as a surprise that some refuse to let go of the old terminology: see Chadwick LJ in *Elvee Ltd v Taykor* TLR 18 December 2001, [47].

[9] S Gee QC, *Commercial Injunctions* (5th edn, Thomson/Sweet and Maxwell, 2004), [17-003]–[17.004].

[10] The Staughton Committee Report was commissioned after concern grew that the *Anton Piller* jurisdiction was being too readily invoked: see *Columbia Picture Industries v Robinson* [1987] Ch 1.

23.16 As set out above, even if all these requirements are met, that does not necessarily mean the court will grant the relief. The Staughton Committee provided the following guidance:

> If any of these . . . pre-conditions is absent, the weight of judicial authority should lead to an application for the grant of an Anton Piller order being refused. If each of these pre-conditions appears to be present, an order will not necessarily be justified. The court will still have to weigh in the balance the plaintiff's need for the order against the injustice to the respondent in making the order ex parte without any opportunity for the respondent to be heard. The judge who hears the application for the order should keep in mind that, in as much as audi alteram partem is a requirement of natural justice, the making of an ex parte mandatory order always risks injustice to the absent and unheard respondent. The order should not be made unless it appears that, without the order, the plaintiff will be likely to suffer a greater injustice than that which the court, by making the order, will be inflicting on the respondent (see *Columbia Picture Industries v Robinson* [1987] 1 Ch at 76 and *Lock International plc v Beswick* [1989] 1 WLR at 1281).

23.17 An applicant should always consider whether there is an alternative form of relief which might serve his interests equally well without needing to make use of the search order.[11]

(1) There must be an extremely strong prima facie case on the merits of the underlying dispute[12]

23.18 Given the applicant is asking the court to proceed in the absence of the putative defendant it is not surprising that the applicant is required to put forward strong evidence in support of the underlying dispute. Otherwise, there would be a real risk that such a draconian order could be abused by being invoked to assist a fishing expedition.

23.19 It is to be noted that this threshold, of an 'extremely strong prima facie case', is higher than that required for a Mareva injunction (which requires only a 'good arguable case'). This no doubt reflects the greater intrusion a search order can have on the private life of a defendant.

23.20 That said, it is important not to fall into the trap of thinking that if one can readily establish the merits of the underlying claim, such that the respondent's wrongdoing is obvious and well founded, this will conclude or even heavily influence the decision to grant Anton Piller relief. It is necessary that *all* the requirements laid down must be met before an applicant is entitled to Anton Piller relief. In *Lock International plc v Beswick*[13] Hoffmann J observed:

> Even in cases in which the plaintiff has strong evidence that an employee has taken what is undoubtedly specified confidential information, such as a list of customers,

---

11 See *Brown v Bennett (No 2)* [2002] 1 WLR 713 (Neuberger J) [8] and [164ff].
12 *Anton Piller KG v Manufacturing Processes* [1976] Ch 55, 62A per Ormrod LJ.
13 [1989] 1 WLR 1268.

the court must employ a graduate response. To borrow a useful concept from the jurisprudence of the European Community, there must be *proportionality* between the perceived threat to the plaintiff's rights and the remedy granted. The fact that there is overwhelming evidence that the defendant has behaved wrongfully in his commercial relationships does not necessarily justify an *Anton Piller* order. People whose commercial morality allows them to take a list of the customers with whom they were in contact while employed will not necessarily disobey an order of the court requiring them to deliver it up.[14]

(2) It must be shown that the defendant's conduct or activities result in very serious potential or actual harm to the claimant's interests[15]

The Anton Piller order is recognized as a draconian power of the court. It can only **23.21** properly be invoked in circumstances where the applicant can readily show, in his evidence, that he would suffer very serious potential or actual harm should no such relief be granted.

It has been suggested that it must be shown that without the relevant documents **23.22** it would not be possible to bring any claim at all.[16] This is discussed below. It suffices to say at this stage that this suggestion probably places the requirement too high.[17] If the defendant deliberately destroys some of the relevant documents but not all, that is going to make the claimant's task of proving his case more difficult than it should be. Indeed, without some documents, the risk is greater that the claimant will fail to persuade the court of his case. That is not a risk the claimant should have to bear given it would have been brought about by the deliberate conduct of the defendant.

(3) There must be clear evidence that the defendant has in his possession incriminating documents or materials

(a) Standard of evidence

The Court of Appeal in *Booker McConnell Plc v Plascow*[18] stressed the need to **23.23** show a 'real possibility' that the defendant has the relevant documents in his possession rather than the usual 'extravagant fears which seem to afflict all plaintiffs who have complaints of breach of confidence, breach of copying or passing off'.

(b) Relevant documents

Intellectual property cases have been at the heart of the development of this relief. **23.24** It is this fact which perhaps explains the manner in which Ormrod LJ sets out this

---

14 ibid, 1281.
15 ibid.
16 *Yousif v Salama* [1980] 1 WLR 1540, 1543D–E per Donaldson LJ dissenting.
17 The other leading cases dealing with Anton Piller orders do not repeat or confirm such a high requirement.
18 [1985] RPC 425, 441.

third requirement. The phrase 'incriminating documents or materials' most aptly covers products infringing various copyrights. But it would be wrong to limit the order to such occasions.

23.25 It is clear that this jurisdiction extends to obtaining documents or materials which assist either in the making of the claim or the pursuit of enforcement procedures after judgment has been obtained.

(c) Documents assisting the making of a claim

23.26 In *Yousif v Salama*[19] the parties had agreed that the claimant would arrange for third parties to place business through the defendant company in return for a share of the profits. The claimant visited the defendant's offices and was shown two files and desk diary containing details of the relevant transactions. Upon the relationship breaking down, the plaintiff sought an Anton Piller order in respect of various documents, which although not in themselves the subject matter of the action, were necessary to preserve as evidence to prove the plaintiff's case. The judge refused the application which was successful on appeal.

23.27 Lord Denning MR said:

> In many cases such an order would not be granted. But in this case there is evidence (if it is accepted) which shows the first defendant to be untrustworthy. The plaintiff has a legitimate fear that the documents will be destroyed. In the circumstances, it seems to me that it would be proper to make an *Anton Piller* order to the effect that the plaintiff's solicitor would be enabled to go and get the documents—take them into his personal custody for a while—make copies of them—and then return the originals to the defendants. The solicitor would have to keep them personally himself and not let them out of his possession. It seems to me that that would be an aid to justice. It would be preserving the evidence in the case. Under RSC Order 29 r 2, there is a far-reaching power for preserving documents which are the subject matter of the action. These files here are not the subject matter of the action. But they are the best possible evidence to prove the plaintiff's case. There is a genuine fear that, if the plaintiff waits till after the application is heard, the first defendant may destroy the documents before the date of the hearing. That is the sort of danger which the *Anton Piller* order is designed to prevent.[20]

23.28 Lord Denning MR went on to vary the terms of the order to be limited to those documents seen during the claimant's visit, namely the two files and the desk diary. To require production of these documents could not possibly cause any harm or difficulty to the defendants and that was an important consideration as far as Lord Denning MR was concerned.

---

19 [1980] 1 WLR 1540.
20 ibid, 1542A–D.

Brightman LJ agreed with Lord Denning MR. His reasoning, with respect, can- **23.29**
not be faulted:

> In my view, the order sought in this case is justified if, but only if, there is prima facie
> evidence that essential documents are at risk. If essential documents are at risk, then
> it seems to me that this court ought to permit the plaintiff to take such steps as are
> necessary to preserve them.
>
> So there are two questions to be asked. First, are the documents sought to be seized
> essential to the plaintiff's case? If so, are such documents at serious risk? Might they
> be dishonestly destroyed?
>
> It is difficult to form any confident view on the merits of the application because
> inevitably the evidence is one-sided. The defendants have had no opportunity to
> answer it. But I think that on the plaintiff's evidence that there are grounds for saying
> that the documents in question are essential to the plaintiff's case. I also think that
> on balance there is sufficient evidence to justify the court in concluding that the docu-
> ments are at risk. . . .[21]

Donaldson LJ however dissented on the basis that this was, as far as he was con- **23.30**
cerned, a typical breakdown in the relationship between accounting parties where
disclosure should take place in the normal way. This was not a situation which
fell within the exceptional ambit of the Anton Piller jurisdiction which was
limited to where (i) there is very clear prima facie case that the defendant will conceal or destroy essential evidence in the grossest possible contempt of the court
and (ii) that if he did so, the whole processes of justice would be frustrated because
the claimant would be left without any evidence to enable him to put forward his
claim. Donaldson LJ went on to hold that the evidence of an intention to destroy
evidence was 'flimsy in the extreme', based, as it was, upon an allegation of forgery
of a cheque. Finally, Donaldson LJ held that even if he was wrong about the state
of the evidence, the documents were not essential to the claimant's case. If the
defendants were unable to produce the necessary accounting documents, then the
court would draw the necessary inferences against them.

Putting aside Donaldson LJ's view on the state of the evidence, the interesting **23.31**
and controversial aspect of his dissenting judgment relates to his view as to when
the Anton Piller jurisdiction can be invoked. In particular, it is submitted that
the second limb of his test places the test too high. A claimant's entitlement to
Anton Piller relief should not, it is submitted, be dependent upon how successfully the defendant destroys relevant documents. In particular, the destruction of
any relevant documents is likely to make the claimant's task of proving his claim
that little more difficult without that evidence. Anton Piller relief should not be

---

[21] ibid, 1544E–G.

and is not limited to those occasions when, without it, no claim at all could be brought.[22]

23.32   In respect of the state of evidence, *Yousif v Salama* was considered as marking a relaxation of the traditional requirements for Anton Piller relief with the court showing a greater willingness to infer the necessary intention to destroy documents.[23] If there was a relaxation in approach, then the Court of Appeal in *Booker McConnell plc v Plascow*[24] re-asserted the traditional strict approach by recognizing the tremendous detrimental impact such an order can have on an individual or company's reputation.

(d)   Documents assisting enforcement of a judgment

23.33   In *Distributori Automatici v Holford Trading Co*[25] Leggatt J held that the Anton Piller jurisdiction extended to documents which were essential for the proper enforcement of a judgment against the defendant.

23.34   In reaching this conclusion, Leggatt J found that the jurisdiction to grant Anton Piller relief extended beyond the narrow ground of the inherent jurisdiction under RSC Order 29, r 2 to a broader principle as enunciated by Lord Denning MR in *Anton Piller* itself:[26]

> such an order can be made by a judge ex parte, but it should only be made where it is essential that the plaintiff should have inspection so that justice can be done between the parties; and when, if the defendant were forewarned, there is a grave danger that vital evidence will be destroyed, that papers will be burnt or lost or hidden, or taken beyond the jurisdiction, and so the ends of justice be defeated: and when the inspection would do no real harm to the defendant or his case.

(4)   There must be a real possibility that such documents or materials may be destroyed before being able to issue an application on notice

23.35   The purpose of this relief is the maintenance of the integrity of the judicial process so that no claimant is put at a disadvantage at trial because the defendant has decided to destroy documents which would otherwise have to be disclosed. Accordingly, it is

---

[22] In *Emanuel v Emanuel* [1982] 1 WLR 669, family divorce proceedings, Wood J granted an Anton Piller order in respect of a husband's documents relating to his assets and general financial position. At p 676, Wood J said: 'The husband is clearly ready to flout the authority of this court and to mislead it if he thinks that it is to his advantage so to do. The normal process of law is liable to be rendered nugatory. I have no doubt that justice in the present matter cannot be achieved without making the present order, and that there is a grave danger that evidence will be removed or destroyed. I cannot think that real harm will be caused to the husband from making the order, as the only documents sought are those which he ought properly to produce, and indeed, ought to have produced in the past.'

[23] See also *Dunlop Holdings Ltd v Staravia Ltd* [1982] Com LR 3.

[24] [1985] RPC 425.

[25] [1985] 1 WLR 1066 (Leggatt J).

[26] [1976] Ch 55, 61.

incumbent upon the claimant to adduce clear evidence of the 'real possibility'[27] that relevant documents may be destroyed prior to trial.

Whilst a slightly more relaxed attitude appeared to have crept into the court's **23.36** approach to inferring the necessary intention to destroy, as seen in cases such as *Yousif v Salama*,[28] the traditional strict approach has been re-asserted in *Booker McConnell plc v Plascow*[29] and *Columbia Picture Industries Inc v Robinson*.[30]

The CPR Practice Direction 25, para 7(3)(2) uses the language of 'probability' **23.37** rather than 'real possibility'. The former is a greater burden to establish than the latter but it must be questionable whether it was in fact really intended to alter the substantive requirements for this relief in a Practice Direction.

(5) The harm likely to be caused by the execution of the Anton Piller order to the respondent and his business affairs must not be excessive or out of proportion to the legitimate object of the order

This additional requirement did not feature in the original requirements as laid **23.38** down by Ormrod LJ in *Anton Piller v Manufacturing Processes*. It derives from the recommendation of the Staughton Committee Report.

It is often not included in the list of pre-conditions or matters to be considered for **23.39** the purposes of an Anton Piller order. It is included in this present list because it is exactly the sort of weighing up exercise a court needs to do in order to determine whether it is appropriate to grant the relief sought.

- With the greater appreciation in the later cases of the tremendous and often irreparable damage that can be caused to the reputation of an individual or a company subject to an Anton Piller order, it is inevitable that the court would wish to enquire into the effect or possible effect such an order would have on the defendant and his reputation and business. The more serious the likely harm to the defendant, the more closely scrutinized any application for such relief against that defendant.

- Under the CPR, the court must consider all applications against the context of the need to conduct litigation in a proportionate manner. This not only includes assessing the application against the needs of other users of the court system but also ensuring no one party is able to use the judicial process to bully the other.[31]

---

[27] The phrase is taken from *Anton Piller KG v Manufacturing Processes* [1976] Ch 55.
[28] [1980] 1 WLR 1540, where the necessary inference was drawn from participation in the forgery of a cheque.
[29] [1985] RPC 425.
[30] [1987] Ch 38.
[31] See A Zuckerman, *Zuckerman on Civil Procedure* (2nd edn, Thomson/Sweet and Maxwell, 2006), [1.17]–[1.22]. See the Overriding Objectives as set out in CPR r 1.1: 'Dealing with a case

D. Duty of Full and Frank Disclosure

23.40 Whether the application is for a freezing injunction or a search order, it is imperative that the claimant prepare for and present his application in accordance with his duty to give full and frank disclosure. The nature and extent of this duty is set out below.

23.41 The imposition of this duty is an imperfect *quid pro quo* for asking the court to proceed to grant relief against the defendant in his absence and therefore without his having been afforded the opportunity to put his side of the case forward. A failure to comply with this duty may lead to the discharge of the relief obtained.[32]

23.42 The duty is examined in some detail in Chapter 24 dealing with freezing injunctions. For convenience sake, Ralph Gibson LJ's succinct set of principles, as laid down in *Brink's Mat Ltd v Elcombe*,[33] is outlined below:

(1) The duty of the applicant is to make 'a full and fair disclosure of all the material facts': see *Rex v. Kensington Income Tax Commissioners, Ex parte Princess Edmond de Polignac*.[34]

(2) The material facts are those which it is material for the judge to know in dealing with the application as made: materiality is to be decided by the court and not by the assessment of the applicant or his legal advisers: see *Rex v. Kensington Income Tax Commissioners*, per Lord Cozens-Hardy M.R.[35] citing *Dalglish v. Jarvie*[36] and Browne-Wilkinson J. in *Thermax Ltd. v. Schott Industrial Glass Ltd.*[37]

(3) The applicant must make proper inquiries before making the application: see *Bank Mellat v. Nikpour*.[38] The duty of disclosure therefore applies not only to material facts known to the applicant but also to any additional facts which he would have known if he had made such inquiries.[39]

(4) The extent of the inquiries which will be held to be proper, and therefore necessary, must depend on all the circumstances of the case including (a) the nature

---

justly includes, so far as is practicable – (a) ensuring that the parties are on an equal footing; (b) saving expense; (c) dealing with the case in ways which are proportionate – (i) to the amount of money involved; (ii) to the importance of the case; (iii) to the complexity of the issues; and (iv) to the financial position of each party; (d) ensuring that it is dealt with expeditiously and fairly . . . '.

[32] *Bank Mellatt v Nikpour* [1985] FSR 87, 92.

[33] [1988] 1 WLR 1350 CA.

[34] [1917] 1 KB 486, 514, per Scrutton LJ.

[35] ibid, 504.

[36] (1850) 2 Mac & G 231, 238.

[37] [1981] FSR 289, 295.

[38] [1985] FSR 87.

[39] The extent of those inquiries will depend on the urgency of the application. That said, the applicant will be expected to have placed before the court any relevant information which can readily be obtained from public sources, particularly the internet.

of the case which the applicant is making when he makes the application; and (b) the order for which application is made and the probable effect of the order on the defendant: see, for example, the examination by Scott J. of the possible effect of an Anton Piller order in *Columbia Picture Industries Inc. v. Robinson*;[40] and (c) the degree of legitimate urgency and the time available for the making of inquiries: see *per* Slade L.J. in *Bank Mellat v. Nikpour*.[41]

(5) If material non-disclosure is established the court will be 'astute to ensure that a plaintiff who obtains [an ex parte injunction] without full disclosure . . . is deprived of any advantage he may have derived by that breach of duty': see *per* Donaldson L.J. in *Bank Mellat v. Nikpour*[42] citing Warrington L.J. in the *Kensington Income Tax Commissioners*' case.[43]

(6) Whether the fact not disclosed is of sufficient materiality to justify or require immediate discharge of the order without examination of the merits depends on the importance of the fact to the issues which were to be decided by the judge on the application. The answer to the question whether the non-disclosure was innocent, in the sense that the fact was not known to the applicant or that its relevance was not perceived, is an important consideration but not decisive by reason of the duty on the applicant to make all proper inquiries and to give careful consideration to the case being presented.

(7) Finally, it 'is not for every omission that the injunction will be automatically discharged. A locus poenitentiae may sometimes be afforded': per Lord Denning M.R. in *Bank Mellat v. Nikpour*.[44] The court has a discretion, notwithstanding proof of material non-disclosure which justifies or requires the immediate discharge of the ex parte order, nevertheless to continue the order, or to make a new order on terms.

'when the whole of the facts, including that of the original non-disclosure, are before [the court, it] may well grant . . . a second injunction if the original non-disclosure was innocent and if an injunction could properly be granted even had the facts been disclosed': *per* Glidewell L.J. in *Lloyds Bowmaker Ltd. v. Britannia Arrow Holdings Plc.*,[45] ante, pp. 1343H–1344A.

E. Cross-undertakings in Damages

As with the freezing injunction, any application for a search order must be accompanied by a willingness to provide a cross-undertaking in damages. Strictly, this is an undertaking to the court, and not to the other party, but it is required to counterbalance the court's willingness to protect the claimant's rights and interests before they have been finally determined at trial. Such an approach always runs the risk that **23.43**

---

[40] [1987] Ch 38.
[41] [1985] FSR 87, 92–3.
[42] ibid, 91.
[43] [1917] 1 KB 486, 509.
[44] [1985] FSR 87, 90.
[45] [1988] 1 WLR 1337.

the defendant's interests might be infringed, thereby causing the defendant some loss. That loss is compensatable via the claimant's cross-undertakings in damages.

23.44 For a more detailed treatment of the cross-undertakings in damages, see Chapter 24, para 24.227 *et seq.*

F. Practice and Procedure

23.45 Any application for a search order or Anton Piller relief must be made to a judge of the High Court or above.[46] There is no jurisdiction in the County Court to grant such relief.

23.46 Since the thrust of this relief is to protect and preserve relevant documents held in the possession of the putative defendant without first giving him a warning by notice that such an order is being sought, all applications for search orders proceed on a 'without notice'[47] basis and the hearing takes place in private.

23.47 Generally, the practice and procedure follows that set out for interim injunctions and requires the applicant to lodge at court ahead of the application the documents identified below.

(a) A claim form

23.48 Ideally the claim form should be issued but if the matter is so urgent it is possible to lodge a draft claim form with an undertaking in the draft Order to issue and serve as soon as possible.

23.49 If it is possible in the time available to prepare Particulars of Claim as well, that will greatly assist the court in identifying what are the real issues in the dispute.

(b) An application notice in form N16A

(c) An affidavit

23.50 Unless the matter is considered so urgent that it is necessary to proceed with an oral application without an affidavit (against an undertaking to file one to support whatever was said in court),[48] an affidavit (or more than one) must be lodged. Witness statements do not suffice.[49]

---

[46] *Schmidt v Wong* [2006] 1 WLR 561.

[47] Or *ex parte* in the old language.

[48] Great care should be taken before deciding to proceed without the benefit of an affidavit. In the absence of a detailed and clearly structured affidavit, the applicant runs the very real risk of omitting important information and/or failing to comply with his duty of full and frank disclosure.

[49] CPR PD (Written Evidence) 32PD para 1.4. This Practice Direction also sets out the form and contents of a typical affidavit.

The affidavit must contain clear evidence to prove the establishment of each of the **23.51**
pre-conditions for this relief.

It is important that the material evidence is placed in the body of the affidavit and **23.52**
not hidden away somewhere in the exhibits. It is to be remembered that a judge
will have limited time to pre-read an urgent application and the applicant should
do all that he can to assist the court by identifying clearly the relevant evidence.
As Lloyd LJ stated in *National Bank of Sharjah v Delborg*:[50]

> If the facts are not fairly stated in the affidavit, it will not assist the plaintiff to be able
> to point to some exhibit from which the facts might be extracted. If they are fairly
> stated then it should not avail the defendant to show that some document, relevant
> on discovery, has been omitted . . .

The affidavit must of course be prepared with the claimant's duty of full and **23.53**
frank disclosure in mind. Any possible but not fanciful defences should be mentioned in the affidavit.

The affidavit must state the name, firm and its address and the experience of the **23.54**
Supervising Solicitor.

(d) Draft order[51]

It is imperative that the official draft order is used, at least as the template for the **23.55**
order placed before the court. Cogent reasons need to be advanced for any departures from that template.

If seeking to make any amendments to the official draft order, the claimant is **23.56**
advised to inform the court of each and every such amendment. One of the easiest
ways of doing that is simply to provide the court with a copy of the official draft
highlighting using the 'tracked changes' system on Microsoft Word. That best
ensures that no amendments are missed out. A failure to bring to the court's attention all deviations from the standard order (whether it be a freezing order or a
search order) can result in a discharge of the order.[52]

(e) Skeleton argument[53]

This is a crucial document in any without notice application. It is the court's guide **23.57**
to the case and will be used by the court to determine what evidence to read, what
issues to consider, etc.

It should be clear and structured in format, identifying all relevant legal author- **23.58**
ities, and setting out any necessary quotations from the case law. In addition to the

---

[50] [1993] 2 Bank LR 109.
[51] The official draft order for the search order is reproduced at Precedent No. 2.
[52] E.g. *A Bank v A Ltd, The Times,* 18 July 2000 (Laddie J). See also *Gadget Shop Ltd v Bug.Com Ltd, The Times,* 28 June 2000 (Rimer J).
[53] *ALG Inc v Uganda Airlines Corporation, The Times,* 31 July 1992.

affidavit, the skeleton argument should also expressly draw the court's attention to matters of full and frank disclosure.[54]

(f) At the hearing

23.59 It goes without saying that the advocate should be fully prepared for the application. He should inquire into precisely what the judge has had an opportunity to read and what he has not read. If necessary, be prepared to ask the court to spend a few minutes reading through an affidavit or the skeleton before proceeding with the oral submissions.

23.60 Without notice applications can be relatively short and there is a danger that if the judge is in favour of granting the order sought, he will be keen to move things on so quickly that it can be difficult to raise adverse matters as required by the duty of full and frank disclosure. Failure to do so will only store up trouble for the *inter partes* hearing on the Return Date.

23.61 Whilst it may strike one as a little odd to suggest that the advocate should insist on raising adverse matters when the judge has indicated he has happy to grant the order sought, nevertheless that is exactly what must be done. On occasion, this may require him to stand firm against a court keen to move on to discuss the terms of the order. It is unlikely such matters will result in any change of heart on the part of the judge but it will at least head off an argument for discharge based upon non-disclosure of a material factor at the *inter partes* Return Date hearing.

23.62 If there has been a departure in any way from the official standard form version of the search order, the advocate must draw this to the court's attention. Any failure to do so may well be considered a material non-disclosure.[55] Best practice suggests taking a 'tracked changes' version of the order as well as a clean copy to be signed by the judge.

23.63 It is essential that a detailed note is taken of the *without notice* hearing as this will need to be provided to the other side prior to the Return Date.[56]

G. Conduct of Execution

23.64 It has already been seen that Anton Piller orders draw a very uneasy line of distinction between a forced search warrant and a consensual search order. Whatever the merit in drawing that distinction, the search order requires great care in its execution.

---

[54] *Memory Corporation plc v Sidhu (No 2)* [2000] 1 WLR 1443.
[55] ibid; *A Bank v A Ltd,* unrep, 18 July 2000 (Laddie J—a Mareva order may be set aside if variation not drawn to court's attention).
[56] *Interoute Telecommunications (UK) Ltd v Fashion Gossip Ltd, The Times,* 10 November 1999 Ch (Lightman J).

(1) By the applicant and Supervising Solicitor

(a) Service

Unless the court otherwise orders,[57] the Supervising Solicitor[58] must serve the **23.65** order personally together with any evidence in support.[59] If any of the supporting evidence is confidential, provision can be made for this to be inspected by the respondent during the visit and limited copies to be taken by the respondent's solicitors.[60]

Only those specifically identified in the order may accompany the Supervising **23.66** Solicitor during the visit. This is to stop the visit from being intimidatory.[61]

It is the responsibility of the Supervising Solicitor to explain, in plain and simple **23.67** terms, the effect of the order and the fact that the respondent has the right to take legal advice and to apply to vary or discharge the order. Importantly, the Supervising Solicitor must also draw to the respondent's attention the fact that he may be entitled to avail himself of legal professional privilege and the privilege against self-incrimination.[62]

Once the order has been explained to the respondent, he must allow entry imme- **23.68** diately unless he wishes to obtain legal advice and/or to ask the court to vary or discharge the order. The Supervising Solicitor may permit a period of two hours without carrying out a search to enable legal advice to be obtained.[63] Should he require longer, the Supervising Solicitor is authorized to grant additional time, although this should only be granted against careful consideration of the fact that the judge has granted this relief because of a real risk the documents might otherwise be destroyed. Even if he gives permission to delay the search, the Supervising Solicitor must be given entry to the premises.[64]

---

[57] If the court orders otherwise, the reason for so doing must be set out in the order itself: CPR 25PD, 7.7.

[58] The Supervising Solicitor must not be an employee or member of the applicant's solicitors: CPR 25PD 7.6.

[59] The use of solicitors closely associated with those assisting the claimant, alternatively use of the claimant directors to effect service of the order, was frowned upon in *Manor Electronics Ltd v Dickson* [1988] RPC 618. The practice of using independent solicitors derives from *Universal Thermosensors Ltd v Hibben* [1992] 1 WLR 840.

[60] CPR 25PD 7.4(1) and (2).

[61] CPR 25PD 7.4(3).

[62] CPR 25PD 7.4(4). A failure by the Supervising Solicitor to explain the effect of the order properly and fairly to the respondent may result in the solicitor being held in contempt of court: *VDU Installations Ltd v Integrated Computer Systems and Cybernetics Ltd* [1989] FSR 378.

[63] Without granting such a period of grace, there would be little point in advising the respondent to take legal advice: *Bhimji v Chatwani* [1991] 1 WLR 989.

[64] See paras 10–12 of the Official Draft Order: Precedent No 2.

23.69 It has been pointed out that the official draft order permits a two-hour delay to the carrying out of the search but does not obviously provide a similar extension of time for delivery up of articles/documents pursuant to paragraphs 16 and 17 of the official draft order.[65]

23.70 If the respondent is an unaccompanied woman, and the Supervising Solicitor is a man, then at least one other member of the individuals entitled to attend on service of the order must be a woman.[66]

23.71 Service of this order can only take place between 9.30 a.m. and 5.30 p.m. Monday to Friday, save where the court orders otherwise.[67] It cannot be carried out at the same time as a police search warrant.[68]

23.72 The respondent runs the risk of being in contempt of court should he fail to comply with the terms of the order. This remains the case even if on the facts the order should be discharged. Unless and until it is discharged, the respondent must comply with its terms.[69]

(b) Search and custody of materials

23.73 The terms of the search order will identify those items or material which can be removed. If it is not referred to in the order it cannot be removed.[70] Any search for those items or material must take place in the presence of the respondent or someone who appears to be a responsible employee of the respondent.[71]

23.74 If any documents are required to be taken to be copied they should be returned within two days. Any material which is taken should be held by the respondent's solicitors on their undertaking to retain it in safekeeping and to produce it at court when required so to do. Before anything is taken it is to be placed on a list by the Supervising Solicitor and, unless the Supervising Solicitor considers this impracticable,[72] the respondent is entitled to a reasonable period of time to check items on the list that are intended to be taken away.[73]

23.75 If any of the identified items are on a computer, the respondent must provide all necessary passwords to gain entry and the Supervising Solicitor, if he has sufficient expertise to do so, must not damage the computer in so doing.[74] Typically, the order will provide for the attendance of an IT specialist to assist in this matter.

---

[65] Gee, *Commercial Injunctions* (5th edn), [17-058].
[66] CPR 25PD 7.4(5).
[67] CPR 25PD 7.4(6).
[68] CPR 25PD 7.8
[69] See e.g. *Wardle Fabrics Ltd v G Myristis Ltd* [1984] FSR 263.
[70] CPR 25PD 7.5(1).
[71] CPR 25PD 7.5(2).
[72] CPR 25PD 7.5(13).
[73] CPR 25PD 7.5(3)–(7).
[74] CPR 25PD 7.5(8)–(10).

If the Supervising Solicitor concludes it is impracticable to await receipt of pass-words, the search may proceed and items removed without compliance with the impracticable requirements.[75]

Finally the Supervising Solicitor must produce a report of the conduct and man- **23.76**
ner of the execution of the order and serve a copy on all parties and the court.[76]

H. Issues of Privilege

A detailed account of the privilege against self-incrimination is beyond the scope **23.77**
of this text. It is necessary, however, to have a proper understanding of this area of
the law as it has an effect on the operation of search orders. The reader is referred
to the leading texts for that detailed understanding.[77]

The starting position is the decision of the Court of Appeal, affirmed on appeal to **23.78**
the House of Lords in *Rank Film Distributors Ltd v Video Information Centre*[78] that
an Anton Piller order should never be made if compliance with it required the
respondent to incriminate himself.[79]

This decision led to the enactment of s 72 of the Supreme Court Act 1981 which **23.79**
provided for the withdrawal of the privilege in civil proceedings relating to the
infringement of intellectual property rights or passing-off. Outside of the ambit
of s 72, the privilege remained and the principle of the *Rank Film* case applied.

Tate Access Floors Inc v Boswell[80] introduced the concept of including within the **23.80**
Anton Piller order wording which explained to the respondent that he had a right
to avail himself of the privilege against self-incrimination and by providing that
certain parts of the order were only to be executed in so far as privilege was not
claimed.[81]

The number of offences for which the privilege against self-incrimination could **23.81**
be claimed has been whittled away by statute. The present position is set out in the
latest version of the draft order. CPR 25 PD 7.9 provides as follows:

7.9 There is no privilege against self-incrimination in:

(1) Intellectual Property cases in respect of a 'related offence' or for the recovery of a
'related penalty' as defined in section 72 Supreme Court Act 1981;

---

[75] CPR 25PD 7.5(13).
[76] CPR 25PD 7.5(11) and (12).
[77] *Zuckerman on Civil Procedure* (2nd edn), ch 17; C Hollander QC, *Documentary Evidence* (9th edn, Thomson/Sweet and Maxwell, 2006), ch 17.
[78] [1982] AC 380 CA and HL.
[79] ibid, 415–16 (Bridge LJ).
[80] [1991] Ch 512.
[81] See also *IBM United Kingdom Ltd v Prima Data International Ltd* [1994] 1 WLR 719.

(2) proceedings for the recovery or administration of any property, for the execution of a trust or for an account of any property or dealings with property, in relation to—

(a) an offence under the Theft Act 1968 (see section 31 of the Theft Act 1968); or

(b) an offence under the Fraud Act 2006 (see section 13 of the Fraud Act 2006) or a related offence within the meaning given by section 13(4) of that Act – that is, conspiracy to defraud or any other offence involving any form of fraudulent conduct or purpose; or

(3) proceedings in which a court is hearing an application for an order under Part IV or Part V of the Children Act 1989 (see section 98 of Children Act 1989).

However, the privilege may still be claimed in relation to material or information required to be disclosed by an order as regards potential criminal proceedings outside those statutory provisions.

23.82 The combination of the Theft Act 1968 and the Fraud Act 2006 means that there are very few fraud-related offences for which the respondent can assert his privilege against incrimination and thereby seek to avoid dealing with the search order.

23.83 It is not necessarily sufficient to rely upon the wording of the standard draft order. In *Den Norske Bank v Antonatos*[82] the Court of Appeal found that no application for a search order should be made if it will require the defendant to incriminate himself. Waller LJ said:

> An Anton Piller order should not be made where it will require the defendant to incriminate himself. The authorities on this aspect are summarized in *Cobra Golf Ltd v Rata* [1998] Ch 109 at 129-128. It is possible to build a mechanism into an order which provides a clear warning to the defendant through, for example, advice from the supervising solicitor. But the authorities summarized by Rimer J in the *Cobra* case show how difficult it is to provide adequate protection and there is no distinction in this regard between an Anton Piller and a Mareva order. Once again, I emphasise that the expedient of ordering a defendant to place incriminating information in the hands of supervising solicitor does not seem to me to provide adequate protection.[83]

23.84 On the facts, the Court of Appeal in *Den Norske Bank* overturned the first instance decision that placing privileged material in the hands of the supervising solicitors maintained privilege.

23.85 The recent Court of Appeal decision in *C plc v P*[84] represents an important extension to the erosion of a defendant's ability to rely upon privilege against self-incrimination when faced with a search order. The facts can be shortly stated. During the course of the execution of a search order, some computers were seized

---

[82] [1998] 3 All ER 74.
[83] ibid, 89.
[84] [2007] EWCA Civ 493, [2007] 3 WLR 437.

and handed over to an IT expert. Whilst examining the computers, the IT expert discovered child pornography, the possession of which is a criminal offence. The expert sought directions from the court. The Court of Appeal held that the expert should hand over the material to the police and that privilege against self-incrimination did not extend to material which had 'an existence independent of the will'. The offending material existed independently of the search order and therefore gave rise to no issues of privilege once in the possession of the IT expert. It was in an altogether different category from 'compelled testimony'. It was simply incriminating material discovered during the process of the execution of a search order. Longmore LJ also indicated that allowing the computer to be taken and given to an IT expert and then asserting a general privilege was not the correct way of asserting privilege. His Lordship indicated that the privilege should have been asserted vis-à-vis the specific computer while it remained in the custody of the Supervising Solicitor. Some disagree with the reasoning, if not the result, in *C v P*.[85]

---

[85] R Moules, 'The Privilege Against Self-Incrimination and Real Evidence' [2007] 66 CLJ 528.

24

FREEZING, PROPRIETARY AND INTERIM INJUNCTIONS

A. Overview of Requirements for Each Injunction

(1) (Worldwide/domestic) freezing injunction in aid of English proceedings

24.01 In order to obtain a freezing injunction the following requirements must be established:

(1) a cause of action justiciable in England and Wales;

(2) a good arguable case on the merits;

(3) prima facie evidence of assets within the jurisdiction (if domestic order) or outside the jurisdiction (if worldwide order);

(4) a real risk that the defendant may dissipate those assets without justification before enforcement of any judgment.

(2) Freezing injunction in aid of foreign proceedings: CJJA 1982 (as amended), s 25(1)

24.02 In order to obtain a freezing injunction under s 25(1) of the Civil Jurisdiction and Judgments Act 1982 (CJJA 1982) in aid of foreign proceedings:

(1) the requirements for a freezing injunction set out above must be satisfied (except (1));

(2) the guidelines set out in *Credit Suisse v Cuoghi*,[1] *Motorola Credit Corporation v Uzan (No 2)*[2] and *Ryan v Friction Dynamics Ltd & Ors* must be followed.[3]

(3) Proprietary injunction

24.03 In order to obtain a proprietary injunction (previously called a tracing injunction) the applicant must satisfy the *American Cyanamid* requirements in respect of a proprietary claim or interest.

(4) Interim injunction

24.04 In order to obtain an interim injunction under the *American Cyanamid* principles,[4] the following must be considered:

(1) that all the facts of the case should be considered, since injunctive relief is discretionary;

(2) relief must be kept flexible;

---

[1] [1998] QB 818.

[2] [2004] 1 WLR 113, 147 [115].

[3] Claim 1998 R No. 6785 Unrep, 2 June 2000.

[4] *American Cyanamid v Ethicon Ltd* [1975] AC 396; *Series 5 Software Ltd v Clarke* [1996] 1 All ER 853.

(3) the court should not attempt to resolve complex issues of fact at the interlocutory hearing: mini-trials are to be avoided;

(4) the extent to which damages are an adequate remedy for either side must be borne in mind and if they are adequate, whether the other side is financially able to pay such damges;

(5) the overall balance of convenience;

(6) maintenance of the status quo pending trial;

(7) if they are extremely clear, the merits may be taken into account.

(5) Writ *ne exeat regno*

The court can prevent a person from leaving the jurisdiction if: **24.05**

(1) there is a good arguable case of a claim in debt (not damages);

(2) it is more than nominal in amount;

(3) there is probable cause to believe that without this relief the defendant will leave the jurisdiction;

(4) any such leaving will have a prejudicial effect on the claimant.

(6) *Bayer v Winter* order

The court has jurisdiction to grant this order taking the passport away from an   **24.06**
individual under s 37 of the Supreme Court Act 1981 whenever it is just and convenient so to do.

B. Introduction

English law does not provide security for judgment. A claimant is not entitled   **24.07**
to ask the court to secure assets belonging to the defendant simply and solely to enable them to be available should the claimant obtain a judgment against the defendant.[5] This principle remains unaltered notwithstanding the strength of the merits of the claim. There always remains a risk, therefore, that a claimant might find, at the conclusion of the trial, that there are few valuable assets against which enforcement of the judgment might take place. Such is considered the normal risk of litigation.[6]

What is not tolerated by English law is where a defendant may take certain steps,   **24.08**
outside of his usual business activities, in order deliberately to dissipate or transfer

---

[5] *Robinson v Pickering* (1881) 16 Ch D 660 per James LJ: 'you cannot get an injunction to restrain a man who is alleged to be a debtor from parting with his property'.

[6] An experienced litigator will typically undertake inquiries early on in the investigation to determine the net worth of a defendant and existence of assets against which enforcement might take place. Such inquiries are commonplace and form an important part of the decision-making process whether to pursue litigation against a certain individual.

his assets so that they will not be available to meet any judgment the English court might award. Such a defendant is not playing by the rules. He is attempting to subvert the judicial process, in the event that judgment is obtained against him. Such conduct is exactly that which attracts the attention of the English court. It should be noted, at the outset, that the court looks to the *effect* of the respondent's conduct and not his motive or intention in carrying out such conduct.

24.09   The difficulty in recent years is that confusion has crept slowly into this area based upon two submissions typically made to the court at an *ex parte* hearing. First, the court is told that it is clear that no nefarious intent need be proven on the part of the defendant. Secondly, the court is provided with the usual extract from *The Ninemia*[7] which talks of needing only to show a real risk the judgment will go unsatisfied.[8] These two submissions, taken together, suggest proving a real risk the judgment may go unsatisfied suffices for the purposes of the freezing order jurisdiction. It does not. With the recent decision of Walker J in *Mobil Cerro Negro Limited v Petroleos de Venezuelas SA*,[9] together with the renewed reliance upon two decisions of the Court of Appeal, *Ketchum International v Group Public Relations Holdings*[10] and *Mediterranean Feeders v Berndt Meyering Schiffahrts*,[11] both of which assert the need to establish unjustifiable dissipation—something more than a mere risk of the judgment going unsatisfied, it is to be hoped that there is a new-found respect for the requirements of this draconian order.

24.10   It is worth noting that even if a freezing injunction is granted, it does not afford the claimant any priority or security over the assets in the event of the insolvency of the defendant. It does not prevent another judgment debtor enforcing his judgment debt against those assets. Irrespective of the existence of the injunction, those assets remain available for distribution in the usual way in the insolvency of the defendant.[12] It is a common misconception that the party who has obtained the freezing injunction has some form of priority over other judgment creditors of the defendant. This is not so.

---

[7] *Ninemia Maritime Corp v Trave Schiffarhrtsgesellschaft GmbH (The Niedersachen)* [1983] 1 WLR 1412, 1422: '. . . the test is whether, on the assumption that the plaintiffs have shown at least "a good arguable case", the court concludes, on the whole of the evidence then before it, that the refusal of a Mareva injunction would involve a real risk that a judgment or award in favour of the plaintiffs would remain unsatisfied.'

[8] On its own, and as will be shown in the text, this oft-quoted extract is misleading. Taken at face value, it would support the granting of Mareva relief whenever there was a risk that a judgment might go unsatisfied. That is not correct.

[9] [2008] EWHC 532, unreported, 20 March 2008 (Comm).

[10] [1997] 1 WLR 4, 10 (Stuart-Smith LJ).

[11] June 1997, unreported.

[12] *A J Bekhor and Co Ltd v Bilton* [1981] QB 923. The consequences of obtaining freezing order relief are discussed in greater detail below.

In addition to the typical freezing injunction, given in aid of English proceedings,   **24.11**
whether on a worldwide or domestic basis, this chapter will also examine three
further principal injunctions.

The first is the freezing injunction in aid of foreign proceedings. Such injunctions   **24.12**
are made available to assist a claimant in foreign proceedings to obtain interim
relief, notably freezing of assets and/or disclosure of information. Whilst the general
criteria for granting freezing order relief remains the same for such injunctions,
there are special considerations which need to be taken into account before the
court is willing to grant such relief.

The second is an injunction in aid of proprietary rights, sometimes better but   **24.13**
somewhat inaccurately known as a tracing injunction. This is a different animal
entirely to the freezing injunction. It is premised upon the existence of a proprietary claim, i.e. an assertion of proprietary interest in certain property or its traceable proceeds. Rather than freezing all assets of the defendant up to a specific level
(i.e. the amount of the overall claim plus a little extra for costs and interest), the
proprietary injunction freezes the specific asset or assets which are the subject matter of the proprietary claim. Such injunctions have different requirements from
the typical freezing injunction and have a different bearing on whether and to
what extent the defendant might be permitted to make use of the frozen asset to
meet ongoing liabilities such as legal fees.

Finally, by way of introduction, this chapter will also briefly examine the interim   **24.14**
injunction. Its main use in a fraud setting relates to performance bonds and bank
guarantees where one party is seeking to prevent the bank from paying out on the
ground of fraud. We shall examine the usual requirements for this type of an injunction and then focus on the specific requirements in the performance bond context.

The various types of interim relief outlined in this chapter feature heavily in   **24.15**
the workload of a commercial fraud litigator. Decisions need to be taken swiftly as
to whether a case is suitable for such relief and if so to have applications issued
without delay—remembering that the first few days of a fraud can be crucial to
the ultimate success of any recoveries of the proceeds of the fraud. All this means
that practitioners within this area must be very familiar with the requirements of
each of the types of relief discussed below and their respective benefits and
disadvantages.

C. Freezing Injunctions in General

(1) Outline of development

Prior to the introduction of the freezing injunction, it was well established in   **24.16**
equity that unless and until an applicant could assert a legal or beneficial interest

in the fund of assets held by a debtor, no injunction would be granted to prevent a debtor from dealing with what amounted to his assets prior to judgment being obtained.[13]

24.17 The modern day freezing injunction jurisdiction was developed in two Court of Appeal cases in 1975, *Nippon Yusen Kaisha v Karageorgis*[14] and the eponymous case of *Mareva Compania Naviera SA v International Bulk Carriers SA*.[15] Both cases concerned defendants resident abroad being prevented from dealing with bank accounts within the jurisdiction. It was once thought that the jurisdiction was limited to foreign defendants but s 37(3) of the Supreme Court Act 1981 makes it clear this is not the case.

24.18 There is now a statutory basis for the granting of what became known as Mareva injunctions derived from what is now s 37(1) of the Supreme Court Act 1981 which provides:

(1) The High Court may by order (whether interlocutory or final) grant an injunction or appoint a receiver in all cases in which it appears to the court to be just and convenient to do so.

(2) Any such order may be made unconditionally or on such terms and conditions as the court thinks just.

(3) The power of the High Court . . . to grant an interlocutory injunction restraining a party to any proceedings from removing from the jurisdiction of the High Court, or otherwise dealing with, assets located within that jurisdiction shall be exercisable in cases where that party is, as well as in cases where he is not, domiciled, resident or present within that jurisdiction.

24.19 The development of the Mareva injunction can be divided into six discrete stages. It is not the purpose of this text to give a history lesson in the development of the freezing order jurisdiction but it is important to know, in outline at least, the various stages, since they have a bearing on how the present-day criteria for this relief is presented.[16]

(1) The establishment of the Mareva jurisdiction in 1975 as an exceptional remedy directed against foreign defendants dealing with their assets within the jurisdiction: *Nippon Yusen Kaisha v Karageorgis*;[17] *Mareva Compania Naviera SA v International Bulk Carriers SA*.[18]

---

[13] *Lister & Co v Stubbs* (1890) 45 Ch D 1; *Siskina v Distos Compania Naviera SA* [1979] AC 210, 260–1. See generally, *Spry's Equitable Remedies* (7th edn, Thomson/Sweet and Maxwell, 2007), 515.

[14] [1975] 1 WLR 1093 CA.

[15] [1975] 2 Lloyd's Rep 509 CA.

[16] See Millett LJ in *Credit Suisse Trust v Cuoghi* [1998] QB 818, 824–5.

[17] [1975] 1 WLR 1093 CA.

[18] [1975] 2 Lloyd's Rep 509 CA.

(2) There was a considerable difference of opinion as to whether the jurisdiction could be exercised over an English defendant.[19] In 1979, the jurisdiction was extended to include English defendants: *Third Chandris Shipping Corporation v Unimarine SA*[20] approving dicta to this effect by the Court of Appeal in *Chartered Bank v Daklouche* [1980] 1 WLR 107.[21]

(3) By 1980, the jurisdiction prevented individuals from dissipating their assets within the jurisdiction as well as removing assets from the jurisdiction: *Rahman (Prince Abdul) bin Turki al Sudaiy v Abu Taha*[22] and *Z Ltd v A-Z*.[23]

(4) By 1982, pursuant to s 25 of the CJJA 1982, the jurisdiction was extended to include providing interim relief in favour of substantive proceedings taking place abroad in a Contracting State to the Brussels or Lugano Conventions.[24]

(5) In 1990, the jurisdiction was extended to include preventing defendants from dealing with their assets both within and without the jurisdiction: *Babanaft International Co SA v Bassatne*.[25]

(6) In 1997, s 25 of the CJJA 1982 was extended by the Civil Jurisdiction and Judgments Act 1982 (Interim Relief) Order 1997 (SI 1997/302) so that it was no longer necessary for the foreign substantive proceedings to take place in a contracting state. This extended the jurisdiction of the freezing order to include providing interim relief in respect of non-contracting states including the USA.

It will not have gone unnoticed that originally the jurisdiction to grant freezing order relief was limited to foreign defendants moving their assets from this jurisdiction. It is precisely because of this limitation (now removed) that some of the cases called for the need to establish the existence of assets within the jurisdiction in order to justify obtaining freezing order relief. Such cases now need to be read in the light of the developments outlined above. **24.20**

---

[19] The 'no' camp included Lloyd J in *Van Weelde v Homeric Marine Services* [1979] 2 Lloyd's Rep 117 and also in *Adler Cosmetica v Minnahurst Ltd* (confirmed on appeal)—both cases cited by S Gee QC in *Commercial Injunctions* (5th edn, Thomson/Sweet and Maxwell, 2004), para 1.017.

[20] [1979] QB 645.

[21] Further support came from Lord Hailsham's dicta in the House of Lords in *Siskina v Distos Compania Naviera SA (The Siskina)* [1979] AC 210. Their Lordships in the event did not need to decide the issue. Conflicting CA dicta remained: *Bank Leumi (UK) Ltd v Ricky George Sportain (UK) Ltd* Transcript No 753 of 1979 (cited by Gee in *Commercial Injunctions*).

[22] [1980] 1 WLR 409.

[23] [1982] QB 558, 585F per Kerr LJ: 'The danger of assets being removed from the jurisdiction is only one facet of the "ploy" of a defendant to make himself "judgment-proof" by taking steps to ensure that there are no available or traceable assets on the day of judgment; not as the result of his using his assets in the ordinary course of his business or for living expenses, but to avoid execution by spiriting his assets away in the interim . . . It is therefore logical to extend the scope of this jurisdiction whenever there is a risk of a judgment which a claimant seems likely to obtain being defeated in this way.'

[24] The House of Lords in *The Siskina* [1979] AC 210 had previously held that no injunctive relief could be granted if the substantive proceedings were taking place abroad.

[25] [1990] Ch 13.

24.21 Most recently, the power to grant freezing order relief has been included within the CPR r 25.1(1)(f) which permits the granting of:

> an order (referred to as a 'freezing injunction')—
> (a) restraining a party from removing from the jurisdiction assets located there; or
> (b) restraining a party from dealing with any assets whether located within the jurisdiction or not.

Sub-paragraph (b) makes it clear that it is no longer considered necessary to show the existence of assets within the UK in order to succeed. This is entirely in accordance with the in personam nature of the injunction.[26] So long as the court has jurisdiction over the defendant, it will be able to assert control, through that defendant, over assets situated beyond the court's jurisdiction.

24.22 It can be seen that this jurisdiction is very well established and forms an important part of the commercial fraud litigator's armoury. If it is to be deployed, time is likely to be of the essence in order to freeze assets before they are spirited away and yet this is one form of interim relief which, being one of the nuclear weapons of civil procedure,[27] demands great care in preparation and execution. This is all the more so where the typical application is made 'without notice' or 'ex parte' in old parlance and so the applicant is under a duty of full and frank disclosure to the court. This duty is addressed below.

(2) Rationale

24.23 The rationale for the development of this jurisdiction, which has been very much judge-driven, can be seen in the various comments and observations made by the judiciary in some of the leading cases in this area. Two themes emerge. The first is that the conduct of the defendant merits court intervention and the second is that the court will not stand by and allow a defendant to render a court order or judgment meaningless.

24.24 In *Ghoth v Ghoth*[28] it was said that the purpose behind the Mareva jurisdiction is to protect a claimant 'from a situation in which the assets of the opposing party are run down, either with the intention of making that party judgment-proof or at least having that effect without reasonable excuse'.[29]

---

[26] Of course, if the freezing order is domestic in nature, ie intended to cover only UK-based assets, the court will need to be persuaded that such assets in fact exist in the UK in order for there to be something that the injunction can bite on.

[27] *Bank Mellatt v Nikpour* [1985] FSR 87, 92 CA (the other one is the search order, formerly known as an Anton Piller order).

[28] [1992] 2 All ER 920, 922. This extract helps support the view expressed in this text that the test laid down in *The Ninemia* is both contrary to principle and authority in not requiring anything other than a real risk the judgment go unsatisfied.

[29] The mere fact that there is a risk that the judgment may go unsatisfied is not without more enough to justify relief. It is necessary to show that this might occur 'without reasonable excuse'.

Similarly, in *PCW (Underwriting Agencies) Ltd v Dixon*,[30] Lloyd J commented: **24.25**

> The purpose of the [Mareva] jurisdiction is not to secure priority for the plaintiff, still less, I would add, to punish the defendant for his alleged misdeeds. The sole purpose or justification for the *Mareva* order is to prevent the plaintiffs being cheated[31] out of the proceeds of their action, should it be successful, by the defendant either transferring his assets abroad or dissipating his assets within the jurisdiction: see *Z v A-Z* per Lord Denning at pp.243 and 294 and per Lord Justice Kerr at pp.251 and 306.[32]

In *CBS United Kingsom Ltd v Lambert*,[33] Lawton LJ remarked: **24.26**

> On the facts put before us this was not a case of a plaintiff seeking to freeze a defendant's assets pending trial in anticipation of getting judgment. It was one which seemed to us to show that the first defendant was conducting his affairs with intent to deprive anyone who got judgment against him of the fruits of victory. The Mareva injunction was brought into use to make this kind of behaviour in commercial cases unprofitable.[34]

In *Derby & CO Ltd v Weldon (No. 3 and No. 4)*[35] Lord Donaldson MR noted the **24.27**
careful balancing exercise to be performed by the freezing order jurisdiction:

> The fundamental principle underlying this jurisdiction is that, within the limits of its powers, no court should permit a defendant to take action designed to ensure that subsequent orders of the court are rendered less effective than would otherwise be the case. On the other hand, it is not its purpose to prevent a defendant carrying on business in the ordinary way, or, if an individual, living his life normally pending the determination of the dispute, nor to impede him in any way in defending himself against the claim. Nor is it its purpose to place the plaintiff in the position of a secured creditor. In a word, whilst one of the hazards facing a plaintiff in litigation is that, come the day of judgment, it may not be possible for him to obtain satisfaction of that judgment, fully or at all, the court should not permit the defendant artificially to create such a situation.[36]

Lord Donaldson MR is clear that the freezing order does not create a security right **24.28**
over the defendant's assets. It does not operate as an attachment which fastens onto particular assets, to ensure that those assets are available for the enforcement of any subsequent judgment. Freezing injunctions operate in personam—against the individual defendant and not his assets specifically. The defendant as owner is

---

30 [1983] 2 Lloyd's Rep 197.
31 Again, note the connotation of doing something untoward, not playing by the rules.
32 ibid, 201, col 1.
33 [1983] Ch 37.
34 ibid, 42A–B.
35 [1990] Ch 65.
36 ibid, 76.

simply prevented from doing various tasks with his own assets.[37] No proprietary interest in the frozen assets is created.[38]

(3) Effects of injunctive relief

24.29 It has already been established that a freezing order does not create any proprietary or security interest in or over the relevant assets which are subject to the order.[39] Nor does it provide the holder of such injunctive relief with any priority over any other debtor's judgment creditors.

24.30 That said, it is a powerful weapon whose practical effects should not be underestimated. It is likely to bring the respondent's banking operations to a grinding halt, since banks, notwithstanding express provision within the standard order for them to be able to continue to operate, typically adopt a cautious approach through concern they do not do anything which might breach the order and place them in contempt of court. This places tremendous pressure on the respondent.

24.31 Trading partners of the respondent are likely to be informed as to the existence and terms of the order. Often they do not understand the full meaning and effect of the order, with the consequence they are reluctant to continue trading with the respondent without insisting on revised and more favourable terms for themselves.

24.32 Perversely, much is made, usually by the claimant, of the stigma to be attached to an individual or business against which such an order has been granted. Credit agencies may review their ratings. Reputations suffer greatly and yet, on the approach advocated in *The Ninemia*, there is no basis for any such stigma to be attached.

24.33 A freezing order is effective on an individual as soon as he has been notified. There is no need for it to have been formally served before it can be effective. That said, by virtue of the manner in which the standard order is drafted, disclosure obligations only take effect after *service* of the order.[40]

---

[37] *Cretanor Maritime Co Ltd v Irish Marine Management Ltd* [1978] 1 WLR 966 (Buckley LJ); see also *Flightline Ltd v Edwards* [2003] EWCA Civ 63, [2003] 1 WLR 1200.

[38] *Cretanor Maritime Co Ltd v Irish Marine Management Ltd* [1978] 1 WLR 966 (Buckley LJ); *Capital Cameras Ltd v Harold Lines Ltd* [1991] 1 WLR 54.

[39] *Cretanor Maritime Co Ltd v Irish Marine Management Ltd* [1978] 1 WLR 966; *Re Multi Guarantee Co Ltd* [1987] BCLC 257; *Bank Mellatt v Kazmi* [1989] QB 541; *Flightline Ltd v Edwards* [2003] 1 WLR 1200. Lord Denning MR had suggested it takes effect in rem: see *Rasu Maritima SA v Perusahaan Pertambangan Minyak Dan Gas Bumi Negara* [1978] QB 644, 657–8; *Z Ltd v A-Z* [1982] QB 558, 573A–C. But Lord Denning MR's comments were per incuriam: *Cretanor Maritime Co Ltd v Irish Marine Ltd*, 974 (Buckley LJ) and see Lord Ackner in *A-G v Times Newspapers Ltd* [1992] 1 AC 191, 215: see A A Zuckerman, *Zuckerman on Civil Procedure* (2nd edn, Thomson/Sweet and Maxwell, 2006), [9.160].

[40] See Clause 9(1): 'Unless paragraph (2) applies, the Respondent must [immediately] [within_____ hours of service of this order]........'.

D. Domestic Freezing Injunction in aid of English Proceedings

This section is concerned with the requirements which need to be satisfied for a **24.34** freezing injunction obtained in aid of English proceedings and concerning assets located within the jurisdiction.

If the applicant requires that the injunction restrain dealings with assets which **24.35** are located both in this jurisdiction *and* abroad, or alternatively just abroad, then in addition to these requirements, the applicant will also need to satisfy the additional requirements of a worldwide freezing injunction (see para 24.98 *et seq* below).

If the applicant is seeking injunctive relief in aid of foreign proceedings and not **24.36** proceedings within this jurisdiction, then his application must, in addition to satisfying the usual requirements for a freezing order set out in this section, also satisfy the additional requirements for relief under s 25 of the CJJA1982 (see para 24.120 *et seq* below).

(1) Accrual of cause of action

Given the existence of the second requirement, namely a good arguable case on **24.37** the merits, it is perhaps not surprising that in order to get a freezing injunction off the ground it is essential (with one possible caveat) that the substantive cause of action has already accrued. If not, and the court is only concerned with a possible future cause of action (which may or may not in fact ever accrue), then no jurisdiction arises.[41]

So, for example, a freezing order over the payment of a purchase price will not be **24.38** considered if the basis of the application is a mere concern, or suspicion that the products, once delivered from the ship, will prove defective.[42] Similarly, freezing order relief is not available prior to the expiry of a contractual period allotted for performance of the respondent's contractual obligations.[43] Until that time has expired, there can be no breach.

This restriction has been criticized at Privy Council level in *Mercedes Benz AG v* **24.39** *Leiduck*[44] by Lord Nicholls[45] who contended that he could see no reason why an

---

[41] *Steamship Mutual v Thakar Shipping Co Ltd* [1986] 2 Lloyd's Rep 439.

[42] *Veracruz Transportation Inc v VC Shipping Co Inc* [1992] 1 Lloyd's Rep 353 criticized LA Collins (1992) 108 LQR 175.

[43] *Zucker v Tyndall Holdings plc* [1993] 1 All ER 124 (relief sought three months before respondent required to transfer shares). See also *The P* [1992] 1 Lloyd's Rep 470; *Re Q's Estate* [1999] 1 Lloyd's Rep 931.

[44] [1996] AC 284, 312.

[45] Lord Nicholls was dissenting on a point not dealt with by the majority.

anticipatory injunction could not be granted and expressed a preference for the Australian authorities on this issue.[46]

24.40 The English authorities which establish the proposition that a contingent cause of action does not suffice for the purposes of obtaining freezing order relief are cases concerning *legal* rights. As *DJ Rowland v Gulfpac*[47] indicates, a rather more fluid approach appears possible when dealing with equitable claims arising under an indemnity.

24.41 In *DJ Rowland*, Rix J stated:

> In law there is no right to Mareva relief unless there is a pre-existing cause of action. Equity, however, will give relief in circumstances where the common law will not and will even give relief in a situation of quia timet before a loss has actually occurred, but only when there is a reasonably good, perhaps clear, evidence that a liability will fall on the party entitled to be indemnified and that the person obliged to indemnify clearly proposes to ignore his obligations. What is needed is a sufficiently clear right to an indemnity even if the cause of action at law is not yet complete, together with a clear indication that the indemnifier is going to ignore his obligations.[48]

It therefore seems to be irrelevant in equity, in the case of a right to an indemnity, that the cause of action at law has not yet been completed, if the equitable right is sufficiently clear and there is clear evidence of a threat by the indemnifier to ignore his obligations.

24.42 The *quia timet* equitable jurisdiction exists to protect an applicant in circumstances where there is a clear *threatened* (but no actual) infringement of his rights. The authorities tend to relate to contracts of indemnity and it is easy to see why. If X has the benefit of an indemnity from Y that X will be held harmless as regards any liability due to Z, then X may be entitled to *quia timet* relief in circumstances where X has threatened not to comply with his obligations to hold X harmless to Z.

24.43 One of the authorities relied upon by Rix J in *DJ Rowland* is the Court of Appeal's decision in *Re Anderson-Berry*[49] where Lord Hanworth described the *quia timet* action as 'a course of procedure which prevents the Court from allowing its action to be stultified'. In other words, the *quia timet* action fills a gap where a strict adherence to the common law need for an accrued cause of action might well result in the applicant being prevented from obtaining any relief at all for the clear wrongdoing of another.

---

[46] See *Patterson v BTR Engineering (Australia) Ltd* (1989) 18 NSWLR 319 (NSWCA); *Dicey & Morris* (14th edn), para 8-009.

[47] [1999] Lloyd's Rep Bank 86; see also *Re Q's Estate* [1999] 1 Lloyd's Rep 931, 939.

[48] [1999] Lloyd's Rep Bank 86, 98.

[49] [1928] 1 Ch 290.

In *Papamichael v National Westminster Bank plc*,[50] his Honour Judge Chambers **24.44**
QC (sitting as a Commercial Court Judge) confirmed the use of the *quia timet*
injunction to circumvent the restrictions of the common law. However, the
judge was keen to emphasize that it would not be correct or helpful to construe
what Rix J said in *D J Rowland v Gulpac* with a 'scholastic rigidity' or too
narrowly.[51]

What needs to be shown is that in the event of the occurrence of the contingency, **24.45**
there will be a right over the person against whom the relief is sought. If this jurisdictional requirement is met, the remainder is a discretionary exercise, balancing
the severity of the relief sought against the degree of the perceived threat.

Subject to the possible application of the *quia timet* jurisdiction, the position **24.46**
remains that an applicant must establish that his cause of action has in fact accrued
prior to applying for freezing order relief.

(2) Cause of action justiciable in England and Wales

The freezing injunction is no more than an interim remedy. It is not in itself a **24.47**
cause of action. It is ancillary to a cause of action and is intended, as we have seen,
to preserve the respondent's assets pending the outcome of the litigation. English
law will not permit the freezing injunction to be self-standing.[52] The injunction
can only exist to support substantive proceedings.

It is important to note that the requirement that the cause of action be justiciable **24.48**
in England and Wales derives, not from some objective requirement of the freezing injunction jurisdiction, but from the simple fact that the type of injunction
being dealt with in this section is one which is in aid of proceedings in England
and Wales. It is true that initially the freezing injunction had been limited to proceedings within this jurisdiction but this is no longer the case.

The grounds upon which the court can take jurisdiction over the various claims **24.49**
which might arise in a commercial fraud are identified and discussed in some
detail in Chapter 19 on jurisdiction.

If the cause of action is not one over which the English court has jurisdiction, the **24.50**
applicant should consider whether the facts merit an application under s 25 of the
CJJA 1982 (see below).

---

[50] [2002] 1 Lloyd's Rep 332.
[51] ibid, [53], [69].
[52] *The Siskina* [1979] AC 210 (HL); *Credit Suisse Fides Trust SA v Cuoghi* [1998] QB 818;
Department of Social Security v Butler [1995] 1 WLR 1528.

(3) A good arguable case on the merits

24.51   In addition to evidencing the existence of a cause of action, the applicant must persuade the court that there is a good arguable case on the merits.[53] This is not a high threshold. It is not to be equated with the test for summary judgment.[54]

24.52   Guidance has been provided by Mustill J in *Ninemia Maritime Corpn v Trave*:[55]

> . . . the [applicant] need not go so far as to persuade the judge that he is likely to win [at trial] . . . The right course is to adopt the test of a good, arguable case, in the sense of a case which is more than barely capable of serious argument, and yet not necessarily one which the judge believes to have a better than fifty per cent chance of success.

24.53   So, while the jurisdictional threshold on the merits is not high, the applicant should well remember that the granting of this relief is discretionary. The more that the court can be persuaded, by the evidence set out in the affidavits sworn in support of the application, that the applicant's case is meritorious, the greater the likelihood that the court would be willing to grant the injunctive relief. That does not mean, however, that a certain claim is guaranteed the protection of a freezing order.

24.54   Of course, the desire of the applicant to show and persuade the court of the merits of his case must be tempered by a realization that the affidavit must be drafted with the applicant's duty of full and frank disclosure very much in mind. There is little point in telling a good story to obtain an injunction at the without notice hearing only for it to be discharged on the Return Date, with the consequence that the client faces the possibility of enforcement of the cross-undertakings in damages for having wrongly obtained an injunction.

(4) Assets held by the respondent

(a) Nature of assets

24.55   A freezing injunction can be granted in respect of a wide range of assets, ranging from tangible assets such as aeroplanes,[56] ships,[57] ships' bunkers,[58] machinery,[59] to

---

[53] *Rasu Maritima SA v Perusahaan* [1978] QB 644.

[54] ibid, 661F–G, 664F.

[55] [1983] 2 Lloyd's Rep 600. Mustill J's view was expressly approved by Kerr LJ on appeal: [1983] 1 WLR 1412.

[56] *Allen v Jambo Holdings* [1980] 1 WLR 1252.

[57] E.g. *The Rena K* [1979] QB 377. Also includes time charterers' bunkers and cargo: *Clipper Maritime Co of Monrovia v Mineralimportexport, The Marie Leonhardt* [1981] 1 WLR 1262.

[58] *Sanko Steamship Co Ltd v D C Commodities (Australasia) Pty Ltd* (1980) WLR 51. This is the fuel oil stored in 'bunkers' on board a vessel.

[59] *Rasu Maritima SA v Perusahaan* [1978] QB 644 (parts for a fertiliser plant—the CA held no injunction appropriate given the minimum scrap value of the assets).

intangible assets including business goodwill,[60] and other choses in action (such as credits or even overdrafts[61] in bank accounts).

Although a cause of action might be viewed as an asset in the hands of a claimant, **24.56** a court will be reluctant to become embroiled in arguments as to whether the settlement of that litigation amounts to a dissipation of assets at an undervalue. In *Normid Housing Association Ltd v Ralphs & Mansell*,[62] Lloyd LJ indicated his view that this would create 'insuperable practicable difficulties' for the court, which would have to familiarize itself as to the merits of the underlying dispute. The better answer if a claimant is concerned as to how a respondent may deal with the claim he has is to obtain a direction that the claimant pursue a watching brief over that litigation and before any settlement takes place, the respondent provides prior written notice to the claimant, who then is able to assess whether the settlement appears at face value to be genuine. It is suggested, following from Lloyd LJ's attitude as exhibited in *Normid Housing* that there would need to be some reasonably clear evidence that the settlement or potential settlement was not at arm's length before the court would become interested.

Again, whilst there can be no doubt that land amounts to an asset, it is a type of **24.57** asset, or tangible immovable, which is not so readily dissipated or transferred out of the jurisdiction. Of course, land can be sold and the freezing order can accommodate the need to catch any proceeds of the sale of the property.[63] A court might be less inclined to grant freezing injunction relief simply in relation to land.

It should also be noted that the freezing injunction is not limited to those assets **24.58** held by the respondent at the time of the injunction having been granted. It also includes all after-acquired assets, subject to the maximum level of the freezing injunction.[64]

A respondent remains free to incur or increase its existing indebtedness by bor- **24.59** rowing further sums notwithstanding being subject to a freezing order.[65]

---

[60] *Darashah v UFAC UK Ltd, The Times,* 30 March 1982.
[61] *Third Chandris Shipping Corporation v Unimarine SA* [1979] QB 645. The court considered that the existence of an overdraft facility might give rise to an inference of the presence of assets within the location, particularly if the overdraft had to be secured.
[62] [1989] 1 Lloyd's Rep 265.
[63] The standard wording in the official draft order is: 'the property known as [address] or the net sale money after payment of any mortgages if it has been sold'.
[64] *TDK Tape Distributor (UK) Ltd v Videochoice Ltd* [1986] 1 WLR 141.
[65] *Cantor Index Ltd v Lister* unrep, 22 November 2001 (Neuberger J); *Anglo Eastern Trust Ltd v Kermanshahci* [2002] EWHC 1702 (Ch) 5 July 2002 unrep (Neuberger J). It is suggested that such additional borrowing should be subject to careful scrutiny by the court and/or the opposing party since that borrowing is likely, ultimately, to lead to the reduction in assets since the borrowing may be repaid via the sale of assets. If the borrowing is out of the ordinary, and is not to cover the usual living expenses or business expenses, the increase in indebtedness and ultimate corresponding reduction in assets is 'unjustifiable'.

(b) Location of assets

24.60 It is sometimes said that it is a condition of entitlement to obtain freezing injunctive relief that the applicant establishes the existence of assets within this jurisdiction.[66] Often those texts can refer to earlier authorities which appear to support that proposition. The actual position, now, is that it is not an essential requirement for an applicant to establish the existence of assets held by the respondent within this jurisdiction. Many of those earlier authorities derive from a time when the freezing injunction was in its early stages of development and was limited to dealing with assets within this jurisdiction. As we have seen, it has moved on significantly since those stages.

24.61 That said, it is undoubtedly the case that the applicant must establish that the respondent has some assets somewhere and additional requirements may need to be established if the only assets of the respondent are said to be located abroad.

24.62 Conversely, if the only assets of the respondent are found to be located within this jurisdiction, that is a good reason for limiting the freezing injunction to a domestic injunction. As Lord Donaldson MR commented in *Derby v Weldon (No 3 and No 4)*:[67]

> . . . the existence of sufficient assets within the jurisdiction is an excellent reason for confining the jurisdiction to such assets, but, other considerations apart, the fewer the assets within the jurisdiction, the greater the necessity for taking protective measures in relation to those outside it.[68]

24.63 The absence of any need to show assets within this jurisdiction became obvious when the freezing injunction jurisdiction was extended to include assets located worldwide [69] and is now expressly recognized by the wording of CPR r 25(1)(g)(b) set out above.

24.64 All this simply supports the obvious fact that freezing injunctions act in personam and not in rem. They are directed towards, and at, the individual and not his assets. The control over the assets is exercised via the control over the individual and so the crucial factor for the success of a freezing injunction is personal jurisdiction by the English court over the respondent. If the court has that, it can

---

[66] E.g. D Bean QC, *Injunctions* (8th edn, Thomson/Sweet and Maxwell, 2004). This is an excellent treatise on injunctive relief and the author does go on to identify the availability of injunctive relief without establishing the existence of assets within this jurisdiction. The issue in the text is whether it is appropriate to say at the outset that an applicant must show assets within the jurisdiction.

[67] [1990] 1 Ch 65, 79.

[68] ibid.

[69] *Babanaft Co SA v Bassatne* [1990] Ch 13; *Republic of Haiti v Duvalier* [1990] 1 QB 202; *Derby & Co Ltd v Weldon* [1990] Ch 48; *Derby & Co Ltd v Weldon (No 3 and No 4)* [1990] Ch 65. See also the excellent discussion of the territorial reach of the freezing injunction by L A Collins, 'The Territorial Reach of Mareva Injunctions' (1989) 105 LQR 262.

even direct that the respondent take steps to transfer certain assets *into* this jurisdiction.[70]

(c) Nature of respondent's interest in assets

The freezing injunction is intended, within limits, to preserve assets from dissipa- **24.65** tion so as to enable the execution of judgment against them. Accordingly, the only relevant assets for present purposes are those against which execution of a judgment obtained against the respondent can be levied.

In general, the respondent must have a legal or equitable interest in the assets sub- **24.66** ject to a freezing injunction since it is only that level of interest which will entitle the judgment debt to be executed against such assets.[71] However, the courts have recently shown a willingness to take bold measures against attempts by defendants to conceal assets behind trusts or shadowy offshore companies or arrangements.

In *Dadourian Group International v Azuri Ltd*[72] the court extended the *Chabra*[73] **24.67** jurisdiction beyond assets held on a bare trust to instances where it was appropriate to prevent evasion of court orders by manipulation of shadowy offshore trusts and companies formed in jurisdictions where there was little regulation and a great deal of secrecy.[74] Ultimately, behind such moves by the court is a belief, generated by evidence of the conduct of the respondent and the relevant third parties, that the respondent's control or apparent control over such assets indicates likely legal or beneficial ownership.

Similarly, in *Marlwood Commercial Incorporated v Viktor Kozeny & Ors*,[75] the court **24.68** was willing to include within the freezing order assets said to belong to his mother. The court's conclusion was based in part on the inconsistencies in the defendant's account of his assets and the lack of disclosure of the type of documentation which one would readily expect to see disclosed. In other words, if the court gains the view that a defendant is failing to comply with its disclosure obligations and/or is trying to be clever and hide behind offshore trusts and companies, it may well simply form the provisional view that certain assets do in fact fall within the terms of the order.

---

[70] *Derby & Co Ltd v Weldon (No 6)* [1990] 1 WLR 1139 CA; N Andrews, *English Civil Procedure* (Oxford University Press, 2003), para 17.104.

[71] *C Inc v L* [2001] 2 Lloyd's Rep 459, 467–8 per Aikens J; *Federal Bank of the Middle East Ltd v Hadkinson* [2000] 2 All ER 395.

[72] [2005] EWHC 1768 (Ch) (Edward Bartley Jones QC).

[73] *TSB Private Bank International v Chabra* [1992] 1 WLR 231.

[74] See *Intenational Credit & Investment Co (Overseas) Ltd v Adham* (1998) BCC 134, 136 (strong comments from Robert Walker J).

[75] [2007] EWHC 950 (Comm). Judge Mackie QC applied *SCF Finance v Masri (No 1)* [1985] 1 WLR 876; *Dadourian Group International v Azuri Ltd* [2005] EWHC 1768 (Ch).

24.69 If the respondent is simply holding those assets for another party, and does not have any legal or equitable interest in them, those assets would not be available to meet any judgment execution and therefore, in principle, should not be included in the order and cannot be made subject to a freezing injunction. So if the respondent is holding assets as a bare trustee, those assets will fall outside the terms of the order (in the standard form: it remains open expressly to include, by way of drafting, assets under the respondent's control).

24.70 The ability to obtain a freezing injunction over assets held by the respondent but purportedly on behalf of a third party is examined separately below.

(d) Assets held or purportedly held on behalf of third parties[76]

24.71 One issue which arises on a regular basis is whether the assets which appear caught by the terms of the freezing order in fact belong, legally or beneficially, to the respondent or an independent third party. If they do not, such assets would not be available to meet any judgment debt and so fall outwith the terms of the standard freezing order.

24.72 So, in *Westpac Banking Corporation v Gill (No 1)*[77] Heron J, in discharging the order vis-à-vis certain assets held by the respondent on trust:

> in which the defendant has some beneficial interest entitling him to deal with them as his own property. It goes without saying, it is against that property the plaintiffs are seeking recourse in the ultimate if judgment is obtained.[78]

> To similar effect is Mummery LJ in *Federal Bank of the Middle East Ltd v Hadkinson*.[79] In *Federal Bank*, Mummery LJ was faced with a standard form order ('his assets and/or funds') and concluded such wording 'naturally refers to assets and funds belonging to the defendant and which are and should remain available to satisfy the claim against him. Assets and funds which belong . . . beneficially to someone else would not be available for that purpose'.[80]

24.73 If it is alleged that the assets in fact belong to a third party, the court is empowered to join that third party to the proceedings and directions may be given for service of evidence and generally to have the issue resolved prior to or at the

---

[76] See generally, P Devonshire, 'The Implications of Third Parties Holding Assets Subject to a Mareva Injunction' [1996] LMCLQ 268; 'Mareva Injunctions and Third Parties: Exposing the Sub-Text' (1999) 62 MLR 539; 'Freezing Orders, Disappearing Assets and the Problem of Enjoining Non-Parties' (2002) 118 LQR 124. *Z Ltd v A-Z* [1982] QB 558; *S C F Finance Co Ltd v Masri* [1985] 1 WLR 876; *Mercantile Group (Europe) AG v Aiyela* [1994] QB 366; *C Inc v L* [2001] Lloyd's Rep 459; *TSB Private Bank v Chabra* [1992] 1 WLR 231.
[77] (1987) 2 PRNZ 52, 56; see also P Devonshire, 'Mareva Injunctions and Third Parties: Exposing the Subtext' (1999) 62 MLR 539.
[78] *Westpac Banking Corporation v Gill (No 1)* (1987) 2 PRNZ 52, 56.
[79] [2000] 1 WLR 1695.
[80] ibid, 1709H.

main trial.[81] *When* the issue is to be resolved will involve a balancing exercise of the various interests and rights and which would be prejudiced the greater by any delay in having the matter resolved.

In *SCF Finance v Masri*,[82] the Court of Appeal laid down the following guidelines: **24.74**

(i) Where a plaintiff invites the court to include within the scope of a Mareva injunction assets which appear on their face to belong to a third party, the court should not accede to the invitation without good reason for supposing that the assets are in truth the assets of the defendants.
(ii) Where the defendant asserts that the assets belong to a third party the court is not obliged to accept that assertion without inquiry, but may do so depending on the circumstances. The same applies where it is the third party who makes the assertion, on an application to intervene.
(iii) In deciding whether to accept the assertion of a defendant or a third party, without further inquiry, the court will be guided by what is just and convenient, not only between the plaintiff and the defendant, but also between the plaintiff, the defendant and the third party.
(iv) Where the court decides not to accept the assertion without further inquiry, it may order an issue to be tried between the plaintiff and the third party in advance of the main action, or it may order that the issue await the outcome of the main action, again depending in each case on what is just and convenient.[83]

In *TSB Private Bank International SA v Chabra*[84] the claimant bank brought pro- **24.75** ceedings against the defendant on the back of a personal guarantee. The defendant was the majority shareholder in a UK company. The claimant obtained a freezing order against the defendant restraining the defendant from removing or disposing of the proceeds of sale of certain business assets belonging to the UK company. Mummery J held that the presence of the UK company was necessary to resolve all issues and so it could be joined as a party to the proceedings. Further, the court held that an injunction against the defendant alone was insufficient to protect the claimant's interests and so it was justifiable extending the order to include the UK company.

(5) A real risk of dissipation—judgment may go unsatisfied

This is the heart of the jurisdiction to grant freezing order relief. It is precisely **24.76** because of the real risk of dissipation of assets that injunctive relief is justified:

> . . . the authorities clearly show that in order to obtain a Mareva injunction, the plaintiffs must show that they would suffer some prejudice as a result of what the

---

[81] *Z Ltd v A-Z* [1982] QB 558; *S C F Finance Co Ltd v Masri* [1985] 1 WLR 876; *Mercantile Group (Europe) AG v Aiyela* [1994] QB 366.
[82] [1985] 1 WLR 876.
[83] ibid, 884.
[84] [1992] 1 WLR 231.

judge referred to in his second question as a 'dissipation of assets' in the event of the injunction being refused. The issue is as to the test which the plaintiffs must satisfy . . . In our view the test is whether, on the assumption that the plaintiffs have shown at least 'a good arguable case', the court concludes, on the whole of the evidence then before it, that the refusal of a Mareva injunction would involve a real risk that a judgment or award in favour of the plaintiffs would remain unsatisfied.[85]

24.77 But it is not every case of dissipation leaving a judgment unsatisfied which justifies injunctive relief. The application of this test involves balancing at least four principles.

(1) That the freezing injunction is not intended to provide security for judgment. If it was, it would cover all and every example of dissipation of assets, whatever the cause. We know that it does not. On that basis alone, the *Ninemia* test cannot be correct.

(2) That the freezing injunction does not prevent the respondent from continuing to carry on normal business transactions and incurring the usual living expenses. The fact that these activities might result in no or reduced assets available for any execution of a judgment is irrelevant.

(3) That the respondent is not entitled to dissipate assets with the consequence that none are available to meet any likely judgment. On its own, this proposition is misleading and requires elaboration.

(4) There is no need to show that the respondent is behaving unconscionably or in bad faith in order to invoke this jurisdiction.[86]

24.78 The difficulty is that once it is accepted that the freezing injunction does not provide security for judgment and there is no requirement to show nefarious intent on the part of the respondent, it is not entirely clear where the line between permissible and impermissible dissipation is to be drawn. One might not unreasonably conclude that if there is no need to show unconscionable conduct on the respondent's part, all forms of dissipation leaving the judgment unsatisfied will suffice. Indeed, the comments quoted above from Kerr LJ would tend to support such a view. But we know because of propositions (1) and (2) that this is not the case.

24.79 The one aspect of the test which is missing from the extract from *The Ninemia* is any reference to the need for the risk of the judgment going unsatisfied to be based on 'unjustifiable conduct'. In the Court of Appeal in *Ketchum International v Group Public Relations Holdings* [1997] 1 WLR 4, Stuart-Smith LJ observed that

---

[85] *Ninemia Maritime Corporation v Trave Schiffahrtsgesellschaft mbH und Co KG* [1983] 1 WLR 1412, 1422E–H per Kerr LJ.

[86] And yet the inference claimants ask third parties and the court to draw, having obtained such an injunction, is precisely that: namely that the respondent was likely to behave badly in respect of his or its assets. It is not a satisfactory state of affairs.

'the court should be able to take steps to ensure that its judgments are not rendered valueless by an unjustifiable disposal of assets'.[87] See similar views expressed by the Court of Appeal in *Mediterranean Feeders v Berndt Meyering Schiffahrts*.[88] Failing to refer to the test of unjustifiable conduct and these two Court of Appeal authorities in particular was one of the grounds upon which Walker J discharged the worldwide freezing order obtained in *Mobil Cerro Negro Ltd v PDVSA* [2008] EWHC 532.

So the conduct leading to the dissipation must be 'unjustifiable' and one way of establishing that is to show that there was a risk that the assets would be dissipated otherwise than for normal and proper commercial purposes. **24.80**

The 'evil' which the court seeks to prevent is any judgment or award remaining unsatisfied because of an *unjustifiable* dissipation of the assets. Although there has been some confusion in the authorities,[89] it is clear now that the court's focus is on the *effect* of the respondent's conduct and not whether the respondent undertook that activity with any intention or design to dissipate assets.[90] **24.81**

Dissipation can take several forms and includes any act of alienation, charging or pledging of property.[91] **24.82**

Very often the evidence of risk of dissipation will need to be carefully collated and presented. It will be a rare day that an applicant can refer to an actual statement on the part of the respondent that he intends to dissipate his assets and so it will usually be necessary to build an inference of that based upon various factors including the following. **24.83**

(1) Is there anything in the nature of the substantive dispute which suggests or supports a concern that the respondent might dissipate his or its assets? For example, if the complaint is that the respondent, as the applicant's finance director, has allegedly misappropriated assets belonging to the applicant, then such material can be relied upon to show a real risk of dissipation.[92]

---

87 [1997] 1 WLR 4, 10.

88 Unreported, June 1997: 'there must be a risk that it [the asset] will be used otherwise than for normal and proper commercial purposes'.

89 It had been suggested in *Derby & Co Ltd v Weldon (No 3 and No 4)* [1990] Ch 65, 76 that the applicant had to show that the respondent intended or had designed to dissipate his assets. This is not considered necessary and Lord Donaldson MR's words have been re-interpreted: *R v Secretary of State for the Home Department ex p Muboyayi* [1992] QB 244, 257H.

90 *The Niedersachsen* [1983] 1 WLR 1412, 1422; *Ketchum International plc v Group Public Relations* [1997] 1 WLR 4, 13A-D; *R v Secretary of State for the Home Department ex p Muboyayi* [1992] QB 244, 257H; Gee, *Commercial Injunctions* (5th edn), [12-032]–[12-033].

91 *CBS UK Ltd v Lambert* [1983] Ch 37, 42 (Lawton LJ); *Z Ltd v A-Z* [1982] 1 QB 558, 571 (Lord Denning MR).

92 *Guinness plc v Saunders*, *Independent*, 15 April 1987.

(2) Is the respondent domiciled in a tax haven or other jurisdiction which has a reputation for weak company legislation or enforcement?

(3) Is it known whether there are any outstanding judgments, awards or other fines which the respondent has failed or refused to pay? Or, does the respondent in fact have an excellent track record of meeting its debts? If so, the applicant's duty of full and frank disclosure requires this to be disclosed to the court.

(4) Does the respondent have a long-standing reputation in business? What does the respondent's credit report reveal? Is the respondent a 'fly-by-night' trader or well established over many years?

(5) Are the respondent's assets of a type which can readily be dissipated or transferred out of the jurisdiction e.g. money, movable chattels as opposed to land or real estate?

(6) What connections does the respondent have to this jurisdiction? Is it his main home? Do his children go to school here? How long has he lived here? Such factors would tend to suggest the respondent was less likely to be willing simply to 'walk away' and leave the judgment unsatisfied.

(7) Has the respondent filed all the necessary accounts and tax returns required by the relevant governing law?

(8) Where are the respondent's assets located? Is it a Judgments Convention state or another jurisdiction such that enforcement of an English judgment would be straightforward?[93]

(9) At the Return Date, has the respondent failed to provide basic information as to its assets which one might reasonably have expected it to provide?

24.84 None of these factors is necessarily decisive in themselves on the issue but they do illustrate the range of material which might be adduced to persuade a court to grant freezing order relief.[94]

24.85 The burden is on the applicant to adduce 'solid evidence' of dissipation[95]—unsupported statements or allegations will not suffice.

---

[93] E.g. *Montecchi v Shimco (UK) Ltd* [1979] 1 WLR 1180. In *Mobil Cerro Negro Ltd v PDVSA* [2008] EWHC 532 Walker J was prepared to accept counsel's submission that: 'There is a real risk of disposal where even an apparently financially solid company transfers its assets outside the jurisdiction if enforcement overseas would cause extra costs and delays: *Stronghold Insurance Co Ltd v Overseas Union Insurance Ltd* [1996] LRLR 13, 18–19, per Potter J. Provided the claimant can demonstrate that the effect of the transfer would be to make the enforcement of any judgment more difficult, it will have discharged the burden of demonstrating a real risk of disposal' [38].

[94] In *Government of Sierra Leone v Davenport* unrep, 11 April 2001 (Ch), Peter Leaver QC, sitting as a deputy judge of the Chancery Division, held that there existed a risk of dissipation on the facts. His conclusion was based, in part, on the respondent's failure to disclose his assets.

[95] *The Niedersachsen* [1983] 2 Lloyd's Rep 600, 606–7.

(6) Discretion

Even if the applicant manages to satisfy each of the above requirements, the court **24.86** retains a discretion whether or not to grant the freezing order. It is impossible to list all factors which go to the court's exercise of that discretion. Such a list will no doubt include:

(1) assessment of merits of underlying claim;
(2) strength of allegation of dissipation;
(3) whether injunctive relief is really necessary;
(4) comparison in value between claim made and assets to be frozen. If the latter is of little value relative to the former, the court might refuse to exercise its discretion.[96] Similarly, the court might consider the value of the claim to be so small that it does not justify the use of such a draconian weapon;[97]
(5) conduct of the applicant;[98]
(6) consequences of granting the relief sought on the applicant and on the respondent. If the respondent is a bank or financial institution whose reputation might collapse once it became known of the imposition of freezing relief, the court will take that into account in determining whether to exercise its discretion.[99]

(7) Ancillary disclosure

The court has jurisdiction to order ancillary disclosure of documents and infor- **24.87** mation relevant to the nature, extent and location of the respondent's assets: CPR r 25.1(1)(g).[100]

Importantly, such disclosure orders are typically not limited to the respondent **24.88** himself but extend to third parties such as the respondent's known bankers.[101]

This jurisdiction is principally designed to assist in the policing of the injunction **24.89** but its importance goes beyond that role. A respondent subject to such a disclosure order is on the back-foot from the moment the order is served. He must fully disclose his assets or run the risk of being cross-examined on his affidavit evidence and/or, worse still, face an application for contempt if he is found not to have given truthful evidence as to the scope of his assets. Knowledge is said to be power

---

[96] E.g. *Rasu Maritima SA v Perusahaan* [1978] QB 644 CA.
[97] *Sions v Price*, *Independent*, 19 December 1988—claim was only £2,000.
[98] As with any equitable remedy, the applicant must come to court 'with clean hands': see *Rasu Maritima SA v Perusahaan* [1978] QB 644 CA.
[99] For the position in respect of a bank see *Polly Peck International plc v Nadir (No 2)* [1992] 4 All ER 769.
[100] E.g. *A J Bekhor & Co v Bilton* [1981] QB 923, 940; *CBS UK Ltd v Lambert* [1983] Ch 37, 42–3.
[101] *A v C* [1981] QB 956. Disclosure may take the form of a bankers trust order (*Bankers Trust Co v Shapira* [1980] 1 WLR 1274 (CA)) or a *Norwich Pharmacal* order (*Norwich Pharmacal Co v Customs and Excise Commissioners* [1974] AC 133.

in some circumstances and it is certainly true in the context of disclosure ancillary to a freezing order.

24.90 CPR r 25(1)(1)(g) gives the court power to order disclosure not only of assets which *are* subject to the freezing injunction but also assets which *may* be subject to such an order. In this situation, the applicant must adduce some credible evidence upon which to base such an application otherwise it will fall foul of being no more than a fishing expedition.[102]

24.91 One of the most controversial aspects of the ancillary disclosure order is that it remains effective and binding notwithstanding an application by the respondent to discharge the whole injunction. In other words, even if a bona fide application to discharge has been lodged, the respondent remains duty-bound to answer the disclosure order.[103]

24.92 It is submitted that whilst there are genuine concerns that any other rule might lead to respondents issuing applications to discharge freezing orders simply as a tactic to delay disclosing assets for enough time to move them undetected, it is not at all clear that an obligation to disclose should be maintained when the whole injunction is the subject of the application to discharge. The disclosure order is one of the most important orders contained within the freezing injunction. On the present understanding of the law, it is possible to obtain such an order without notice and, let us assume, wholly unjustifiably so,[104] and the respondent is given no chance to respond to such a without notice order or in any way to challenge its validity before it is expected to take effect. That cannot be right. This is all the more so where the information and documentation, once disclosed, will always be known to the claimant. That information cannot be taken back.

24.93 This is an unsatisfactory aspect of the present freezing injunction jurisdiction. There must be a better way of identifying bogus or non-genuine applications to discharge at an early stage which have been issued simply to delay the inevitable disclosure of assets. Perhaps consideration could be given to the lodging of some security pending the hearing of the discharge application. Perhaps a judge could examine on paper the application to discharge as a means of ensuring there was something there to merit the application.

24.94 One final word on this aspect. The duty to provide disclosure, and in particular the time for so doing, usually starts to run after the injunction order has been *served*. In *Mobil Cerro v PDVSA*, the process of service in Venezuela was a little

---

[102] *Parker v CS Structured Credit Fund Ltd* [2003] EWHC 391 (Ch).

[103] *Motorola Credit Corporation v Uzan* [2002] EWCA Civ 989, [2002] 2 All ER (Comm) 945; *Federal Republic of Nigeria v Union Bank of Nigeria*, 18 October 2001 unrep (Laddie J).

[104] So the injunction and with it, the disclosure order would be discharged at the inter partes hearing.

convoluted and slow but the respondent was held entitled to rely upon that means of service being effected first before any duty to disclosure arises. This is something to bear in mind for the future, particularly if there is to be no improvement on the question of suspension of disclosure obligations pending determination of a discharge application.

It is of course open in certain limited circumstances to a respondent to refuse to answer disclosure requests on the grounds of privilege.[105] **24.95**

Difficult issues may arise if disclosure is sought against the respondent's bank which has already made a money laundering report about the activities of the defendant customer. In such circumstances, problems of 'tipping off' arise under the money laundering legislation.[106] **24.96**

(8) The standard order

A copy of the official draft order is to be found in the Appendix.[107] Whilst a party is free to depart from its terms, it is essential that any amendment is brought to the court's attention at the ex parte hearing. **24.97**

E. Worldwide Freezing Injunction in Aid of English Proceedings

Section D above was concerned with the requirements for obtaining a domestic freezing injunction i.e. one that is limited to restraining the respondent from dealing with or dissipating assets within the jurisdiction. Sometimes, a respondent's assets are spread across several jurisdictions such that insufficient funds or assets appear to be located within this jurisdiction to justify applying for only a domestic freezing injunction. It is precisely to deal with such a situation that the court extended the jurisdiction of freezing injunctions to worldwide freezing injunctions.[108] **24.98**

Some of the earlier authorities granting worldwide relief suggested that it would only be available in exceptional circumstances or would be only rarely available.[109] Whilst it remains true that one should not lightly apply for worldwide relief, **24.99**

---

105 See *Den Norske Bank ASA v Antonatos* [1999] QB 271.
106 See *C v S (Money Laundering: Discovery of Documents)* [1999] 1 WLR 1551. This issue is dealt more specifically in Chapter 22 on disclosure.
107 Precedent No 1.
108 See *Babanaft International SA v Bassatne* [1990] Ch 13 (worldwide injunction granted post-judgment); *Republic of Haiti v Duvalier* [1990] QB 202; *Derby v Weldon* [1990] Ch 48; *Derby v Weldon (Nos 3 and 4)* [1990] Ch 65.
109 *Babanaft International SA v Bassatne* [1990] Ch 13; *Republic of Haiti v Duvalier* [1990] QB 202; *Derby v Weldon* [1990] Ch 48.

so long as the factors justify the granting of this relief, it does not appear as though these comments in the earlier authorities survive as an additional barrier to obtaining this relief. Indeed, in *Derby v Weldon (Nos 3 and 4)*[110] Lord Donaldson MR said that 'once the court is concerned with an international operator, the position may well be different'.[111]

24.100 The general requirements for a worldwide freezing injunction remain the same as for a domestic freezing injunction. In other words, the applicant must establish a good arguable case on the merits and a real risk of dissipation of assets should no injunctive relief be granted. There are, however, certain additional factors which come into play with a worldwide freezing injunction given the extra-territorial effect of the injunction.

24.101 One main additional factor is the obvious fact that this injunction purports to take effect on a worldwide basis and not just in this jurisdiction. This immediately creates potential conflicts, particularly for banks and other financial institutions, between complying with the terms of the order whilst at the same time not placing oneself in a breach of contractual or other obligations in the foreign jurisdiction. It is for this reason that the worldwide freezing order must contain certain provisos for the protection of third parties. A copy of the official standard draft for worldwide relief is to be found in the Appendix.[112]

(1) Relevance of location of assets

24.102 Unlike a domestic injunction, it is not necessary to establish the location of any assets of the respondent within the jurisdiction. It suffices if the respondent's only assets are abroad. Indeed, there would be little point to a worldwide freezing injunction if the respondent did not have any assets outside the jurisdiction.

24.103 If, however, the respondent has sufficient assets within the jurisdiction to meet the quantum of the claim, then it would generally be inappropriate (as well as unnecessary) to apply for a worldwide injunction.[113]

(2) The *Babanaft* proviso

24.104 One obvious difference between a worldwide injunction and a domestic injunction is that the former is intended to take effect outside of the jurisdiction whereas the latter is limited to operating within the jurisdiction. This creates a difficulty for third parties who may become unsure whether they should comply with the order or with their contractual obligations.

---

[110] [1990] Ch 65.
[111] ibid, 79.
[112] Precedent No 1.
[113] *Derby and Co Ltd v Weldon (Nos 3 and 4)* [1990] Ch 65.

Strictly, the English court has no jurisdiction over the foreign-based third parties **24.105** and so they would not be bound by the terms of the worldwide freezing order. However, since clarity is an essential aspect of the freezing injunction, the court has seen fit to ensure that the third parties are well aware that the terms of the order do not bind them unless and until the local courts enforce those terms. It has been said that the inclusion of such a clause, whilst strictly unnecessary, may well encourage foreign courts to enforce the orders, should the application be made to do so.[114]

Accordingly, the court in *Babanaft International Co SA v Bassatne*[115] insisted that **24.106** a worldwide freezing injunction must contain what has become known as a *Babanaft* proviso, which protects third parties by stating that the order will not bite on them unless and until it has been recognized, registered or enforced by the relevant (local) foreign court.[116]

This has now been incorporated into the standard wording for a worldwide **24.107** injunction.

Example of *Babanaft* proviso

19 Persons outside England and Wales

(1) Except as provided in paragraph (2) below, the terms of this order do not affect or concern anyone outside the jurisdiction of this court.
(2) The terms of this order will affect the following persons in a country or state outside the jurisdiction of this court—
    (a) the Respondent or his officer or agent appointed by power of attorney;
(3) any person who—
    (i) is subject to the jurisdiction of this court;
    (ii) has been given written notice of this order at his residence or place of business within the jurisdiction of this court; and
    (iii) is able to prevent acts or omissions outside the jurisdiction of this court which constitute or assist in a breach of the terms of this order; and
    (b) any other person, only to the extent that this order is declared enforceable by or is enforced by a court in that country or state.[117]

It is to be noted that the *Babanaft* proviso had been the subject of one revision **24.108** by Lord Donaldson MR in *Derby & Co Ltd v Weldon (Nos 3 and 4)*[118] to include what became known as the *Derby v Weldon* proviso. This added the requirement that persons who were subject to the jurisdiction of the English court with notice of the order were required to prevent breaches of its terms if they were able to do so.

---

[114] *Republic of Haiti v Duvalier* [1990] 1 QB 202 (Staughton LJ).
[115] [1990] Ch 13.
[116] For the official wording, see Cl 19(2)(c) of the standard order. Appendix: Precedent No 1.
[117] Clause 19(2)(c) represents the *Babanaft* proviso.
[118] [1990] Ch 65.

24.109   The *Derby v Weldon* proviso, however, caused difficulties in application. In his 1993 End of Year Statement as Judge in Charge of the Commercial Court, Saville J had this to say:

> A problem emerged earlier this year which was of great concern to those banks which are subject to the jurisdiction of both the English court and the courts of the country or countries where they may be holding assets of the defendant which are made the subject of a worldwide [freezing order]. Certain countries may not recognize or give effect to ex parte orders made in this jurisdiction and indeed may make inconsistent orders. In such cases third party banks can be put in an impossible position, being required to do something by a court in this country and the opposite by a court abroad. The *Derby v Weldon* proviso does not seem to help as it does not apply to persons who are subject to the jurisdiction which of course is the case with most major banks. To solve this problem of double jeopardy we would suggest in appropriate cases that something along the lines of the [*Baltic*] provision be added to the order.[119]

24.110   As set out below, the Court of Appeal in *Bank of China v NBM LLC*[120] endorsed Saville J's conclusion that the *Baltic* proviso should be included in the standard draft order.[121]

24.111   Third parties located abroad are also assisted by the standard undertaking not to enforce abroad without first seeking permission from the English court. See paras 24.117–24.119 below.

(3) The *Baltic* proviso[122]

24.112   The genesis of this proviso was a concern that non-parties, such as banks, should not be placed in an invidious position whereby they faced conflicting duties: if they complied with their contractual obligation abroad, that might result in a breach of the terms of the freezing order granted by the English court.

24.113   The problem is particularly acute with banks having a branch within this jurisdiction being asked to restrain dealings with assets held at other branches abroad. In *Baltic Shipping*, Clarke J granted an application by the third party bank to vary the standard worldwide freezing order so as to include what has become known as the *Baltic* proviso. Clarke J went on to explain his reasoning:

> In general plaintiffs should recognize this difficulty and apply to the local Court as soon as they possibly can, either at the same time or as soon as may be after a worldwide Mareva has been granted. It appears to me that if the bank's proviso is adopted the plaintiff has reasonable protection because the bank can only act on reasonable belief. In forming that belief it will have to act on the information available to it. So if in a particular case the plaintiff has the powerful opinion of a lawyer to the effect that there would be no breach of local law if a payment out were to be made then the

---

[119] Cited and quoted by Tuckey LJ in *Bank of China v NBM LLC* [2002] 1 WLR 844, 849.
[120] ibid, 852 [22]–[23].
[121] See Clause 20 of the standard order. Appendix: Precedent No 1.
[122] *Baltic Shipping v Translink Shipping Ltd* [1995] 1 Lloyd's Rep 673.

bank will have to take the opinion into account in forming its belief. If the belief is not reasonable than the bank will be at risk.[123]

The *Baltic* proviso was perceived as the means by which to mitigate the problems **24.114** caused by the *Derby v Weldon* proviso and referred to by Saville J in the 1993 End of Year Statement as Judge in Charge of the Commercial Court (see above).

To like effect were the comments of the Court of Appeal in *Bank of China v NBM* **24.115** *LLC*:[124]

> 22 So, like the three experienced commercial judges who have previously had to consider this point, I conclude that the need to avoid unwarranted extraterritorial jurisdiction, the need to provide reasonable protection for third parties affected by freezing orders and the need to clarify the *Derby v Weldon* proviso will usually entitle third parties to have the *Baltic* proviso added to the worldwide freezing order unless the court considers on the particular facts of the case that this is inappropriate. As third parties are not represented when the order is first made, I think the *Baltic* proviso should be included in the standard form.
>
> 23 I see no reason for not including the *Baltic* proviso in this case. The claimant deserved the best protection which this court can give, not least because it does not know where the defendant's assets, if any, are. . . .

The *Baltic* proviso is now embodied in the standard draft worldwide freezing **24.116** order, clause 20, which reads:

> **20 Assets located outside England and Wales.**
>
> (4) Nothing in this order shall, in respect of assets located outside England and Wales, prevent any third party from complying with—
>
> (1) what it reasonably believes to be its obligations, contractual or otherwise, under the laws and obligations of the country or state in which those assets are situated or under the proper law of any contract between itself and the Respondent; and
>
> (2) any orders of the courts of that country or state, provided that reasonable notice of any application for such an order is given to the Applicant's solicitors.

(4) Undertakings not to enforce

As further protection for third parties outside of the jurisdiction, an applicant is **24.117** required to seek the court's approval before seeking to have the worldwide freezing injunction enforced in a foreign jurisdiction.

This undertaking has also now become part of the standard wording for a draft **24.118** worldwide order, in the form of Schedule B, Undertakings to the Court by the Applicant, clause 10 of which reads:

> (10) The Applicant will not without the permission of the court seek to enforce this order in any country outside England and Wales [or seek an order of a similar nature

---

[123] *Baltic Shipping v Translink Shipping Ltd* [1995] 1 Lloyd's Rep 673, 679 (Clarke J).
[124] [2002] 1 WLR 844, 852 [22]–[23] Tuckey LJ.

including orders conferring a charge or other security against the Respondent or the Respondent's assets].

24.119 The manner in which the court will exercise its discretion in favour of permitting enforcement abroad has been the subject of what are now known as the *Dadourian Guidelines* as provided by the Court of Appeal in *Dadourian Group International Inc v Simms (Practice Note)*.[125] The Court of Appeal rejected the submission that the permission should never be granted in circumstances where it was possible to bring the party holding the assets before the English court. The Court emphasized that it had a discretion and that was to be exercised on the basis of the following factors:

(1) The principle that applies to the grant of permission to enforce a worldwide freezing order abroad is that the grant of that permission should be just and convenient for the purpose of ensuring the effectiveness of the order, and in addition that it is not oppressive to the parties to the English proceedings or to third parties who may be joined to the foreign proceedings.

(2) All the relevant circumstances and options need to be considered. In particular consideration should be given to granting relief on terms, for example, terms as to the extension to third parties of the undertaking to compensate for costs incurred as a result of the order and as to the type of proceedings that may be commenced abroad. Consideration should also be given to the proportionality of the steps proposed to be taken abroad, and in addition to the form of any order.

(3) The interests of the applicant should be balanced against the interests of the other parties to the proceedings and any new party likely to be joined to the foreign proceedings.

(4) Permission should not normally be given in terms that would enable the applicant to obtain relief in the foreign proceedings which is superior to the relief given by the worldwide freezing order.

(5) The evidence in support of the application for permission should contain all the information (so far as it can reasonably be obtained in the time available) necessary to assist the judge to reach an informed decision, including evidence as to the applicable law and practice in the foreign court, evidence as to the nature of the proposed proceedings to be commenced and evidence as to the assets believed to be located in the jurisdiction of the foreign court and the names of the parties by whom such assets are held.

(6) The standard of proof as to the existence of assets that are both within the worldwide freezing order and within the jurisdiction of the foreign court is a

---

[125] [2006] EWCA Civ 399, [2006] 1 WLR 2499.

real prospect, that is the applicant must show that there is a real prospect that such assets are located within the jurisdiction of the foreign court in question.

(7) There must be evidence of a risk of dissipation of the assets in question.

(8) Normally the application should be made on notice to the respondent, but in cases of urgency, where it is just to do so, the permission may be given without notice to the party against whom relief will be sought in the foreign proceedings but that party should have the earliest practicable opportunity of having the matter reconsidered by the court at a hearing of which he is given notice.

F. Freezing Injunction in Aid of Foreign Proceedings—CJJA 1982, s 25

It has already been established that originally a freezing injunction could not exist **24.120** without being ancillary to a substantive cause of action. Further, prior to 1982, the only relevant substantive causes of action to which the freezing injunction could be ancillary, were causes of action which were justiciable in England and Wales: *The Siskina*.

Section 25 of the CJJA 1982 changed all that. It provides as follows: **24.121**

(1) The High Court in England and Wales or Northern Ireland shall have power to grant interim relief where—
  (a) proceedings have been or are to be commenced in a [Brussels or Lugano Contracting State] other than the United Kingdom or in a part of the United Kingdom other than that in which the High Court in question exercises jurisdiction; and
  (b) they are or will be proceedings whose subject-matter is within the scope of the 1968 Convention as determined by Article 1 (whether or not [that or any other Convention] has effect in relation to the proceedings).

(2) On an application for any interim relief under subsection (1) the court may refuse to grant that relief if, in the opinion of the court, the fact that the court has no jurisdiction apart from this section in relation to the subject-matter of the proceedings in question makes it inexpedient for the court to grant it.

Section 25 of the CJJA 1982 removed the jurisdictional restriction, imposed by **24.122** *The Siskina*, that injunctive relief had to be in favour of substantive proceedings taking place within this jurisdiction. By so doing, Parliament created the circumstances where the English courts were able to take advantage of the entitlement to grant interim relief in aid of substantive proceedings taking place in a contract state.

The range of interim relief available is limited to that which is ordinarily available **24.123** under the domestic laws of the contracting state. So, if that contracting state included a freezing injunction within its list of interim remedies available in domestic claims then it would also be available under Article 24.[126] There is no uniform list of interim remedies available in all contracting states.

24.124 Section 25 of the CJJA 1982 was initially limited to giving the English court jurisdiction to grant a freezing injunction in aid of proceedings taking place in another contracting state under the Brussels or Lugano Conventions. It was thus not possible to rely upon s 25 of the CJJA 1982 to obtain a freezing injunction in aid of US proceedings or any foreign proceedings taking place outside of a contracting state. A further limitation was that it was also limited to the scope of the subject matter of the relevant Conventions which excluded, for example, any matter relating to arbitrations. On 31 January 2007, Schedule 3 of the Arbitration Act 1996 came into force, repealing s 25(3)(c) and s 25(5) of the CJJA 1982. The former was the express power to extend s 25(1) to arbitrations and the latter contained certain amendments under the old arbitration law which would need to take place to implement any extension of s 25(1) to arbitrations. As a consequence, the possibility of extending s 25 of the CJJA 1982 to include arbitration proceedings was repealed in favour of the new regime for similar relief under s 44 of the Arbitration Act 1996.[127]

24.125 In 1997, s 25 of the CJJA 1982 was extended by the Civil Jurisdiction and Judgments Act 1982 (Interim Relief) Order 1997 (SI 1997/302)[128] so as to give the English court jurisdiction to grant interim relief, including freezing order relief, in aid of proceedings taking place in any foreign jurisdiction as well as proceedings falling outside the definition of 'civil or commercial matter' for the purposes of Regulations.[129] As Millett LJ noted in one case:

> the position has now been reached, therefore, that the High Court has power to grant interim relief in aid of substantive proceedings elsewhere of whatever kind and wherever taking place.[130]

---

[126] CJJA 1982, s 25(7) defines 'interim relief' as follows: 'means interim relief of any kind which [the High Court] has power to grant in proceedings relating to matters within its jurisdiction, other than—(a) a warrant for the arrest of property; or (b) provision for obtaining evidence.'

[127] See *Euro Telecom International NV v Republic of Bolivia* [2008] EWHC 1689 (Comm) (Andrew Smith J); aff'd on appeal [2008] EWCA Civ 880.

[128] Interim Relief Order 1997 reads, in material part: 'The High Court in England and Wales or Northern Ireland shall have the power to grant interim relief under section 25(1) . . . in relation to proceedings of the following descriptions, namely – (a) proceedings commenced or to be commenced otherwise than in a Brussels or Lugano Contracting State; (b) proceedings whose subject-matter is not within the scope of the 1968 Convention.'

[129] It was argued in *ETI v Republic of Bolivia* [2008] EWHC 1689 (Comm) that the 1997 Order in Council extended s 25(1) to arbitration proceedings by virtue of the removal of the restriction that proceedings had to fall within the scope of the Regulations (arbitrations having been excluded). Andrew Smith J rejected that argument. It ignored the repeal of s 25(3)(c) by the 1996 Act, which showed clearly that (i) arbitrations fell within s 25(3)(c) and not within s 25(3)(b); (ii) s 25 was not to be extended to arbitrations because (iii) s 44 of the Arbitration Act 1996 was to provide the necessary regime for interim relief in aid of arbitrations.

[130] *Credit Suisse Fides Trust SA v Cuoghi* [1998] QB 818, 825 per Millett LJ.

Whilst the court now has jurisdiction to grant freezing order relief in aid of any **24.126** foreign proceedings, it has a discretion to do so only when it is considered just and convenient so to do. Indeed, s 25(2) of the CJJA 1982 provides that the court may decide not to grant any interim relief in the circumstances where the fact that the court lacks jurisdiction over the substantive proceedings makes it 'inexpedient' for the court to grant interim relief.

The general two-stage approach to be adopted to any application under s 25 of the **24.127** CJJA 1982 was laid down in *Refco v Eastern Trading Co*.[131] The court there held that the first stage is that the court should consider whether it would grant the relief if the matter was proceeding in this jurisdiction.[132] Once that is done, at the second stage, the court can then consider whether the fact it does not have substantive jurisdiction renders it inexpedient to grant the relief.

As regards the overall exercise of discretion under s 25 of the CJJA 1982 there are **24.128** three important authorities, *Credit Suisse Fides Trust SA v Cuoghi*,[133] *Motorola Credit Corporation v Uzan (No 2)*[134] and *Ryan v Friction Dynamics Ltd & Ors*[135] which need to be considered in some detail as they have each laid out general principles for the proper determination of s 25 applications. Finally, practitioners should pay regard to the observations made by Morison J in *Indosuez International Finance BV v National Reserve Bank*[136] of the dangers of focusing too heavily on widely-drafted general principles.

In *Credit Suisse Fides Trust SA v Cuoghi*,[137] the Court of Appeal dismissed an appeal **24.129** against the granting of a freezing injunction in aid of civil proceedings taking place in Switzerland. In so doing, Millett LJ and Lord Bingham CJ laid down certain guidelines as to how the court should carry out its discretion under s 25 of the CJJA 1982.

(1) If a defendant and his assets are located outside the jurisdiction of the court conducting the substantive proceedings, 'it is . . . most appropriate that protective measures should be granted by those courts best able to make their orders effective. In relation to orders taking direct effect against the assets, this means the courts of the state where the assets are located; and in relation to orders in personam, including orders for disclosure, this means the courts of the state where the person enjoined resides.'[138]

---

[131] [1999] 1 Lloyd's Rep 159.
[132] I.e. the applicant must first establish the usual requirements for, say, a freezing order.
[133] [1998] QB 818.
[134] [2004] 1 WLR 113, 147 [115].
[135] Claim 1998 R No. 6785 unrep, 2 June 2000.
[136] [2002] EWHC 774 (Comm Court—Morison J).
[137] [1998] QB 818.
[138] ibid, 827C–D per Millett LJ.

(2) An ancillary jurisdiction should be exercised with caution and care should be taken not to make orders which conflict with those of the court seized of the substantive proceedings.

(3) Avoidance of conflict does not mean that this court's jurisdiction to award interim relief is limited by what is available in the court seized of substantive proceedings. Indeed, Article 24 of the Brussels Convention (now Article 31 of the Regulations) provides that the court should provide such interim relief as would be available if its own court were seized of the substantive proceedings.[139]

(4) 'In other areas of law, such as cross-border insolvency, commercial necessity has encouraged national courts to provide assistance to each other without waiting for such co-operation to be sanctioned by international convention. International fraud requires a similar response. It is becoming widely accepted that comity between the courts of different countries requires mutual respect for the territorial integrity of each other's jurisdiction, but that this should not inhibit a court in one jurisdiction from rendering whatever assistance it properly can to a court in another in respect of assets located or persons resident within the territory of the former.'[140]

(5) A 'regrettable gloss' has been placed on the words of s 25(2). 'The question for consideration is not whether the circumstances are exceptional or very exceptional but whether it would be inexpedient to the make the order.'[141]

(6) 'Where an application is made for *in personam* relief in ancillary proceedings, two considerations which are highly material are the place where the person sought to be enjoined is domiciled and the likely reaction of the court which is seised of the substantive dispute. Where a similar order has been applied for and has been refused by that court, it would generally be wrong for us to interfere. But where the other court lacks jurisdiction to make an effective order against a defendant because he is resident in England, it does not at all follow that it would find our order objectionable.'[142]

(7) '. . . it would obviously weigh heavily, probably conclusively, against the grant of interim relief if such grant would obstruct or hamper the management of the case by the court seized of the substantive proceedings ("the primary court") or give rise to a risk of conflicting, inconsistent or overlapping orders in other courts.'[143]

---

[139] See *Alltrans Inc v Interdom Holdings Ltd* [1991] 4 All ER 458. Millett LJ was keen to stress that by granting relief not available in, say, Switzerland, the court was not thereby attempting to remedy any procedural gaps or omissions in Swiss law.

[140] [1998] QB 818, 827G per Millett LJ.

[141] ibid, 829D–E per Millett LJ.

[142] ibid, 829 per Millett LJ.

[143] ibid, 831H per Lord Bingham CJ.

(8) 'It may weigh against the grant of relief by this court that the primary court could have granted such relief and has not done so, particularly if the primary court has been asked to grant such relief and declined.'[144]

(9) 'On the other hand, it may be thought to weigh in favour of granting such relief that a defendant is present in this country and so liable to effective enforcement of an order made in personam, always provided that by granting such relief this court does not tread on the toes of the primary court or any other court involved in the case.'[145]

(10) When acting under s 25, this court must always remember its role is subordinate to and must be supportive of that of the primary court.[146]

24.130 Applying these factors to the facts of the case, the Court of Appeal held that the injunction should be maintained and dismissed the appeal. The Swiss court was not empowered to make a similar order and the terms of the injunction did not conflict with any orders of the Swiss court. The order was in personam against a defendant domiciled and resident in this jurisdiction. Even though the order extended to assets within Switzerland that could not be enforced without an order of the Swiss court, thus ensuring that the primary court maintained control over these proceedings.

24.131 Further guidance has been provided by the Court of Appeal in *Motorola Credit Corporation v Uzan (No 2)*[147] where the Court held that five issues for consideration could be derived from the authorities on the question of whether it is expedient to grant the order:

(1) whether the making of the order will interfere with the management of the case in the primary court, e.g. where the order is inconsistent with an order of the primary court or overlaps with it;

(2) whether it is the policy in the primary jurisdiction not itself to make worldwide freezing/disclosure orders;

(3) whether there is a danger that the orders made will give rise to disharmony or confusion and/or risk of conflicting inconsistent or overlapping orders in other jurisdictions, in particular the courts of the state where the person

---

144 ibid, 832A per Lord Bingham CJ.

145 ibid, 832A–B per Lord Bingham CJ.

146 The reason why the English court is subordinate to another 'primary court' is because that other court is determining the rights between the parties—it is dealing with the substantive dispute—whereas, under s 25, the English court is only ever providing interim relief to assist the primary court. In *ETI v Republic of Bolivia* [2008] EWHC 1689, the Commercial Court held that there could be no interim relief from an English court in aid of interim attachment proceedings in New York, where both interim proceedings were in aid, not of each other, but of the underlying ICSID arbitration, where the substantive dispute was likely to be resolved, and where there was no basis for maintaining that the New York proceedings were in fact the primary proceedings.

147 [2004] 1 WLR 113, 147 [115].

enjoined resides or where the assets affected are located. If so, then respect for the territorial jurisdiction of that state should discourage the English court from using its unusually wide powers against a foreign defendant;

(4) whether at the time the order is sought there is likely to be a potential conflict as to jurisdiction rendering it inappropriate and inexpedient to make a world-wide order;

(5) whether in a case where jurisdiction is resisted and disobedience to be expected, the court will be making an order which it cannot enforce.

24.132 On the facts of *Motorola*, the Court of Appeal found that no real sanction would exist if two of the defendants disobeyed the order and therefore it was inexpedient to grant the order against them, whereas it was expedient to grant that order against the first defendant because in the event of his disobedience, such an order could be effectively enforced.

24.133 Having analysed the guidance given in both *Credit Suisse* and *Motorola* as set out above, Neuberger J in *Ryan v Friction Dynamics Ltd & Ors*[148] set out his version of the relevant principles to be derived from these authorities as to the exercise of discretion under s 25 of the CJJA 1982. They are worth setting out in full:

(1) The court should always exercise caution before granting any freezing order. The decision and observation of the US Supreme Court in the *Grupo Mexicano* case emphasizes the potentially draconian nature of a freezing order in personam, but, before the court has ruled definitively on the parties' rights, it can be said that such an order is obviously potentially harsh, even when it is made on a pro-prietary basis.

(2) As Millett LJ indicated in *Cuoghi*, particular caution is appropriate where a freezing order is sought under section 25. The fact that the primary forum for the litigation is abroad means that this court is likely to be even less fully appraised of all the facts than in a case where it is exercising primary jurisdiction. See also the observations in *Refco v Eastern Trading Co* [1999] 1 Lloyd's Rep 159 of Rix J at p.164.

(3) However, factors such as comity and the need to stop international fraud mean that this court should not be timid about granting an injunction under section 25, if satisfied that good grounds exist. It should be remembered, as pointed out in *Cuoghi*, that section 25(2) indicates that an order should be made unless it is 'inexpedient' to do so.

(4) Just as when exercising its primary jurisdiction to grant a freezing order, the court should not make such an order under section 25 unless the basic requirements are satisfied, namely that the claimant has a good arguable case and there is a real risk of dissipation. See *Refco* at p.164 per Rix J, and at p.171 per Morritt LJ.

(5) Where a foreign court has refused to grant a freezing order then this court should be slow to grant a freezing order. However, as is clear from the majority view in

---

[148] Claim 1998 R No 6785 unrep, 2 June 2000.

Refco, it may be appropriate nonetheless for this court to grant a freezing order under s.25: see per Morritt LJ at 173 and Potter LJ at 174.

(6) The fact that there is a worldwide freezing order granted by the principal foreign court does not prevent this court from granting a freezing order, at least in relation to British assets and/or against a defendant resident and domiciled within the jurisdiction. . . . Worldwide freezing orders are frequently granted by this court, as the primary court, on terms which specifically envisage that the claimant will apply for freezing orders in the courts of the Channel Islands, or the Isle of Man, or Gibraltar in respect of assets within their jurisdiction. Further, to hold otherwise would involve implying an absolute fetter on a statutory jurisdiction which on its face appears to be intended to give a wide and flexible discretion.

(7) However, before such an overlapping freezing order is made under s.25, the court should expect to be given cogent reasons to justify it. Overlapping orders mean overlapping applications, which in turn result in substantial increased costs and court time. . . . Furthermore, overlapping injunctions in different jurisdictions can lead to a risk of double jeopardy for defendants and the opportunity for forum shopping by a claimant. In *Re BCCI SA* [1994] 1 WLR 708, at 713, Dillon LJ said that a freezing order in this country should not be 'enforced oppressively by a multiplicity of applications in different countries throughout the world.' If anything, there is an even stronger case for discouraging a multiplicity of applications for overlapping freezing orders against the same defendants in respect of the same assets in different jurisdictions. No doubt Lord Bingham had that in mind in *Cuoghi*.

(8) Where it is appropriate to grant a freezing order under s.25 in respect of British assets, and the order overlaps with a worldwide or similar freezing order of the foreign court with primary jurisdiction, it is sensible to have some indication as to which court is to have the primary role for enforcing the overlapping injunctions. This would at least substantially reduce the risk of double jeopardy and forum shopping. In general, I would have thought that, save where there is good reason to the contrary, it should be the foreign court to which such applications should normally be made.

(9) Where an overlapping order is made under s.25, it is in general desirable that it should track the terms of the order made by the foreign court. Any inconsistency could lead to uncertainty and extra complications for a defendant, which would be unfair. Worse, it could in some cases lead to a position where a defendant finds itself bound to be in breach of one order or the other. I derive support for this view from the decision of Jacob J, *The State of Brunei Darussalam v Prince Jefri Bolkah* (unreported) 20th March 2000. . . . I should add that, of course, there may be good reasons in a particular case why an order made under s.25 should be in different terms from the order made by the primary court.

Applying these principles to the facts of *Ryan*, Neuberger J refused to discharge **24.134** the injunction but allowed the application that the terms of the injunction be varied to fall into line with those of the US court.

Finally, this section has contained a good deal of guidance by way of general prin- **24.135** ciples as to how the court will face the issue of exercise of discretion under s 25. It is noteworthy, however, that not all judges consider setting out such wide-ranging general principles as a guide is particularly helpful. In *Indosuez International Finance BV v National Reserve Bank*[149] Morison J noted, in respect of the nine principles provided by Neuberger J:

> Helpful though his analysis is, I have to say that there is a danger in a judge formulating general principles when its discretionary powers are being invoked. The danger is that in a subsequent case the advocates will concentrate on looking at each of the principles as though each was a requirement that needed to be fulfilled. Further, some of the principles are couched in such wide-terms as to amount to no discernible principle at all. Thus, the 7th numbered principle is that the court should expect to be given cogent reasons to justify making what was called an overlapping order, as here. Before exercising its discretion the court will always expect to be provided with cogent reasons for its exercise in whatever jurisdiction it is acting.[150]

24.136 It is accepted that there is always a tendency within litigators to treat and construe what are no more than general principles or guidelines as if they were contained within a statute. The consequence is that the whole flexibility of the exercise of the discretion can be lost if this occurs. With that caveat in mind, it is suggested that it is preferable for a practitioner to have the benefit of these court-generated general principles than for it to be left languishing trying to sort out what evidence is required without any such guidance at all.

G. Proprietary Injunctions

24.137 So far this chapter has examined the freezing order in both its domestic and worldwide nature. A proprietary injunction[151] is intended to remedy the same evil as does a freezing injunction, namely the dissipation of assets, but contains the additional feature that the applicant asserts that certain assets held by the respondent are in fact owned by the applicant. The proprietary injunction, therefore, focuses in on these certain assets in an effort to secure them in the event that the applicant succeeds on its substantive claims.

24.138 The original basis for the jurisdiction of proprietary injunctions was equity's concern to preserve a trust fund:

> A court of equity has never hesitated to use the strongest powers to protect and preserve a trust fund in interlocutory proceedings on the basis that, if the trust fund disappears by the time the actions comes to trial, equity will have been invoked in vain.[152]

---

149 [2002] 2 EWHC 774 (Comm)—Morison J, 26 April 2002.
150 [2002] 2 EWHC 774 (Comm) [18].
151 Previously, this would have been called a tracing injunction. Given our better understanding that tracing is simply a means of identifying the location of value, and not a claim in itself, it is more accurate to describe the injunction as a proprietary injunction.
152 *Mediterranea Raffineria Siciliana Petroli SpA v Mabanaft GmbH* CA (Civ Div) Transcript No 816 of 1978 (1 December 1978), per Templeman LJ cited in *Bankers Trust Co v Shapira*

That jurisdiction remains and has been supplemented by the introduction of CPR r 25(1)(c) which is concerned about protecting property which is the subject matter of a claim or as to which a question may arise on a claim and by CPR r 25.1(1)(g), which directs a party to provide information about the location of relevant property or assets or to provide information about relevant property or assets which are or may be the subject of an application for a freezing injunction: CPR r25(1)(2).

24.139 It has also been held that if the proprietary claim is in respect of assets located outside of the jurisdiction, s 37(1) of the Supreme Court Act 1981 conferred jurisdiction on the court to grant an injunction in respect of such a claim.[153]

24.140 It has been recognized that the basis for the grant of this relief differs significantly from that underpinning the Mareva jurisdiction. In *Polly Peck International plc v Nadir (No 2)*,[154] the Court of Appeal was facing an application by the bank to have the freezing and proprietary injunctions discharged. The Court held that the freezing injunction should be discharged on the basis that it should, in principle, not be granted against a bank if it was going to interfere with the ordinary course of business of the bank. Turning to the more limited proprietary injunction in relation to £8.9m on deposit, Scott LJ stated:

> I now come to the question whether a limited injunction preserving, pending trial, the £8.9m should be granted. This would not be a Mareva injunction. It would not be subject to provisos enabling the use of the money for normal business purposes, or for the payment of legal fees, or the like. There is, in general, no reason why a defendant should be permitted to use money belonging to another in order to pay his legal costs or other expenses The objection in principle to the grant of the Mareva injunction . . . does not apply to an injunction to preserve a fund that, in the contention of PPI, belongs to PPI.

24.141 Scott LJ continued and made it clear that one applies the *American Cyanamid* principles to this type of injunction:

> In deciding whether or not an interlocutory injunction to protect the £8.9m should be granted, the approach prescribed by *American Cyanamid Co v Ethicon Ltd* [1975] AC 396 should be followed. First, PPI must show an arguable case. If an arguable case is shown then the balance of convenience should be applied. If the scale appears very evenly balanced it is then legitimate to take into account the strength or weakness of PPI's case.[155]

[1980] 1 WLR 1274, 1280H–1281D, per Lord Denning MR; *London and Counties Securities Ltd (in Liquidation) v Caplan* unrep, 26 May 1978 (Templeman J); see also *Bekhor v Bilton* [1981] QB 923, esp 937–8; *PCW (Underwriting Agencies) Ltd v Dixon* [1983] 2 Lloyd's Rep 197.

[153] *Ashtiani v Kashi* [1987] QB 888, 901.
[154] [1992] 4 All ER 769 (CA).
[155] ibid, 784 (Scott LJ), 787 (Lord Donaldson).

24.142 So an additional requirement for a proprietary injunction is the need to persuade the court of the applicant's entitlement to assert a proprietary interest in the identified assets. This will involve the court not only in a consideration of the merits of the claim being brought by the applicant but also an examination of the tracing exercise pursuant to which the assets have been identified.

24.143 If the court is persuaded of the merits of the proprietary claim, it is generally perceived that injunctive and disclosure relief will be more readily and widely granted.[156]

24.144 It is not unusual, and represents good litigation practice, to combine the freezing and proprietary injunctions so as to have the best of both worlds and not be restricted to the limitations of either.[157] It is essential, however, that the terms of the order are clear and unambiguous as to what the respondent can do vis-à-vis his assets since ambiguity and uncertainty is unacceptable in an order containing a penal clause.

24.145 As made clear in *Polly Peck International plc v Nadir*,[158] a proprietary injunction is based, essentially, upon the *American Cyanamid* principles. These are discussed in detail elsewhere.[159]

24.146 It will be necessary to establish a good arguable case on the merits of the existence of the proprietary claim underlying the injunction but there is no need to establish a risk of dissipation in order to justify the injunctive relief.

24.147 The court also has jurisdiction to grant interim relief in respect of specific property under CPR r 25.1(1)(c)(i) for the detention, custody or preservation of relevant property.

(1) Ancillary dislosure order

24.148 In addition to the injunctive relief, the applicant will almost certainly want to obtain disclosure from the respondent and/or his banks or financial advisers as to the present location, as best known, of the particular assets over which he asserts a proprietary interest.

24.149 The jurisdiction to grant the disclosure order is often viewed as an extension of the *Norwich Pharmacal* jurisdiction. It is true that Lord Denning MR did cite *Norwich*

---

[156] *Republic of Haiti v Duvalier* [1989] 2 WLR 261, 270 (CA) per Staughton LJ; see M Hapgood QC (ed), *Paget's Law of Banking* (13th edn, Butterworths, 2006), [26.27].

[157] This was done by Robert Goff J in *A v C* [1981] QB 956 (Note), [1980] 2 All ER 347. Here the judge granted a proprietary injunction in respect of the specified amount of the claim over certain bank accounts and also granted a freezing order over the same accounts to a much higher figure to include the large sum accounts.

[158] [1992] 4 All ER 769.

[159] See para 24.152 *et seq.*

Pharmacal in *Bankers Trust Company v Shapira* [1980] 1 WLR 1274 in support of his view that a bank could be ordered to provide disclosure of cheque books, correspondence and other documents relating to accounts in the name of individuals who had allegedly stolen US$1m from the claimant. However, Lord Denning MR also relied upon equity's traditional power to order disclosure to assist in locating a trust fund.[160]

Further, in *Murphy v Murphy*[161] Neuberger J traced the two distinct lines of **24.150** authorities. Whilst recognizing a potential for them to overlap he was clear that they were two distinct lines of cases.

In *Arab Monetary Fund v Hashim (No 5),* Hoffmann J provided certain guidelines **24.151** as to the availability of this type of relief. He first examined the underlying principles and concluded that this jurisdiction rested on the proposition that unless the assets in question can be located and secured, the ultimate determination of ownership of those assets may be frustrated by their removal or dissipation and there would be no point in calling on a third party at trial to give evidence. He went on:

- The claimant must demonstrate a real prospect that the information may lead to the location or preservation of the assets. If there has been delay which would seriously undermine the chase of the assets that could be fatal.

- Disclosure should be more limited than normal disclosure and should condescend to particulars. It is unclear whether this represents the present position.[162]

H. Interim Injunctions[163]

Interim injunctions are invoked in many varied factual situations and the prin- **24.152** ciples underlying the grant of relief typically vary from one type of situation to another. The requirements for a mandatory injunction will vary from that of neighbours disputing whether one can fell an overhanging tree to obtaining such relief in order to prevent a fraudulent call on a performance bond. We are not here concerned with a general review of all such interim injunctions but rather a detailed examination of when such relief may be invoked in a commercial fraud setting.

---

[160] Lord Denning MR cited *A v C* [1981] QB 956 and *Mediterrania v Mabanaft* [1978] CA Transcript.

[161] [1998] 3 All ER 1.

[162] See C Hollander, *Documentary Evidence* (9th edn, Thomson/Sweet and Maxwell, 2006), [5-33].

[163] It is worth noting that prior to the CPR, a distinction existed between interlocutory injunctions (i.e. injunctions which were to continue until trial or judgment) and interim injunctions (i.e. injunctions which were to continue until a stated inter partes hearing date or return day). Post-CPR, both sorts of injunctions fall under the umbrella of 'interim injunctions'. On the distinction, see Spry, *Equitable Remedies* (7th edn, Law Book Co of Australasia, 2007), 446 and 508.

24.153 The general principles governing the *American Cyanamid* approach to interim injunctions will first be set out briefly. Thereafter, the application of those principles in the context of performance bonds, etc. will be scrutinized.

(1) General principles

24.154 The overriding principle guiding when an interim injunction will be granted is set out in s 37(1) of the Supreme Court Act 1981 which provides:

> The High Court may by order (whether interlocutory or final) grant an injunction or appoint a receiver in all cases in which it appears to the court to be just and convenient to do so.[164]

24.155 Provision is made for obtaining an interim injunction under CPR r 25(1)(a) and that it can be sought pre-action: CPR r 25(2) so long as it is either urgent or in the interests of justice so to do.

24.156 The leading case in this area is undoubtedly the House of Lords decision in *American Cyanamid Co v Ethicon Ltd*,[165] where Lord Diplock set out some general principles governing interim injunctions as well certain specific requirements which must be met. The whole thrust of Lord Diplock's approach is premised upon an assumption that the issues at hand are ultimately to be resolved at trial and that the interim injunction is simply a means of holding the position till then. There is also a danger to accord Lord Diplock's guidelines the status of statutory principles. It must not be forgotten that the general statutory test is the granting of injunctive relief whenever it is considered 'just and convenient' so to do under s 37(1) of the Supreme Court Act 1981.

24.157 In this regard, it is as well to consider the warning laid down by Kerr LJ in *Cambridge Nutrition Ltd v BBC*:[166]

> It is important to bear in mind that the *American Cyanamid* case contains no principle of universal application. The only such principle is the statutory power of the court to grant injunctions when it is just and convenient to do so. The *American Cyanamid* case is no more than a set of useful guidelines which apply in many cases. It must never be used as a rule of thumb. Let alone as a straitjacket . . . The *American Cyanamid* case provides an authoritative and most helpful approach to cases where the function of the court in relation to the grant or refusal of interim injunctions is to hold the balance as justly as possible in situations where the substantial issues between the parties can only be resolved by a trial. In my view . . . the present case is

---

[164] There is some suggestion that the introduction of the Human Rights Act 1998 may have altered the test to 'just and proportionate': *South Buckinghamshire District Council v Porter* [2003] 2 AC 558.

[165] [1975] AC 396.

[166] [1990] 3 All ER 523.

not in that category. Neither side is interested in monetary compensation, and once the interim decision has been given little, if anything, will remain in practice.[167]

(a) Overview of Lord Diplock's requirements

Lord Diplock laid down certain general requirements or observations about **24.158** the nature of interim injunctive relief and what it requires. The following is a summary.

(1) The object of the interlocutory injunction is to protect the plaintiff against injury by violation of his right for which he could not be adequately compensated in damages recoverable in the action if the uncertainty were resolved in his favour at the trial; but the plaintiff's need for such protection must be weighed against the corresponding need of the defendant to be protected against injury resulting from his having been prevented from exercising his own legal rights for which he could not be adequately compensated under the plaintiff's undertaking in damages if the uncertainty were resolved in the defendant's favour at the trial. The court must weigh one need against another and determine where 'the balance of convenience' lies.

(2) The threshold test is that the claim must not be frivolous or vexatious. There must be a serious question to be tried.

(3) It is not part of the court's function at this stage of the litigation to try to resolve conflicts of evidence on affidavit as to facts nor to decide difficult questions of law which call for detailed argument and mature considerations.

(4) One of the reasons for introducing the practice of requiring an undertaking as to damages upon the grant of an interlocutory injunction was that 'it aided the court in doing that which was its great object, viz, abstaining from expressing any opinion upon the merits of the case until the hearing': *Wakefield v Duke of Buccleugh* (1865) 12 LT 628, 629.

(5) So unless the material available to the court at the hearing of the application for an interlocutory injunction fails to disclose that the plaintiff has any real prospect of succeeding in his claim for a permanent injunction, the court should go on to consider whether the balance of convenience lies in favour of granting or refusing the interlocutory relief.

(6) The court should first consider whether, if the plaintiff were to succeed at the trial in establishing his right to a permanent injunction, he would be adequately compensated by an award of damages for the loss he would have sustained as a result of the defendant's continuing to do what was sought to be enjoined between the time of the application and the time of the trial. If damages in the measure recoverable at common law would be adequate remedy and the defendant would be in a financial position to pay them, no interlocutory

---

[167] ibid, 534j.

injunction should normally be granted, however strong the plaintiff's claim appeared to be.

(7) If damages would not provide an adequate remedy, the court should consider whether, on the contrary hypothesis that the defendant were to succeed in establishing his right to do that which was sought to be enjoined, he would be adequately compensated under the plaintiff's undertaking as to damages for the loss he would have sustained by being prevented from doing so between the application and the trial. If damages would be an adequate remedy and the plaintiff would be in a financial position to pay them, there would be no reason to refuse an interlocutory injunction.

(8) The question of balance of convenience arises if there is doubt as to the adequacy of the damages to either part.

(9) If the factors underlying the general balance of convenience are evenly balanced, the court is likely to take steps to preserve the status quo.

(2) Serious issue to be tried

24.159   It is no function of the court, on an interlocutory hearing, to be engaged in mini-trials. The evidence is limited in nature, on paper and typically not the subject of any cross-examination. In other words, the usual machinery employed by the court at a trial to determine the merits of a claim are simply not available at an interlocutory hearing. Lord Diplock in *American Cyanamid* recognized this fact and wanted to take steps to move away from any determination of the merits at the interlocutory stage.

24.160   It is quite surprising what a difference even a small lowering of the merit threshold can have on the nature and extent of arguments raised in interlocutory proceedings. Whilst parties might still consider it worth arguing over the merits in Anton Piller applications, where the merit threshold is higher than most other interlocutory applications, they will not bother to undergo the same exercise for a Mareva injunction, where 'good arguable case' is considered not a difficult threshold to overcome. The sound advice typically given in respect of a Return Date hearing of a Mareva is unless it is obviously a bad case, there is little point arguing the issues on the merits. That saves a tremendous amount of preparation and court time.

24.161   Accordingly, Lord Diplock laid down a test based upon the need to establish a serious issue to be tried. This 'can only arise if there is evidential backing for it'.[168] So if the matter relates to a foreign law issue, which needs to be proved as fact in English proceedings, expert evidence of that law must be adduced.

---

[168] *Tetrosyl Ltd v Silver Paint and Lacqueur Co Ltd* [1979] CAT No 599, reported in *New Law Journal,* 28 August 1980.

Some further guidance on what 'serious issue to be tried' means was given in   **24.162**
Mothercare Ltd v Robson Books Ltd[169] where Sir Robert Megarry V-C said:

> The prospects of the plaintiff's success are to be investigated to a limited extent, but
> they are not to be weighed against his prospects of failure. All that has to be seen is
> whether the plaintiff has prospects of success which, in substance and reality, exist.
> Odds against success no longer defeat the plaintiff, unless they are so long that the
> plaintiff can have no expectation of success, but only a hope. If his prospects of suc-
> cess are so small that they lack substance and reality, then the plaintiff fails, for he can
> point to no question to be tried which can be called 'serious' and no prospect of suc-
> cess which can be called 'real'.[170]

A good illustration of just how low the merit threshold can be gained from Megaw   **24.163**
LJ's observation in *Alfred Dunhill Ltd v Sunoptics SA*:[171]

> It is irrelevant whether the court thinks that the plaintiff's chances of success in estab-
> lishing liability are 90 per cent or 20 per cent.

A 20% chance of success is very low indeed and yet that will suffice for the purposes of passing this initial test.

(3) Adequacy of damages

Once a serious issue to be tried has been shown, the applicant must then persuade   **24.164**
the court that he will not be adequately compensated for by damages:

> If damages in the measure recoverable at common law would be an adequate remedy
> and the defendant would be in a financial position to pay them, no [interim] injunc-
> tion should normally be granted.[172]

This requirement is not surprising. Injunctive relief is equitable in nature and   **24.165**
equity traditionally was called upon to fill the gaps left by the common law remedies. It is thus essential for an applicant to show that a common law award of
damages would be an inadequate remedy to justify invoking equity.[173]

However, the court must weigh-up the need to ensure, so far as possible, that   **24.166**
the defendant is able to pay the damages awarded against a desire not to create a
system which unduly favours those best able to pay damages. If too much weight
is accorded this requirement, it will result in wealthy applicants being able to rely
upon the impecuniosity of defendants to obtain injunctive relief. In *Vernon & Co*

---

[169] [1979] FSR 466.
[170] ibid, 474.
[171] [1979] FSR 373.
[172] *American Cyanamid Co v Ethicon Ltd* [1975] AC 396, 408 (Lord Diplock).
[173] *London and Blackwall Railway Co v Cross* (1886) 31 Ch D 354; *Beswick v Beswick* [1968]
AC 58.

(Pulp Products) Ltd v Universal Pulp Containers Ltd,[174] Sir Robert Megarry V-C remarked:

> It would be intolerable if the Cyanamid case was allowed to become a charter of success for all the rich companies who seek interlocutory injunctions against poor companies in cases in which damages would be an adequate remedy, enabling them to obtain an injunction merely on showing that there is a serious question to be tried.

24.167   The Vice-Chancellor went on to set out his concerns that unless carefully scrutinized, there was a danger that the injunctive process could be used to send the impecunious defendant into insolvency by effectively preventing it from trading out of its difficulties.

24.168   In a similar vein, Megarry V-C in *Apply Corps v Lingasong*[175] stated:

> This argument seems to lead towards the conclusion that whenever affluent plaintiffs claim an interlocutory injunction against defendants with slender resources, the balance of convenience points towards granting the injunction. I would regret such conclusion. I accept that there are circumstances in which the means of the defendant will be relevant in considering whether to grant an injunction: but I do not think the term 'balance of convenience' was ever intended to produce the result that the prosperous could go far to obtain interlocutory injunctions against defendants of modest means merely by pointing to the financial disparity.[176]

24.169   The court will therefore be astute to prevent the financial circumstances of a party from having a conclusive effect on his entitlement to obtain injunctive relief. It will be taken as just one of several factors to be borne in mind in determining how best to proceed.[177]

(4) Undertaking in damages adequate protection to respondent

24.170   If the applicant would not be adequately compensated for by an award of damages but the respondent would be and the applicant is able to pay out under a cross-undertaking in damages, ordinarily an injunction should be granted. In *American Cyanamid,* Lord Diplock said:

> If damages in the measure recoverable under such an undertaking would be an adequate remedy and the [claimant] would be in a financial position to pay them, there would be no reason upon this ground to refuse an [interim] injunction. It is where there is doubt as to the adequacy of the respective remedies in damages available to either party or to both, that the question of balance of convenience arises.[178]

---

[174] [1980] FSR 179.
[175] [1977] FSR 345.
[176] ibid, 352.
[177] See Zuckerman, *Zuckerman on Civil Procedure* (2nd edn), [9.83].
[178] [1975] AC 396, 408.

If the applicant is not in a financial position to meet his obligations under the **24.171**
cross-undertakings in damages, injunctive relief will normally[179] but not always[180]
be refused.

(5) Balance of convenience

The court only reaches this stage in circumstances where neither party is able to **24.172**
prove that the other will be adequately compensated for by an award of damages.

In *Cayne v Global Natural Resources plc*,[181] May LJ commented on the 'balance of **24.173**
convenience' as follows:

> That is the phrase which, of course is always used in this type of application. It is, if I
> may say so, a useful shorthand but in truth . . . the balance that one is seeking to make
> is more fundamental, more weighty, than mere 'convenience'. I think that it is quite
> clear from both cases that, although the phrase may well be substantially less elegant,
> the 'balance of the risk of doing an injustice' better describes the process involved.[182]

Lord Diplock refused to be drawn on a definitive list of matters and the weight to **24.174**
be attached to them that should be taken into account when considering the overall balance of convenience. He considered they would vary from case to case.[183]
He did however consider three such factors in *American Cyanamid*: (i) status quo;
(ii) relative strength of cases; (iii) special factors.

(a) Status quo

Lord Diplock stated: 'Where other factors appear to be evenly balanced it is a **24.175**
counsel of prudence to take such measures as are calculated to preserve the status
quo.'[184] Such a test clearly favours established activities over new ventures.

Although there are conflicting decisions, the status quo is a reference to that period **24.176**
existing immediately prior to the commencement of the proceedings or the application notice if substantially later.[185]

(b) Relative strength of cases

Having done his best to remove detailed inquiry into the merits of the case at the **24.177**
outset of applications for injunctive relief, Lord Diplock opened the door to

---

[179] *Morning Star Co-Operative Society Ltd v Express Newspapers Ltd* [1979] FSR 113.
[180] *Allen v Jambo Holdings Ltd* [1980] 1 WLR 1252.
[181] [1984] 1 All ER 225.
[182] ibid, 237H. In *Francome v Mirror Group Newspapers Ltd* [1984] 1 WLR 892, Sir John
Donaldson MR used the phrase 'a balance of justice'.
[183] [1975] AC 396, 408.
[184] ibid. See Zuckerman, *Zuckerman on Civil Procedure* (2nd edn) for an interesting discussion
on the difficulties of using injunctive relief to maintain the status quo: [9.12]–[9.20].
[185] *Garden Cottage Foods Ltd v Milk Marketing Board* [1984] AC 130, 140; *Snell's Equity* (17th
edn), [16-23].

exactly such inquiries, albeit at a later stage in the investigation into whether or not to grant relief. He said:

> . . . it may not be improper to take into account in tipping the balance the relative strength of each party's case as revealed by the affidavit evidence adduced on the hearing of the application. This, however, should be done only where it is apparent upon the facts disclosed by evidence as to which there is no credible dispute that the strength of one party's case is disproportionate to that of the other party. The court is not justified in embarking upon anything resembling a trial of the action upon conflicting affidavits in order to evaluate the strength of either party's case.

It is evident that Lord Diplock is not advocating a detailed inquiry into the relative merits of each party's case. But if from the documents, it is apparent there is a marked difference in their strengths, that is something that can be taken into account. A court should therefore be retiscent to allow detailed submissions be made on this point by counsel. Either the difference is obvious or it does not qualify to be taken into account.[186]

(c) *Special factors*

24.178 These factors are peculiar to the fact situation of each individual case. In the case of *American Cyanamid*, the special factor was that if the injunction had been refused but the claimant had succeeded at trial, it would have been extremely difficult to have insisted on the defendant's sutures being withdrawn and replaced by the claimant's since the doctors would, by that point, have become well used to the defendant's products.

I. Interim Injunctions: Performance Bonds[187]

24.179 The availability of interim injunctive relief in respect of performance bonds and/or demand guarantees gives rise to unique factors and issues which call for separate consideration.[188] It is once again an area of discrete case law of which a commercial fraud litigator must have a detailed knowledge.

---

[186] See *Cambridge Nutrition Ltd v BBC* [1990] 3 All ER 523 for an example of the court taking into account the relative strengths of each party's case; see also *The Quaker Oats Co v Alltrades Distributors Ltd* [1981] FSR 9, 13, 14; *Series 5 Software v Clarke* [1996] 1 All ER 853.

[187] The leading texts include M Hapgood QC (ed), *Paget's Law of Banking* (13th edn, LexisNexis Butterworths, 2007), ch 34; M Brindle QC and R Cox QC (eds), *Law of Bank Payments* (3rd edn, Thomson/Sweet and Maxwell, 2004), [8.87]–[8.99]; Jack, Malek and Quest, *Documentary Credits* (3rd edn, LexisNexis, 2000).

[188] For the purposes of the text, no distinction is drawn between performance bonds, performance guarantees or demand guarantees. The terms are used interchangeably in practice: See G Andrews QC and R Millett QC, *Law of Guarantees* (5th edn, Thomson/Sweet and Maxwell, 2008), [16-001].

Before examining any possible fraud exception to the enforcement of such bonds, **24.180**
it is essential that one fully understands the nature of these instruments and crucial role they play in modern commerce. They are, after all, 'the life-blood of
international commerce'[189] and consequently the courts will be very astute to
ensure that it will be rare for their operation to be prevented by the grant of
injunctive relief.

When analysing the case law it is important to distinguish three distinct scenarios: **24.181**

(a) where a bank decides not to pay out under a letter of credit because of a fraudu-
    lent demand;
(b) where a customer tries to injunct a bank from paying out under a letter of
    credit because of a fraudulent demand; and
(c) where a bank refuses to pay out because it is concerned that the instrument
    itself (whether it be a letter of credit or performance bond) is tainted by
    fraud.

Distinct principles are at play in these three scenarios. **24.182**

• Scenario (a) involves the issue of whether the bank has an obligation to pay out
  in a case of established fraud.

• Scenario (b) relates to whether the vendor can injunct the bank from paying out
  under the letter of credit on the basis that the demand is fraudulent. This raises
  specific issues about balance of convenience and how it operates on these facts.
  It will be seen that the general view is that it will be extremely rare that the balance of convenience will favour the grant of injunctive relief.

• Finally, scenario (c) is entirely distinct again since the fraud here is said to taint
  not merely the demand but the whole instrument itself. In such circumstances,
  the general principles, expressed above, about such instruments being the life-
  blood of commerce and so should not be interfered with simply do not apply.
  It will be seen that the court adopts a wholly different approach.

(1) Nature of letters of credit, performance bonds or demand guarantees

Performance bonds or demand guarantees are unconditional undertakings to pay to **24.183**
an identified beneficiary on a particular demand being made or certain documents
being produced. So long as the condition precedent for liability to pay is satisfied,[190]

---

[189] *R D Harbottle (Mercantile) Ltd v National Westminster Bank Ltd* [1978] QB 146, 155 per Kerr
J. His views were adopted by Lord Denning MR in *Edward Owen Engineering Ltd v Barclays Bank
International Ltd* [1978] QB 159, 171.
[190] I.e. either the correct demand has been made or the correct demand with accompanying
documents.

the bank need not and should not concern itself with any disputes which may have arisen in respect of the underlying dispute:

> The unique value of such a letter, bond or guarantee is that the beneficiary can be completely satisfied that whatever disputes may thereafter arise between him and the bank's customer in relation to the performance or indeed existence of the underlying contract, the bank is personally undertaking to pay him provided that the specified conditions are met. In requesting his bank to issue such a letter, bond or guarantee, the customer is seeking to take advantage of this unique characteristic.[191]

24.184 To similar effect is Lord Denning MR in *Edward Owen Engineering Ltd v Barclays Bank International Ltd*[192] who, having described performance bonds as 'virtually promissory notes on demand'[193] went on to say:

> A bank which gives a performance guarantee must honour that guarantee according to its terms. It is not concerned in the least with the relations between the supplier and the customer; nor with the question whether the supplier has performed his contracted obligation or not; nor with the question whether the supplier is in default or not. The bank must pay according to its guarantee, on demand, if so stipulated, without proof or conditions.[194]

24.185 It is thus evident that it will be a rare occasion which would justify a court preventing a bank from complying with its obligations under performance bond.

(2) Scenario (a): where a bank decides whether to pay out in the face of a fraudulent demand under valid instruments

24.186 In this situation, there is in existence a valid letter of credit, performance bond or demand guarantee. As such, the principles, expressed above, about such instruments being the life-blood of commerce apply and it is therefore necessary to find a good enough reason to circumvent such principles and refuse to pay out.

24.187 The fraud exception to the payment out under an otherwise valid instrument was first recognized in English law by Megarry J in *Discount Records Ltd v Barclays Bank Ltd*[195] and then by the Court of Appeal in *Edward Owen Engineering Ltd v Barclays Bank International Ltd.*[196] The House of Lords soon followed with Lord

---

[191] *Bolivinter Oil SA v Chase Manhattan Bank NA* [1984] 1 WLR 392, 393, per Sir John Donaldson MR. See also *IE Contractors v Lloyds Bank plc and Rafidain Bank* [1990] 2 Lloyd's Rep 496.

[192] [1978] 1 QB 159.

[193] ibid, 170.

[194] ibid, 171. See also *Gulf Bank KSC v Mitsubishi Heavy Industries Ltd* [1994] 2 Lloyd's Rep 145.

[195] [1975] 1 Lloyd's Rep 444. The injunction was refused on the basis that since there had already been a discounting of the draft not yet due, the fraudsters would already have received the monies and an injunction would simply have prevented the bank from honouring its obligations: see 447–8.

[196] [1978] QB 159.

Diplock making the following well-known observation in *United City Merchants (Investments) Ltd v Royal Bank of Canada*:[197]

> To this general statement of principle as to the contractual obligations of the confirming bank to the seller, there is one established exception: that is, where the seller, for the purpose of drawing on the credit, fraudulently presents to the confirming bank documents that contain, expressly or by implication, material representations of fact that to his knowledge are untrue. Although there does not appear among the English authorities any case in which this exception has been applied, it is well established in the American cases of which the leading or 'landmark' case is *Sztejn v J Henry Schroder Banking Corpn* 31 NYS 2d 631 (1941). This judgment of the New York Court of Appeals was referred to with approval by the English Court of Appeal in *Edward Owen Engineering Ltd v Barclays Bank International Ltd* [1978] QB 159, though this was actually a case about a performance bond under which a bank assumes obligations to a buyer analogous to those assumed by a confirming bank to the seller under a documentary credit. The exception for fraud on the part of the beneficiary seeking to avail himself of the credit is a clear application of the maxim ex turpi causa non oritur action or, if plain English is to be preferred, 'fraud unravels all'. The courts will not allow their process to be used by a dishonest person to carry out a fraud.[198]

(a) Beneficiary's fraudulent demand

24.188 We are here concerned with the beneficiary making a fraudulent demand under the performance bond. Two criteria must be satisfied.

- First, and perhaps pretty obviously, that the beneficiary has no entitlement to any payment under the underlying contract.

- Secondly, the beneficiary knows or has no genuine belief in its entitlement to make the demand.[199] If the beneficiary genuinely but mistakenly believes he is entitled to make the demand it is not a fraudulent demand and cannot therefore be prevented by injunctive relief.

24.189 Even satisfaction of these two criteria will not suffice in preventing payment out. In other words, if a bank had a mere suspicion of the true position but was unsure, that would not justify not paying out even if it subsequently was proved that the beneficiary was knowingly making a fraudulent demand.

24.190 This point casts some doubt on those who favour the approach that in order to overcome the obvious lack of cause of action in any application for injunctive relief by a seller and a *confirming* bank (with whom the seller has no contractual

---

[197] [1983] 1 AC 168.
[198] ibid, 183.
[199] *State Trading Corpn of India Ltd v E D & F Man (Sugar) Ltd* [1981] Com LR 235.

relationship) one can simply argue the injunctive relief is obtained on the basis to prevent an abuse of process.[200]

(b) Level of knowledge on the part of the bank

24.191 If a bank is going to refuse to pay out this can only be where it has clear knowledge of the beneficiary's fraud.[201] A good indication of the level of knowledge required is that the bank must know enough that it would be able to plead such an allegation.[202] Mere suspicion or say-so of the customer will not suffice.

24.192 Given the bank is not itself involved in the underlying contractual dispute, it is entirely reliant upon its customer to provide documentary proof of the existence of a fraud. Once presented, the authorities suggest that the bank should afford the beneficiary an opportunity to try and explain its position. After all, the bank's lack of involvement in the underlying events makes it vulnerable simply to believing whatever its customer tells it. If the explanation from the beneficiary is not satisfactory and that together with the documentary evidence provided by the customer give rise to an irresistible inference of fraud, then the bank will be justified in refusing to pay out.[203]

24.193 The Court of Appeal in *United Trading Corp v Allied Arab Bank Ltd*[204] has provided some guidance as to the standard of proof required:

> The evidence of fraud must be clear, both as to the fact of fraud and as to the bank's knowledge. There mere assertion or allegation of fraud would not be sufficient (see [*Bolivinter*] at p.257). We would expect the Court to require strong corroborative evidence of the allegation, usually in the form of contemporary documents, particular those emanating from the buyer. In general, for the evidence of fraud to be clear, we would also expect the buyer to have been given an opportunity to answer the allegation and to have failed to provide any, or any adequate answer in circumstances where one could properly be expected. If the Court considers on the material before it that the only realistic inference to draw is that of fraud, then the seller would have made out a sufficient case of fraud. Whilst accepting that letters of credit and performance bonds are part of the essential machinery of international commerce . . . the strength of this proposition can be over-emphasised. As Mr Just Neil observed in the judgment under appeal, it cannot be in the interests of international commerce or of the banking community as a whole that this important machinery that is provided

---

[200] See *Czarnikow-Rionda v Standard Bank* [1999] 2 Lloyd's Rep 187, 203 per Rix J: 'If the source of the power to injunct were purely the law's interest in preventing the beneficiary from benefiting from his own fraud, I do not see why there should be the added requirement that the fraud be patent to the bank.'

[201] *Edward Owen (Engineering) Ltd v Barclays Bank International Ltd* [1978] QB 159.

[202] See Saville J's reaction to a failure so to do in *Society of Lloyd's v Canadian Imperial Bank of Commerce* [1993] 2 Lloyd's Rep 579.

[203] *Bolivinter Oil SA v Chase Manhattan Bank* [1984] 1 Lloyd's Rep 251, 257; see generally Hapgood, *Paget's Law of Banking* (13th edn), [34.10].

[204] [1985] 2 Lloyd's Rep 554.

for traders should be misused for the purposes of fraud...Moreover, we would find it an unsatisfactory position if, having established an important exception to what had previously been thought an absolute rule, the Courts in practice were to adopt so restrictive an approach to the evidence required as to prevent themselves from intervening. Were this to be the case, impressive and high-sounding phrases such as 'fraud unravels all' would become meaningless.

Ultimately, applying the principles of *American Cyanamid*, the Court of Appeal concluded that the relevant question was: have the claimants established that it is seriously arguable that, on the material available, the only realistic inference is that the seller could not honestly have believed in the validity of its demands on the performance bonds?[205] **24.194**

(3) Scenario (b): injunctive relief preventing payment out of fraudulent demand

It will come as no surprise that the very limited circumstances in which a bank is justified in refusing to pay out under a performance bond are mirrored in the limited circumstances available for injunctive relief. **24.195**

The Court of Appeal in *Bolivinter Oil SA v Chase Manhattan Bank*[206] made the following observations as to the limited nature of the circumstances justifying such relief being granted in respect of instruments such as performance bonds: **24.196**

> The unique value of such a letter, bond or guarantee is that the beneficiary can be completely satisfied that whatever disputes may thereafter arise between him and the bank's customer in relation to the performance or indeed existence of the underlying contract, the bank is personally undertaking to pay him provided that the specified conditions are met. In requesting his bank to issue such a letter, bond or guarantee, the customer is seeking to take advantage of this unique characteristic. If, save in the most exceptional cases, he is to be allowed to derogate from the bank's personal and irrevocable undertaking, given be it again noted at his request, by obtaining an injunction restraining the bank from honouring that undertaking, he will undermine what is the bank's greatest asset, however large and rich it may be, namely its reputation for financial and contractual probity. Furthermore, if this happens at all frequently, the value of all irrevocable letters of credit and performance bonds and guarantees will be undermined.
>
> Judges who are asked, often at short notice and *ex parte*, to issue an injunction restraining payment by a bank under an irrevocable letter of credit or performance bond or guarantee should ask whether there is any challenge to the validity of the letter, bond or guarantee itself. If there is not or if the challenge is not substantial, prima facie no injunction should be granted and the bank should be left free to honour its contractual obligation, although restrictions may well be imposed upon the freedom

---

[205] [1985] 2 Lloyd's Rep 554, 565.
[206] [1984] 1 Lloyd's Rep 251.

of the beneficiary to deal with the money after it has received it.[207] The wholly exceptional case where an injunction may be granted is where it is proved that the bank knows that any demand for payment already made or which may thereafter be made will clearly be fraudulent. But the evidence must be clear, both as to the fact of fraud and as to the bank's knowledge. It would certainly not normally be sufficient that this rests upon the uncorroborated statement of the customer, for irreparable damage can be done to a bank's credit in the relatively brief time which must elapse between the granting of such an injunction and an application by the bank to have it discharged.

(a) Balance of convenience—an insurmountable problem?

24.197 Assuming that the evidence satisfies the above requirements for a bank to refuse to pay out, there remains a major hurdle in a seller obtaining an injunction to prevent the bank from paying out (as opposed to the bank being entitled, of its own volition, to determine not to pay out) and that is the *Amercian Cyanamid* requirement of showing that the balance of convenience is in favour of granting the injunctive relief.

24.198 The difficulty is that in such circumstances, where the bank is aware of a clear fraud on the part of the beneficiary, the issuing bank would be under no contractual obligation to make that payment. Accordingly, the bank should make no payment out in any event, irrespective of the grant of an injunction. If it did, it would be doing so in breach of mandate and, if the issuing bank, would be liable in damages to the buyer alternatively would not be able to claim an indemnity from the buyer. Indeed, if it did, it would be in breach of his mandate. Having raised the issue of the importance of these instruments as the life-blood of commerce, Kerr J put the point as follows:

> However, let it be assumed in the plaintiff's favour that these considerations would not by themselves preclude the court from continuing the injunctions against the bank. The plaintiffs then still face what seems to me to be an insuperable difficulty. They are seeking to prevent the bank from paying and debiting their account. It must then follow that if the bank pays and debits the plaintiffs' account, it is either entitled to do so or not to do so. To do so would either be in accordance with the contract, then the plaintiffs have no cause of action against the bank and, as it seems to me, no possible basis for an injunction against it. Alternatively, if the threatened payment is in breach of contract . . . then the plaintiffs would have good claims for damages against the bank. In that event the injunctions would be inappropriate, because they interfere with the bank's obligations to the Egyptian banks, because they might cause greater damage to the bank than the plaintiffs could pay on their undertaking in damages, and because the plaintiffs would then have an adequate remedy in damages.

---

[207] This is a reference to the alternative course of action which a victim of a fraud could adopt: namely, to freeze the proceeds of payment out as opposed to preventing the bank from making the payment out. It has the very distinct advantage of not asking the court to interfere with the operation of instruments such as performance bonds.

The balance of convenience would in that event be hopelessly weighted against the plaintiffs.[208]

After an extensive and illuminating review of the authorities in this area in **24.199** *Czarnikow-Rionda v Standard Bank*,[209] Rix J commented on this 'insuperable difficulty' in terms which serve only to reiterate and highlight just how rare a successful application for injunctive relief is likely to be:

> I do not know that it can be affirmatively stated that a Court would never, as a matter of balance of convenience, injunct a bank from making payment under its letter of credit or performance guarantee obligations in circumstances where a good claim within the fraud exception was accepted by the Court at a pre-trial stage. I do not regard Mr Justice Kerr and the other Courts which have approved or applied the logic of his 'insuperable difficulty' as necessarily saying that it could *never* be done. It is perhaps wise to expect the unexpected, even the presently unforeseeable. All that can be said is that the circumstances in which it should be done have not so far presented themselves, and that it would of necessity take extraordinary facts to surmount this difficulty.[210]

An important factor to be considered when dealing with balance of convenience **24.200** is that it would be open to the customer to apply for Mareva relief against the proceeds of payment out and thereby avoid interfering with the bank's obligations under the instrument to pay out. It is accepted that this would not give priority in any insolvency but nevertheless it would ensure that the monies could not be dissipated by the fraudsters.[211]

(4) Scenario (c): fraud tainting the instrument itself

It will be recalled that in *Bolivinter*, a distinction was drawn between a fraudulent **24.201** demand under an otherwise valid instrument and a demand under an instrument itself tainted with fraud. This distinction became important in the Court of Appeal case of *Solo Industries UK Ltd v Canara Bank*.[212]

In this case, Solo Industries, an English company, was the beneficiary of a per- **24.202** formance bond issued by the Indian bank. The bank had alleged that the bond had been procured by fraudulent misrepresentation and conspiracy to which Solo Industries was said to be a party. Solo sought summary judgment against the bank. The court refused the application on the grounds that the bank had a real prospect of justifying its avoidance. On appeal, the issue was whether the court

---

[208] *R D Harbottle (Mercantile) Ltd v National Westminster Bank Ltd* [1978] QB 146, 155. This passage was applied by the Court of Appeal in *United Trading Corporation SA v Allied Arab Bank Ltd* [1985] 2 Lloyd's Rep 554, 565–6.

[209] [1999] 2 Lloyd's Rep 187.

[210] ibid, 204.

[211] See *Czarnikow-Rionda v Standard Bank* [1999] 2 Lloyd's Rep 187, 203 per Rix J.

[212] [2001] EWCA Civ 1059, [2001] 2 All ER (Comm) 217.

had applied the correct test bearing in mind the fact that such instruments are often considered the same as cash.

24.203 Mance LJ, giving the leading judgment, held that the principles set out above which restrict the availability of injunctive relief preventing fraudulent demands on valid instruments did not apply to instruments which were themselves tainted by fraud. Risks which a bank may take to pay out under a valid instrument against a fraudulent demand do not arise when the bank has itself been fraudulently mis-led into agreeing to issue the instrument. There was therefore no reason why the bank's defence should be subject to anything other than normal contractual prin-ciples, without needing to rely upon the more restrictive approach. On the facts, it was for the bank to show that it had a real prospect of defending the claim under CPR r 24.2(a)(ii) by justifying its claim to have avoided the bond. On the facts, it was held the bank satisfied this burden.

J. Orders Restricting Movement Abroad—Writ *ne exeat regno* and *Bayer AG v Winter* order

24.204 This section is concerned with two discrete orders which will restrict the ability of an individual to leave the jurisdiction.

(1) Writ *ne exeat regno*

24.205 The first, the writ *ne exeat regno* is, as its name suggests, of ancient origin (13th century). In *Blackstone's Commentaries*,[213] it was said that the purpose of the writ, as used in Chancery was:

> exactly the same as an arrest at law in the commencement of an action, viz, to prevent the party from withdrawing his person and property beyond the jurisdiction of the court, before a judgment could be obtained and carried into execution; so where there is a suit in equity for a demand, for which the defendant cannot be arrested in an action at law, upon an affidavit made that there is reason to apprehend that he will leave the kingdom before the conclusion of the suit, the chancellor by this writ will stop him . . .

24.206 In *Felton v Callis*,[214] after a review of the history of this writ, Megarry J held that four conditions needed to be established before such a writ could be issued.

(1) The action is one in which the defendant would formerly (i.e. before the Debtors Act 1869) have been liable to arrest at law.

---

213 Vol 1, 15th edn, 1809, 266n.
214 [1969] 1 QB 200. *Allied Arab Bank Ltd v Hajjar* [1988] QB 787.

- This would include a claim in debt including money had and received/unjust enrichment;
- It does not include a claim for damages for fraudulent conspiracy: *Allied Arab Bank v Hajjar* [1988] QB 787.

(2) A good cause of action for at least £50 is established. The threshold figure will no doubt be a good deal more nowadays. Given the draconian nature of the relief sought, the court is likely to require a reasonably substantial claim in debt to justify invoking the procedure. So, for example, it is rare to see the Mareva jurisdiction invoked for claims below £50,000 and perhaps a similar approach might be adopted in this respect.

(3) There is 'probable cause' for believing that the defendant is 'about to quit England' unless he is arrested.

(4) 'The absence of the defendant from England will materially prejudice the plaintiff in the prosecution of his action.'[215]
- This requirement is limited to prejudice being caused to the prosecution of the claim and hence the writ is limited to pre-judgment. It is not available post-judgment in aid of execution: *Lipkin Gorman v Cass*[216] authorities suggest that the debtor is entitled to be released after judgment has been given.
- 'In the present case I have no evidence whatever before me to show that the defendant's absence from England would materially prejudice the plaintiffs in the prosecution of their action. I can well see that his absence may very materially prejudice the plaintiffs in obtaining the fruits of their action; but that is not the test.'[217]

In addition, Megarry J emphasized two overriding principles: **24.207**

- whether or not the four conditions are satisfied, entitlement to such relief remains discretionary;
- the standard of proof is high: 'the court must be convinced'.

Given the limitations on the type of claim which falls within ambit of this writ, **24.208**
and the strict application of the other criteria, it may well be that the commercial fraud litigator will find greater assistance from the *Bayer AG v Winter* order.

(2) *Bayer AG v Winter* order

This order derives from s 37 of the Supreme Court Act 1981 and is based upon **24.209**
the court's powers to grant injunctive relief whenever it is just and convenient so

---

[215] ibid, 211.
[216] *The Times,* 29 May 1985.
[217] *Felton v Callis* [1969] 1 QB 200, 214.

to do. It is not an order in aid of specific legal or equitable rights and so does not require the existence of a cause of action.[218]

24.210 In *Bayer AG v Winter*,[219] the claimant was a pharmaceutical company which manufactured an insecticide. The claimant alleged that the defendants were marketing a counterfeit product. The judge granted various orders requiring the defendants to disclose information and documentation relating to the counterfeit outfit and operation. But he refused to grant an order restraining the defendant from leaving London or to give up his passport.

24.211 On appeal, the Court of Appeal held that the court has jurisdiction to grant such orders. Fox LJ noted:

> Therefore, it seems to me that the court is faced with a situation in which there is a risk to the plaintiffs that they may not obtain the information ordered to be disclosed, unless the order which is now sought is granted; while, at the same time, any risk of hardship to the first defendant is dealt with by his capacity to apply to a judge to vary or discharge the order.[220]

24.212 The Court of Appeal granted the injunction but held that it should last only so long as it was necessary to enable the plaintiffs to serve the Mareva and Anton Piller orders and try to obtain the necessary information identified in the orders.

K. Practice and Procedure[221]

(1) Applying for injunctive relief

(a) Nature of application

24.213 There is usually limited time between initial instructions and the time when it is necessary to make the application so it is important that the practitioner is well aware of all the issues that his instructions must cover and the information that is needed to be provided to the court.

24.214 The application is before a judge and typically proceeds by way of an initial 'without notice' application i.e. without notifying the respondent that the application has been made.

24.215 The application is one of the few remaining applications which must be supported by evidence in the form of an affidavit as opposed to a witness statement.[222]

---

218 *In Re Oriental Credit Ltd* [1988] 1 Ch 204, 207–8 (Harman J).
219 [1986] 1 WLR 497 CA.
220 ibid, 502H.
221 This section on practice and procedure will cover all the applications referred to in the text.
222 See Practice Direction 25, para 3.1

Of course, in cases of extreme urgency, a draft affidavit together with an undertaking to swear it in that form may suffice.

In preparing the written evidence and in presenting it to the court, it is of the **24.216** utmost importance that the advocate ensures full compliance with his duty of full and frank disclosure to the court. He must therefore bring to the court's attention any adverse facts which may undermine his entitlement to injunctive relief. The details of this duty are examined separately below. Failure to adhere to this duty can result in the discharge of the injunction and an enforcement of the cross-undertakings in damages.

The *quid pro quo* for being permitted to proceed in the absence of the respondent **24.217** is that the court will require the applicant to provide an effective cross-undertaking in damages to be enforced by the court in the event that it subsequently proves that the injunction should never have been granted in the first place. It is now usual that the court will ask that the applicant fortify the cross-undertakings in damages with security.

(b) Duty of full and frank disclosure

The initial application for a freezing injunction takes place in the absence of the **24.218** respondent at a without notice hearing. As such, it involves a denial of that respondent's fundamental right to be heard before the court makes an initial determination of the applicant's entitlement to a freezing injunction. That denial is justified only on the basis that had proper notice been given, there was a real likelihood that the injunction would be rendered worthless since the prior-informed respondent would have taken steps to place those assets beyond the court's reach.

Notwithstanding the justification for proceeding in the absence of the respond- **24.219** ent, the court is concerned that it acts on the basis of a proper understanding of the dispute—one which involves both parties' points of view. There is thus placed on the applicant a duty of full and frank disclosure of all facts and matters including those which are favourable to the respondent when making a without notice application.[223]

The importance of this duty and the need for the applicant to comply fully with **24.220** it cannot be over-emphasized. A failure to comply with this duty may lead to the discharge of the injunction even in circumstances where compliance might not have made any difference to the court's view on the merits.

---

[223] *R v Kensington Income Tax Comrs ex p Princess Edmond de Polignac* [1917] 1 KB 486, 509; *Castelli v Cook* (1849) 7 Hare 89, 94; *Dalglish v Jarvie* (1850) 2 Mac & G 231, 238; *The Andria* [1984] QB 477; *Bank Mellat v Nikpour* [1985] FSR 87, 89.

24.221 The following relevant legal principles were set out by Ralph Gibson LJ in *Brink's Mat Ltd v Elcombe*:[224]

(1) The duty of the applicant is to make 'a full and fair disclosure of all the material facts' see *R v Kensington Income Tax Commissioners, Ex parte Princess Edmond de Polignac* [1917] 1 KB 486, 514 per Scrutton LJ.

(2) The material facts are those which it is material for the judge to know in dealing with the application as made: materiality is to be decided by the court and not by the assessment of the applicant or his legal advisers: see *R v Kensington Income Tax Commissioners Ex parte Princess Edmond de Polignac*, per Cozens-Hardy MR at p.504, citing *Dalglish v Jarvie* (1850) 2 Mac & G 231, 238 and Browne-Wilkinson J in *Thermax Ltd v Schott Industrial Glass Ltd* [1981] FSR 289, 295.

(3) The applicant must make proper inquiries before making the application: see *Bank Mellatt v Nikpour (Mohammad Ebrahaim)* [1985] FSR 87. The duty of disclosure therefore applies not only to material facts known to the applicant but also to any additional facts which he would have known if he had made such inquiries.

(4) The extent of the inquiries which will be held to be proper, and therefore necessary, must depend on all the circumstances of the case including (a) the nature of the case which the applicant is making when he makes the application; and (b) the order for which application is made and the probable effect of the order on the defendant: see, for example, the examination by Scott J of the possible effect of an Anton Piller order in *Columbia Picture Industries v Robinson* [1987] Ch 38; and (c) the degree of legitimate urgency and the time available for the making of inquiries: see per Slade LJ in *Bank Mellett v Nikpour (Mohammad Ebrahaim)* [1985] FSR 87, 92-93.

(5) If material non-disclosure is established the court will be 'astute to ensure that a plaintiff who obtains [a without notice injunction] without full disclosure. . . .is deprived of any advantage he may have derived by that breach of duty:' see per Donaldson LJ in *Bank Mellatt v Nikpour*. . . at p 91 citing Warrington LJ in *R v Kensington Income Tax Commissioners, Ex parte princess Edmond de Polignac* [1917] KB 486, 509.

(6) Whether the fact not disclosed is of sufficient materiality to justify or require immediate discharge of the order without examination of the merits depends on the importance of the fact to the issues which were to be decided by the judge on the application. The answer to the question whether the non-disclosure was innocent, in the sense that the fact was not known to the applicant or that its relevance was not perceived, is an important consideration but not decisive by reason of the duty on the applicant to make all proper inquiries and to give careful consideration to the case being presented.

(7) Finally, it 'is not for every omission that the injunction will be automatically discharged. A *locus poentitentiae* may sometimes be afforded:' per Lord Denning MR in *Bank Mellat v Mikpour*. . .[1985] FSR 87,90. The court has a discretion, notwithstanding proof of material non-disclosure which justifies or requires the immediate discharge of the ex parte order, or to make a new order on terms.

---

[224] [1988] 1 WLR 1350, 1356–7.

The duty of full and frank disclosure extends from the exhibiting of all relevant **24.222** documents to the manner in which the evidence is orally presented at court. The duty demands that adverse documents are expressly pointed out by counsel and not simply left by the court to be found as exhibits to affidavits, some of which time will not have permitted the judge to read. There is a limit, of course, as to what can be expected of a solicitor, in preparing the evidence, and of counsel, in presenting it, in terms of effectively standing in the shoes of the absent respondent.[225] No one pretends that it makes up for the denial of the respondent's right to be heard but it represents the next best thing.

In *O'Regan v Iambic Production*,[226] Peter Pain J remarked: **24.223**

> It is clearly the duty of Counsel and of the solicitor to point out to the Judge any points which are to their clients' disadvantage, which the Judge should take into account in considering whether or not to grant the injunction. It is difficult for a Judge upon an ex parte application at short notice to grasp all the relevant points. In this context it is prudent to remind myself of the following dicta of Bingham J in *Spore Trade SA v Compel Commodities Ltd* [1986] 2 Lloyd's Rep 428 at 437:
>
> '[The applicant must] identify the crucial points for and against the application, and not rely upon the mere exhibiting of numerous documents.'

Similarly, in *Memory Corpn Plc v Sidhu*[227] Mummery LJ emphasized the role to be **24.224** played by the advocate at the without notice hearing:

> It cannot be emphasized too strongly that at an urgent without notice hearing for a freezing injunction, as well as for a search order or any other form of interim injunction, there is a high duty to make full, fair, an accurate disclosure of material information to the court and to draw the court's attention to significant factual, legal and procedural aspects of the case. It is the particular duty of the advocate to see that the correct legal procedures and forms are used; that a written skeleton argument and a properly drafted order are prepared by him personally and lodged with the court before the oral hearing; and that at the hearing the court's attention is drawn by him to unusual features of the evidence adduced, to the applicable law and to the formalities and procedure to be observed . . . It is unsatisfactory for an advocate to hand to the court for the first time during the course of an urgent hearing a long and complex draft order which requires close reading and careful scrutiny by the court. If the advocate is unable to produce a draft order for the judge to read before the oral hearing starts then the application should not be made, save in the most exceptional circumstances, until the order has been drafted and lodged.

---

[225] *Columbia Picture Industries v Robinson* [1987] Ch 38, 75; *Amanuel v Alexander Shipping Co* [1986] QB 464, 469. The inadequacies of the duty, when compared with the absence of the respondent's actual right to be heard, should not however lull any applicant for without notice relief into the belief that the duty demands anything less than 100% compliance: see Sir John Donaldson MR in *Eastglen International Corpn v Monpare SA* (1987) 137 NLJ Rep 56 cited and quoted in this respect in *Lloyds Bowmaker Ltd v Britannia Arrow* [1988] 1 1337, 1343.

[226] (1989) 139 New LJ 1378.

[227] [2000] 1 WLR 1443; *Gadget Shop Ltd v Bug Com Ltd* [2001] FSR 383.

24.225 It is good practice to have a section both in the affidavit and in the Skeleton Argument which is expressly headed 'Duty of Full and Frank Disclosure' listing all of the factors that are considered relevant which might be adverse to the case. This will focus the minds of those preparing the evidence as well as that of the advocate of the need to consider matters which might be adverse the application. Otherwise, one can too readily be carried along with the rush to court on the back of what appears to be a clear case of fraudulent conduct. It is essential that the practitioner, both solicitor and counsel, act as a barrier to that rush to court to ensure that the client has provided *all* relevant information.

24.226 Further, the judge might well consider that your clients have an obvious case for injunctive relief. This can result in the court indicating a desire to move on to sorting out the terms of the draft order before counsel has had an opportunity to raise any adverse points. Nevertheless, it is incumbent upon counsel to ensure that time is taken by the court to listen to those factors which are adverse to the claim or application. It will be no answer to a subsequent application to discharge the injunction for the applicant to contend that he assumed the judge must have read the adverse factors in the Skeleton Argument or that the court wanted to hurry the application along. None of this justifies the advocate's failure orally to raise adverse factors. Be prepared to insist that the court hears your submissions on issues of full and frank disclosure.

(c) Cross-undertakings in damages[228]

24.227 An applicant for without notice interim injunctive relief will nearly always[229] be required to give a cross-undertaking in damages as a condition of his entitlement to that relief. The standard wording is an 'undertaking . . . to the court to pay any damages which the respondent(s) (or any other party served with or notified of the order) sustain which the court considers the applicant should pay'.

24.228 The justification for the cross-undertaking is the fact that the court is being asked to proceed to grant relief without a full examination of the evidence or proper determination of the issues. Such a process runs the obvious risk of the court reaching the wrong conclusion and granting relief in circumstances where ultimately it is shown that none is justified. Accordingly, in order to cover the circumstances where it is proved that an injunction has been wrongly obtained, the court requires an applicant to provide a cross-undertaking in damages[230] to protect the respondent's interests.

---

[228] *Zuckerman on Civil Procedure* (2nd edn), 337 *et seq.*
[229] ibid, [9.110].
[230] See *F Hoffman-La Roche & Co AG v Secretary of State for Trade and Industry* [1975] AC 295; *Smithkline Beecham Plc v Apotex Europe Ltd* [2005] EWHC 1655; [2006] 1 WLR 872; AAS Zuckerman, 'Dispensation with Undertaking in Damages—an Elementary Injustice' (1993) 12 CJQ 268; AAS Zuckerman, 'Interlocutory Injunctions in Quest of Procedural Fairness' (1993) 56 MLR 325.

An applicant will be deemed to have provided an undertaking in damages even if **24.229** it is not included in the relevant order.[231] That said, if an applicant expressly refuses to provide an undertaking in damages, he cannot be made by the court to provide one.[232] The proper course for the court to take is simply to refuse the interim relief.

The undertaking is given to the court and not to the other party.[233] It follows that **24.230** in the event that it is subsequently discovered that the injunction had been wrongly granted, no cause of action under the undertakings immediately vests in the respondent or non-party identified in the cross-undertakings.

In order to ensure that the cross-undertakings in damages represent a real benefit **24.231** to the respondent, the court has shown a greater willingness in recent times to insist on its fortification by some form of security, such as the provision of a bank guarantee. The standard wording of the draft freezing injunction, schedule B, dealing with undertakings, contains wording for the provision of a bank guarantee in support. It is imperative that counsel ensure that he has obtained proper instructions on this issue prior to the hearing, as the judge may well raise it as a condition of entitlement to interim relief. If the client is very keen to avoid giving any such security, he will need to ensure that the affidavit contains detailed information as to his net worth[234] and the location of assets within the jurisdiction in order to have any chance of persuading a court not to require fortification.

Consistent with the duty of full and frank disclosure, which continues after the **24.232** initial without notice hearing, it is incumbent upon the applicant to keep the court informed of any material changes in his financial condition which may affect the enforceability of the cross-undertakings in damages.[235]

That said, the court will not impose a condition which cannot be complied with. **24.233** If the applicant lacks the funds to support such an undertaking by way of security, that will not automatically bar the client from pursuit of the application but it is

---

[231] *Spanish General Agency Corpn v Spanish Corpn* (1890) LT 161; *Colledge v Crossley, The Times* 18 March 1975. Laddie J in *Bank of Scotland v A Ltd* [2001] C P Rep 14 (Ch) noted the potential for omission of the undertaking given the time pressures placed on court and remarked that it would be wrong if the protection granted to protect the respondent's interests should depend on whether the court remembers specifically to include such an undertaking in the terms of the order. See also Zuckerman, *Civil Procedure* (2nd edn), [9.96].

[232] *Smithkline Beecham Plc v Apotex Europe Ltd* [2006] EWCA Civ 658, [2007] Ch 71. Other than requiring a cross-undertaking in damages, the Court of Appeal denied that the Court had a general power in restitution to order the applicant to cover any losses a third party may have suffered as a result of the injunction.

[233] See Schedule B of the standard draft order in Part 25 PD Interim Injunctions; *F Hoffman-La Roche & Co AG v Secretary of State for Trade and Industry* [1975] AC 295, 361.

[234] *Staines v Walsh* [2003] EWHC 1486; *The Times,* 1 August 2003; *Sinclair Investment Holdings SA v Cushnie* [2004] EWHC 218 (Ch).

[235] *Staines v Walsh* [2003] EWHC 1486; *The Times,* 1 August 2003.

submitted that it is likely to make the task that much harder. The court will need to take that into account in deciding whether to exercise its discretion in favour of the applicant. In the case of a freezing injunction which can have catastrophic effects on the reputation of a businessman, the court will need to be heavily persuaded as to the merits of the application before exposing the respondent to injunctive relief where no adequate enforcement of undertakings can take place.

24.234　There is no automatic entitlement to damages in the event that the injunction is discharged. An application to the court must be made. If the court decides to enforce the undertakings, directions will be given for the hearing of the application. The measure of damages is the contract measure.[236]

(2)　Challenging the relief

(a)　Preparatory steps

24.235　Whatever the form of injunctive relief, the starting point must be not to rush back to court. That will be the temptation and that will be the pressure from the client. It is necessary first and foremost to consider the issues and decide whether there truly is any basis for challenging the relief obtained.

24.236　One important aspect of considering the issues is to ensure that the applicant for the interim relief has provided all the papers necessary for a proper determination. This includes the order, the evidence relied upon including exhibits, the Skeleton Argument, any authorities bundle and a note of the without notice hearing. If a transcript is available, that should be requested as well. If additional affidavits had to be sworn as a result of anything said at the hearing, these need to be drafted and provided.

24.237　Thereafter, these papers should be properly considered. Clients will naturally be anxious to get going but it is essential to resist that pressure to ensure a clear-headed decision is made. If you decide against making any challenge, you must do so understanding that the other side will no doubt make much of that every time your client attends court. But if there truly is no basis to challenge, do not make one just for the sake of it. Such conduct may only result in the court making more adverse comments about the case and clients.

(b)　Potential grounds for discharge

24.238　Ultimately, these will depend on the nature of the relief obtained against the client. Typical candidates include an attack on the underlying merits, that there has been a material non-disclosure or some other element of the requirements for the relief is not satisfied.

---

[236] *Smith v Day* (1882) 21 Ch D 421, 428; *Hunt v Hunt* (1884) 54 LJ CH 289; *Triodos Bank NV v Dobbs* [2005] EWHC 108 (Ch).

It is not often that an attack on the underlying merits will succeed. The burden to **24.239** overcome is not particularly high and the court will not want to become engaged in a detailed examination of the merits at this stage. Such a challenge is more likely to succeed if it is made on the basis of some technical legal argument (e.g. no proprietary claim can arise *as a matter of legal principle* on the facts alleged) rather than a dispute about factual events.

Material non-disclosure is a very typical application to make. The duty (examined **24.240** above) is a high one and so it is usually quite easy to find departures. Often, it is considered little more than a last ditch effort by the respondent to get rid of the relief. If the application is to be made on this basis, think about it carefully—why is the missing information important? To what issue or issues does the missing information relate? If the court had this missing information, why would that have resulted in it changing its mind?

As set out above, the challenge could be based on any aspect of the initial applic- **24.241** ation. It may be that the court has been misled as to the existence of assets or their value or the respondent's conduct in respect of those assets has been mischaracterized as giving rise to a risk of dissipation. Has the applicant complied with all their undertakings to the court, both those given orally at the without notice hearing as well as those contained in the order itself? A failure to comply with such undertakings will place the applicant seriously on the back foot.

Be selective. Any application to challenge based on everything and the kitchen **24.242** sink will soon lose credibility before the court.

(c) *Variation*

After very careful consideration, it may be decided that there is no basis to chal- **24.243** lenge in principle the order obtained. However, it may be that some form of variation will be needed. Consider carefully whether the client's business can operate properly. If not, what variation might assist? Has an adequate allowance been given for living expenses and legal fees? It is not for the claimant to impose a reduced lifestyle on the respondent. Any attempt to increase allowances is only likely to succeed once full disclosure has been made.

(d) *Provision of security*

If the client is in a position so to do, and wishes to avoid giving full disclosure of **24.244** his assets, it is possible to have the interim relief discharged on the back of the provision of adequate security

APPENDIX 1

Precedent No. 1: Freezing Injunction

Forms of Freezing Injunction and Search Order
adapted for use in the Commercial Court

*** FREEZING INJUNCTION ***
[Note: The footnotes in this Precedent have been inserted by the author.]

IN THE HIGH COURT OF JUSTICE
QUEEN'S BENCH DIVISION
COMMERCIAL COURT

Before The Honourable Mr Justice [   ]

Claim No.

BETWEEN

Claimant(s)

– and –

Defendant(s)

Applicant(s)

Respondent(s)

PENAL NOTICE

If you [   ]¹ disobey this order you may be held to be in contempt of court and may be imprisoned, fined or have your assets seized.

Any other person who knows of this order and does anything which helps or permits the Respondent to breach the terms of this order may also be held to be in contempt of court and may be imprisoned, fined or have their assets seized.

THIS ORDER

1. This is a Freezing Injunction made against [   ] ('the Respondent') on [   ] by Mr Justice [   ] on the application of [   ] ('the Applicant'). The Judge read the Affidavits listed in Schedule A and accepted the undertakings set out in Schedule B at the end of this Order.
2. This order was made at a hearing without notice to the Respondent. The Respondent has a right to apply to the court to vary or discharge the order—see paragraph 13 below.

---

¹ Insert name of Respondent(s).

3. There will be a further hearing in respect of this order on [   ] ('the return date').[2]

4. If there is more than one Respondent—

   (a) unless otherwise stated, references in this order to "the Respondent" mean both or all of them; and

   (b) this order is effective against any Respondent on whom it is served or who is given notice of it.

FREEZING INJUNCTION

[For injunction limited to assets in England and Wales]

5. Until the return date or further order of the court, the Respondent must not remove from England and Wales or in any way dispose of, deal with or diminish the value of any of his assets which are in England and Wales up to the value of £   .

[For worldwide injunction]

5. Until the return date or further order of the court, the Respondent must not—

   (1) remove from England and Wales any of his assets which are in England and Wales up to the value of £   ; or

   (2) in any way dispose of, deal with or diminish the value of any of his assets whether they are in or outside England and Wales up to the same value.

[For either form of injunction]

6. Paragraph 5 applies to all the Respondent's assets whether or not they are in his own name and whether they are solely or jointly owned. For the purpose of this order the Respondent's assets include any asset which he has the power, directly or indirectly, to dispose of or deal with as if it were his own. The Respondent is to be regarded as having such power if a third party holds or controls the asset in accordance with his direct or indirect instructions.[3]

7. This prohibition includes the following assets in particular—

   (a) the property known as *[title/address]* or the net sale money after payment of any mortgages if it has been sold;

   (b) the property and assets of the Respondent's business [known as *[name]*] [carried on at *[address]*] or the sale money if any of them have been sold; and

   (c) any money in the account numbered *[account number]* at *[title/address]*.

[For injunction limited to assets in England and Wales]

8. If the total value free of charges or other securities ('unencumbered value') of the Respondent's assets in England and Wales exceeds £   , the Respondent may remove any of those assets from England and Wales or may dispose of or deal with them so long as the total unencumbered value of his assets still in England and Wales remains above £   .

[For worldwide injunction]

8. (1) If the total value free of charges or other securities ('unencumbered value') of the Respondent's assets in England and Wales exceeds £   , the Respondent may remove any of those assets from England and Wales or may dispose of or deal with them so long as the

---

[2] This will usually be one or two weeks after the without notice hearing. The court is always keen to ensure maintenance of control over the order but often, in complex fraud cases, the return date is far too early for the Respondent to be able to mount any application to challenge the order.

[3] If the Applicant wishes to rely upon assets held in the name of third parties as nominees for the Respondent then (i) the third party should be joined so that it can raise such objection as it wishes *(C Inc PLC v L* [2001] 2 Lloyd's Rep 113), and (ii) care should be taken to ensure that the requirements for such relief are satisfied *(SCF Finance v Masri* [1985] 1 WLR 876; *Mercantile Group (Europe) AC v Aiyela* [1994] QBB QB 366; *TSB Private Bank International SA v Chabra* [1992] 1 WLR 231). The court may need to consider giving directions for the resolution of the issue in a hearing before trial.

total unencumbered value of the Respondent's assets still in England and Wales remains above £   .[4]

(2) If the total unencumbered value of the Respondent's assets in England and Wales does not exceed £   , the Respondent must not remove any of those assets from England and Wales and must not dispose of or deal with any of them. If the Respondent has other assets outside England and Wales, he may dispose of or deal with those assets outside England and Wales so long as the total unencumbered value of all his assets whether in or outside England and Wales remains above £   .

PROVISION OF INFORMATION

9. (1) Unless paragraph (2) applies, the Respondent must [immediately] [within hours of service of this order][5] and to the best of his ability inform the Applicant's solicitors of all his assets [in England and Wales] [worldwide] [exceeding £   in value] whether in his own name or not and whether solely or jointly owned, giving the value, location and details of all such assets.[6]

(2) If the provision of any of this information is likely to incriminate the Respondent, he may be entitled to refuse to provide it, but is recommended to take legal advice before refusing to provide the information. Wrongful refusal to provide the information is contempt of court and may render the Respondent liable to be imprisoned, fined or have his assets seized.

10. Within [   ] working days after being served with this order, the Respondent must swear and serve on the Applicant's solicitors an affidavit setting out the above information.[7]

EXCEPTIONS TO THIS ORDER

11. (1) This order does not prohibit the Respondent from spending £   a week towards his ordinary living expenses and also £   [*or*   a reasonable sum] on legal advice and representation. [But before spending any money the Respondent must tell the Applicant's legal representatives where the money is to come from.][8]

[(2) This order does not prohibit the Respondent from dealing with or disposing of any of his assets in the ordinary and proper course of business.][9]

---

[4] The meaning of this clause is tolerably clear. However, this provision can make enforcement and policing of the injunction difficult in circumstances where, as in *Mobil Cerro Negro Ltd v Petroleos de Venezuelas SA* [2008] 1 Lloyd's Rep 684, the respondent has assets substantially in excess of those frozen. The excess can be moved about without restriction.

[5] The standard order offers two options. The first is that the information be provided 'immediately' which, given the usual number of questions being asked, seems a little ridiculous. But once one moves to offering say, five hours, to get the information together complaints are raised that this is not a sufficient amount of time. The parties should not forget that this is simply stage one of a two-stage disclosure exercise. The first stage is premised on 'to the best of his ability'. Mistakes can happen. It is the second stage which involves confirming the accuracy of the information provided on affidavit.

[6] It would be sensible to ensure that the definition of assets mirrors that used in para 6 for the purposes of the injunctive relief. Further, it may well be worth spelling out what is included in assets to avoid argument at a later date. For example, some Respondents take the view that they need not disclose their bank accounts which are in overdraft since they represent 'an asset'. An appropriately worded definition of assets, expressly including matters such as bank accounts, should be considered.

[7] This is usually seven working days.

[8] The brackets are usually removed. This ensures that the Respondent must first inform the Applicant where the monies are coming from before he can engage in any serious discussion as to increasing the amounts to spend. Note, it is not for the Applicant to impose a lower level of living on the Respondent. If he genuinely has outgoings of £10k per week and is able to afford it, there is not a great deal that can be done about that.

[9] This clause typically requires a great deal of co-operation as between solicitors for the Applicant and for the Respondent. Unless co-operation and common sense prevails, this aspect can be found to take up a lot of the solicitors' time on both sides.

(3) The Respondent may agree with the Applicant's legal representatives that the above spending limits should be increased or that this order should be varied in any other respect, but any agreement must be in writing.

(4) The order will cease to have effect if the Respondent—

(a) provides security by paying the sum of £   into court, to be held to the order of the court; or

(b) makes provision for security in that sum by another method agreed with the Applicant's legal representatives.

COSTS

12. The costs of this application are reserved to the judge hearing the application on the return date.

VARIATION OR DISCHARGE OF THIS ORDER

13. Anyone served with or notified of this order may apply to the court at any time to vary or discharge this order (or so much of it as affects that person), but they must first inform the Applicant's solicitors. If any evidence is to be relied upon in support of the application, the substance of it must be communicated in writing to the Applicant's solicitors in advance.[10]

INTERPRETATION OF THIS ORDER

14. A Respondent who is an individual who is ordered not to do something must not do it himself or in any other way. He must not do it through others acting on his behalf or on his instructions or with his encouragement.

15. A Respondent which is not an individual which is ordered not to do something must not do it itself or by its directors, officers, partners, employees or agents or in any other way.

PARTIES OTHER THAN THE APPLICANT AND RESPONDENT

16. **Effect of this order**

It is a contempt of court for any person notified of this order knowingly to assist in or permit a breach of this order. Any person doing so may be imprisoned, fined or have their assets seized.

17. **Set off by banks**

This injunction does not prevent any bank from exercising any right of set off it may have in respect of any facility which it gave to the respondent before it was notified of this order.

18. **Withdrawals by the Respondent**

No bank need enquire as to the application or proposed application of any money withdrawn by the Respondent if the withdrawal appears to be permitted by this order.

[For worldwide injunction]

19. **Persons outside England and Wales**

(1) Except as provided in paragraph (2) below, the terms of this order do not affect or concern anyone outside the jurisdiction of this court.

(2) The terms of this order will affect the following persons in a country or state outside the jurisdiction of this court—

(a) the Respondent or his officer or agent appointed by power of attorney;

(b) any person who—

(i) is subject to the jurisdiction of this court;

(ii) has been given written notice of this order at his residence or place of business within the jurisdiction of this court; and

---

[10] It is advisable to insert a time frame such as '72 hours' written notice' of such an application.

      (iii) is able to prevent acts or omissions outside the jurisdiction of this court which constitute or assist in a breach of the terms of this order; and

    (c) any other person, only to the extent that this order is declared enforceable by or is enforced by a court in that country or state.[11]

[For worldwide injunction]

20. Assets located outside England and Wales

Nothing in this order shall, in respect of assets located outside England and Wales, prevent any third party from complying with—

(1) what it reasonably believes to be its obligations, contractual or otherwise, under the laws and obligations of the country or state in which those assets are situated or under the proper law of any contract between itself and the Respondent; and

(2) any orders of the courts of that country or state, provided that reasonable notice of any application for such an order is given to the Applicant's solicitors.[12]

COMMUNICATIONS WITH THE COURT

All communications to the court about this order should be sent to Room EB09, Royal Courts of Justice, Strand, London WC2A 2LL quoting the case number. The telephone number is 020 7947 6826.

The offices are open between 10 a.m. and 4.30 p.m. Monday to Friday.

SCHEDULE A

AFFIDAVITS

The Applicant relied on the following affidavits—

      [name]   [number of affidavit]   [date sworn]   [filed on behalf of]

(1)

(2)

SCHEDULE B

UNDERTAKINGS GIVEN TO THE COURT BY THE APPLICANT

(1) If the court later finds that this order has caused loss to the Respondent, and decides that the Respondent should be compensated for that loss, the Applicant will comply with any order the court may make.

[(2) The Applicant will—

    (a) on or before *[date]* cause a written guarantee in the sum of £   to be issued from a bank with a place of business within England or Wales, in respect of any order the court may make pursuant to paragraph (1) above; and

---

[11]   This is the *Babanaft* proviso (see *Babanaft International Co SA v Bassatne* [1990] Ch 13). This is standard in a worldwide freezing order as it protects a third party operating in another jurisdiction. That third party knows that unless and until the order is recognized or enforced in that other country, it has no effect over the third party. The applicant also gives an undertaking in Sch B not to enforce in a foreign jurisdiction without seeking the court's permission: the guidelines for permission are set out in *Dadourian Group International Inc v Simms* [2006] 1 WLR 2499.

[12]   This is known as the *Baltic* proviso. This enables third parties to comply with what they understand to be their obligations under a third jurisdiction. See *Bank of China v NBM L* [2002] 1 WLR 844.

(b) immediately upon issue of the guarantee, cause a copy of it to be served on the Respondent.][13]

(3)   As soon as practicable the Applicant will issue and serve a claim form [in the form of the draft produced to the court] [claiming the appropriate relief].

(4)   The Applicant will [swear and file an affidavit] [cause an affidavit to be sworn and filed] [substantially in the terms of the draft affidavit produced to the court] [confirming the substance of what was said to the court by the Applicant's counsel/solicitors].

(5)   The Applicant will serve upon the Respondent [together with this order] [as soon as practicable]—

(i) copies of the affidavits and exhibits containing the evidence relied upon by the Applicant, and any other documents provided to the court on the making of the application;

(ii) the claim form; and

(iii) an application notice for continuation of the order.

[(6)   Anyone notified of this order will be given a copy of it by the Applicant's legal representatives.]

(7)   The Applicant will pay the reasonable costs of anyone other than the Respondent which have been incurred as a result of this order including the costs of finding out whether that person holds any of the Respondent's assets and if the court later finds that this order has caused such person loss, and decides that such person should be compensated for that loss, the Applicant will comply with any order the court may make.

(8)   If this order ceases to have effect (for example, if the Respondent provides security or the Applicant does not provide a bank guarantee as provided for above) the Applicant will immediately take all reasonable steps to inform in writing anyone to whom he has given notice of this order, or who he has reasonable grounds for supposing may act upon this order, that it has ceased to have effect.

[(9)   The Applicant will not without the permission of the court use any information obtained as a result of this order for the purpose of any civil or criminal proceedings, either in England and Wales or in any other jurisdiction, other than this claim.]

[(10) The Applicant will not without the permission of the court seek to enforce this order in any country outside England and Wales [or seek an order of a similar nature including orders conferring a charge or other security against the Respondent or the Respondent's assets].]

NAME AND ADDRESS OF APPLICANT'S LEGAL REPRESENTATIVES

The Applicant's legal representatives are—

[Name, address, reference, fax and telephone numbers both in and out of office hours and e-mail]

---

[13]   The court is likely to require some form of fortification of the undertakings.

APPENDIX 2

Precedent No. 2: Search Order

SEARCH ORDER

IN THE HIGH COURT OF JUSTICE
QUEEN'S BENCH DIVISION
COMMERCIAL COURT
Before The Honourable Mr Justice [   ]

Claim No.

BETWEEN

Claimant(s)

– and –

Defendant(s)

_____

Applicant(s)

Respondent(s)

PENAL NOTICE

If you [   ][1] disobey this order you may be held to be in contempt of court and may be imprisoned, fined or have your assets seized.

Any other person who knows of this Order and does anything which helps or permits the Respondent to breach the terms of this Order may also be held to be in contempt of court and may be imprisoned, fined or have their assets seized.

THIS ORDER

1. This is a Search Order made against [   ] ('the Respondent') on [   ] by Mr Justice [   ] on the application of [   ] ('the Applicant'). The Judge read the Affidavits listed in Schedule F and accepted the undertakings set out in Schedules C, D and E at the end of this order.
2. This order was made at a hearing without notice to the Respondent. The Respondent has a right to apply to the court to vary or discharge the order—see paragraph 27 below.
3. There will be a further hearing in respect of this order on [   ] ('the return date').
4. If there is more than one Respondent—
   (a) unless otherwise stated, references in this order to 'the Respondent' mean both or all of them; and
   (b) this order is effective against any Respondent on whom it is served or who is given notice of it.

---

[1] Insert name of Respondent(s).

5. This order must be complied with by—
   (a) the Respondent;
   (b) any director, officer, partner or responsible employee of the Respondent; and
   (c) if the Respondent is an individual, any other person having responsible control of the premises to be searched.

THE SEARCH

6. **The Respondent must permit the following persons—**[2]
   (a) [   ] ('the Supervising Solicitor');
   (b) [   ], a solicitor in the firm of [   ], the Applicant's solicitors; and
   (c) up to [   ] other persons[3] being [*their identity or capacity*] accompanying them,

   (together 'the search party'), to enter the premises mentioned in Schedule A to this order and any other premises of the Respondent disclosed under paragraph 18 below and any vehicles under the Respondent's control on or around the premises ('the premises') so that they can search for, inspect, photograph or photocopy, and deliver into the safekeeping of the Applicant's solicitors all the documents and articles which are listed in Schedule B to this order ('the listed items').

7. Having permitted the search party to enter the premises, the Respondent must allow the search party to remain on the premises until the search is complete. In the event that it becomes necessary for any of those persons to leave the premises before the search is complete, the Respondent must allow them to re-enter the premises immediately upon their seeking re-entry on the same or the following day in order to complete the search.

RESTRICTIONS ON SEARCH

8. This order may not be carried out at the same time as a police search warrant.
9. Before the Respondent allows anybody onto the premises to carry out this order, he is entitled to have the Supervising Solicitor explain to him what it means in everyday language.
10. The Respondent is entitled to seek legal advice and to ask the court to vary or discharge this order. Whilst doing so, he may ask the Supervising Solicitor to delay starting the search for up to 2 hours or such other longer period as the Supervising Solicitor may permit. However, the Respondent must—
    (a) comply with the terms of paragraph 27 below;
    (b) not disturb or remove any listed items; and
    (c) permit the Supervising Solicitor to enter, but not start to search.
11. Before permitting entry to the premises by any person other than the Supervising Solicitor, the Respondent may, for a short time (not to exceed two hours, unless the Supervising Solicitor agrees to a longer period), gather together any documents he believes may be [incriminating or][4] privileged and hand them to the Supervising Solicitor for him to assess whether they are [incriminating or] privileged as claimed. If the Supervising Solicitor decides that any of the documents may be [incriminating or] privileged or is in any doubt as to their status, he will exclude them from the search and retain them in his possession pending further order of the court.

---

[2] Where the premises are likely to be occupied by an unaccompanied woman and the Supervising Solicitor is a man, at least one of the persons accompanying him should be a woman.
[3] None of these persons should be people who could gain personally or commercially from anything they might read or see on the premises, unless their presence is essential.
[4] References to incriminating documents should be omitted from orders made in intellectual property proceedings, where the privilege against self-incrimination does not apply—see paragraph 8.4 of the Practice Direction.

12. If the Respondent wishes to take legal advice and gather documents as permitted, he must first inform the Supervising Solicitor and keep him informed of the steps being taken.

13. No item may be removed from the premises until a list of the items to be removed has been prepared, and a copy of the list has been supplied to the Respondent, and he has been given a reasonable opportunity to check the list.

14. The premises must not be searched, and items must not be removed from them, except in the presence of the Respondent.

15. If the Supervising Solicitor is satisfied that full compliance with paragraphs 13 or 14 is not practicable, he may permit the search to proceed and items to be removed without fully complying with them.

DELIVERY UP OF ARTICLES/DOCUMENTS

16. The Respondent must immediately hand over to the Applicant's solicitors any of the listed items, which are in his possession or under his control, save for any computer or hard disk integral to any computer. Any items the subject of a dispute as to whether they are listed items must immediately be handed over to the Supervising Solicitor for safe keeping pending resolution of the dispute or further order of the court.

17. The Respondent must immediately give the search party effective access to the computers on the premises, with all necessary passwords, to enable the computers to be searched. If they contain any listed items the Respondent must cause the listed items to be displayed so that they can be read and copied.[5] The Respondent must provide the Applicant's Solicitors with copies of all listed items contained in the computers. All reasonable steps shall be taken by the Applicant and the Applicant's solicitors to ensure that no damage is done to any computer or data. The Applicant and his representatives may not themselves search the Respondent's computers unless they have sufficient expertise to do so without damaging the Respondent's system.

PROVISION OF INFORMATION

18. The Respondent must immediately inform the Applicant's Solicitors (in the presence of the Supervising Solicitor) so far as he is aware—
    (a) where all the listed items are;
    (b) the name and address of everyone who has supplied him, or offered to supply him, with listed items;
    (c) the name and address of everyone to whom he has supplied, or offered to supply, listed items; and
    (d) full details of the dates and quantities of every such supply and offer.

19. Within [   ] working days after being served with this order the Respondent must swear and serve an affidavit setting out the above information.[6]

PROHIBITED ACTS

20. Except for the purpose of obtaining legal advice, the Respondent must not directly or indirectly inform anyone of these proceedings or of the contents of this order, or warn anyone that proceedings have been or may be brought against him by the Applicant until 4.30 p.m. on the return date or further order of the court.

---

[5] If it is envisaged that the Respondent's computers are to be imaged (i.e. the hard drives are to be copied wholesale, thereby reproducing listed items and other items indiscriminately), special provision needs to be made and independent computer specialists need to be appointed, who should be required to give undertakings to the court.

[6] The period should ordinarily be longer than the period in paragraph (2) of Schedule D, if any of the information is likely to be included in listed items taken away of which the Respondent does not have copies.

21. Until 4.30 p.m. on the return date the Respondent must not destroy, tamper with, cancel or part with possession, power, custody or control of the listed items otherwise than in accordance with the terms of this order.
22. [Insert any negative injunctions.]
23. [Insert any further order.]

COSTS

24. The costs of this application are reserved to the judge hearing the application on the return date.

RESTRICTIONS ON SERVICE

25. This order may only be served between [   ] a.m./p.m. and [   ] a.m./p.m. [and on a weekday].[7]
26. This order must be served by the Supervising Solicitor, and paragraph 6 of the order must be carried out in his presence and under his supervision.

VARIATION AND DISCHARGE OF THIS ORDER

27. Anyone served with or notified of this order may apply to the court at any time to vary or discharge this order (or so much of it as affects that person), but they must first inform the Applicant's solicitors. If any evidence is to be relied upon in support of the application, the substance of it must be communicated in writing to the Applicant's solicitors in advance.

INTERPRETATION OF THIS ORDER

28. Any requirement that something shall be done to or in the presence of the Respondent means—
    (a) if there is more than one Respondent, to or in the presence of any one of them; and
    (b) if a Respondent is not an individual, to or in the presence of a director, officer, partner or responsible employee.
29. A Respondent who is an individual who is ordered not to do something must not do it himself or in any other way. He must not do it through others acting on his behalf or on his instructions or with his encouragement.
30. A Respondent which is not an individual which is ordered not to do something must not do it itself or by its directors, officers, partners, employees or agents or in any other way.

COMMUNICATIONS WITH THE COURT

All communications to the court about this order should be sent to Room EB09, Royal Courts of Justice, Strand, London WC2A 2LL quoting the case number. The telephone number is 020 7947 6826.

The offices are open between 10 a.m. and 4.30 p.m. Monday to Friday.

SCHEDULE A
THE PREMISES

SCHEDULE B
THE LISTED ITEMS

---

[7] Normally, the order should be served in the morning (not before 9.30 a.m.) and on a weekday to enable the Respondent more readily to obtain legal advice.

SCHEDULE C
UNDERTAKINGS GIVEN TO THE COURT BY THE APPLICANT

(1)   If the court later finds that this order or carrying it out has caused loss to the Respondent, and decides that the Respondent should be compensated for that loss, the Applicant will comply with any order the court may make. Further if the carrying out of this order has been in breach of the terms of this order or otherwise in a manner inconsistent with the Applicant's solicitors' duties as officers of the court, the Applicant will comply with any order for damages the court may make.

[(2)   As soon as practicable the Applicant will issue a claim form [in the form of the draft produced to the court] [claiming the appropriate relief].]

(3)   The Applicant will [swear and file an affidavit] [cause an affidavit to be sworn and filed] [substantially in the terms of the draft affidavit produced to the court] [confirming the substance of what was said to the court by the Applicant's counsel/solicitors].

(4)   The Applicant will not, without the permission of the court use any information or documents obtained as a result of carrying out this order nor inform anyone else of these proceedings except for the purposes of these proceedings (including adding further Respondents) or commencing civil proceedings in relation to the same or related subject matter to these proceedings until after the return date.

[(5)   The Applicant will maintain pending further order the sum of £ [   ] in an account controlled by the Applicant's solicitors.]

[(6)   The Applicant will insure the items removed from the premises.]

SCHEDULE D
UNDERTAKINGS GIVEN BY THE APPLICANT'S SOLICITORS

(1)   The Applicant's solicitors will provide to the Supervising Solicitor for service on the Respondent—
   (i) a service copy of this order;
   (ii) the claim form (with defendant's response pack) or, if not issued, the draft produced to the court;
   (iii) an application for hearing on the return date;
   (iv) copies of the affidavits *[or draft affidavits]* and exhibits capable of being copied containing the evidence relied upon by the applicant;
   (v) a note of any allegation of fact made orally to the court where such allegation is not contained in the affidavits or draft affidavits read by the judge; and
   (vi) a copy of the skeleton argument produced to the court by the Applicant's [counsel/solicitors].

(2)   The Applicant's solicitors will answer at once to the best of their ability any question whether a particular item is a listed item.

(3)   Subject as provided below the Applicant's solicitors will retain in their own safe keeping all items obtained as a result of this order until the court directs otherwise.

(4)   The Applicant's solicitors will return the originals of all documents obtained as a result of this order (except original documents which belong to the Applicant) as soon as possible and in any event within [two] working days of their removal.

SCHEDULE E
UNDERTAKINGS GIVEN BY THE SUPERVISING SOLICITOR

(1)   The Supervising Solicitor will use his best endeavours to serve this order upon the Respondent and at the same time to serve upon the Respondent the other documents required to be served and referred to in paragraph (1) of Schedule D.

(2)　The Supervising Solicitor will offer to explain to the person served with the order its meaning and effect fairly and in everyday language, and to inform him of his right to take legal advice (such advice to include an explanation that the Respondent may be entitled to avail himself of [the privilege against self-incrimination or] [legal professional privilege]) and to apply to vary or discharge this order as mentioned in paragraph 27 above.

(3)　The Supervising Solicitor will retain in the safe keeping of his firm all items retained by him as a result of this order until the court directs otherwise.

(4)　Within [48] hours of completion of the search the Supervising Solicitor will make and provide to the Applicant's solicitors, the Respondent or his solicitors and to the judge who made this order (for the purposes of the court file) a written report on the carrying out of the order.

Schedule F

Affidavits

The Applicant relied on the following affidavits—

　　　　　[name]　　[number of affidavit]　　[date sworn]　　[filed on behalf of]

(1)

(2)

NAME AND ADDRESS OF APPLICANT'S SOLICITORS

The Applicant's solicitors are—

[Name, address, reference, fax and telephone numbers both in and out of office hours.]

664

INDEX